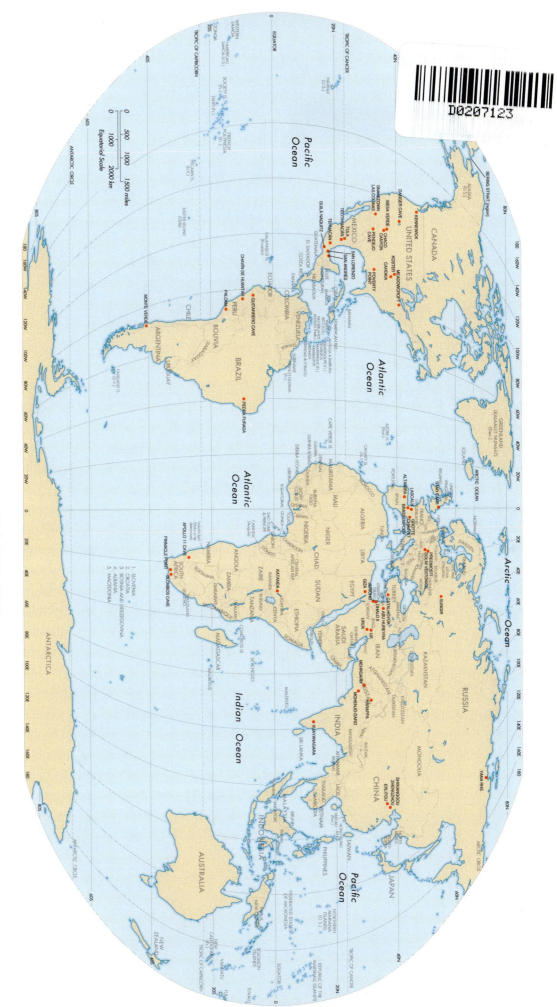

MAJOR ARCHAEOLOGICAL SITES

Understanding Humans

Introduction to Physical Anthropology and Archaeology

TENTH EDITION

Barry Lewis

Professor Emeritus, University of Illinois at Urbana–Champaign

Robert Jurmain

Professor Emeritus, San Jose State University

Lynn Kilgore

University of Colorado, Boulder

WADSWORTH
CENGAGE Learning™

Australia • Brazil • Japan • Korea • Mexico • Singapore
Spain • United Kingdom • United States

Understanding Humans: Introduction to Physical Anthropology and Archaeology, **Tenth Edition**
Barry Lewis, Robert Jurmain, and Lynn Kilgore

Editorial Director, West Coast: Marcus Boggs

Development Editor: Lin Marshall Gaylord

Assistant Editor: Liana Monari

Editorial Assistant: Arwen Petty

Marketing Communications Manager: Tami Strang

Project Manager, Editorial Production: Jerilyn Emori

Creative Director: Rob Hugel

Art Director: Caryl Gorska

Print Buyer: Judy Inouye

Permissions Editor: Roberta Broyer

Production Service and Photo Researcher: Patti Zeman, Hespenheide Design

Text Designer: Norman Baugher

Copy Editor: Janet Greenblatt

Cover Designer: Bartay Studio

Cover Image: www.KevinMoloney.com

Compositor: Hespenheide Design

© 2010, 2007 Wadsworth, Cengage Learning

For product information and technology assistance, contact us at
Cengage Learning Customer & Sales Support, 1-800-354-9706.

For permission to use material from this text or product, submit all requests online at **www.cengage.com/permissions**. Further permissions questions can be e-mailed to **permissionrequest@cengage.com**.

Library of Congress Control Number: 2008937639

Student Edition:
ISBN-13: 978-0-495-60474-7
ISBN-10: 0-495-60474-7

Wadsworth
10 Davis Drive
Belmont, CA 94002-3098
USA

Cengage Learning is a leading provider of customized learning solutions with office locations around the globe, including Singapore, the United Kingdom, Australia, Mexico, Brazil, and Japan. Locate your local office at **www.cengage.com/international**.

Cengage Learning products are represented in Canada by Nelson Education, Ltd.

To learn more about Wadsworth, visit **www.cengage.com/Wadsworth**

Purchase any of our products at your local college store or at our preferred online store **www.ichapters.com**.

Printed in the United States of America
1 2 3 4 5 6 7 12 11 10 09 08

Brief Contents

Contents

Lynn Kilgore

Anthropology

Heredity and Evolution

Lynn Kilgore

L. G. Moore

Primates

San Francisco Zoo

Paleoanthropology/Fossil Hominins

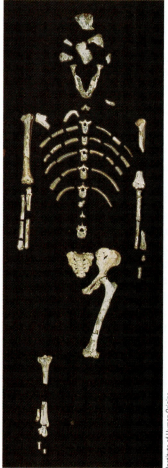

Institute of Human Origins

© Russell Ciochon

David Lordkipanidze

© Russell Ciochon

Archaeology

William Turnbaugh

CHAPTER 15
The First Civilizations

Dr. Robert Clouse

Mark A. Gutchen

Preface

The tenth edition of *Understanding Humans: Introduction to Physical Anthropology and Archaeology* is a major change from previous editions. We've worked hard to respond to the many constructive comments and suggestions of instructors and students who used the ninth edition in the classroom, and we think that you'll like the new edition as much as we do. We improved and updated its content, tightened up its coverage of key topics, changed the book's design, enhanced the quality of its pictures and graphs, and made it shorter in the process. Cengage, our publisher, also worked hard to make this textbook more affordable, while at the same time improving the quality of its production. In the end, we made so many changes that we decided the book also needed a new title!

The tenth edition of *Understanding Humans: Introduction to Physical Anthropology and Archaeology* stays true to our long tradition of providing introductory students and their instructors with a current and comprehensive understanding of human biological and cultural development from an evolutionary point of view. As always, the most compelling justification for a new edition is simply that the story of the human past and the approaches and methods by which it is studied change rapidly. New discoveries, fresh theories, new methods and technologies force revisions, sometimes fundamental revisions, in the understanding of how the world around us works.

Although every edition of this text is committed to providing up-to-date subject content for students and their instructors, we authors are also teachers and even sometimes students ourselves. We know that instructional software, the Internet, multimedia, new teaching approaches, and a host of other factors (including technologically adept students!) are reshaping classrooms and the ways in which students and instructors engage the course material. To meet the pedagogical challenges of today's classrooms, we enhance each edition with in-chapter learning aids (see "In-Chapter Learning Aids," p. xii) to help ensure that learning and teaching the course material continue to be positive and productive experiences.

What's New in the Tenth Edition?

Much is new. First, we made several major organizational changes. For example, the two chapters in the ninth edition on the world's earliest civilizations were combined into one chapter (Chapter 15), a decision that created a more balanced treatment of this important cultural development and reduced the number of chapters from 16 to 15.

Primatologists continue to report new examples of tool use in nonhuman primates, including the recent observation that female chimpanzees in one population sometimes use sharpened sticks to kill prey (covered in Chapter 7). Unfortunately, nonhuman primates continue to decline in numbers, and in Chapter 6 we provide current information from central Africa of just how seriously threatened is the continued existence of mountain gorillas there and elsewhere.

We have also expanded the sections that deal with the archaeology of fossil hominins in Chapters 9 through 12 to ensure that students receive a clear understanding of the development of the earliest human technology and the combined effects of biocultural processes on human evolution.

There have also been a number of crucial new discoveries relating to the fossil hominins themselves. Some of these, as discussed in Chapter 9, are quite old, including a 3-million-year-old infant skeleton from Ethiopia. In Chapter 10, we discuss new evidence regarding the body size of some of the earliest hominins to leave Africa (discovered in the Republic of Georgia) as well as discoveries of 1.2-million-year-old fossils from northern Spain that are the earliest western European hominins yet found.

We have also introduced what may seem like a small change in terminology regarding the way the human lineage is classified. In place of the former term *hominid*, we now use the term *hominin*. This new terminology, in fact, reflects a major change in how the human lineage is now classified relative to the great apes, especially our *very* close cousins, the chimpanzee and gorilla.

Moreover, there have been astounding breakthroughs in the study of ancient DNA—derived from minuscule fragments preserved in partially fossilized hominin bones dating as far back as 50,000 years ago. We cover these new discoveries in Chapters 11 and 12. In late 2006, two teams of researchers announced that they had sequenced large sections of Neandertal DNA from the vast portion found in the nucleus of cells (that is, nuclear DNA). It's interesting, too, that the scientific assessment of just how different we are from Neandertals is made much more accurate by taking into account the newly available information regarding the chimpanzee genome (also published since our last edition). Indeed, exciting new work has helped identify specific Neandertal genes that may tell us about the Neandertal aptitude for language as well as other genes that provide evidence about their skin color!

Then, too, there are the "little people" from an island in Indonesia, whom the press refer to as "hobbits." These unusual hominins were discussed in our last edition, but since then, anthropologists have intensely debated what sort of hominins these fossils represent. The debate continues and is discussed in some detail in Chapter 12; as you'll see, the latest and most detailed studies provide more conclusive evidence than was previously available.

We also updated the focus questions, "At a Glance" boxes, and other learning aids in every chapter to help students more easily master the sometimes complex material. And lastly, the photos and artwork have been substantially expanded and updated, not just to make the book more visually appealing, but also to provide a better sense of what physical anthropologists and archaeologists do and why they enjoy doing it! For those familiar with earlier editions, you'll notice that all the maps have been redrawn, as has much of the other artwork. In addition, many photos have been replaced with upgraded versions and new ones added.

In-Chapter Learning Aids

- **Chapter outlines**, at the beginning of each chapter, list all major topics covered.

- **Focus Questions** appear at the beginning of each chapter, highlighting the central topic of that chapter.

- A **running glossary** in the margins provides definitions of important terms on the page where the term is first introduced. A **full glossary** is provided at the back of the book.

- **At a Glance** features briefly summarize complex or controversial material in a visually understandable fashion.

- **Figures**, including numerous photographs, line drawings, and maps, most in full color, are carefully selected to clarify and support discussion in the text.

- **Critical Thinking Questions**, at the end of each chapter, have been completely revised to reinforce key concepts and encourage students to think critically about what they have read.

- **What's Important Tables** that summarize the most significant fossil discoveries and archaeological sites discussed are included at the end of relevant chapters to help students as they review the chapter material.

- **Full bibliographical citations** throughout the book provide sources from which the materials are drawn. This type of documentation guides students to published source materials and illustrates for them the proper use of referencing. All cited sources are listed in the comprehensive bibliography at the back of the book.

- A "**Click**" icon at the beginning of each chapter directs students to the media relevant to that chapter. One or more of the following media will be listed when appropriate: Online Virtual Laboratories for Physical Anthropology, Version 4.0; Genetics in Anthropology: Principles and Applications CD-ROM, Version 2.0; and Hominid Fossils: An Interactive Atlas CD-ROM.

Acknowledgments

We wish to thank the team at Cengage Learning: Marcus Boggs, Lin Marshall Gaylord, Arwen Petty, Liana Monari, and Jerilyn Emori. Moreover, for their unflagging expertise and patience, we are grateful to our copy editor, Janet Greenblatt, our production coordinator, Gary Hespenheide, and his skilled staff at Hespenheide Design: Patti Zeman, Bridget Neumayr, and Randy Miyake.

To the many friends and colleagues who have generously provided photographs, comments, and criticism, we are greatly appreciative: Brenda Benefit, Colin Betts, Jonathan Bloch, C. K. Brain, Günter Bräuer, Joanna Casey, Desmond Clark, Ron Clarke, Robert Clouse, Raymond Dart, Louis de Bonis, Tom Emerson, Denis Etler, Andy Fortier, Diane France, David Frayer, Kathleen Galvin, Michael Hargrave, Eve Hargrave, David Haring, Nancy Hawkins, Almut Hoffman, Ellen Ingmanson, Fred Jacobs, Peter Jones, John Kappelman, Richard Kay, William Kimbel, Kenneth Kelly, Leslie Knapp, Laura Kozuch, Arlene Kruse, Richard Leakey, Hannah Lewis, Susan Lewis, Carol Lofton, Giorgio Manzi, Monte McCrossin, Lorna Moore, Stephen Nash, Xijum Ni, John Oates, Bonnie Pedersen, Lorna Pierce, David Pilbeam, Dolores Piperno, William Pratt, Judith Regensteiner, Debra Rich, Jeffrey Schwartz, Sastrohamijoyo Sartono, Eugenie Scott, Rose Sevick, Helaine Silverman, Elwyn Simons, Meredith Small, Fred Smith, Thierry Smith, Suzanne Spencer-Wood, Lisa Cordani-Stevenson, Li Tianyuan, Philip Tobias, Erik Trinkaus, Shane Vanderford, Richard VanderHoek, Alan Walker, Dietrich Wegner, James Westgate, Milford Wolpoff, and Xinzhi Wu.

November 2008
Barry Lewis
Robert Jurmain
Lynn Kilgore

Supplements

Understanding Humans: Introduction to Physical Anthropology and Archaeology, **Tenth Edition**, comes with a strong supplements program to help instructors create an effective learning environment both inside and outside the classroom and to aid students in mastering the material.

Supplements for Instructors

Online Instructor's Manual with Test Bank   The Instructor's Manual offers detailed chapter outlines, lecture suggestions, key terms, and student activities such as *InfoTrac College Edition* exercises and Internet exercises. In addition, each chapter offers over 50 test questions, including multiple-choice, true-false, fill-in-the-blank, short-answer, and essay questions. Contact your local Cengage Learning sales representative for access.

PowerLecture with ExamView for *Understanding Humans: Introduction to Physical Anthropology and Archaeology* **0-495-60336-8**   A complete all-in-one reference for instructors, the PowerLecture CD contains Microsoft® PowerPoint® slides of images from the text, zoomable art, image library, PowerPoint lecture slides that outline the main points of each chapter, lecture launcher photos and interviews, Microsoft® Word files of the Test Bank and Instructor's Manual, and ExamView testing software that allows instructors to create, deliver, and customize tests and study guides (both print and online) in minutes.

Cengage Anthropology Video Library   Qualified adopters may select full-length videos from an extensive library of offerings drawn from such excellent educational video sources as *Films for the Humanities and Sciences*.

ABC Anthropology Video Series   This exclusive video series was created jointly by Cengage and ABC for the anthropology course. Each video contains approximately 45 minutes of footage originally broadcast on ABC within the past several years. The videos are broken into short 2- to 7-minute segments, perfect for classroom use as lecture launchers or to illustrate key anthropological concepts. An annotated table of contents accompanies each video, providing descriptions of the segments and suggestions for their possible use within the course.

Online Resources for Instructors and Students

Companion website for *Understanding Humans: Introduction to Physical Anthropology and Archaeology* (*www.cengage* *.com/anthropology/Lewis/Understanding10e*)   This companion website offers an in-depth and interactive study experience that will help students make their grade. Some of the chapter resources include:

- **Access to web resources such as Earthwatch Journal and The Latest Dirt**, allowing students to explore more topics in-depth
- **Flash Cards, Glossary, and Crossword Puzzles** that help students improve their anthropological vocabulary
- **Tutorial Quizzes** with feedback
- **Essay Questions** that can be answered and e-mailed to instructors
- **Instructor resources** such as PowerPoint lecture slides

Anthropology Resource Center   This online center offers a wealth of information and useful tools for both instructors and students in all four fields of anthropology. It includes interactive maps, learning modules, video exercises, and breaking news in anthropology. To get started with the Anthropology Resource Center, students are directed to www.cengage.com/sso, where they can create an account through Single Sign On. Access to this rich resource is free when packaged with new books.

InfoTrac College Edition   InfoTrac College Edition is an online library that offers full-length articles from thousands of scholarly and popular publications. Among the journals available are *American Anthropologist*, *Current Anthropology*, and *Canadian Review of Sociology and Anthropology*. To get started with InfoTrac, students are directed to http://infotrac.cengagelearning.com/, where they can create an account.

Supplements for Students

Hominid Fossils: An Interactive Atlas CD-ROM, by James Ahern   The interactive atlas CD-ROM includes over 75 key fossils important for a clear understanding of human evolution. The QuickTime Virtual Reality (QTVR) "object" movie format for each fossil enables students to have a near-authentic experience of working with these important finds by allowing them to rotate the fossil 360°. Unlike some VR media, QTVR objects are made using actual photographs of the real objects and thus better preserve details of color and texture. The fossils used are high-quality research casts and real fossils. The organization of the atlas is nonlinear, with three levels and multiple paths, enabling students to see how the fossil fits into the map of human evolution in terms of geography, time, and evolution. The CD-ROM offers students an inviting, authentic learning environment, one that contains a dynamic quizzing feature that allows students to test their knowledge of fossil and species identification as well as providing more detailed information about the fossil record. Available at a discount with the text upon request.

Online Virtual Laboratories for Physical Anthropology, Version 4.0, by John Kappelman www.cengage.com /sso Through the use of video segments, interactive exercises, quizzes, 3-D animations, sound, and digital images, students can actively participate in 12 labs on their own terms—at home, in the library—at any time! Recent fossil discoveries are included, as well as exercises in behavior and archaeology and critical thinking and problem-solving activities. When you order Virtual Laboratories on the web-based CengageNOW platform, a powerful course management component allows you to reorder the labs, move content within the labs, utilize the pre-lab and post-lab tests for each lab, and track how much time students spend on each lab. Virtual Laboratories includes web links, outstanding fossil images, exercises, a notebook feature, and a post-lab self-quiz. This supplement is also available on CD-ROM (with a portion of the features and functionality of the online version).

Genetics in Anthropology: Principles and Applications CD-ROM, Version 2.0, by Robert Jurmain and Lynn Kilgore This student CD-ROM expands on basic biological concepts covered in the book, focusing on biological inheritance (such as genes and DNA sequencing) and its applications to modern human populations. Interactive animations and simulations bring these important concepts to life so that students can fully understand the essential biological principles underlying human evolution. Also available are quizzes and interactive flash cards for further study.

Readings and Case Studies

Cengage Modules in Physical Anthropology series Each free-standing module is actually a complete text chapter, featuring the same quality of pedagogy and illustration contained in Cengage's physical anthropology texts.

Evolution of the Brain: Neuroanatomy, Development, and Paleontology, by Daniel D. White The human species is the only species that has ever created a symphony, written a poem, developed a mathematical equation, or studied its own origins. The biological structure that has enabled humans to perform these feats of intelligence is the human brain. This module explores the basics of neuroanatomy, brain development, later-

alization, and sexual dimorphism and provides the fossil evidence for hominin brain evolution. This module in chapter-like print format can be packaged free with the text.

Human-Environment Interactions: New Directions in Human Ecology, by Kathy Galvin This module begins with a brief discussion of the history and core concepts of the field of human ecology, the study of how humans interact with the natural environment, before looking in depth at how the environment influences cultural practices (environmental determinism) as well as how aspects of culture, in turn, affect the environment. Human behavioral ecology is presented within the context of natural selection, examining how ecological factors influence the development of cultural and behavioral traits and how people subsist in different environments. The module concludes with a discussion of resilience and global change as a result of human-environment interactions. This module in chapter-like print format can be packaged free with the text.

Forensics Anthropology Module: A Brief Review, by Diane France The forensic application of physical anthropology is exploding in popularity. This module explores the myths and realities of the search for human remains in crime scenes, what can be expected from a forensic anthropology expert in the courtroom, some of the special challenges in responding to mass fatalities, and the issues a student should consider if they're thinking of pursuing a career in forensic anthropology. This module in chapter-like print format can be packaged free with the text.

Molecular Anthropology Module, by Leslie Knapp This module explores how molecular genetic methods are used to understand the organization and expression of genetic information in humans and nonhuman primates. Students will learn about the common laboratory methods used to study genetic variation and evolution in molecular anthropology. Examples are drawn from up-to-date research on human evolutionary origins and comparative primate genomics to demonstrate that scientific research is an ongoing process with theories frequently being questioned and reevaluated. Mitochondrial DNA and the human-chimp biological connection are also examined in this fascinating and timely module. This module in chapter-like print format can be packaged free with the text.

NEW Classic and Contemporary Readings in Physical Anthropology, edited by Mary K. Sandford and Eileen M. Jackson This first-edition reader includes 23 selections that help students examine the question, What does it mean to be human? Mirroring the organization of most introductory courses in biological anthropology, the book covers five main areas of interest: the nature of science, evolution and heredity, primate behavior, human evolution, and modern human variation. The book's collection of classic and contemporary readings reflects Sandford and Jackson's careful consideration of the available literature, stressing the importance of scientific principles and methods as well as the historical development of physical anthropology and the applications of new technology to the discipline.

Case Studies in Archaeology, edited by Jeffrey Quilter   These engaging accounts of cutting-edge archaeological techniques, issues, and solutions—as well as studies discussing the collec-tion of material remains—range from site-specific excavations to types of archaeology practiced.

These resources are available to qualified adopters, and order-ing options for student supplements are flexible. Please consult your local Cengage sales representative for more information or to evaluate examination copies of any of these resources or receive product demonstrations. You may also contact the Cengage Academic Resource Center at 800-423-0563 or visit us at **www.cengage.com**. Additional information is also available at **www.cengage.com/anthropology/lewis**.

About the Authors

Barry Lewis has joined Robert Jurmain and Lynn Kilgore once again for the tenth edition of *Understanding Humans: Introduction to Physical Anthropology and Archaeology*. While the authors have their particular areas of expertise and have made distinct contributions to the text, their effort has truly been a collaborative one!

Barry Lewis

Barry Lewis received his Ph.D. from the University of Illinois at Urbana-Champaign, where he is currently Professor Emeritus of Anthropology. During his 27-year tenure as a professor of anthropology at the University of Illinois, he taught courses on introductory archaeology, quantitative methods in archaeology, geographic information systems, and social science research methods. He has published extensively on his research concerning late prehistoric Native American towns and villages in the southeastern United States. His recent research centers on the archaeology and history of early modern kingdoms and chiefdoms in South India.

Robert Jurmain

Robert Jurmain received an A.B. in anthropology from UCLA and a Ph.D. in biological anthropology from Harvard University. He taught at San Jose State University from 1975 to 2004 and is now Professor Emeritus there. During his teaching career, he taught courses in all major branches of physical anthropology, including osteology and human evolution, with the greatest concentration in general education teaching for introductory students. His areas of research interest include the skeletal biology of humans and nonhuman primates; paleopathology; and paleoanthropology. In addition to his three textbooks, which together have appeared in 28 editions, he is author of numerous articles in research journals as well as the book *Stories from the Skeleton: Behavioral Reconstruction in Human Osteology* (1999, Gordon & Breach Publishers).

Lynn Kilgore

Lynn Kilgore earned her Ph.D. from the University of Colorado, Boulder, where she currently is an adjunct Assistant Professor. Her primary research interests are osteology and paleopathology. She has taught numerous undergraduate and graduate courses in human osteology, primate behavior, human heredity and evolution, and general physical anthropology. Her research focuses on developmental defects, disease, and trauma in human and great ape skeletons.

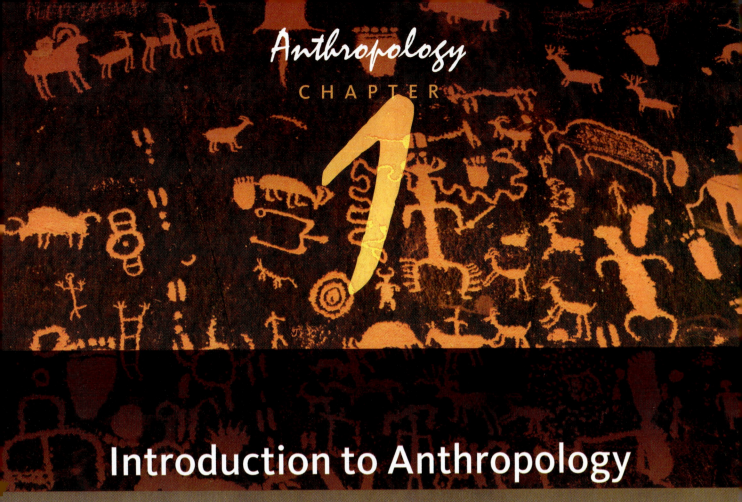

Anthropology

CHAPTER

1

Introduction to Anthropology

Click!

Go to the following media for interactive activities and exercises on topics covered in this chapter:

- Online Virtual Laboratories for Physical Anthropology, Version 4.0

- Genetics in Anthropology: Principles and Applications CD-ROM, Version 2.0

- Hominid Fossils: An Interactive Atlas CD-ROM

evolution A change in the genetic structure of a population from one generation to the next. The term is also frequently used to refer to the appearance of a new species.

anthropology The field of inquiry that studies human culture and evolutionary aspects of human biology; includes cultural anthropology, archaeology, linguistics, and physical anthropology.

scientific method An approach to research whereby a problem is identified, a hypothesis (or hypothetical explanation) is stated, and that hypothesis is tested through the collection and analysis of data.

Introduction

A trip along the northern coast of New Guinea would be high adventure for most of us. We'd be treated to great natural beauty, welcoming people, and at least one remarkable observation that we probably wouldn't anticipate—an extraordinary diversity of local languages (Fig. 1-1). The inhabitants of villages separated by only a few miles may speak different languages. Language diversity is nearly as great in the rest of New Guinea; on an island only a little bigger than the state of Texas, more than 800 languages are spoken—or roughly 15 percent of the world's languages (Wurm, 1994, p. 93).

But why should anyone care how many languages are spoken on the island of New Guinea? Mostly because language diversity is a good rough measure of cultural diversity, and humans exhibit an enormous range of cultural diversity. But biologically, human populations from around the world are very similar to each other. In fact, regardless of their extraordinary cultural diversity, humans show less genetic variation than can be found in a group of wild chimpanzees (Pagel and Mace, 2004).

The main point of this example is that modern humans are cultural *and* biological beings, and we cannot be adequately understood without examining ourselves from both perspectives. Moreover humans are probably unique among animals in the capacity to ask the question "why?" These points illustrate fundamental motivations for the field of anthropology and for this book as an introduction to the biocultural perspective of human **evolution**.

Anthropology addresses the entire scope of the human experience, past and present. It's often described as a holistic discipline, which means that it brings multiple perspectives to bear on the study of all aspects of what it is to be human. Such a broad focus encompasses all topics related to behavior, including social relationships (for example, kinship and marriage patterns), religion, ritual, technology, subsistence, and economic and political systems. Anthropology is also concerned with the numerous biological and evolutionary dimensions of our species, such as genetics, anatomy, skeletal structure, adaptation to disease and other environmental factors, growth, nutrition, and, ultimately, all the evolutionary processes that resulted in the development of modern humans.

In contrast, an economist, for example, might study market systems—the production, distribution, and consumption of goods—and only rarely, if ever, consider the effects of genetics, evolutionary factors, religion, or kinship on economic systems. But anthropology's holistic approach recognizes that many factors contribute to whatever we humans do, even including economic transactions. Indeed, anthropologists incorporate findings from many academic fields (for example, psychology, biology, history, and religious studies) as they seek to understand and explain what being human is all about. In a practical sense, however, no single anthropologist can hope to encompass the entire discipline.

In keeping with anthropology's commitment to a holistic perspective, aspects of this discipline rest firmly in both science and the humanities: Anthropologists answer many questions by applying the **scientific method**, but they also apply interpretive methods to achieve an understanding of such human qualities as love, individual or group identity, compassion, and ethnicity.

Figure **1-1**

Modern humans are products of both culture and biology, and human culture can be amazingly diverse. These market vendors at Wewak, on Papua New Guinea's northern coast, may find that their customers speak a different language even if they come from only a few towns away.

The Biocultural Approach

The concept of **biocultural evolution** helps give all anthropologists a shared perspective. Humans are the product of the combined influences of biology and **culture** that have shaped our evolutionary history over the last several million years. It is by tracing the changing interaction between biology and culture and understanding *how* the process worked in the past and how it continues to work today that we are able to come to grips scientifically with what we are and how we came to be.

As we'll emphasize in this book, humans have occupied center stage in only one short scene of life's evolutionary play. Our role is fascinating; but because of cultural factors, we have also become a threat to many life-forms, including ourselves. Culture is therefore an extremely important concept, not only as it pertains to modern humans but also in terms of its critical role in human evolution.

Viewed in an evolutionary perspective, human culture can be described as the strategy people use in adapting to the natural and social environments in which they live. Culture includes technologies that range from stone tools to computers; subsistence patterns ranging from hunting and gathering to agribusiness on a global scale; housing types from thatched huts to skyscrapers; and clothing from animal skins to synthetic fibers (Fig. 1-2). Because religion, values, social organization, language, kinship, marriage rules, gender roles, and so on, are all aspects of culture, each culture shapes people's perceptions of the external environment, or worldview, in particular ways that distinguish that culture from all others. One fundamental point to remember is that culture is *learned* and not biologically determined. In other words, we inherit genes that influence our biological characteristics, but those genes have no impact on cultural behavior.

For example,* if a young South Indian girl is raised in New Orleans by Italian American parents, she'll acquire, through the process called **enculturation**, all those aspects

---

*These examples draw upon two very different enculturation experiences to illustrate what enculturation is all about. If, like most readers, you didn't grow up in either of these cultural webs, you may find them impenetrable because you're an outsider. It's okay. The main point here is that enculturation plays an enormous role in shaping who we are. Need a quick guide to some of the terms? In New Orleans (aka the Big Easy), red beans and rice are a traditional Monday dish; a roux is flour browned in oil and used as the base for many South Louisiana dishes; many people view the choupic as a "trash fish" and won't eat it; a court bouillon is a fish stew, often made with redfish. In Mysore, a city in South India, Kannada is the local language; *filmi gana* is Hindi for "movie music," an extremely popular music genre throughout South Asia; and idli are steamed cakes made of fermented rice or *rava* (farina) and typically served with onion sambar, a spicy dal soup.

biocultural evolution The mutual, interactive evolution of human biology and culture; the concept that biology makes culture possible and that developing culture further influences the direction of biological evolution; a basic concept in understanding the unique components of human evolution.

culture All aspects of human adaptation, including technology, traditions, language, religion, and social roles. Culture is a set of learned behaviors; it is transmitted from one generation to the next through learning and not by biological or genetic means.

enculturation The process by which individuals, generally as children, learn the values and beliefs of the family, peer groups, and society in which they are raised.

(a)

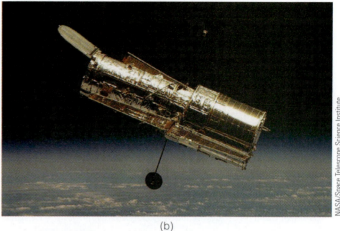

(b)

(c)

(d)

Figure **1-2**

(a) An early stone tool from East Africa. This type of tool was used there about 1.5 million years ago. (b) Hubble space telescope against the earth's horizon. (c) A Samburu woman building a simple, traditional dwelling of stems, plant fibers, and mud. (d) These Hong Kong skyscrapers are typical of cities in industrialized countries today.

species A group of organisms that can interbreed to produce fertile offspring. Members of one species are reproductively isolated from members of all other species (i.e., they can't mate with them to produce fertile offspring).

of growing up in the Big Easy, including a distinctive dialect of American English, a sense of surprise when she discovers that Mardi Gras is not a national holiday, how to make a roux, and the understanding that red beans go with Mondays and a choupic court bouillon is a joke. Alternatively, an Italian American girl raised in Mysore by South Indian parents will just as likely grow up speaking Kannada as her first language, experience a sense of surprise when she learns that the chili pepper is not native to India, know all the latest and best Kannada and Hindi *filmi gana*, and understand that onion sambar goes with idli. In short, both girls' perspectives will be strongly shaped by their respective enculturation experiences, not their genetic ancestry. We are all products of the culture in which we are socialized, and since most human behavior is learned, it clearly is also culturally patterned.

But as biological beings, humans are subject to the same evolutionary forces as all other species. On hearing the term *evolution*, many people think of the appearance of new **species**. Certainly, new species formation is one consequence of evolution; however, biologists see evolution as an ongoing process with a precise genetic meaning. Quite simply, *evolution* is a change in the genetic makeup of a population from one generation to the next. It's the accumulation of such changes over considerable periods of time that can result in the appearance of a new species. So, evolution can be defined and studied at two different levels. At one level there are genetic alterations *within* populations. Although this kind of change may not lead to the development of new species, it frequently does result in variation between populations with regard to the frequency of certain traits. Evolution at this level is referred to as *microevolution*. The other level involves long-term genetic change that does lead to the appearance of new species. Evolution at this level is called *macroevolution* or *speciation*. Both types of evolution will be addressed in this textbook.

In the course of human evolution, biocultural interactions have resulted in such anatomical, biological, and behavioral changes as increased brain size, reorganization of neurological structures, decreased tooth size, and development of language, to list a few. Biocultural interactions are still critically important today, and, among other things, they are changing patterns of disease worldwide. As one example, changing social and sexual mores in many countries may have influenced the evolutionary rate of HIV, the virus that causes AIDS. Certainly, these cultural factors are influencing the spread of HIV throughout populations in both developed and developing countries.

Biologists study all the biological aspects of humankind, including **adaptation** and evolution, but when such research also considers the role of cultural factors, it falls within the discipline of anthropology. This approach recognizes that the human predisposition to assimilate a culture and to function within it is influenced by biological factors. But in the course of human evolution, as you'll see, the role of culture has increasingly assumed an added importance. In this respect, humans are unique.

What Is Anthropology?

Stated ambitiously but simply, anthropology is the study of humankind. The term itself is derived from the Greek words *anthropos*, meaning "human," and *logos*, meaning "word" or "study of." Clearly, anthropologists aren't the only scientists who study humans, and the goals of anthropology are shared by other disciplines within the social, behavioral, and biological sciences. As we noted earlier, the main difference between anthropology and other related fields is anthropology's holistic perspective, which integrates the findings of many disciplines, including sociology, economics, history, psychology, and biology.

In the United States, anthropology comprises three main subfields: cultural, or social, anthropology; archaeology; and physical, or biological, anthropology. Additionally, many universities include linguistic anthropology as a fourth subfield. Each of these subdisciplines, in turn, is divided into more specialized areas of interest. The following is a brief discussion of the main subdisciplines of anthropology.

CULTURAL ANTHROPOLOGY

Cultural anthropology is the study of all aspects of human behavior. Its beginnings are rooted in the **Enlightenment** of the eighteenth century, which exerted considerable influence on how Europeans viewed the place of humans in nature, questioned the extent to which there exists a knowable order to the natural world, and introduced fresh concepts of "primitive," or traditional, societies. These changes in political and social philosophy were particularly felt in the spread of European colonial powers between 1500 and 1900.

The interest in traditional societies led many early anthropologists to study and record lifeways that are now mostly extinct. These studies yielded descriptive **ethnographies** that later became the basis for comparisons between cultures. Early ethnographies were narratives emphasizing such phenomena as religion, ritual, myth, use of symbols, subsistence and dietary preferences, technology, gender roles, child-rearing practices, taboos, medical practices, and how kinship was reckoned.

The focus of cultural anthropology changed considerably with the global social, political, and economic upheavals of the twentieth century. Researchers using traditional ethnographic methods still spend months or years living in and studying various societies, but the nature of the study groups has changed. For example, in recent decades,

adaptation Functional response of organisms or populations to the environment. Adaptation results from evolutionary change (specifically, as a result of natural selection).

Enlightenment An eighteenth-century philosophical movement in western Europe that assumed a knowable order to the natural world and the interpretive value of reason as the primary means of identifying and explaining this order.

ethnographies Detailed descriptive studies of human societies. In cultural anthropology, *ethnography* is traditionally the study of non-Western societies.

ethnographic techniques have been applied to the study of diverse subcultures and their interactions with one another in contemporary metropolitan areas. The subfield of cultural anthropology that deals with issues of inner cities is appropriately called *urban anthropology*. Among the many issues addressed by urban anthropologists are relationships between various ethnic groups, those aspects of traditional cultures that are maintained by immigrant populations, poverty, labor relations, homelessness, access to health care, and problems facing the elderly.

Medical anthropology is the subfield that explores the relationship between various cultural attributes and health and disease. Areas of interest include how different groups view disease processes and how these views affect treatment or the willingness to accept treatment. When medical anthropologists focus on the social dimensions of disease, they may collaborate with physicians and physical anthropologists. Indeed, many medical anthropologists receive much of their training in physical anthropology.

Many subfields of cultural anthropology have practical applications and are pursued by anthropologists working both within and outside the university setting. This approach is aptly termed *applied anthropology*. Although most applied anthropologists regard themselves as cultural anthropologists, the designation is also sometimes used to describe the activities of archaeologists and physical anthropologists. Indeed, the various fields of anthropology, as they are practiced in the United States, overlap to a considerable degree. After all, that was the rationale for combining them under the umbrella of anthropology in the first place.

PHYSICAL ANTHROPOLOGY

Physical anthropology is the study of human biology within the framework of evolution and with an emphasis on the interaction between biology and culture. This subdiscipline is also referred to as *biological anthropology*, and you will find the terms used interchangeably. *Physical anthropology* is the original term, and it reflects the initial interests of anthropologists in describing human physical variation. The American Association of Physical Anthropologists, its journal, many college courses, and numerous publications retain this term. The designation *biological anthropology* reflects the shift in emphasis to more biologically oriented topics, such as **genetics**, evolutionary biology, nutrition, physiological adaptation, and growth and development. This shift has occurred largely due to advances in the field of genetics since the late 1950s. Although we use the traditional term in the title of this textbook, you will find that all the major topics in physical anthropology pertain to biological issues.

The origins of physical anthropology are found in two main areas of interest among nineteenth-century scholars. First, there was increasing curiosity among many scientists (at the time called *natural historians*) regarding the mechanisms by which modern species had come to be. In other words, they were beginning to doubt the literal, biblical interpretation of creation. Although most scientists weren't prepared to believe that humans had evolved from earlier forms, discoveries of several Neandertal fossils in the 1800s raised questions about the origins and antiquity of the human species.

The sparks of interest in biological change over time were fueled into flames by the publication of Charles Darwin's *On the Origin of Species* in 1859. Today, **paleoanthropology**, or the study of human evolution, particularly as revealed in the fossil record, is a major subfield of physical anthropology (Fig. 1-3). There are now thousands of specimens of human ancestors housed in research collections. Taken together, these fossils span at least 4 million years of human prehistory; and although incomplete, they provide us with significantly more knowledge than was available just 10 years ago. The ultimate goal of paleoanthropological research is to identify the various early **hominin** species, establish a chronological sequence of relationships among them, and gain insights into their adapta-

genetics The study of gene structure and action and of the patterns of inheritance of traits from parent to offspring. Genetic mechanisms are the underlying foundation for evolutionary change.

paleoanthropology The interdisciplinary approach to the study of earlier hominins—their chronology, physical structure, archaeological remains, habitats, etc.

hominin Colloquial term for members of the tribe Hominini, the evolutionary group that includes modern humans and now-extinct bipedal relatives.

tion and behavior. Only then will there emerge a clear picture of how and when humankind came into being.

Observable physical variation was another nineteenth-century interest that had direct relevance to anthropology. Enormous effort was aimed at describing and explaining the biological differences among human populations. Although some endeavors were misguided and even racist, they gave birth to literally thousands of body measurements that could be used to compare people. Physical anthropologists use many of the techniques of **anthropometry** today, not only to study living groups but also to study skeletal remains from archaeological sites (Fig. 1-4). Moreover, anthropometric techniques have considerable application in the design of everything from airplane cockpits to office furniture.

Today, anthropologists are concerned with human variation because of its *adaptive significance* and because they want to identify the evolutionary factors that have produced variability. In other words, some traits evolved as biological adaptations to local environmental conditions, including infectious disease. Others may simply be the results of geographical isolation or the descent of populations from small founding groups.

Some physical anthropologists examine other aspects of human variation, including how various groups respond physiologically to different kinds of environmentally induced stress (Fig. 1-5). Examples of such stresses include high altitude, cold, and heat. Others conduct nutritional studies, investigating the relationships between various dietary components, cultural practices, physiology, and certain aspects of health and disease (Fig. 1-6). Investigations of human fertility, growth, and development are closely related to the topic of nutrition and are fundamental to studies of adaptation in modern human populations.

© Russell L. Ciochon

Figure **1-3**

Paleoanthropological research at Omo, Ethiopia.

Lynn Kilgore

Figure **1-4**

This anthropology student is measuring the length of a human cranium with spreading calipers.

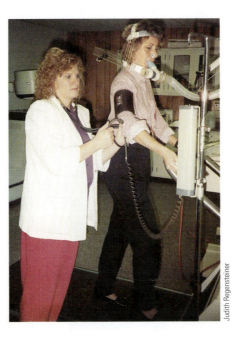

Judith Regensteiner

Figure **1-5**

Researcher using a treadmill test to assess a subject's heart rate, blood pressure, and oxygen consumption.

anthropometry Measurement of human body parts. When osteologists measure skeletal elements, the term *osteometry* is often used.

Figure 1-6

Kathleen Galvin measures upper arm circumference in a young Maasai boy in Tanzania. Data derived from various body measurements, including height and weight, were used in a health and nutrition study of groups of Maasai cattle herders.

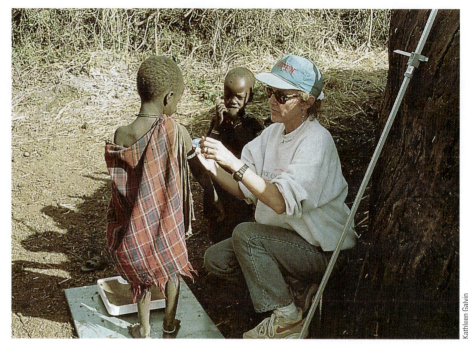

Kathleen Galvin

primates Members of the mammalian order Primates (pronounced "pry-may´-tees"), which includes prosimians, monkeys, apes, and humans.

primatology The study of the biology and behavior of nonhuman primates (prosimians, monkeys, and apes).

Figure 1-7

Cloning and DNA-sequencing methods are frequently used to identify genes in humans and nonhuman primates. This graduate student identifies a genetically modified bacterial clone.

Robert Jurmain

It would be impossible to study evolutionary processes without an understanding of genetic principles. For this reason and others, genetics is a crucial field for physical anthropologists. Modern physical anthropology wouldn't exist as an evolutionary science if not for rapidly developing advances in the understanding of genetic mechanisms.

Molecular anthropologists use cutting-edge technologies to investigate evolutionary relationships between human populations as well as between humans and nonhuman **primates**. To do this, they examine similarities and differences in DNA sequences between individuals, populations, and species. In addition, by extracting DNA from certain fossils, they've contributed to our understanding of relationships between extinct and living species. As genetic technologies continue to improve, molecular anthropologists will play a key role in explaining human evolution, adaptation, and our biological relationships with other species (Fig. 1-7).

Primatology, the study of nonhuman primates, has become increasingly important since the late 1950s (Fig. 1-8). Behavioral studies, especially when conducted in the wild, have implications for numerous scientific disciplines. Because nonhuman primates are our closest living relatives, the identification of underlying factors related to social behavior, communication, infant care, reproductive behavior, and so on, helps us develop a better understanding of the natural forces that have shaped so many aspects of modern human behavior.

But an even more important reason to study non-human primates is that most species are threatened or seriously endangered. Only through research will scientists be able to recommend policies that can better ensure the survival of many nonhuman primates and thousands of other species as well.

Primate paleontology, the study of the primate fossil record, has implications not only for nonhuman primates but also for hominins. Virtually every year, fossil-bearing beds in North America, Africa, Asia, and Europe yield important new discoveries. By studying fossil primates and comparing them with anatomically similar living species, primate paleontologists can learn a great deal about such things as diet or locomotion in earlier life-forms. They can also make assumptions about social behavior in some extinct primates and attempt to clarify what we know about evolutionary relationships between extinct and living species, including ourselves.

Osteology, the study of the skeleton, is central to physical anthropology. In fact, it's so important that when many people think of biological anthropology, the first thing that comes to mind is bones. The emphasis on osteology is due partly to the importance of fossil analysis, which requires a thorough knowledge of the structure and function of the skeleton.

Bone biology and physiology are of major importance to many other aspects of physical anthropology. Many osteologists specialize in studies that emphasize various measurements of skeletal elements. This type of research is essential, for example, to the identification of stature and growth patterns in archaeological populations.

One subdiscipline of osteology is the study of disease and trauma in skeletons from archaeological sites. **Paleopathology** is a prominent subfield that investigates the prevalence of trauma, certain infectious diseases (such as syphilis and tuberculosis), nutritional deficiencies, and many other conditions that may leave evidence in bone (Fig. 1-9). This research tells us a great deal about the lives of individuals and populations in the past. Paleopathology also provides information pertaining to the history of certain disease processes, making it of interest to scientists in biomedical fields.

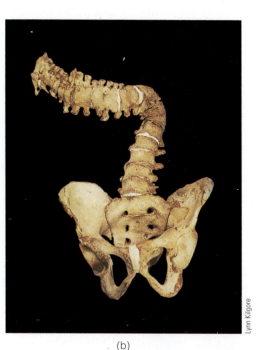

Julie Lesnik

Figure **1-8**

Primatologist Jill Pruetz follows chimpanzees in Senegal.

osteology The study of skeletal material. Human osteology focuses on the interpretation of the skeletal remains of past groups. Some of the same techniques are used in paleoanthropology to study early hominins.

paleopathology The branch of osteology that studies the traces of disease and injury in human skeletal (or, occasionally, mummified) remains.

(a)   (b)

Lynn Kilgore

Figure **1-9**

(a) A partially healed fracture of the femur (thigh bone) from a child's skeleton (estimated age at death is 6 years). Cause of death was probably an infection resulting from this injury. (b) Very severe congenital scoliosis in an adult male from Nubia. The curves are due to several developmental defects that affect individual vertebrae. (This is not the most common form of scoliosis.)

Forensic anthropology is directly related to osteology and paleopathology. Technically, this approach is the application of anthropological (usually osteological and sometimes archaeological) techniques to legal issues (Fig. 1-10). Forensic anthropologists are routinely called on to help identify skeletal remains in cases of mass disaster or other situations where a human body has been found.

Forensic anthropologists have been involved in numerous cases having important legal, historical, and human consequences. These scientists played a prominent role in identifying the skeletons of most of the Russian imperial family, whose members were executed in 1918. Forensic anthropologists also participated in the process of

Lorna Pierce/Judy Suchey

Figure 1-10

Physical anthropologists Lorna Pierce (left) and Judy Suchey (center) working as forensic consultants. The dog has just located a concealed human cranium during a training session.

identifying missing American soldiers in Southeast Asia. And more recently, many forensic anthropologists participated in the overwhelming task of trying to identify human remains in the aftermath of the September 11, 2001, terrorist attacks in the United States.

Anatomical studies are another area of interest for physical anthropologists. In living organisms, bones and teeth are intimately linked to the muscles and other tissues that surround and act on them. Consequently, a thorough knowledge of soft tissue anatomy is essential to the understanding of biomechanical relationships involved in movement. Knowledge of such relationships is fundamental to the accurate interpretation of the structure and function of limbs and other structures in extinct animals now represented only by fossilized remains. For such reasons, many physical anthropologists specialize in anatomical studies. In fact, several physical anthropologists hold professorships in anatomy departments at universities and medical schools (Fig. 1-11).

Figure 1-11

Dr. Linda Levitch teaching a human anatomy class at the University of North Carolina School of Medicine.

forensic anthropology An applied anthropological approach dealing with legal matters. Forensic anthropologists work with coroners and law enforcement agencies in the recovery, analysis, and identification of human remains.

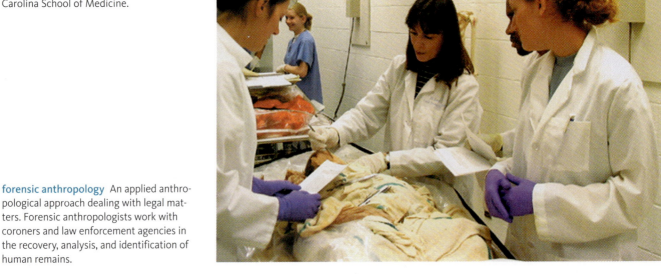

Linda Levitch

ARCHAEOLOGY

Stripped to its basics, archaeology is a body of methods designed to understand the human past through the examination and study of its material remains. Its primary data are the **artifacts** and other **material culture**, associations, and contextual information created by past peoples and preserved to the extent that they can be reliably identified and interpreted by modern researchers. From this, it should be clear that archaeologists don't study the fossils of nonprimate species such as dinosaurs or mammoths, a field properly claimed by **paleontologists**.

Given that archaeology is just a body of methods, you won't be surprised to learn that there are lots of different kinds of archaeology. For example, *classical archaeologists* study the Mediterranean world's "classical" civilizations, such as those created by the Romans and Greeks (Fig. 1-12). These archaeologists tend to be found in departments of art history, classics, and architecture rather than anthropology. To these examples we could also add battlefield archaeology, industrial archaeology, underwater archaeology (Fig. 1-13), and many more; but you get the picture.

Anthropological archaeology, which is the kind of archaeology dealt with in this book, refers to the application of archaeological methods to the understanding of the origins and diversity of modern humans. As such, its domain covers the entire span of the **archaeological record**—from the earliest identifiable hominin tools, and the **sites** in which these implements were deposited, to the trash cans in our kitchens.

Archaeology exists as a discipline because researchers can justify a key assumption: Many human activities and their by-products tend to enter the archaeological record in

Figure 1-12

Classical archaeologists recording the mosaic floor of a Roman brick and timber building buried deep underneath a modern office structure near St. Paul's Cathedral in London, England. The building dates between A.D. 100 and 200, when London was the Roman settlement of Londinium.

Figure 1-13

An underwater archaeologist maps artifact locations at the site of an ancient Greek shipwreck in the Mediterranean Sea off the southern coast of France. The white pipes in the background are part of the excavation grid that the archaeologists constructed across the site when they began their fieldwork.

artifact Objects or materials made or modified for use by hominins. The earliest artifacts tend to be tools made of stone or, occasionally, bone.

material culture The physical manifestations of human activities, such as tools, art, and structures. As the most durable aspects of culture, material remains make up the majority of archaeological evidence of past societies.

paleontologists Scientists whose study of ancient life-forms is based on fossilized remains of extinct animals and plants.

archaeological record The material remains of the human past and the physical contexts of these remains (e.g., stratigraphic relationships, association with other remains).

sites Locations of past human activity, often associated with artifacts and features.

patterned, knowable ways that reflect the behaviors, values, and beliefs of the individuals who created them. Given this assumption, archaeologists can study events and processes that are far removed in time from the modern world and interpret developments in the human past that happened at rates ranging from months to millennia. This perspective of the human past is unique to archaeology.

Archaeology is a historical science, much like geology and evolutionary biology. It is scientific because it answers many research questions by applying the scientific method, and it's inherently historical because its primary data cannot be divorced from their context in space and time. The past, as the late paleontologist and evolutionary biologist Stephen Jay Gould (1989) liked to remind us, happened, and it won't happen again. Consequently, archaeology differs in several fundamental aspects from research in such fields as physics and chemistry, where primary data are not anchored firmly in time and space (Dunnell, 1982).

As we've mentioned, archaeology is also firmly rooted in the humanities. Archaeology in general—and anthropological archaeology in particular—tries to answer many questions about the past that go beyond the search for explanations of general trends and patterns. Understanding certain cognitive and symbolic aspects of the past require additional interpretive tools from such humanities disciplines as history, art history, architecture, and comparative literature.

Anthropological archaeologists (from here on, simply called archaeologists) traditionally differ from other anthropologists in their emphasis on the archaeological record as their primary data source. But the boundaries between anthropological subfields are not sharply drawn. Some archaeologists mainly study cultures that existed before the invention of writing (the era commonly known as **prehistory**). Other specialists, sometimes called **historical archaeologists**, examine the archaeological and documentary record of past cultures that left written evidence (Fig. 1-14). And **ethnoarchaeologists** blur the past-present dichotomy between archaeology and cultural anthropology by conducting ethnographic research with modern peoples in projects designed to achieve archaeological objectives.

Like the other anthropological subfields, modern archaeology largely grew out of the Enlightenment in Europe. Although European awareness of the past can be traced to

Figure **1-14**

Archaeologists expose the foundation of a nineteenth-century farmstead in Illinois.

prehistory The several million years between the emergence of bipedal hominins and the availability of written records.

historical archaeologists Archaeologists who study past societies for which a contemporary written record also exists.

ethnoarchaeologists Archaeologists who use ethnographic methods to study modern peoples so that they can better understand and explain patterning in the archaeological record.

Roman times, it wasn't until the eighteenth and nineteenth centuries that some scholars began to accept evidence that the existence of living things, including humans, must be considerably older than previously thought. They also began to devise instruments for measuring time as it's reflected in the archaeological and fossil records. Once these factors came together with emerging evolutionary ideas in the mid-nineteenth century, the stage was set for the development of archaeology as the primary means by which the human past can be discovered.

Although the rise of American archaeology was greatly influenced by events in western Europe, it didn't develop along precisely the same lines. In North America, early **antiquarian** interests were fueled by the desire to explain the relationship between contemporary Native Americans and the archaeological record. Although this relationship seems obvious to us in the twenty-first century, it was by no means clear to colonists from the Old World or their descendants, even into the early twentieth century. In the United States, curiosity about the possible solution to this problem motivated what is generally agreed to be the earliest systematically conducted archaeological excavation, conducted in 1782 by Thomas Jefferson (Fig. 1-15). He excavated a prehistoric burial mound on his property in Virginia not to find artifacts, but to discover how it was constructed. Therefore, he took careful notes on what he found and on the **stratigraphic** relationships. He then published an account of his work and concluded that the mound had been built by the ancestors of modern Native Americans (Jefferson, 1853).

Few of Jefferson's contemporaries on either side of the Atlantic took such care in their excavations, which is hardly surprising: For most early archaeologists, the questions that motivated their excavations were nearly as crude as their methods. By the early twentieth century, this situation had changed; archaeologists began to exploit the patterned nature of the archaeological record as a way to measure the relative sequence of events in the human past and to explain how and why past cultures changed.

Archaeology reached a certain methodological maturity in the second half of the twentieth century. This process was greatly facilitated by the development of new dating techniques, such as radiocarbon dating, and by technological possibilities created by the advent of computers in the 1960s and 1970s. The breadth of questions asked of the archaeological record also expanded greatly throughout the twentieth century in response to theoretical changes in anthropology as a whole. In 1900, many archaeologists were satisfied simply to describe what their excavations revealed and perhaps to arrange these remains in time and space frameworks. By 2000, they also sought to understand how the people who created these sites lived. They asked how or why these people differed culturally from one another, what similarities they shared, and even why they held particular beliefs about themselves, each other, and the cosmos—all this while simultaneously controlling for time and space in the archaeological record.

In addition to the social science perspective of anthropology, archaeology established itself as a scientific discipline in the twentieth century, and it maintains strong ties with the natural and physical sciences. Contemporary archaeological research often involves the specialized expertise of many disciplines. Remote-sensing technology, including everything from GPS (global positioning system) handhelds to ground-penetrating radar, may be used to locate or define sites. Geologists, soil scientists, and others assist in reconstructing a site's ancient environment. In the subfield of **archaeometry**, archaeologists work with physicists, chemists, engineers, and other scientists to apply the methods and techniques of their respective disciplines to the analysis of ancient materials.

Bioarchaeologists examine human skeletal remains for the overall health status, diet, and physical traits of ancient individuals (Fig. 1-16). Many archaeology students combine their studies with training that prepares them to conduct specialized analyses of ancient plant and animal remains, GIS (geographical information system) spatial data, stable isotopes, ceramics, textiles, and other materials from the archaeological record.

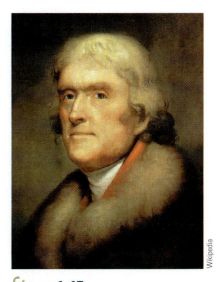

Wikipedia

Figure **1-15**

Long before he became the third president of the United States in 1801, Thomas Jefferson conducted the earliest systematic archaeological excavations in North America and published his results.

antiquarian Relating to an interest in things and texts of the past.

stratigraphic Pertaining to the depositional levels, or strata, of an archaeological site.

archaeometry Application of the methods of the natural and physical sciences to the investigation of archaeological materials.

bioarchaeologists Physical anthropologists who specialize in the analysis and interpretation of human skeletal remains that are discovered at archaeological sites.

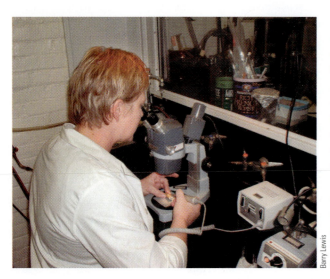

Barry Lewis

Figure **1-16**

Bioarchaeologist Kris Hedman processing a bone sample for analysis of strontium levels in prehistoric human skeletons.

In the late twentieth century, **public archaeology** emerged as an important development in American archaeology. This field includes efforts to reach out to communities and involve wider audiences through education and the media. Most public archaeologists are engaged in cultural resource management (CRM) and other heritage management programs. As mandated by government environmental legislation since the 1970s, CRM archaeologists evaluate sites that may be threatened with damage from development and construction on public lands and in connection with private land projects that receive federal funds or are licensed or regulated by a federal agency (Fig. 1-17). CRM work utilizes a wide range of archaeological expertise, including that of prehistorians, historical archaeologists, field technicians, archaeological illustrators and writers, and laboratory specialists. Many archaeologists in the CRM field are affiliated with environmental research and engineering firms, and others are employed by state or federal agencies or by educational institutions. About 40 percent of the respondents in a 1994 membership survey conducted by the Society for American Archaeology fill such positions (Zeder, 1997), and the long-term trend is for this area of archaeology to continue to grow.

A commitment to the scientific method is also evident in the field of *experimental archaeology*, where researchers attempt to replicate ancient techniques and processes under controlled conditions so that they can better understand the past. Using these approaches, archaeologists have reproduced the entire range of ancient stone tools and employed them in many tasks that replicate the tool wear and breakage patterns on similar tools made and used by prehistoric peoples.

Archaeology's goals also continue to broaden as anthropology changes and as we learn more about the past. Today, anthropological archaeology has several primary goals. The first goal is to reconstruct culture history: This task orders the archaeological record in time and space and creates the archaeological equivalent of the chronologies of history. The second goal is to reconstruct and describe ancient lifeways, and the third is to understand the general processes of culture change and explain how and why past cultures changed in patterned ways. Finally, as an emerging area of research, archaeologists aim to examine and interpret the cognitive and symbolic aspects of past cultures (Demarrais et al., 2005).

As we should expect of any field in which basic goals continue to unfold, archaeologists are engaged in an ongoing negotiation of the discipline's research priorities, the bodies of theory that motivate research, and even the philosophical underpinnings of these theories. No single approach commands a clear consensus in archaeology; but this is a good sign of a healthy, growing, scholarly discipline, not an indication that something is broken. Every option—from ways of knowing about the past to the inevitable conflict between what C. P. Snow (1965) called the "Two Cultures" of science and humanism—is on the table, and the early twenty-first century is an exciting time to be an archaeologist.

LINGUISTIC ANTHROPOLOGY

Linguistic anthropology is the study of human speech and language, including the origins of language in general as well as specific languages. By examining similarities between contemporary languages, linguists have been able to trace historical ties between languages and groups of languages; in this way, linguistic anthropologists can identify language families and past relationships between human populations.

There is also much interest in the relationship between language and culture: how language reflects the way members of a society perceive phenomena and how the use of language shapes perceptions in different cultures. For example, language dialects can encode many meanings, including geographical origins, identity, and social

public archaeology A broad term that covers archaeological research conducted for the public good as part of cultural resource management and heritage management programs; a major growth area of world archaeology.

class. Such encoded meanings influence how a person is treated by those who do or do not speak the same dialects of this or a closely related language. For example, a teacher who speaks Southern American English with the slow cadence or drawl of Vicksburg, Mississippi, may not be taken seriously by students in Minneapolis or Chicago, where the stereotypical image of the speakers of such dialects is that of hillbillies. However, in Southampton, England, or Adelaide, Australia, the same teacher's voice may simply be viewed as wonderfully exotic, the main difference being cultural—in this case, the social meanings associated with the tones and cadence of speech.

Because the spontaneous acquisition and use of language is a uniquely human characteristic, the topic holds considerable interest for linguistic anthropologists, who, along with specialists in other fields, study the process of language acquisition in infants. This research is also important to physical anthropologists because insights into the process may well have implications for the development of language skills in human evolution.

Illinois Transportation Archaeological Research Program, University of Illinois

Figure **1-17**

An archaeological field crew excavates the remains of late prehistoric houses (the outlines of which are marked by lines of white dots in the excavation) and other village features in advance of highway construction. The St. Louis, Missouri, skyline can be seen in the distance.

The Scientific Method

Science is a process of understanding phenomena through observation, generalization, verification, and refutation. By this we mean that there is an objective, **empirical** approach to gaining information through the use of systematic and explicit techniques. Because physical anthropologists and archaeologists are engaged in scientific pursuits, they adhere to the principles of the *scientific method*, whereby a research question is identified and information is subsequently gathered, analyzed, and interpreted to provide an answer.

The gathering of information is referred to as **data** collection, and when researchers use a rigorously controlled approach, they can precisely describe their techniques and results in a manner that facilitates comparisons with the work of others. For example, when scientists collect data on tooth size in hominin fossils, they must specify precisely which teeth are being measured, how they are measured, the validity and reliability of these measures, and what the results of the measurements are (expressed numerically, or **quantitatively**). Subsequently, it's up to the investigators to analyze, interpret, and draw inferences about these measurements. This body of information then becomes the basis of future studies—possibly by other researchers, who can compare their own results with those already obtained. The eventual outcome of this type of inquiry is the acceptance or rejection of proposed answers to the questions that motivated the research.

Once observations have been made, scientists attempt to explain them. First, a **hypothesis**, or provisional explanation of some aspect of the natural world, is developed. To be analytically useful, a hypothesis must be tested by means of data collection and analysis. Indeed, the testing of hypotheses with the possibility of proving them false is the very basis of the scientific method. Everything that scientists accept as true is always a "working" or "conditional" truth, because subsequent testing may demonstrate it to be false.

In anthropology, the **scientific testing** of hypotheses may take several years or longer and may involve researchers who weren't connected with the original work. In

science A body of knowledge gained through observation and experimentation; from the Latin *scientia*, meaning "knowledge."

empirical Relying on experiment or observation; from the Latin *empiricus*, meaning "experienced."

data (*sing.*, datum) Facts from which conclusions can be drawn; scientific information.

quantitatively (quantitative) Pertaining to measurements of quantity and including such properties as size, number, and capacity.

hypothesis (*pl.*, hypotheses) A provisional explanation of a phenomenon. Hypotheses require repeated testing.

scientific testing The precise repetition of an experiment or expansion of observed data to provide verification; the procedure by which hypotheses and theories are verified, modified, or discarded.

subsequent studies, other investigators may achieve similar results, or their findings may be incompatible with those of the initial study. For example, the archaeologist V. Gordon Childe argued in the early 1950s that the earliest prehistoric Near Eastern plant and animal domestication events took place soon after the end of the last Ice Age around the oases, or water holes, of the region (Childe, 1928). Later, Robert Braidwood (Braidwood and Howe, 1960) tested Childe's hypothesis in the field and found that the oldest evidence of Near Eastern plant domestication was actually to be found not around the oases, as Childe's hypothesis predicted, but in village sites scattered among the foothills of the Zagros Mountains in Iraq and Iran. Braidwood's research effectively refuted Childe's hypothesis (just as Braidwood's tentative explanation was itself refuted by subsequent research, which is a story that we'll take up in more detail in Chapter 14). This example illustrates that although it's easier to repeat original studies conducted in laboratory settings, it's no less important to verify research results based on data collected outside of tightly controlled laboratory situations.

After repeated testing, some hypotheses become so well accepted that they're unlikely to be changed by new evidence. At this point, such hypotheses, perhaps combined with others, are accepted as **theories**. In common everyday usage, the word *theory* often means a hunch or guess. But in scientific terms, a theory is a statement or explanation that hasn't been falsified, or shown to be false, by currently available evidence. Of course, theories, or parts of theories, may be altered over time as new technologies and information allow for repeated testing, but in general, they're sustained. For example, it's a fact that when you drop a stone it falls to the ground. That fact is explained by Isaac Newton's theory of gravity, proposed in 1687. But if you were on board the space shuttle and you dropped a stone, it would seem to float because, even though it would still be influenced by the earth's gravitational field, that field would be weaker on the shuttle than it is on earth. Since 1687, Newton's theory has been enhanced by a greater understanding of the attraction of masses to one another as expressed mathematically. But even after more than 300 years, the theory of gravity remains intact with little modification.

Use of the scientific method permits the development and testing of hypotheses, and it also permits various types of *bias* to be addressed and controlled. It's important to realize that bias occurs in all studies. Sources of bias include the researcher's personal values; how the investigator was trained and by whom; what particular questions interest the researcher; what specific skills and talents he or she possesses; what earlier results (if any) have been established in this realm of study and by whom (for example, the researcher, close colleagues, or those with rival approaches); and what sources of data are available (for example, accessible countries or museums) and thus what samples can be collected.

Bias cannot be entirely eliminated from research, but it's possible to minimize its effects through careful research design, in which the researcher consciously works to identify and control for possible bias effects. Anthropologists, like all researchers, strive to minimize bias in their research outcomes as well as in the articles and books they write.

Science is an approach—indeed, a *tool*—used to minimize bias, enable the replication of relevant tests by other researchers, and maximize the validity and reliability of the results. Application of the scientific method thus requires vigilance by all who practice it. The goal isn't to establish "truth" in any absolute sense, but rather to generate ever more accurate and consistent explanations of how the world around us works.

At its very heart, scientific methodology is an exercise in rational thought and critical thinking. The development of critical thinking skills is an important and lasting benefit of a college education. Such skills enable people to evaluate, compare, analyze, critique, and synthesize information so they won't accept everything they hear at face value. A good example of the need for critical thinking in everyday life is how we evaluate advertising claims. For example, people spend billions of dollars every year on "natural" dietary supplements, basing their purchasing decisions on marketing claims that in fact may not have been tested. So when a salesperson tells you that, for example, extracts made from the roots of echinacea help prevent colds, ask if that statement has been scientifically tested—and if so, how, when,

theories Well-substantiated explanations of natural phenomena, supported by hypothesis testing and by evidence gathered over time. Theories also allow scientists to make predictions about as yet unobserved phenomena. Some theories are so well established that no new evidence is likely to alter them substantially.

and by whom and how valid and reliable the test results are—before you decide to try this herbal remedy. Similarly, when politicians make claims in 30-second sound bites, check those claims before you accept them as truth. In other words, be skeptical.

The Anthropological Perspective

Perhaps the most important benefit you will derive from this textbook (and this course) is a wider appreciation of the human experience. To better understand human beings and how our species came to be, we need to broaden our viewpoint across space (comparing individuals, populations, and even species) and through time (considering the past, with special emphasis on evolutionary factors). All branches of anthropology seek to achieve this in a holistic approach we call the *anthropological perspective*.

From the overview presented in this chapter, we can see that physical anthropologists focus on varied aspects of the biological nature of *Homo sapiens* and that archaeologists discover and interpret the cultural evidence of hominin (including modern human) behavior from sites ranging in age from over 2 million years old up to the present day. Modern humans are products of the same forces that produced all life on earth. As such, we represent one contemporary component of a vast biological continuum at one point in time. Yes, we're just another animal, but we're also an extraordinary form of life. Like many other organisms, we've been biologically successful when viewed across the depths of evolutionary time. Unlike other organisms, we are conscious of that fact, aware of the responsibilities that our success engenders, and compelled to learn more about how and why it happened.

This question—*How* and *why* did humans become so successful?—is the main motivation for this textbook. Humans are the only species to develop complex culture as a means of buffering the challenges posed by nature, and we're the only species that spontaneously acquires and uses spoken language as a very complex form of communication. Consequently, physical anthropologists are keenly interested in how humans differ from and are similar to other animals, especially nonhuman primates. For example, in Chapters 4 and 14, we will discuss how aspects of human nutrition have been influenced by evolutionary factors. Today, most of the foods people eat are derived from domesticated plants and animals; but these dietary items were unavailable prior to the development of agriculture more than 10,000 years ago. And yet, human physiological mechanisms for chewing and digesting, as well as the types of foods humans are predisposed to eat, are variations of patterns that were well established in nonhuman primate ancestors long before 10,000 years ago. Indeed, these adaptations probably go back millions of years.

In addition to differences in diet prior to the development of agriculture, earlier hominins might well have differed from modern humans in average body size, metabolism, and activity patterns. How, then, does the basic evolutionary "equipment" (that is, physiology) inherited from our hominin and prehominin forebears accommodate our modern diets? Clearly, the way to understand such processes is not simply to look at contemporary human responses, but to place them within the context of evolution and adaptation through time. Indeed, throughout this book, we'll focus on the biocultural interactions that came about after the development of agriculture, an event that was one of the most fundamental revolutions in all of human prehistory. By studying human behavior and anatomy from the broader perspective provided by an evolutionary context, we're better able to understand the factors leading to the development of the human species.

Archaeologists trace the evolution of culture and its ever-expanding role in human affairs over the past 2.5 million years. Information from archaeological research is frequently combined with biological data to explain how cultural and biological factors interacted in the past to produce variations in human adaptive response, disease patterns, and even the genetic diversity that we see today. From such a perspective, we can begin to appreciate the diversity of the human experience and, in so doing, more fully understand human constraints and potentials. Furthermore, by extending the breadth of our knowledge, it's easier to avoid the **ethnocentric** pitfalls inherent in a more limited view of humanity, a view that isolates modern humans from other human groups and places them outside the context of evolution.

We hope that the following pages will help you develop a better understanding of the similarities we share with other organisms as well as the biocultural processes that shaped the traits that make us unique. We live in what may well be the most crucial period for our planet in the last 65 million years. We are members of the one species that, through the very agency of culture, has wrought such changes in ecological systems that we must now alter our technologies or face potentially disastrous consequences. In such a time, it's vital that we attempt to gain the best possible understanding of what it means to be human. We believe that the study of physical anthropology and archaeology is one endeavor that aids in this attempt, and that is indeed the goal of this text.

Summary

In this chapter, we've introduced the fields of physical anthropology and archaeology and placed them within the overall context of anthropology, a social science discipline that also includes cultural anthropology and linguistics as major subfields.

Physical anthropology studies aspects of human biology (emphasizing evolutionary perspectives), nonhuman primates, and the hominin fossil record. Physical anthropologists are interested in how hominins came to possess culture and how this process influenced the direction of human evolution. Especially regarding the study of early hominins, physical anthropologists work in close collaboration with many specialists from archaeology, geology, chemistry, and other disciplines that form the interdisciplinary field of paleoanthropology.

Archaeology provides time depth for our understanding of humans as biocultural organisms. Systematic examination of the archaeological record provides the basis for archaeologists' interpretations of extinct lifeways as well as the construction of cultural chronologies, explanations for observable cultural changes, and interpretations of the cognitive and symbolic patterns that mark our past. As with paleoanthropology (of which prehistoric archaeology is a key component), archaeological research involves input from many related disciplines. This collaborative examination of the archaeological record yields nearly all we know, if not all we are likely to ever know, about prehistoric human behavior and activities.

Critical Thinking Questions

1. Why does American anthropology describe itself as a three- (often four-) field discipline that includes cultural (social) anthropology, physical (biological) anthropology, and archaeology?
2. Is it important to you, personally, to know about human evolution? Why or why not?
3. Why is the biocultural perspective important to understanding human evolution?
4. What fundamental assumption about the relationship between human behavior and the archaeological record makes archaeology's study of the human past possible? Can archaeology exist as a valid and reliable source of understanding the past if this assumption is true only sometimes or only under certain conditions?
5. Do you think that understanding the scientific method and developing critical thinking skills can benefit you personally? Why?

ethnocentric Viewing other cultures from the inherently biased perspective of one's own culture. Ethnocentrism often results in other cultures being seen as inferior to one's own.

Heredity and Evolution

CHAPTER

2

The Development of Evolutionary Theory

Focus Questions

What are the basic premises of natural selection?

What were the technological and philosophical changes that led people to accept notions of evolutionary change?

Click!

Go to the following media for interactive activities and exercises on topics covered in this chapter:

- Online Virtual Laboratories for Physical Anthropology, Version 4.0
- Genetics in Anthropology: Principles and Applications CD-ROM, Version 2.0

Introduction

Has anyone ever asked you, "If humans evolved from monkeys, then why do we still have monkeys?" Or perhaps, "If evolution happens, then why don't we ever see new species?" These are the kinds of questions people sometimes ask if they don't understand evolutionary processes or they don't believe those processes exist. Evolution is one of the most fundamental of biological processes, and yet it's one of the most misunderstood. The explanation for the misunderstanding is simple. Evolution isn't taught in most primary and secondary schools, and in fact, it's frequently avoided. In colleges and universities, evolution is covered only in classes that directly relate to it. Indeed, if you're not an anthropology or biology major and you're taking a class in biological anthropology mainly to fill a science requirement, you'll probably never study evolution again.

By the end of this course, you'll know the answers to the questions that opened the previous paragraph. Briefly, no one who studies evolution would ever say that humans evolved from monkeys, because they didn't. They didn't evolve from chimpanzees either. The earliest human ancestors evolved from a species that lived some 5 to 8 million years ago (mya). That ancestral species was the *last common ancestor* we share with chimpanzees. In turn, the lineage that led to the apes and ourselves separated from a monkey-like ancestor some 20 mya, and monkeys are still around because as lineages diverged from a common ancestor, each group went its separate way. Over time, some of these groups became extinct, while others evolved into the species we see today. Therefore, each living species is the current product of processes that go back millions of years. Because evolution takes time, and lots of it, we rarely witness the appearance of new species except in microorganisms. But we do see *microevolutionary* changes in many species.

The subject of evolution is controversial, especially in the United States, because some people think that evolutionary statements run counter to biblical teachings. Indeed, as you're probably aware, there is strong opposition to the teaching of evolution in public schools.

People who deny that evolution happens often say that "evolution is only a theory," implying that evolution is nothing more than supposition. Actually, referring to a concept as "theory" supports it. As we discussed in Chapter 1, theories are hypotheses that have been tested and subjected to verification through accumulated evidence. Evolution *is* a theory, one that has increasingly been supported by a mounting body of genetic evidence. It's a theory that has stood the test of time, and today it stands as the most fundamental unifying force in biological science.

Because physical anthropology is concerned with all aspects of how humans came to be and how we adapt physiologically to the external environment, understanding the details of the evolutionary process is crucial. Therefore, it's beneficial to know how the mechanics of the process came to be discovered. Also, if we want to appreciate the nature of the controversy that still surrounds the issue, we need to see how social and political events influenced the discovery of evolutionary principles.

A Brief History of Evolutionary Thought

The discovery of evolutionary principles first took place in western Europe and was made possible by advances in scientific thinking that date back to the sixteenth century. Having said this, we must recognize that Western science could not have developed without writings from other cultures, especially the Arabs, Indians, and Chinese. In fact, intellectuals in these cultures and in ancient Greece had notions of biological evolution (Teresi, 2002), but they never formulated them into a cohesive theory.

Charles Darwin was the first person to explain the basic mechanics of the evolutionary process. But while he was developing his theory of **natural selection**, a Scottish naturalist named Alfred Russel Wallace independently reached the same conclusion. The fact that natural selection, the single most important force of evolutionary change, should be proposed at more or less the same time by two British men in the mid-nineteenth century may seem like a strange coincidence. But if Darwin and Wallace hadn't made their simultaneous discoveries, someone else soon would have, and that someone would probably have been British or French. That's because the groundwork had already been laid in Britain and France, and many scientists there were prepared to accept explanations of biological change that would have been unacceptable even 25 years before.

Like other human endeavors, scientific knowledge is usually gained through a series of small steps rather than giant leaps, and just as technological change is based on past achievements, scientific knowledge builds on previously developed theories. For this reason, it's informative to examine the development of ideas that led Darwin and Wallace to independently develop the theory of evolution by natural selection.

Throughout the Middle Ages, one predominant feature of the European worldview was that all aspects of nature, including all forms of life and their relationships to one another, never changed. This view was partly shaped by a feudal society that was itself a hierarchical, rigid class system that hadn't changed much for centuries. It was also influenced by an extremely powerful religious system, and the teachings of Christianity were taken literally. Consequently, it was generally accepted that all life on earth had been created by God exactly as it existed in the present, and the belief that life-forms couldn't change came to be known as **fixity of species**.

The plan of the entire universe was viewed as God's design. In what is called the "argument from design," anatomical structures were engineered to meet the purpose for which they were required. Wings, arms, and eyes fit the functions they performed, and nature was a deliberate plan of the Grand Designer who was believed to have completed his works fairly recently. In fact, an Irish archbishop named James Ussher (1581–1656) analyzed the "begat" chapter of Genesis and concluded that the earth was created in 4004 B.C. Archbishop Ussher wasn't the first person to suggest a recent origin of the earth, but he was the first to propose a precise date for it.

The prevailing notion of the earth's brief existence, together with fixity of species, posed a huge obstacle to the development of evolutionary theory because evolution requires time, and the idea of immense geological time, which today we take for granted, simply didn't exist. In fact, until the concepts of fixity and time were fundamentally altered, it was impossible to conceive of evolution by means of natural selection.

THE SCIENTIFIC REVOLUTION

So, what transformed centuries-old beliefs in a rigid, static universe to a view of worlds in continuous motion? How did the earth's brief history become an immense expanse of incomprehensible time? How did the scientific method as we know it today develop? These are important questions, but it would be equally appropriate to ask why it took so

natural selection The most critical mechanism of evolutionary change, first articulated by Charles Darwin; refers to genetic change or changes in the frequencies of certain traits in populations due to differential reproductive success between individuals.

fixity of species The notion that species, once created, can never change; an idea diametrically opposed to theories of biological evolution.

J. van (Johannes) Loon/Wikimedia Commons

Figure **2-1**

This beautifully illustrated seventeenth-century map shows the earth at the center of the solar system. Around it are seven concentric circles depicting the orbits of the moon, the sun, and the five planets that were known at the time. (Note also the signs of the zodiac.)

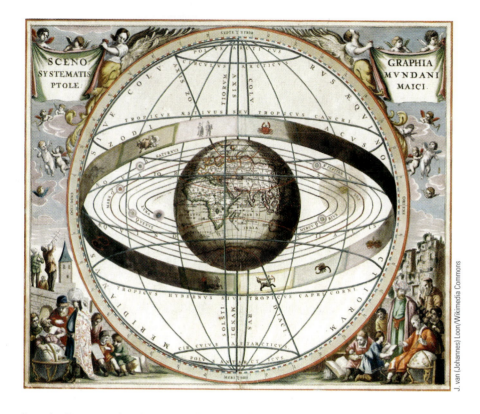

long for Europe to break from traditional belief systems when Arab and Indian scholars had developed concepts of planetary motion centuries earlier.

For Europeans, the discovery of the New World and circumnavigation of the globe in the fifteenth century overturned some very basic ideas about the planet. For one thing, the earth could no longer be thought of as flat. Also, as Europeans began to explore the New World, their awareness of biological diversity was greatly expanded as they became aware of plants and animals they hadn't seen before.

There were other attacks on traditional beliefs. In 1514, a Polish mathematician named Copernicus challenged the notion, proposed more than 1,800 years earlier by the Greek philosopher Aristotle, that the earth, circled by the sun, moon, and stars, was the center of the universe (Fig. 2-1). In fact, Indian scholars had figured out that the sun was the center of the solar system long before Copernicus did; but Copernicus is generally credited with removing the earth as the center of all things.

Copernicus' theory didn't attract much attention at the time; however, in the early 1600s, it was restated by an Italian mathematician named Galileo Galilei. To his misfortune, Galileo came into confrontation with the Pope over his publications, and he spent the last nine years of his life under house arrest. Still, in intellectual circles, the universe had changed from earth-centered to sun-centered. Throughout the sixteenth and seventeenth centuries, European scholars developed methods and theories that revolutionized scientific thought. Their technological advances, such as the invention of the telescope, permitted investigations of natural phenomena and opened up entire new worlds for discoveries such as never before had been imagined. But even with these advances, the idea that living forms could change over time simply didn't occur to people.

PRECURSORS TO THE THEORY OF EVOLUTION

Before early naturalists could begin to understand the many forms of organic life, it was necessary to list and describe them. And as research progressed, scholars were increasingly impressed with the amount of biological diversity they saw.

John Ray It wasn't until the seventeenth century that John Ray (1627–1705), a minister educated at Cambridge University, developed the concept of species. He was the first person to recognize that groups of plants and animals could be distinguished from other groups by their ability to mate with one another and produce offspring. He placed such groups of reproductively isolated organisms into a single category, which he called the *species* (*pl.*, species). Thus, by the late 1600s, the biological criterion of reproduction was used to define species, much as it is today (Young, 1992). Ray also recognized that species frequently shared similarities with other species, and he grouped these together in a second level of classification he called the *genus* (*pl.*, genera). He was the first to use the labels *genus* and *species* in this way, and they're the terms we still use today.

Carolus Linnaeus The Swedish naturalist Carolus Linnaeus (1707–1778) is best known for developing a method of classifying plants and animals. In his famous work, *Systema Naturae* (Systems of Nature), first published in 1735, he standardized Ray's use of genus and species terminology and established the system of **binomial nomenclature**. He also added two more categories: class and order. Linnaeus' four-level system became the basis for **taxonomy**, the system of classification we continue to use today.

Another of Linnaeus' innovations was to include humans in his classification of animals, placing them in the genus *Homo* and species *sapiens*. Including humans in this scheme was controversial because it defied contemporary thought that humans, made in God's image, should be considered unique and separate from the animal kingdom.

Linnaeus also believed in fixity of species, although in later years, faced with mounting evidence to the contrary, he came to question it. Indeed, fixity was being challenged on many fronts, especially in France, where voices were being raised in favor of a universe based on change—and, more to the point, in favor of a biological relationship between similar species based on descent from a common ancestor.

Georges-Louis Leclerc de Buffon Buffon (1707–1788) was Keeper of the King's Gardens in Paris. Unlike others, he recognized the dynamic relationship between the external environment and living forms. In his *Natural History*, first published in 1749, he repeatedly stressed the importance of change in the universe and in the changing nature of species.

Buffon believed that when groups of organisms migrated to new areas, they were gradually altered as a result of adaptation to a somewhat different environment. Buffon's recognition of the external environment as an agent of change in species was an important innovation; however, he rejected the idea that one species could give rise to another.

Erasmus Darwin Today, Erasmus Darwin (1731–1802) is best known as Charles Darwin's grandfather. But he was also a physician, inventor, naturalist, philosopher, poet, and leading member of a well-known intellectual community in Lichfield, England. Living in the English midlands, birthplace of the industrial revolution—which was in full swing—Darwin counted among his friends some of the leading figures of this time of rapid technological and social change.

During his lifetime, Erasmus Darwin became famous as a poet. In his most famous work, he publicly expressed his views that life had originated in the seas and that all species had descended from a common ancestor. From letters and other sources, we know that Charles Darwin read his grandfather's writings; but the degree to which his theories were influenced by Erasmus isn't known.

Jean-Baptiste Lamarck Neither Buffon nor Erasmus Darwin attempted to *explain* the evolutionary process. The first scientist to do this was a French naturalist named Jean-Baptiste Lamarck (1744–1829). Lamarck (Fig. 2-2), like Buffon, suggested a dynamic relationship between species and the environment such that if the external environment changed, an animal's activity patterns would also change to accommodate the new

binomial nomenclature (*binomial*, meaning "two names") In taxonomy, the convention established by Carolus Linnaeus whereby genus and species names are used to refer to species. For example, *Homo sapiens* refers to human beings.

taxonomy The branch of science concerned with the rules of classifying organisms on the basis of evolutionary relationships.

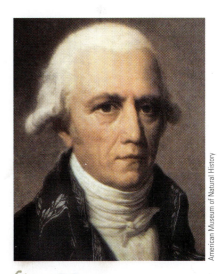

American Museum of Natural History

Figure **2-2**

Lamarck believed that species change was influenced by environmental change. He is best known for his theory of the inheritance of acquired characteristics.

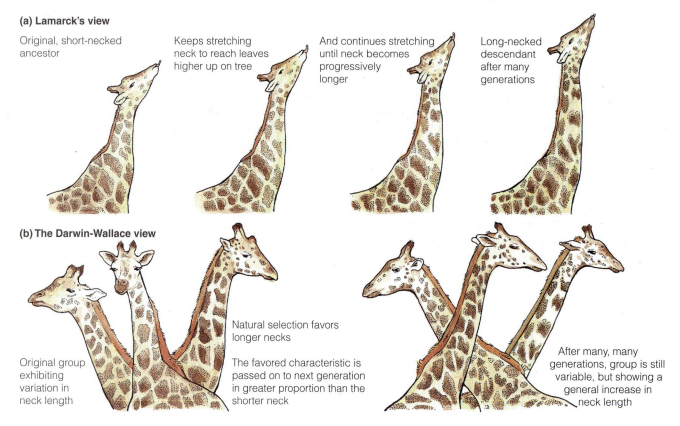

(a) Lamarck's view

Original, short-necked ancestor

Keeps stretching neck to reach leaves higher up on tree

And continues stretching until neck becomes progressively longer

Long-necked descendant after many generations

(b) The Darwin-Wallace view

Original group exhibiting variation in neck length

Natural selection favors longer necks

The favored characteristic is passed on to next generation in greater proportion than the shorter neck

After many, many generations, group is still variable, but showing a general increase in neck length

Figure **2-3**

Contrasting ideas about the mechanism of evolution. (a) Lamarck's theory holds that acquired characteristics can be passed to subsequent generations. Short-necked giraffes stretched their necks to reach higher into trees for food. Consequently their necks became longer and, according to Lamarck, this acquired trait was passed on to offspring, who were born with longer necks. (b) The Darwin-Wallace theory of natural selection states that among giraffes there is variation in neck length. If having a longer neck provides an advantage for feeding, the trait will be passed on to a greater number of offspring, leading to an overall increase in the length of giraffe necks over many generations.

circumstances. This would result in the increased or decreased use of certain body parts, and consequently, those body parts would be modified. According to Lamarck, these physical changes would occur in response to bodily "needs," so that if a particular part of the body felt a certain need, "fluids and forces" would be directed to that point and the structure would be modified. Because the alteration would make the animal better suited to its habitat, the new trait would be passed on to its offspring. This theory is known as the *inheritance of acquired characteristics*, or the *use-disuse* theory.

One of the most frequently given hypothetical examples of Lamarck's theory is that of the giraffe, which, having stripped all the leaves from the lower branches of a tree (environmental change), tries to reach leaves on upper branches. As "vital forces" move to tissues of the neck, it becomes slightly longer, and the giraffe can reach higher. The longer neck is then passed on to offspring, with the eventual result that all giraffes have longer necks than their predecessors had (Fig. 2-3). Thus, according to this theory, *a trait acquired by an animal during its lifetime can be passed on to offspring.* Today we know that this explanation is wrong, because only those traits that are influenced by genetic information contained within sex cells (eggs and sperm) can be inherited (see Chapter 3).

Because Lamarck's explanation of species change isn't genetically correct, it's been made fun of and dismissed. But actually, Lamarck deserves a lot of credit because he emphasized the importance of interactions between organisms and the external environment and tried to explain them. Moreover, he coined the term *biology* to refer to studies of living organisms.

Georges Cuvier Georges Cuvier (1769–1832), the most vehement opponent of Lamarck, was a French vertebrate paleontologist who introduced the concept of extinction to explain the disappearance of animals represented by fossils (Fig. 2-4). Although a brilliant anatomist, Cuvier never grasped the dynamic concept of nature, and he insisted on the fixity of species. So, rather than assume that similarities between certain fossil forms and living species indicated evolutionary relationships, he suggested a variation of a theory known as **catastrophism**.

Catastrophism was the belief that the earth's geological features are the results of sudden, worldwide cataclysmic events like the Noah flood. Cuvier's version of catastrophism suggested that a series of regional disasters had destroyed most or all of the plant and animal life in various places. These areas were then restocked with new, similar forms that migrated in from unaffected regions. But Cuvier needed to be consistent with emerging fossil evidence that indicated organisms had become more complex over time, so he suggested that after each disaster, the incoming migrants had a more modern appearance because they were the results of more recent creation events. (The last of these events was the one described in Genesis.) So Cuvier's explanation of increased complexity over time avoided any notion of evolution while still being able to account for the evidence for change that was preserved in the fossil record.

Thomas Malthus In 1798, Thomas Malthus (1766–1834), an English clergyman and economist, wrote *An Essay on the Principle of Population*, which inspired both Charles Darwin and Alfred Wallace in their separate discoveries of natural selection (Fig. 2-5). In his essay, Malthus argued for limits to human population growth and pointed out that human populations could double in size every 25 years if they weren't kept in check by limited food supplies. Of course, humans, unlike other species, can increase their food supplies and aren't dependent on natural sources, but Malthus warned that increased numbers of humans would eventually lead to famine.

Darwin and Wallace accepted Malthus' proposition that population size increases exponentially while food supplies remain relatively constant, and they extended it to all organisms. But what impressed them the most was something Malthus hadn't written about. They both recognized the important fact that when population size is limited by the availability of resources, there must be constant competition for food and water. And competition between individuals is the ultimate key to understanding natural selection.

Charles Lyell Charles Lyell (1797–1875), the son of Scottish landowners, is considered the founder of modern geology (Fig. 2-6). He was a barrister, a geologist, and for many years Charles Darwin's friend and mentor. Before meeting Darwin in 1836, Lyell had earned acceptance in Europe's most prestigious scientific circles, thanks to his highly praised *Principles of Geology*, first published during the years 1830–1833.

In this immensely important work, Lyell argued that the geological processes observed in the present are the same as those that occurred in the past. This theory, called **uniformitarianism**, didn't originate entirely with Lyell, having been proposed by James Hutton in the late 1700s. Even so, it was Lyell who demonstrated that such forces as wind, water erosion, local flooding, frost, decomposition of vegetation, volcanoes, earthquakes, and glacial movements had all contributed in the past to produce the geological landscape that exists in the present. What's more, the fact that these processes still occurred indicated that geological change was still happening and that the forces driving such change were consistent, or *uniform*, over time. In other words, although various aspects of the earth's surface (for example, climate, plants, animals, and land surfaces) are variable through time, the *underlying processes* that influence them are constant.

Wikipedia

Figure **2-4**
Cuvier explained the fossil record as the result of a succession of catastrophes followed by new creation events.

With permission from the Master of Haileybury

Figure **2-5**
Thomas Malthus' *Essay on the Principle of Population* led both Darwin and Wallace to the principle of natural selection.

catastrophism The view that the earth's geological landscape is the result of violent cataclysmic events. This view was promoted by Cuvier, especially in opposition to Lamarck.

uniformitarianism The theory that the earth's features are the result of long-term processes that continue to operate in the present as they did in the past. Elaborated on by Lyell, this theory opposed catastrophism and contributed strongly to the concept of immense geological time.

Figure 2-6
Portrait of Charles Lyell.

transmutation The change of one species to another. The term *evolution* did not assume its current meaning until the late nineteenth century.

Figure 2-7
Black-and-white photograph of Charles Darwin taken five years before the publication of *Origin of Species*.

The theory of uniformitarianism flew in the face of Cuvier's catastrophism. Additionally, Lyell emphasized the obvious: namely, that for such slow-acting forces to produce momentous change, the earth would have to be far older than anyone had previously suspected. By providing an immense time scale and thereby altering perceptions of earth's history from a few thousand to many millions of years, Lyell changed the framework within which scientists viewed the geological past. Thus, the concept of "deep time" (Gould, 1987) remains one of Lyell's most significant contributions to the discovery of evolutionary principles. The immensity of geological time permitted the necessary time depth for the inherently slow process of evolutionary change.

THE DISCOVERY OF NATURAL SELECTION

Charles Darwin Having already been introduced to Erasmus Darwin, you shouldn't be surprised that his grandson Charles grew up in an educated family with ties to intellectual circles. Charles Darwin (1809–1882) was one of six children of Dr. Robert and Susanna Darwin (Fig. 2-7). Being the grandson not only of Erasmus Darwin but also of the wealthy Josiah Wedgwood (of Wedgwood china fame), Charles grew up enjoying the comfortable lifestyle of the landed gentry in rural England.

As a boy, he had a keen interest in nature and spent his days fishing and collecting shells, birds' eggs, rocks, and so forth. However, this interest in natural history didn't dispel the generally held view of family and friends that he was in no way remarkable. In fact, his performance at school was no more than ordinary.

After the death of his mother when he was eight years old, Darwin was raised by his father and his older sisters. Because he showed little interest in anything except hunting, shooting, and perhaps science, his father sent him to Edinburgh University to study medicine. It was there that Darwin first became acquainted with the evolutionary theories of Lamarck and others.

During that time (the 1820s), notions of evolution were becoming feared in England and elsewhere. Anything identifiable with postrevolutionary France was viewed with suspicion by the established order in England. Lamarck, partly because he was French, was especially vilified by British scientists.

It was also a time of growing political unrest in Britain. The Reform Movement, which sought to undo many of the wrongs of the traditional class system, was under way; and like most social movements, this one had a radical faction. Because many of the radicals were atheists and socialists who also supported Lamarck's ideas, many people came to associate evolution with atheism and political subversion. Such was the growing fear of evolutionary ideas that many believed that if they were generally accepted, "the Church would crash, the moral fabric of society would be torn apart, and civilized man would return to savagery" (Desmond and Moore, 1991, p. 34). It's unfortunate that some of the most outspoken early proponents of **transmutation** were so vehemently anti-Christian, because their rhetoric helped establish the entrenched suspicion and misunderstanding of evolutionary theory that persist today.

While at Edinburgh, young Darwin studied with professors who were outspoken supporters of Lamarck. Therefore, although he hated medicine and left Edinburgh after two years, his experience there was a formative period in his intellectual development.

Even though Darwin was fairly indifferent to religion, he next went to Christ's College, Cambridge, to study theology. It was during his Cambridge years that he seriously cultivated his interests in natural science, immersing himself in botany and geology. It's no wonder that following his graduation in 1831, he was invited to join a scientific expedition that would circle the globe. And so it was that Darwin set sail aboard

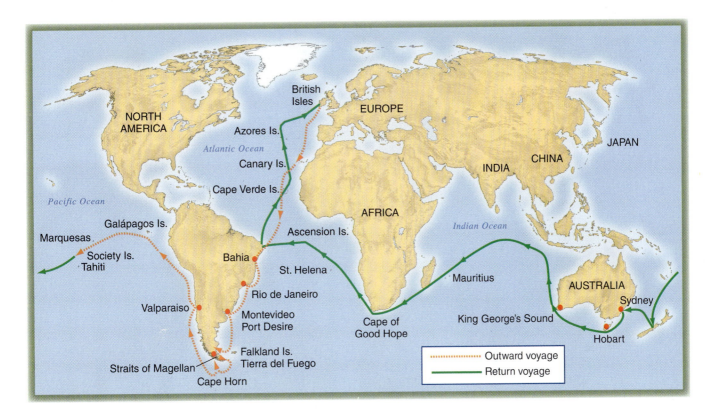

Figure **2-8**

The route of HMS *Beagle*.

the HMS *Beagle* on December 17, 1831. The famous voyage of the *Beagle* would take almost five years and would forever change not only the course of Darwin's life but also the history of biological science.

Darwin went aboard the *Beagle* believing in fixity of species. But during the voyage, he privately began to have doubts. For example, he came across fossils of ancient giant animals that, except for size, looked very much like species that still lived in the same vicinity, and he wondered if the fossils represented ancestors of those living forms.

During the famous stopover at the Galápagos Islands (Fig. 2-8), Darwin noticed that the vegetation and animals (especially birds) shared many similarities with those on the mainland of South America. But they weren't identical to them. What's more, the birds on one island were somewhat different from those living on another. Darwin collected 13 different varieties of Galápagos finches, and it was clear that they represented a closely affiliated group; but they differed with regard to certain physical traits, particularly the shape and size of their beaks (Fig. 2-9). He also collected finches from the mainland, and these appeared to represent only one group, or species.

The insight that Darwin gained from the finches is legendary. He recognized that the various Galápagos finches had all descended from a common mainland ancestor and had been modified over time in response to different island habitats and dietary preferences.

Figure **2-9**

Beak variation in Darwin's Galápagos finches.

(a) Ground finch
Main food: seeds
Beak: heavy

(b) Tree finch
Main food: leaves, buds, blossoms, fruits
Beak: thick, short

(c) Tree finch (called woodpecker finch)
Main food: insects
Beak: stout, straight

(d) Ground finch (known as warbler finch)
Main food: insects
Beak: slender

Wolf: John Giustina/Getty Images   Dogs surrounding wolf: Lynn Kilgore and Lin Marshall

Figure 2-10

All domestic dog breeds share a common ancestor, the wolf. The extreme variation exhibited by dog breeds today has been achieved in a relatively short time through artificial selection. In this situation, humans allow only certain dogs to breed to emphasize specific characteristics. (We should note that not all traits desired by human breeders are advantageous to the dogs themselves.)

But actually, it wasn't until *after* he returned to England that he recognized the significance of the variation in beak structure. In fact, during the voyage, he had paid little attention to the finches. It was only later that he considered the factors that could lead to the modification of one species into 13 (Gould, 1985; Desmond and Moore, 1991).

Darwin arrived back in England in October 1836 and was immediately accepted into the most prestigious scientific circles. He married his cousin, Emma Wedgwood, and moved to the village of Down, near London, where he spent the rest of his life writing on topics ranging from fossils to orchids. But the question of species change was his overriding passion.

At Down, Darwin began to develop his views on what he called *natural selection*. This concept was borrowed from animal breeders, who choose, or "select," as breeding stock those animals that possess certain traits they want to emphasize in offspring. Animals with undesirable traits are "selected against," or prevented from breeding. A dramatic example of the effects of selective breeding can be seen in the various domestic dog breeds shown in Figure 2-10. Darwin applied his knowledge of domesticated species to naturally occurring ones, recognizing that in undomesticated organisms, the selective agent is nature, not humans.

By the late 1830s, Darwin had realized that biological variation within a species (that is, differences among individuals) was crucial. Furthermore, he recognized that sexual reproduction increased variation, although he didn't know why. Then, in 1838, he read Malthus' essay, and there he found the answer to the question of how new species came to be. He accepted from Malthus that populations increase at a faster rate than do resources, and he recognized that in nonhuman animals, increase in population size is continuously restricted by limited food supplies. He also accepted that in nature there is a constant "struggle for existence." The idea that in each generation more offspring are born than survive to adulthood, coupled with the notions of competition for resources and biological diversity, was all Darwin needed to develop his theory of natural selection. He wrote: "It at once struck me that under these circumstances favourable variations would tend to be preserved, and unfavourable ones to be destroyed. The result of this would be the formation of a new species" (F. Darwin, 1950, pp. 53–54). Basically, this quotation summarizes the entire theory of natural selection.

By 1844, Darwin had written a short summary of his views on natural selection, but he didn't think he had enough data to support his hypothesis, so he continued his research without publishing. He also had other reasons for not publishing what he knew would be, to say the least, a highly controversial work. He was deeply troubled by the fact that his wife, Emma, saw his ideas as running counter to her strong religious convictions (Keynes, 2001). Also, as a member of the established order, he knew that many of his friends and associates were concerned with threats to the status quo, and evolutionary theory was viewed as a very serious threat. So he waited.

Alfred Russel Wallace Unlike Darwin, Alfred Russel Wallace (1823–1913) was born into a family of modest means (Fig. 2-11). He went to work at the age of 14, and with little formal education, he moved from one job to the next. He became interested in collecting plants and animals, and in 1848 he joined an expedition to the Amazon, where he acquired firsthand knowledge of many natural phenomena. Then, in 1854, he sailed for Southeast Asia and the Malay Peninsula to collect bird and insect specimens.

Figure **2-11**

Alfred Russel Wallace independently discovered the key to the evolutionary process.

In 1855, Wallace published a paper suggesting that species were descended from other species and that the appearance of new species was influenced by environmental factors. The Wallace paper caused Lyell and others to urge Darwin to publish, but still he hesitated.

Then, in 1858, Wallace sent Darwin another paper, "On the Tendency of Varieties to Depart Indefinitely from the Original Type." In it, Wallace described evolution as a process driven by competition and natural selection. Once he read it Darwin feared that Wallace might get credit for a theory (natural selection) that he himself had developed. He quickly wrote a paper presenting his ideas, and both papers were read before the Linnean Society of London. Neither author was present. Wallace was out of the country, and Darwin was mourning the recent death of his young son.

The papers received little notice at the time; but when Darwin completed and published his greatest work, *On the Origin of Species,** in December 1859, the storm broke, and it still hasn't abated. Although public opinion was negative, there was much scholarly praise for the book, and scientific opinion gradually came to Darwin's support. The riddle of species was now explained: Species were mutable, not fixed; and they evolved from other species through the mechanism of natural selection.

NATURAL SELECTION

Early in his research, Darwin had realized that natural selection was the key to evolution. With the help of Malthus' ideas, he saw *how* selection in nature could be explained. In the struggle for existence, those *individuals* with favorable variations would survive and reproduce, but those with unfavorable variations wouldn't. For Darwin, the explanation of evolution was simple. The basic processes, as he understood them, are as follows:

1. All species are capable of producing offspring at a faster rate than food supplies increase.
2. There is biological variation within all species. (Today we know that except for identical twins, no two individuals are genetically the same.)

---

*The full title is *On the Origin of Species by Means of Natural Selection, or the Preservation of Favoured Races in the Struggle for Life.*

3. Since in each generation more offspring are produced than can survive, and owing to limited resources, there is competition between individuals. (*Note*: This statement doesn't mean that there is constant fierce fighting.)

4. Individuals who possess favorable variations or traits (for example, speed, resistance to disease, protective coloration) have an advantage over those who don't have them. In other words, favorable traits increase the likelihood of survival and reproduction.

5. The environmental context determines whether or not a trait is beneficial. What is favorable in one setting may be a liability in another. Consequently, the traits that become most advantageous are the result of a natural process.

6. Traits are inherited and passed on to the next generation. Because individuals who possess favorable traits contribute more offspring to the next generation than individuals who don't, over time, such characteristics become more common in the population; less favorable traits aren't passed on as frequently, and they become less common, or are "weeded out." Individuals who produce more offspring in comparison to others are said to have greater **reproductive success**.

7. Over long periods of geological time, successful variations accumulate in a population, so that later generations may be distinct from ancestral ones. Thus, in time, a new species may appear.

8. Geographical isolation also contributes to the formation of new species. As populations of a species become geographically isolated from one another, for whatever reasons, they begin to adapt to different environments. Over time, as populations continue to respond to different **selective pressures** (that is, different ecological circumstances), they may become distinct species. The 13 species of Galápagos finches are presumably all descended from a common ancestor on the South American mainland, and they provide an example of the role of geographical isolation.

Before Darwin, individual members of species weren't considered important, so they weren't studied. But as we've seen, Darwin recognized the uniqueness of individuals and realized that variation among them could explain how selection occurs. Favorable variations are selected, or chosen, for survival by nature; unfavorable ones are eliminated. *Natural selection operates on individuals*, favorably or unfavorably, but *it's the population that evolves*. The unit of natural selection is the individual; the unit of evolution is the population (because individuals don't change genetically, but over time, populations do).

Natural Selection in Action

The most frequently cited example of natural selection concerns changes in the coloration of "peppered" moths around Manchester, England. In recent years, the moth story has come under some criticism; but the basic premise remains valid, so we use it to illustrate how natural selection works.

Before the nineteenth century, the most common variety of the peppered moth was a mottled gray color. During the day, as moths rested on lichen-covered tree trunks, their coloration provided camouflage (Fig. 2-12). There was also a dark gray variety of the same species, but since the dark moths weren't camouflaged, they were eaten by birds more frequently and so they were less common. (In this example, the birds are the *selective agent*, and they apply *selective pressure* on the moths.) Therefore, the dark moths produced fewer offspring than the camouflaged moths. Yet, by the end of the nineteenth century, the common gray form had been almost completely replaced by the darker one.

The cause of this change was the changing environment of industrialized nineteenth-century England. Coal dust from factories and fireplaces settled on trees, turning them dark gray and killing the lichen. The moths continued to rest on the trees, but the light gray ones became more conspicuous as the trees became darker, and they were

reproductive success The number of offspring an individual produces and rears to reproductive age; an individual's genetic contribution to the next generation.

selective pressures Factors in the environment that influence reproductive success in individuals.

(a)   (b)

Michael Tweedie/Photo Researchers

Breck P. Kent/Animals Animals

increasingly targeted by birds. Since fewer of the light gray moths were living long enough to reproduce, they contributed fewer genes to the next generation than the darker moths did, and the proportion of lighter moths decreased while the dark moths became more common. A similar color shift had also occurred in North America. But when the advent of clean air acts in both Britain and the United States reduced the amount of air pollution (at least from coal), the predominant color of the peppered moth once again became the light mottled gray. This kind of evolutionary shift in response to environmental change is called *adaptation*.

Another example of natural selection is provided by the medium ground finch of the Galápagos Islands. In 1977, drought killed many of the plants that produced the smaller, softer seeds favored by these birds. This forced a population of finches on one of the islands to feed on larger, harder seeds. Even before 1977, some birds had smaller, less robust beaks than others (that is, there was variation); and during the drought, because they were less able to process the larger seeds, more smaller-beaked birds died than larger-beaked birds. Therefore, although overall population size declined, average beak thickness in the survivors and their offspring increased, simply because thicker-beaked individuals were surviving in greater numbers and producing more offspring. In other words, they had greater reproductive success. But during heavy rains in 1982–1983, smaller seeds became more plentiful again and the pattern in beak size reversed itself, demonstrating how reproductive success is related to environmental conditions (Grant, 1975, 1986; Ridley, 1993).

The best illustration of natural selection, however, and certainly one with potentially grave consequences for humans, is the recent increase in resistant strains of disease-causing microorganisms. When antibiotics were first introduced in the 1940s, they were hailed as the cure for bacterial disease. But that optimistic view didn't take into account the fact that bacteria, like other organisms, possess genetic variability. Although an antibiotic will kill most bacteria in an infected person, any bacterium with an inherited resistance to that particular therapy will survive. Subsequently, the survivors reproduce and pass their drug resistance to future generations, so that eventually, the population is mostly made up of bacteria that don't respond to treatment. What's more, because bacteria produce new generations every few hours, antibiotic-resistant strains are continuously being produced. As a result, many types of infection no longer respond to treatment. For example, tuberculosis was once thought to be well controlled, but it has seen a resurgence in recent years because the bacterium that causes it is now resistant to many antibiotics.

These three examples provide the following insights into the fundamentals of evolutionary change produced by natural selection:

1. *A trait must be inherited if natural selection is to act on it.* A characteristic that isn't hereditary (such as a temporary change in hair color produced by the hairdresser)

Figure 2-12

Variation in the peppered moth. (a) The dark form is more visible on the light, lichen-covered tree. (b) On trees darkened by pollution, the lighter form is more visible.

won't be passed on to succeeding generations. In finches, for example, beak size is a hereditary trait.

2. *Natural selection can't occur without population variation in inherited characteristics.* If, for example, all the peppered moths had initially been gray (you will recall that some dark forms were always present) and the trees had become darker, the survival and reproduction of all moths could have been so low that the population might have become extinct. *Selection can work only with variation that already exists.*

3. **Fitness** *is a relative measure that changes as the environment changes.* Fitness is simply *differential reproductive success.* In the initial stage, the lighter moths were more fit because they produced more offspring. But as the environment changed, the dark gray moths became more fit, and a further change reversed the adaptive pattern. Likewise, the majority of Galápagos finches will have larger or smaller beaks, depending on external conditions. So it should be obvious that statements regarding the "most fit" mean nothing without reference to specific environments.

4. *Natural selection can act only on traits that affect reproduction.* If a characteristic isn't expressed until later in life, after organisms have reproduced, then natural selection can't influence it. This is because the inherited components of the trait have already been passed on to offspring. Many forms of cancer and cardiovascular disease are influenced by hereditary factors, but because these diseases usually affect people after they've had children, natural selection can't act against them. By the same token, if a condition usually kills or compromises the individual before he or she reproduces, natural selection acts against it because the trait won't be passed on.

So far, our examples have shown how different death rates influence natural selection (for example, moths or finches that die early leave fewer offspring). But mortality isn't the complete picture. Another important aspect of natural selection is fertility, because an animal that gives birth to more young passes its genes on at a faster rate than one that bears fewer offspring. However, fertility isn't the entire story either, because the crucial element is the number of young raised successfully to the point at which they themselves reproduce. We call this *differential net reproductive success.* The way this mechanism works can be demonstrated through yet another example.

In swifts (small birds that resemble swallows), data show that producing more offspring doesn't necessarily guarantee that more young will be successfully raised. The number of eggs hatched in a breeding season is a measure of fertility. The number of birds that mature and are eventually able to leave the nest is a measure of net reproductive success, or offspring successfully raised. The following table shows the correlation between the number of eggs hatched (fertility) and the number of young that leave the nest (reproductive success), averaged over four breeding seasons (Lack, 1966):

Number of eggs hatched (fertility)	2 eggs	3 eggs	4 eggs
Average number of young raised (reproductive success)	1.92	2.54	1.76
Sample size (number of nests)	72	20	16

As you can see, the most efficient number of eggs is three, because that number yields the highest reproductive success. Raising two offspring is less beneficial to the parents, since the end result isn't as successful as with three eggs. Trying to raise more than three is actually detrimental, since the parents may not be able to provide enough nourishment for any of the offspring. In evolutionary terms, offspring that die before reaching reproductive age are equivalent to never being born. Actually, death of an offspring can be a minus to the parents, because before it dies, it drains parental resources. It may even inhibit their ability to raise other offspring, thereby reducing their reproductive success even further. Selection favors those genetic traits that yield the maximum net reproductive success. If the number of eggs laid is a genetic trait in birds (and it seems to be), natural selection in swifts should act to favor the laying of three eggs as opposed to two or four.

fitness Pertaining to natural selection, a measure of the *relative* reproductive success of individuals. Fitness can be measured by an individual's genetic contribution to the next generation compared to that of other individuals. The terms *genetic fitness, reproductive fitness,* and *differential reproductive success* are also used.

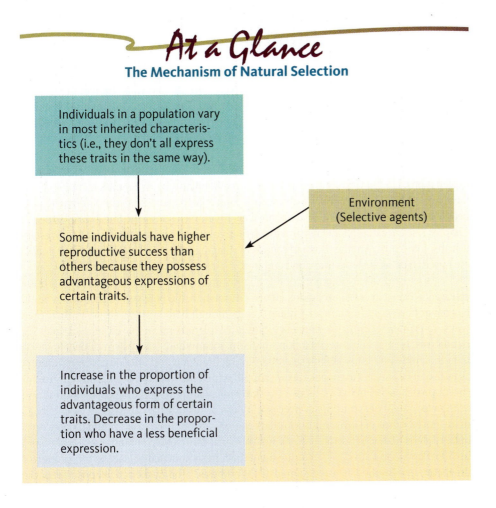

At a Glance

The Mechanism of Natural Selection

Individuals in a population vary in most inherited characteristics (i.e., they don't all express these traits in the same way).

Environment (Selective agents)

Some individuals have higher reproductive success than others because they possess advantageous expressions of certain traits.

Increase in the proportion of individuals who express the advantageous form of certain traits. Decrease in the proportion who have a less beneficial expression.

Constraints on Nineteenth-Century Evolutionary Theory

Darwin argued for the concept of evolution in general and the role of natural selection in particular, but he didn't understand the mechanisms of evolutionary change. As we have seen, natural selection acts on variation within species. But neither Darwin nor anyone else in the nineteenth century understood the actual source of variation. Also, no one understood how parents pass traits to offspring. Almost without exception, nineteenth-century scholars believed that inheritance was a *blending* process in which parental characteristics were mixed together to produce intermediate expressions in offspring. Given this notion, we can see why the true nature of genes was unimaginable, and with no alternative explanations, Darwin accepted it. As it turns out, a contemporary of Darwin's had actually worked out the rules of heredity. However, the work of this Augustinian monk named Gregor Mendel (whom you will meet in Chapter 3) wasn't recognized until the beginning of the twentieth century.

The first three decades of the twentieth century saw the merger of Mendel's discoveries and natural selection. This was a crucial development because until then, scientists thought that these concepts were unrelated. Then, in 1953, the structure of **deoxyribonucleic acid (DNA)** was discovered. This landmark achievement has been followed by even more amazing advances in the field of genetics, including the sequencing of the human **genome**. We may finally be on the threshold of revealing the remaining secrets of the evolutionary process. If only Darwin could know!

deoxyribonucleic acid (DNA) The double-stranded molecule that contains the genetic code.

genome The entire genetic makeup of an individual or species.

Opposition to Evolution

Almost 150 years after the publication of *Origin of Species*, the debate over evolution is far from over. For the vast majority of scientists today, evolution is indisputable. The genetic evidence for it is solid and accumulating daily. Anyone who appreciates and understands genetic mechanisms can't avoid the conclusion that populations and species evolve. But surveys consistently show that about half of all Americans don't believe that evolution occurs. There are a number of reasons for this.

The mechanisms of evolution are complex and don't lend themselves to simple explanations. Understanding them requires some familiarity with genetics and biology—a familiarity that people don't have unless they took related courses in school. What's more, people tend to want definitive, clear-cut answers to complex questions. But as you learned in Chapter 1, science doesn't always provide definitive answers to questions, nor does it establish absolute truths. Another thing to consider is that regardless of their culture, most people are raised in belief systems that don't emphasize **biological continuity** between species.

As we said at the beginning of this chapter, much of the opposition to evolutionary concepts is based in certain religious views. The relationship between science and religion has never been easy (remember Galileo). Even though both systems serve, in their own ways, to explain various phenomena, scientific explanations are based in data analysis, hypothesis testing, and interpretation. Religion, meanwhile, is a system of beliefs based in faith, and it isn't amenable to scientific testing. Religion and science concern different aspects of the human experience and we should remember that they aren't mutually exclusive approaches. Belief in God doesn't exclude the possibility of biological evolution; and acknowledgment of evolutionary processes doesn't preclude the existence of God. What's more, not all forms of Christianity or other religions are opposed to evolutionary concepts. Some years ago, the Vatican hosted an international conference on human evolution; and in 1996, Pope John Paul II issued a statement that "fresh knowledge leads to recognition of the theory of evolution as more than just a hypothesis." Today, the official position of the Catholic Church is that evolutionary processes occur, but that the human soul is of divine creation and not subject to evolutionary processes. Likewise, mainstream Protestants don't generally see a conflict. But those who believe absolutely in a literal interpretation of the bible (called fundamentalists) accept no compromise.

In 1925, a law banning the teaching of evolution in public schools was passed in Tennessee. To test the validity of the law, the American Civil Liberties Union persuaded a high school teacher named John Scopes to allow himself to be arrested and tried for teaching evolution. The subsequent trial (called the Scopes Monkey Trial) was a 1920s equivalent of current celebrity trials, and in the end, Scopes was convicted and fined $100. In the more than 80 years since that trial, Christian fundamentalists have continued to try to remove evolution from public school curricula. Known as "creationists" because they explain the existence of the universe as the result of a sudden creation event that occurred no more than 10,000 years ago, they are determined either to eliminate the teaching of evolution or to introduce antievolutionary material into public school classes. In the past 20 years, creationists have insisted that what they used to call "creation science" is as valid a scientific endeavor as is the study of evolution. They argue that in the interest of fairness, a balanced view should be offered: If evolution is taught as science, then creationism should also be taught as science. Superficially, this argument would sound fair to most people, but "creation science" is not science for the simple reason that creationists insist that their view is absolute and infallible. Consequently, creationism isn't a hypothesis that can be tested, nor is it amenable to falsification. Because hypothesis testing is the basis of all science, creationism, by its very nature, cannot be considered science.

Still, creationists remain active in state legislatures, promoting laws that mandate the teaching of creationism in public schools. In 1981, the Arkansas state legislature passed

biological continuity Refers to a biological continuum—the idea that organisms are related through common ancestry and that traits present in one species are also seen to varying degrees in others. When expressions of a phenomenon continuously grade into one another so that there are no discrete categories, they exist on a continuum. Color is one such phenomenon, and life-forms are another.

one such law but it was overturned in 1982. In his ruling against the state, the judge stated that "a theory that is by its own terms dogmatic, absolutist and never subject to revision is not a scientific theory." And he added: "Since creation is not science, the conclusion is inescapable that the only real effect of [this law] is the advancement of religion."

Since that time, numerous similar laws have been passed, only to be overturned because they violate the principle of separation of church and state as provided in the First Amendment to the U.S. Constitution. The First Amendment states, "Congress shall make no law respecting an establishment of religion, or prohibiting the free exercise thereof...." This "establishment clause" was initially proposed to ensure that the government could neither promote nor restrict any particular religious view, as it did in England at the time the Constitution was written. Since then, state and federal courts have consistently interpreted this sentence to mean that institutions (such as public schools) that are funded by public money, which is derived from taxes, cannot be used to promote religion. Of course, this doesn't mean that people can't pray in public buildings, but it does prohibit organized events that promote a particular religion in such places. (It's worth mentioning that the establishment clause also exempts churches from paying property taxes.)

But court rulings haven't stopped the creationists, who encourage teachers to claim "academic freedom" to teach creationism. They've also dropped the word *creationism* in favor of the less religious-sounding term *intelligent design theory*, which harkens back to the argument from design (see p. 21). The term *intelligent design* is based on the notion that most biological functions and anatomical traits (for example, the eye) are too complex to be explained by a theory that doesn't include the presence of a creator or designer. To avoid objections based on the guarantee of separation of church and state, proponents of intelligent design claim that they don't emphasize any particular religion. But this argument still doesn't speak to the essential point that promoting *any* religious view in a publicly funded school constitutes a violation of the U.S. Constitution.

Antievolution feeling also remains strong among many politicians, particularly those with strong support from Christian fundamentalists. The president of the United States (as of this writing) has publicly supported teaching intelligent design in public schools; and in 1999, one very powerful former U.S. congressman went so far as to state that the teaching of evolution is one of the factors behind violence in America today! Now, that's a stretch!

Summary

Our current understanding of evolutionary processes is directly traceable to developments in intellectual thought in western Europe over the last 300 years. Many people contributed to this shift in perspective, and we've named only a few. Linnaeus placed humans in the same taxonomic scheme as all other animals. Importantly, Lamarck and Buffon both recognized that species could change in response to environmental circumstances, but Lamarck also attempted to explain *how* the changes occurred. He proposed the idea of *inheritance of acquired characteristics*, which was later discredited. Lyell, in his theory of uniformitarianism, provided the necessary expanse of time for evolution to occur, and Malthus discussed how population size is kept in check by the availability of resources. Darwin and Wallace, influenced by their predecessors, independently recognized that because of competition for resources, individuals with favorable characteristics tend to survive and pass those traits on to offspring. Those lacking beneficial traits produce fewer offspring, if they survive to reproductive age at all. That is, they have lower reproductive success and reduced fitness. Thus, over time, advantageous characteristics accumulate in a population (because they have been selected for) while disadvantageous ones are eliminated (selected against). This, in a nutshell, is the theory of evolution by means of natural selection.

Critical Thinking Questions

1. After having read this chapter, how would you respond to the question, "If humans evolved from monkeys, why do we still have monkeys?"

2. What are selective agents? Can you think of some examples we didn't discuss? Why did Darwin look at domesticated species as models for natural selection, and what is the selective agent in artificial selection? List some examples of artificial selection that we didn't discuss.

3. Given what you've read about the scientific method, how would you explain the differences between science and religion as methods of explaining natural phenomena? Do you personally see a conflict between evolutionary and religious explanations of how species came to be? Why or why not?

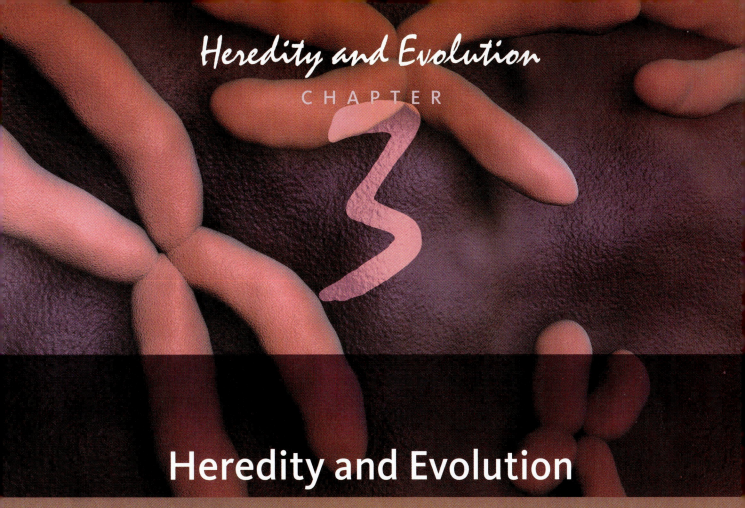

Heredity and Evolution

CHAPTER

3

Heredity and Evolution

Focus Questions

How does knowing about the mechanisms of heredity help to understand how human beings fit into a biological continuum?

Why is it important to know the basic mechanisms of inheritance to understand the processes of evolution?

Click!

Go to the following media for interactive activities and exercises on topics covered in this chapter:

- Genetics in Anthropology: Principles and Applications CD-ROM, Version 2.0

Introduction

Have you ever seen a cat with five, six, or even seven toes? Or maybe you've known someone with an extra finger or toe, because it's not unheard of in people. Anne Boleyn, mother of England's Queen Elizabeth I and the first of Henry VIII's wives to lose her head, apparently had an extra little finger. (Of course, this had nothing to do with her early demise—that's another story.)

Having extra fingers or toes (digits) is called polydactyly (Fig. 3-1), and it's fairly certain that one of Anne Boleyn's parents was also polydactylous. It's also likely that any polydactylous cat has a parent with extra toes. But how do we know this? Actually, it's fairly simple. Polydactyly is a Mendelian trait, meaning that its pattern of inheritance follows principles discovered almost 150 years ago by a monk named Gregor Mendel. And by the time you finish reading this chapter, you'll understand these principles and be able to explain how we know that cats and people with extra digits probably have a polydactylous parent, even if we've never seen their parents.

For at least 10,000 years, beginning with the domestication of plants and animals, people have tried to explain how offspring inherit characteristics from their parents. One common belief was that traits of offspring resulted from the blending of parental characteristics. We now know that this isn't true; in fact, thanks to genetic research, mostly in the twentieth century, we actually know a lot about how traits are inherited.

As you already know, this book is partly about human evolution and adaptation, both of which are intimately linked to life processes that involve cells, the replication and decoding of genetic information, and the transmission of this information between generations. So, to present human evolution and adaptation in the broad sense, we need to examine the fundamental principles of genetics. **Genetics** is the study of how traits are transmitted from one generation to the next, and even though many physical anthropologists don't actually specialize in genetics, it's genetics that ultimately links the various subdisciplines of biological anthropology.

Figure 3-1

Polydactyly in a human infant (a) and in a cat (b).

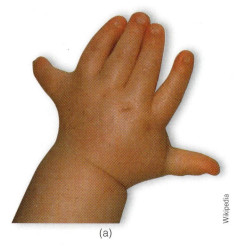

(a)

(b)

genetics The study of gene structure and action and of the patterns of inheritance of traits from parent to offspring. Genetic mechanisms are the underlying foundation for evolutionary change.

The Cell

To discuss genetic and evolutionary principles, we first need to know how cells function. Cells are the basic units of life in all living things. In some forms, such as bacteria, a single cell constitutes the entire organism. However, more complex *multicellular forms*, such as plants, insects, birds, and mammals, are composed of billions of cells. Indeed, an adult human is made up of perhaps as many as 1,000 billion (1,000,000,000,000) cells, all functioning in complex ways to promote the survival of the individual.

Life on earth can be traced back at least 3.7 billion years, to the form of *prokaryotic* cells. Prokaryotes are single-celled organisms, represented today by bacteria and blue-green algae. Structurally more complex cells appeared approximately 1.2 billion years ago, and these are called *eukaryotic* cells. Because eukaryotic cells are found in all multicellular organisms, they're the focus of this discussion. Despite the numerous differences between various life-forms and the cells that constitute them, it's important to understand that the cells of all living organisms share many similarities because they share a common evolutionary history.

In general, a eukaryotic cell is a three-dimensional structure that contains a variety of structures, called organelles, enclosed within a *cell membrane* (Fig. 3-2). One of these organelles is the **nucleus** (*pl.*, nuclei), a discrete unit surrounded by a thin nuclear membrane. Within the nucleus are two acids that contain the genetic information that controls the cell's functions: **deoxyribonucleic acid (DNA)** and **ribonucleic acid (RNA)**. The nucleus is surrounded by a gel-like fluid called the **cytoplasm**, which contains several other types of organelles (see p. 000). These organelles are involved in various activities, such as breaking down nutrients and converting them to other substances, storing and releasing energy, eliminating waste, and manufacturing **proteins** (a process called **protein synthesis**).

There are basically two types of cells: **somatic cells** and **gametes**. Somatic cells are the cellular components of body tissues, such as muscles, bones, skin, nerves, heart, and

nucleus A structure (organelle) found in all eukaryotic cells. The nucleus contains chromosomes (nuclear DNA).

deoxyribonucleic acid (DNA) The double-stranded molecule that contains the genetic code. DNA is a main component of chromosomes.

ribonucleic acid (RNA) A molecule similar in structure to DNA. Three different single-stranded forms of RNA are essential to protein synthesis.

cytoplasm The portion of the cell contained within the cell membrane, excluding the nucleus. The cytoplasm consists of a semifluid material and contains numerous structures involved with cell function.

proteins Three-dimensional molecules that serve a wide variety of functions through their ability to bind to other molecules.

protein synthesis The assembly of chains of amino acids into functional protein molecules. The process is directed by DNA.

somatic cells Basically, all the cells in the body except those involved with reproduction.

gametes Reproductive cells (eggs and sperm in animals) developed from precursor cells in ovaries and testes.

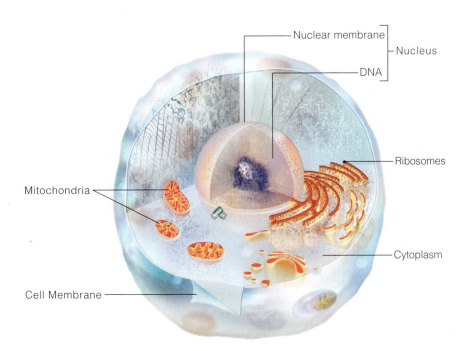

Figure 3-2

Structure of a generalized eukaryotic cell, illustrating the cell's three-dimensional nature. Various organelles are shown, but for simplicity only those we discuss are labeled.

brain. Gametes, or sex cells, are specifically involved in reproduction and are not structural components of the body. There are two types of gametes: egg cells, produced in the ovaries in females; and sperm, which develop in male testes. The sole function of a sex cell is to unite with a gamete from another individual to form a **zygote**, which has the potential to develop into an entire new individual. In this way, gametes transmit genetic information from parent to offspring.

DNA Structure and Function

As already mentioned, cellular functions are directed by DNA. If we want to understand these functions and how traits are inherited, we must first know something about the structure and function of DNA.

The DNA **molecule** is composed of two chains of even smaller molecules called **nucleotides**. A nucleotide, in turn, is made up of three components: a sugar molecule (deoxyribose), a phosphate unit, and one of four bases (Fig. 3-3). In DNA, nucleotides are stacked on top of one another to form a chain that is bonded along its bases to another nucleotide chain. Together the two twist to form a spiral, or helical, shape. The resulting DNA molecule, then, is two-stranded and is described as forming a *double helix* that resembles a twisted ladder. If we follow the twisted ladder analogy, the sugars and phosphates represent the two sides, while the bases and the bonds that join them form the rungs.

The four bases are the key to how DNA works. These bases are named *adenine, guanine, thymine,* and *cytosine,* but they're usually referred to by their initial letters: A, G, T, and C. In the formation of the double helix, one type of base can pair, or bond, with only one other type; therefore, base pairs can form only between adenine and thymine and between guanine and cytosine (see Fig. 3-3). This specificity is essential to the DNA molecule's ability to replicate, or make an exact copy of itself.

zygote A cell formed by the union of an egg and a sperm cell. It contains the full complement of chromosomes (in humans, 46) and has the potential to develop into an entire organism.

molecule A structure made up of two or more atoms. Molecules can combine with other molecules to form more complex structures.

nucleotides Basic units of the DNA molecule, composed of a sugar, a phosphate unit, and one of four DNA bases.

Figure **3-3**

Part of a DNA molecule. The illustration shows the two DNA strands with the sugar and phosphate backbone and the bases extending toward the center.

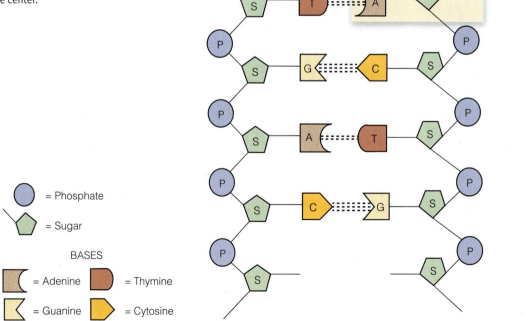

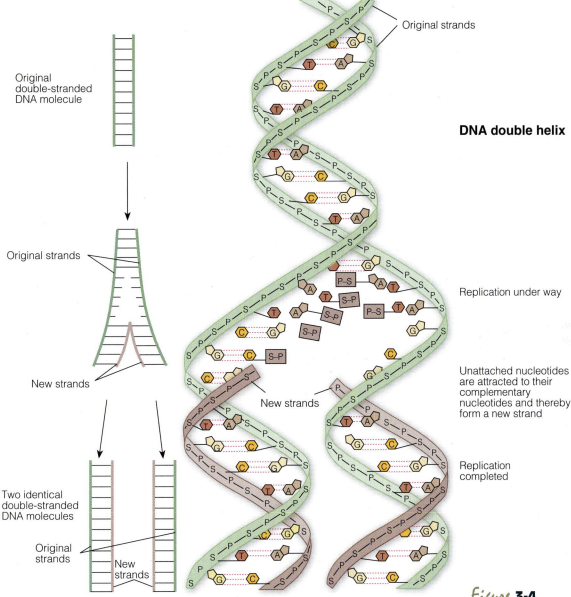

Original double-stranded DNA molecule

Original strands

New strands

Two identical double-stranded DNA molecules

Original strands

New strands

Original strands

DNA double helix

Replication under way

Unattached nucleotides are attracted to their complementary nucleotides and thereby form a new strand

New strands

Replication completed

Figure **3-4**

DNA replication. During DNA replication, the two strands of the DNA molecule are separated, and each strand serves as a template for the formation of a new strand. When replication is complete, there are two DNA molecules. Each molecule consists of one new and one original DNA strand.

enzymes Specialized proteins that initiate and direct chemical reactions in the body.

complementary Referring to the fact that DNA bases form base pairs in a precise manner. For example, adenine can bond only to thymine. These two bases are said to be complementary because one requires the other to form a complete DNA base pair.

DNA REPLICATION

Cells multiply by dividing to make exact copies of themselves. This, in turn, enables organisms to grow and injured tissues to heal. There are two kinds of cell division. In the simpler form, cells divide in a way that ensures that each new cell receives a full set of genetic material. This is important, because a cell can't function properly without the appropriate amount of DNA. But before a cell can divide, its DNA must replicate.

Prior to cell division, **enzymes** break the bonds between bases in the DNA molecule, leaving the two previously joined strands of nucleotides with their bases exposed (Fig. 3-4). The exposed bases then attract unattached nucleotides that are constantly being manufactured elsewhere in the cell nucleus. Because one base can be joined to only one other, the attraction between bases occurs in a **complementary** way. Consequently, each of the two previously joined parental nucleotide chains serve as models, or *templates*, for the formation of a new strand of nucleotides. As each new strand is formed, its bases are joined to the bases of an original strand. When the process is completed, there are two double-stranded DNA molecules exactly like the original, and each new molecule consists of one original nucleotide chain joined to a newly formed chain (see Fig. 3-4).

PROTEIN SYNTHESIS

One of the most important functions of DNA is to direct the manufacture of proteins (protein synthesis) within the cell. Proteins are complex, three-dimensional molecules that function through their ability to bind to other molecules. For example, the protein **hemoglobin**, found in red blood cells, is able to bind to oxygen, which it transports to cells throughout the body.

Proteins function in countless ways. Some are structural components of tissues. Collagen, for example, is the most common protein in the body, and it's a major component of all connective tissues. Enzymes are also proteins, and they regulate chemical reactions. For instance, a digestive enzyme called *lactase* breaks down *lactose*, or milk sugar, into two simpler sugars. Another class of proteins includes many kinds of **hormones**. Specialized cells produce and release hormones into the bloodstream to circulate to other areas of the body, where they produce specific effects in tissues and organs. For example, insulin is a hormone produced by cells in the pancreas, and it causes cells in the liver to absorb energy-producing glucose (sugar) from the blood. Lastly, many kinds of proteins can actually enter a cell's nucleus and attach directly to the DNA. These proteins are called regulatory proteins or molecules, because when they bind to the DNA, they can switch genes on and off, thereby influencing how the genes function. As you can see, proteins make us what we are, so it's critical that protein synthesis occur accurately. If it doesn't, physiological development and activities can be disrupted or even prevented.

hemoglobin A protein molecule that occurs in red blood cells and binds to oxygen molecules.

hormones Substances (usually proteins) that are produced by specialized cells and travel to other parts of the body, where they influence chemical reactions and regulate various cellular functions.

Table 3-1   **The Genetic Code**

Amino Acid Symbol	Amino Acid	mRNA Codon	DNA Triplet
Ala	Alanine	GCU, GCC, GCA, GCG	CGA, CGG, CGT, CGC
Arg	Arginine	CGU, CGC, CGA, CGG, AGA, AGG	GCA, GCG, GCT, GCC, TCT, TCC
Asn	Asparagine	AAU, AAC	TTA, TTG
Asp	Aspartic acid	GAU, GAC	CTA, CTG
Cys	Cysteine	UGU, UGC	ACA, ACG
Gln	Glutamine	CAA, CAG	GTT, GTC
Glu	Glutamic acid	GAA, GAG	CTT, CTC
Gly	Glycine	GGU, GGC, GGA, GGG	CCA, CCG, CCT, CCC
His	Histidine	CAU, CAC	GTA, GTG
Ile	Isoleucine	AUU, AUC, AUA	TAA, TAG, TAT
Leu	Leucine	UUA, UUG, CUU, CUC, CUA, CUG	AAT, AAC, GAA, GAG, GAT, GAC
Lys	Lysine	AAA, AAG	TTT, TTC
Met	Methionine	AUG	TAC
Phe	Phenylalanine	UUU, UUC	AAA, AAG
Pro	Proline	CCU, CCC, CCA, CCG	GGA, GGG, GGT, GGC
Ser	Serine	UCU, UCC, UCA, UCG, AGU, AGC	AGA, AGG, AGT, AGC, TCA, TCG
Thr	Threonine	ACU, ACC, ACA, ACG	TGA, TGG, TGT, TGC
Trp	Tryptophan	UGG	ACC
Tyr	Tyrosine	UAU, UAC	ATA, ATG
Val	Valine	GUU, GUC, GUA, GUG	CAA, CAG, CAT, CAC
Terminating triplets		UAA, UAG, UGA	ATT, ATC, ACT

Proteins are made up of chains of smaller molecules called **amino acids**. In all, there are 20 amino acids, which are combined in different amounts and sequences to produce potentially millions of proteins. What makes proteins different from one another is the number of amino acids involved and the sequence in which they are arranged. This means that a protein can't function correctly unless its amino acids are arranged in the proper order.

DNA serves as a recipe for making a protein, because it's the sequence of DNA bases that ultimately determines the order of amino acids in a protein molecule. In the DNA instructions, a *triplet*, or group of three bases, specifies a particular amino acid. For example, if a triplet consists of the base sequence cytosine, guanine, and adenine (CGA), it specifies the amino acid *alanine* (Table 3-1). So, a small portion of the DNA recipe might look like this (except there wouldn't be spaces between the triplets): AGA CGA ACA ACC TAC TTT TTC CTT AAG GTC.

Protein synthesis is a little more complicated than the last paragraph suggests, and it involves an additional molecule similar to DNA called RNA (ribonucleic acid). While DNA provides the instructions for protein synthesis, it's RNA that reads the instructions and actually assembles amino acids to form proteins.

The entire sequence of DNA bases responsible for the synthesis of a protein or, in some cases, part of a protein, is referred to as a **gene**. Or, to put it another way, a gene is a segment of DNA that dictates the sequence of amino acids in a particular protein. A gene may consist of only a few hundred bases, or it may be composed of thousands. If the sequence of DNA bases is changed by a **mutation**, some proteins may not be manufactured, and the cell (or indeed the organism) may not function properly, if at all.

This definition of a gene is technically correct. But it's important to emphasize that gene action is complex and only partly understood. For example, the DNA segments that ultimately are translated into amino acids are called *exons*. But most of the DNA in a gene isn't expressed during protein synthesis, and these unexpressed segments are called *introns* (Fig. 3-5). Even though introns aren't involved in protein manufacture, they may have other functions, and it's the combination of introns and exons interspersed along a DNA strand that makes up the unit we call a gene.

We usually think of genes as coding for the production of proteins that make up body tissues. But many genes, called **regulatory genes**, make proteins that switch other genes on and off, so they influence how those genes work. Obviously, regulatory genes are critical for individual organisms, and they also play an important role in evolution. For example, many of the anatomical differences between humans and chimpanzees are the results of evolutionary changes in regulatory genes in both lineages.

Homeobox genes, or *Hox* genes, are extremely important regulatory genes. *Hox* genes direct early segmentation of embryonic tissues, including those that give rise to the spine and thoracic muscles. They also interact with other genes to determine the identity and characteristics of developing body segments and structures, but not their actual development. For example, homeobox genes determine where limb buds will appear in a developing embryo. They also establish the number and overall pattern of the different types of vertebrae, the bones that make up the spine (Fig. 3-6).

Homeobox genes are highly conserved, meaning they've been maintained pretty much throughout evolutionary history. They're present in all invertebrates (such as worms and insects) and vertebrates, and they don't vary greatly from species to species. This type of conservation means not only that these genes are vitally important, but also that they evolved from genes that were present in some of the earliest forms of life. Moreover,

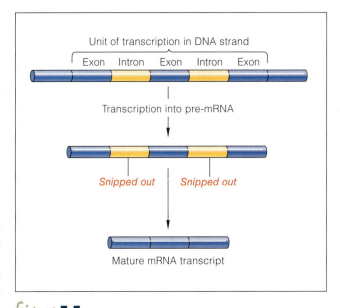

Figure 3-5

Diagram of a DNA sequence being transcribed. The introns are deleted from the pre-mRNA before it leaves the cell nucleus. The remaining mature mRNA contains only exons.

amino acids Small molecules that are the components of proteins.

gene A sequence of DNA bases that specifies the order of amino acids in an entire protein or, in many cases, a portion of a protein, or any functional product. A gene may be made up of hundreds or thousands of DNA bases.

mutation A change in DNA. The term can refer to changes in DNA bases as well as changes in chromosome number or structure.

regulatory genes Genes that code for the production of proteins that can bind to DNA and modify the action of genes. Many are active only during certain stages of development.

homeobox (*Hox*) genes An evolutionary ancient family of regulatory genes. *Hox* genes direct the segmentation and patterning of the overall body plan during embryonic development.

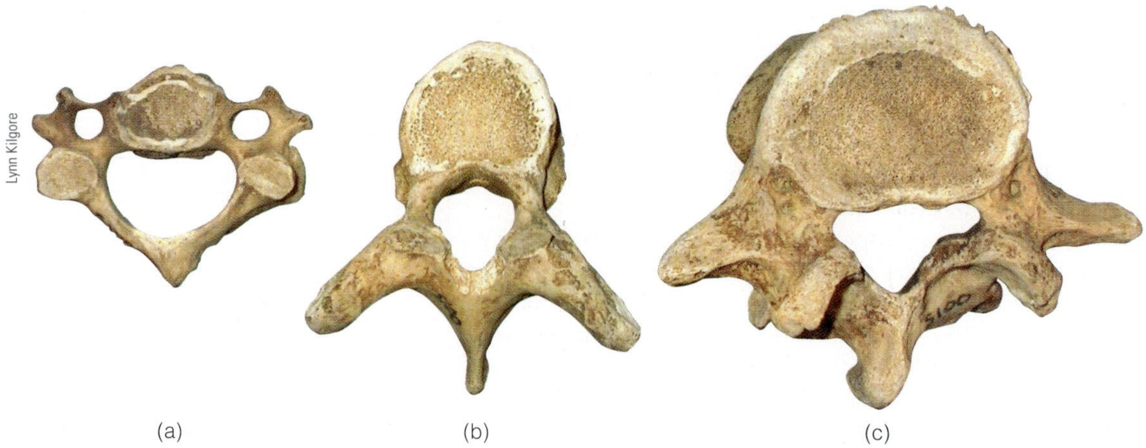

Lynn Kilgore

(a)   (b)   (c)

Figure **3-6**

The differences in these three vertebrae, from different regions of the spine, are caused by the action of *Hox* genes during embryonic development. The cervical (neck) vertebrae (a) have characteristics that differentiate them from the thoracic vertebrae (which are attached to the ribs) (b) and also from the lumbar vertebrae of the lower back (c). *Hox* genes determine the overall pattern not only of each type of vertebra but also of each individual vertebra.

changes in the behavior of homeobox genes are responsible for various physical differences between species.

A final point is that the genetic code is universal; at least on earth, DNA is the genetic material in all forms of life. The DNA of all organisms, from bacteria to oak trees to human beings, is composed of the same molecules using the same kinds of instructions. Consequently, the DNA triplet CGA, for example, specifies the amino acid alanine, regardless of species. These similarities imply biological relationships among, and an ultimate common ancestry for, all forms of life. What makes oak trees different from humans isn't differences in their DNA material, but differences in how that material is arranged and regulated.

Cell Division: Mitosis and Meiosis

Throughout much of a cell's life, its DNA exists as an uncoiled, threadlike substance. (Incredibly, the nuclei of every one of your somatic cells contain an estimated 6 feet of DNA!) However, at various times in the life of most types of cells, normal functions are interrupted and the cell divides. Cell division results in the production of new cells, and during this process, the DNA becomes tightly coiled and is visible under a light microscope as a set of discrete structures called **chromosomes** (Fig. 3-7).

A chromosome is composed of a DNA molecule and associated proteins (Fig. 3-8). If chromosomes were visible during normal cell function, they would appear as single-stranded structures. However, during the early stages of cell division, they are made up of two strands, or two DNA molecules, joined together at a constricted area called the **centromere**. The reason there are two strands is simple: The DNA molecules have *replicated* and one strand is an exact copy of the other.

Every species is characterized by a specific number of chromosomes in somatic cells (Table 3-2). In humans there are 46 chromosomes, organized into 23 pairs. Chimpanzees and gorillas have 48, or 24 pairs. This difference in chromosome number doesn't necessarily mean that humans have less DNA; it only indicates that the DNA is packaged differently in the three species.

chromosomes Discrete structures, composed of DNA and protein, found only in the nuclei of cells. Chromosomes are visible only under magnification during certain stages of cell division.

centromere The constricted portion of a chromosome. After replication, the two strands of a double-stranded chromosome are joined at the centromere.

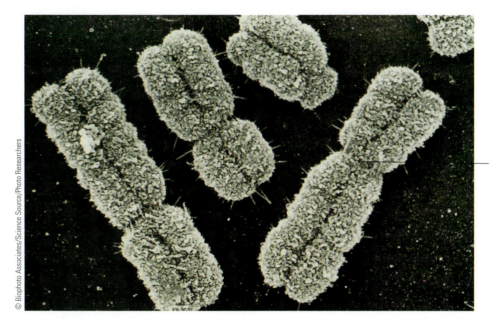

Figure **3-7**

Scanning electron micrograph of human chromosomes during cell division. Note that these chromosomes are composed of two strands, or two DNA molecules.

Centromere

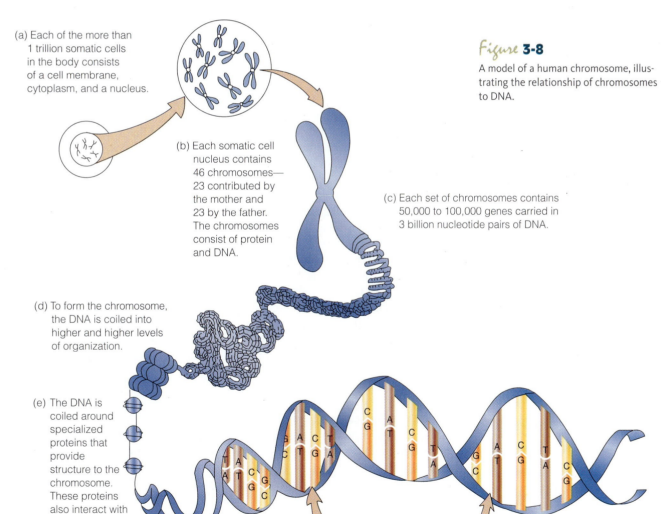

(a) Each of the more than 1 trillion somatic cells in the body consists of a cell membrane, cytoplasm, and a nucleus.

Figure **3-8**

A model of a human chromosome, illustrating the relationship of chromosomes to DNA.

(b) Each somatic cell nucleus contains 46 chromosomes—23 contributed by the mother and 23 by the father. The chromosomes consist of protein and DNA.

(c) Each set of chromosomes contains 50,000 to 100,000 genes carried in 3 billion nucleotide pairs of DNA.

(d) To form the chromosome, the DNA is coiled into higher and higher levels of organization.

(e) The DNA is coiled around specialized proteins that provide structure to the chromosome. These proteins also interact with the DNA.

(f) A specific sequence of nucleotide base pairs constitutes a gene.

Table 3-2 **Standard Chromosomal Complement in Various Organisms**

Organism	Chromosome Number in Somatic Cells	Chromosome Number in Gametes
Human (*Homo sapiens*)	46	23
Chimpanzee (*Pan troglodytes*)	48	24
Gorilla (*Gorilla gorilla*)	48	24
Dog (*Canis familiaris*)	78	39
Chicken (*Gallus domesticus*)	78	39
Frog (*Rana pipiens*)	26	13
Housefly (*Musca domestica*)	12	6
Onion (*Allium cepa*)	16	8
Corn (*Zea mays*)	20	10
Tobacco (*Nicotiana tabacum*)	48	24

Source: Cummings, 2000, p. 16.

One member of each chromosomal pair is inherited from the father (paternal), and the other member is inherited from the mother (maternal). Members of chromosomal pairs are alike in size and position of the centromere, but this doesn't mean that partner chromosomes are genetically identical because they aren't; but they do influence the same traits.

There are two basic types of chromosomes: **autosomes** and **sex chromosomes**. Autosomes carry genetic information that governs all physical characteristics except primary sex determination. The two sex chromosomes are the X and Y chromosomes, and the Y chromosome is directly involved in determining maleness. Although the X chromosome is called a sex chromosome, it really functions more like an autosome, since it isn't involved in primary sex determination and it carries genes that influence a number of other traits. In mammals, all genetically normal males have one X and one Y chromosome (XY). However, all genetically normal females have two X chromosomes (XX), and they're female simply because they don't have a Y chromosome. Actually, you could say that femaleness is the default setting.

It's extremely important to understand that *all* autosomes occur in pairs. Normal human somatic cells have 22 pairs of autosomes and one pair of sex chromosomes. It's also important to know that abnormal numbers of autosomes, with few exceptions, are fatal to the individual—usually soon after conception. Although abnormal numbers of sex chromosomes aren't usually fatal, they may result in sterility and can also have other consequences. This means that to function normally, a human cell must possess both members of each chromosomal pair, or a total of 46 chromosomes.

MITOSIS

Cell division in somatic cells is called **mitosis**. Mitosis is the way somatic cells reproduce, and the reproduction of somatic cells is essential to growth and development. In addition, mitosis is the mechanism by which injured tissues heal and older cells are replaced.

In the early stages of mitosis, a cell contains 46 double-stranded chromosomes, which line up in random order along the center of the cell (Fig. 3-9). As the cell wall begins to constrict at the center, the chromosomes split apart at the centromere, so that the two

autosomes All chromosomes except the sex chromosomes.

sex chromosomes The X and Y chromosomes. The Y chromosome determines maleness; in its absence, an embryo develops as a female.

mitosis Simple cell division; the process by which somatic cells divide to produce two identical daughter cells.

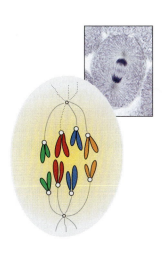

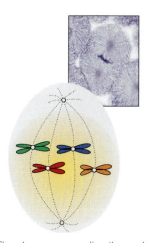

(a) The cell is involved in metabolic activities. DNA replication occurs, but chromosomes are not visible.

(b) The nuclear membrane disappears, and double-stranded chromosomes are visible.

(c) The chromosomes align themselves at the center of the cell.

(d) The chromosomes split at the centromere, and the strands separate and move to opposite ends of the dividing cell.

(e) The cell membrane pinches in as the cell continues to divide. The chromosomes begin to uncoil (not shown here).

(f) After mitosis is complete, there are two identical daughter cells. The nuclear membrane is present, and chromosomes are no longer visible.

strands are separated. Once the two strands are apart, they pull away from each other and move to opposite ends of the dividing cell. At this point, each strand is now a distinct chromosome, *composed of one DNA molecule*. Following the separation of chromosome strands, the cell wall pinches in and becomes sealed, so that two new cells are formed, each with a full complement of DNA, or 46 chromosomes.

Mitosis is referred to as "simple cell division" because a somatic cell divides one time to produce two daughter cells that are genetically identical to each other and to the original cell. In mitosis, the original cell possesses 46 chromosomes, and each new daughter cell inherits an exact copy of all 46. This precise arrangement is made possible by the ability of the DNA molecule to replicate. Thus, DNA replication ensures that the amount of genetic material remains constant from one generation of cells to the next.

Figure **3-9**

A diagrammatic representation of mitosis. Above four of the illustrations are photomicrographs of the actual events depicted in the drawings.

MEIOSIS

While mitosis produces new cells, **meiosis** can lead to the development of an entire new organism because it produces reproductive cells. Although meiosis is similar to mitosis, it's a more complicated process, because in meiosis there are two divisions instead of one. Also, meiosis produces four daughter cells, not two, and each of these four cells contains only half the original number of chromosomes (Fig. 3-10).

During meiosis, specialized cells in male testes and female ovaries divide and eventually develop into sperm and egg cells. Initially, these cells contain the full complement of chromosomes (46 in humans), but after the first division (called "reduction division"), the number of chromosomes in the two daughter cells is 23, or half the original number (Fig. 3-10). This reduction in chromosome number is crucial because the resulting gamete, with its 23 chromosomes, may eventually unite with another gamete that also has 23 chromosomes. The product of this union is a *zygote*, or fertilized egg, in which the original number of chromosomes (46) has been restored. In other words, a zygote inherits the exact amount of DNA it needs (half from each parent) to develop and function normally. But if it weren't for *reduction division* in meiosis, it wouldn't be possible to maintain the correct number of chromosomes from one generation to the next.

During the first division of meiosis, partner chromosomes come together to form pairs of double-stranded chromosomes. Then the *pairs* of chromosomes line up along the cell's equator (see Fig. 3-10). Pairing of partner chromosomes is extremely important, because while they're together, the members of each pair exchange genetic information in a critical process called **recombination** or *crossing over*. Pairing is also important because it facilitates the accurate reduction of chromosome number by ensuring that each new daughter cell receives only one member of each pair.

As a cell begins to divide, the chromosomes themselves remain intact (that is, double-stranded), but *members of pairs* pull apart and move to opposite ends of the cell. After the first division, there are two new daughter cells, but they aren't identical to each other or to the parent cell. They're different because each cell contains only one member of each chromosome pair and therefore only 23 chromosomes. But all the chromosomes still have two strands (see Fig. 3-10).

The second meiotic division happens pretty much the same way it does in mitosis. In the two newly formed cells, the 23 double-stranded chromosomes line up at the cell's center and, as in mitosis, the strands of each chromosome separate at the centromere and move apart. Once this second division is completed, there are four daughter cells, each with 23 single-stranded chromosomes. (For a diagrammatic representation of the differences between mitosis and meiosis, see Fig. 3-11.)

The Evolutionary Significance of Meiosis Meiosis occurs in all sexually reproducing organisms, and it's an extremely important evolutionary innovation because it increases genetic variation in populations. Members of sexually reproducing species aren't genetically identical **clones** of other individuals because they inherit a combination of genes from two parents. As a result, each individual represents a unique combination of genes that, in all likelihood, has never occurred before and will never occur again. The genetic uniqueness of individuals is further increased by recombination between partner chromosomes during meiosis, because recombination ensures that chromosomes aren't transmitted intact from one generation to the next. Instead, in every generation, parental contributions are reshuffled in an almost infinite number of combinations, altering the genetic composition of chromosomes even before they are passed on.

As we mentioned in Chapter 2, natural selection acts on genetic variation in populations. If all individuals in a population were genetically identical from one generation to the next, natural selection (and evolution) couldn't occur. Although there are other sources of variation (mutation being the only source of *new* variation), sexual reproduction and meiosis are of major evolutionary importance because they enhance the role of natural selection in populations.

meiosis Cell division in specialized cells in ovaries and testes. Meiosis involves two divisions and results in four daughter cells, each containing only half the original number of chromosomes. These cells can develop into gametes.

recombination The exchange of DNA between paired chromosomes during meiosis; also called *crossing over*.

clones A clone is an organism that is genetically identical to another organism. In addition to entire organisms, the term may also be used to refer to genetically identical DNA segments and molecules.

Chromosomes are not visible as DNA replication occurs in a cell preparing to divide.

Figure **3-10**

A diagrammatic representation of meiosis. The five circles are photomicrographs of the stages being illustrated.

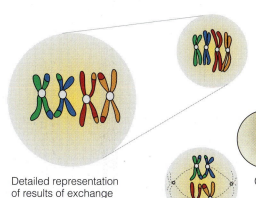

Double-stranded chromosomes become visible, and partner chromosomes exchange genetic material in a process called recombination or crossing over.

Detailed representation of results of exchange of genetic material during recombination

Chromosome pairs migrate to the center of the cell.

FIRST DIVISION (reduction division)

Partner chromosomes separate, and members of each pair move to opposite ends of the dividing cell. This results in only half the original number of chromosomes in each new daughter cell.

After the first meiotic division, there are two daughter cells, each containing only one member of each original chromosomal pair, or 23 nonpartner chromosomes.

SECOND DIVISION

In this division, the chromosomes split at the centromere, and the strands move to opposite sides of the cell.

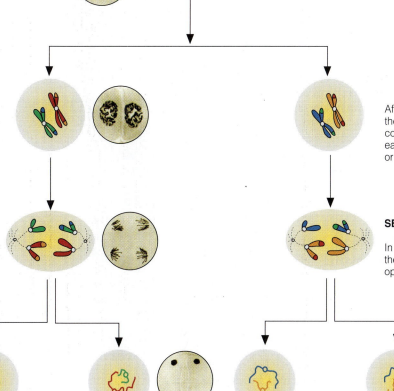

After the second division, meiosis results in four daughter cells. These may mature to become functional gametes, containing only half the DNA in the original cell.

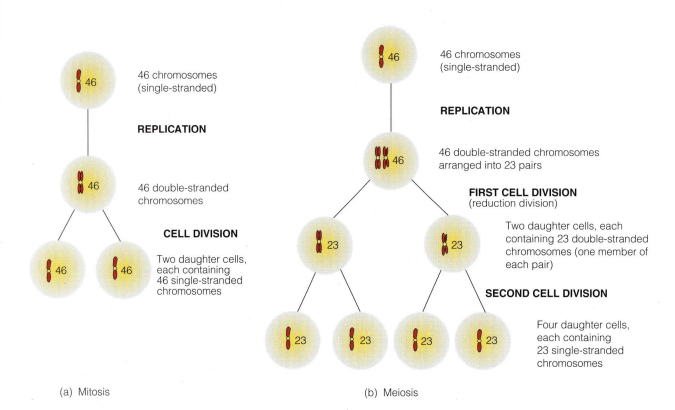

46 chromosomes
(single-stranded)

REPLICATION

46 double-stranded
chromosomes

CELL DIVISION

Two daughter cells,
each containing
46 single-stranded
chromosomes

(a) Mitosis

46 chromosomes
(single-stranded)

REPLICATION

46 double-stranded chromosomes
arranged into 23 pairs

FIRST CELL DIVISION
(reduction division)

Two daughter cells, each
containing 23 double-stranded
chromosomes (one member of
each pair)

SECOND CELL DIVISION

Four daughter cells,
each containing
23 single-stranded
chromosomes

(b) Meiosis

Figure **3-11**

Mitosis and meiosis compared. (a) In mitosis, one division produces two daughter cells, each of which contains 46 chromosomes. (b) Meiosis is characterized by two divisions. After the first, there are two cells, each containing only 23 chromosomes (one member of each original chromosome pair). Each daughter cell divides again, so that the final result is four cells, each with only half the original number of chromosomes.

hybrids Offspring of mixed ancestry; heterozygotes.

The Genetic Principles Discovered by Mendel

It wasn't until Gregor Mendel (1822–1884) addressed the question of heredity that it began to be resolved (Fig. 3-12). Mendel was a monk living in an abbey in what is now the Czech Republic. At the time he began his research, he had already studied botany, physics, and mathematics at the University of Vienna, and he also had performed various experiments in the monastery gardens. These experiments led him to explore the various ways in which physical traits, such as color or height, could be expressed in plant **hybrids**.

Mendel worked with garden peas, concentrating on seven different traits, each of which could be expressed in two different ways (Fig. 3-13). We want to emphasize that the principles Mendel discovered apply to all biological organisms, not just peas; so we discuss Mendel's pea experiments only to illustrate the basic rules of inheritance.

MENDEL'S PRINCIPLE OF SEGREGATION

Mendel began by crossing parent (P) plants that produced only tall plants with others that produced only short ones (Fig. 3-14). Blending theories of inheritance would have predicted that the hybrid offspring of the initial crosses (called the F$_1$ plants) would be intermediate in height, but they weren't. Instead, they were all tall.

Figure **3-12**

Portrait of Gregor Mendel.

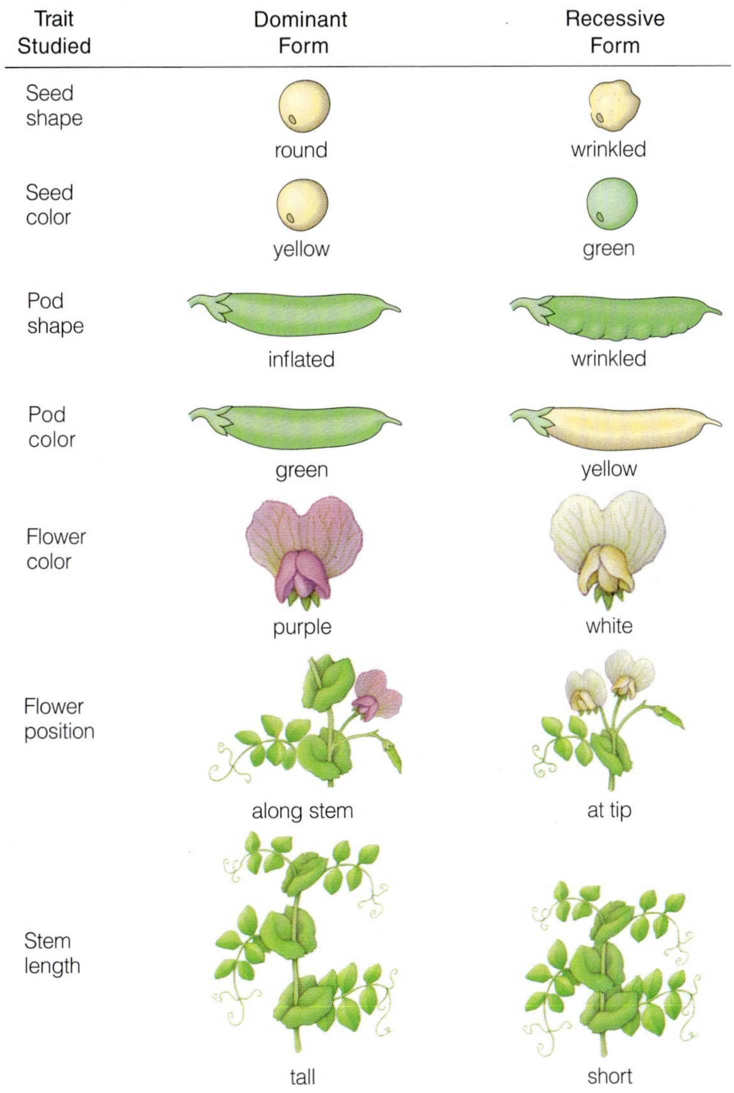

Trait Studied	Dominant Form	Recessive Form
Seed shape	round	wrinkled
Seed color	yellow	green
Pod shape	inflated	wrinkled
Pod color	green	yellow
Flower color	purple	white
Flower position	along stem	at tip
Stem length	tall	short

Figure **3-13**

The traits Mendel studied in peas.

Next, he allowed the F_1 plants to self-fertilize and produce a second generation (the F_2 generation). But this time, only about ¾ of the offspring were tall, and the remaining ¼ were short. One expression (shortness) of the trait (height) had completely disappeared in the F_1 plants and reappeared in the F_2 plants. Moreover, the expression that was present in all the F_1 generation was more common in the F_2 generation, occurring in a ratio of approximately 3:1, or three tall plants for every short one.

To Mendel, these results suggested that different expressions of a trait are controlled by discrete *units* or particles, which we would call genes. The units occur in pairs, and offspring inherit one unit from each parent. Mendel also realized that the members of a pair of units separate into different sex cells and were again united with another member during fertilization of the egg. This discovery was the basis of Mendel's *first principle of inheritance*, known as the **principle of segregation**.

Today we know that meiosis explains Mendel's principle of segregation. You will remember that during meiosis, paired chromosomes, and the genes they carry, separate from each other and are distributed to different gametes. However, in the zygote, the full complement of chromosomes is restored, and both members of each chromosome pair are present in the offspring.

principle of segregation Genes (alleles) occur in pairs (because chromosomes occur in pairs). During gamete production, the members of each gene pair separate, so that each gamete contains one member of each pair. During fertilization, the full number of chromosomes is restored, and members of gene pairs (alleles) are reunited.

Figure 3-14

Results of crosses when only one trait at a time is considered.

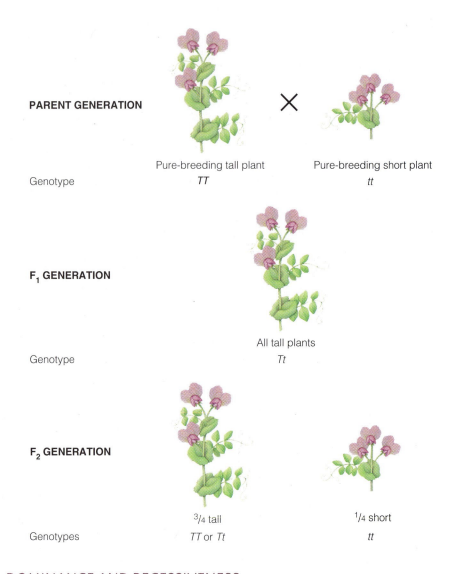

PARENT GENERATION

Pure-breeding tall plant   Pure-breeding short plant

Genotype   *TT*   *tt*

F₁ GENERATION

All tall plants

Genotype   *Tt*

F₂ GENERATION

³/₄ tall   ¹/₄ short

Genotypes   *TT* or *Tt*   *tt*

recessive Describing a trait that is not expressed in heterozygotes; also refers to the allele that governs the trait. For a recessive allele to be expressed, there must be two copies of the allele (i.e., the individual must be homozygous).

dominant Describing a trait governed by an allele that can be expressed in the presence of another, different allele (i.e., in heterozygotes). Dominant alleles prevent the expression of recessive alleles in heterozygotes. (*Note*: This is the definition of *complete* dominance.)

locus (*pl.*, loci) (lo´-kus, lo-sigh´) The position on a chromosome where a given gene occurs. The term is sometimes used interchangeably with *gene*.

alleles Alternate forms of a gene. Alleles occur at the same locus on paired chromosomes and thus govern the same trait. However, because they are different, their action may result in different expressions of that trait. The term *allele* is often used synonymously with *gene*.

homozygous Having the same allele at the same locus on both members of a chromosome pair.

DOMINANCE AND RECESSIVENESS

Mendel also realized that the expression that was absent in the first generation hadn't actually disappeared at all. It was still there but it was masked somehow and couldn't be expressed. He described the trait that seemed to disappear as **recessive**, and he called the expressed trait **dominant**. With this fact in mind, Mendel developed the important principles of *recessiveness* and *dominance*, and they're still important concepts in the field of genetics.

As you already know, a *gene* is a segment of DNA that directs the production of a specific protein, part of a protein, or any functional element. Each gene has a specific location on a chromosome, and that position is called its **locus** (*pl.*, loci). At numerous genetic loci, however, there may be more than one possible form of the gene, and these variations of genes at specific loci are called **alleles** (Fig. 3-15). Simply stated, alleles are different forms of a gene, each of which can direct the cell to make a slightly different version of the same protein and, ultimately, a different expression of a trait.

As it turns out, plant height in garden peas is controlled by two different alleles at one genetic locus. The allele that determines that a plant will be tall is dominant to the allele for short. (It's worth mentioning that height isn't governed this way in all plants.) In Mendel's experiments, all the parent (P) plants had two copies of the same allele, either dominant or recessive, depending on whether they were tall or short. When two copies of the same allele are present, the individual is said to be **homozygous**. Thus, all the tall parent plants were homozygous for the dominant allele, and all the short parent plants were homozygous for the recessive allele. (This explains why tall plants crossed with tall plants produced only tall offspring, and short plants crossed with short plants produced only short offspring; they were all homozygous, so they lacked genetic variation at this locus.) However, all the hybrid F_1 plants had inherited one allele from each parent plant, and therefore, they all possessed two different alleles at specific loci. Individuals that possess two different alleles at a locus are **heterozygous**.

Figure 3-14 illustrates the crosses that Mendel initially performed. Uppercase letters refer to dominant alleles (or dominant traits), and lowercase letters refer to recessive alleles (or recessive traits). Therefore,

T = the allele for tallness
t = the allele for shortness

The same symbols are combined to describe an individual's actual genetic makeup, or **genotype**. The term *genotype* can be used to refer to an organism's entire genetic makeup or to the alleles at a specific genetic locus. Thus, the genotypes of the plants in Mendel's experiments were

TT = homozygous tall plants
Tt = heterozygous tall plants
tt = homozygous short plants

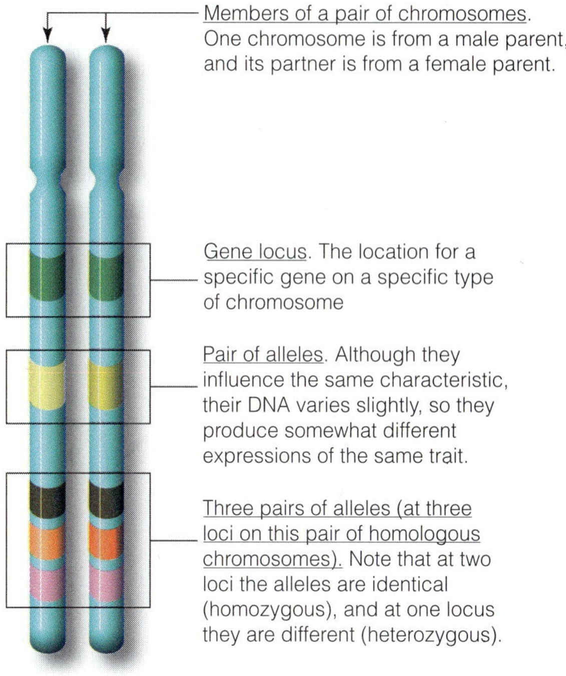

Figure 3-16 is a *Punnett square*. It represents the different ways the alleles can be combined when the F_1 plants are self-fertilized to produce an F_2 generation. In this way, the figure shows the genotypes that are possible in the F_2 generation, and it also demonstrates that approximately ¼ of the F_2 plants are homozygous dominant (TT); ½ are heterozygous (Tt); and the remaining ¼ are homozygous recessive (tt).

The Punnett square also shows the proportions of F_2 **phenotypes**, or the observed physical manifestations of genes, and it illustrates why Mendel saw three tall plants for every short plant in the F_2 generation. By examining the Punnett square, you can see that ¼ of the F_2 plants will be tall because they have the TT genotype. An additional ½ of the plants, which are heterozygous (Tt), will also be tall because T is dominant to t and will therefore be expressed in the phenotype. The remaining ¼ are homozygous recessive (tt), and they will be short because no dominant allele is present. It's important to note that the *only* way a recessive allele can be expressed is if it occurs with another recessive allele—that is, if the individual is homozygous recessive at the particular locus in question.

Members of a pair of chromosomes. One chromosome is from a male parent, and its partner is from a female parent.

Gene locus. The location for a specific gene on a specific type of chromosome

Pair of alleles. Although they influence the same characteristic, their DNA varies slightly, so they produce somewhat different expressions of the same trait.

Three pairs of alleles (at three loci on this pair of homologous chromosomes). Note that at two loci the alleles are identical (homozygous), and at one locus they are different (heterozygous).

Figure 3-15

As this diagram illustrates, alleles are located at the same locus on paired chromosomes, but they aren't always identical. For the sake of simplicity, they are shown here on single-stranded chromosomes.

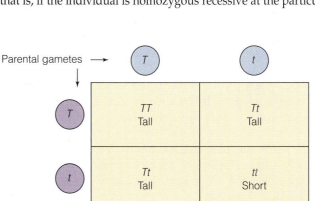

Figure 3-16

Punnett square representing possible genotypes and phenotypes and their proportions in the F_2 generation. The circles across the top and at the left of the Punnett square represent the gametes of the F_1 parents. The four squares illustrate that ¼ of the F_2 plants can be expected to be homozygous tall (TT); another ½ also can be expected to be tall but will be heterozygous (Tt); and the remaining ¼ can be expected to be short (tt). Thus, ¾ can be expected to be tall and ¼ to be short.

heterozygous Having different alleles at the same locus on members of a chromosome pair.

genotype The genetic makeup of an individual. Genotype can refer to an organism's entire genetic makeup or to the alleles at a particular locus.

phenotypes The observable or detectable physical characteristics of an organism; the detectable expressions of genotypes.

MENDEL'S PRINCIPLE OF INDEPENDENT ASSORTMENT

Mendel also showed that traits aren't necessarily inherited together by demonstrating that plant height and seed color are independent of each other. In other words, he proposed that any tall plant had a 50-50 chance of producing either yellow or green seeds (peas). This relationship, called the **principle of independent assortment**, says that the units (genes) that code for different traits assort independently of one another during gamete formation. Today we know that this happens because the genes that control plant height and seed color are located on different chromosomes, and during meiosis, the chromosomes travel to newly forming cells independently of one another. But if Mendel had used just *any* two traits, his results would have sometimes been different. For example, if the two traits in question were influenced by genes located on the same chromosome, then they would more likely be inherited together, in which case they wouldn't conform to Mendel's ratios. The ratios came out as he predicted because the loci governing most of the traits he chose were carried on different chromosomes. Even though Mendel didn't know about chromosomes, he was certainly aware that all traits weren't independent of one another in the F_2 generation, so he appears to have reported only on those characteristics that did in fact illustrate independent assortment.

In 1866, Mendel's results were published, but their methodology and statistical nature were beyond the thinking of the time, and the significance of his work wasn't appreciated. However, by the end of the nineteenth century, several investigators had made important contributions to the understanding of chromosomes and cell division. These discoveries paved the way for the acceptance of Mendel's work by 1900, when three different groups of scientists came across his paper. Unfortunately, Mendel had died 16 years earlier and never saw his work substantiated.

Mendelian Inheritance in Humans

Mendelian traits (also referred to as *discrete traits* or *traits of simple inheritance*) are controlled by alleles at *one* genetic locus). The most comprehensive listing of Mendelian traits in humans is V. A. McKusick's (1998) *Mendelian Inheritance in Man*. This volume, as well as its continuously updated online version (www.ncbi.nlm.nih.gov/omim/), currently lists almost 18,000 characteristics that are inherited according to Mendelian principles.

Although some Mendelian traits have a visible phenotypic expression, most don't. Most are biochemical in nature, and many genetic disorders (some of which do produce visible phenotypic abnormalities) result from harmful alleles inherited in Mendelian fashion (Table 3-3). So if it seems like textbooks overemphasize genetic disease when they discuss Mendelian traits, it's because many of the known Mendelian characteristics are the results of harmful alleles.

Blood groups, like the ABO system, provide some of the best examples of Mendelian traits in humans. The ABO system is governed by three alleles, *A*, *B*, and *O*, that occur at the ABO locus on the ninth chromosome.* Although three alleles are present in populations, an individual can possess only two. These alleles determine which ABO blood type a person has by coding for the production of special substances, called **antigens**, on the surface of red blood cells. If only antigen A is present, the blood type (phenotype) is A; if only B is present, the blood type is B; if both are present, the blood type is AB; and when neither is present, the blood type is O (Table 3-4).

Dominance and recessiveness are clearly illustrated by the ABO system. The *O* allele is recessive to both *A* and *B*; therefore, if a person has type O blood, he or she must be homozygous (*OO*) for the *O* allele. Since both *A* and *B* are dominant to *O*, an individual

principle of independent assortment The distribution of one pair of alleles into gametes does not influence the distribution of another pair. The genes controlling different traits are inherited independently of one another.

Mendelian traits Characteristics that are influenced by alleles at only one genetic locus. Examples include many blood types, such as ABO. Many genetic disorders, including sickle-cell anemia and Tay-Sachs disease, are also Mendelian traits.

antigens Large molecules found on the surface of cells. Several different loci governing antigens on red and white blood cells are known. (Foreign antigens provoke an immune response in individuals.)

---

* Human chromosomes are numbered in order of size of the autosomes 1 through 22) plus X and Y.

Table 3-3   Some Mendelian Traits in Humans

Dominant Traits Condition	Manifestations	Recessive Traits Condition	Manifestations
Achondroplasia	Dwarfism due to growth defects involving the long bones of the arms and legs; trunk and head size usually normal.	Cystic fibrosis	Among the most common genetic (Mendelian) disorders among European Americans; abnormal secretions of the exocrine glands, with pronounced involvement of the pancreas; most patients develop obstructive lung disease. Until the recent development of new treatments, only about half of all patients survived to early adulthood.
Brachydactyly	Shortened fingers and toes.		
Familial hyper-cholesterolemia	Elevated cholesterol levels and cholesterol plaque deposition; a leading cause of heart disease, with death frequently occurring by middle age.		
Neurofibromatosis	Symptoms range from the appearance of abnormal skin pigmentation to large tumors resulting in severe deformities; can, in extreme cases, lead to paralysis, blindness, and death.	Tay-Sachs disease	Most common among Ashkenazi Jews; degeneration of the nervous system beginning at about 6 months of age; lethal by age 2 or 3 years.
Marfan syndrome	The eyes and cardiovascular and skeletal systems are affected; symptoms include greater than average height, long arms and legs, eye problems, and enlargement of the aorta; death due to rupture of the aorta is common. Abraham Lincoln may have had Marfan syndrome.	Phenylketonuria (PKU)	Inability to metabolize the amino acid phenylalanine; results in mental retardation if left untreated during childhood; treatment involves strict dietary management and some supplementation.
Huntington disease	Progressive degeneration of the nervous system accompanied by dementia and seizures; age of onset variable but commonly between 30 and 40 years.	Albinism	Inability to produce normal amounts of the pigment melanin; results in very fair, untannable skin, light blond hair, and light eyes; may also be associated with vision problems. (There is more than one form of albinism.)
Camptodactyly	Malformation of the hands whereby the fingers, usually the little finger, is permanently contracted.	Sickle-cell anemia	Abnormal form of hemoglobin (Hb^S) that results in collapsed red blood cells, blockage of capillaries, reduced blood flow to organs, and, without treatment, death.
Hypodontia of upper lateral incisors	Upper lateral incisors are absent or only partially formed (peg-shaped). Pegged incisors are a partial expression of the allele.	Thalassemia	A group of disorders characterized by reduced or absent alpha or beta chains in the hemoglobin molecule; results in severe anemia and, in some forms, death.
Cleft chin	Dimple or depression in the middle of the chin; less prominent in females than in males.	Absence of permanent dentition	Failure of the permanent dentition to erupt. The primary dentition is not affected.
PTC tasting	The ability to taste the bitter substance phenylthiocarbamide (PTC). Tasting thresholds vary, suggesting that alleles at another locus may also exert an influence.		

with blood type A can have one of two genotypes: *AA* or *AO*. The same is true of type B, which results from the genotypes *BB* and *BO*. However, type AB presents a slightly different situation and is an example of **codominance**.

Codominance is seen when two different alleles occur in heterozygotes, but instead of one having the ability to mask the expression of the other, the products of *both* are expressed in the phenotype. So, when both *A* and *B* alleles are present, both A and B antigens can be detected on the surface of red blood cells, and the blood type is AB.

Several genetic disorders are inherited as dominant traits (see Table 3-3). This means that if a person inherits only one copy of a harmful dominant allele, the condition it causes will be present, regardless of the existence of a different, recessive allele on the partner chromosome.

codominance The expression of both alleles in heterozygotes. In this situation, neither is dominant or recessive; thus, both influence the phenotype.

Table 3-4   ABO Genotypes and Associated Phenotypes

Genotype	Antigens on Red Blood Cells	ABO Blood Type (Phenotype)
AA, AO	A	A
BB, BO	B	B
AB	A and B	AB
OO	None	O

Recessive conditions (see Table 3-3) are commonly associated with the lack of a substance, usually an enzyme. For a person actually to have a recessive disorder, he or she must have *two* copies of the recessive allele that causes it. Heterozygotes who have only one copy of a harmful recessive allele are unaffected, but they're frequently called carriers.

Although carriers don't actually have the recessive condition they carry, they can pass the allele that causes it to their children. (Remember, half their gametes will carry the recessive allele.) If the carrier's mate is also a carrier, then it's possible for them to have a child who has two copies of the allele, and that child will be affected. In fact, in a mating between two carriers, the risk of having an affected child is 25 percent (see Fig. 3-16).

Misconceptions Regarding Dominance and Recessiveness

Traditional methods of teaching genetics have led to some misunderstanding of dominance and recessiveness. Thus, most people have the impression that these phenomena are all-or-nothing situations. This misconception especially pertains to recessive alleles, and the general view is that when these alleles occur in carriers, they have absolutely no effect on the phenotype. That is, they are completely inactivated by the other allele. Certainly, this is how it appeared to Gregor Mendel and, until the last two or three decades, to most geneticists.

However, modern biochemical techniques have shown that recessive alleles actually do have some effect on the phenotype, although these effects aren't always apparent through simple observation. It turns out that in heterozygotes, many recessive alleles act to reduce, but not eliminate, the gene products they influence. In fact, it's now clear that our *perception* of recessive alleles greatly depends on whether we examine them at the directly observable phenotypic level or the biochemical level.

Similar misconceptions also relate to dominant alleles. Most people see dominant alleles as somehow "stronger" or "better," and there is always the mistaken notion that dominant alleles are more common in populations. These misconceptions undoubtedly stem from the label "dominant" and some of its connotations. However, in genetic usage, those connotations are misleading. If dominant alleles were always more common, then a majority of people would have such conditions as achondroplasia and Marfan syndrome (see Table 3-3). But, as you know, most people don't.

The relationships between recessive and dominant alleles and their functions are more complicated than they first appeared to be. Previously held views of dominance and recessiveness were guided by available technologies; as genetic technologies continue to change, new theories will emerge, and our perceptions will be further altered. (This is another example of how new techniques and continued hypothesis testing can lead to a revision of hypotheses and theories.) In fact, although dominance and recessiveness will remain important factors in genetics, it's clear that the ways in which these concepts will be taught will be adapted to accommodate new discoveries.

Polygenic Inheritance

Mendelian traits are said to be *discrete*, or *discontinuous*, because their phenotypic expressions don't overlap; instead, they fall into clearly defined categories (Fig. 3-17a). For example, Mendel's pea plants were either short or tall, but none was intermediate in height. In the ABO system, the four phenotypes are completely distinct from one another; there is no intermediate form between type A and type B to represent a gradation between the two. In other words, Mendelian traits don't show *continuous* variation.

However, many traits do have a wide range of phenotypic expressions that form a graded series. These are called **polygenic**, or *continuous*, traits (Fig. 3-17b). While Mendelian traits are governed by only one genetic locus, polygenic characteristics are governed by two or more loci, with each locus making a contribution to the phenotype. For example,

polygenic Referring to traits that are influenced by genes at two or more loci. Examples of such traits are stature, skin color, and eye color. Many polygenic traits are also influenced by environmental factors.

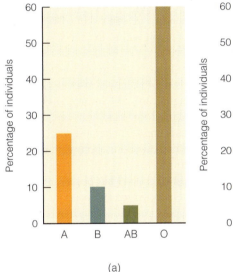

(a)

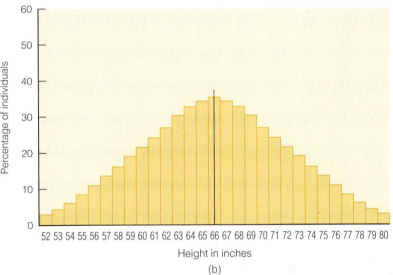

(b)

Figure **3-17**

(a) This bar chart shows the discontinuous distribution of a Mendelian trait (ABO blood type) in a hypothetical population. Expression of the trait is described in terms of frequencies. (b) This histogram represents the continuous expression of a polygenic trait (height) in a large group of people. Notice that the percentage of extremely short or tall individuals is low; most people are closer to the mean, or average, height, represented by the vertical line at the center of the distribution. (c) A group of male students arranged according to height. The most common height is 70 inches (5´10˝), which is the mean, or average, for this group.

Ray Carson, University of Florida News and Public Affairs

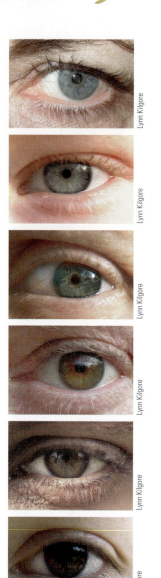

Lynn Kilgore

Lynn Kilgore

Lynn Kilgore

Lynn Kilgore

Lynn Kilgore

Lynn Kilgore

Robert Jurmain

Figure 3-18

Examples of the continuous variation seen in human eye color.

one of the most frequently cited examples of polygenic inheritance in humans is skin color, and the single most important factor influencing skin color is the amount of melanin that is present.

Melanin is a pigment that's produced by specialized cells in the skin, and its production is influenced by several different loci, some of which have been identified (Lamason et al., 2005). The traditional view has been that each locus has at least two alleles. Given that there are several loci and alleles involved, there are numerous ways in which these alleles can combine to influence skin color. If a person inherits 11 alleles coding for maximum pigmentation and only 1 for reduced melanin production, his or her skin will be very dark. Someone who inherits a higher proportion of reduced pigmentation alleles will have lighter skin. This is because in this system, as in some other polygenic systems, there's an *additive effect*. This means that each allele that codes for melanin production makes a contribution to increased amounts of melanin (although for many characteristics the contributions of the alleles aren't all equal). Likewise, each allele coding for reduced melanin production contributes to lighter skin. The effect of multiple alleles at several loci, each making a contribution to a person's skin color, is to produce continuous variation from very dark to very fair skin within the species. (Skin color is also discussed in Chapter 4.)

The additive effects of several alleles at different loci are still believed to play a critical role in human skin color. But a recent study by Lamason et al. (2005) showed that one single gene with two alleles makes a significant, and perhaps disproportionate, contribution to the amount of melanin that cells produce. In addition, at least four other pigmentation genes have been identified, and this is important because until recently, none had been. Thus, it appears that many long-standing questions about variation in human skin color may be answered in the foreseeable future.

Polygenic traits actually account for most of the readily observable phenotypic variation seen in humans, and they have traditionally served as a basis for racial classification (see Chapter 4). In addition to skin color, polygenic inheritance in humans is seen in hair color, weight, stature, eye color (Fig. 3-18), fingerprint pattern and shape of the face. Because they exhibit continuous variation, most polygenic traits can be measured on a scale composed of equal increments (see Fig. 3-17b). For example, height (stature) is measured in feet and inches (or meters and centimeters). If we were to measure height in a large number of individuals, the distribution of measurements would continue uninterrupted from the shortest extreme to the tallest. That's what is meant by the term *continuous traits*.

Because polygenic traits can usually be measured in some way, physical anthropologists treat them statistically. (Incidentally, *all* physical traits measured and discussed in fossils are polygenic.) By using simple summary statistics, such as the *mean* (average) or *standard deviation* (a measure of variation within a group), scientists can create basic descriptions of, and make comparisons between, populations. For example, a researcher might be interested in average height in two different populations and whether any differences between the two are significant, and if so, why. However, the types of statistical tests that would be used in such a study can't be used to examine Mendelian traits, because they can't be measured in the same way. Mendelian traits are either present or they aren't. Or they're expressed one way or another (for example, blood type A or blood type O). Nevertheless, Mendelian characteristics can be described in terms of frequency within populations, and this permits between-group comparisons regarding prevalence. For example, a majority of people in one population may have blood type A, but in another population, type A may be very rare. Mendelian traits can also be analyzed for mode of inheritance (dominant or recessive). Finally, for many Mendelian traits, the approximate or exact positions of genes have been identified, and this makes it possible to examine the mechanisms and patterns of inheritance at these loci. Because polygenic characters are influenced by several loci, they can't, as yet, be traced to specific loci.

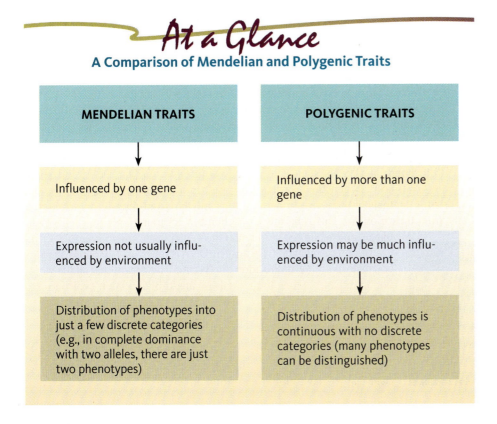

At a Glance

A Comparison of Mendelian and Polygenic Traits

MENDELIAN TRAITS	POLYGENIC TRAITS
Influenced by one gene	Influenced by more than one gene
Expression not usually influenced by environment	Expression may be much influenced by environment
Distribution of phenotypes into just a few discrete categories (e.g., in complete dominance with two alleles, there are just two phenotypes)	Distribution of phenotypes is continuous with no discrete categories (many phenotypes can be distinguished)

Genetic and Environmental Factors

By now, you may have the impression that phenotypes are solely the expressions of genotypes, but that's not true. (Here we use the terms *genotype* and *phenotype* in a broader sense to refer to an individual's entire genetic makeup and physical characteristics, respectively.) The genotype sets limits and potentials for development, but it also interacts with the environment, and this genetic-environmental interaction influences many aspects of the phenotype. However, it's usually not possible to identify which specific environmental factors are affecting the phenotype.

Many polygenic traits are influenced by environmental factors. Adult height, for example, is strongly affected by nutrition during growth and development. Other important environmental factors that affect various phenotypes include exposure to altitude, temperature, and, unfortunately, increasing levels of exposure to toxic waste and airborne pollutants. All these, and many more, contribute in complex ways to the continuous phenotypic variation seen in characteristics governed by several loci.

Mendelian traits are less likely to be influenced by environmental factors. For example, ABO blood type is determined at fertilization and remains fixed throughout an individual's lifetime, regardless of diet, exposure to ultraviolet radiation, temperature, and so forth.

Mendelian and polygenic inheritance produce different kinds of phenotypic variation. In the former, variation occurs in discrete categories, while in the latter, it's continuous. However, it's important to understand that even for polygenic characteristics, Mendelian principles still apply at individual loci. In other words, if a trait is influenced by genes at seven loci, each one of those loci may have two or more alleles, with one perhaps being dominant to the other or with the alleles being codominant. It's the combined action of the alleles at all seven loci, interacting with the environment, that results in observable phenotypic expression.

Mitochondrial Inheritance

Another component of inheritance involves cellular organelles called **mitochondria** (Fig. 3-19). All cells contain hundreds of these oval-shaped structures that convert energy (derived from the breakdown of nutrients) to a form that cells can use.

Each mitochondrion contains several copies of a DNA molecule. While **mitochondrial DNA (mtDNA)** is distinct from the DNA found within cell nuclei, its molecular structure and functions are the same. The entire molecule has been sequenced and is known to contain around 40 genes that direct the conversion of energy within the cell.

Mitochondrial DNA is subject to mutations just like nuclear DNA, and some mutations cause certain genetic disorders that result from impaired energy conversion. Importantly, animals of both sexes inherit all their mtDNA, and thus all mitochondrial traits, from their mothers. This is because mitochondria are found only in a cell's cytoplasm, and while egg cells retain their cytoplasm, sperm cells lose theirs just prior to fertilization. Because mtDNA is inherited from only one parent, meiosis and recombination don't occur. This means that all the variation in mtDNA among individuals is caused by mutation, which makes mtDNA extremely useful for studying genetic change over time. So far, geneticists have used mutation rates in mtDNA to investigate evolutionary relationships between species, to trace ancestral relationships within the human lineage, and to study genetic variability among individuals and/or populations. While these techniques are still being refined, it's clear that we have a lot to learn from mtDNA.

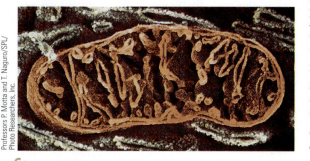

Professors P. Motta and T. Naguro/SPL/ Photo Researchers, Inc.

Figure 3-19

Scanning electron micrograph of a mitochondrion.

New Frontiers

Since the discovery of DNA structure and function in the 1950s, the field of genetics has revolutionized biological science and reshaped our understanding of inheritance, genetic disease, and evolutionary processes. For example, a technique developed in 1986, called **polymerase chain reaction (PCR)**, enables scientists to make thousands of copies of small samples of DNA that can then be analyzed. In the past, DNA samples such as those from crime scenes or from fossils were too small to be studied. But PCR has made it possible to examine nucleotide sequences in, for example, Neandertal fossils and Egyptian mummies. As you can imagine, PCR has limitless potential for many disciplines, including forensic science, medicine, and paleoanthropology.

Another application of PCR allows scientists to identify *DNA fingerprints*, so called because they appear as patterns of repeated DNA sequences that are unique to each individual. For example, one person might have a segment of six bases such as ATTCTA repeated 3 times, while another person might have the same sequence repeated 10 times (Fig. 3-20).

DNA fingerprinting is perhaps the most powerful tool available for human identification. Scientists have used it to identify scores of unidentified remains, including members of the Russian royal family murdered in 1918 and victims of the September 11, 2001, terrorist attacks. It also provided the DNA evidence in the O. J. Simpson murder trial. Moreover, the technique has been used to exonerate many innocent people wrongly convicted of crimes—in some cases decades after they were imprisoned.

Over the last two decades, scientists have used the techniques of **recombinant DNA technology** to transfer genes from the cells of one species into those of another. The most common method has been to insert human genes that direct the production of various proteins into bacterial cells. The altered bacteria can then produce human gene products such as insulin. Until the early 1980s, diabetic patients relied on insulin derived from nonhuman animals. However, this insulin wasn't plentiful, and some patients developed allergies to

mitochondria (*sing.*, mitochondrion) (my´-tow-kond´-dree-uh) Structures contained within the cytoplasm of eukaryotic cells that convert energy, derived from nutrients, to a form that is used by the cell.

mitochondrial DNA (mtDNA) DNA found in mitochondria. mtDNA is inherited only from the mother.

polymerase chain reaction (PCR) A method of producing copies of a DNA segment using the enzyme DNA polymerase.

recombinant DNA technology A process in which genes from the cell of one species are transferred to somatic cells or gametes of another species.

it. But since 1982, abundant supplies of human insulin, produced by bacteria, have been available; and bacteria-derived insulin doesn't cause allergic reactions.

In recent years, genetic manipulation has become increasingly controversial because of questions related to product safety, environmental concerns, animal welfare, and concern over the experimental use of human embryos. For example, the insertion of bacterial DNA into certain crops has made them toxic to leaf-eating insects, thus reducing the need for pesticides. Cattle and pigs are commonly treated with antibiotics and genetically engineered growth hormone to increase growth rates. There's no current evidence that humans are susceptible to the insect-repelling bacterial DNA or harmed by eating meat and dairy products from animals treated with growth hormone. But there are concerns over the unknown effects of long-term exposure.

No matter how contentious these new techniques may be, nothing has generated as much controversy as cloning. The controversy escalated in 1997 with the birth of Dolly, a **clone** of a female sheep (Wilmut et al., 1997). Actually, cloning isn't as new as you might think. Anyone who has ever taken a cutting from a plant and rooted it to grow a new one has produced a clone. Currently, the list of cloned mammals includes mice, rats, rabbits, cats, sheep, cattle, horses, a mule, and a dog.

How successful cloning will be hasn't been determined yet. Dolly, who had developed health problems, was euthanized in February 2003 at the age of 6 years (Giles and Knight, 2003). Long-term studies have yet to show whether cloned animals live out their normal life span, but some evidence from mice suggests that they don't.

As exciting as these innovations are, probably the single most important advance in genetics has been the progress made by the **Human Genome Project**. The goal of this international effort, begun in 1990, was to sequence the entire human **genome**, which consists of some 3 billion bases comprising approximately 25,000 genes. In 2003, the project was completed; now, all human chromosomes have been provisionally mapped. The next step is to sort out which DNA segments operate as functional genes and which don't. It will also be several years before scientists identify the functions of many of the proteins produced by these genes. It's one thing to know a gene's chemical makeup but quite another to know what it does. Still, the magnitude and importance of the achievement can't be overstated; it will ultimately transform biomedical and pharmaceutical research, changing forever the way many human diseases are diagnosed and treated.

The potential for anthropological applications is also enormous. While scientists were sequencing human genes, the genomes of other organisms were also being studied. As of now, the genomes of hundreds of species have been sequenced. In December 2002, the mouse genome had been completely sequenced (Waterston et al., 2002). The sequence of the chimpanzee genome was announced in 2005 (Chimpanzee Sequencing and Analysis Consortium, 2005). Moreover, two different groups are also currently working to reveal the Neandertal genome (Green et al., 2006; Noonan et al., 2006). The availability of these genomes, and many others, will allow comparisons between human DNA and the DNA of Neandertals and nonhuman primates. This research, called *comparative genomics*, has implications not only for biomedical research but also for studies of evolutionary relationships among species, including ourselves.

Eventually, comparative genome analysis should provide a thorough assessment of genetic similarities and differences, and thus the evolutionary relationships, between humans and other primates. What's more, we can already look at human variation in an entirely different light than we could even 10 years ago (see Chapter 4). Among other things, genetic comparisons between human groups can inform us about population movements in the past and give us further insight as to the selective pressures that may have been exerted on different populations to produce some of the variability we see. We may even be able to speculate on patterns of infectious disease in the past. The possibilities are extraordinary, and it wouldn't be exaggerating to say that this is the most exciting time in the history of evolutionary biology since Darwin published *On the Origin of Species* 150 years ago.

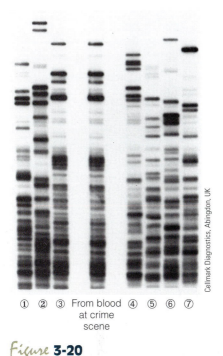

① ② ③ From blood at crime scene ④ ⑤ ⑥ ⑦

Figure **3-20**

Eight DNA fingerprints, one of which is from a blood sample left at an actual crime scene. The other seven are from suspects. By comparing the banding patterns, it is easy to identify the guilty person.

Human Genome Project An international effort that has mapped the entire human genome.

genome The entire genetic makeup of an individual or species. In humans, it is estimated that each person possesses approximately 3 billion DNA nucleotides.

Modern Evolutionary Theory

By the beginning of the twentieth century, the foundations for evolutionary theory had already been developed. Darwin and Wallace had described natural selection 40 years earlier, and the rediscovery of Mendelian genetics in 1900 contributed the other major component, a mechanism for inheritance. We might expect that these two basic contributions would have been combined into a consistent theory of evolution, but they weren't. For the first 30 years of the twentieth century, some scientists argued that mutation was the main factor in evolution, while others emphasized natural selection. What they really needed was a merger of both views (not an either-or situation), but that didn't happen until the mid-1930s.

THE MODERN SYNTHESIS

In the 1920s and early 1930s, biologists realized that mutation and natural selection weren't opposing processes and that both actually contributed to biological evolution. The two major foundations of the biological sciences were thus brought together in what a scientist named Julian Huxley called the Modern Synthesis. From such a "modern" (that is, middle of the twentieth century onward) perspective, we define evolution as a two-stage process:

1. The production and redistribution of **variation** (inherited differences among organisms)
2. *Natural selection* acting on this variation, whereby inherited differences, or variation, among individuals differentially affect their ability to successfully reproduce

A CURRENT DEFINITION OF EVOLUTION

As we discussed in Chapter 2, Darwin saw **evolution** as the gradual unfolding of new varieties of life from previous forms over long periods of time. And this is indeed one result of the evolutionary process. But these long-term effects can come about only through the accumulation of many small genetic changes occurring over generations; and today, we can show how evolution works by examining some of these intergenerational genetic changes. From this modern genetic perspective, we define *evolution* as a change in **allele frequency** from one generation to the next.

Allele frequencies are indicators of the genetic makeup of an interbreeding group of individuals known as a **population**. To show how allele frequencies change, we'll use a simplified example of an inherited characteristic, again the ABO blood groups (see p. 54). (*Note*: In addition to ABO, several other blood type systems are controlled by many other loci.)

Let's assume that the students in your anthropology class represent a population, an interbreeding group of individuals, and that we've determined the ABO blood type of each member. (To be considered a population, individuals must choose mates more often from *within* the group than from outside it. Obviously, your class won't meet this requirement, but we'll overlook this point for now.) The proportions of the *A*, *B*, and *O* alleles are the allele frequencies for this trait. Therefore, if 50 percent of all the ABO alleles in your class are *A*, 40 percent are *B*, and 10 percent are *O*, then the frequencies of these alleles are *A* = .50, *B* = .40, and *O* = .10.

Since the frequencies for these alleles represent only proportions of a total, it's obvious that allele frequencies can refer only to groups of individuals—that is, populations. Individuals don't have allele frequencies; they have either *A*, *B*, or *O* in any combination of two. Also, from conception onward, a person's genetic composition is fixed. If you start out with blood type A, you'll always have type A. Therefore, only a population can evolve over time; individuals can't.

variation In genetics, inherited differences among individuals; the basis of all evolutionary change.

evolution (modern genetic definition) A change in the frequency of alleles from one generation to the next.

allele frequency In a population, the percentage of all the alleles at a locus accounted for by one specific allele.

population Within a species, a community of individuals where mates are usually found.

Assume that 25 years from now, we calculate the frequencies of the ABO alleles for the offspring of our classroom population and find the following: $A = .30$, $B = .40$, and $O = .30$. We can see that the relative proportions have changed: A has decreased, O has increased, and B has remained the same. This wouldn't really be a big deal, but in a biological sense, these kinds of apparently minor changes constitute evolution. Over the short span of just a few generations, such changes in inherited traits may be very small; but if they continue to happen, and particularly if they consistently go in one direction as a result of natural selection, they can produce new adaptations and even new species.

Whether we're talking about the short-term effects (as in our classroom population) from one generation to the next, which is sometimes called **microevolution**, or the long-term effects through time, called speciation or **macroevolution**, the basic evolutionary mechanisms are similar. But how do allele frequencies change? Or, to put it another way, what causes evolution? As we've already seen, evolution is a two-stage process. Genetic variation must first be produced by mutation, and then it can be acted on by natural selection.

Factors That Produce and Redistribute Variation

We've emphasized the importance of genetic variation to the process of evolution and pointed out that mutation is the only source of new variation, because when a gene changes, a new allele is produced. We've also mentioned natural selection several times. But to really understand how evolution works, we need to consider these two factors in greater detail; and we also have to consider a few other mechanisms that contribute to the process.

MUTATION

You've already learned that a change in DNA is one kind of mutation. Many genes can occur in one of several alternative forms, which we've defined as alleles (A, B, or O, for example). If one allele changes to another—that is, if the gene itself is altered—a mutation has occurred. Even the substitution of one single DNA base for another, called a *point mutation*, can cause an allele to change. But point mutations have to occur in sex cells if they're going to be important to the evolutionary process. This is because evolution is a change in allele frequencies *between* generations, and mutations that occur in somatic cells, but not in gametes, aren't passed on to offspring. If, however, a genetic change occurs in the sperm or egg of one of the students in our classroom (A mutates to B, for instance), the offspring's blood type will be different from that of the parent, causing a minute shift in the allele frequencies of the next generation.

Actually, it would be rare to see evolution occurring by mutation alone, except in microorganisms. Mutation rates for any given trait are usually low, so we wouldn't really expect to see a mutation at the ABO locus in so small a population as your class. In larger populations, mutations might be observed in, say, 1 individual out of 10,000; but by themselves, the mutations wouldn't affect allele frequencies. However, when mutation is combined with natural selection, not only can evolutionary changes occur, but they can occur more rapidly.

It's important to remember that mutation is the basic creative force in evolution, since it's the *only* way to produce *new* genes (that is, variation). Its role in the production of variation is the key to the first stage of the evolutionary process.

microevolution Small changes occurring within species, such as a change in allele frequencies.

macroevolution Changes produced only after many generations, such as the appearance of a new species.

CHAPTER 7

GENE FLOW

Gene flow is the exchange of genes between populations. The term *migration* is also frequently used; but strictly speaking, migration means movement of people, whereas gene flow refers to the exchange of *genes* between groups, and this can happen only if the migrants interbreed. Also, even if individuals move temporarily and mate in a new population (thus leaving a genetic contribution), they don't necessarily remain in the population. For example, the offspring of U.S. soldiers and Vietnamese women (born during the Vietnam War) represent gene flow, even though the fathers returned to their native population.

Population movements (particularly in the last 500 years) have reached unprecedented levels, and few breeding isolates remain. Significant population movements also occurred in the past, although not at current levels. Migration between populations has been a consistent feature of hominin evolution since the first dispersal of our genus, and gene flow between populations (even though sometimes limited) helps explain why, in the last million years, speciation has been rare.

An interesting example of how gene flow influences microevolutionary changes in modern human populations is seen in African Americans. African Americans in the United States are largely of West African descent, but there has also been considerable genetic admixture with European Americans. By measuring allele frequencies for specific genetic loci, we can estimate the amount of migration of European alleles into the African American **gene pool**. Data from northern and western U.S. cities (including New York, Detroit, and Oakland) have shown the migration rate (that is, the proportion of *non-African* genes in the African American gene pool) at 20 to 25 percent (Cummings, 2000). However, more restricted data from the southern United States (Charleston and rural Georgia) have suggested a lower degree of gene flow (4 to 11 percent).

Gene flow doesn't require large-scale movements of entire groups. In fact, significant changes in allele frequencies can come about through long-term patterns of mate selection whereby members of a group obtain mates from one or more other groups. If mate exchange consistently moves in one direction (for example, village A obtains mates from village B, but not vice versa) over a long period of time, allele frequencies in village A will eventually change.

GENETIC DRIFT AND FOUNDER EFFECT

Genetic drift is the random factor in evolution, and it's directly related to population size. *Drift occurs because the population is small.* If an allele is rare in a population comprised of, say, a few hundred individuals, then there is a chance that it may not be passed on to offspring. In this type of situation, such an allele can eventually disappear altogether from the population. This may seem like a minor thing, but in effect, genetic variability in this population has been reduced (Fig. 3-21a).

One particular kind of genetic drift is called **founder effect**, and we can see its results today in many modern human and nonhuman populations (Fig. 3-21b). Founder effect can occur when a small migrant band of "founders" leaves its parent group and forms a new colony somewhere else. Over time, a new population will be established, and as long as mates are chosen only from within this population, all of its members will be descended from the small group of founders. In effect, all the genes in the expanding group will have come from a few original colonists. In such a case, an allele that was rare in the founders' parent population, but that is carried by even one of the founders, can eventually become common in succeeding generations. This is because a high proportion of members of later generations are all descended from that one founder.

Colonization isn't the only way founder effect can happen. Small founding groups may consist of a few survivors of a large group that, at some time in the past, was decimated by some type of disaster. The small founder population (the survivors) possesses

gene flow Exchange of genes between populations.

gene pool The total complement of genes shared by the reproductive members of a population.

genetic drift Evolutionary changes—that is, changes in allele frequencies—produced by random factors. Genetic drift is a result of small population size.

founder effect A type of genetic drift in which allele frequencies are altered in small populations that are taken from, or are remnants of, larger populations.

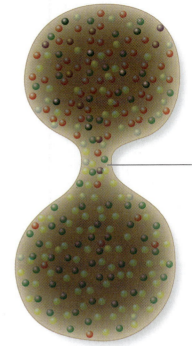

Time

A small population with considerable genetic variability. Note that the dark green and light blue alleles are less common than the other alleles.

After just a few generations, the population is approximately the same size, but genetic variation has been reduced. Both the dark green and blue alleles have been lost. Also, the red allele is less common and the frequency of the light green allele has increased.

Population size

(a)

Original population with considerable genetic variation

A small group leaves to colonize a new area or a bottleneck occurs, so that population size decreases and genetic variation is reduced.

Population size is restored, but the dark green and purple alleles have been lost. The frequencies of the red and yellow alleles have also changed.

Population size

(b)

Figure **3-21**

Small populations are subject to genetic drift where rare alleles can be lost because, just by chance, they weren't passed to offspring. Also, although more common alleles may not be lost, their frequencies may change for the same reason. (a) This diagram represents six alleles (different-colored dots) that occur at one genetic locus in a small population. You can see that in a fairly short period of time (three or four generations), rare alleles can be lost and genetic diversity consequently reduced. (b) This diagram illustrates founder effect, a form of genetic drift where diversity is lost because a large population is drastically reduced in size and consequently passes through a genetic "bottleneck." Founder effect also happens when a small group leaves the larger group and "founds" a new population elsewhere. (In this case, the group of founders is represented by the bottleneck.) Those individuals that survive (the founders) and the alleles they carry represent only a sample of the variation that was present in the original population. Future generations, all descended from the survivors (founders), will therefore have less variability.

only a sample of all the alleles that were present in the original group. Just by chance alone, some alleles may be completely removed from the gene pool. Other alleles may become the only allele at a locus that previously had two or more. Whatever the cause, the outcome is reduced genetic diversity, and the allele frequencies of succeeding generations may be substantially different from those of the original large population. The loss of genetic diversity in this type of situation is called a *genetic bottleneck*, and its effects can be very detrimental to a species (Fig. 3-21b).

There are many known examples of species or populations that have passed through genetic bottlenecks. Genetically, cheetahs (Fig. 3-22) are an extremely uniform species, and biologists believe that at some point in the past, these magnificent cats suffered a catastrophic decline in numbers. For reasons we don't know but that are related to the species-wide loss of numerous alleles, male cheetahs produce a high percentage of defective sperm compared to other cat species.

Decreased reproductive potential, greatly reduced genetic diversity, and other factors (including human hunting) have combined to jeopardize the continued existence

Figure **3-22**

Cheetahs, like many other species, have passed through a genetic bottleneck. Consequently, as a species they have little genetic variation.

of this species. Other examples include California elephant seals, sea otters, and condors. Indeed, our own species is genetically uniform, compared to chimpanzees, and it appears that all modern human populations are the descendants of a few small groups (see p. 80).

Many examples of founder effect in human populations have been documented in small, usually isolated populations (for example, island groups or small agricultural villages in New Guinea or South America). Even larger populations descended from fairly small groups of founders can show the effects of genetic drift many generations later. For example, French Canadians in Quebec, who currently number close to 6 million, are all descended from about 8,500 founders who left France during the sixteenth and seventeenth centuries. Because the genes carried by the initial founders represented only a sample of the gene pool from which they were derived, just by chance a number of alleles now occur in different frequencies from those of the current population of France. These differences include an increased presence of several harmful alleles (see Table 3-3), including cystic fibrosis, a variety of Tay-Sachs, thalassemia, and PKU (Scriver, 2001).

In small populations, drift plays a major evolutionary role because fairly sudden fluctuations in allele frequency occur solely because of small population size. Throughout much of human evolution (at least the last 4 to 5 million years), hominins probably lived in small groups, and drift would have had significant impact. But even though genetic drift has caused evolutionary change in certain circumstances, its effects have been irregular. That's because drift isn't directional; that is, it doesn't consistently increase or decrease the frequency of a given allele. But by altering allele frequencies in small populations, drift can provide significantly greater opportunities for natural selection, the only truly directional force in evolution.

As we've seen, both gene flow and genetic drift can produce some evolutionary changes by themselves. However, these changes are usually *microevolutionary* ones; that is, they produce changes within species over the short term. To have the kind of evolutionary changes that ultimately result in entire new groups (for example, the diversification of the first primates or the appearance of the hominins), natural selection would be necessary. But natural selection can't operate independently of the other evolutionary factors—mutation, gene flow, and genetic drift.

SEXUAL REPRODUCTION AND RECOMBINATION

As we saw earlier in this chapter, in sexually reproducing species both parents contribute genes to offspring. Also, during meiosis, members of chromosomal pairs exchange segments of DNA. Thus, genetic information is reshuffled every generation. Although these processes won't change allele frequencies (that is, cause evolution), they do produce different combinations of genes that natural selection may be able to act on. In fact, the reshuffling of chromosomes during meiosis can produce literally trillions of gene combinations, making every human being genetically unique.

Natural Selection Acts on Variation

directional change In a genetic sense, the nonrandom change in allele frequencies caused by natural selection. The change is directional because the frequencies of alleles consistently increase or decrease (they change in one direction), depending on environmental circumstances and the selective pressures involved.

The evolutionary factors just discussed—mutation, gene flow, genetic drift, and sexual reproduction and recombination—interact to produce variation and to distribute genes within and between populations. But there is no long-term *direction* to any of these factors. So how do populations adapt? The answer is natural selection, which causes **directional change** in allele frequencies. This means that natural selection can increase or decrease the frequency of certain alleles over time in ways that are beneficial in specific environmental settings. If you recall the moth example on page 31, the increase in frequency of dark or light moths depended on environmental change. Such a functional shift in allele frequen-

Table 3-5   Levels of Organization in the Evolutionary Process

Evolutionary Factor	Level	Evolutionary Process	Technique of Study
Mutation	DNA	Storage of genetic information; ability to replicate; influences phenotype by production of proteins	Biochemistry, electron microscope, recombinant DNA
Mutation	Chromosome	A vehicle for packaging and transmitting genetic material (DNA)	Light or electron microscope
Recombination (sex cells only)	Cell	The basic unit of life that contains the chromosomes and divides for growth and for production of sex cells	Light or electron microscope
Natural selection	Organism	The unit, composed of cells, that reproduces and which we observe for phenotypic traits	Visual study, biochemistry
Drift, gene flow	Population	A group of interbreeding organisms; changes in allele frequencies between generations; it's the population that evolves	Statistical analysis

cies is what we mean by *adaptation*. If there are long-term environmental changes in a consistent direction, then allele frequencies should also shift gradually in each generation. The levels of organization in the evolutionary process are summarized in Table 3-5.

In Chapter 2, we discussed the general principles underlying natural selection and gave some nonhuman examples. The best-documented example of natural selection in humans involves hemoglobin S (Hb^S), an abnormal form of hemoglobin that results from a point mutation in the gene that produces part of the hemoglobin molecule. The allele for hemoglobin S, *Hb^S*, is recessive to the allele for normal hemoglobin, *Hb^A*. Most people are homozygous for the *Hb^A* allele, and they produce normal hemoglobin. But people who inherit the recessive allele from both parents (that is, they are homozygous with the genotype *Hb^S/Hb^S*) produce no normal hemoglobin and have a very serious condition called sickle-cell anemia. People who have one copy of each allele (that is, they're heterozygotes with the *Hb^A/Hb^S* genotype) have a condition called *sickle-cell trait*, and although some of their hemoglobin is abnormal, enough of it is normal to enable them to function normally under most circumstances.

Sickle-cell anemia has numerous manifestations, but basically, the abnormal hemoglobin reduces the ability of red blood cells to transport oxygen. When people with sickle-cell anemia increase their body's demand for oxygen (for example, while exercising or traveling to high altitude), their red blood cells collapse and form a shape similar to a sickle (Fig. 3-23). These sickled cells can't carry adequate amounts of oxygen; moreover, they clump together and block small capillaries. The result is that vital organs are deprived of oxygen. Even with treatment, life expectancy in the United States today is less than 45 years for patients with sickle-cell anemia. Worldwide, sickle-cell anemia causes an estimated 100,000 deaths each year; in the United States, approximately 40,000 to 50,000 individuals, mostly of African descent, suffer from this disease.

The *Hb^S* mutation occurs at pretty much the same rate in all human populations. In some populations, however, especially in western and central Africa, the *Hb^S* allele is more common than elsewhere, with frequencies as high as 20 percent. It's also fairly common in parts of Greece and India (Fig. 3-24). Given the devastating effects of *Hb^S* in homozygotes, you might wonder why it's so common in some populations. It seems like natural selection would act against it, but it doesn't. How do we explain its higher prevalence in some populations? The explanation for this situation can be summed up in one word: malaria.

Malaria is an infectious disease that kills an estimated one to three million people each year worldwide. It's caused by a single-celled organism that is transmitted to humans

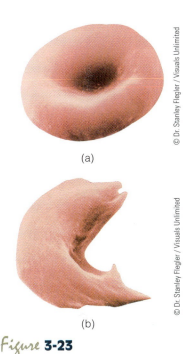

(a)

(b)

Figure **3-23**

(a) Scanning electron micrograph of a normal, fully oxygenated red blood cell.
(b) Scanning electron micrograph of a collapsed, sickle-shaped red blood cell that contains Hb^S.

© Dr. Stanley Flegler / Visuals Unlimited

Figure **3-24**

The distribution of the sickle-cell allele in the Old World.

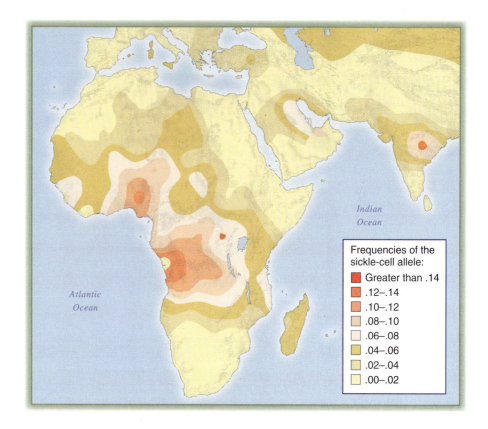

Frequencies of the sickle-cell allele:

- Greater than .14
- .12–.14
- .10–.12
- .08–.10
- .06–.08
- .04–.06
- .02–.04
- .00–.02

Indian Ocean

Atlantic Ocean

by mosquitoes. Very briefly, after an infected mosquito bite, these parasites invade red blood cells, where they get the oxygen they need for reproduction. The consequences of this infection to the human host include fever, chills, headache, nausea, vomiting, and frequently death. In parts of western and central Africa, where malaria is always present, children bear the burden of the disease, with as many as 50 to 75 percent of 2- to 9-year-olds being affected.

In the mid-twentieth century, the geographical correlation between malaria and the distribution of the sickle-cell allele (Hb^S) was the only evidence of a biological relationship between the two (Figs. 3-24 and 3-25). But now we know that people with sickle-cell trait have greater resistance to malaria than people who have only normal hemoglobin. This is because people with sickle-cell trait have some red blood cells that contain hemoglobin S, and these cells don't provide a suitable environment for the malarial parasite. In other words, having some hemoglobin S is beneficial because it affords some protection from malaria. So, in malarial areas, malaria acts as a selective agent that favors the heterozygous phenotype, since individuals with sickle-cell trait have higher reproductive success than those with normal hemoglobin, who may die of malaria. But selection for heterozygotes means that the Hb^S allele will be maintained in the population. Thus, there will always be some people with sickle-cell anemia, and they, of course, have the lowest reproductive success, since without treatment, most die before reaching adulthood.

The relationship between malaria and Hb^S provides one of the best examples we have of natural selection in contemporary humans. In this case, natural selection has favored the heterozygous phenotype, thus increasing the frequency of Hb^S, an allele that in homozygotes causes severe disease and early death.

There are many other examples of how disease has been a selective force throughout the course of human evolution and how it has contributed to small, but important, genetic differences between individuals and populations. But the relationship between malaria and the sickle-cell trait is the best single example we have to demonstrate microevolution

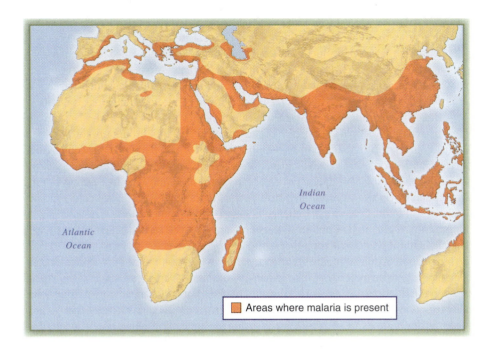

Areas where malaria is present

Figure **3-25**
The distribution of malaria in the Old World.

in humans. If you understand this discussion of the complex relationship between environmental factors (mosquitoes), disease, and one slight difference in the gene that governs hemoglobin production, you will comprehend how evolutionary change occurs.

Summary

The topics we've covered in this chapter relate almost entirely to discoveries made after Darwin and Wallace described the fundamentals of natural selection. But all the issues presented here are basic to an understanding of biological evolution, adaptation, and human variation.

We have shown that cells are the fundamental units of life and that they are essentially classified into two types. Somatic cells make up body tissues, while gametes (eggs and sperm) are reproductive cells that transmit genetic information from parent to offspring.

Genetic information is contained in the DNA molecule, found in the nuclei of cells. The DNA molecule is capable of replication, or making copies of itself, and during mitosis and meiosis, this key factor makes it possible for daughter cells to receive the correct amount of DNA that allows them to function properly. DNA also controls protein synthesis by directing cells to arrange amino acids in the proper sequence for each particular type of protein. Also involved in the process of protein synthesis is another, similar molecule called RNA.

Cells multiply by dividing, and during cell division, DNA is visible under a microscope in the form of chromosomes. In humans, there are 46 chromosomes, or 23 pairs.

Somatic cells divide during growth or tissue repair or to replace old or damaged cells. Somatic cell division is called mitosis. During mitosis, a cell divides one time to produce two daughter cells, each possessing a full and identical set of chromosomes.

Sex cells are produced when specialized cells in the ovaries and testes divide during meiosis. Unlike mitosis, meiosis is characterized by two divisions that produce four nonidentical daughter cells, each having only half the amount of DNA (23 chromosomes) contained within the original cell.

We've also discussed how Gregor Mendel discovered the principles of segregation, independent assortment, and dominance and recessiveness by doing experiments with pea plants. Characteristics influenced by only one genetic locus are called Mendelian traits, and the ABO blood type system is one example of a human Mendelian trait. In contrast, many characteristics, such as stature and skin color, are polygenic, meaning that they're influenced by more than one genetic locus and show a continuous range of expression.

Building on fundamental nineteenth-century contributions by Charles Darwin and the rediscovery of Mendel's work in 1900, advances in genetics throughout the twentieth century contributed to contemporary evolutionary thought. In particular, the combination of natural selection with Mendel's principles of inheritance and experimental evidence concerning the nature of mutation have all been synthesized into a modern understanding of evolutionary change, appropriately termed the Modern Synthesis. In this contemporary theory of evolution, evolutionary change is seen as a two-stage process. The first stage is the production and redistribution of genetic variation. The second stage is the process whereby natural selection acts on that variation.

Mutation is crucial to all evolutionary change because it's the only source of completely new genetic material (which increases variation). Natural selection is the crucial factor that influences the long-term direction of evolutionary change. How natural selection works can best be explained as differential net reproductive success—that is, how successful individuals are in producing offspring for succeeding generations. Genetic drift (the random loss of alleles due to small population size) and gene flow (the exchange of genes between populations) are also very important to evolutionary change.

The expression of all biological traits is, to varying degrees, under genetic control. Genes, then, can be said to set limits and potentials for human growth, development, and achievement. However, these limits and potentials aren't written in stone, so to speak, because many characteristics are also very much influenced by such environmental factors as temperature, diet, and sunlight. So ultimately, it's the interaction between genetic and environmental factors that produces phenotypic variation and evolutionary change in all species, including *Homo sapiens*.

Critical Thinking Questions

1. Before reading this chapter, were you aware that your DNA is structurally the same as in all other organisms? How do you see this fact as having potential to clarify some of the many questions we still have regarding biological evolution?
2. Has this chapter changed your understanding of genetics and evolution? If so, how?
3. Many people have the misconception that sickle-cell anemia affects only people of African descent. Explain why this isn't true.
4. Give some examples of how selection, gene flow, genetic drift, and mutation have acted on populations or species in the past. Try to think of at least one human and one nonhuman example that weren't mentioned in this chapter. Why do you think genetic drift might be important today to endangered species?
5. Did the discussion of misconceptions about dominance and recessiveness change your perceptions of these phenomena? If so, how?
6. Did this chapter change your views about human variation? If so, how?

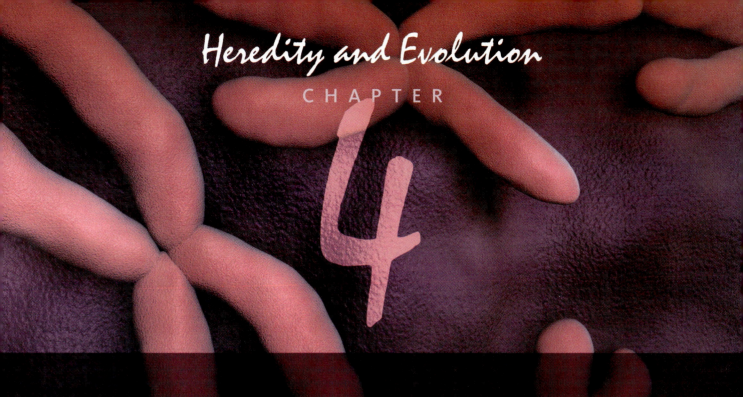

Heredity and Evolution

CHAPTER

4

Modern Human Variation and Adaptation

Focus Question

How does the contemporary evolutionary-based approach to understanding human diversity differ from the traditional nineteenth-century approach?

 Click!

Go to the following media for interactive activities and exercises on topics covered in this chapter:

- Online Virtual Laboratories for Physical Anthropology, Version 4.0
- Genetics in Anthropology: Principles and Applications CD-ROM, Version 2.0

Introduction

At some time or other, you've probably been asked to specify your ethnicity on an application form. Did that bother you, and if so, why? Usually, you can choose from a variety of racial/ethnic categories. Was it easy to pick one? Where would your parents and grandparents fit in?

Notions about human diversity have played a large role in human relations for at least a few thousand years, and they still influence political and social perceptions. While we'd like to believe that informed views have become almost universal, the gruesome tally of genocidal/ethnic cleansing atrocities in recent years tells us that worldwide, we have a long way to go before tolerance becomes the norm.

Most people don't seem to understand the nature of human diversity, and many seem unwilling to accept what science has to contribute on the subject. Many of the misconceptions, especially those regarding how race is defined and categorized, are rooted in cultural history over the last few centuries. Indeed, the way most people view themselves and their relationship to other peoples is a legacy of racial interpretations that developed in the last 400 years.

In Chapter 3, we saw how physical characteristics are influenced by the DNA in our cells. We went on to discuss how individuals inherit genes from parents and how variations in genes (alleles) can produce different expressions of traits. We also focused on how the basic principles of inheritance are related to evolutionary change.

In this chapter, we'll continue to discuss topics that directly relate to genetics—namely, biological diversity in humans and how humans adapt physically to environmental challenges. After discussing historical attempts to explain human phenotypic diversity and racial classification, we'll examine contemporary methods of interpreting diversity. In recent years, several new techniques have emerged that permit direct examination of the DNA molecule, revealing differences between individuals even at the level of single nucleotides. But as discoveries of different levels of diversity emerge, geneticists have also shown that our species is remarkably uniform genetically, particularly when compared with other species.

Historical Views of Human Variation

The first step toward understanding diversity in nature is to organize it into categories that can then be named, discussed, and perhaps studied. Historically, when different groups of people came into contact with one another, they tried to account for the physical differences they saw. Because skin color was so noticeable, it was one of the more frequently explained traits, and most systems of racial classification were based on it.

As early as 1350 B.C., the ancient Egyptians had classified humans based on their skin color: red for Egyptian, yellow for people to the east, white for those to the north, and black for sub-Saharan Africans (Gossett, 1963). In the sixteenth century, after the discovery of the New World, several European countries embarked on a period of intense exploration and colonization in both the New and Old Worlds. One result of this contact was an increased awareness of human diversity.

Throughout the eighteenth and nineteenth centuries, European and American scientists concentrated primarily on describing and classifying the biological variation in both humans and nonhuman species. The first scientific attempt to describe the newly discovered variation among human populations was Linnaeus' taxonomic classification (see p. 23), which placed humans into four separate categories (Linnaeus, 1758). Linnaeus assigned behavioral and intellectual qualities to each group, with the least complimentary descriptions going to sub-Saharan, dark-skinned Africans. This ranking was typical of the period and reflected the almost universal European ethnocentric view that Europeans were superior to everyone else.

Johann Friedrich Blumenbach (1752–1840), a German anatomist, classified humans into five races. Although Blumenbach's categories came to be described simply as white, yellow, red, black, and brown, he also used criteria other than skin color. Blumenbach emphasized that categories based on skin color were arbitrary and that many traits, including skin color, weren't discrete phenomena and that their expression often overlapped between groups. He also pointed out that classifying all humans using such a system would omit all those who didn't neatly fall into a specific category.

Nevertheless, by the mid-nineteenth century, populations were ranked essentially on a scale based on skin color (along with size and shape of the head), with sub-Saharan Africans at the bottom. The Europeans themselves were also ranked, so that northern, light-skinned populations were considered superior to their southern, somewhat darker-skinned neighbors from Italy and Greece.

To many Europeans, non-Europeans weren't "civilized" because their cultures were different, and this fact implied an even more basic inferiority of character and intellect. This view was rooted in a concept called **biological determinism**, which in part holds that there is an association between physical characteristics and such attributes as intelligence, morals, values, abilities, and even social and economic status. In other words, cultural variations are *inherited* in the same way that biological differences are. It follows, then, that there are inherent behavioral and cognitive differences between groups and that, by nature, some groups are superior to others. Following this logic, it's fairly easy to justify the persecution and even enslavement of other peoples simply because their outward appearance differs from what's familiar.

After 1850, biological determinism was a predominant theme underlying common thinking as well as scientific research in Europe and the United States. Most people, including such notable figures as Thomas Jefferson, Georges Cuvier, Benjamin Franklin, Charles Lyell, Abraham Lincoln, Charles Darwin, and Oliver Wendell Holmes, held deterministic (and what today we'd call racist) views. Commenting on this usually de-emphasized characteristic of many respected historical figures, the late evolutionary biologist Stephen J. Gould (1981, p. 32) remarked that "all American culture heroes embraced racial attitudes that would embarrass public-school mythmakers."

Francis Galton (1822–1911), Charles Darwin's cousin, shared an increasingly common fear among nineteenth-century Europeans that "civilized society" was being weakened by the failure of natural selection to completely eliminate unfit and inferior members (Greene, 1981, p. 107). Galton wrote and lectured on the necessity of "race improvement" and suggested government regulation of marriage and family size, an approach he called **eugenics**. Although eugenics had its share of critics, its popularity flourished throughout the 1930s. Nowhere was this viewpoint more attractive than in Germany, where it took a horrifying turn. The false idea of pure races was increasingly extolled as a means of reestablishing a strong and prosperous state, and eugenics was seen as scientific justification for purging Germany of its "unfit." In Nazi Germany, many scientists continued to support the ideologies of racial purity and eugenics, even when these policies served as excuses for condemning millions of people to death (Proctor, 1988, p. 143).

biological determinism The concept that various aspects of behavior (e.g., intelligence, values, morals), are governed by biological (genetic) factors; the inaccurate association of various behavioral attributes with certain biological traits, such as skin color.

eugenics The philosophy of "race improvement" through the forced sterilization of members of some groups and increased reproduction among others; an overly simplified, often racist, view that is now discredited.

But at the same time, many scientists were turning away from racial typologies and classification in favor of a more evolutionary approach. For some, this shift was no doubt motivated by growing concerns over the goals of the eugenics movement. However, the merger of Darwin's theories of natural selection and genetics in the 1930s had an even greater impact. As discussed in Chapter 3, this breakthrough influenced all the biological sciences, and some physical anthropologists soon began applying evolutionary principles to the study of human variation.

The Concept of Race

All contemporary humans are members of the same **polytypic** species, *Homo sapiens*. A polytypic species is composed of local populations that differ in the expression of one or more traits. Even *within* local populations, there's a great deal of genotypic and phenotypic variation among individuals.

In discussions of human variation, people have traditionally classified populations according to how various traits such as skin color, hair color, hair form (curly or straight), eye color, and shape of the face and nose are combined. People with particular combinations of these and other traits have been placed together in categories associated with specific geographical localities. Such categories are called *races*.

We all think we know what we mean by the word *race*, but in reality, the term has had various meanings since the 1500s, when it first appeared in the English language. Race has been used synonymously with *species*, as in "the human race." Since the 1600s, race has also referred to various culturally defined groups, and this usage is still common. For example, you'll hear people say, "the English race" or "the Japanese race," when they actually mean nationality. Another phrase you've probably heard is "the Jewish race," when the speaker is really talking about an ethnic and religious identity.

So even though *race* is usually a term with biological connotations, it also has enormous social significance. And there's still a widespread perception that certain physical traits (skin color, in particular) are associated with numerous cultural attributes, such as language, occupational preferences, or even morality (however it's defined). As a result, in many cultural contexts, a person's social identity is strongly influenced by the way he or she expresses those physical traits traditionally used to define "racial groups." Characteristics such as skin color are highly visible, and they make it easy to superficially place people into socially defined categories. However, so-called racial traits aren't the only phenotypic expressions that contribute to social identity. Sex and age are also critically important. But aside from these two variables, an individual's biological and/or ethnic background is still inevitably a factor that influences how he or she is initially perceived and judged by others.

References to national origin (for example, African or Asian) as substitutes for racial labels have become more common in recent years, both within and outside anthropology. Within anthropology, the term *ethnicity* was proposed in the early 1950s to avoid the more emotionally charged term *race*. Strictly speaking, ethnicity refers to cultural factors, but the fact that the words *ethnicity* and *race* are used interchangeably reflects the social importance of phenotypic expression and demonstrates once again how phenotype is mistakenly associated with culturally defined variables.

In its most common biological usage, the term *race* refers to geographically patterned phenotypic variation within a species. By the seventeenth century, naturalists were beginning to describe races in plants and nonhuman animals. They had recognized that when populations of a species occupied different regions, they sometimes differed from one another in the expression of one or more traits. But even today, there are no established criteria for assessing races of plants and animals, including humans.

polytypic Referring to species composed of populations that differ with regard to the expression of one or more traits.

Before World War II, most studies of human variation focused on visible phenotypic variation between large, geographically defined populations, and these studies were largely descriptive. Since World War II, the emphasis has shifted to examining differences in allele frequencies within and between populations, as well as considering the adaptive significance of phenotypic and genotypic variation. This shift in focus occurred partly because of the Modern Synthesis in biology and partly because of further advances in genetics.

In the second half of the twentieth century, the application of evolutionary principles to the study of modern human variation replaced the superficial nineteenth-century view of race *based solely on observed phenotype*. Additionally, the genetic emphasis dispelled previously held misconceptions that races are fixed biological entities that don't change over time and that are composed of individuals who all conform to a particular *type*. Clearly, there are phenotypic differences between humans, and some of these differences roughly correspond to particular geographical locations. But certain questions must be asked. Do readily observable phenotypic variations, like skin color, have adaptive significance? Is genetic drift a factor? What is the degree of underlying genetic variation that influences phenotypic variation? These questions are founded in a completely different perspective from that of 50 years ago and they place considerations of human variation within a contemporary evolutionary framework.

Although biological anthropology is partly rooted in attempts to explain human diversity, no contemporary anthropologist subscribes to pre-Darwinian and pre–Modern Synthesis concepts of races (human or nonhuman) as fixed biological entities. Also, anthropologists recognize that race isn't a valid concept, especially from a genetic perspective, because the amount of genetic variation accounted for by differences *between* groups is vastly exceeded by the variation that exists *within* groups. Many physical anthropologists also argue that race is an outdated creation of the human mind that attempts to simplify biological complexity by organizing it into categories. Therefore, human races are a product of the human tendency to impose order on complex natural phenomena. In this view, simplistic classification may have been an understandable approach some 150 years ago, but given the current state of genetic and evolutionary science, it's absolutely meaningless today.

Even so, some anthropologists continue to view outwardly expressed phenotypic variations as having the potential to yield information about population adaptation, genetic drift, mutation, and gene flow. Forensic anthropologists, in particular, find the phenotypic criteria associated with a person's ancestry (especially in the skeleton) to have practical applications. Law enforcement agencies frequently call upon them to help identify human skeletal remains. Because unidentified human remains are often those of crime victims, identification must be as accurate as possible. The most important variables in such identification are the individual's sex, age, stature, and ancestry ("racial" and ethnic background). Using metric and nonmetric criteria, forensic anthropologists use various techniques for establishing broad population affinity (that is, a likely relationship) for that individual.

In addition to genetic reasons, biological anthropologists object to racial taxonomies because traditional classification schemes are *typological*, meaning that categories are distinct and based on stereotypes or ideals that comprise a specific set of traits. So typologies are inherently misleading, because any grouping always includes many individuals who don't conform to all aspects of a particular type. In any so-called racial group, there will be people who fall into the normal range of variation for another population based on one or several characteristics. For example, two people of different ancestry might have different skin color, but they could share any number of other traits, including height, head shape, hair color, eye color, and ABO blood type. In fact, they could easily share more similarities with each other than they do with many members of their own populations.

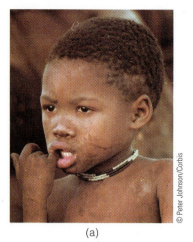

(a)

(b)

© Peter Johnson/Corbis

© Charles & Josette Lenars/Corbis

(c)

(d)

© Gallo Images/Corbis

© Otto Lang/Corbis

(e)

Lynn Kilgore

Figure 4-1

Some examples of phenotypic variation among Africans.
(a) San (South African).
(b) West African (Bantu).
(c) Ethiopian.
(d) Ituri (Central African).
(e) North African (Tunisia).

The characteristics that have traditionally been used to define races are *polygenic* and therefore exhibit a continuous range of expression. So it's difficult, if not impossible, to draw distinct boundaries between populations with regard to many traits. This limitation becomes clear if you ask yourself, "At what point is hair color no longer dark brown but medium brown, or no longer light brown but dark blond?" (You may want to refer back to Figure 3-18, p. 58, to see how eye color exhibits continuous gradations from light blue to dark brown.)

Our understanding of human variation will continue to change as we learn more about the genetic diversity (and also the uniformity) of our species. Given the rapid changes in genome studies, and because very few genes contribute to outward expressions of phenotype, dividing the human species into racial categories isn't a biologically meaningful way to look at human variation. But among the general public, race will undoubtedly continue to be the most common view. With this in mind, it falls to anthropologists and biologists to continue exploring the issue so that, to the best of our abilities, accurate information about human variation is available to anyone who seeks informed explanations of complex phenomena (Fig. 4-1).

Racism

Racism is based on the previously mentioned false belief that along with physical characteristics, humans inherit such factors as intellect and various cultural attributes. Such beliefs also commonly rest on the assumption that one's own group is superior to other groups.

Since we've already alluded to certain aspects of racism, such as the eugenics movement and persecution of people based on racial or ethnic misconceptions, we won't belabor the point here. It's important, though, to point out that racism is hardly a thing of the past, and it's not restricted to Europeans and North Americans of European descent. Racism is a cultural phenomenon, and it's found worldwide.

We end this brief discussion of racism with an excerpt from "The Study of Race," an article by the late Sherwood Washburn, a well-known physical anthropologist who taught at the University of California, Berkeley. Although written many years ago, the statement is as relevant today as it was then:

> Races are products of the past. They are relics of times and conditions which have long ceased to exist. Racism is equally a relic supported by no phase of modern science. We may not know how to interpret the form of the Mongoloid face, or why Rh is of high incidence in Africa, but we do know the benefits of education and of economic progress. We . . . know that the roots of happiness lie in the biology of the whole species and that the potential of the species can only be realized in a culture, in a social system. It is knowledge and the social system which give life or take it away, and in so doing change the gene frequencies and continue the million-year-old interaction of culture and biology. Human biology finds its realization in a culturally determined way of life, and the infinite variety of genetic combinations can only express themselves efficiently in a free and open society. (Washburn, 1963, p. 531)

Intelligence

As we've shown, belief in the relationship between physical characteristics and specific behavioral attributes is common even today, but there's no scientific evidence to show that personality or any other behavioral trait differs genetically *between* human groups. Most scientists would agree with this last statement, but one question that produces controversy inside scientific circles and in the general public is whether or not there is a relationship between population affinity and **intelligence**.

Genetic and environmental factors contribute to intelligence, although it's not possible to accurately measure the proportion each contributes. What can be said is that IQ scores and intelligence aren't the same thing. IQ scores can change during a person's lifetime, and average IQ scores of different populations overlap. Such differences in average IQ scores that do exist between groups are difficult to interpret, given the problems inherent in the design of the IQ tests. What's more, complex cognitive abilities, however they're measured, are influenced by multiple loci and are thus polygenic.

Innate factors set limits and define potentials for behavior and cognitive ability in any species. In humans, the limits are broad and the potentials aren't fully known. Individual abilities result from complex interactions between genetic and environmental factors. One product of this interaction is learning, and the ability to learn is influenced by genetic and other biological components. Undeniably, there are differences among individuals regarding these factors, but it's probably impossible to determine what proportion of the variation in test scores is due to biological factors. Besides, innate differences in abilities reflect individual variation *within* populations, not inherent differences *between* them. Comparing populations based on the results of IQ tests is a misuse of testing procedures. There's no convincing evidence *whatsoever* that populations vary in their cognitive abilities, regardless of what some popular books may suggest. Unfortunately, racist attitudes toward intelligence continue to flourish, despite the lack of evidence of mental inferiority of some populations and mental superiority of others and despite the questionable validity of IQ tests.

Contemporary Interpretations of Human Variation

Because the physical characteristics (such as skin color and hair form) used to define race are *polygenic*, measuring the genetic influence on them hasn't been possible. So physical anthropologists and other biologists who study modern human variation have largely abandoned the traditional perspective of describing superficial phenotypic characteristics in favor of *measuring* actual *genetic* characteristics.

Beginning in the 1950s, studies of modern human variation focused on the various components of blood as well as other aspects of body chemistry. Such traits as the ABO blood types are *phenotypes*, but they are *direct* products of the genotype. (Recall that protein-coding genes direct cells to make proteins, and the antigens on blood cells and many components of blood serum are partly composed of proteins; Fig. 4-2). During the twentieth century, this perspective met with a great deal of success, as eventually dozens of loci were identified and the frequencies of many specific alleles were obtained from numerous human populations. Nevertheless, in all these cases, it was the phenotype that was observed, and information about the underlying genotype remained largely unobtainable. But beginning in the 1990s, with the advent of genomic studies, new techniques were developed. Now that we can directly sequence DNA, we can actually identify entire genes and even larger DNA segments and make comparisons between individuals and populations. A decade ago, only a small portion of the human genome was accessible to physical

intelligence Mental capacity; ability to learn, reason, or comprehend and interpret information, facts, relationships, and meanings; the capacity to solve problems, whether through the application of previously acquired knowledge or through insight.

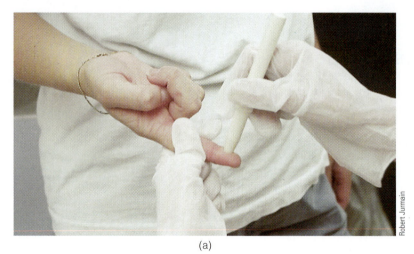

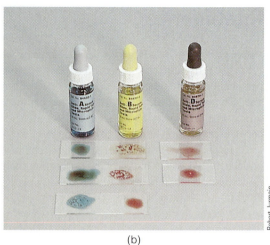

Robert Jurmain

(a)   (b)

Figure **4-2**

(a) A blood sample is drawn. (b) To determine an individual's blood type, a few drops of blood are treated with antigens contained in the three bottles. The blue bottle contains anti-A antigens, which will cause red blood cells in type A blood to clump together. The yellow bottle contains anti-B antigens, and they will cause the same effect in type B blood. The blood on the top two glass slides under the blue and yellow bottles is from the same person and is type AB, as indicated by the clumping of red blood cells when exposed to both types of antigens; the blood in the middle row is type B because it has responded only to the anti-B antigens; and the blood in the bottom row is type A because it has reacted to the anti-A antigens. Type O blood does not react to either antigen. The two samples to the right depict Rh-negative blood (top) and Rh-positive blood (bottom).

polymorphisms Loci with more than one allele. Polymorphisms can be expressed in the phenotype as the result of gene action (as in ABO), or they can exist solely at the DNA level within noncoding regions.

cline A gradual change in the frequency of genotypes and phenotypes from one geographical region to another.

anthropologists, but now we have the capacity to obtain DNA profiles for virtually every human population on earth. And we can expect that in the next decade, our understanding and knowledge of human biological variation and adaptation will dramatically increase.

HUMAN POLYMORPHISMS

Traits that differ in expression are called **polymorphisms**, and they're the main focus of human variation studies. A genetic trait is *polymorphic* if the locus that governs it has two or more alleles. (Refer to p. 54 for a discussion of the ABO blood group system governed by three alleles at one locus.) Since new alleles arise by mutation and their frequency increases or decreases as a result of natural selection, understanding polymorphisms requires evolutionary explanations. Therefore, by studying polymorphisms and comparing allele frequencies between different populations, we can begin to reconstruct the evolutionary events that have caused certain human genetic differences.

By the 1960s, the study of *clinal distributions* of individual polymorphisms had become a popular alternative to the racial approach to human diversity. A **cline** is a gradual change in the frequency of a trait or allele in populations dispersed over geographical space. In humans, the various expressions of many polymorphic traits exhibit a more or less continuous distribution from one region to another, and most of the traits that have been shown to have a clinal distribution are Mendelian. The distribution of the *B* allele in the Old World provides a good example of a clinal distribution (Fig. 4-3). Clinal distributions are generally thought to reflect microevolutionary influences of natural selection and/or gene flow. Consequently, clinal distributions are explained in evolutionary terms.

The ABO system is interesting from an anthropological perspective because the frequencies of the *A*, *B*, and *O* alleles vary tremendously among humans. In most groups, *A* and *B* are rarely found in frequencies greater than 50 percent, and usually their frequencies are much lower. Still, most human groups are polymorphic for all three alleles, but there are exceptions. For example, in native South American Indians, frequencies of the *O* allele reach 100 percent. (Actually, you could say that in these groups, the ABO system isn't polymorphic.) Exceptionally high frequencies of *O* are also found in northern Australia, and some islands off the Australian coast show frequencies exceeding 90 percent. In these populations, the high frequencies of the *O* allele are probably due to genetic drift (founder effect), although the influence of natural selection can't be entirely ruled out.

Examining single traits can be informative regarding potential influences of natural selection or gene flow. This approach, however, is limited when we try to sort out population relationships, since the study of single traits, by themselves, can lead to confusing interpretations regarding likely population relationships. A more meaningful approach is to study several traits simultaneously.

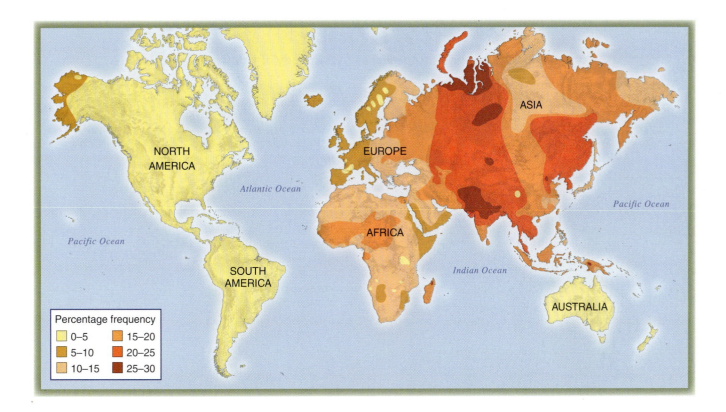

Figure **4-3**

ABO blood group system. Distribution of the *B* allele in the indigenous populations of the world. (After Mourant et al., 1976.)

POLYMORPHISMS AT THE DNA LEVEL

As a result of the Human Genome Project, we've gained considerable insight regarding human variation at the DNA level. Molecular biologists have recently discovered many variations in DNA in the human genome. For example, there are hundreds of sites where DNA segments are repeated, in some cases just a few times, and in other cases hundreds of times. These areas of nucleotide repetitions are called *microsatellites*, and they vary tremendously from person to person. In fact, every person has their own unique arrangement that defines their distinctive "DNA fingerprint." In Chapter 3, you saw how forensic scientists can now use PCR (see p. 60) to make copies of DNA contained in, for example, a drop of blood, a hair, or a semen stain and then study the "DNA fingerprints" to identify specific individuals.

Finally, researchers are now mapping patterns of variation in individual nucleotides. Of course, it's been recognized for some time that changes of individual DNA bases (called "point mutations") occur in protein-coding genes. The sickle-cell allele at the hemoglobin beta locus is the best-known example of a point mutation in humans. But now we know that point mutations also occur in noncoding DNA segments, and these, together with those in coding regions of DNA, are all referred to as *single nucleotide polymorphisms (SNPs)*. Already, more than a million SNPs have been recognized, 96 percent of which are in noncoding DNA (International SNP Map Working Group, 2001). Thus, at the beginning of the twenty-first century, geneticists have gained access to a vast biological "library," documenting the population patterning and genetic history of our species.

Biologists have collected DNA samples from contemporary human populations from around the world and examined over 600,000 loci (mostly SNPs). Their results show that African populations are significantly more variable than all those outside Africa (Grayson et al., 2008; Jacobsson et al., 2008) . This pattern is explained by the fact that modern *Homo sapiens* first appeared in Africa, then subsequently migrated out of Africa to other areas at various times (see Chapter 12 for further discussion). Because the migrating

At a Glance

Former and Contemporary Approaches to the Study of Human Variation

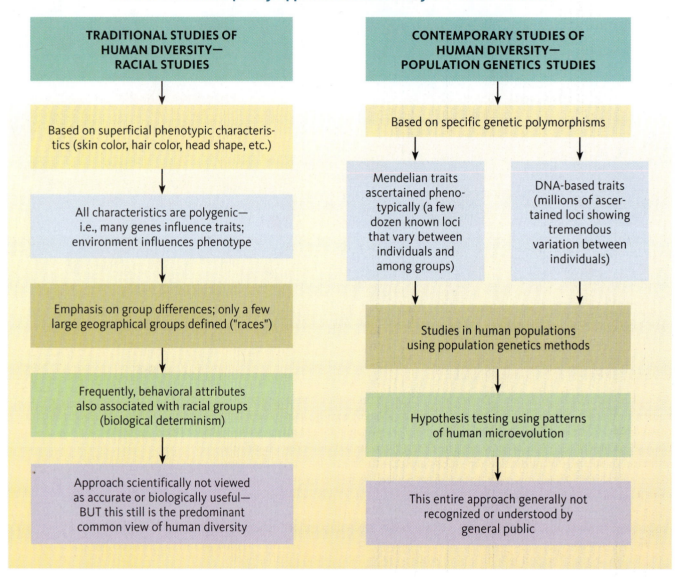

TRADITIONAL STUDIES OF HUMAN DIVERSITY— RACIAL STUDIES

↓

Based on superficial phenotypic characteristics (skin color, hair color, head shape, etc.)

↓

All characteristics are polygenic— i.e., many genes influence traits; environment influences phenotype

↓

Emphasis on group differences; only a few large geographical groups defined ("races")

↓

Frequently, behavioral attributes also associated with racial groups (biological determinism)

↓

Approach scientifically not viewed as accurate or biologically useful— BUT this still is the predominant common view of human diversity

CONTEMPORARY STUDIES OF HUMAN DIVERSITY— POPULATION GENETICS STUDIES

↓

Based on specific genetic polymorphisms

↓

Mendelian traits ascertained phenotypically (a few dozen known loci that vary between individuals and among groups)

DNA-based traits (millions of ascertained loci showing tremendous variation between individuals)

↓

Studies in human populations using population genetics methods

↓

Hypothesis testing using patterns of human microevolution

↓

This entire approach generally not recognized or understood by general public

groups were small, founder effect over the last 50,000 to 100,000 years probably accounts for much of the genetic variation we see among human populations today. There are many reasons to study this newly discovered variation, and one of these is that genetic differences between populations influence the risk of certain diseases in particular groups (Lohmueller et al., 2008).

Until recently, our understanding of polygenic traits has been inadequate because we didn't know the locations of the genes that contribute to them. But now, geneticists can identify specific loci, and soon they'll be able to isolate particular gene variants that contribute to skin color, stature, hypertension, and many other human traits that haven't been well understood. For example, with the publication of the chimpanzee genome and the first opportunity to compare human gene sequences with those seen in our closest relatives, geneticists have identified specific alleles that probably contribute to coronary artery disease and diabetes (The Chimpanzee Sequencing and Analysis Consortium, 2005).

As you can see, the recently developed tools now used by geneticists permit the study of human genetic variation at a level never before conceived. Such research will have a profound influence on our changing views of human diversity in the coming years. Moreover, through the use of these new techniques, the broader history of our species is coming under closer genetic scrutiny.

Human Biocultural Evolution

We've defined culture as a human strategy of adaptation to the natural environment. Humans live in cultural environments that are continually modified by their own activities; thus, evolutionary processes are understandable only within this *cultural* context. You will recall that natural selection pressures operate within specific environmental settings. For humans and many of our hominin ancestors, this means an environment dominated by culture. For example, you learned in Chapter 3 that the altered form of hemoglobin called Hb^S confers resistance to malaria. But the sickle-cell allele hasn't always been an important factor in human populations. Before the development of agriculture, humans rarely, if ever, lived close to mosquito-breeding areas for long periods of time. But with the spread in Africa of **slash-and-burn agriculture**, perhaps in just the last 2,000 years, penetration and clearing of tropical forests occurred. As a result, rainwater was left to stand in open, stagnant pools that provided mosquito-breeding areas near human settlements. DNA analyses have further confirmed such a recent origin and spread of the sickle-cell allele in a population from Senegal, in West Africa. One recent study estimates the origin of the Hb^S mutation in this group at between 1,250 and 2,100 ya (Currat et al., 2002). Thus, it appears that at least in some areas, malaria began to have an impact on human populations only recently. But once it did, it became a powerful selective force.

The increase in the frequency of the sickle-cell allele is a biological adaptation to an environmental change (see p. 67). However, as you learned in Chapter 3, this type of adaptation comes with a huge cost. Heterozygotes (people with sickle-cell trait) have increased resistance to malaria and presumably higher reproductive success, but prior to modern medical treatment, some of their offspring died from the genetic disease sickle-cell anemia; indeed, this situation still persists in much of the developing world. So there is a counterbalance between selective forces with an advantage for carriers *only* in malarial environments. (The genetic patterns of recessive traits such as sickle-cell anemia are discussed in Chapter 3.)

Following World War II, extensive DDT spraying by the World Health Organization began to control mosquitoes in the tropics. Forty years of DDT spraying killed millions of mosquitoes (and had devastating consequences for some local bird populations); but natural selection, acting on these insect populations, produced several DDT-resistant strains (Fig. 4-4). Accordingly, malaria is again on the rise, with several hundred thousand new cases reported annually in India, Africa, and Central America.

Lactose intolerance, which involves an individual's ability to digest milk, is another example of human biocultural evolution. In all human populations, infants and young children are able to digest milk, an obvious necessity for any young mammal. One ingredient of milk is *lactose*, a sugar that's broken down by the enzyme *lactase*. In most mammals, including many humans, the gene that codes for lactase production "switches off" in adolescence. Once this happens, if a person drinks fresh milk, the lactose ferments in the large intestine, leading to diarrhea and severe gastrointestinal upset. So, as you might expect, adults stop drinking fresh milk. Among many African and Asian populations (a majority of humankind today), most adults are lactose-intolerant (Table 4-1). But in other populations, including some Africans and Europeans, adults continue to produce lactase and are able to digest fresh milk. This continued production of lactase is called **lactase persistence**.

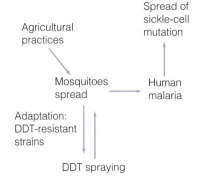

Figure **4-4**

Evolutionary interactions affecting the frequency of the sickle-cell allele.

Table **4-1** **Frequencies of Lactose Intolerance**

Population Group	Percent
U.S. whites	2–19
Finnish	18
Swiss	12
Swedish	4
U.S. blacks	70–77
Ibos	99
Bantu	90
Fulani	22
Thais	99
Asian Americans	95–100
Native Americans	85

Source: Lerner and Libby, 1976, p. 327.

slash-and-burn agriculture A traditional land-clearing practice whereby trees and vegetation are cut and burned. Fields are usually abandoned after a few years and another area subsequently cleared.

lactase persistence The ability to continue to produce the enzyme lactase in adults. Most mammals, including humans, lose this ability after they are weaned.

Throughout most of hominin evolution, milk was unavailable after weaning, so there may be a selective advantage to switching off the gene that codes for lactase production. So why can some adults (the majority in some populations) tolerate milk? The distribution of lactose-tolerant populations may provide an answer to this question, and it suggests a powerful cultural influence on this trait.

Europeans, who are generally lactose-tolerant, are partly descended from Middle Eastern populations. Often economically dependent on pastoralism, these groups raised cows and/or goats and probably drank considerable quantities of milk. In such a cultural environment, strong selection pressures would favor lactose tolerance, and modern European descendants of these populations apparently retain this ancient ability. Genetic evidence from north-central Europe has recently supported this interpretation. DNA analysis of both cattle and humans suggest that these species have influenced each other genetically. This interaction between humans and cattle resulted in cattle that produce high-quality milk and humans with the genetic capacity to digest it (Beja-Pereira et al., 2003). In other words, more than 5,000 years ago, populations of north-central Europe were selectively breeding cattle for higher milk yields. And as these populations were increasing their dependence on fresh milk, they were inadvertently selecting for the gene that produces lactase persistence in themselves.

But perhaps even more informative is the distribution of lactose tolerance in Africa, where the majority of people are lactose-intolerant. Groups such as the Fulani and Tutsi, who have been pastoralists for perhaps thousands of years, have much higher rates of lactose persistence than nonpastoralists. Presumably, like their European counterparts, they've retained the ability to produce lactase because of their continued consumption of fresh milk (Powell et al., 2003).

As we've seen, the geographical distribution of lactase persistence is related to a history of cultural dependence on fresh milk products. There are, however, some populations that rely on dairying but don't have high rates of lactase persistence (Fig. 4-5). It's been suggested that such populations traditionally have consumed their milk in the form of cheese and yogurt, in which the lactose has been broken down by bacterial action (Durham, 1981).

The interaction of human cultural environments and changes in lactose tolerance in human populations is another example of biocultural evolution. In the last few thousand years, cultural factors have initiated specific evolutionary changes in human groups. Such cultural factors have probably influenced the course of human evolution for at least 3 million years, and today they're of paramount importance.

Figure **4-5**

Natives of Mongolia rely heavily on milk products from goats and sheep, but mostly consume these foods in the form of cheese and yogurt.

Population Genetics

Physical anthropologists use the approach of **population genetics** to interpret microevolutionary patterns of human variation. Population genetics is the area of research that, among other things, examines allele frequencies in populations and attempts to identify the various factors that cause allele frequencies to change in specific groups. As we defined it in Chapter 3, a *population* is a group of interbreeding individuals that share a common **gene pool**. As a rule, a population is the group within which individuals are most likely to find mates.

In theory, this is a straightforward concept. In every generation, the genes (alleles) in a gene pool are mixed by recombination and then reunited with their counterparts (located on paired chromosomes) through mating. What emerges in the next generation is a direct product of the genes going into the pool, which in turn is a product of who is mating with whom.

Factors that determine mate choice are geographical, ecological, and social. If people are isolated on a remote island in the middle of the Pacific, there's not much chance they'll find a mate outside the immediate vicinity. Such **breeding isolates** are fairly easily defined and are a favorite subject of microevolutionary studies. Geography plays a dominant role in producing these isolates by strictly determining the range of available mates. But even within these limits, cultural rules can play a deciding role by prescribing who is most appropriate among those who are potentially available.

Today, most humans aren't so clearly defined as members of particular populations as they would be if they belonged to a breeding isolate. Inhabitants of large cities may appear to be members of a single population, but within the city, socioeconomic, ethnic, and religious boundaries crosscut in complex ways to form smaller population segments. In addition to being members of these local population groupings, we're also members of overlapping gradations of larger populations: the immediate geographical region (a metropolitan area or perhaps a state), a section of the country, a nation, and ultimately the entire species.

Once specific human populations have been identified, the next step is to ascertain what evolutionary forces, if any, are operating on them. To determine whether evolution is occurring at a given locus, population geneticists measure allele frequencies for specific traits. Then they compare these observed frequencies with those predicted by a mathematical model called the **Hardy-Weinberg equilibrium** equation. Just how the equation is used is illustrated in Appendix C. The Hardy-Weinberg formula provides a tool to establish whether allele frequencies in a population are indeed changing. In Chapter 3, we discussed several factors that act to change allele frequencies, including:

1. New variation (new alleles produced by mutation)
2. Redistributed variation (recombination, gene flow, or genetic drift)
3. Selection of "advantageous" allele combinations that promote reproductive success (natural selection)

The Adaptive Significance of Human Variation

Today, biological anthropologists view human variation as the result of the evolutionary factors we've already named: mutation; genetic drift (including founder effect), gene flow; and natural selection (the latter is especially seen in adaptations to environmental conditions, both past and present). As we've emphasized, cultural adaptations have also played an important role in the evolution of our species, and although in this discussion

population genetics The study of the frequency of alleles, genotypes, and phenotypes in populations from a microevolutionary perspective.

gene pool The total complement of genes shared by the reproductive members of a population.

breeding isolates Populations that are clearly isolated geographically or socially from other breeding groups.

Hardy-Weinberg equilibrium A mathematical formula that calculates the predicted allele frequencies at one genetic locus in a population in which no evolution is occurring. For evolution not to occur, there must be no genetic drift, gene flow, or natural selection.

we're primarily concerned with biological issues, we must still consider the influence of cultural practices on human adaptive responses.

To survive, all organisms must maintain the normal functions of internal organs, tissues, and cells within the context of an ever-changing environment. Even during the course of a single, seemingly uneventful day, there are numerous fluctuations in temperature, wind, solar radiation, humidity, and so on. Physical activity also places **stress** on physiological mechanisms. The body must accommodate all these changes by compensating in some manner to maintain internal constancy, or **homeostasis**, and all life-forms have evolved physiological mechanisms that, within limits, achieve this goal.

Physiological response to environmental change is influenced by genetic factors. We've already defined adaptation as a functional response to environmental conditions in populations and individuals. In a narrower sense, adaptation refers to *long-term* evolutionary (that is, genetic) changes that characterize all individuals within a population or species.

Examples of long-term adaptations in humans include some physiological responses to heat (sweating) or excessive levels of ultraviolet (UV) light (deeply pigmented skin in tropical regions). Such characteristics are the results of evolutionary change in species or populations, and they don't vary as the result of short-term environmental change. For example, the ability to sweat isn't lost in people who spend their entire lives in predominantly cool areas. Likewise, people born with dark skin won't become lighter even if they're never exposed to intense sunlight.

Acclimatization is another kind of physiological response to environmental conditions, and it can be short-term, long-term, or even permanent. These responses to environmental factors are partially influenced by genes, but some can also be affected by the duration and severity of the exposure, technological buffers (such as shelter or clothing), and individual behavior, weight, and overall body size.

The simplest type of acclimatization is a temporary and rapid adjustment to an environmental change (Hanna, 1999). Tanning, which can occur in almost everyone, is an example of this kind of acclimatization. Another example (one you've probably experienced but don't know it) is the very rapid increase in hemoglobin production that occurs when people who live at low elevations travel to higher ones. This increase provides the body with more oxygen in an environment where oxygen is less available. In both these examples, the physiological change is temporary. Tans fade once exposure to sunlight is reduced, and hemoglobin production drops to original levels following a return to a lower elevation.

On the other hand, *developmental acclimatization* is irreversible and results from exposure to an environmental challenge during growth and development. Lifelong residents of high altitude exhibit certain expressions of developmental acclimatization.

In the following discussion, we present some examples of how humans respond to environmental challenges. Some of these examples characterize the entire species. Others illustrate adaptations seen in only some populations. And still others illustrate the more short-term process of acclimatization.

SOLAR RADIATION, VITAMIN D, AND SKIN COLOR

Skin color is often cited as an example of adaptation through natural selection in humans. In general, prior to European contact, skin color in populations followed a largely predictable geographical distribution, especially in the Old World (Fig. 4-6) Populations with the greatest amount of pigmentation are found in the tropics, while lighter skin color is associated with more northern latitudes, particularly the inhabitants of northwestern Europe.

Skin color is mostly influenced by the pigment *melanin*, a granular substance produced by specialized cells (*melanocytes*) in the epidermis (see Fig. 4-8 on page 86). All humans have approximately the same number of melanocytes. It's the amount of melanin and the size of the melanin granules that vary. Melanin is important because it acts as a

stress In a physiological context, any factor that acts to disrupt homeostasis; more precisely, the body's response to any factor that threatens its ability to maintain homeostasis.

homeostasis A condition of balance, or stability, within a biological system, maintained by the interaction of physiological mechanisms that compensate for changes (both external and internal).

acclimatization Physiological responses to changes in the environment that occur during an individual's lifetime. Such responses may be temporary or permanent, depending on the duration of the environmental change and when in the individual's life it occurs. The capacity for acclimatization may typify an entire species or population, and because it's under genetic influence, it's subject to evolutionary factors such as natural selection or genetic drift.

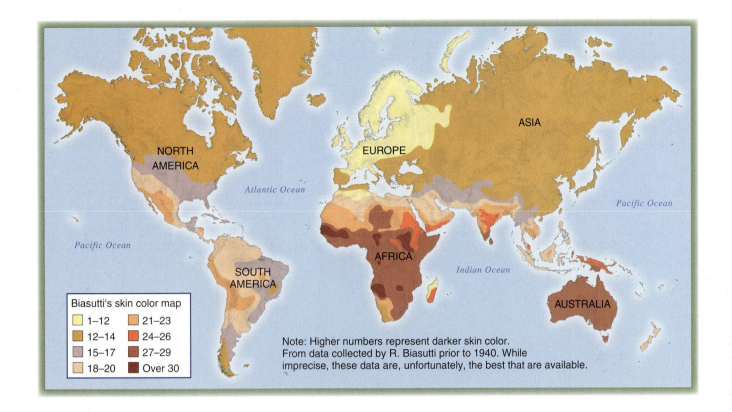

Biasutti's skin color map

1–12	21–23
12–14	24–26
15–17	27–29
18–20	Over 30

Note: Higher numbers represent darker skin color. From data collected by R. Biasutti prior to 1940. While imprecise, these data are, unfortunately, the best that are available.

Figure **4-6**

Geographical distribution of skin color in indigenous human populations. (After Biasutti, 1959.)

built-in sunscreen by absorbing potentially dangerous UV rays present (although not visible) in sunlight. So melanin protects us from overexposure to UV radiation, which can cause genetic mutations in skin cells. These mutations may lead to skin cancer, which, if left untreated, can eventually spread to other organs and result in death.

As we previously mentioned, exposure to sunlight triggers a protective mechanism in the form of tanning, the result of temporarily increased melanin production (acclimatization). This response occurs in all humans except albinos, who have a genetic mutation that prevents their melanocytes from producing melanin (Fig. 4-7). But even people who do produce melanin differ in their ability to tan. For instance, many people of northern European descent have very fair skin, blue eyes, and light hair. Their melanocytes produce small amounts of melanin, but when exposed to sunlight, they have little ability to increase production. And in all populations, women tend not to tan as deeply as men.

Natural selection has favored dark skin in areas nearest the equator, where the sun's rays are most direct and thus where exposure to UV light is most intense. In considering the cancer-causing effects of UV radiation from an *evolutionary* perspective, three points must be kept in mind:

1. Early hominins lived in the tropics, where solar radiation is more intense than in temperate areas to the north and south.
2. Unlike modern city dwellers, early hominins spent their days outdoors.
3. Early hominins didn't wear clothing that would have protected them from the sun.

Given these conditions, UV radiation was probably a powerful agent selecting for high levels of melanin production in early humans.

Jablonski (1992) and Jablonski and Chaplin (2000) offer an additional explanation for the distribution of skin color, one that focuses on the role of UV radiation in the degradation of folate. Folate is a B vitamin that isn't stored in the body and therefore must be replenished through dietary sources. Folate deficiencies in pregnant women are associated with numerous complications, including maternal death; and in children they can lead to retarded

Figure **4-7**

An African albino. This young man has a much greater chance of developing skin cancer than the man standing next to him.

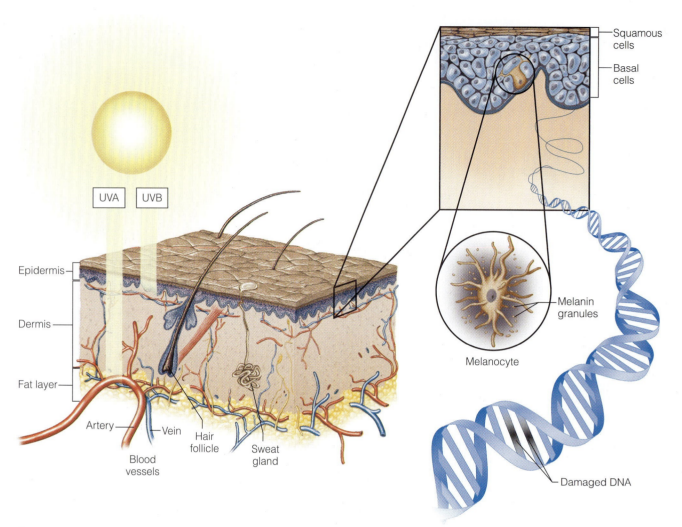

Squamous cells

Basal cells

Melanin granules

Melanocyte

Damaged DNA

Epidermis

Dermis

Fat layer

Artery   Vein

Blood vessels

Hair follicle   Sweat gland

Figure **4-8**

Ultraviolet rays penetrate the skin and can eventually damage DNA within skin cells. The three major types of cells that can be affected are squamous cells, basal cells, and melanocytes.

neural tube In early embryonic development, the anatomical structure that develops to form the brain and spinal cord.

spina bifida A condition in which the arch of one or more vertebrae fails to fuse and form a protective barrier around the spinal cord.

growth and other serious conditions. Folate also plays a crucial role in **neural tube** development very early in embryonic development, and deficiencies can lead to defects, including various expressions of **spina bifida**. The consequences of severe neural tube defects can include pain, infection, paralysis, and even death. It goes without saying that neural tube defects can dramatically reduce the reproductive success of affected individuals.

Some studies have shown that UV radiation rapidly depletes folate serum levels both in laboratory experiments and in fair-skinned individuals. These findings have implications for pregnant women and children and also for the evolution of dark skin in hominins. Jablonski and Chaplin suggest that the earliest hominins may have had light body skin covered with dark hair, as is seen in chimpanzees and gorillas. (Both have darker skin on exposed body parts.) But as loss of body hair in hominins occurred, dark skin evolved rather quickly as a protective response to the damaging effects of UV radiation on folate.

As hominins migrated out of Africa into Europe and Asia, they faced new selective pressures. Not only were they moving away from the tropics, where ultraviolet rays were most direct, but they were also moving into areas where winters were cold and cloudy. Bear in mind, too, that physiological adaptations weren't sufficient to meet the demands of living in colder climates. Therefore, we assume that these populations were wearing animal skins or other types of clothing at least part of the year. Although clothing would have added necessary warmth, it would also have blocked sunlight. Consequently, the advantages provided by deeply pigmented skin in the tropics were no longer important, and selection for darker skin may have been relaxed (Brace and Montagu, 1977).

However, relaxed selection for dark skin isn't sufficient to explain the very depigmented skin seen especially in some northern Europeans. Perhaps another factor, the need for adequate amounts of vitamin D, was also critical. The theory concerning the possible role of vitamin D, known as the *vitamin D hypothesis*, offers the following explanation.

Vitamin D is produced in the body partly as a result of the interaction between ultraviolet radiation and a substance similar to cholesterol. It's also available in some foods, including liver, fish oils, egg yolk, butter, and cream. Vitamin D is necessary for normal bone growth and mineralization, and some exposure to ultraviolet radiation is therefore essential. Insufficient amounts of vitamin D during childhood result in *rickets*, a condition that often leads to bowing of the long bones of the legs and deformation of the pelvis (Fig. 4-9). Pelvic deformities are of particular concern for women, because they can lead to a narrowing of the birth canal, which, in the absence of surgical intervention, frequently results in the death of both mother and infant during childbirth.

Rickets may have been a significant selective factor that favored lighter skin in regions with less sunlight. Reduced levels of UV light and the increased use of clothing could have been detrimental to dark-skinned individuals in more northern latitudes. In these people, melanin would have blocked absorption of the already reduced amounts of available ultraviolet radiation required for vitamin D synthesis. Therefore, selection pressures would have shifted over time to favor lighter skin. There is substantial evidence, both historically and in contemporary populations, to support this theory.

During the latter decades of the nineteenth century in the United States, African American inhabitants of northern cities suffered a higher incidence of rickets than whites. (The solution to this problem was fairly simple: the supplementation of milk with vitamin D.) Another example is seen in Britain, where darker-skinned East Indians and Pakistanis show a higher incidence of rickets than people with lighter skin (Molnar, 1983).

Jablonski and Chaplin (2000) have also looked at the *potential* for vitamin D synthesis in people with different skin color based on the yearly average UV radiation at various latitudes (Fig. 4-10). Their conclusions support the vitamin D hypothesis to the point of stating that the requirement for vitamin D synthesis in northern latitudes was as important to natural selection as the need for protection from UV radiation in tropical regions.

Except for a person's sex, more social importance has been attached to variation in skin color than to any other single human biological trait. But aside from its probable adaptive significance relative to UV radiation, skin color is no more important physiologically than many other characteristics. However, from an evolutionary perspective, it provides a good example of how the forces of natural selection have produced geographically patterned variation as the consequence of two competing selective forces: the need for protection from overexposure to UV radiation (which can lead to folate depletion and skin cancer) on the one hand, and the necessity for adequate UV exposure to promote vitamin D synthesis on the other.

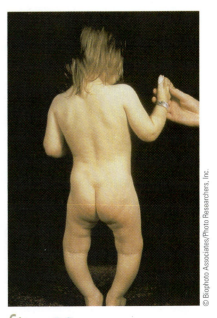

Figure **4-9**
A child with rickets.

THE THERMAL ENVIRONMENT

Mammals and birds have evolved complex mechanisms to maintain a constant internal body temperature. While reptiles rely on exposure to external heat sources to raise body temperature and energy levels, mammals and birds have physiological mechanisms that, within certain limits, increase or reduce the loss of body heat. The optimum internal body temperature for normal cellular functions is species-specific, and for humans it's approximately 98.6°F.

People are found in a wide variety of habitats, with temperatures ranging from over 120°F to less than −60°F. In these extremes, human life wouldn't be possible without cultural innovations. But even accounting for the artificial environments in which we live, such external conditions place the human body under enormous stress.

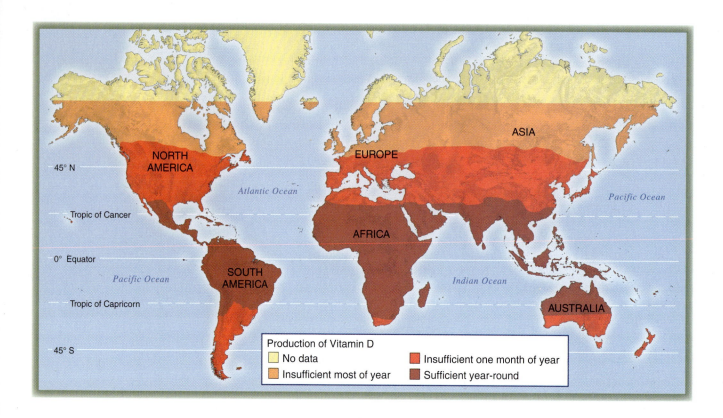

Figure 4-10

Populations indigenous to the tropics received enough UV radiation for vitamin D synthesis year-round. In other areas, people have moderately melanized skin and don't receive enough UV light for vitamin D synthesis for one month of the year. In still other areas, even light skin doesn't receive enough UV light for vitamin D synthesis during most of the year. (Adapted from Jablonski and Chaplin, 2000, 2002.)

vasodilation Expansion of blood vessels, permitting increased blood flow to the skin. Vasodilation permits warming of the skin and also facilitates radiation of warmth as a means of cooling. Vasodilation is an involuntary response to warm temperatures, various drugs, and even emotional states (blushing).

Response to Heat All available evidence suggests that the earliest hominins evolved in the warm-to-hot savannas of East Africa. The fact that humans cope better with heat than they do with cold is testimony to the long-term adaptations to heat that evolved in our ancestors.

In humans, as well as certain other species, such as horses, sweat glands are distributed throughout the skin. This wide distribution of sweat glands makes it possible to lose heat at the body surface through evaporative cooling, a mechanism that has evolved to the greatest degree in humans. The ability to dissipate heat by sweating is seen in all humans to an almost equal degree, with the average number of sweat glands per individual (approximately 1.6 million) being fairly constant. However, people who aren't generally exposed to hot conditions do experience a period of acclimatization that initially involves significantly increased perspiration rates (Frisancho, 1993). An additional factor that enhances the cooling effects of sweating is increased exposure of the skin because of reduced amounts of body hair. We don't know when in our evolutionary history we began to lose body hair, but it represents a species-wide adaptation.

Although effective, heat reduction through evaporation can be expensive, and indeed dangerous, in terms of water and sodium loss. Up to 3 liters of water can be lost by a human engaged in heavy work in high heat. You can appreciate the importance of this fact if you consider that losing 1 liter of water is approximately equal to losing 1.5 percent of total body weight, and quickly losing 10 percent of body weight can be life threatening. This is why water must be continuously replaced when you exercise on a hot day.

Another mechanism for radiating body heat is **vasodilation**, which occurs when capillaries near the skin's surface widen to permit increased blood flow to the skin. The visible effect of vasodilation is flushing, or increased redness and warming of the skin, particularly of the face. But the physiological effect is to permit heat, carried by the blood from the interior of the body, to be radiated from the skin's surface to the surrounding air. (Some drugs, including alcohol, also produce vasodilation, which accounts for the redder and warmer face some people have after a couple of drinks.)

Body size and proportions are also important in regulating body temperature. Indeed, there seems to be a general relationship between climate and body size and shape in birds and mammals. In general, within a species, body size (weight) increases as distance from the equator increases. In humans, this relationship holds up fairly well, but there are numerous exceptions.

Two rules that pertain to the relationship between body size, body proportions, and climate are *Bergmann's rule* and *Allen's rule*.

1. *Bergmann's rule concerns the relationship of body mass or volume to surface area.* In mammals, body size tends to be greater in populations that live in colder climates. This is because as mass increases, the relative amount of surface area decreases proportionately. Because heat is lost at the surface, it follows that increased mass allows for greater heat retention and reduced heat loss.

2. *Allen's rule concerns shape of the body, especially appendages.* In colder climates, shorter appendages, with increased mass-to-surface ratios, are adaptive because they're more effective at preventing heat loss. Conversely, longer appendages, with increased surface area relative to mass, are more adaptive in warmer climates because they promote heat loss.

According to these rules, the most suitable body shape in hot climates is linear with long arms and legs. In a cold climate, a more suitable body type is stocky with shorter limbs. Several studies have shown that human populations generally conform to these principles. In colder climates, body mass tends, on average, to be greater and characterized by a larger trunk relative to arms and legs (Roberts, 1973). People living in the Arctic tend to be short and stocky, while many sub-Saharan Africans, especially East African pastoralists, are, on average, tall and linear (Fig. 4-11). But there's a great deal of variability regarding human body proportions, and not all populations conform so readily to Bergmann's and Allen's rules.

Response to Cold Human physiological responses to cold combine factors that increase heat production with those that enhance heat retention. Of the two, heat retention is more efficient because it requires less energy. This is an important point because energy is

(a)   (b)

Figure **4-11**

(a) This African woman has the linear proportions characteristic of many inhabitants of sub-Saharan Africa. (b) By comparison, the Inuit woman is short and stocky. These two individuals serve as good examples of Bergmann's and Allen's rules.

Renee Lynn/Photo Researchers

George Holton/Photo Researchers

derived from food. Unless resources are abundant, and in winter they frequently aren't, any factor that conserves energy can have adaptive value.

Short-term responses to cold include increased metabolic rate and shivering, both of which generate body heat, at least for a short time. **Vasoconstriction**, another short-term response, restricts heat loss and conserves energy. Humans also have a subcutaneous (beneath the skin) fat layer that provides an insulative layer throughout the body. Behavioral modifications include increased activity, wearing warmer clothing, increased food consumption, and even curling up into a ball.

Increases in metabolic rate (the rate at which cells break up nutrients into their components) release energy in the form of heat. Shivering also generates muscle heat, as does voluntary exercise. But these methods of heat production are expensive because they require an increased intake of nutrients to provide energy. (Perhaps this explains why we tend to have a heartier appetite during the winter and frequently eat more fats and carbohydrates, the very sources of energy our body requires.)

In general, people exposed to chronic cold (meaning much or most of the year) maintain higher metabolic rates than those living in warmer climates. The Inuit (Eskimo) people living in the Arctic maintain metabolic rates between 13 and 45 percent higher than that observed in non-Inuit control subjects (Frisancho, 1993). Moreover, the highest metabolic rates are seen in inland Inuit, who are exposed to even greater cold stress than coastal populations. Traditionally, the Inuit had the highest animal protein and fat diet of any human population in the world. Their diet was dictated by the available resource base (fish and mammals but little to no vegetable material), and it served to maintain the high metabolic rates required by exposure to chronic cold.

Vasoconstriction (the opposite of vasodilation) restricts capillary blood flow to the surface of the skin, thus reducing heat loss at the body surface. Because retaining body heat is more economical than creating it, vasoconstriction is very efficient, provided temperatures don't drop below freezing. If temperatures do fall below freezing, continued vasoconstriction can allow the skin's temperature to decline to the point of frostbite or worse.

Long-term responses to cold vary among human groups. For example, in the past, desert-dwelling native Australian populations were exposed to wide temperature fluctuations from day to night. Since they wore no clothing and didn't build shelters, their only protection from temperatures that hovered only a few degrees above freezing was provided by sleeping fires. They also experienced continuous vasoconstriction throughout the night, and this permitted a degree of skin cooling most people would find extremely uncomfortable. But, as there was no threat of frostbite, continued vasoconstriction was an efficient adaptation that helped prevent excessive internal heat loss.

By contrast, the Inuit experience intermittent periods of vasoconstriction and vasodilation. This compromise provides periodic warmth to the skin that helps prevent frostbite in subfreezing temperatures. At the same time, because vasodilation is intermittent, energy loss is restricted, with more heat retained at the body's core.

These examples illustrate two of the ways that adaptations to cold vary among human populations. Obviously, winter conditions exceed our ability to adapt physiologically in many parts of the world. So if they hadn't developed cultural innovations, our ancestors would have remained in the tropics.

HIGH ALTITUDE

Studies of high-altitude residents have greatly contributed to our understanding of physiological adaptation. As you would expect, altitude studies have focused on inhabited mountainous regions, particularly in the Himalayas, Andes, and Rocky Mountains. Of these three areas, permanent human habitation probably has the longest history in the Himalayas (Moore et al., 1998). Today, perhaps as many as 25 million people live at alti-

vasoconstriction Narrowing of blood vessels to reduce blood flow to the skin. Vasoconstriction is an involuntary response to cold and reduces heat loss at the skin's surface.

L. G. Moore

(a)

William Pratt

(b)

Figure **4-12**

(a) A household in northern Tibet, situated at an elevation of over 15,000 feet above sea level. (b) La Paz, Bolivia, at just over 12,000 feet above sea level, is home to more than 1 million people.

tudes above 10,000 feet. In Tibet, permanent settlements exist above 15,000 feet, and in the Andes, they can be found as high as 17,000 feet (Fig. 4-12).

Because the mechanisms that maintain homeostasis in humans evolved at lower altitudes, we're compromised by conditions at higher elevations. At high altitudes, many factors produce stress on the human body. These include **hypoxia** (reduced available oxygen), more intense solar radiation, cold, low humidity, wind (which increases cold stress), a reduced nutritional base, and rough terrain. Of these, hypoxia exerts the greatest amount of stress on human physiological systems, especially the heart, lungs, and brain.

Hypoxia results from reduced barometric pressure. It's not that there's less oxygen in the atmosphere at high altitudes; it's just less concentrated. Therefore, to obtain the same amount of oxygen at 9,000 feet as at sea level, people must make certain physiological alterations that increase the body's ability to transport and efficiently use the oxygen that's available.

At high altitudes, reproduction, in particular, is affected through increased infant mortality rates, miscarriage, low birth weights, and premature birth. An early study (Moore and Regensteiner, 1983) reported that in Colorado, infant deaths are almost twice as common above 8,200 feet (2,500 m) than at lower elevations. One cause of fetal and maternal death is preeclampsia, a severe elevation of blood pressure in pregnant women after the twentieth gestational week. In another Colorado study, Palmer et al. (1999) reported that among pregnant women living at elevations over 10,000 feet, the prevalence of preeclampsia was 16 percent, compared to 3 percent at around 4,000 feet. In general, the problems related to childbearing are attributed to issues that compromise the vascular supply (and thus oxygen transport) to the fetus.

People born at lower altitudes differ from high-altitude natives in how they adapt to hypoxia. In people born at low elevations, acclimatization begins to occur within hours of exposure to high altitude. The responses may be short-term modifications, depending on duration of stay. These changes include an increase in respiration rate, heart rate, and production of red blood cells. (Red blood cells contain hemoglobin, the protein responsible for transporting oxygen to organs and tissues.)

Developmental acclimatization occurs in high-altitude natives during growth and development. This type of acclimatization is present only in people who grow up in high-altitude areas, not in those who moved there as adults. Compared with populations at

hypoxia Lack of oxygen. Hypoxia can refer to reduced amounts of available oxygen in the atmosphere (due to lowered barometric pressure) or to insufficient amounts of oxygen in the body.

lower elevations, lifelong residents of high altitudes grow somewhat more slowly and mature later. Other differences include greater lung capacity and a relatively larger heart. And people born at high altitudes are more efficient than migrants at diffusing oxygen from blood to body tissues. Developmental acclimatization to high-altitude hypoxia serves as a good example of physiological plasticity by illustrating how, within the limits set by genetic factors, development can be influenced by environment.

There is evidence that entire *populations* have also genetically adapted to high altitudes. Indigenous peoples of Tibet who have inhabited regions higher than 12,000 feet for around 25,000 years may have made genetic (that is, evolutionary) accommodations to hypoxia. Altitude doesn't appear to affect reproduction in these people to the degree it does in other populations. Infants have birth weights as high as those of lowland Tibetan groups and higher than those of recent (20 to 30 years) Chinese immigrants. This fact may be the result of alterations in maternal blood flow to the uterus during pregnancy (Moore et al., 1991; Moore et al., 2005).

Another line of evidence concerns how the body processes glucose (blood sugar). Glucose is critical because it's the only source of energy used by the brain, and it's also used, although not exclusively, by the heart. Both highland Tibetans and the Quechua (inhabitants of high-altitude regions of the Peruvian Andes) burn glucose in a way that permits more efficient use of oxygen. This implies the presence of genetic mutations in the mitochondrial DNA (mtDNA directs how cells use glucose). It also implies that natural selection has acted to increase the frequency of these advantageous mutations in these groups.

As yet, there's no certain evidence that Tibetans and Quechua have made evolutionary changes to accommodate high-altitude hypoxia (since specific genetic mechanisms that underlie these populations' unique abilities have not been identified). But the data suggest that selection has operated to produce evolutionary change in these two groups. If further study supports these findings, we have an excellent example of evolution in action producing long-term adaptation at the population level.

INFECTIOUS DISEASE

Infection, as opposed to other disease categories, such as degenerative or genetic disease, includes pathological conditions caused by microorganisms (viruses, bacteria, and fungi). Throughout the course of human evolution, infectious disease has exerted enormous selective pressures on populations and consequently has influenced the frequency of certain alleles that affect the immune response. In fact, it would be difficult to overstate the importance of infectious disease as an agent of natural selection in human populations. But as important as infectious disease has been, its role isn't very well documented.

The effects of infectious disease on humans are mediated culturally as well as biologically. Innumerable cultural factors, such as architectural styles, subsistence techniques, exposure to domesticated animals, and even religious practices, all affect how infectious disease develops and persists within and between populations.

Until about 10,000 to 12,000 years ago, all humans lived in small nomadic hunting and gathering groups. These groups rarely remained in one location for long, so they had minimal contact with refuse heaps that house disease **vectors**. But with the domestication of plants and animals, people became more sedentary and began living in small villages. Gradually, villages became towns, and towns, in turn, developed into densely crowded, unsanitary cities.

As long as humans lived in small bands, there was little opportunity for infectious disease to have much impact on large numbers of people. Even if an entire local group or band were wiped out, the effect on the overall population in a given area would have been negligible. Moreover, for a disease to become **endemic** in a population, sufficient numbers of people must be present. Therefore, small bands of hunter-gatherers weren't faced with continuous exposure to endemic disease.

vectors Agents that transmit disease from one carrier to another. Mosquitoes are vectors for malaria, just as fleas are vectors for bubonic plague.

endemic Continuously present in a population.

But with the advent of settled living and close proximity to domesticated animals, opportunities for disease greatly increased. As sedentary life permitted larger group size, it became possible for diseases to become permanently established in some populations. Moreover, exposure to domestic animals, such as cattle and fowl, provided an opportune environment for the spread of several **zoonotic** diseases, such as tuberculosis. Humans had no doubt always contracted diseases occasionally from the animals they hunted; but when they began to live with domesticated animals, they were faced with an entire array of new infectious conditions. Also, the crowded, unsanitary conditions that characterized parts of all cities until the late nineteenth century and that persist in much of the world today further added to the disease burden borne by human inhabitants.

AIDS (acquired immunodeficiency syndrome) provides an excellent example of the influence of human infectious disease as a selective agent. In the United States, the first cases of AIDS were reported in 1981. Since that time, perhaps as many as 1.5 million Americans have been infected by HIV (human immunodeficiency virus), the agent that causes AIDS. However, most of the burden of AIDS is borne by developing countries, where 95 percent of all HIV-infected people live. By the end of 2007, an estimated 33 million people worldwide were living with HIV infection, and at least 23 million had died.

HIV is transmitted from person to person through the exchange of body fluids, usually blood or semen. It's not spread through casual contact with an infected person. Within six months of infection, most people test positive for anti-HIV antibodies, meaning that their immune system has recognized the presence of foreign antigens and has responded by producing antibodies. However, serious HIV-related symptoms may not appear for years. HIV is a "slow virus" that may persist in a person's body for several years before the onset of severe illness. This asymptomatic state is called a "latency period," and the average latency period in the United States is more than 11 years.

Like all viruses, HIV must invade certain types of cells and alter the functions of those cells to produce more virus particles in a process that eventually leads to cell destruction. HIV can attack various types of cells, but it especially targets so-called T4 helper cells, which are major components of the immune system. As HIV infection spreads and T4 cells are destroyed, the patient's immune system begins to fail. Consequently, he or she develops symptoms caused by various **pathogens** that are commonly present but usually kept in check by a normal immune response. When an HIV-infected person's T cell count drops to a level indicating that immunity has been suppressed, and when symptoms of "opportunistic" infections appear, the patient is said to have AIDS.

By the early 1990s, scientists were aware of a number of patients who had been HIV positive for 10 to 15 years but continued to show few if any symptoms. Researchers began to suspect that some individuals possess a natural immunity or resistance to HIV infection. This was shown to be true in late 1996 with the publication of two different studies (Dean et al., 1996; Samson et al., 1996) that demonstrated a mechanism for HIV resistance.

These two reports describe a genetic mutation that involves a major "receptor site" on the surface of certain immune cells, including T4 cells. (Receptor sites are protein molecules that enable HIV and other viruses to invade cells.) As a result of the mutation, the receptor site doesn't function properly and HIV can't enter the cell. Current evidence suggests that people who are homozygous for a particular (mutant) allele may be completely resistant to many types of HIV infection. In heterozygotes, infection may still occur, but the course of HIV disease is slowed.

For unknown reasons, the mutant allele occurs mainly in people of European descent, among whom its frequency is about 10 percent. Samson and colleagues (1996) reported that in the Japanese and West African groups they studied, the mutation was absent, but Dean and colleagues (1996) reported an allele frequency of about 2 percent among African Americans. They speculated that the presence of the allele in African Americans may be entirely due to genetic admixture (gene flow) with European Americans. They also suggested that this polymorphism exists in Europeans as a result of selective pressures favoring

zoonotic (zoh-oh-no´-tic) Pertaining to a zoonosis (*pl.*, zoonoses), a disease that is transmitted to humans through contact with nonhuman animals.

pathogens Any agents, especially microorganisms such as viruses, bacteria, or fungi, that infect a host and cause disease.

an allele that originally occurred as a rare mutation. But we should point out that the original selective agent was *not* HIV. Instead, it was some other, as yet unidentified pathogen that requires the same receptor site as HIV, and some researchers (Lalani et al., 1999) have suggested that it may have been the virus that causes smallpox. (Lalani et al.,1999, reported that a virus related to the smallpox virus can use the same receptor site as HIV.) While this conclusion hasn't been proved, it offers an exciting avenue of research. It may reveal how a mutation that originally was favored by selection because it provides protection against one type of infection (smallpox) can also increase resistance to another (AIDS).

The best-known epidemic in history was the Black Death (bubonic plague) in the mid-fourteenth century. Bubonic plague is caused by a bacterium and is transmitted from rodents to humans by fleas. In just a few years, this deadly disease had spread (following trade routes and facilitated by rodent-infested ship cargoes) from the Caspian Sea throughout the Mediterranean area to northern Europe. During the initial exposure to this disease, as many as one-third of the inhabitants of Europe died.

A lesser-known but even more devastating example was the influenza **pandemic** that broke out in 1918 at the end of World War I. This was actually one of a series of influenza outbreaks, but it has remained notable for its still unexplained virulence and the fact that it accounted for the death of over 21 million people worldwide.

While we have no clear-cut evidence of a selective role for bubonic plague or influenza, this doesn't mean that one doesn't exist. The tremendous mortality that these diseases (and others) are capable of causing certainly increases the likelihood that they influenced the development of human adaptive responses in ways we haven't yet discovered.

The Continuing Impact of Infectious Disease

It's important to understand that humans and pathogens exert selective pressures on each other, creating a dynamic relationship between disease organisms and their human (and nonhuman) hosts. Just as disease exerts selective pressures on host populations to adapt, microorganisms also evolve and adapt to various pressures exerted on them by their hosts.

Evolutionarily speaking, it's to the advantage of any pathogen not to be so virulent as to kill its host too quickly. If the host dies soon after becoming infected, the viral or bacterial agent may not have time to reproduce and infect other hosts. Thus, selection sometimes acts to produce resistance in host populations and/or to reduce the virulence of disease organisms, to the benefit of both. However, members of populations exposed for the first time to a new disease frequently die in huge numbers. This type of exposure was a major factor in the decimation of indigenous New World populations after contact with Europeans introduced smallpox into Native American groups. This has also been the case with the current worldwide spread of HIV.

Of the known disease-causing organisms, HIV provides the best-documented example of evolution and adaptation in a pathogen. It's also one of several examples of interspecies transfer of infection. HIV is the most mutable and genetically variable virus known. The type of HIV responsible for the AIDS epidemic is HIV-1, which in turn is divided into three major subtypes (Hu et al., 1996; Gao, 1999). Another far less common type is HIV-2, which is present only in populations of West Africa. HIV-2 also exhibits a wide range of genetic diversity, and while some strains cause AIDS, others are far less virulent.

Since the late 1980s, researchers have been comparing the DNA sequences of HIV and a closely related virus called *simian immunodeficiency virus (SIV)*. SIV is found in chimpanzees and several African monkey species. Like HIV, SIV is genetically variable, and each strain appears to be specific to a given species and even subspecies of primate. SIV produces no symptoms in the African monkeys and chimpanzees that are its traditional

pandemic An extensive outbreak of disease affecting large numbers of individuals over a wide area; potentially a worldwide phenomenon.

hosts. This finding indicates that the various forms of SIV have shared a long evolutionary history (perhaps several hundred thousand years) with a number of African primate species and that the latter are able to accommodate this virus. Moreover, these results substantiate long-held hypotheses that SIV and HIV evolved in Africa.

Comparisons of the DNA sequences of HIV-2 and the form of SIV found in one monkey species (the sooty mangabey) revealed that, genetically, these two viruses are almost identical. These findings led to the generally accepted conclusion that HIV-2 evolved from sooty mangabey SIV. Moreover, sooty mangabeys are hunted for food and also kept as pets in western central Africa, and the transmission of SIV to humans probably occurred through bites and the butchering of monkey carcasses.

A group of medical researchers (Gao et al., 1999) also compared DNA sequences of HIV-1 and the form of SIV found in chimpanzees indigenous to western central Africa. Their results showed that HIV-1 almost certainly evolved from the strain of chimpanzee SIV that infects the central African subspecies *Pan troglodytes troglodytes*.

Unfortunately for both species, chimpanzees are routinely hunted by humans for food in parts of West Africa (see p. 144). Consequently, the most probable explanation for the transmission of SIV from chimpanzees to humans is, as with sooty mangabeys, the hunting and butchering of chimpanzees (Gao et al., 1999; Weiss and Wrangham, 1999; Fig. 4-13). Hence, HIV/AIDS is a zoonotic disease. The DNA evidence further suggests that there were at least three separate human exposures to chimpanzee SIV, and at some point the virus was altered to the form we call HIV. When chimpanzee SIV was first transmitted to humans is unknown. The oldest evidence of human infection is a frozen HIV-positive blood sample taken from a West African patient in 1959. There are also a few documented cases of AIDS infection by the late 1960s and early 1970s. Therefore, although human exposure to SIV/HIV probably occurred many times in the past, the virus didn't become firmly established in humans until the latter half of the twentieth century.

From this SIV/HIV example, you can appreciate how, through the adoption of various cultural practices, humans have radically altered patterns of infectious disease. The interaction of cultural and biological factors has influenced microevolutionary change in humans, as in the example of sickle-cell anemia (see p. 81), to accommodate altered relationships with disease organisms.

Karl Ammann

Figure 4-13

These people, selling butchered chimpanzees, may not realize that by handling this meat they could be exposing themselves to HIV.

At a Glance
Zoonoses and Human Infectious Disease

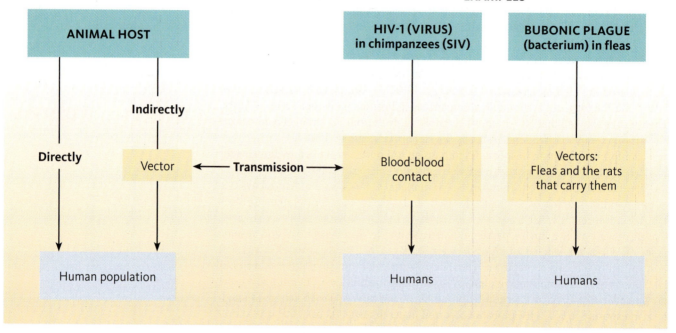

EXAMPLES

Until the twentieth century, infectious disease was the number one cause of death in all human populations. Even today, in many developing countries, as much as half of all mortality is due to infectious disease, compared to only about 10 percent in the United States. For example, malaria is a disease of the poor in developing nations. Annually, there are an estimated 1 million deaths due to malaria. That figure computes to one malaria-related death every 30 seconds (Weiss, 2002)! Ninety percent of these deaths occur in sub-Saharan Africa, where 5 percent of children die of malaria before age 5 (Greenwood and Mutabingwa, 2002; Weiss, 2002). In the United States and other developing nations, with improved living conditions and sanitation and especially with the widespread use of antibiotics and pesticides beginning in the late 1940s, infectious disease has given way to heart disease and cancer as the leading causes of death.

Optimistic predictions held that infectious disease would be a thing of the past in developed countries and, with the introduction of antibiotics and better living standards, in developing nations too. But between 1980 and 1992, the number of deaths in the United States in which infectious disease was the underlying cause rose from 41 to 65 per 100,000, an increase of 58 percent (Pinner et al., 1996).

Obviously, AIDS contributed substantially to the increase in mortality due to infectious disease in the United States between 1980 and 1992. By 1992, AIDS was the leading cause of death in men aged 25 to 44 years. As of 1998, mortality due to AIDS had decreased significantly; still, even when subtracting the effect of AIDS in mortality rates, there was a 22 percent increase in mortality rates due to infectious disease between 1980 and 1992 (Pinner et al., 1996).

This increase may partly be due to the overuse of antibiotics. It's estimated that half of all antibiotics prescribed in the United States are used to treat viral conditions such as colds and flu. Because antibiotics are completely ineffective against viruses, such therapy not only is useless, but may also have dangerous long-term consequences. There's considerable concern in the biomedical community over the indiscriminate use of antibiotics since the 1950s. Antibiotics have exerted selective pressures on bacterial species that have, over time, developed antibiotic-resistant strains (an excellent example of natural selection). So, in the past few years we've seen the *reemergence* of many bacterial diseases, including influenza, pneumonia, cholera, and tuberculosis (TB), in forms that are less responsive to treatment.

The World Health Organization now lists tuberculosis as the world's leading killer of adults (Colwell, 1996). In fact, the number of tuberculosis cases has risen 28 percent worldwide since the mid-1980s, with an estimated 10 million people infected in the United States alone. Although not all infected people develop active disease, in the 1990s an estimated 30 million persons worldwide are believed to have died from TB. One very troubling aspect of the increase in tuberculosis infection is that newly developed strains of *Mycobacterium tuberculosis*, the bacterium that causes TB, are resistant to antibiotics and other treatments.

Various treatments for nonbacterial conditions have also become ineffective. One such example is the appearance of chloroquin-resistant malaria, which has rendered chloroquin (the traditional preventive medication) virtually useless in some parts of Africa. And many insect species have also developed resistance to commonly used pesticides.

In addition to threats posed by resistant strains of pathogens, there are other factors that may contribute to the emergence (or reemergence) of infectious disease. Political leaders in some (mostly European) countries and the overwhelming majority of scientists worldwide are becoming increasingly concerned over the potential for global warming to expand the geographical range of numerous tropical disease vectors, such as mosquitoes. Moreover, the destruction of natural environments not only contributes to global warming, but also facilitates the spread of disease vectors from formerly restricted local areas to new habitats.

Fundamental to all these factors is human population size, which, as it continues to soar, creates more environmental disturbance and, through additional human activity, adds further to global warming. Moreover, in developing countries, where as much as 50 percent of mortality is due to infectious disease, overcrowding and unsanitary conditions increasingly contribute to increased rates of communicable illness. One could scarcely conceive of a better set of circumstances for the appearance and spread of communicable disease, and it remains to be seen if scientific innovation and medical technology are able to meet the challenge.

Summary

In this chapter, we investigated some of the ways in which humans differ from one another, both within and between populations. We first explored how this variation was approached in the past, in terms of racial categories. We then discussed contemporary approaches that describe simple genetic polymorphisms for which allele frequencies may be calculated, and we emphasized new techniques in which genetic data are obtained from direct analyses of mitochondrial and nuclear DNA. Moreover, we reviewed the theoretical basis of the population genetics approach, the subdiscipline of physical anthropology that seeks to measure genetic diversity among humans. Data on polymorphic traits can be used to understand aspects of human microevolution. For humans, of course, culture also plays a crucial evolutionary role, and the sickle-cell trait and lactase persistence are thus viewed from a biocultural perspective.

We also considered how populations vary with regard to physiological adaptations to a number of environmental conditions, including solar radiation, heat, cold, and high altitude. We also focused on how infectious disease influences evolutionary processes, and we particularly emphasized AIDS/HIV and the dynamic relationship between pathogens and human hosts.

The topic of human variation is very complicated, and the biological and cultural factors that have contributed to that variation and that continue to influence it are manifold. But from an explicitly evolutionary perspective, it is through the investigation of changes in allele frequencies in response to environmental conditions that we will continue to elucidate the diverse adaptive potential that characterizes our species.

Critical Thinking Questions

1. Imagine you're with some friends talking about variation and how many races there are. One person says that there are three, and another thinks that there are five. Would you agree with either one? Why or why not?

2. For the same group of friends in question 1 (none of whom have had a course in biological anthropology), how would you explain how scientific knowledge doesn't support their preconceived notions about human races?

3. In the twentieth century, how did the scientific study of human diversity change from the more traditional approach?

4. Why can we say that variations in human skin color are the result of natural selection in different environments? Why can we say that less-pigmented skin is a result of conflicting selective factors?

5. We know that infectious disease has played an important role in human evolution. Do you think it still plays a role in human adaptation today?

6. How have human cultural practices influenced the patterns of infectious disease seen today? Provide as many examples as you can, including some not discussed in this chapter.

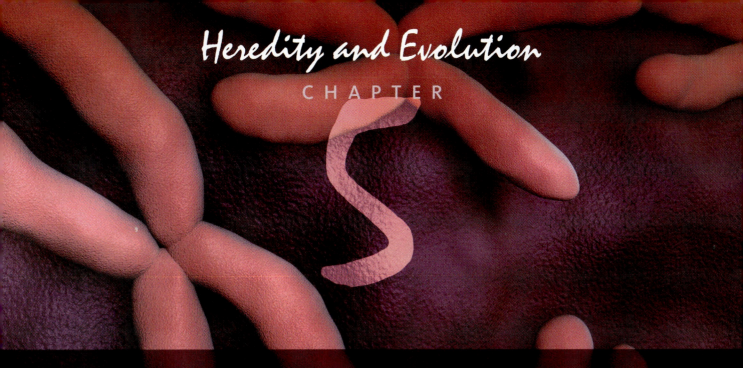

Heredity and Evolution

CHAPTER

5

Macroevolution: Processes of Vertebrate and Mammalian Evolution

Focus Question

In what ways do humans fit into a biological continuum (as vertebrates and as mammals)?

Introduction

Many people think of paleontology as pretty boring and only interesting to overly serious academics. But have you ever been to a natural history museum—or perhaps to one of the larger, more elaborate toy stores? If so, you may have seen a full-size mock-up of *Tyrannosaurus rex*, one that might even have moved its head and arms and screamed threateningly. These displays are usually encircled by flocks of noisy children who seem anything but bored.

The study of the history of life on earth is full of mystery and adventure. The bits and pieces of fossils are the remains of once living, breathing animals (some of them extremely large and dangerous). Searching for these fossils in remote corners of the globe is not a task for the faint of heart. Piecing together the tiny clues and ultimately reconstructing what *Tyrannosaurus rex* (or, for that matter, a small, 50-million-year-old primate) looked like and how it might have behaved is really much like detective work. Sure, it can be serious; but it's also a lot of fun.

In this chapter, we review the evolution of vertebrates and, more specifically, mammals. It's important to understand these more general aspects of evolutionary history so that we can place our species in its proper biological context. *Homo sapiens* is only one of millions of species that have evolved. More than that, humans have been around for just an instant in the vast expanse of time that life has existed, and we want to know where we fit in this long and complex story of life on earth. To discover where humans belong in this continuum of evolving life on earth, we also discuss some contemporary issues relating to evolutionary theory. In particular, we emphasize concepts relating to large-scale evolutionary processes, that is, *macroevolution* (in contrast to the microevolutionary focus of Chapters 3 and 4). The fundamental perspectives reviewed here concern geological history, principles of classification, and modes of evolutionary change. These perspectives will serve as a basis for topics covered throughout much of the remainder of this book.

The Human Place in the Organic World

There are millions of species living today; if we were to include microorganisms, the total would likely exceed tens of millions. And if we added in the multitudes of species that are now extinct, the total would be staggering—perhaps *hundreds* of millions!

How do we deal scientifically with all this diversity? As humans, biologists approach complexity by simplifying it. One way to do this is to develop a system of **classification** that organizes diversity into categories and at the same time indicates evolutionary relationships.

Multicellular organisms that move about and ingest food (but don't photosynthesize, as do plants) are called animals (Fig. 5-1). Within the Kingdom Animalia, there are more than 20 major groups called *phyla* (*sing.*, phylum). One of these phyla is **Chordata**, containing animals with a nerve cord, gill slits (at some stage of development), and a supporting cord along the back. In turn, most (but not all) chordates are **vertebrates**—so

classification In biology, the ordering of organisms into categories, such as orders, families, and genera, to show evolutionary relationships.

Chordata The phylum of the animal kingdom that includes vertebrates.

vertebrates Animals with segmented, bony spinal columns; traditionally includes fishes, amphibians, reptiles, birds, and mammals.

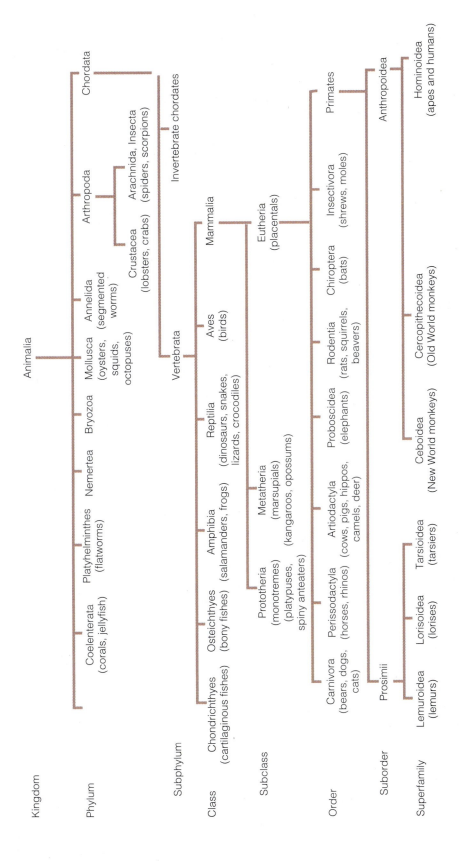

Figure 5-1

In this classification chart, modified from Linnaeus, all animals are placed in certain categories based on structural similarities. Not all members of categories are shown; for example, there are up to 20 orders of placental mammals (8 are depicted). Chapter 6 presents a more comprehensive classification of the primate order.

called because they have a vertebral column. Vertebrates also have a developed brain and paired sensory structures for sight, smell, and balance.

The vertebrates themselves are traditionally subdivided into six classes: cartilaginous fishes, bony fishes, amphibians, reptiles, birds, and mammals. We'll discuss mammalian classification later in this chapter. A further point we should make is that more rigorous contemporary classifications group reptiles and birds together in one class.

By putting organisms into increasingly narrow groupings, this hierarchical arrangement organizes diversity into categories. It also makes statements about evolutionary and genetic relationships between species and groups of species. Further dividing mammals into orders makes the statement that, for example, all carnivores (Carnivora) are more closely related to each other than they are to any species placed in another order. Consequently, bears, dogs, and cats are more closely related to each other than they are to cattle, pigs, or deer (Artiodactyla). At each succeeding level (suborder, superfamily, family, subfamily, genus, and species), finer distinctions are made between categories until, at the species level, only those animals that can potentially interbreed and produce viable offspring are included.

Principles of Classification

Before we go any further, we need to discuss the basis of animal classification. The field that specializes in establishing the rules of classification is called *taxonomy*. Organisms are classified first, and most traditionally, according to their physical similarities. Such was the basis of the first systematic classification devised by Linnaeus in the eighteenth century (see Chapter 2).

Today, basic physical similarities are still considered a good starting point. But for similarities to be useful, they *must* reflect evolutionary descent. For example, the bones of the forelimb of all air-breathing vertebrates initially adapted to land (terrestrial) environments are so similar in number and form (Fig. 5-2) that the obvious explanation for the striking resemblance is that all four kinds of these "four-footed" (tetrapod) vertebrates ultimately derived their forelimb structure from a common ancestor. What's more, recent discoveries of remarkably well-preserved fossils from Canada have provided exciting new evidence of how the transition from aquatic to land living took place and what the earliest land vertebrates looked like (Daeschler et al., 2006; Shubin et al., 2006).

How could such seemingly major evolutionary modifications in structure occur? They quite likely began with only relatively minor genetic changes. For example, recent research shows that forelimb development in all vertebrates is directed by just a few regulatory genes, called *Hox* genes (Shubin et al., 1997; Riddle and Tabin, 1999). A few mutations in certain *Hox* genes in early vertebrates led to the basic limb plan seen in all subsequent vertebrates. With additional small mutations in these genes (or in the genes they regulate), the varied structures that make up the wing of a chicken, the flipper of a porpoise, and the upper limb of a human developed. You should recognize that *basic genetic regulatory mechanisms are highly conserved in animals*; that is, they've been maintained relatively unchanged for hundreds of millions of years. Like a musical score with a basic theme, small variations on the pattern can produce the different "tunes" that define one organism from another. This is the essential genetic foundation for most macroevolutionary change. Large anatomical modifications, therefore, don't always require major genetic rearrangements.

Structures shared by species on the basis of descent from a common ancestor are called **homologies**. Homologies alone are reliable indicators of evolutionary relationship, but we have to be careful not to draw hasty conclusions from superficial similarities. For example, both birds and butterflies have wings, but they shouldn't be grouped together on the basis of this single characteristic; butterflies (as insects) differ dramatically from

homologies Similarities between organisms based on descent from a common ancestor.

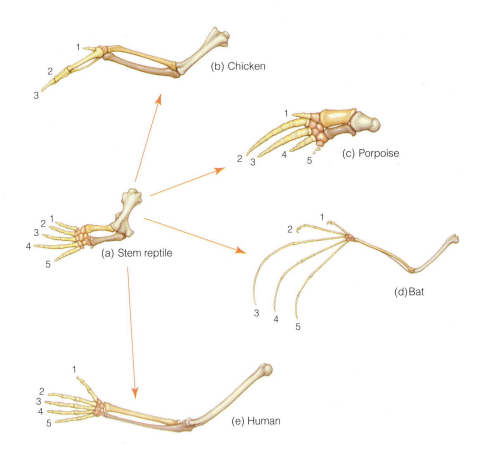

Figure 5-2
Homologies. Similarities in the forelimb bones of these animals can be most easily explained by descent from a common ancestor.

birds in several other, even more fundamental ways. (For example, birds have an internal skeleton, central nervous system, and four limbs; insects don't.)

Here's what's happened in evolutionary history: From quite distant ancestors, both butterflies and birds have developed wings *independently*. So their superficial similarities are a product of separate evolutionary responses to roughly similar functional demands. Such similarities, based on independent functional adaptation and not on shared evolutionary descent, are called **analogies**. The process that leads to the development of analogies (also called analogous structures) such as wings in birds and butterflies is termed **homoplasy**. In the case of butterflies and birds, the homoplasy has occurred in evolutionary lines that share only very remote ancestry. Here, homoplasy has produced analogous structures separately from any homology. In some cases, however, homoplasy can occur in lineages that are more closely related (and share considerable homology as well). Homoplasy in closely related lineages is evident among the primates (for example, New and Old World monkeys show considerable homoplasy, as do the great apes; see Chapter 6).

CONSTRUCTING CLASSIFICATIONS AND INTERPRETING EVOLUTIONARY RELATIONSHIPS

Evolutionary biologists typically use two major approaches, or "schools," when interpreting evolutionary relationships with the goal of producing classifications. The first approach, called **evolutionary systematics**, is the more traditional. The second approach, called **cladistics**, has emerged primarily in the last two decades. While aspects of both approaches are still used by most evolutionary biologists, in recent years cladistic methodologies have predominated among anthropologists. Indeed, one noted primate evolutionist commented that "virtually all current studies of primate phylogeny involve the methods and terminology" of cladistics (Fleagle, 1999, p. 1).

analogies Similarities between organisms based strictly on common function, with no assumed common evolutionary descent.

homoplasy (*homo*, meaning "same," and *plasy*, meaning "growth") The separate evolutionary development of similar characteristics in different groups of organisms.

evolutionary systematics A traditional approach to classification (and evolutionary interpretation) in which presumed ancestors and descendants are traced in time by analysis of homologous characters.

cladistics An approach to classification that attempts to make rigorous evolutionary interpretations based solely on analysis of certain types of homologous characters (those considered to be derived characters).

Before we begin drawing distinctions between these two approaches, it's first helpful to note features shared by both evolutionary systematics and cladistics. First, both schools are interested in tracing evolutionary relationships and in constructing classifications that reflect these relationships. Second, both schools recognize that organisms must be compared using specific features (called *characters*) and that some of these characters are more informative than others. And third (deriving directly from the previous two points), both approaches focus exclusively on homologies.

But these approaches also have some significant differences—in how characters are chosen, which groups are compared, and how the results are interpreted and eventually incorporated into evolutionary schemes and classifications. The primary difference is that cladistics more explicitly and more rigorously defines the kinds of homologies that yield the most useful information. For example, at a very basic level, all life (except for some viruses) shares DNA as the molecule underlying all organic processes. However, beyond inferring that all life most likely derives from a single origin (a most intriguing point), the mere presence of DNA tells us nothing further regarding more specific relationships among different kinds of life-forms. To draw further conclusions, we need to look at particular characters that certain groups share as the result of more recent ancestry.

This perspective emphasizes an important point: Some homologous characters are much more informative than others. We saw earlier that all terrestrial vertebrates share homologies in the number and basic arrangement of bones in the forelimb. Even though these similarities are broadly useful in showing that these large evolutionary groups (amphibians, birds/reptiles, and mammals) are all related through a distant ancestor, they don't provide information we can use to distinguish one group from another (a reptile from a mammal, for example). These kinds of characters (also called traits) that are shared through such remote ancestry are said to be **ancestral**, or **primitive**. We prefer the term *ancestral* because it doesn't reflect negatively on the evolutionary value of the character in question. In biological anthropology, the term *primitive* or *ancestral* simply means that a character seen in two organisms is inherited in both of them from a distant ancestor.

In most cases, analyzing ancestral characters doesn't supply enough information to make accurate evolutionary interpretations of relationships between different groups. In fact, misinterpretation of ancestral characters can easily lead to quite inaccurate evolutionary conclusions. Cladistics focuses on traits that distinguish particular evolutionary lineages; such traits are far more informative than ancestral traits. Lineages that share a common ancestor are called a **clade**, giving the name *cladistics* to the field that seeks to identify and interpret these groups. The characters of interest are said to be **derived**, or **modified**. Thus, while the general ancestral bony pattern of the forelimb in land vertebrates doesn't allow us to distinguish among them, the further modification of this pattern in certain groups (as hooves, flippers, or wings, for instance) does.

A simplified example might help clarify the basic principles used in cladistic analysis. Figure 5-3a shows a hypothetical "lineage" of passenger vehicles. All of the "descendant" vehicles share a common ancestor, the prototype passenger vehicle. The first major division (I) differentiates passenger cars from trucks. The second split (that is, diversification) is between luxury cars and sports cars (you could, of course, imagine many other subcategories). Modified (derived) traits that distinguish trucks from cars might include type of frame, suspension, wheel size, and, in some forms, an open cargo bed. Derived characters that might distinguish sports cars from luxury cars could include engine size and type, wheel base size, and a decorative racing stripe.

Now let's assume that you're presented with an "unknown" vehicle (meaning one as yet unclassified). How do you decide what kind of vehicle it is? You might note such features as four wheels, a steering wheel, and a seat for the driver, but these are *ancestral* characters (found in the common ancestor) of all passenger vehicles. If, however, you note that the vehicle lacks a cargo bed and raised suspension (so it's not a truck) but has a racing stripe, you might conclude that it's a car, and more than that, a sports car (since it has a derived feature presumably of *only* that group).

ancestral (primitive) Referring to characters inherited by a group of organisms from a remote ancestor and thus not diagnostic of groups (lineages) that diverged after the character first appeared.

clade A group of organisms sharing a common ancestor. The group includes the common ancestor and all descendants.

derived (modified) Referring to characters that are modified from the ancestral condition and thus are diagnostic of particular evolutionary lineages.

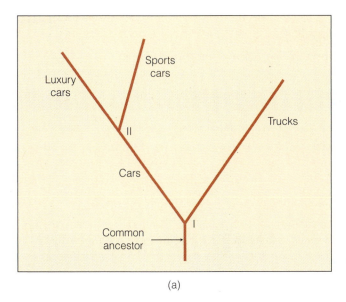

(a)

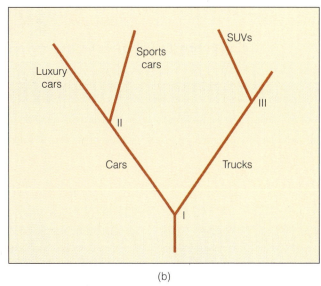

(b)

From a common ancestor of all passenger vehicles, the first major divergence is that between cars and trucks (I). A later divergence also occurs between luxury cars and sports cars (II). Derived features of each grouping ("lineage") appear only after its divergence from other groups (e.g., cargo beds are found only in trucks, cushioned suspension only in cars; likewise, only sports cars have a decorative racing stripe).

In this "tree," SUVs diverge from trucks, but like sports cars, they have a decorative racing stripe. This feature is a homoplasy and does not make SUVs sports cars. The message is that classifications based on just one characteristic that can appear independently in different groups can lead to an incorrect conclusion. *Note:* In (a), two clades are defined (I and II), while in (b), three clades (I, II, and III) are recognized.

Figure **5-3**
Evolutionary "trees" showing development of passenger vehicles.

All this seems fairly obvious, and you've probably noticed that this simple type of decision making characterizes much of human mental organization. Still, we frequently deal with complications that aren't so obvious. What if you're presented with a sports utility vehicle (SUV) with a racing stripe (Fig. 5-3b)? SUVs are basically trucks, but the presence of the racing stripe could be seen as a homoplasy with sports cars. The lesson here is that we need to be careful, look at several traits, decide which are ancestral and which are derived, and finally try to recognize the complexity (and confusion) introduced by homoplasy.

Our example of passenger vehicles is useful up to a point. Because it concerns human inventions, the groupings possess characters that humans can add and delete in almost any combination. Naturally occurring organic systems are more limited in this respect. Any species can possess only those characters that have been inherited from its ancestor or that have been subsequently modified (derived) from those shared with the ancestor. So any modification in *any* species is constrained by that species' evolutionary legacy—that is, what the species starts out with.

One last point needs to be mentioned. Traditional evolutionary systematics illustrates the hypothesized evolutionary relationships using a *phylogeny*, more properly called a **phylogenetic tree**. Strict cladistic analysis, however, shows relationships in a **cladogram**. A phylogenetic tree incorporates the dimension of time. A cladogram doesn't indicate time; all forms (fossil and modern) are shown along one dimension. Phylogenetic trees usually attempt to make some hypotheses regarding ancestor-descendant relationships. Cladistic analysis (through cladograms) makes no attempt whatsoever to discern ancestor-descendant relationships. In fact, strict cladists are quite skeptical that the evidence really permits such specific evolutionary hypotheses to be scientifically confirmed (since there are many more extinct species than living ones).

In practice, most physical anthropologists (and other evolutionary biologists) utilize cladistic analysis to identify and assess the utility of traits and to make testable hypotheses regarding the relationships between groups of organisms. They also frequently extend this

phylogenetic tree A chart showing evolutionary relationships as determined by evolutionary systematics. It contains a time component and implies ancestor-descendant relationships.

cladogram A chart showing evolutionary relationships as determined by cladistic analysis. It's based solely on interpretation of derived characters. It contains no time component and does not imply ancestor-descendant relationships.

At a Glance

Comparing Two Approaches to Interpretations of Evolutionary Relationships

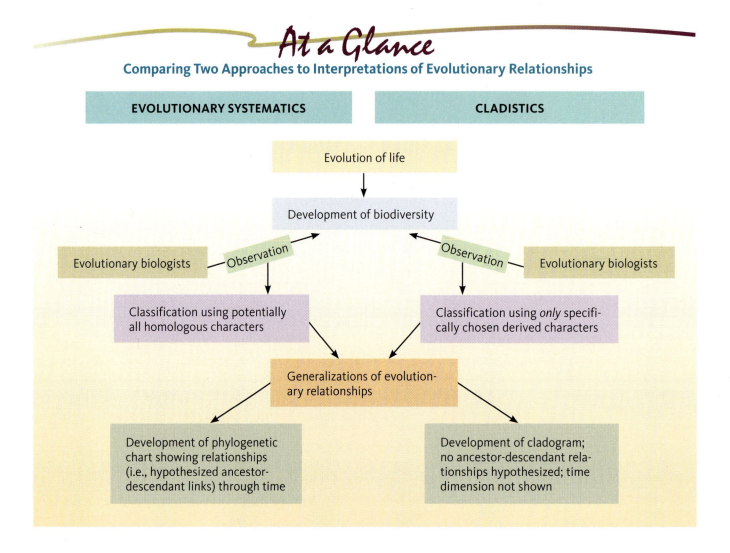

basic cladistic methodology to further hypothesize likely ancestor-descendant relationships shown relative to a time scale (that is, in a phylogenetic tree). In this way, aspects of both traditional evolutionary systematics and cladistic analysis are combined to produce a more complete picture of evolutionary history.

Definition of Species

Whether biologists are doing a cladistic or more traditional phylogenetic analysis, they're comparing groups of organisms—that is, different species, genera (*sing.*, genus), families, orders, and so forth. Fundamental to all these levels of classification is the most basic, the species. It's appropriate, then, to ask just how biologists define species. We addressed this issue briefly in Chapter 1, where we used the most common definition, one that emphasizes interbreeding and reproductive isolation. While it's not the only definition of species (others are discussed shortly), this view, called the **biological species concept** (Mayr, 1970), is the one preferred by most zoologists.

To understand what species are, you might consider how they come about in the first place—what Darwin called the "origin of species." This most fundamental of macro-

biological species concept A depiction of species as groups of individuals capable of fertile interbreeding but reproductively isolated from other such groups.

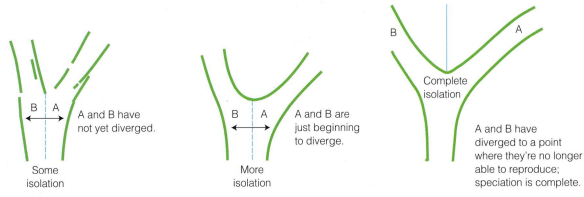

B | A — A and B have not yet diverged.

Some isolation

B | A — A and B are just beginning to diverge.

More isolation

B   A

Complete isolation

A and B have diverged to a point where they're no longer able to reproduce; speciation is complete.

Figure **5-4**

This speciation model illustrates branching evolution, pushed along through the influence of increasing reproductive isolation.

evolutionary processes is called **speciation**. According to the biological species concept, the way new species are first produced involves some form of isolation. Picture a single species (baboons, for example) composed of several populations distributed over a wide geographical area. Gene exchange between populations (gene flow) will be limited if a geographical barrier, such as an ocean or mountain range, effectively separates these populations. This extremely important form of isolating mechanism is called *geographical isolation*.

If one baboon population (A) is separated from another baboon population (B) by a mountain range, individual baboons of population A will not mate with individuals from B (Fig. 5-4). As time passes (perhaps hundreds or thousands of generations), genetic differences will accumulate in both populations. If population size is small, we can assume that genetic drift will also cause allele frequencies to change in both populations. And since drift is *random*, we wouldn't expect the effects to be the same. Consequently, the two populations will begin to diverge genetically.

As long as gene exchange is limited, the populations can only become more genetically different over time. What's more, further difference can be expected if the baboon groups are occupying slightly different habitats. These additional genetic differences would be incorporated through the process of natural selection. Certain individuals in population A would be more reproductively fit in their own environment, but they would show less reproductive success in the environment occupied by population B. So allele frequencies will shift further, resulting in even greater divergence between the two groups.

With the cumulative effects of genetic drift and natural selection acting over many generations, the result will be two populations that—even if they were to come back into geographical contact—could no longer interbreed. More than just geographical isolation might now apply. There may, for instance, be behavioral differences that interfere with courtship—what we call *behavioral isolation*. Using our *biological* definition of species, we would now recognize two distinct species where initially only one existed.

While most biologists today accept the biological species concept as the most workable definition of species (see, for example, Wilson, 2002), they still don't completely agree on the best approach for defining species. Some biologists have thus proposed alternative definitions, two of which are most relevant to our discussion. One of these definitions emphasizes mate recognition and breeding, while the other is based on ecological separation. It's important to remember, however, that these varied approaches to defining species are not mutually exclusive. Indeed, aspects of all three concepts could potentially interact in the formation of new species. For example, some species isolation could *begin* the process of speciation and then be further reinforced by selective breeding (that is, mate recognition) as well as ecological separation.

speciation The process by which a new species evolves from an earlier species. Speciation is the most basic process in macroevolution.

INTERPRETING SPECIES AND OTHER GROUPS IN THE FOSSIL RECORD

Throughout much of this text, we'll be using various taxonomic terms for fossil primates (including fossil hominins). You'll be introduced to such terms as *Ardipithecus*, *Australopithecus*, and *Homo*. Of course, *Homo* is still a living primate. But it's especially difficult to make these types of designations from the remains of animals that are long dead (and only partially preserved as skeletal remains). So, what do such names mean in evolutionary terms?

Our goal when applying species, genus, or other taxonomic labels to groups of organisms is to make meaningful biological statements about the variation that's represented. When looking at populations of living or long-extinct animals, we certainly are going to see variation; this happens in *any* sexually reproducing organism because of recombination (see Chapter 3). As a result of recombination, each individual organism is a unique combination of genetic material, and that uniqueness is usually reflected to some extent in the phenotype.

Besides such *individual variation*, we see other kinds of systematic variation in all biological populations. *Age changes* alter overall body size, as well as shape, in many mammals. One pertinent example for fossil human and ape studies is the change in number, size, and shape of teeth from deciduous (also known as baby or milk) teeth (only 20 teeth are present) to the permanent dentition (32 are present). It would be an obvious error to differentiate fossil forms based solely on such age-dependent criteria. If one individual were represented just by milk teeth and another (seemingly very different) individual were represented just by adult teeth, they easily could be different-aged individuals from the *same* population. Variation due to sex also plays an important role in influencing differences among individuals observed in biological populations. Differences in physical characteristics between males and females of the same species, called **sexual dimorphism**, can result in marked variation in body size and proportions in adults of the same species (we'll discuss this important topic in more detail in Chapter 6).

Recognition of Fossil Species Keeping in mind all the types of variation present within interbreeding groups of organisms, the minimum biological category we'd like to define in fossil primate samples is the *species*. As already defined (according to the biological species concept), a species is a group of interbreeding or potentially interbreeding organisms that is reproductively isolated from other such groups. In modern organisms, this concept is theoretically testable by observations of reproductive behavior. In animals long extinct, such observations are obviously impossible. Our only way, then, of getting a handle on the variation we see in fossil groups is to refer to living animals.

When studying a fossil group, we may observe obvious variation, such as some individuals being larger and with bigger teeth than others. The question then becomes: What is the biological significance of this variation? Two possibilities come to mind. Either the variation is accounted for by individual, age, and sex differences seen *within* every biological species (that is, it is **intraspecific**), or the variation represents differences *between* reproductively isolated groups (that is, it is **interspecific**). How do we decide which answer is correct? To do this, we have to look at contemporary species.

If the amount of variation we observe in fossil samples is comparable to that seen today *within species of closely related forms*, then we shouldn't "split" our sample into more than one species. We must, however, be careful in choosing modern analogues, because rates of evolution vary among different groups of mammals. So, for example, when studying extinct fossil primates, we need to compare them with well-known modern primates. Even so, studies of living groups have shown that defining exactly where species boundaries begin and end is often difficult. In dealing with extinct species, the uncertainties are even greater. In addition to the overlapping patterns of variation *spatially* (over space), variation also occurs *temporally* (through time). In other words, even more variation will

sexual dimorphism Differences in physical characteristics between males and females of the same species. For example, humans are slightly sexually dimorphic for body size, with males being taller, on average, than females of the same population.

intraspecific Within species; refers to variation seen within the same species.

interspecific Between species; refers to variation beyond that seen within the same species to include additional aspects seen between two different species.

be seen in **paleospecies**, since individuals may be separated by thousands or even millions of years. Applying strict Linnaean taxonomy to such a situation presents an unavoidable dilemma. Standard Linnaean classification, designed to take account of variation present at any given time, describes a static situation. But when we deal with paleospecies, the time frame is expanded and the situation can be dynamic (that is, later forms might be different from earlier forms). In such a fluid situation, taxonomic decisions (where to draw species boundaries) are ultimately going to be somewhat arbitrary.

Because the task of interpreting paleospecies is so difficult, paleoanthropologists have sought various solutions. Most researchers today define species using clusters of derived traits (identified cladistically). But owing to the ambiguity of how many derived characters are required to identify a fully distinct species (as opposed to a subspecies), the frequent mixing of characters into novel combinations, and the always difficult problem of homoplasy, there continues to be disagreement. A good deal of the dispute is driven by philosophical orientation. Exactly how much diversity should one *expect* among fossil primates, especially among fossil hominins?

Some researchers, called "splitters," claim that speciation occurred frequently during hominin evolution, and they often identify numerous fossil hominin species in a sample being studied. As the nickname suggests, these scientists are inclined to split groups into many species. Others, called "lumpers," assume that speciation was less common and see much variation as being intraspecific. These scientists lump groups together, so that fewer hominin species are identified, named, and eventually plugged into evolutionary schemes. As you'll see in the following chapters, debates of this sort pervade paleoanthropology, perhaps more than in any other branch of evolutionary biology.

Recognition of Fossil Genera The next and broader level of taxonomic classification, the **genus** (*pl.*, genera), presents another problem. To have more than one genus, we obviously must have at least two species (reproductively isolated groups), and the species of one genus must differ in a basic way from the species of another genus. A genus is therefore defined as a group of species composed of members more closely related to each other than they are to species from any other genus.

Grouping species into genera can be quite subjective and is often much debated by biologists. One possible test for contemporary animals is to check for results of hybridization between individuals of different species—rare in nature, but quite common in captivity. If members of two normally separate species interbreed and produce live (though not necessarily fertile) offspring, the two parental species probably are not too different genetically and should therefore be grouped in the same genus. A well-known example of such a cross is horses with donkeys (*Equus caballus* × *Equus asinus*), which normally produces live but sterile offspring (mules).

As previously mentioned, we can't perform breeding experiments with extinct animals, which is why another definition of genus becomes highly relevant. Species that are members of the same genus share the same broad adaptive zone. An adaptive zone represents a general ecological lifestyle more basic than the narrower ecological niches characteristic of individual species. This ecological definition of genus can be an immense aid in interpreting fossil primates. Teeth are the most frequently preserved parts, and they often can provide excellent general ecological inferences. Cladistic analysis also helps scientists to make judgments about evolutionary relationships. That is, members of the same genus should all share derived characters not seen in members of other genera.

As a final comment, we should stress that classification by genus is not always a straightforward decision. For instance, in emphasizing the very close genetic similarities between humans (*Homo sapiens*) and chimpanzees (*Pan troglodytes*), some current researchers (Wildman et al., 2003) place both in the same genus (*Homo sapiens, Homo troglodytes*). This philosophy has even been argued by some to advocate extension of basic human rights to great apes. Such thinking underscores the point that when it gets this close to home, it's often difficult to remain objective!

paleospecies Species defined from fossil evidence, often covering a long time span.

genus (*pl.*, genera) A group of closely related species.

Vertebrate Evolutionary History: A Brief Summary

Besides the staggering array of living and extinct life-forms, biologists must also contend with the vast amount of time that life has been evolving on earth. Again, scientists have devised simplified schemes—but in this case to organize *time*, not biological diversity.

To this end, geologists have formulated the **geological time scale** (Fig. 5-5), in which very large time spans are organized into eras that include one or more periods. Periods, in turn, can be broken down into epochs. For the time span encompassing vertebrate evolution, there are three eras: the Paleozoic, the Mesozoic, and the Cenozoic. The first vertebrates are present in the fossil record dating to early in the Paleozoic at 500 mya, and their origins probably go back considerably further. It's the vertebrates' capacity to form bone that accounts for their more complete fossil record *after* 500 mya.

During the Paleozoic, several varieties of fishes (including the ancestors of modern sharks and bony fishes), amphibians, and reptiles appeared. At the end of the Paleozoic,

Figure **5-5**
Geological time scale.

ERA	PERIOD	(Began mya)	EPOCH	(Began mya)
CENOZOIC	Quaternary	1.8	Holocene Pleistocene	0.01 1.8
CENOZOIC	Tertiary	65	Pliocene Miocene Oligocene Eocene Paleocene	5 23 33 55 65
MESOZOIC	Cretaceous	136		
MESOZOIC	Jurassic	190		
MESOZOIC	Triassic	225		
PALEOZOIC	Permian	280		
PALEOZOIC	Carboniferous	345		
PALEOZOIC	Devonian	395		
PALEOZOIC	Silurian	430		
PALEOZOIC	Ordovician	500		
PALEOZOIC	Cambrian	570		
PRE-CAMBRIAN				

geological time scale The organization of earth history into eras, periods, and epochs; commonly used by geologists and paleoanthropologists.

close to 250 mya, several varieties of mammal-like reptiles were also diversifying. It's generally thought that some of these forms ultimately gave rise to the mammals.

The evolutionary history of vertebrates and other organisms during the Paleozoic and Mesozoic was profoundly influenced by geographical events. We know that the positions of the earth's continents have dramatically shifted during the last several hundred million years. This process, called **continental drift**, is explained by the geological theory of *plate tectonics*, which states that the earth's crust is a series of gigantic moving and colliding plates. Such massive geological movements can induce volcanic activity (as, for example, all around the Pacific rim), mountain building (for example, the Himalayas), and earthquakes. Living on the juncture of the Pacific and North American plates, residents of the Pacific coast of the United States are acutely aware of some of these consequences, as illustrated by the explosive volcanic eruption of Mt. St. Helens and the frequent earthquakes in Alaska and California.

While reconstructing the earth's physical history, geologists have established the prior, much altered positions of major continental landmasses. During the late Paleozoic, the continents came together to form a single colossal landmass called *Pangea.* (In reality, the continents had been drifting on plates, coming together and separating, long before the end of the Paleozoic around 225 mya.) During the early Mesozoic, the southern continents (South America, Africa, Antarctica, Australia, and India) began to split off from Pangea, forming a large southern continent called *Gondwanaland* (Fig. 5-6a). Similarly, the northern continents (North America, Greenland, Europe, and Asia) were consolidated into a northern landmass called *Laurasia.* During the Mesozoic, Gondwanaland and Laurasia continued to drift apart and to break up into smaller segments. By the end of the Mesozoic (about 65 mya), the continents were beginning to assume their current positions (Fig. 5-6b).

The evolutionary ramifications of this long-term continental drift were profound. Groups of land animals became effectively isolated from each other by oceans, significantly influencing the distribution of reptiles and mammals. These continental movements continued in the Cenozoic and indeed are still happening, although without such dramatic results.

During most of the Mesozoic, reptiles were the dominant land vertebrates, and they exhibited a broad expansion into a variety of **ecological niches**, which included aerial and marine habitats. The most famous of these highly successful Mesozoic reptiles were the dinosaurs, which themselves evolved into a wide array of sizes and species and adapted to a variety of lifestyles. Dinosaur paleontology, never a boring field, has advanced several startling notions in recent years: that many dinosaurs were "warm-blooded" (see p. 113); that some varieties were quite social and probably also engaged in considerable parental care; that many forms became extinct because of major climatic changes to the earth's atmosphere

continental drift The movement of continents on sliding plates of the earth's surface. As a result, the positions of large landmasses have shifted drastically during the earth's history.

ecological niches Positions of species within their physical and biological environments. A species' ecological niche is defined by such components as diet, terrain, vegetation, type of predators, relationships with other species, and activity patterns, and each niche is unique to a given species. Together, ecological niches make up an ecosystem.

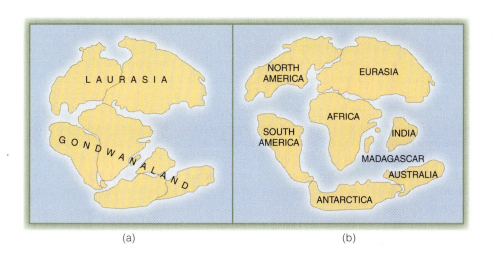

(a)   (b)

Figure **5-6**

Continental drift. (a) Positions of the continents during the Mesozoic (ca. 125 mya). Pangea is breaking up into a northern landmass (Laurasia) and a southern landmass (Gondwanaland). (b) Positions of the continents at the beginning of the Cenozoic (ca. 65 mya).

PALEOZOIC						MESOZOIC		
Cambrian	Ordovician	Silurian	Devonian	Carbon-iferous	Permian	Triassic	Jurassic	Cretaceous
Trilobites abundant; also brachiopods, jellyfish, worms, and other invertebrates	First fishes; trilobites still abundant; graptolites and corals become plentiful; possible land plants	Jawed fishes appear; first air-breathing animals; definite land plants	Age of Fishes; first amphibians and first forests	First reptiles; radiation of amphibians; modern insects diversify	Reptile radiation; mammal-like reptiles	Reptiles further radiate; first dinosaurs; egg-laying mammals	Great Age of Dinosaurs; flying and swimming dinosaurs; first toothed birds	Placental and marsupial mammals; first modern birds

Major extinction event (between Permian and Triassic)
Major extinction event (after Cretaceous)

| 570 mya | 500 mya | 430 mya | 395 mya | 345 mya | 280 mya | 225 mya | 190 mya | 136 mya | 65 mya |

Figure **5-7**

This time line depicts major events in early vertebrate evolution.

from collisions with comets or asteroids; and finally, that not all dinosaurs became entirely extinct and have many descendants still living today (that is, all modern birds). (See Fig. 5-7 for a summary of major events in early vertebrate evolutionary history.)

The Cenozoic is divided into two periods, the Tertiary (about 63 million years duration) and the Quaternary, from about 1.8 mya up to and including the present (see Fig. 5-5). Paleontologists often refer to the next, more precise level of subdivision within the Cenozoic as the **epochs**. There are seven epochs within the Cenozoic: the Paleocene, Eocene, Oligocene, Miocene, Pliocene, Pleistocene, and Holocene, the last often referred to as the Recent epoch.

Mammalian Evolution

We can learn about mammalian evolution from fossils as well as from studying the DNA of living species (Bininda-Emonds et al., 2007). Studies using both of these approaches suggest that all the living groups of mammals (that is, all the orders; see p. 101) had diverged by 75 mya. Later, only after several million years following the beginning of the Cenozoic, did the various current mammalian subgroups (that is, the particular families) begin to diversify.

Today, there are over 4,000 species of mammals, and we could call the Cenozoic the Age of Mammals. It is during this era that, along with birds, mammals replaced reptiles as the dominant land-living vertebrates.

How do we account for the relatively rapid success of the mammals during the late Mesozoic and early Cenozoic? Several characteristics relating to learning and general flexibility of behavior are of prime importance. To process more information, mammals were selected for larger brains than those typically found in reptiles. In particular, the cerebrum became generally enlarged, especially the outer covering, the neocortex, which controls higher brain functions (Fig. 5-8). In some mammals, the cerebrum expanded so much that it came to comprise most of the brain volume; the number of surface convolutions also increased, creating more surface area and thus providing space for even more nerve cells (neurons). As we'll soon see in Chapter 6, this is a trend even further emphasized among the primates.

For such a large and complex organ as the mammalian brain to develop, a longer, more intense period of growth is required. Slower development can occur internally (*in*

epochs Categories of the geological time scale; subdivisions of periods. In the Cenozoic, epochs include the Paleocene, Eocene, Oligocene, Miocene, and Pliocene (from the Tertiary) and the Pleistocene and Holocene (from the Quaternary).

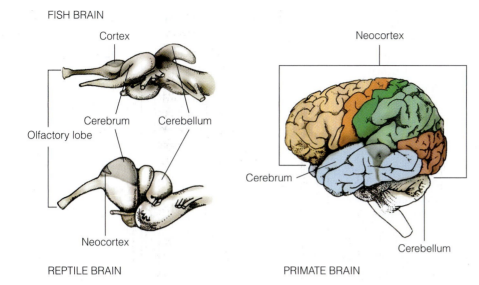

FISH BRAIN

Cortex

Cerebrum   Cerebellum

Olfactory lobe

Neocortex

REPTILE BRAIN

Neocortex

Cerebrum

Cerebellum

PRIMATE BRAIN

Figure **5-8**

Lateral view of the brain in fishes, reptiles, and primates. You can see the increased size of the cerebral cortex, also called the neocortex, of the primate brain. The cerebral cortex integrates sensory information and selects responses.

utero) as well as after birth. Internal fertilization and internal development aren't unique to mammals, but the latter is a major innovation among terrestrial vertebrates. Other forms (birds, most fishes, and reptiles) incubate their young externally by laying eggs, while mammals, with very few exceptions, give birth to live young. Even among mammals, however, there's considerable variation among the major groups in how mature the young are at birth. As you'll see, it is in mammals like us—the **placental** forms—that *in utero* development goes farthest.

Another distinctive feature of mammals is seen in the dentition. While living reptiles consistently have similarly shaped teeth (called a *homodont* dentition), mammals have differently shaped teeth (Fig. 5-9). This varied pattern, termed a **heterodont** dentition, is reflected in the ancestral (primitive) mammalian array of dental elements, which includes 3 incisors, 1 canine, 4 premolars, and 3 molars in each quarter of the mouth. Since the upper and lower jaws are usually the same and are symmetrical for both sides, the "dental formula" is conventionally illustrated by dental quarter (see p. 126 for a more complete discussion of dental patterns as they apply to primates). So with 11 teeth in each quarter of the mouth, the ancestral mammalian dental complement includes a total of 44 teeth. Such a heterodont arrangement allows mammals to process a wide variety of foods. Incisors can be used for cutting, canines for grasping and piercing, and premolars and molars for crushing and grinding.

A final point regarding teeth relates to their disproportionate representation in the fossil record. As the hardest, most durable portion of a vertebrate skeleton, teeth have the greatest likelihood of becoming fossilized (that is, mineralized, since teeth are predominantly mineral to begin with). As a result, the vast majority of available fossil data (particularly early on) for most vertebrates, including primates, consists of teeth.

Another major adaptive complex that distinguishes contemporary mammals from reptiles is the maintenance of a constant internal body temperature. Known colloquially (and incorrectly) as warm-bloodedness, this crucial physiological adaptation is also seen in contemporary birds (and may have characterized many dinosaurs as well). In fact, many contemporary reptiles are able to approximate a constant internal body temperature through behavioral means (especially by regulating activity and exposing the body to the sun). In this sense, reptiles (along with birds and mammals) could be said to be *homeothermic*. So a more useful distinction is to see how the energy to maintain body temperature is produced. In reptiles, it's obtained directly from exposure to the sun; reptiles are thus said to be *ectothermic*. In mammals and birds, however, the energy is generated *internally* through metabolic activity (by processing food or by muscle action); for this reason, mammals and birds are referred to as **endothermic**.

(a) Reptilian (alligator): homodont

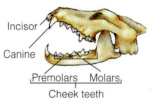

Incisor

Canine

Premolars   Molars

Cheek teeth

(b) Mammalian: heterodont

Figure **5-9**

Reptilian and mammalian teeth.

placental A type (subclass) of mammal. During the Cenozoic, placentals became the most widespread and numerous mammals and today are represented by upward of 20 orders, including the primates.

heterodont Having different kinds of teeth; characteristic of mammals, whose teeth consist of incisors, canines, premolars, and molars.

endothermic (*endo*, meaning "within" or "internal") Able to maintain internal body temperature by producing energy through metabolic processes within cells; characteristic of mammals, birds, and perhaps some dinosaurs.

Figure **5-10**

A wallaby with an infant in the pouch (marsupials).

J. C. Stevenson/Animals Animals

The Emergence of Major Mammalian Groups

There are three major subgroups of living mammals: the egg-laying mammals, or monotremes; the pouched mammals, or marsupials (Fig. 5-10); and the placental mammals. The monotremes (of which the platypus and wallaby are two examples) are extremely primitive and are considered more distinct from marsupials or placentals than these two subgroups are from each other.

The most notable difference between marsupials and placentals concerns fetal development. In marsupials, the young are born extremely immature and must complete development in an external pouch. But placental mammals develop over a longer period of time *in utero*, made possible by the evolutionary development of a specialized tissue (the placenta) that provides for fetal nourishment.

With a longer gestation period, the central nervous system develops more completely in the placental fetus. What's more, after birth, the "bond of milk" between mother and young allows more time for complex neural structures to form. We should also emphasize that from a *biosocial* perspective, this dependency period not only allows for adequate physiological development but also provides for a wider range of learning stimuli. That is, a vast amount of information is channeled to the young mammalian brain through observation of the mother's behavior and through play with age-mates. It's not enough to have evolved a brain capable of learning. Collateral evolution of mammalian social systems has ensured that young mammal brains are provided with ample learning opportunities and are thus put to good use.

Processes of Macroevolution

As we noted earlier, evolution operates at both microevolutionary and macroevolutionary levels. We discussed evolution primarily from a microevolutionary perspective in Chapters 3 and 4; in this chapter, our focus is on macroevolution. Macroevolutionary mechanisms operate more on the whole species than on individuals or populations, and they take much longer than microevolutionary processes to have a noticeable impact.

ADAPTIVE RADIATION

As we mentioned in Chapter 2, the potential capacity of a group of organisms to multiply is practically unlimited, but its ability to increase its numbers is regulated largely by the availability of resources (food, water, shelter, and space). As population size increases, access to resources decreases, and the environment will ultimately prove inadequate. Depleted resources induce some members of a population to seek an environment in which competition is reduced and the opportunities for survival and reproductive success are increased. This evolutionary tendency to exploit unoccupied habitats may eventually produce an abundance of diverse species.

This story has been played out countless times during the history of life, and some groups have expanded extremely rapidly. This evolutionary process, known as **adaptive radiation**, can be seen in the divergence of the stem reptiles into the profusion of different forms of the late Paleozoic and especially those of the Mesozoic. It's a process that takes place when a life-form rapidly takes advantage, so to speak, of the many newly available ecological niches.

The principle of evolution illustrated by adaptive radiation is fairly simple, but important. It may be stated this way: A species, or group of species, will diverge into as many variations as two factors allow. These factors are (1) its adaptive potential and (2) the adaptive opportunities of the available niches.

adaptive radiation The relatively rapid expansion and diversification of life-forms into new ecological niches.

In the case of reptiles, there was little divergence in the very early stages of evolution, when the ancestral form was little more than one among a variety of amphibian water dwellers. Later, a more efficient egg (one that could incubate out of water) developed in reptiles; this new egg, with a hard, watertight shell, had great adaptive potential, but initially there were few zones to invade. When reptiles became fully terrestrial, however, a wide array of ecological niches became accessible to them. Once freed from their attachment to water, reptiles were able to exploit landmasses with no serious competition from any other animal. They moved into the many different ecological niches on land (and to some extent in the air and sea), and as they adapted to these areas, they diversified into a large number of species. This spectacular radiation burst forth with such evolutionary speed that it may well be termed an adaptive explosion.

Of course, the rapid expansion of placental mammals during the late Mesozoic and throughout the Cenozoic is another excellent example of adaptive radiation.

GENERALIZED AND SPECIALIZED CHARACTERISTICS

Another aspect of evolution closely related to adaptive radiation involves the transition from *generalized* characteristics to *specialized* characteristics. These two terms refer to the adaptive potential of a particular trait. A trait that's adapted for many functions is said to be generalized, while one that's limited to a narrow set of functions is said to be specialized.

For example, a generalized mammalian limb has five fairly flexible digits, adapted for many possible functions (grasping, weight support, and digging). In this respect, human hands are still quite generalized. On the other hand (or foot), there have been many structural modifications in our feet to make them suited for the specialized function of stable weight support in an upright posture.

The terms *generalized* and *specialized* are also sometimes used when speaking of the adaptive potential of whole organisms. Consider, for example, the aye-aye of Madagascar, an unusual primate species. The aye-aye is a highly specialized animal, structurally adapted to a narrow, rodent/woodpecker-like econiche—digging holes with prominent incisors and removing insect larvae with an elongated bony finger.

It's important to note that only a generalized ancestor can provide the flexible evolutionary basis for rapid diversification. Only a generalized species with potential for adaptation to varied ecological niches can lead to all the later diversification and specialization of forms into particular ecological niches.

An issue that we've already raised also bears on this discussion: the relationship of ancestral and derived characters. It's not always the case, but ancestral characters *usually* tend to be more generalized. And specialized characteristics are nearly always derived ones as well.

Summary

In this chapter, we've surveyed the basics of vertebrate and mammalian evolution, emphasizing a macroevolutionary perspective. Given the huge amount of organic diversity displayed, as well as the vast amount of time involved, two major organizing perspectives prove indispensable: (1) schemes of formal classification to organize organic diversity and (2) the geological time scale to organize geological time. We reviewed the principles of classification in some detail, contrasting two differing approaches: evolutionary systematics and cladistics. Because primates are vertebrates and, more specifically, mammals, we briefly reviewed these broader organic groups, emphasizing major evolutionary trends.

Theoretical perspectives relating to contemporary understanding of macroevolutionary processes (especially the concepts of species and speciation) are crucial to any

interpretation of long-term aspects of evolutionary history, be it vertebrate, mammalian, or primate.

Since genus and species designation is the common form of reference for both living and extinct organisms (and we use it frequently throughout the text), we discussed its biological significance in depth.

Critical Thinking Questions

1. What are the two goals of classification? What happens when meeting both goals simultaneously becomes difficult or even impossible?

2. Remains of a fossil mammal have been found on your campus. If you adopt a cladistic approach, how would you determine (a) that it's a mammal rather than some other kind of vertebrate (discuss specific characters), (b) what kind of mammal it is (again, discuss specific characters), and (c) how it *might* be related to one or more living mammals (again, discuss specific characters)?

3. For the same fossil find (and your interpretation) in question 2, draw an interpretive figure using cladistic analysis (that is, draw a cladogram). Next, using more traditional evolutionary systematics, construct a phylogeny. Lastly, explain the differences between the cladogram and the phylogeny (be sure to emphasize the fundamental ways the two schemes differ).

4. a. Humans are fairly generalized mammals. What do we mean by this, and what specific features (characters) would you select to illustrate this statement?

    b. More precisely, humans are *placental* mammals. How do humans, and generally all placental mammals, differ from the other two major groups of mammals?

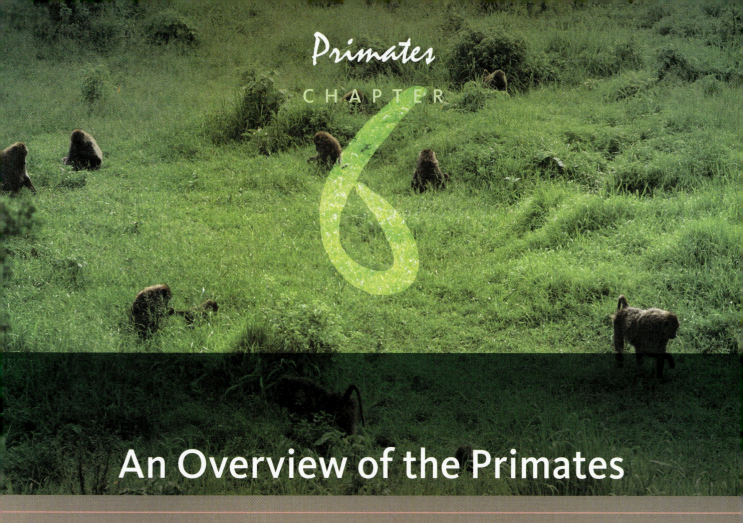

Primates

CHAPTER

6

An Overview of the Primates

Focus Questions

What are the major characteristics of primates?

Why are humans considered primates?

 Click!

Go to the following media for interactive activities and exercises on topics covered in this chapter:

- Online Virtual Laboratories for Physical Anthropology, Version 4.0

Introduction

Chimpanzees aren't monkeys. Neither are gorillas and orangutans. They're apes, and even though most people think they're basically the same, they aren't. Yet, how many times have you seen a greeting card or advertisement with a picture of a chimpanzee and a phrase that goes something like, "Don't monkey around"? Or maybe you've seen people at zoos making fun of captive primates. While these things might seem trivial, they aren't, because they show how little most people know about our closest relatives. This is unfortunate, because by better understanding these relatives, we can learn a great deal about ourselves. Also, we need this knowledge if we want to save the many primate species that are now critically endangered.

One way to better understand any organism is to compare its anatomy and behavior with the anatomy and behavior of other, closely related species. This comparative approach helps explain how and why physiological and behavioral systems evolved as adaptive responses to various selective pressures throughout the course of evolution. This statement applies to human beings just as it does to any other species. So if we want to identify the components that have shaped the evolution of our species, a good starting point is to compare ourselves with our closest living relatives, the approximately 230 species of nonhuman primates (**prosimians**, monkeys, and apes). (Groves, 2001b, suggests that there may be as many as 350 primate species.)

This chapter describes the physical characteristics that define the order Primates; gives a brief overview of the major groups of living primates; and introduces some methods of comparing living primates through genetic data. (For a comparison of human and nonhuman skeletons, see Appendix A.) But before we go any further, we again want to call attention to a few common misunderstandings about evolutionary processes.

Evolution isn't a goal-directed process. Therefore, the fact that lemurs and lorises evolved before **anthropoids** doesn't mean that they "progressed," or "advanced," to become anthropoids. Living primate species aren't in any way "superior" to their predecessors or to one another. Consequently, discussions of major groupings of contemporary nonhuman primates don't imply that any of these groups is superior or inferior to any other group. Each lineage or species has come to possess unique qualities that make it better suited to a particular habitat and lifestyle. Given that all living organisms are "successful" results of the evolutionary process, it's best to completely avoid using such loaded terms as *superior* and *inferior*. Finally, you shouldn't make the mistake of thinking that contemporary primates (including humans) necessarily represent the final stage or apex of a lineage. Actually, the only species that represent final evolutionary stages of particular lineages are the ones that become extinct.

Primate Characteristics

All primates share many characteristics with other mammals. Some of these basic mammalian traits are body hair; a relatively long gestation period followed by live birth; mammary glands (thus the term *mammal*); different types of teeth (incisors, canines,

prosimians Members of a suborder of Primates, the suborder Prosimii (pronounced "pro-sim´-ee-eye"). Traditionally, the suborder includes lemurs, lorises, and tarsiers.

anthropoids Members of a suborder of Primates, the suborder Anthropoidea (pronounced "ann-throw-poid´-ee-uh"). Traditionally, the suborder includes monkeys, apes, and humans.

premolars, and molars); the ability to maintain a constant internal body temperature through physiological means, or *endothermy*; increased brain size; and a considerable capacity for learning and behavioral flexibility. Therefore, to differentiate primates, as a group, from other mammals, we need to describe those characteristics that, taken together, set primates apart.

Identifying single traits that define the primate order isn't easy because compared to many mammals, primates have remained quite *generalized*. That is, primates have retained many ancestral mammalian traits that some other mammals have lost over time. In response to particular selective pressures, many mammalian groups have become increasingly **specialized**, or derived. For example, through the course of evolution, horses and cattle have undergone a reduction of the number of digits (fingers and toes) from the ancestral pattern of five to one and two, respectively. Moreover, these species have developed hard, protective coverings over their feet in the form of hooves (Fig. 6-1a). This limb structure is adaptive in prey species, whose survival depends on speed and stability, but it restricts them to only one type of locomotion. Moreover, limb function is limited entirely to support and movement, while the ability to manipulate objects is completely lost.

Primates can't be defined by one or even a few traits they share in common because they *aren't* so specialized. Therefore, anthropologists have drawn attention to a group of characteristics that, taken together, more or less typify the entire primate order. But these are a set of *general* tendencies that aren't equally expressed in all primates. In addition, while some of these traits are unique to primates, many others are

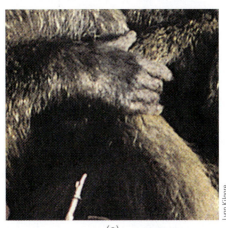
(a)

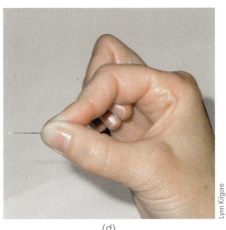
(b)

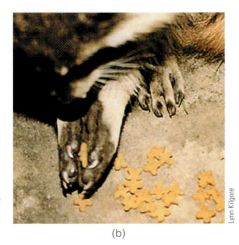

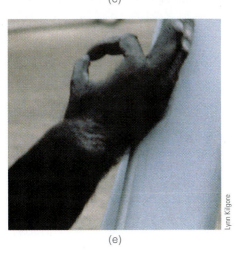
(c)

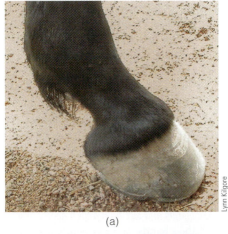
(d)

(e)

Figure **6-1**

(a) A horse's front foot, homologous with a human hand, has undergone reduction from five digits to one. (b) While raccoons are capable of considerable manual dexterity and can readily pick up small objects with one hand, they have no opposable thumb. (c) Many monkeys are able to grasp objects with an opposable thumb, while others have very reduced thumbs. (d) Humans are capable of a "precision grip." (e) Chimpanzees, with their reduced thumbs, are also capable of a precision grip, but they frequently use a modified form.

retained primitive mammalian characteristics shared with other mammals. So the following list is meant to give an overall structural and behavioral picture of the primates in general, and it emphasizes the characteristics that tend to set primates apart from other mammals. Concentrating on certain ancestral mammalian traits along with more specific derived ones has been the traditional approach of **primatologists**, and it's still used today. In their limbs and locomotion, teeth and diet, senses, brain, and behaviors, primates reflect a common evolutionary history with adaptations to similar environmental challenges, mostly as highly social, arboreal animals.

specialized Evolved for a particular function; usually refers to a specific trait (e.g., incisor teeth), but may also refer to the entire way of life of an organism.

primatologists Scientists who study the evolution, anatomy, and behavior of nonhuman primates. Those who study behavior in noncaptive animals are usually trained as physical anthropologists.

A. *Limbs and locomotion*

1. *A tendency toward erect posture (especially in the upper body).* Present to some degree in almost all primates, this tendency is variously associated with sitting, leaping, standing, and, occasionally, bipedal walking.

2. *A flexible, generalized limb structure, which allows most primates to practice a number of locomotor behaviors.* Primates have retained some bones (for example, the clavicle, or collarbone) and certain abilities (like rotation of the forearm) that have been lost in some more specialized mammals. Various aspects of hip and shoulder anatomy also provide primates with a wide range of limb movement and function (for example, walking on four or sometimes two limbs, climbing, and hanging by the hands or feet from tree branches. Thus, by maintaining a generalized locomotor anatomy, primates aren't restricted to one form of movement, such as quadrupedalism.

3. *Hands and feet with a high degree of **prehensility** (grasping ability).* All primates use their hands, and frequently their feet, to grasp and manipulate objects (Fig. 6-1b through e). This is variably expressed and is enhanced by a number of characteristics, including:

   a. *Retention of five digits on hands and feet.* This characteristic varies somewhat throughout the order, with some species showing reduction or absence of the thumb or second digit (first finger).

   b. *An opposable thumb and, in most species, a divergent and partially opposable big toe.* Most primates are capable of moving the thumb so that it comes in contact (in some fashion) with the second digit or the palm of the hand (see Fig. 6-1c through 6-1e).

   c. *Nails instead of claws.* This characteristic is seen in all primates except some New World monkeys. All prosimians also have a claw on one digit.

   d. *Tactile pads enriched with sensory nerve fibers at the ends of digits.* This enhances the sense of touch.

B. *Diet and teeth*

1. *Lack of dietary specialization.* This is typical of most primates, who tend to eat a wide assortment of food items. In general, primates are **omnivorous**.

2. *A generalized dentition.* The teeth aren't specialized for processing only one type of food, a pattern related to the lack of dietary specialization.

C. *The senses and the brain.* Primates, especially **diurnal** ones, rely heavily on vision and less on the sense of smell. This emphasis is reflected in evolutionary changes in the skull, eyes, and brain.

1. *Color vision.* This is a characteristic of all diurnal primates. **Nocturnal** primates don't have color vision.

2. *Depth perception.* **Stereoscopic vision**, or the ability to perceive objects in three dimensions, is made possible through a variety of mechanisms, including:

   a. *Eyes positioned toward the front of the face (not to the sides).* This provides for overlapping visual fields, or **binocular vision** (Fig. 6-2).

   b. *Visual information from each eye transmitted to visual centers in both **hemispheres** of the brain.* In nonprimate mammals, most optic nerve fibers cross to the opposite hemisphere through a structure at the base of the brain. In primates, about 40 percent of the fibers remain on the same side, so that each hemisphere receives information from both eyes (see Fig. 6-2).

   c. *Visual information organized into three-dimensional images by specialized structures in the brain itself.* The capacity for stereoscopic vision depends on overlapping visual fields and on each hemisphere of the brain receiving visual information from both eyes.

3. *Decreased reliance on the sense of smell (olfaction).* This trend is expressed in an overall reduction in the size of olfactory structures in the brain (see next page).

---

prehensility Grasping with the hands and, in many primates, also the feet.

omnivorous Having a diet consisting of many kinds of foods, such as plant materials (seeds, fruits, leaves), meat, and insects.

diurnal Active during the day.

nocturnal Active during the night.

stereoscopic vision The condition whereby visual images are, to varying degrees, superimposed on one another. This provides for depth perception, or the perception of the external environment in three dimensions. Stereoscopic vision is partly a function of structures in the brain.

binocular vision Vision characterized by overlapping visual fields provided for by forward-facing eyes. Binocular vision is essential to depth perception.

hemispheres The two halves of the cerebrum that are connected by a dense mass of fibers. (The cerebrum is the large rounded outer portion of the brain.)

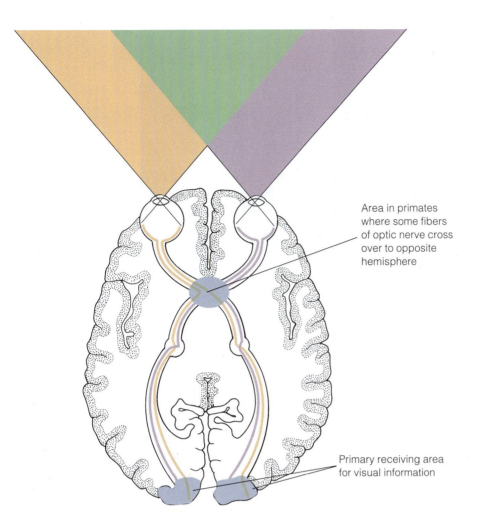

Figure **6-2**

Simplified diagram showing overlapping visual fields that permit binocular vision in primates with eyes positioned at the front of the face. (The green shaded area represents the area of overlap.) Stereoscopic vision (three-dimensional vision) is provided in part by binocular vision and in part by the transmission of visual stimuli from each eye to *both* hemispheres of the brain. (In nonprimate mammals, most, if not all, visual information crosses over to the hemisphere opposite the eye in which it was initially received.)

Area in primates where some fibers of optic nerve cross over to opposite hemisphere

Primary receiving area for visual information

Figure **6-3**

The skull of a male baboon (a) compared with that of a red wolf (b). Note the forward-facing eyes positioned above the snout in the baboon, compared with the lateral position of the eyes at the sides of the wolf's face. Also, the baboon's large muzzle doesn't reflect a heavy reliance on the sense of smell. Rather, it supports the roots of the large canine teeth, which curve back through the bone for as much as 1½ inches.

Corresponding reduction of the entire olfactory apparatus has also resulted in decreased size of the snout. In some species, such as baboons, the large muzzle isn't related to olfaction, but to the presence of large teeth, especially the canines (Fig. 6-3).

4. *Expansion and increased complexity of the brain.* This is a general trend among placental mammals, but it's especially true of primates (Fig. 6-4). In primates, this

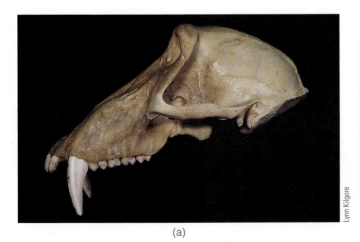

(a)

Lynn Kilgore

(b)

Lynn Kilgore

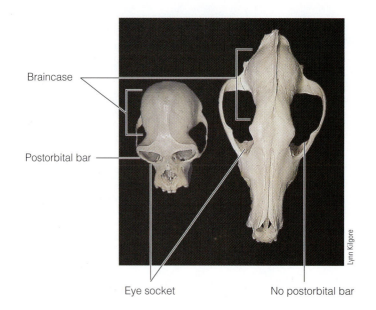

Figure 6-4

The skull of a gibbon (left) compared with that of a red wolf (right). Note that the absolute size of the braincase in the gibbon is slightly larger than that of the wolf, even though the wolf (at about 80 to 100 pounds) is six times the size of the gibbon (about 15 pounds).

Braincase

Postorbital bar

Eye socket

No postorbital bar

Lynn Kilgore

expansion is most evident in the visual and association areas of the **neocortex** (portions of the brain where information from different **sensory modalities** is integrated).

D. *Maturation, learning, and behavior*

1. *A more efficient means of fetal nourishment, longer periods of gestation, reduced numbers of offspring (with single births the norm), delayed maturation, and longer life span.*

2. *A greater dependence on flexible, learned behavior.* This trend is correlated with delayed maturation and longer periods of infant and childhood dependency on at least one parent. As a result of both these trends, parental investment in each offspring is increased, so that although fewer offspring are born, they receive more intense rearing.

3. *The tendency to live in social groups and the permanent association of adult males with the group.* Except for some nocturnal species, primates tend to associate with other individuals. The permanent association of adult males with the group is uncommon in most mammals but widespread in primates.

4. *The tendency toward diurnal activity patterns.* This is seen in most primates; only one New World monkey species and some prosimians are nocturnal.

neocortex The more recently evolved portions of the brain's cortex that are involved with higher mental functions and composed of areas that integrate incoming information from different sensory modalities.

sensory modalities Different forms of sensation (e.g., touch, pain, pressure, heat, cold, vision, taste, hearing, and smell).

arboreal Tree-living; adapted to life in the trees.

adaptive niche The entire way of life of an organism: where it lives, what it eats, how it gets food, how it avoids predators, etc.

Primate Adaptations

In this section, we'll consider how primate anatomical traits evolved as adaptations to environmental circumstances. It's important to remember that the term *environmental circumstances* refers to several interrelated variables, including climate, diet, habitat (such as woodland, grassland, forest), and predation.

EVOLUTIONARY FACTORS

Traditionally, the suite of characteristics shared by primates has been explained as the result of adaptation to **arboreal** living. While other placental mammals were adapting to various ground-dwelling lifestyles and even marine environments, the primates found their **adaptive niche** in the trees. Some other mammals were also adapting to arboreal living, but while many of them nested in trees, they continued to feed on the ground. But throughout the course of evolution, primates increasingly found food (leaves, seeds, fruits, nuts, insects, birds' eggs, and small mammals) in the branches themselves. Over time, this dietary shift enhanced a general trend toward increased *omnivory*; and this trend in turn led to the retention of the generalized dentition we see in primates today.

This adaptive process is also reflected in how heavily primates rely on vision. In a complex, three-dimensional environment with uncertain footholds, color vision and depth perception are, to say the least, extremely beneficial. Grasping hands and feet also reflect an adaptation to living in the trees. Obviously, grasping hands aren't essential to climbing, as many animals (such as cats, squirrels, and raccoons) demonstrate quite effectively. Nevertheless, most early primates adopted a technique of grasping branches with prehensile hands and feet (and tails in some species), and grasping abilities were further enhanced with the appearance of flattened nails instead of claws.

It has also been suggested that primates became increasingly more dependent on vision as a result of hunting small prey (Cartmill, 1972, 1992). This explanation is based on the fact that highly visual predators like cats and owls have eyes positioned at the front of the face. Moreover, early primates may not have even been arboreal. Instead, they may have begun to exploit shrubs after the appearance of flowering plants and only later moved into the trees (Sussman, 1991). The appearance of flowering plants certainly opened up entire new econiches and eventually provided foods such as nectar, fruits, berries, and insects, all of which could be exploited by animals that were adapting to a wide variety of foods and a generalized resource base. These hypotheses aren't mutually exclusive. The complex of primate characteristics might well have begun in nonarboreal settings, but at some point, the primates did take to the trees, and that's where most of them still live today.

GEOGRAPHICAL DISTRIBUTION AND HABITATS

With just a couple of exceptions, primates are found in tropical or semitropical areas of the New and Old Worlds. In the New World, these areas include southern Mexico, Central America, and parts of South America. Old World primates are found in Africa, India, Southeast Asia (including numerous islands), parts of China, and Japan (Fig. 6-5).

While the majority of primates are mostly arboreal and live in forest or woodland habitats, some Old World monkeys (for example, baboons) have adapted to life on the ground in places where trees are sparsely distributed. Moreover, the African apes (gorillas, chimpanzees, and bonobos) spend a lot of time on the ground in forested and wooded habitats. Nevertheless, no nonhuman primate is adapted to a fully terrestrial lifestyle, so they all spend some time in the trees.

DIET AND TEETH

Omnivory is one example of the overall lack of specialization in primates. Although the majority of primate species tend to emphasize some foods over others, most eat a combination of fruits, nuts, seeds, leaves, other plant materials, and insects. Many also get animal protein from birds and amphibians, and some occasionally kill and eat small mammals, including other primates. Others, such as African colobus monkeys and the leaf-eating monkeys (langurs) of India and Southeast Asia, have become more specialized and mostly feed on leaves. Such a wide array of choices is highly adaptive, even in fairly predictable environments.

Like the majority of other mammals, most primates have four kinds of teeth: incisors and canines for biting and cutting, and premolars and molars for chewing. Biologists use what's called a *dental formula* to describe the number of each type of tooth a species

Howler species
(Central and South
America)

Spider monkeys
and muriquis
(Central and South
America)

Prince Bernhard's titi
(Brazil, Amazon
rain forest)

Uakari
(Brazil, near Jurua River)

Squirrel monkeys
(South America)

White-faced
capuchins
(South America)

Muriqui
(southeastern Brazil)

Marmosets and
tamarins
(South America)

Figure **6-5**

Geographical distribution of living nonhuman primates.
Much original habitat is now very fragmented.

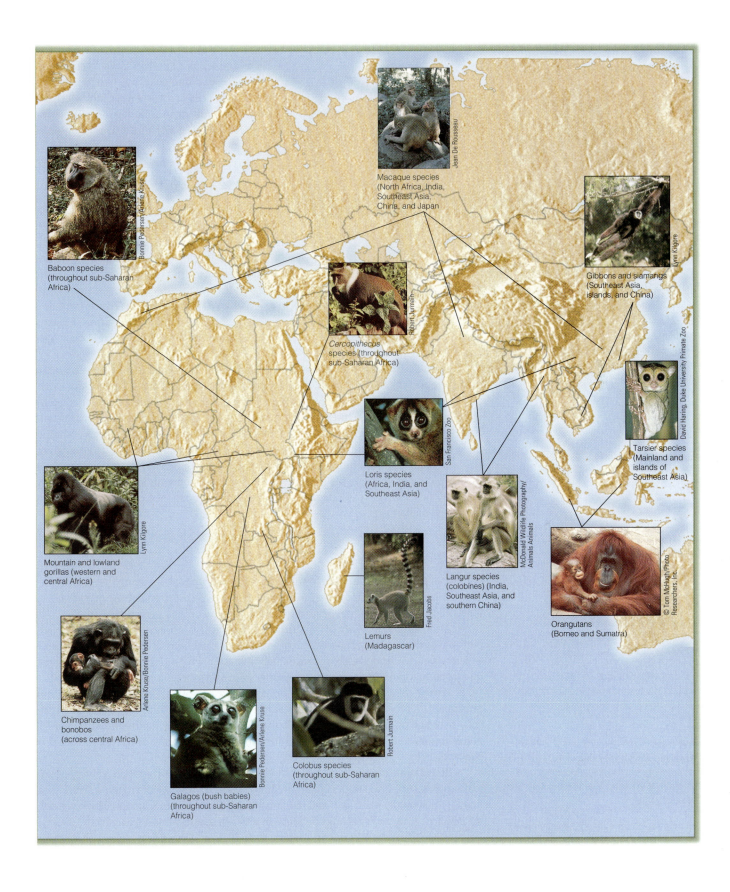

Macaque species (North Africa, India, Southeast Asia, China, and Japan)

Baboon species (throughout sub-Saharan Africa)

Gibbons and siamangs (Southeast Asia, islands, and China)

Cercopithecus species (throughout sub-Saharan Africa)

Tarsier species (Mainland and islands of Southeast Asia)

Loris species (Africa, India, and Southeast Asia)

Mountain and lowland gorillas (western and central Africa)

Langur species (colobines) (India, Southeast Asia, and southern China)

Lemurs (Madagascar)

Orangutans (Borneo and Sumatra)

Chimpanzees and bonobos (across central Africa)

Galagos (bush babies) (throughout sub-Saharan Africa)

Colobus species (throughout sub-Saharan Africa)

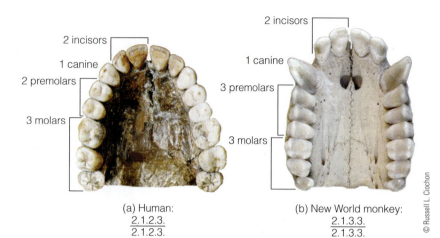

2 incisors
1 canine
2 premolars

3 molars

(a) Human:
2.1.2.3.
2.1.2.3.

2 incisors
1 canine
3 premolars

3 molars

(b) New World monkey:
2.1.3.3.
2.1.3.3.

© Russell L. Ciochon

Figure 6-6

The human maxilla (a) illustrates a dental formula of $\frac{2.1.2.3.}{2.1.2.3.}$ characteristic of all Old World monkeys, apes, and humans. The *Cebus* maxilla (b) shows the $\frac{2.1.3.3.}{2.1.3.3.}$ dental formula that is typical of most New World monkeys. (Not to scale.)

midline An anatomical term referring to a hypothetical line that divides the body into right and left halves.

cusps The bumps on the chewing surfaces of premolar and molar teeth.

morphology The form (shape, size) of anatomical structures; can also refer to the entire organism.

quadrupedal Using all four limbs to support the body during locomotion; the basic mammalian (and primate) form of locomotion.

macaques (muh-kaks´) A group of Old World monkeys comprising several species, including rhesus monkeys. Most macaque species live in India, other parts of Asia, and nearby islands.

brachiation A form of locomotion in which the body is suspended beneath the hands, and support is alternated from one forelimb to the other; arm swinging.

has in each quadrant of the mouth (Fig. 6-6). For example, all Old World *anthropoids* (monkeys, apes, and humans) have two incisors, one canine, two premolars, and three molars on each side of the **midline** in both the upper and lower jaws, for a total of 32 teeth. This is represented as a dental formula of

2.1.2.3 (upper)
2.1.2.3 (lower)

The dental formula for a generalized placental mammal is 3.1.4.3 (three incisors, one canine, four premolars, and three molars). But primates have fewer teeth than this ancestral pattern because of an evolutionary trend toward fewer teeth in many mammal groups. Moreover, the number of each type of tooth varies among primate lineages. For example, in most New World monkeys, the dental formula is 2.1.3.3 (two incisors, one canine, three premolars, and three molars). In contrast, humans, apes, and all Old World monkeys all have a dental formula of 2.1.2.3; that is, they have one fewer premolar than most New World monkeys.

The lack of dietary specialization in primates is reflected in the lack of specialization in the size and shape of the teeth, because tooth form is directly related to diet. For example, carnivores typically have premolars and molars with high pointed **cusps** adapted for tearing meat (refer back to the wolf cranium in Fig. 4-4); but herbivores, such as cattle and horses, have molars with broad, flat surfaces suited to chewing tough grasses and other plant materials. Most primates have premolars and molars with low, rounded cusps, and this kind of molar **morphology** allows them to process most types of foods. So throughout their evolutionary history, the primates have developed a dentition adapted to a varied diet, and their ability to exploit many foods has contributed to their overall success during the last 50 million years.

LOCOMOTION

Almost all primates are, at least to some degree, **quadrupedal**, meaning they use all four limbs to support the body during locomotion. However, most primates use more than one form of locomotion, and they're able to do this because of their generalized anatomy.

Although the majority of quadrupedal primates are arboreal, terrestrial quadrupedalism is fairly common and is typical of some lemurs, baboons, and **macaques**. The limbs of terrestrial quadrupeds are approximately the same length (Fig. 6-7a), but in arboreal quadrupeds, forelimbs are somewhat shorter (Fig. 6-7b).

Vertical clinging and leaping, another form of locomotion, is characteristic of many prosimians. As the term implies, vertical clingers and leapers support themselves vertically by grasping onto tree trunks with their knees and ankles tightly flexed (Fig. 6-7c). Forceful extension of their long hind limbs allows them to spring powerfully forward or backward.

Brachiation, or arm swinging, is another type of primate locomotion where the body is alternately supported under either forelimb (Fig. 6-7d). Because of anatomical modifications at the shoulder joint, apes and humans are capable of true brachiation. However, only the small gibbons and siamangs of Southeast Asia brachiate almost exclusively.

Species that brachiate tend to have arms that are longer than legs, a short stable lower back, long curved fingers, and shortened thumbs. Because these are traits seen in all the apes, it's believed that although none of the great apes (orangutans, gorillas, bonobos,

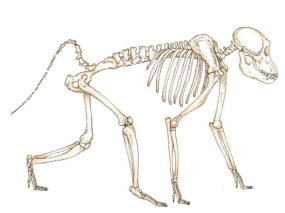

(a) Skeleton of a terrestrial quadruped (savanna baboon).

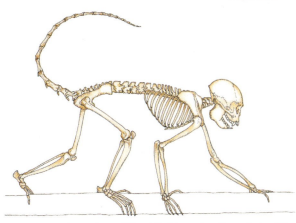

(b) Skeleton of an arboreal New World monkey (bearded saki).

(c) Skeleton of a vertical clinger and leaper (indri).

(d) Skeleton of a brachiator (gibbon).

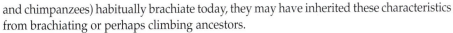

Figure 6-7

Differences in skeletal anatomy and limb proportions reflect differences in locomotor patterns. (Redrawn from original art by Stephen Nash in John G. Fleagle, *Primate Adaptation and Evolution*, 2nd ed., 1999. Reprinted by permission of publisher and Stephen Nash.)

Figure 6-8

Chimpanzee knuckle walking. Note how the weight of the upper body is supported on the knuckles and not on the palm of the hand.

and chimpanzees) habitually brachiate today, they may have inherited these characteristics from brachiating or perhaps climbing ancestors.

Some New World monkeys (for example, muriquis and spider monkeys) are called *semibrachiators*, as they practice a combination of leaping with some arm swinging. Also, some New World species enhance arm swinging and other suspensory behaviors by using a *prehensile tail*, which in effect serves as a grasping fifth hand. It's important to mention that none of the Old World monkeys have prehensile tails.

Lastly, all the apes (to varying degrees) have arms that are longer than their legs, and some (gorillas, bonobos, and chimpanzees) practice a special form of quadrupedalism called knuckle walking. Because their arms are so long relative to their legs, instead of walking with the palms of their hands flat on the ground like some monkeys do, they support the weight of their upper body on the back surfaces of their bent fingers (Fig. 6-8).

127

Primate Classification

The living primates are commonly categorized into their respective subgroups as shown in Figure 6-9. This taxonomy is based on the system originally established by Linnaeus. (Remember that the primate order, which includes a diverse array of approximately 230 species, belongs to a larger group, the class Mammalia.)

As you learned in Chapter 5, in any taxonomic system, animals are organized into increasingly specific categories. For example, the order Primates includes *all* primates. But at the next level down, the *suborder*, primates have conventionally been divided into two large categories, Prosimii (all the prosimians: lemurs, lorises, and, customarily, the tarsiers) and Anthropoidea (all the monkeys, apes, and humans). Therefore, as you can see, the suborder distinction is more specific than the order.

At the suborder level, the prosimians are distinct, as a group, from all the other primates. This distinction is important because it makes the biological and evolutionary statement that all the prosimian species are more closely related to each other than they are to any of the anthropoids. Likewise, all anthropoid species are more closely related to one another than they are to the prosimians.

Traditionally, taxonomies were based on physical similarities between species and lineages. However, this approach isn't foolproof because two species that resemble each other anatomically (for example, some New and Old World monkeys) may not be closely related at all. By looking only at physical characteristics, it's possible to overlook the unknown effects of separate evolutionary history (see our discussion of homoplasy on p. 000). Fortunately, we're able to overcome this problem through the use of genetic technologies. For example, since the mid-1990s, genetic research has shown that humans are even more closely related to the great apes (especially the African great apes) than previously thought. Primate classification is currently in a state of transition, mainly because of genetic evidence that has emerged over the past few years. In particular, the DNA-sequencing techniques used in the Human Genome Project have made it possible to make direct between-species comparisons of DNA sequences. This approach is called *comparative genomics*.

A complete draft sequence of the chimpanzee genome was completed in 2005 (The Chimpanzee Sequencing and Analysis Consortium, 2005), and it represents a major advance in human comparative genomics. But even prior to this, molecular anthropologists had already compared the sequences of a number of chimpanzee and human genes. For example, Wildman et al. (2003) compared nearly 100 human genes with their chimpanzee, gorilla, and orangutan counterparts and determined that humans are most closely related to chimpanzees and that their "functional elements," or **coding DNA sequences**, are between 98.4 and 99.4 percent identical. These results are consistent with the findings of several other previous studies that suggested a genetic difference between chimpanzees and ourselves of approximately 1.2 percent (Chen et al., 2001). Other studies have substantiated these figures, but they've also revealed more variation in **noncoding DNA segments** and portions that have been inserted, deleted, or duplicated. So when the *entire* genome is considered, reported differences between chimpanzees and humans range from 2.7 percent (Cheng et al., 2005) to 6.4 percent (Demuth et al., 2006).

Genetic similarities and fossil evidence together suggest that humans and chimpanzees last shared a common ancestor around 6–8 mya. These facts have caused many primatologists to consider changing how they classify the hominoids (Goodman et al., 1998; Wildman et al., 2003). Most biological anthropologists now support placing all the great apes in the family Hominidae along with humans. Traditionally, the great apes have been placed in a separate family from ourselves. But including the African great apes in the same family as humans reflects the fact that they are even more closely related to us than was previously thought (see Fig. 6-9 and At a Glance, p. 130).

coding DNA sequences DNA sequences that code for the production of a protein.

noncoding DNA sequences Sequences that don't code for identifiable proteins but in many cases produce molecules that influence the actions of coding sequences. (The terminology is somewhat confusing. Currently, geneticists use the term *coding* to refer to sequences that code for proteins that are fairly easy to detect. *Noncoding* currently refers to sequences that seem not to have any function or that code for proteins that regulate the actions of other genes.)

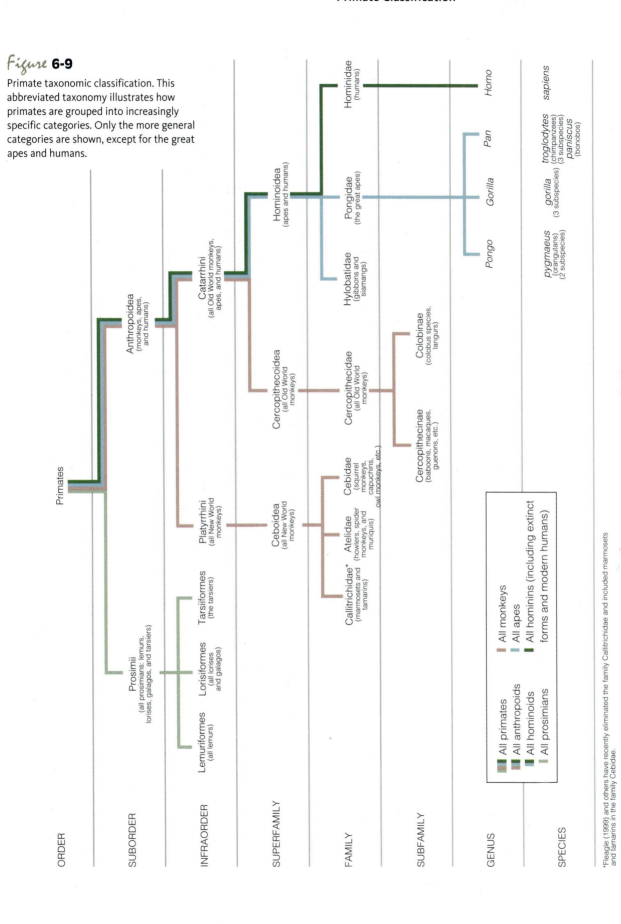

Figure 6-9

Primate taxonomic classification. This abbreviated taxonomy illustrates how primates are grouped into increasingly specific categories. Only the more general categories are shown, except for the great apes and humans.

*Fleagle (1999) and others have recently eliminated the family Callitrichidae and included marmosets and tamarins in the family Cebidae.

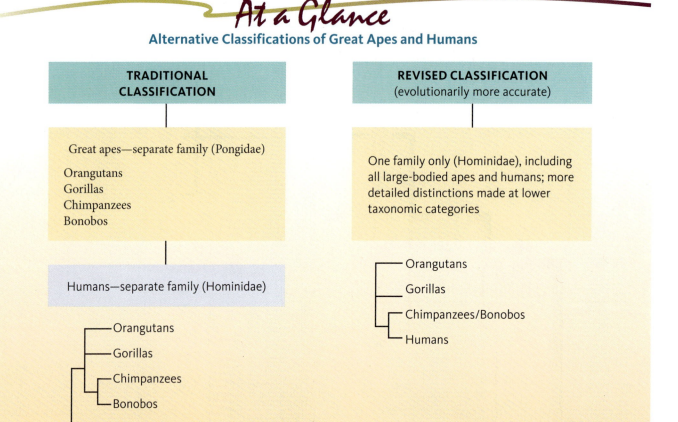

At a Glance

Alternative Classifications of Great Apes and Humans

TRADITIONAL CLASSIFICATION	REVISED CLASSIFICATION (evolutionarily more accurate)
Great apes—separate family (Pongidae) Orangutans Gorillas Chimpanzees Bonobos	One family only (Hominidae), including all large-bodied apes and humans; more detailed distinctions made at lower taxonomic categories

Humans—separate family (Hominidae)

Orangutans
Gorillas
Chimpanzees
Bonobos

Humans

Orangutans
Gorillas
Chimpanzees/Bonobos
Humans

Another area where changes have been suggested concerns tarsiers (see p. 133). Tarsiers are highly specialized animals that display several unique physical characteristics. Because they possess a number of prosimian traits, tarsiers have traditionally been classified as prosimians (with lemurs and lorises). But they also have certain anthropoid features, and they're more similar to the anthropoids biochemically (Dene et al., 1976).

Primatologists who maintain that tarsiers are more closely related to anthropoids have supported a reclassification. Instead of simply moving tarsiers into the suborder Anthropoidea, one scheme (Fig. 6-10) places lemurs and lorises in a different suborder, Strepsirhini, instead of Prosimii, while tarsiers are included with monkeys, apes, and humans in another suborder, Haplorhini (Szaley and Delson, 1979). In this classification, the traditionally named suborders Prosimii and Anthropoidea are replaced by Strepsirhini and Haplorhini, respectively. This designation hasn't been universally accepted. Nevertheless, the terminology is common, especially in technical publications. So if you see the term *strepsirhine*, you know that the author is referring specifically to lemurs and lorises.

 6-10

Revised partial classification of the primates. In this system, the names Prosimii and Anthropoidea would be replaced by Strepsirhini and Haplorhini, respectively. Tarsiers would be included in the same suborder as monkeys, apes, and humans to reflect a closer relationship with these species than with lemurs and lorises. (Compare with Fig. 6-9.)

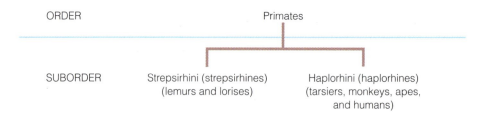

ORDER — Primates

SUBORDER — Strepsirhini (strepsirhines) (lemurs and lorises) | Haplorhini (haplorhines) (tarsiers, monkeys, apes, and humans)

Lynn Kilgore

Lynn Kilgore

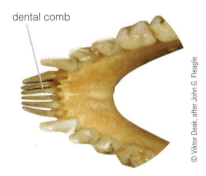

© Viktor Deak, after John G. Fleagle

Figure **6-11**

As you can see, rhinaria come in different shapes and sizes, but they all serve to enhance an animal's sense of smell.

A Survey of the Living Primates

In this section, we discuss the major primate subgroups. Since it's beyond the scope of this book to cover any species in detail, we present a brief description of each major grouping. Then we take a closer look at the apes.

LEMURS AND LORISES

The most primitive primates are the lemurs and lorises. Remember that by "primitive" we mean that they're more similar to their earlier mammalian ancestors than are the other primates (tarsiers, monkeys, apes, and humans). For example, they retain certain more ancestral characteristics, such as a more pronounced reliance on the sense of smell. Their greater olfactory capabilities (compared to other primates) are reflected in the presence of a moist, fleshy pad, or **rhinarium**, at the end of the nose and in a relatively long snout (Fig. 6-11). Lemurs and lorises also mark their territories with scent in a manner not seen in most other primates.

Many other characteristics distinguish lemurs and lorises from the haplorhines, including eyes placed more to the side of the face, differences in reproductive physiology, and shorter gestation and maturation periods. Lemurs and lorises also have a unique trait called a "dental comb" (Fig. 6-12). The dental comb is formed by forward-projecting lower incisors and canines, and together these modified teeth are used in grooming and feeding. Another characteristic that sets lemurs and lorises apart from anthropoids is the retention of a claw (called a "grooming claw") on the second toe.

Lemurs Lemurs are found only on the island of Madagascar and nearby islands off the east coast of Africa (Fig. 6-13). As the only nonhuman primates on Madagascar, lemurs diversified into numerous and varied ecological niches without competition from monkeys and apes. Thus, the approximately 60 surviving lemur species represent an evolutionary pattern that has vanished elsewhere.

Lemurs range in size from the small mouse lemur, with a body length (head and trunk) of only 5 inches, to the indri, with a body length of 2 to 3 feet (Nowak, 1999). While the larger lemurs are diurnal and exploit a wide variety of dietary items, such as leaves, fruits, buds, bark, and shoots, the smaller species (mouse and dwarf lemurs) are nocturnal and insectivorous.

Lemurs display considerable variation regarding numerous other aspects of behavior. Some are mostly arboreal, but others, such as the ring-tailed lemur (Fig. 6-14), are more terrestrial. Some arboreal species are quadrupeds, and others (sifakas and indris) are vertical clingers and leapers (Fig. 6-15). Socially, several species, such as ring-tailed lemurs and sifakas, are gregarious and live in groups of 10 to 25 animals composed of males and

Figure **6-12**

Prosimian dental comb, formed by forward-projecting incisors and canines.

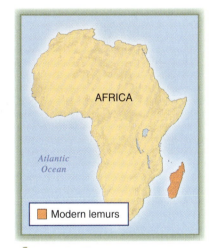

AFRICA

Atlantic Ocean

☐ Modern lemurs

Figure **6-13**

Geographical distribution of modern lemurs.

rhinarium (rine-air´-ee-um) (*pl.*, rhinaria) The moist, hairless pad at the end of the nose seen in most mammals. The rhinarium enhances an animal's ability to smell.

Figure **6-14**
Ring-tailed lemur.

Figure **6-15**
Sifakas.

females of all ages. Others (the indris) live in family units composed of a mated pair and their offspring; and several nocturnal forms are mostly solitary.

Lorises Lorises (Fig. 6-16), which resemble lemurs, were able to survive in mainland areas by becoming nocturnal when most other prosimians became extinct. In this way, they were (and are) able to avoid competition with more recently evolved primates, the diurnal monkeys.

There are at least eight loris species, all of which are found in tropical forest and woodland habitats of India, Sri Lanka, Southeast Asia, and Africa. Also included in the same general category are six to nine (Bearder, 1987; Nowak, 1999) galago species (Fig. 6-17), which are widely distributed throughout most of the forested and woodland savanna areas of sub-Saharan Africa.

Locomotion in some, but not all, lorises is a slow climbing form of quadrupedalism. All galagos are highly agile vertical clingers and leapers. Some lorises and galagos are almost entirely insectivorous; others supplement their diet with fruits, leaves, gums, and slugs. Lorises and galagos frequently forage for food alone, and unlike other primates,

Figure **6-16**
Slow loris.

Figure **6-17**
Galago, or "bush baby."

Figure **6-18**

Tarsier.

females leave infants behind in nests until they are older. Feeding ranges overlap, and two or more females occasionally forage together or share the same sleeping nest.

TARSIERS

There are five recognized tarsier species (Nowak, 1999; Fig. 6-18), all of which are restricted to island areas in Southeast Asia (Fig. 6-19), where they inhabit a wide range of habitats, from tropical forest to backyard gardens. Tarsiers are nocturnal insectivores that leap from lower branches and shrubs onto prey (which may include small vertebrates). They appear to form stable pair bonds, and the basic tarsier social unit is a mated pair and their young offspring (MacKinnon and MacKinnon, 1980).

As we have already mentioned, tarsiers present a complex blend of characteristics not seen in other primates. One of the most obvious differences is their enormous eyes, which dominate much of the face and cannot move within their sockets. To compensate for the inability to move their eyes, tarsiers (like owls) are able to rotate their heads 180°.

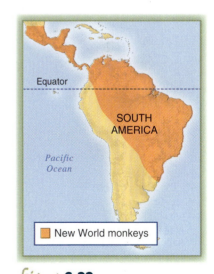

Figure **6-19**

Geographical distribution of tarsiers.

ANTHROPOIDS (MONKEYS, APES, AND HUMANS)

There's a great deal of variation among anthropoids, but they share certain features that, when taken together, distinguish them as a group from prosimians (and most other placental mammals). Here's a partial list of these traits:

1. Generally larger body size
2. Larger brain (in absolute terms and relative to body weight)
3. Reduced dependence on the sense of smell, as indicated by absence of a rhinarium
4. Increased reliance on vision, with forward-facing eyes at the front of the face
5. Greater degree of color vision
6. Back of eye socket formed by a bony plate
7. Blood supply to brain different from that of prosimians
8. Fusion of the two sides of the mandible at the midline to form one bone (in prosimians they are two bones joined by fibrous tissue)
9. Less specialized dentition, as seen in the lack of a dental comb and some other features
10. Differences in female internal reproductive anatomy
11. Longer gestation and maturation periods
12. Increased parental care
13. More mutual grooming

Approximately 85 percent of all primates are monkeys (about 195 species). Monkeys are divided into two groups separated by geographical area (New World and Old World), as well as by several million years of separate evolutionary history.

New World Monkeys There are approximately 70 New World monkey species and they exhibit considerable variation in size, diet, and ecological adaptation (Fig. 6-20). They are found throughout most forested areas of southern Mexico and Central and South America (Fig. 6-21). In size, they range from the tiny marmosets and tamarins (about 12 ounces) to the 20-pound howler monkeys (Figs. 6-22 and 6-23). New World monkeys are almost

Figure **6-20**

Geographical distribution of modern New World monkeys.

Figure **6-21**

A pair of golden lion tamarins.

Figure **6-22**

Howler monkeys.

exclusively arboreal, and some never come to the ground. Like Old World monkeys, all except one species (the owl monkey) are diurnal.

New World monkeys have traditionally been divided into two families: **Callitrichidae** (marmosets and tamarins) and **Cebidae** (all others). But molecular data along with recently reported fossil evidence indicate that a major regrouping of New World monkeys is in order (Fleagle, 1999).

Marmosets and tamarins are the smallest of the New World monkeys, and they're distinct in several ways. They're arboreal quadrupeds, but instead of nails, they have claws, which they use for climbing. Their diet consists largely of insects, although marmosets eat gums from trees, and tamarins eat fruits. Socially, these small monkeys live in family groups usually composed of a mated pair, or a female and two adult males, and their offspring. Unlike other primates, marmosets and tamarins usually give birth to twins, and they're among the few primate species in which males are extensively involved in infant care.

Cebids range in size from squirrel monkeys (body length 12 inches) to howlers (body length 24 inches). Diet varies, but most eat a combination of fruits and leaves supplemented, to varying degrees, by insects. Most cebids are quadrupedal; but some, such as muriquis and spider monkeys (Fig. 6-24), are semibrachiators. Muriquis, howlers, and spider monkeys also have prehensile tails that are used not only in locomotion but also for suspension under branches. Socially, most cebids are found in groups of both sexes and all age categories. Some (for example, titis) form monogamous pairs and live with their subadult offspring.

Callitrichidae (kal-eh-trick´-eh-dee)

Cebidae (see´-bid-ee)

Cercopithecidae (serk-oh-pith´-eh-sid-ee)

cercopithecines (serk-oh-pith´-eh-seens) The subfamily of Old World monkeys that includes baboons, macaques, and guenons.

colobines (kole´-uh-beans) The subfamily of Old World monkeys that includes the African colobus monkeys and Asian langurs.

Old World Monkeys Except for humans, Old World monkeys are the most widely distributed of all living primates. They are found throughout sub-Saharan Africa and southern Asia, ranging from tropical jungle habitats to semiarid desert and even to seasonally snow-covered areas in northern Japan (Fig. 6-25).

All Old World monkeys are placed in one taxonomic family: **Cercopithecidae**; in turn, this family is divided into two subfamilies: the **cercopithecines** and **colobines**. Most Old World monkeys are quadrupedal and primarily arboreal, but some (baboons, macaques, and langurs) spend much of the day on the ground and return to the trees in the evening to sleep.

The cercopithecines are the more generalized of the two groups: They're more omnivorous, and they have cheek pouches for storing food (like hamsters). As a group,

Squirrel monkeys

Figure **6-23**

New World monkeys.

Female muriqui with infant

Prince Bernhard's titi monkey (discovered in 2002)

Male uakari

White-faced capuchins

135

Figure 6-24

Spider monkey. Note the prehensile tail.

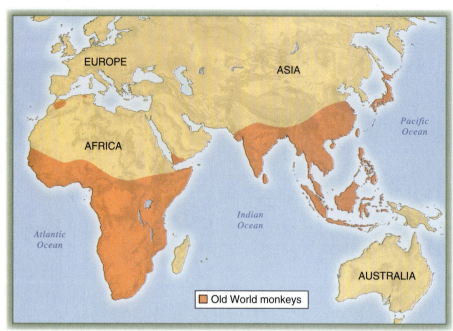

Figure 6-25

Geographical distribution of modern Old World monkeys.

the cercopithecines eat almost anything, including fruits, seeds, leaves, grasses, tubers, roots, nuts, insects, birds' eggs, amphibians, small reptiles, and small mammals (the last seen in baboons).

The majority of cercopithecine species, such as the mostly arboreal guenons (Fig. 6-26) and the more terrestrial savanna and hamadryas baboons, are found in Africa (Fig. 6-27). However, all but one of the several macaque species, which include the well-known rhesus monkey, are distributed across southern Asia and India.

Colobine species have a narrower range of food preferences and mainly eat mature leaves, which is why they're also called "leaf-eating monkeys." The colobines are found

Figure 6-26

Adult male sykes monkey, one of several guenon species.

(a)   (b)

Bonnie Pedersen/Arlene Kruse

Bonnie Pedersen/Arlene Kruse

Figure **6-27**
Savanna baboons. (a) Male. (b) Female.

mainly in Asia, but both red colobus and black-and-white colobus are exclusively African (Fig. 6-28). Other colobines include several Asian langur species and the proboscis monkey of Borneo.

Marked differences in body size or shape between the sexes, referred to as **sexual dimorphism**, are typical of some terrestrial species and are particularly pronounced in baboons. In these species, male body weight (up to 80 pounds in baboons) may be twice that of females.

Females of several species, especially baboons and some macaques, have pronounced cyclical changes of the external genitalia. These changes, including swelling and redness, are associated with **estrus**, a hormonally initiated period of sexual receptivity in female nonhuman mammals correlated with ovulation.

Old World monkeys live in a few different kinds of social groups, and there are uncertainties about some species. Colobines tend to live in small groups, with only one or two adult males. Savanna baboons and most macaque species are found in large social units comprising several adults of both sexes and offspring of all ages. Monogamous pairing is uncommon in Old World monkeys, but is seen in a few langurs and possibly one or two guenon species.

Lynn Kilgore

Figure **6-28**
Black-and-white colobus monkey.

sexual dimorphism Differences in physical characteristics between males and females of the same species. For example, humans are slightly sexually dimorphic for body size, with males being taller, on average, than females of the same population.

estrus (es´-truss) Period of sexual receptivity in female mammals (except humans), correlated with ovulation. When used as an adjective, the word is spelled "estrous."

Orangutans
Gibbons

Pacific Ocean

Figure **6-29**

Geographical distribution of modern Asian apes.

HOMINOIDS (APES AND HUMANS)

The other large grouping of anthropoids, the hominoids, includes apes and humans, and today, apes are found in Asia and Africa. The small-bodied gibbons and siamangs live in Southeast Asia, and the two orangutan subspecies live on the islands of Borneo and Sumatra (Fig. 6-29). In Africa, until the mid- to late twentieth century, gorillas, chimpanzees and bonobos occupied the forested areas of western, central, and eastern Africa, but their habitat is now extremely fragmented, and all are now threatened or highly endangered (see pp. 144–147). Apes and humans differ from monkeys in numerous ways:

1. Generally larger body size, except for gibbons and siamangs
2. Absence of a tail
3. Shorter and more stable lower back
4. Arms longer than legs (apes only)
5. Differences in position and musculature of the shoulder joint, which is adapted for suspensory behaviors (brachiation and/or feeding)
6. Generally more complex behavior
7. More complex brain and enhanced cognitive abilities
8. Increased period of infant development and dependency

Gibbons and Siamangs The eight gibbon species and the closely related siamangs are the smallest of the apes, weighing around 13 and 25 pounds, respectively. Their most distinctive anatomical features are adaptations to feeding while hanging beneath branches and brachiation, at which gibbons and siamangs excel (Fig. 6-30). In fact, gibbons and siamangs are more dedicated to brachiation than any other primate, and this fact is reflected in their extremely long arms, permanently curved fingers, short thumbs, and powerful shoulder muscles. (Their arms are so long that when they're on the ground, they can't walk quadrupedally, so instead, they walk bipedally with their arms raised to the side.) Gibbons and siamangs mostly eat fruits, although both (especially siamangs) consume a variety of leaves, flowers, and insects.

The basic social unit of gibbons and siamangs is an adult male and female with dependent offspring, and like other species that live in male-female pairs, they aren't sexually dimorphic. Although they've been described as monogamous, in reality, members of pairs sometimes do mate with other individuals. Like marmosets and tamarins,

Figure **6-30**

White-handed gibbon brachiating. Note the long curved fingers, long arms, and heavily muscled shoulders..

Lynn Kilgore

Noel Rowe

(a)

Lynn Kilgore

(b)

Figure **6-31**

Orangutans. (a) Female. (b) Male.

male gibbons and siamangs are very involved in rearing their young. Both males and females are highly territorial and protect their territories with elaborate whoops and siren-like "songs."

Orangutans Orangutans (*Pongo pygmaeus*) (Fig. 6-31) are represented by two subspecies found today only in heavily forested areas on the Indonesian islands of Borneo and Sumatra (see Fig. 6-29). Due to poaching by humans and continuing habitat loss on both islands, orangutans are severely threatened with extinction in the wild.

Orangutans are very large animals with pronounced sexual dimorphism (males may weigh 200 pounds or more and females less than 100 pounds). In the wild, they lead largely solitary lives, although adult females are usually accompanied by one or two dependent offspring. They're primarily **frugivorous**, but may also eat bark, leaves, insects, and meat (on rare occasions). Orangutans are slow, cautious climbers whose locomotor behavior can best be described as "four-handed," since they tend to use all four limbs for grasping and support. Although they're almost completely arboreal, males in particular also travel quadrupedally on the ground.

Gorillas The largest of all living primates, gorillas (*Gorilla gorilla*) are today confined to forested areas of western and eastern equatorial Africa (Fig. 6-32). There are four generally recognized subspecies, the most numerous of which are the western lowland gorillas, found in several countries of western central Africa (Fig. 6-33). In 1998, Doran and McNeilage reported an estimated population size of perhaps 110,000. However, a recently published report (Walsh et al., 2003) suggests that numbers are far lower.

The Cross River gorilla, a western lowland gorilla subspecies, was identified in the early 1900s but was subsequently thought to be extinct until the 1980s, when primatologists became aware of a few small populations in Nigeria and Cameroon (Sarmiento and Oates, 2000). Primatologists believe that there are only about 250 to 300 of these animals; thus, Cross River gorillas are among the most endangered of all primates. Currently, the International Union for the Conservation of Nature and Natural Resources (IUCN) is developing plans to protect this vulnerable and little-known subspecies (Oates et al., 2007).

Eastern lowland gorillas, which haven't really been studied, are found near the eastern border of the Democratic Republic of the Congo (DRC—formerly Zaire), a region that unfortunately is prone to warfare. At present, their numbers are unknown; researchers fear that many have been killed, but it's impossible to know how many.

AFRICA

Atlantic Ocean

■ Chimpanzees
■ Bonobos
□ Gorillas

Figure **6-32**

Geographical distribution of modern African apes.

frugivorous (fru-give´-or-us) Having a diet composed primarily of fruits.

(a)

(b)

Figure **6-33**

Western lowland gorillas. (a) Male. (b) Female.

Figure **6-34**

Mountain gorillas. (a) Male. (b) Female.

Mountain gorillas (Fig. 6-34), the most extensively studied of the four subspecies, are restricted to the mountainous areas of central Africa in Rwanda, the DRC, and Uganda. Mountain gorillas have probably never been very numerous, and today they're critically endangered, numbering only about 700. Tragically, in September 2007, rebel forces moved into the gorilla sector of the DRC, which is home to at least 300 gorillas. Since that time (at least as of this writing, July 2008), it's been impossible to monitor the gorillas' activities or to protect them.

Gorillas exhibit marked sexual dimorphism, with males weighing up to 400 pounds and females around 150 to 200 pounds. Because of their weight, adult gorillas, especially males, are primarily terrestrial and adopt a quadrupedal knuckle-walking posture on the ground.

Mountain gorillas live in groups consisting of one, or sometimes two, large *silverback* males, a variable number of adult females, and their subadult offspring. The term

(a)

(b)

silverback refers to the saddle of white hair across the back of full adult (at least 12 or 13 years of age) male gorillas. Silverback males may tolerate the presence of one or more young adult *blackback* males, probably their sons. Typically, but not always, both females and males leave their **natal group** as young adults. Females join other groups, but males, who appear to be less likely to emigrate, may live alone for a while, or they may join up with other males before eventually forming their own group.

Systematic studies of free-ranging western lowland gorillas weren't begun until the mid-1980s, and not as much is known about them, even though they're the only gorillas you'll see in zoos. The social structure of western lowland gorillas is similar to that of mountain gorillas, but groups are smaller and somewhat less cohesive.

All gorillas are almost exclusively vegetarian. Mountain and western lowland gorillas concentrate primarily on leaves, pith, and stalks, but the latter also eat more fruit. Also, western lowland gorillas, unlike mountain gorillas, which avoid water, frequently wade through swamps and forage on aquatic plants (Doran and MacNeilage, 1998).

Because of their large body size and enormous strength, gorillas have long been considered ferocious, but in fact they're usually shy and gentle. However, this doesn't mean that gorillas are never aggressive. Among males, competition for females can be extremely violent, and when threatened, males will attack and defend their group from any perceived danger, whether it's another male gorilla or a human hunter. Still, the reputation of gorillas as murderous beasts is nothing but a myth.

Chimpanzees Although chimpanzees are probably the best known of all nonhuman primates (Fig. 6-35), they're often misunderstood because of zoo exhibits, advertising, and television. The true nature of chimpanzees didn't become known until years of fieldwork with wild groups provided a more accurate picture. Today, chimpanzees are found in equatorial Africa, in an area that stretches from the Atlantic Ocean in the west to Lake Tanganyika in the east. But within this large area, their range is very patchy, and it's becoming even more so with continued forest clearing.

natal group The group in which animals are born and raised. (*Natal* pertains to birth.)

Figure 6-35

Chimpanzees. (a) Male. (b) Female.

(a)

(b)

In many ways, chimpanzees are anatomically similar to gorillas, with corresponding limb proportions and upper-body shape. However, the ecological adaptations of chimpanzees and gorillas differ in many ways, and chimpanzees are more arboreal than gorillas. Moreover, while gorillas are typically placid and quiet, chimpanzees are highly excitable, active, and noisy.

Chimpanzees are smaller than orangutans and gorillas, and although they're sexually dimorphic, differences between the sexes aren't as pronounced. While male chimpanzees may weigh over 100 pounds, females can weigh at least 80.

In addition to quadrupedal knuckle walking, chimpanzees (particularly youngsters) may brachiate when they're in the trees. Chimpanzees also sometimes walk bipedally for short distances when carrying food or other objects.

Chimpanzees eat a huge variety of foods, including fruits, leaves, insects, nuts, birds' eggs, berries, caterpillars, and small mammals. Moreover, both males and females occasionally take part in group efforts to hunt and kill small mammals such as red colobus monkeys, young baboons, bushpigs, and antelope. When hunts are successful, the group (especially members of the hunting party) share the prey.

Chimpanzees live in large, fluid communities ranging in size from 10 to as many as 100 individuals. A group of closely bonded males forms the core of chimpanzee communities, especially in East Africa (Goodall, 1986; Wrangham and Smuts, 1980; Wrangham et al., 1992). But for some West African groups, females appear to be more central to the community (Boesch, 1996; Boesch and Boesch-Ackerman, 2000; Vigilant et al., 2001). Relationships among closely bonded males aren't always peaceful or stable; yet these males cooperatively defend their territory and are highly intolerant of unfamiliar chimpanzees, especially males.

Even though chimpanzees are said to live in communities, it's rare for all members to be together at the same time. Rather, they tend to come and go, so that the individuals they encounter vary from day to day. Adult females usually forage alone or in the company of their offspring, a grouping that might include several individuals, since females with infants sometimes accompany their own mothers and their younger siblings. These associations have been reported at Gombe National Park, Tanzania, where about 40 percent of females remain in the group they were born in (Williams, 1999). But at most other locations, females leave their natal group to join another community. This behavioral pattern may reduce the risk of mating with close relatives, since males apparently never leave the group in which they were born.

Chimpanzee social behavior is complex, and individuals can form lifelong attachments with friends and relatives. Indeed, the bond between mothers and infants can remain strong until one of them dies. This may be a considerable period, because many wild chimpanzees live into their 40s or even longer.

Bonobos Bonobos (*Pan paniscus*) are found only in an area south of the Zaire River in the DRC (Fig. 6-36). Not officially recognized by European scientists until the 1920s, they remain among the least studied of the great apes. Although ongoing field studies have produced much information (Susman, 1984; Kano, 1992), research has been hampered by more or less continuous civil war. There are no accurate counts of bonobos, but their numbers are believed to be between 10,000 and 20,000 (IUCN, 1996), and they're highly threatened by human hunting, warfare, and habitat loss.

Because bonobos bear a strong resemblance to chimpanzees but are slightly smaller, they've been called "pygmy chimpanzees." However, that term isn't commonly used by primatologists and size differences aren't that great. But, there are some anatomical differences between bonobos and chimpanzees; bonobos have a more linear body build, longer legs relative to arms, a relatively smaller head, a dark face from birth, and tufts of hair at the sides of the face.

Bonobos are more arboreal than chimpanzees, and they're less excitable and aggressive. While aggression isn't unknown, it appears that physical violence both

Figure **6-36**
Female bonobos with young.

within and between groups is uncommon. Like chimpanzees, bonobos live in geographically based, fluid communities, and they eat many of the same foods, including occasional meat derived from small mammals (Badrian and Malinky, 1984). But bonobo communities aren't centered around a group of closely bonded males. Instead, male-female bonding is more important than in chimpanzees (and most other nonhuman primates), and females aren't peripheral to the group (Badrian and Badrian, 1984). This may be related to bonobo sexuality, which differs from that of other nonhuman primates in that copulation is very frequent and occurs throughout a female's estrous cycle, so sex isn't entirely linked to reproduction. In fact, bonobos are famous for their sexual behavior, engaging in sex frequently and using it to defuse potentially tense situations. Sexual behavior between members of the same sex is also common (Kano, 1992; de Waal and Lanting, 1997).

HUMANS

We humans exhibit our primate heritage in our overall anatomy and genetic makeup and in many aspects of behavior. With the exception of reduced canine size, human teeth are typical primate (especially ape) teeth. The human dependence on vision and decreased reliance on olfaction, as well as flexible limbs and grasping hands, are rooted in our primate, arboreal past. Humans can even brachiate, as many of us demonstrated during childhood.

In general, humans are omnivorous, although all societies observe certain culturally based dietary restrictions. Even so, as a species with a rather generalized digestive system, we are physiologically adapted to digest an extremely wide assortment of foods. Perhaps to our detriment, we also share with our relatives a fondness for sweets that originates from the importance of high-energy fruits in the diets of many nonhuman primates.

But quite obviously, humans are unique among primates and indeed among all animals. For example, no other species has the ability to write or think about issues such as how they differ from other life-forms. This ability is rooted in the fact that human evolution, during the last 800,000 years or so, has been characterized by dramatic increases in brain size and other neurological changes.

Humans are also completely dependent on culture. Without cultural innovation, we would never have been able to leave the tropics. As it is, humans inhabit every corner of the planet with the exception of Antarctica, and we've even established outposts there. And lest we forget, a fortunate few have even walked on the moon. None of the technologies (indeed, none of the other aspects of culture) that humans have developed over the last several thousand years would have been possible without the highly developed cognitive abilities that we alone possess. Nevertheless, the neurological basis for **intelligence** is rooted in our evolutionary past, and it's something we share with other primates. Indeed, research has demonstrated that several nonhuman primate species (most notably chimpanzees, bonobos, and gorillas) display a level of problem solving and insight that most people would have considered impossible 25 years ago (see Chapter 7).

Humans are uniquely predisposed to use spoken language, and for the last 5,000 years or so, we've also used written language. This ability exists because during the course of human evolution, certain neurological and anatomical structures have been modified in ways not seen in any other species. But while nonhuman primates aren't anatomically capable of producing speech, research has shown that to varying degrees, the great apes can communicate by using symbols, which is a foundation for language that humans and the great apes (to a more limited degree) have in common.

Aside from cognitive abilities, the one other trait that sets humans apart from other primates is our unique (among mammals) form of *habitual* bipedal locomotion. This particular trait appeared early in the evolution of our lineage, and over time, we have become more efficient at it because of related changes in the musculoskeletal anatomy of the pelvis, leg, and foot (see Chapter 9). Still, while it's certainly true that human beings are unique intellectually and in some ways anatomically, we are still primates. In fact, fundamentally, humans are somewhat exaggerated African apes.

Endangered Primates

In September 2000, scientists announced that a subspecies of red colobus, named Miss Waldron's red colobus, had officially been declared extinct. This announcement came after a 6-year search for the 20-pound monkey that hadn't been seen for 20 years (Oates et al., 2000). Thus, this species, indigenous to the West African countries of Ghana and the Ivory Coast, has the distinction of being the first nonhuman primate to be declared extinct in the twenty-first century. But it won't be the last. In fact, as of this writing, over half of all nonhuman primate species are now in jeopardy, and some face almost immediate extinction in the wild.

There are three basic reasons for the worldwide depletion of nonhuman primates: habitat destruction, hunting for food, and live capture for export or local trade. Underlying these three causes is one major factor: unprecedented human population growth, particularly in developing countries, which are also home to over 90 percent of all nonhuman primate species. These countries, aided in no small part by the United States, China, and the industrialized countries of Europe, are cutting their forests at a rate of about 30 million acres per year. Unbelievably, in the year 2002, deforestation of the Amazon increased by 40 percent over that of 2001. This increase was largely due to land clearing for the cultivation of soybeans. In Brazil, the Atlantic rain forest originally covered some 385,000 square miles. Today, an estimated 7 percent is all that remains of what was once home to countless New World monkeys and thousands of other species.

The motivation behind rain forest destruction is, of course, economic: the short-term gains from clearing forests to create immediately available (but poor) farmland or ranchland; the use of trees for lumber and paper products; and large-scale mining operations (with their necessary roads, digging, and so forth, all of which cause habitat destruction). Furthermore, the demand for tropical hardwoods (such as mahogany, teak, and rosewood) in the United States, Europe, and Japan continues unabated, creating an enormously profitable market for rain forest products.

intelligence Mental capacity; ability to learn, reason, or comprehend and interpret information, facts, relationships, and meanings; the capacity to solve problems, whether through the appplication of previously acquired knowledge or through insight.

THE BUSHMEAT CRISIS

In many areas, habitat loss has been, and continues to be, the single greatest cause of declining numbers of nonhuman primates. But in the past few years, human hunting has posed an even greater threat. During the 1990s, primatologists and conservationists became aware of a rapidly developing trade in *bushmeat*, meat from wild animals, especially in Africa (Fig. 6-37). The current slaughter, which now accounts for the loss of tens of thousands of nonhuman primates (and other animals) annually, has been compared to the near extinction of the American bison in the nineteenth century.

Wherever primates live, people have always hunted them for food. But in the past, subsistence hunting wasn't a serious threat to nonhuman primate populations, and certainly not to entire species. But now, hunters armed with automatic rifles can, and do, wipe out an entire group of monkeys or gorillas in minutes. It's impossible to know how many animals are killed each year, but the estimates are staggering. The Society for Conservation Biology estimates that about 6,000 kg (13,228 pounds) of bushmeat is taken through just seven western cities (New York, London, Toronto, Paris, Montreal, Chicago, and Brussels) every month. No one knows how much of this meat is from primates, but this figure represents only a tiny fraction of all the animals being slaughtered because much smuggled meat isn't detected at ports of entry. If this weren't enough, the international trade is thought to account for only about 1 percent of the total (Marris, 2006).

Quite clearly, many primate species, which number only a few hundred or thousand animals, cannot and will not survive this onslaught for more than a few years. In addition, hundreds of infants are orphaned and sold in markets as pets. Although a few of these traumatized orphans make it to sanctuaries, most die within days or weeks of capture (Fig. 6-38).

One major factor in the development of the bushmeat trade has been logging. The construction of logging roads, mainly by French, German, and Belgian lumber companies, has opened up vast tracts of previously inaccessible forest to hunters. What has emerged is a multimillion-dollar trade in bushmeat, a trade in which logging company employees and local government officials participate with hunters, villagers, market vendors, and smugglers who cater to local and overseas markets. In other words, the hunting of wild animals for food, particularly in Africa, has quickly shifted from a subsistence activity to a commercial enterprise of international scope.

John Oates

Figure **6-37**

Red-eared guenons (with red tails) and Preuss' guenons for sale in bushmeat market, Malabo, Equatorial Guinea.

Figure **6-38**

These orphaned chimpanzee infants are being bottle-fed at a sanctuary near Pointe Noir, Congo. They will probably never be returned to the wild, and they face an uncertain future.

Although the slaughter may be best known in Africa, it's by no means limited to that continent. In South America, for example, hunting nonhuman primates for food is common. One report documents that in less than two years, one family of Brazilian rubber tappers killed almost 500 members of various large-bodied species, including spider monkeys, woolly monkeys, and howler monkeys (Peres, 1990). And live capture and illegal trade in endangered primate species continue unabated in China and Southeast Asia, where nonhuman primates are not only eaten but are also funneled into the exotic pet trade. Moreover, primate body parts are extensively used in traditional medicines, and with increasing human population size, the enormous demand for these products (and for products from nonprimate species, such as tigers) has placed many species in extreme jeopardy.

MOUNTAIN GORILLAS AT GREAT RISK

Mountain gorillas are one of the most endangered of all nonhuman primate species. All of the approximately 700 mountain gorillas alive today are restricted to a heavily forested area in and around the Virunga mountains (the Virunga Volcanoes Conservation Area) shared by three countries: Uganda, Rwanda, and the DRC. This entire area is a UNESCO (United Nations Educational, Scientific, and Cultural Organization) World Heritage Site. In addition, there is a separate, noncontiguous park in Uganda—the Bwindi Impenetrable Forest, that is also home to some of these gorillas. Tourism has been the only real hope of salvation for these magnificent animals, and for this reason, several gorilla groups have been habituated to humans and are heavily protected by park rangers. Nevertheless, poaching, civil war, and land clearing have continued to take a toll on these small populations.

Between January and late July 2007, eleven mountain gorillas were slaughtered in the DRC. In addition, two infants, orphaned in the attacks, were rescued and taken to a veterinary clinic where, as of this writing (July, 2008), they are in good condition (Newport, pers. comm.).

Six of the victims, including the silverback male (Fig. 6-39), were members of one family group of 12. The remnant of this group consists of four immature males and one immature female, and without a silverback, their future is uncertain.

These gorillas weren't shot for meat or because they were raiding crops. They were killed because their existence in the park is an obstacle to people who would destroy what little remains of the gorillas' forest home. One of the many reasons for cutting the forests is the manufacture of charcoal, a major source of fuel in rural Rwanda and the DRC.

In 2007, paleoanthropologist Richard Leakey and a colleague, Emanuelle de Merode, established WildlifeDirect.org to help support conservationists and especially the rangers who work to protect the mountain gorillas. You may want to go to their website (www. wildlifedirect.org), where you can read updates and see photographs and videos posted daily by the rangers. These communications offer fascinating insights into their efforts, conditions in the forest, and updates on gorillas and other species.

There are several other conservation groups that work to protect mountain gorillas. And in 2000, the United Nations Environmental Program established the Great Ape Survival Project (GRASP). GRASP is an alliance of many of the world's major great ape conservation and research organizations. In 2003, GRASP appealed for $25 million to be used in protecting the great apes from extinction. The money (a paltry sum) would be used to enforce laws that regulate hunting and illegal logging. It goes without saying that GRASP and other organizations must succeed if the great apes are to survive in the wild for even 20 more years!

But GRASP and the various conservation organizations face a formidable task just to save mountain gorillas, not to mention the dozens of other primate species at risk. In early September 2007, rebel forces in the gorilla sector of the DRC attacked a ranger station, where they killed one ranger. Consequently, WildlifeDirect evacuated all rangers from the area, leaving the gorillas unprotected. As of this writing (July, 2008), fighting has stopped, but the rangers still can't return to the area, so the status of the gorillas is uncertain.

As a note of optimism, in November 2007, the DRC government and the Bonobo Conservation Initiative, in Washington, D.C., created a bonobo reserve consisting of 30,500 square kilometers. This amounts to about 10 percent of the land in the DRC, and the government has stated that its goal is to set aside an additional 5 percent for wildlife protection (News in Brief, 2007). This is a huge step forward, but it remains to be seen how protection will be enforced.

Figure **6-39**

Congolese villagers carrying the body of the silverback gorilla killed in July, 2007. His body was buried with the other members of his group who were also shot.

WildlifeDirect.org

If you are in your 20s or 30s, you will certainly live to hear of the extinction of some of our marvelous cousins. Many more will slip away unnoticed. Tragically, this will occur, in most cases, before we've even gotten to know them. Each species on earth is the current result of a unique set of evolutionary events that, over millions of years, has produced a finely adapted component of a diverse ecosystem. When it becomes extinct, that adaptation and that part of biodiversity is lost forever. What a tragedy it will be if, through our own mismanagement and greed, we awaken to a world without chimpanzees, mountain gorillas, or the tiny, exquisite lion tamarin. When this day comes, we truly will have lost a part of ourselves, and we will certainly be the poorer for it.

Summary

In this chapter, we introduced you to the primates, the mammalian order that includes prosimians, monkeys, apes, and humans. We discussed how primates, including humans, have retained a number of ancestral characteristics that have permitted them, as a group, to be generalized in terms of diet and locomotor patterns. We also presented a general outline of traits that differentiate primates from other mammals.

You also became acquainted with the major groups of nonhuman primates, especially with regard to their basic social structure, diet, and locomotor patterns. Most primates are diurnal and live in social groups. The only nocturnal primates are lorises, galagos, some lemurs, tarsiers, and owl monkeys. Nocturnal species tend to forage for food alone or with offspring and one or two other animals. Diurnal primates live in a variety of social groupings, including male-female pairs and groups consisting of one male with several females and offspring or those composed of several males and females and offspring.

Finally, we talked about the precarious existence of most nonhuman primates today as they face hunting, capture, and habitat loss. These threats are all imposed by only one primate species, one that arrived fairly late on the evolutionary stage: *Homo sapiens*.

Critical Thinking Questions

1. How does a classification scheme reflect biological and evolutionary changes in a lineage?
2. How do you think continued advances in genetic research will influence how we look at our species' relationship with nonhuman primates 10 or 15 years from now?
3. What factors are threatening the existence of nonhuman primates in the wild? What can you do to help in the efforts to save nonhuman primates from extinction?

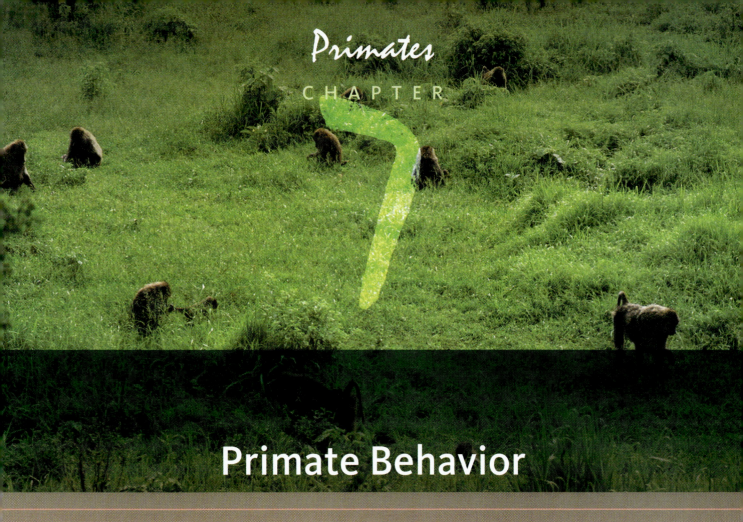

Primates

Primate Behavior

Focus Question

How can behavior be a product of evolutionary processes, and what is one example of a behavior that has been influenced by evolution?

Click!

Go to the following media for interactive activities and exercises on topics covered in this chapter:

- Online Virtual Laboratories for Physical Anthropology, Version 4.0

Introduction

Do you think cats are cruel when they play with mice before they kill them? Or if you've ever fallen off a horse when it leaped aside for no apparent reason, did you think the horse deliberately tried to throw you? If you answered yes to either of these questions, you're not alone. To most people, it does seem cruel for a cat to torment a mouse for no obvious reason. And more than one rider has thought that a horse's eagerness to rid itself of a burden was deliberate mischief (and, admittedly, sometimes it may be). But these views generally demonstrate how little most people really know about nonhuman animal **behavior**.

Especially in mammals and birds, behavior is extremely complex because it's been shaped over evolutionary time by interactions between genetic and environmental factors. But few people give this much thought, and even those who do don't necessarily accept this basic premise. For example, many social scientists object to the notion of genetic influences on human behavior because of concerns that behaviors will be viewed as fixed and can't be changed by experience (that is, learning). This concern has some validity because the notion of fixed behaviors could be used to support racist and sexist ideologies.

Most people also share the common belief that there's a fundamental division between humans and all other animals. In some cultures, this view is fostered by religion; but even when religion isn't a factor, most people see themselves as uniquely set apart from all other species. But at the same time, and in obvious contradiction, they may judge other species from a strictly human perspective and explain certain behaviors in terms of human motivations (for example, cats are cruel to play with mice). Of course, this isn't a valid thing to do for the simple reason that other animals aren't human. Cats sometimes play with mice before they kill them because that's how, as kittens, they learn to hunt. Cruelty doesn't enter into it though, because the cat has no concept of cruelty and no idea of what it's like to be the mouse. Likewise, the horse doesn't deliberately throw you off when it hears leaves rattling in a shrub. It leaps aside and maybe even runs away because its behavior has been shaped by thousands of generations of horse ancestors who jumped first and asked questions later. It's important to understand that just as cats evolved as predators, horses evolved as prey animals, and their evolutionary history is littered with unfortunate animals that didn't jump at a sound in a shrub. In many cases, those ancestral horses learned, too late, that the sound wasn't caused by a breeze at all. This is a mistake that prey animals don't usually survive, and those that don't leap first leave few descendants.

Of course, this chapter isn't about cats and horses. It's about what we know and hypothesize about the individual and social behaviors of nonhuman primates. But we begin with the familiar examples of cats and horses because we want to point out that many basic behaviors have been shaped by a species' evolutionary history. Also, the same factors that have influenced many behaviors in nonprimate animals also apply to primates. So if we want to discover the underlying principles of behavioral evolution, including that of humans, we first need to identify the interactions between a number of environmental and physiological variables.

behavior Anything organisms do that involves action in response to internal or external stimuli; the response of an individual, group, or species to its environment. Such responses may or may not be deliberate, and they aren't necessarily the result of conscious decision making

The Evolution of Behavior

Scientists study behavior in free-ranging primates from an **ecological** and evolutionary perspective, meaning that they focus on the relationship between behaviors, the natural environment, and various physiological traits of the species in question. This approach is called **behavioral ecology**, and it's based on the underlying assumption that all of the biological components of ecological systems (animals, plants, and even microorganisms) evolved together. Therefore, behaviors are adaptations to environmental circumstances that existed in the past as much as in the present.

Briefly, the cornerstone of this perspective is that *behaviors have evolved through the operation of natural selection.* That is, since certain behaviors are influenced by genes, they're subject to natural selection in the same way physical characteristics are. (Remember that within a specific environmental context, natural selection favors traits that provide a reproductive advantage to the individuals who possess them.) Therefore, behavior constitutes a phenotype, and individuals whose behavioral phenotypes increase reproductive fitness will pass on their genes at a faster rate than those who don't have those favorable behaviors. But this doesn't mean that primatologists think that genes code for specific behaviors, such as a gene for aggression, another for cooperation, and so on. Examining complex behaviors from an evolutionary viewpoint doesn't imply a one gene–one behavior relationship, nor does it suggest that behaviors that are influenced by genes can't be modified through learning.

Much of the behavior of insects and other invertebrates is largely under genetic control. In other words, most behavioral patterns in those species aren't learned; they're innate. But in many vertebrates, especially birds and mammals, the proportion of behavior that's due to learning is substantially increased, and the proportion under genetic control is reduced. This is especially true of primates; and in humans, who are so much a product of culture, most behavior is learned. But at the same time, we know that in mammals and birds, some behaviors are at least partly influenced by certain gene products such as hormones. For example, you're probably aware that increased levels of testosterone increase aggression in many species. You may also know that some forms of depression, schizophrenia, and bipolar disorder are caused by abnormal levels of certain chemicals produced by brain cells.

Behavioral genetics, or the study of how genes influence behavior, is a fairly new field, and we currently don't know how much genes influence behavior in humans or even other species. But we do know that behavior must be viewed as the product of *complex interactions between genetic and environmental factors.* There's a great deal of variability among species in the limits and potentials for learning and for behavioral **plasticity**, or flexibility. In some, the potentials are extremely broad; in others, they aren't. Ultimately, those limits and potentials are set by genetic factors that natural selection has favored throughout the evolutionary history of every species. That history, in turn, has been shaped by the ecological setting not only of living species, *but also of their ancestors.*

One of the major goals of primatology is to determine how behaviors influence reproductive fitness and how ecological factors have shaped the evolution of these behaviors. While the actual mechanics of behavioral evolution aren't yet fully understood, new technologies are beginning to help scientists answer many questions. For example, genetic analysis has recently been used to establish paternity in a few primate groups, and this has helped support hypotheses about some behaviors (see p. 163). But in general, an evolutionary approach to the study of behavior doesn't provide definitive answers to many research questions. Rather, it provides a framework within which primatologists analyze data to generate and test hypotheses concerning behavioral patterns.

Because primates are among the most social of animals, social behavior is one of the major topics in primate research. This is a broad subject that includes *all* aspects of behavior that occur in social groupings, even some you may not think of as social

ecological Pertaining to the relationships between organisms and all aspects of their environment (temperature, predators, non-predators, vegetation, availability of food and water, types of food, disease organisms, parasites, etc.).

behavioral ecology The study of the evolution of behavior, emphasizing the role of ecological factors as agents of natural selection. Behaviors and behavioral patterns have been favored because they increase the reproductive fitness of individuals (i.e., they are adaptive) in specific environmental contexts.

plasticity The capacity to change; in a behavioral context, the ability of animals to modify behaviors in response to differing circumstances

behaviors, like feeding or mating. To understand the function of one behavioral element, it's necessary to determine how it's influenced by numerous interrelated factors. As an example, we'll discuss some of the more important variables that influence **social structure**.

SOME FACTORS THAT INFLUENCE SOCIAL STRUCTURE

Body Size As a general rule, larger animals require fewer calories per unit of weight than smaller animals because they have a smaller ratio of surface area to mass than smaller animals. Since body heat is lost at the surface, larger animals can retain heat more efficiently, and so they require less energy overall.

Basal Metabolic Rate (BMR) The BMR concerns **metabolism**, the rate at which the body uses energy to maintain all body functions while in a resting state. It's closely correlated with body size; in general, smaller animals have a higher BMR than larger ones (Fig. 7-1). Consequently, smaller primates, like galagos, tarsiers, marmosets, and tamarins, require an energy-rich diet high in protein (insects), fats (nuts and seeds), and carbohydrates (fruits and seeds). Some larger primates, which tend to have a lower BMR and reduced energy requirements relative to body size, can do well with less energy-rich foods, such as leaves.

Diet Since the nutritional requirements of animals are related to the previous two factors, all three have evolved together. Therefore, when primatologists study the relationships between diet and behavior, they consider the benefits in terms of energy (calories) derived from various food items against the costs (energy expended) of obtaining and digesting them. While small-bodied primates focus on high-energy foods, larger ones don't necessarily need to. For instance, gorillas eat leaves, pith from bamboo stems, and other types of vegetation, and they don't need to use much energy searching for food, since they are frequently surrounded by it (Fig. 7-2).

Distribution of Resources Various types of foods are distributed in different ways. Leaves can be plentiful and dense and will therefore support large groups of animals. Insects, on the other hand, may be widely scattered, and the animals that rely on them usually feed alone or in small groups of two or three.

Fruits, nuts, and berries in dispersed trees and shrubs occur in clumps. These can most efficiently be exploited by smaller groups of animals, so large groups frequently break up into smaller subunits while feeding. Such subunits may consist of one-male–multifemale groups (some baboons) or **matrilines** (macaques). Species that feed on abundantly distributed resources may also live in one-male–multifemale groups, and because food is plentiful, these units are able to join with others to form large, stable communities (for example, howlers, some colobines, and some baboons). To the casual observer, these communities can appear to be **multimale-multifemale groups**.

Some species that rely on foods distributed in small clumps are protective of resources, especially if their feeding area is small enough to be defended. Some live in small groups composed of a mated pair (siamangs) or a female with one or two males (marmosets and tamarins). Naturally, dependent offspring are also included. Lastly, many kinds of food are only seasonally available. These include fruits, nuts, seeds, and berries. Primates that rely on seasonally available foods must exploit a number of different food types and must move about in order to have enough to eat throughout the year. This is another factor that tends to favor smaller feeding groups.

Russ Mittermeir

Figure 7-1

This tiny dwarf mouse lemur has a high BMR and requires an energy-rich diet of insects and other forms of animal protein.

social structure The composition, size, and sex ratio of a group of animals. The social structure of a species is, in part, the result of natural selection in a specific habitat, and it guides individual interactions and social relationships.

metabolism The chemical processes within cells that break down nutrients and release energy. (When nutrients are broken down into their component parts, such as amino acids, energy is released and made available for the cell to use.)

matrilines Groups that consist of a female, her daughters, and their offspring. Matrilineal groups are common in macaques.

"multimale-multifemale" groups Social groups composed of several adults and subadults of both sexes.

Predation Primates, depending on their size, are vulnerable to many types of predators, including snakes, birds of prey, leopards, wild dogs, lions, and even other primates. Their responses to predation depend on their body size, social structure, and the type of predator. Typically, where predation pressure is high and body size is small, large communities are advantageous. These may be multimale-multifemale groups or congregations of one-male–multifemale groups.

Relationships with Other, Nonpredatory Species Many primate species associate with other primate and nonprimate species for various reasons, including predator avoidance. When they share habitats with other species, they exploit somewhat different resources.

Dispersal Dispersal is another factor that influences social structure and relationships within groups. As is true of most mammals (and indeed, most vertebrates), members of one sex leave the group in which they were born (their *natal group*) about the time they reach puberty. Male dispersal is the most common pattern in primates (ring-tailed lemurs, vervets, and macaques, to name a few). (This is generally true for other animals, too.) Female dispersal is seen in some colobus species, hamadryas baboons, chimpanzees, and mountain gorillas.

Dispersal may have more than one outcome. When females leave, they join another group. When males leave, they may live alone for a while or temporarily join an all-male "bachelor" group until they're able to establish a group of their own (a pattern seen in gorillas). But one common theme is that individuals who disperse usually find mates outside their natal group. This commonality has led primatologists to conclude that the most valid explanations for dispersal are probably related to two major factors: reduced competition for mates (particularly between males) and, perhaps even more important, the decreased likelihood of close inbreeding.

Life Histories **Life history traits** are characteristics or developmental stages that typify members of a given species and influence potential reproductive rates. Examples of life history traits include length of gestation, length of time between pregnancies (interbirth interval), period of infant dependency, age at weaning, age at sexual maturity, and life expectancy.

Life history traits have important consequences for many aspects of social life and social structure, and they can also be critical to species survival. Shorter life histories are advantageous to species that live in marginal or unpredictable habitats (Strier, 2003). Since these species mature early and have short interbirth intervals, they can reproduce at a relatively fast rate. Conversely, species with extended life histories, such as gorillas, are better suited to stable environmental conditions. The extended life spans of the great apes in particular, characterized by later sexual maturation and long interbirth intervals (three to five years), mean that most females will raise only three or four offspring to maturity. This slow reproductive rate is a detriment to species that are threatened with extinction.

Distribution and Types of Sleeping Sites Gorillas are the only nonhuman primates that sleep on the ground. Primate sleeping sites can be in trees or on cliff faces, and their spacing can be related to social structure and predator avoidance.

Activity Patterns As you already know, most primates are diurnal, but several small-bodied prosimians and one New World monkey (the owl monkey) are nocturnal.

Figure **7-2**
This male mountain gorilla has only to reach out to find something to eat.

life history traits Characteristics and developmental stages that influence reproductive rates. Examples include longevity, age at sexual maturity, and length of time between births.

Nocturnal primates tend to forage for food alone or in groups of two or three, and many hide to avoid predators.

Human Activities Virtually all nonhuman primate populations are now impacted by human hunting and forest clearing. These activities disrupt and isolate groups, reduce numbers, decrease food supplies, change behavior, and eventually cause extinction.

Why Be Social?

Group living exposes animals to competition with other group members for resources, so why don't they live alone? After all, competition can lead to injury or even death, and it's costly in terms of energy expenditure. One widely accepted answer to this question is that the costs of competition are offset by the benefits of predator defense provided by associating with others. Groups made up of several adult males and females (multimale-multifemale groups) are advantageous in areas where predation pressure is high, particularly in mixed woodlands and on open savannas. Leopards are the most significant predator of terrestrial primates (Fig. 7-3). Where members of prey species occur in larger groups, the chances of early predator detection and avoidance are increased simply because there are more pairs of eyes looking about. There really is safety in numbers.

Savanna baboons have long been used as an example of these principles. They're found in semiarid grassland and broken woodland habitats throughout sub-Saharan Africa. To avoid nocturnal predators, savanna baboons sleep in trees, but during the day, they spend much of their time on the ground foraging for food. If a nonhuman predator appears, baboons flee back into the trees, but if they're some distance from safety, adult males (and sometimes females) may join forces to chase the intruder. The effectiveness of male baboons in this regard shouldn't be underestimated, since they've been known to kill domestic dogs and even to attack leopards and lions.

There is probably no single answer to the question of why primates live in groups. More than likely, predator avoidance is a major factor but not the only one. Group living evolved as an adaptive response to a number of ecological variables, and it has served primates well for a very long time.

Figure **7-3**

When a baboon strays too far from its troop, as this one has done, it's more likely to fall prey to predators. Leopards are the most serious nonhuman threat to terrestrial primates.

Time Life Pictures/Getty Images

Primates (and other animals) also communicate through **displays**, which are more complicated, frequently elaborate combinations of behaviors. For example, the exaggerated courtship dances of many male birds, often enhanced by colorful plumage, are displays. Chest slapping and tearing vegetation are common gorilla threat displays.

All nonhuman animals use various body postures, vocalizations, and facial expressions to transmit information. But the array of communicative devices is much richer among nonhuman primates, even though they don't use language the way humans do. Communication is important, because it makes social living possible. Through submissive gestures, aggression is reduced and physical violence is less likely. Likewise, friendly intentions and relationships are reinforced through physical contact and grooming. Indeed, we humans can see ourselves in other primate species most clearly in their use of nonverbal communication, particularly because some of their gestures and facial expressions carry the same meaning as ours do.

Lynn Kilgore

Figure **7-6**

Adolescent savanna baboons holding hands.

AGGRESSIVE INTERACTIONS

Within primate societies, there is an interplay between aggressive behaviors, which can lead to group disruption, and **affiliative** behaviors, which promote group cohesion. Conflict within a group frequently develops out of competition for resources, including mating partners or food. Instead of actual attacks or fighting, most aggression occurs in the form of various signals and displays, frequently within the context of a dominance hierarchy. Therefore, the majority of tense situations are resolved through various submissive and appeasement behaviors. However, not all conflicts are resolved peacefully. Competition between males for mates can result in injury and even death. Females also compete with each other, frequently for resources, and especially low-ranking females may starve when food supplies are short (Silk et al., 2003).

Between groups, aggression is used to protect resources or **territories**. Primate groups are associated with a *home range* where they remain permanently. (Although individuals may leave their home range and join another community, the group itself remains in a particular area.) Within the home range is a portion called the **core area**, which contains the highest concentration of predictable resources, and it's where the group is most

displays Sequences of repetitious behaviors that serve to communicate an animal's emotional state. Nonhuman primate displays are most frequently associated with reproductive or agonistic behavior, and examples include chest slapping in gorillas or, in male chimpanzees, dragging and waving branches while charging and threatening other animals.

affiliative Pertaining to amicable associations between individuals. Affiliative behaviors, such as grooming, reinforce social bonds and promote group cohesion.

territories Portions of an individual's or group's home range that are actively defended against intrusion, especially by members of the same species.

core area The portion of a home range containing the highest concentration and most reliable supplies of food and water. The core area is defended.

Figure **7-7**

Chimpanzee facial expressions.

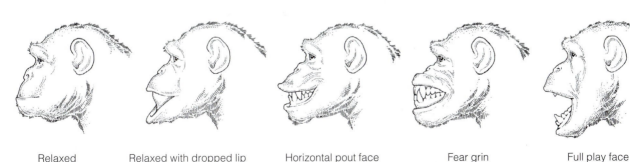

| Relaxed | Relaxed with dropped lip | Horizontal pout face (distress) | Fear grin (fear/excitement) | Full play face |

Curt Busse

Figure **7-8**

Members of a chimpanzee "border patrol" at Gombe survey their territory from a tree.

frequently found. Although parts of a group's home range may overlap the with home ranges of other groups, core areas of adjacent groups don't overlap. The core area can also be said to be a group's territory, and it's the portion of the home range defended against intrusion.

Not all primates are territorial. In general, territoriality is typical of species whose ranges are small enough to be patrolled and protected (for example, gibbons and vervets). Moreover, in many species, group encounters are frequently nonaggressive. Male chimpanzees, however, are highly intolerant of unfamiliar chimpanzees, especially other males, and they fiercely defend their territories and resources (Fig. 7-8). Therefore, interactions between different chimpanzee groups almost always include aggressive displays, chasing, and frequently actual fighting.

Beginning in 1974, Jane Goodall and her colleagues saw at least five unprovoked and extremely brutal attacks by groups of chimpanzees on other chimpanzees. To explain these attacks, it's necessary to point out that by 1973, the original Gombe chimpanzee community had divided into two distinct groups, one located in the north and the other in the south of what had once been the original group's home range. In effect, the smaller offshoot group had denied the others access to part of their former home range.

By 1977, all seven males and one female of the splinter group were either known or suspected to have been killed. All observed incidents involved several animals, usually adult males, who brutally attacked lone individuals. Although it isn't possible to know exactly what motivated the attackers, it was clear that they intended to incapacitate their victims (Goodall, 1986).

A similar situation was also reported for a chimpanzee group in the Mahale Mountains south of Gombe. Over a 17-year period, all the males of a small community disappeared. Although no attacks were actually observed, there was circumstantial evidence that most of these males met the same fate as the Gombe attack victims (Nishida et al., 1985, 1990).

Even though the precise reasons for aggression between chimpanzee groups may never be fully understood, it appears that acquiring and protecting resources (including females) are involved (Nishida et al., 1985, 1990; Goodall, 1986; Manson and Wrangham, 1991; Nishida, 1991). Through careful examination of shared aspects of human and chimpanzee social life, we can develop hypotheses regarding how conflict between groups may have arisen in our own lineage. Early hominins and chimpanzees may have inherited from a common ancestor the predispositions that lead to similar patterns of strife between populations. It's not possible to draw direct comparisons between chimpanzee conflict and modern human warfare owing to later human elaborations of culture, use of symbols (for example, national flags), and language. But it's important to speculate on the fundamental issues that may have led to the development of similar patterns in both species.

AFFILIATION AND ALTRUISM

As you've just seen, even though it can be destructive, a certain amount of aggression helps maintain order within groups and protect resources. Fortunately, to minimize actual violence and to defuse potentially dangerous situations, there are many behaviors that

(a)

(b)

(c)

(d)

Robert Jurmain

Meredith Small

Arlene Kruse/Bonnie Pedersen

Arlene Kruse/Bonnie Pedersen

reinforce bonds between individuals and enhance group stability. Common affiliative behaviors include reconciliation, consolation, and simple amicable interactions between friends and relatives. These involve various forms of physical contact; in fact, physical contact is one of the most important factors in primate development, and it's crucial in promoting peaceful relationships in many primate social groups.

Grooming is one of the most important affiliative behaviors in many primate species, so much so that primatologist Alison Jolly (1985) called it the "social cement" of primate societies. Although grooming occurs in other animal species, social grooming is mostly a primate activity, and it plays an important role in day-to-day life (Fig. 7-9). Because grooming involves using the fingers to pick through the fur of another individual (or one's own) to remove insects, dirt, and other materials, it serves hygienic functions. But it's also an immensely pleasurable activity that members of some species (especially chimpanzees) engage in for long periods of time.

Grooming occurs in a variety of contexts. Mothers groom infants. Males groom sexually receptive females. Subordinate animals groom dominant ones, sometimes to gain favor; and friends groom friends. In general, grooming is comforting. It restores peaceful relationships between animals who've quarreled and provides reassurance during tense situations. In short, grooming reinforces social bonds and consequently helps strengthen and maintain the structure of the group.

Figure **7-9**

Grooming primates. (a) Patas monkeys; female grooming male. (b) Longtail macaques. (c) Savanna baboons. (d) Chimpanzees.

grooming Picking through fur to remove dirt, parasites, and other materials that may be present. Social grooming is common among primates and reinforces social relationships.

Conflict resolution through reconciliation is another important aspect of primate social behavior. Following a conflict, chimpanzee opponents frequently move within minutes to reconcile (de Waal, 1982). Reconciliation takes many forms, including hugging, kissing, and grooming. Even uninvolved individuals may take part, either grooming one or both participants or forming their own grooming parties. In addition, bonobos are unique in their use of sex to promote group cohesion, restore peace after conflicts, and relieve tension within the group (de Waal, 1987, 1989).

Social relationships are crucial to nonhuman primates, and the bonds between individuals can last a lifetime. These relationships serve a variety of functions. Individuals of many species form alliances in which members support each other against outsiders. Alliances, or coalitions, as they are also called, can be used to enhance the status of members. For example, at Gombe, the male chimpanzee Figan achieved alpha status because of support from his brother (Goodall, 1986, p. 424). In fact, chimpanzees so heavily rely on coalitions and are so skillful politically that an entire book, appropriately titled *Chimpanzee Politics* (de Waal, 1982), is devoted to the topic.

Altruism, behavior that benefits another while involving some risk or sacrifice to the performer, is common in many primate species, and altruistic acts sometimes contain elements of what might be interpreted as compassion and cooperation. The most fundamental of altruistic behaviors, the protection of dependent offspring, is ubiquitous among mammals and birds, and in the majority of species, altruistic acts are confined to this context.

Evolutionary explanations of altruism are usually based on one of two premises. The first is that individuals perform acts that benefit others because they share genes with the recipient; thus, by helping a relative, the performer is helping to ensure the survival of the genes they have in common. The second explanation, sometimes called "reciprocal altruism," is that one individual helps another to increase the chances that, at a future date, the recipient might return the favor.

Among primates, however, recipients of altruistic acts may include individuals who aren't offspring and who may not even be closely related to the performer. Stelzner and Strier (1982) witnessed a female baboon chasing a hyena that was chasing a young adult male baboon. This female's unsuccessful rescue attempt was intriguing because not only was she too small to engage the hyena, but she was also unrelated to the victim. Chimpanzees routinely come to the aid of relatives and friends; female langurs join forces to protect infants from infanticidal males; and male baboons protect infants and cooperate to chase predators. In fact, the primate literature is full of examples of altruistic acts, whereby individuals place themselves at some risk to protect others.

Adoption of orphans is a form of altruism that has been reported for macaques, baboons, and gorillas, and it's common in chimpanzees. When chimpanzee youngsters are orphaned, they're almost always adopted, usually by older siblings who are solicitous and highly protective. Adoption is crucial to the survival of orphans, who certainly wouldn't survive on their own.

There are now hundreds of documented examples of cooperation and altruism in nonhuman primates, especially chimpanzees. This fact has caused some primatologists to consider the possibility that the common ancestor of humans and chimpanzees had a propensity for cooperation and helping others, at least in certain circumstances (Warneken and Tomasello, 2006).

Empathy, or the ability to identify with the feelings and thoughts of another individual, is required for altruistic behavior, and the degree to which chimpanzees (and other primates) are capable of empathy is debated by primatologists. Some believe there is substantial evidence for it (deWaal, 1996, 2007), but others remain unconvinced (Silk et al., 2005).

altruism Behavior that benefits another individual but at some potential risk or cost to oneself.

Reproduction and Reproductive Behaviors

In most primate species, sexual behavior is tied to the female's reproductive cycle, with females being receptive to males only when they're in estrus. Estrus is characterized by behavioral changes that indicate that a female is receptive. In Old World monkeys and apes that live in multimale-multifemale groups, estrus is also accompanied by swelling and changes in color of the skin around the genital area. These changes serve as visual cues of a female's readiness to mate (Fig 7-10).

Permanent bonding between males and females isn't common among nonhuman primates. However, male and female savanna baboons and chimpanzees sometimes form mating *consortships*. These temporary relationships last while the female is in estrus, and the two spend most of their time together, mating frequently. Consortships are common in bonobos, and male and female bonobos may spend several weeks primarily in each other's company. During this time, they mate often, even when the female isn't in estrus. These relationships of longer duration aren't typical of chimpanzees (*Pan troglodytes*).

Such a male-female bond may result in increased reproductive success for both sexes. For the male, there is the increased likelihood that he will be the father of any infant the female conceives. At the same time, the female potentially gains protection from predators or other members of her group; and she may also gain some help in caring for offspring she may already have.

FEMALE AND MALE REPRODUCTIVE STRATEGIES

Reproductive strategies, and especially how they differ between the sexes, have been a primary focus of primate research. The goal of these strategies is to produce and successfully rear to adulthood as many offspring as possible.

Primates are among the most **K-selected** of mammals. By this we mean that individuals produce only a few young, in whom they invest a tremendous amount of parental care. This pattern is contrasted with **r-selected** species, where large numbers of offspring are produced but parents invest little or no energy in infant care. Good examples of r-selected species include insects, most fishes, and, among mammals, mice and rabbits.

Considering the degree of care required by young, dependent primate offspring, it's clear that enormous investment by at least one parent is necessary, and in a majority of species, the mother carries most of the burden, both before and after birth. Primates are completely helpless at birth, and because they develop slowly, they're exposed to expanded learning opportunities within a *social* environment. This trend has been elaborated most dramatically in great apes and humans, especially the latter. So what we see in ourselves and our close primate relatives (and presumably in our more recent ancestors) is a strategy in which at least one parent, usually the mother, makes an extraordinary investment to produce a few "high-quality," slowly maturing offspring.

Finding food and mates, avoiding predators, and caring for and protecting dependent young are difficult challenges for nonhuman primates. Moreover, in most species, males and females use different strategies to meet these challenges. Female primates spend almost all their adult lives either pregnant, lactating, and/or caring for offspring, and the resulting metabolic demands are enormous. A pregnant or lactating female, although perhaps only half the size of her male counterpart, may require about the same number of calories per day. Even if these demands are met, her physical resources may be drained. For example, analysis of chimpanzee skeletons from Gombe showed significant loss of bone and bone mineral in older females (Sumner et al., 1989).

Given these physiological costs and the fact that her reproductive potential is limited by lengthy intervals between births, a female's best strategy is to maximize

Figure **7-10**
Estrous swelling of genital tissues in a female baboon.

Alexander Klemm/iStockphoto.com

reproductive strategies The complex of behavioral patterns that contributes to individual reproductive success. The behaviors need not be deliberate, and they can vary considerably between males and females.

K-selected Pertaining to an adaptive strategy whereby individuals produce relatively few offspring, in whom they invest increased parental care. Although only a few infants are born, chances of survival are increased for each one because of parental investments in time and energy. Examples of K-selected nonprimate species are birds and canids (e.g., wolves, coyotes, and dogs).

r-selected An adaptive strategy that emphasizes relatively large numbers of offspring and reduced parental care (compared to K-selected species). *K-selection* and *r-selection* are relative terms; e.g., mice are r-selected compared to primates but K-selected compared to fish.

the amount of resources available to her and her offspring. Indeed, as we just discussed, females of many species (gibbons, marmosets, and macaques, to name a few) are competitive with other females and aggressively protect resources and territories. In other species, females distance themselves from others to avoid competition. Males, however, face a separate set of challenges. Having little investment in the rearing of offspring and the continuous production of sperm, it's to the male's advantage to secure as many mates and produce as many offspring as possible. One way of doing this is to compete with other males for mating partners.

SEXUAL SELECTION

Sexual selection, a phenomenon first described by Charles Darwin, is one outcome of different mating strategies. Sexual selection is a type of selection that operates on only one sex, usually males. The selective agent is male competition for mates and, in some species, mate choice by females. The long-term effect of sexual selection is to increase the frequency of certain traits in males that lead to greater success in acquiring mates.

In the animal kingdom, numerous male attributes are the result of sexual selection. For example, female birds of many species are attracted to males with more vividly colored plumage. Selection has thus increased the frequency of alleles that influence brighter coloration in males, and in these species, such as peacocks, males are more colorful than females.

Sexual selection in primates is most common in species in which mating is polygynous and there is considerable male competition for females. In these species, sexual selection produces dimorphism with regard to a number of traits, most noticeably body size. Conversely, in species that live in pairs (such as gibbons) or where male competition is reduced, sexual dimorphism is either reduced or nonexistent. For this reason, the presence or absence of sexual dimorphism in a species can be a reasonably good indicator of mating structure.

INFANTICIDE AS A REPRODUCTIVE STRATEGY?

One way males may increase their chances of reproducing is by killing infants fathered by other males. This explanation was first offered in an early study of Hanuman langurs in India (Hrdy, 1977). Hanuman langurs (Fig. 7-11) typically live in groups composed of one adult male, several females, and their offspring. Other males without mates form "bachelor" groups that frequently forage within sight of the one-male associations. These peripheral males occasionally attack and defeat a reproductive male and drive him from his group. Sometimes, following such a takeover, the new male kills some or all of the group's infants (fathered by the previous male).

This behavior would appear to be counterproductive, especially for a species as a whole. However, individuals act to increase their *own* reproductive success, no matter what effect their behavior may have on the group or even the species. By killing infants fathered by other animals, male langurs may in fact increase their own chances of fathering offspring, even if they don't really know it. This is because while a female is producing milk and nursing an infant, she doesn't come into estrus and therefore isn't sexually available. But when an infant dies, its mother resumes cycling and becomes sexually receptive. So by killing nursing infants, a new male avoids waiting two to three years for them to be weaned before he can mate with their mothers. This could be advantageous for him because there's a good chance that he won't even be in the group for two or three years. Also, he doesn't expend energy and put himself at risk defending infants who don't carry his genes.

Figure **7-11**

Hanuman langurs.

McDonald Wildlife Photography/Animals Animals

sexual selection A type of natural selection that operates on only one sex in a species. It's the result of competition for mates, and it can lead to sexual dimorphism with regard to one or more traits.

Hanuman langurs aren't the only primates that practice infanticide. Infanticide has been observed (or surmised) in many species, such as redtail monkeys, red colobus, blue monkeys, savanna baboons, howlers, orangutans, gorillas, chimpanzees (Struhsaker and Leyland, 1987), and humans. (It should also be noted that infanticide occurs in numerous nonprimate species, including rodents, cats, and horses, to name a few.) In the majority of reported nonhuman primate examples, infanticide coincides with the transfer of a new male into a group or, as in chimpanzees, an encounter with an unfamiliar female and infant.

Numerous objections to this explanation of infanticide have been raised. Alternative explanations have included competition for resources (Rudran, 1973), aberrant behaviors related to human-induced overcrowding (Curtin and Dohlinow, 1978), and inadvertent killing during aggressive episodes, where it wasn't clear that the infant was actually the target animal (Bartlett et al., 1993). Sussman and colleagues (1995), as well as others, have questioned the actual prevalence of infanticide, arguing that although it does occur, it's not particularly common. These authors have also suggested that if indeed male reproductive fitness is increased through the killing of infants, such increases are negligible. Yet others (Struhsaker and Leyland, 1987; Hrdy et al, 1995) maintain that the incidence and patterning of infanticide by males are not only significant, but consistent with the assumptions established by theories of behavioral evolution.

Henzi and Barrett (2003) have reported that when chacma baboon males migrate into a new group, they "deliberately single out females with young infants and hunt them down" (Fig. 7-12). The importance of these findings is the conclusion that, at least in chacma baboons, newly arrived males consistently try to kill infants, and their attacks are highly aggressive and purposeful. However, such reports don't prove that infanticide increases a male's reproductive fitness. To do this, primatologists must demonstrate two crucial facts:

1. Infanticidal males *don't* kill their own offspring.
2. Once a male has killed an infant, he subsequently fathers another infant with the victim's mother.

Borries and colleagues (1999) collected DNA samples from the feces of infanticidal males and their victims in several groups of free-ranging Hanuman langurs specifically to determine if these males killed their own offspring. Their results showed that in all 16 cases where infant and male DNA was available, the males weren't related to the infants they either attacked or killed. Moreover, DNA analysis also showed that in four out of five cases where a victim's mother subsequently gave birth, the new infant was fathered by the infanticidal male. Although still more evidence is needed, this DNA evidence strongly suggests that by practicing infanticide, a male may increase his chances of fathering offspring.

Figure **7-12**

An immigrant male chacma baboon chases a terrified female and her infant (clinging to her back). Resident males interceded to stop the chase.

© Peter Henzi

Figure **7-13**

Infant macaque clinging to cloth mother.

Mothers, Fathers, and Infants

The basic social unit among all primates is the female and her offspring (Fig. 7-15 on the following page), and except in those species in which monogamy or **polyandry** occurs, males usually don't directly participate in the rearing of offspring. The mother-infant bond begins at birth. Although the exact nature of the bonding process isn't fully known, there appear to be predisposing innate factors that strongly attract the female to her infant, so long as she herself has had a sufficiently normal experience with her own mother. This doesn't mean that primate mothers automatically know how to take care of an infant. In fact, they don't. Monkeys and apes reared in captivity without contact with their own mothers not only don't know how care for a newborn infant; they may be afraid of it and attack or even kill it. Thus, learning is critically important in the establishment of a mother's attraction to her infant.

The role of bonding between primate mothers and infants was clearly demonstrated in a famous series of experiments at the University of Wisconsin. Psychologist Harry Harlow (1959) raised infant monkeys with *surrogate* mothers made of wire or a combination of wire and cloth. Other monkeys were raised with no mother at all. In one experiment, infants retained an attachment to their cloth-covered surrogate mother (Fig. 7-13). But those raised with no mother were incapable of forming lasting **affectional** ties. These deprived monkeys sat passively in their cages and stared vacantly into space. None of the motherless males ever successfully copulated, and those females who were (somewhat artificially) impregnated either paid little attention to their infants or were aggressive toward them (Harlow and Harlow, 1961). The point is that the monkeys reared in isolation were denied opportunities to *learn* the rules of social and maternal behavior. Moreover, and just as essential, they were denied the all-important physical contact so necessary for normal primate psychological and emotional development.

The importance of a normal relationship with the mother is demonstrated by field studies as well. From birth, infant primates are able to cling to their mother's fur, and they're in more or less constant physical contact with her for several months. During this critical period, infants develop a closeness with their mothers that doesn't always end with weaning. It may even be maintained throughout life (especially among some Old World monkeys). In fact, mothers and infants may remain close until one or the other dies.

In some species, presumed fathers also participate in infant care (Fig. 7-14). Male siamangs are actively involved, and marmoset and tamarin infants are usually carried on the father's back and transferred to their mother only for nursing.

Figure **7-14**

This male savanna baboon with a youngster on his back is exhibiting infant care, but he may not be the father.

polyandry A mating system wherein a female continuously associates with more than one male (usually two or three) with whom she mates. Among nonhuman primates, polyandry is seen only in marmosets and tamarins. It also occurs in a few human societies.

affectional A term used in psychology that refers to bonding or attachments between individuals, especially mothers and their infants.

Figure **7-15**

Primate mothers with young.
(a) Mongoose lemur. (b) Chimpanzee.
(c) Patas monkey. (d) Sykes monkey.
(e) Orangutan.

(a)

(b)

(c)

(d)

(e)

David Haring, Duke University Primate Center

Arlene Kruse/Bonnie Pedersen

Robert Jurmain

Robert Jurmain

© Tom McHugh/Photo Researchers, Inc.

Primate Cultural Behavior

One important trait that makes primates, and especially chimpanzees and bonobos, attractive as models for behavior in early hominins may be called *cultural behavior*. Although many cultural anthropologists and others prefer to use the term *culture* to refer specifically to human activities, most biological anthropologists consider it appropriate to use the term in reference to nonhuman primates too (McGrew, 1992, 1998; de Waal, 1999; Whiten et al., 1999).

Undeniably, most aspects of culture are uniquely human, and one must be cautious when interpreting nonhuman animal behavior. But again, since humans are products of the same evolutionary forces that have produced other species, they can be expected to show some of the same *behavioral patterns* seen in other primates. However, because of increased brain size and learning capacities, humans express many characteristics to a greater degree. We would argue that the *aptitude for culture* as a means of adapting to the natural environment is one such characteristic.

Among other things, cultural behavior is *learned*; it's passed from generation to generation not by genes, but through learning. Whereas humans deliberately teach their young, free-ranging nonhuman primates (with the exception of a few reports) don't appear to do so. But at the same time, like young nonhuman primates, human children also acquire a tremendous amount of knowledge through observation rather than instruction (Fig. 7-16a). Nonhuman primate infants, through observing their mothers and others, learn about food items, appropriate behaviors, and how to use and modify objects to achieve certain ends (Fig. 7-16b). In turn, their own offspring will observe their activities. What emerges is a *cultural tradition* that may eventually come to typify an entire group or even a species.

The earliest reported example of cultural behavior concerned a study group of Japanese macaques on Koshima Island. In 1952, researchers began giving sweet potatoes to the macaques. The following year, a young female named Imo began washing her potatoes in a freshwater stream before she ate them. Within three years, several monkeys had adopted the practice, but they had switched from using the stream to taking their potatoes to the ocean nearby. Maybe they just liked the salt!

The researchers pointed out that dietary habits and food preferences are learned and that potato washing was an example of nonhuman culture. Because the practice arose as

Figure 7-16

(a) This little girl is learning basic computer skills by watching her older sister.
(b) A chimpanzee learns the art of termiting through intense observation.

(a)

(b)

an innovative solution to a problem (removing dirt) and gradually spread through the troop until it became a tradition, it was seen as containing elements of human culture.

A study of orangutans in six areas identified 19 behaviors that showed sufficient regional variation to be classed as "very likely cultural variants" (van Schaik et al., 2003). Four of these were differences in how nests were used or built. Other behaviors that varied included the use of branches to swat insects and pressing leaves or hands to the mouth to amplify sounds This is a very important point, because traditionally, tool use (along with language) was said to distinguish humans from other animals..

Breuer and colleagues (2005) reported seeing two female lowland gorillas in the DRC using branches as tools. In one case, a gorilla used the branch to test the depth of a pool of water. Then, as she waded through the pool bipedally, she used the branch again, this time as a walking stick.

Chimpanzees exhibit even more elaborate examples of *tool use*. They insert twigs and grass blades into termite mounds in a practice called "termite fishing." When termites grab the twig, the chimpanzee withdraws it and eats them. Chimpanzees also modify some of their stems and twigs, in effect making tools from the natural material. For example, a chimpanzee will choose a piece of vine or stem and modify it by removing leaves and then breaking pieces off until it's the appropriate length. Chimpanzees have also been seen making these tools even before the termite mound is in sight.

All this preparation has several implications. First, the chimpanzees are involved in an activity that prepares them for a future task at a somewhat distant location, and this fact implies planning and forethought. Second, attention to the shape and size of the raw material indicates that chimpanzees have a preconceived idea of what the finished product needs to be in order to be useful. To produce even a simple tool based on a concept is an extremely complex behavior that isn't the exclusive domain of humans. Chimpanzees also crumple and chew handfuls of leaves, which they dip into tree hollows where water accumulates; then they suck the water from their newly made "leaf sponges." They also use leaves to wipe substances from their fur, and they use twigs as toothpicks. Chimpanzees may use stones as weapons, and they drag or roll various objects, such as branches and stones, to enhance displays.

The recent discovery that chimpanzees also modify and use tools for hunting came as a surprise to primatologists. Preutz and Bertolani (2007) report that savanna chimpanzees in Senegal, West Africa, use sharpened sticks to hunt galagos. Ten different animals (adult males, females, and subadults) repeatedly jabbed sticks into cavities in tree branches and trunks to pull galagos from their sleeping nests. In much the same way that they modify termiting sticks, these chimpanzees had stripped off side twigs and leaves. But they'd also chewed the ends to sharpen them, in effect producing a small thrusting spear. Only one galago was actually seen to be retrieved and eaten, and although it wasn't moving or vocalizing, it was unclear if it had actually been killed by the "spear" (Preutz and Bertolani, 2007).

Chimpanzees in several West African study groups use hammer stones along with platform stones to crack nuts and hard-shelled fruits (Boesch et al., 1994; (Fig. 7-17). However, neither the hammer stone nor the platform stone is deliberately manufactured. Like chimpanzees, wild capuchin monkeys use leaves to get water from cavities in trees (Phillips, 1998), and they smash objects against stones (Izawa and Mizuno, 1977). Their use of stones in captivity (both as hammers and anvils) has also been reported (Visalberghi, 1990). But chimpanzees are the only nonhuman primate that consistently and habitually makes and uses tools (McGrew, 1992).

Tetsuro Matsuzawa

Figure **7-17**

Chimpanzees in Bossou, Guinea, West Africa, use a pair of stones as hammer and anvil to crack oil palm nuts. Although the youngster isn't being taught to use stone tools, it's learning about them through observation.

Importantly, chimpanzees show regional variation regarding both the types and methods of tool use. Stone hammers and platforms are used only in West African groups. And at central and eastern African sites, chimpanzees "fish" for termites with stems and sticks, but they don't at some West African locations (McGrew, 1992).

Chimpanzees also show regional dietary preferences (Nishida et al., 1983; McGrew, 1992, 1998). For example, oil palm fruits and nuts are eaten at many locations, including Gombe, but even though these same foods are also available in the Mahale Mountains, they aren't eaten by the chimpanzees there. Such regional patterns in tool use and food preferences that aren't related to availability are reminiscent of the cultural variations seen in humans.

Using sticks, twigs, and stones enhances chimpanzees' ability to exploit resources. They learn these behaviors during infancy and childhood, partly as a result of prolonged contact with the mother. It's also important that exposure to other members of a social group provide additional learning opportunities. These statements can also be appropriately applied to early hominins. While sticks and unmodified stones don't remain to tell tales, our early ancestors surely used these same objects as tools in much the same way chimpanzees do today.

While wild chimpanzees haven't been observed modifying the stones they use, a male bonobo named Kanzi (see also p. 171) learned to strike two stones together to produce sharp-edged flakes. In a study conducted by psychologist Sue Savage-Rumbaugh and archaeologist Nicholas Toth, Kanzi was allowed to watch as Toth produced stone flakes, which were then used to open a transparent plastic food container (Savage-Rumbaugh and Lewin, 1994). Although bonobos don't commonly use objects as tools in the wild, Kanzi readily appreciated the usefulness of the flakes in obtaining food. What's more, he was able to master the basic technique of producing flakes without being taught, although at first his progress was slow. Finally, Kanzi realized that if he threw the stone onto a hard floor, it would shatter and he would have an abundance of cutting tools. Although his solution wasn't the one that Savage-Rumbaugh and Toth expected, it was perhaps even more significant because it provided an excellent example of bonobo insight and problem-solving ability. Moreover, Kanzi did eventually learn to produce flakes by striking two stones together, and then he used the flakes to obtain food. These behaviors aren't just examples of tool manufacture and use, albeit in a captive situation; they're also very sophisticated goal-directed activities.

Culture has become the environment in which modern humans live. Quite clearly, the use of sticks in termite fishing and hammer stones to crack nuts is hardly comparable to modern human technology. However, modern human technology had its beginnings in these very types of behaviors. But this doesn't mean that nonhuman primates are "on their way" to becoming human. Remember, evolution isn't goal directed, and even if it were, there's nothing to dictate that modern humans necessarily constitute an evolutionary goal. Such a conclusion is a purely **anthropocentric** view and has no validity in discussions of evolutionary processes.

Language

One of the most significant events in human evolution was the development of language. We've already described several behaviors and autonomic responses that convey information in primates. But although we emphasized the importance of communication to nonhuman primate social life, we also said that nonhuman primates don't use language the way humans do.

The view traditionally held by most linguists and behavioral psychologists has been that nonhuman communication consists of mostly involuntary vocalizations and actions that convey information solely about the emotional state of the animal (anger, fear, and so

anthropocentric Viewing nonhuman animals in terms of human motives, experiences, and capabilities; emphasizing the importance of humans over everything else.

Lynn Kilgore

Figure **7-18**
Group of free-ranging vervets.

on). Nonhuman animals haven't been considered capable of communicating about external events, objects, or other animals, either in close proximity or removed in space or time. For example, when a startled baboon barks, other group members know only that it's startled. They don't know why it barked, so they have to look around to see what provoked it. In general, then, it's been assumed that in nonhuman animals, including primates, vocalizations, facial expressions, body postures, and so on, don't refer to *specific* external phenomena.

But for several years, these views have been challenged (Steklis, 1985; King, 1994, 2004). For example, vervet monkeys (Fig. 7-18) use specific vocalizations to refer to particular categories of predators, such as snakes, birds of prey, and leopards (Struhsaker, 1967; Seyfarth, Cheney, and Marler, 1980a, 1980b). When researchers made tape recordings of various vervet alarm calls and played them back within hearing distance of free-ranging vervets, they saw different responses to various calls. When the vervets heard leopard-alarm calls, they climbed trees; they looked up when they heard eagle-alarm calls; and they responded to snake-alarm calls by looking around at the ground.

These results show that vervets use distinct vocalizations to refer to specific types of predators. These calls aren't involuntary, and they don't refer solely to the emotional state (alarm) of the individual, although this information is also conveyed. While these findings dispel certain long-held misconceptions about nonhuman communication (at least for some species), they also indicate certain limitations. Vervet communication is restricted to the present; as far as we know, no vervet can communicate about a predator it saw yesterday or one it might see in the future.

Other studies have demonstrated that numerous nonhuman primates, including cottontop tamarins (Cleveland and Snowdon, 1982), Goeldi's monkeys (Masataka, 1983), red colobus (Struhsaker, 1975), and gibbons (Tenaza and Tilson, 1977), produce distinct calls that have specific references. There is also growing evidence that many birds and some nonprimate mammals use specific predator alarm calls (Seyfarth, 1987).

Humans use *language*, a set of written and/or spoken symbols that refer to concepts, other people, objects, and so on. This set of symbols is said to be *arbitrary* because the symbol itself has no inherent relationship with whatever it stands for. For example, the English word *flower*, when written or spoken, neither looks, sounds, smells, nor feels like the thing it represents. Humans can also recombine their linguistic symbols in an infinite number of ways to create new meanings, and we can use language to refer to events, places, objects, and people far removed in both space and time. For these reasons, language is described as a form of communication based on the human ability to think symbolically.

Language, as distinct from other forms of communication, has always been considered a uniquely human achievement, setting humans apart from the rest of the animal kingdom. But work with captive apes has raised some doubts about certain aspects of this notion. Although many people were skeptical about the capacity of nonhuman primates to use language, reports from psychologists, especially those who work with chimpanzees, leave little doubt that apes can learn to interpret visual signs and use them in communication. Other than humans, no mammal can speak. However, the fact that apes can't speak has less to do with lack of intelligence than to differences in the anatomy of the vocal tract and language-related structures in the brain.

Because of unsuccessful attempts by others to teach young chimpanzees to speak, psychologists Beatrice and Allen Gardner designed a study to test language capabilities in chimpanzees by teaching an infant female named Washoe to use ASL (American Sign Language for the deaf). The project began in 1966, and in three years, Washoe acquired at least 132 signs. "She asked for goods and services, and she also asked questions about the world of objects and events around her" (Gardner et al., 1989, p. 6).

Years later, an infant chimpanzee named Loulis was placed in Washoe's care. Psychologist Roger Fouts and colleagues wanted to know if Loulis would acquire signing skills from Washoe and other chimpanzees in the study group. Within just eight days, Loulis began to imitate the signs of others. Moreover, Washoe deliberately *taught* Loulis how to make certain signs. In 1980, Dr. Fouts moved Washoe and Loulis to a facility at Central Washington University where the language studies are ongoing. It was there that Washoe, the first signing chimpanzee, died in 2007 at the age of 42.

Dr. Francine Patterson, who taught ASL to Koko, a female lowland gorilla, reports that Koko uses more than 500 signs. Furthermore, Michael, an adult male gorilla who was also involved in the study until his death in 2000, had a considerable sign vocabulary, and the two gorillas regularly communicated with each other using sign language.

In the late 1970s, a 2-year-old male orangutan named Chantek began to use signs after one month of training. Eventually, he acquired approximately 140 signs, which were sometimes used to refer to objects (and people) that weren't present. Chantek also

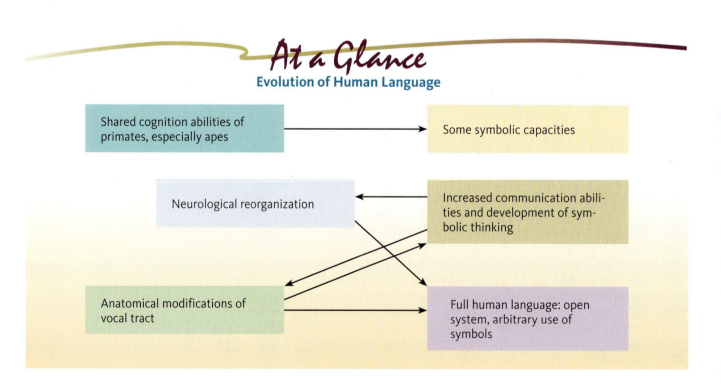

At a Glance
Evolution of Human Language

Shared cognition abilities of primates, especially apes → Some symbolic capacities

Neurological reorganization

Increased communication abilities and development of symbolic thinking

Anatomical modifications of vocal tract

Full human language: open system, arbitrary use of symbols

Rose A. Sevcik, Language Research Center, Georgia State University; photo by Elizabeth Pugh

Figure **7-19**

The bonobo Kanzi, as a youngster, using lexigrams to communicate with human observers.

invented signs and recombined them in novel ways, and he appeared to understand that his signs were *representations* of items, actions, and people (Miles, 1990).

Questions have been raised about this type of research. Do the apes really understand the signs they learn, or are they merely imitating their trainers? Do they learn that a symbol is a name for an object or simply that using it will produce that object?

Partly in an effort to address some of these questions and criticisms, Sue Savage-Rumbaugh taught two chimpanzees named Sherman and Austin to use symbols to categorize *classes* of objects, such as "food" or "tool." This was done in recognition of the fact that in previous studies, apes had been taught symbols for *specific* items. Savage-Rumbaugh recognized that using a symbol as a label isn't the same thing as understanding the *representational value* of the symbol. But if the chimpanzees could classify things into groups, it would indicate that they can use symbols referentially.

Sherman and Austin were taught to recognize familiar food items, for which they routinely used symbols, as belonging to a broader category referred to by yet another symbol, "food." Then they were introduced to unfamiliar food items they had no symbols for to see if they would put them in the food category. The fact that they both had perfect or nearly perfect scores further substantiated that they could categorize unfamiliar objects. More importantly, it was clear that they were capable of assigning symbols to indicate an object's membership in a broader grouping. This ability was a strong indication that the chimpanzees understood that the symbols were being used referentially. However, subsequent work has shown that the manner in which chimpanzees are introduced to language influences their ability to understand the representational value of symbols.

Throughout the relatively brief history of ape language studies, a major assumption has been that young chimpanzees must be *taught* to use symbols, in contrast to the ability of human children to learn language through exposure, without being taught. Therefore, it was significant when Savage-Rumbaugh and her colleagues reported that the young bonobo Kanzi, before his tool making days, was *spontaneously* acquiring and using symbols when he was just 2½ years old (Savage-Rumbaugh et al., 1986; Fig. 7-19). His younger half-sister began to use symbols spontaneously when she was only 11 months old. Both animals had been exposed to the use of lexigrams, or illustrated symbols that represent words, when they accompanied their mother to training sessions. But neither had actually been taught and weren't even involved in these sessions.

While the language studies with great apes have shown that they have the ability to use language to a certain degree and that they have a remarkable degree of cognitive complexity, it nevertheless remains evident that apes don't acquire and use language the same way humans do. It also appears that not all signing apes understand the referential relationship between symbol and object, person, or action. Nonetheless, there's now abundant evidence that humans aren't the only species capable of some degree of symbolic thought and complex communication.

The Primate Continuum

It's an unfortunate fact that humans generally view themselves as separate from the rest of the animal kingdom. This perspective is, in no small measure, due to a prevailing lack of knowledge of the behavior and abilities of other species. Moreover, these notions are continuously reinforced through exposure to advertising, movies, and television (Fig. 7-20).

For decades, behavioral psychology taught that animal behavior represents nothing more than a series of conditioned responses to specific stimuli. (This perspective is very convenient for those who wish to use nonhuman animals, for whatever purposes, and remain guilt-free.) Fortunately, this attitude has begun to change in recent years to reflect a growing awareness that humans, although in many ways unquestionably unique, are nevertheless part of a **biological continuum**. Indeed, we are also a part of a behavioral continuum.

Where do humans fit in this biological continuum? Are we at the top? The answer depends on the criteria used. Certainly, we're the most intelligent species if we define intelligence in terms of problem-solving abilities and abstract thought. However, if we

Figure **7-20**

This unfortunate advertising display is a good example of how humans misunderstand and thus misrepresent our closest relatives.

biological continuum Refers to the fact that organisms are related through common ancestry and that behaviors and traits seen in one species are also seen in others to varying degrees. (When expressions of a phenomenon continuously grade into one another so that there are no discrete categories, they are said to exist on a continuum. Color is such a phenomenon.)

Lynn Kilgore

look more closely, we recognize that the differences between ourselves and our primate relatives, especially chimpanzees and bonobos, are primarily quantitative and not qualitative.

Although the human brain is absolutely and relatively larger, neurological processes are functionally the same. The necessity of close bonding with at least one parent and the need for physical contact are essentially the same. Developmental stages and dependence on learning are strikingly similar. Indeed, even in the capacity for cruelty and aggression combined with compassion, tenderness, and altruism exhibited by chimpanzees, we see a close parallel to the dichotomy between "evil" and "good" so long recognized in ourselves. The main difference between how chimpanzees and humans express these qualities (and therefore the dichotomy) is one of degree. Humans are much more adept at cruelty and compassion, and we can reflect on our behavior in ways that chimpanzees can't. Like the cat that plays with a mouse, chimpanzees don't seem to understand the suffering they inflict on others. But humans do. Likewise, while an adult chimpanzee may sit next to a dying relative, it doesn't seem to feel the intense grief a human normally does in the same situation.

To arrive at any understanding of what it is to be human, it's important to recognize that many of our behaviors are elaborate extensions of those of our hominin ancestors and close primate relatives. The fact that so many of us prefer to bask in the warmth of the "sun belt" with literally millions of others reflects our heritage as social animals adapted to life in the tropics. And the sweet tooth that afflicts so many of us is a result of our earlier primate ancestors' predilection for high-energy sugar contained in sweet, ripe fruit. Thus, it's important to recognize our primate heritage as we explore how humans came to be and how we continue to adapt.

Summary

In this chapter, we've presented the major theoretical models for the evolution of behavior in primates, and we've discussed some of the evidence, including some reports that use genetic data to support these models. The subject of the evolution of behavior is extremely complex because it requires research into the interactions of dozens, if not hundreds, of ecological and physiological variables.

The fundamental principle of behavioral evolution is that aspects of behavior (including social behavior) are influenced by genetic factors. And because some behavioral elements are therefore inherited, natural selection can act on them in the same way it acts on physical and anatomical characteristics. We pointed out that in mammals and birds, the proportion of behavior that's due to learning is much greater than it is in insects and most other invertebrates, in which a high proportion of behavior is directly influenced by genes.

Behavioral ecology is the discipline that examines behavior from the perspective of complex ecological relationships and the role of natural selection as it favors behaviors that increase reproductive fitness. This approach generates many models of behavioral evolution that can be applied to all species, including humans. Members of each species inherit a genome that is species-specific, and some part of that genome influences behaviors. But in more complex animals, the genome allows for greater degrees of behavioral flexibility and learning. And in humans, who rely on cultural adaptations for survival, most behavior is learned.

Life history traits or strategies (developmental stages that characterize a species) are important to the reproductive success of individuals. These include length of gestation, number of offspring per birth, interbirth interval, age of sexual maturity, and longevity. Although these characters are strongly influenced by the genome of any species, they're also influenced by environmental and social factors such as nutrition and social status. In turn, nutritional requirements are affected by body size, diet, and basal metabolic rate (BMR).

We discussed numerous examples of cultural behaviors that have been documented for the great apes. These include different types of tool use, which youngsters learn by watching adults. There are also food preferences that vary from one area to another, even though the same types of food are available. These examples represent cultural traditions that may be similar to those that were present among the earliest hominins.

Lastly, we talked about the biological and behavioral continuity within the primate order. Although nonhuman primate cultural behavior and communication are in no way as elaborate as they are in humans, they can be seen as behaviors that are variably expressed throughout the primate order and especially among the great apes and humans.

Critical Thinking Questions

1. Apply some of the topics presented in this chapter to some nonprimate species you are familiar with. Can you develop some hypotheses to explain the behavior of some domestic species? You might want to speculate on how behavior in domestic animals may differ from that of their wild ancestors. (Chapter 2 might help you here.)

2. Speculate on how the behavioral ecology of nonhuman primates may be helpful in explaining some human behaviors.

3. How might infanticide be seen as a reproductive strategy for males? If this concept were to be applied to human males, do you think some people would object? Why or why not?

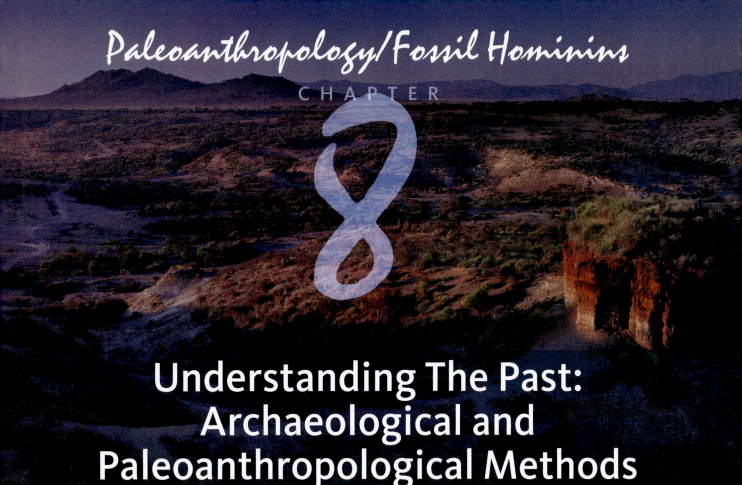

Understanding The Past: Archaeological and Paleoanthropological Methods

Focus Questions

What are the central aspects of paleoanthropology in general? Of archaeology in particular?

Why, from a biocultural perspective, do we want to learn about both the behavior and the anatomy of ancient hominins?

 Click!

Go to the following media for interactive activities and exercises on topics covered in this chapter:

- Hominid Fossils: An Interactive Atlas CD-ROM

Introduction

A portion of a pig's tusk, a small sample of volcanic sediment, a battered cobble, a primate's molar tooth: What do these seemingly unremarkable remains have in common, and more to the point, why are they of interest to paleoanthropologists and archaeologists? First of all, if they are all discovered at certain sites in Africa or Eurasia, they may be quite ancient—perhaps millions of years old. Further, some of these materials actually inform scientists directly of accurate and precise dating of the finds. Last, and most exciting, some of these finds may have been modified, used, and discarded by creatures who looked and behaved in some ways like us, but were, in other respects, very different. And what of that molar tooth? Is it a fossilized remnant of an ancient **hominin**? These are the kinds of questions asked by paleoanthropologists and archaeologists, and to answer them, these researchers travel to remote locales in the Old World.

How do we identify possible hominins from other types of animals, especially when all we may have to study are fragmentary fossil remains from just a small portion of a skeleton? How do humans and our most distant ancestors compare with other animals? In the last three chapters, we've seen how humans are classified as primates, both structurally and behaviorally, and how our evolutionary history coincides with that of other mammals and, specifically, other primates. But we are a unique kind of primate, and our ancestors have been adapted to a particular lifestyle for several million years. Some primitive hominoid probably began this process close to 7 mya, but with better-preserved fossil discoveries, scientists now have more definitive evidence of hominins shortly after 5 mya.

The hominin nature of these remains is revealed by more than the structure of teeth and bones; we know that these animals are hominins also because of the way they behaved—emphasizing once again the biocultural nature of human evolution. Most of our understanding of these events and changes is the result of paleoanthropological, and especially archaeological, research. In this chapter, we describe the basic concepts of these interrelated lines of investigation so that you can approach the rest of the book with a solid grounding in the research methods on which reconstruction of the human past is based. We'll begin with the broader aspects of paleoanthropology, which, in addition to archaeology, examines early hominin behavior and ecology through the study of fossil remains. This sets the stage for Chapters 9 through 12, in which we examine the fossil evidence of human ancestors and near relatives.

As part of paleoanthropology, some archaeologists specialize in studying the early phases of human biocultural development. This work certainly makes archaeology a major component of paleoanthropological research, but in this chapter we'll also cover a variety of research perspectives and methods that are practiced by *all* archaeologists (including those investigating later phases of prehistory as well as historical contexts). Our more specific focus on archaeology emphasizes it as a body of methods related to those used by other paleoanthropologists. But while archaeology explores similar questions about the human past, it does so primarily through examination of material remains. The importance of archaeological methods increases gradually throughout Chapters 9 through 12 and becomes the dominant source of information in Chapters 13 through 15. Toward the

hominin Colloquial term for a member of the Tribe Hominini, the evolutionary group that includes modern humans and now-extinct bipedal relatives.

end of this chapter, you'll be able to appreciate the close partnership of paleoanthropology and archaeology in the study of the early human past by reading about the best-known early hominin site locality in the world: Olduvai Gorge, in East Africa.

Biocultural Evolution: The Human Capacity for Culture

One of the most distinctive behavioral features of humans is our extraordinary elaboration of and dependence on culture. Certainly other primates, and many other animals, for that matter, modify their environments. As we saw in Chapter 7, chimpanzees especially are known for such behaviors as using termite sticks, and some even carry rocks to use for crushing nuts. Because of such observations, we're on tenuous ground when it comes to drawing a sharp line between early hominin toolmaking behavior and that exhibited by other animals.

Another point to remember is that human culture, at least as it's defined in contemporary contexts, involves much more than toolmaking capacity. For humans, culture integrates an entire adaptive strategy involving cognitive, political, social, and economic components. The *material culture*, the tools humans use, is but a small portion of this cultural complex.

Nevertheless, when we examine the archaeological record of earlier hominins, what is available for study is almost exclusively limited to material culture, especially residues of stone tool manufacture. So it's extremely difficult to learn anything about the earliest stages of hominin cultural development before the regular manufacture of stone tools. As you will see, this most crucial cultural development has been traced to approximately 2.6 mya (Semaw et al., 2003). Yet, hominins were undoubtedly using other kinds of tools (made of perishable materials) and displaying a whole array of other cultural behaviors long before then. However, without any "hard" evidence preserved in the archaeological record, our understanding of the early development of these nonmaterial cultural components remains elusive.

The fundamental basis for human cultural success relates directly to cognitive abilities. Again, we're not dealing with an absolute distinction, but a relative one. As you have already learned, other primates, as documented in chimpanzees and bonobos, have some of the language capabilities exhibited by humans. Even so, modern humans display these abilities in a complexity several orders of magnitude beyond that of any other animal. And only humans are so completely dependent on symbolic communication and its cultural by-products that contemporary *Homo sapiens* could not survive without them.

At this point, you may be wondering just when the unique combination of cognitive, social, and material cultural adaptations become prominent in human evolution. In answering that question, we must be careful to recognize the manifold nature of culture; we can't expect it to always contain the same elements across species (as when comparing ourselves with nonhuman primates) or through time (when trying to reconstruct ancient hominin behavior). Richard Potts (1993) has critiqued such overly simplistic perspectives and suggests instead a more dynamic approach, one that incorporates many subcomponents (including aspects of behavior, cognition, and social interaction).

We know that the earliest hominins almost certainly did not regularly manufacture stone tools (at least, none that have been found and identified as such). These earliest members of the hominin lineage, dating back to approximately 7–5 mya, could be referred to as **protohominins**. These protohominins may have carried objects such as naturally sharp stones or stone flakes, parts of carcasses, and pieces of wood around their home ranges. At the very least, we would expect them to have displayed these behaviors to at least the same degree as that exhibited in living chimpanzees.

protohominins The earliest members of the hominin lineage, as yet only poorly represented in the fossil record; thus, the reconstruction of their structure and behavior is largely hypothetical.

As you'll soon see, by at least 5 mya and perhaps even by 7 mya, hominins had developed one crucial advantage: They were bipedal and could therefore much more easily carry all manner of objects from place to place.

What we know for sure is that over a period of several million years, during the formative stages of hominin emergence, many components interacted, but not all of them developed simultaneously. As cognitive abilities developed, more efficient means of communication and learning resulted. Largely because of consequent neurological reorganization, more elaborate tools and social relationships also emerged. These, in turn, selected for greater intelligence, which in turn selected for further neural elaboration. Quite clearly, then, these mutual dynamic interactions are at the very heart of what we call hominin *biocultural* evolution.

Paleoanthropology

To adequately understand human evolution, we obviously need a broad base of information. It's the paleoanthropologist's task to recover and interpret all the clues left by early hominins. *Paleoanthropology* is defined as the overall study of fossil hominins. As such, it's a diverse **multidisciplinary** pursuit seeking to reconstruct every possible bit of information concerning the dating, structure, behavior, and ecology of our hominin ancestors. In the last few decades, the study of early humans has marshaled the specialized skills of many different kinds of scientists. Included in this growing and exciting adventure are geologists, archaeologists, physical anthropologists, and paleoecologists (Table 8-1).

Geologists, usually working with anthropologists, do the initial surveys to locate potential early hominin sites. Many sophisticated techniques aid in this search, including the analysis of aerial and satellite imagery (Fig. 8-1). Paleontologists are usually involved in this early survey work, for they can help find fossil beds containing faunal remains. Where conditions are favorable for the preservation of bone from such species as pigs and elephants, hominin remains may also be preserved. In addition, paleontologists can (through comparison with known faunal sequences) give approximate age estimates of fossil sites without having to wait for the results of more time-consuming analyses.

Fossil beds likely to contain hominin finds are subjected to extensive field surveying. For some sites, generally those postdating 2.6 mya (roughly the age of the oldest identified human artifacts), archaeologists take over in the search for hominin material traces. We don't necessarily have to find remains of early hominins themselves to know that they consistently occupied a particular area. Such material clues as **artifacts** also inform us directly about early hominin activities. Modifying rocks according to a consistent plan or simply carrying them around from one place to another over fairly long distances (assuming the

multidisciplinary Pertaining to research that involves the mutual contributions and cooperation of experts from various scientific fields (i.e., disciplines)

artifacts Objects or materials made or modified for use by hominins. The earliest artifacts are usually made of stone or, occasionally, bone.

Table **8-1** **Contributing Scientific Fields to Paleoanthropology**

Physical Sciences	Biological Sciences	Social Sciences
Geology	Physical anthropology	Archaeology
Stratigraphy	Ecology	Ethnoarchaeology
Petrology (rocks, minerals)	Paleontology (fossil animals)	Cultural anthropology
Pedology (soils)	Palynology (fossil pollen)	Ethnography
Geomorphology	Primatology	Psychology
Geophysics		
Chemistry		
Taphonomy		

NASA Goddard Space Flight Center

Figure **8-1**

Satellite photo of East Africa taken by the space shuttle. In the center you can see a volcanic crater with a small lake inside.

action can't be explained by natural means, such as streams or glaciers) is characteristic of no other animal but a hominin. So, when we see such material evidence at a site, we know absolutely that hominins were present.

Because organic materials such as wooden and bone tools aren't usually preserved in the archaeological record of the oldest hominins, we have no solid evidence of the earliest stages of hominin cultural modifications. On the other hand, our ancestors at some point showed a veritable fascination with stones, because they provided not only easily accessible and transportable materials (to use as convenient objects for throwing or for holding down other objects, such as skins and windbreaks) but also the most durable and sharpest cutting edges available at that time. Luckily for us, stone is almost indestructible, and some early hominin sites are strewn with thousands of stone artifacts. The earliest artifact sites now documented are from the Gona and Bouri areas in northeastern Ethiopia, dating to close to 2.6 mya (Semaw et al., 1997; de Heinzelin et al., 1999). Other contenders for the "earliest" stone assemblage come from the adjacent Hadar and Middle Awash areas, immediately to the south in Ethiopia, dated 2.5–2 mya.

If an area is clearly demonstrated to be a hominin site, much more concentrated research will then begin. We should point out that a more mundane but very significant aspect of paleoanthropology not reflected in Table 8-1 is the financial one. But once the financial hurdle has been cleared, a coordinated research project can begin. Usually headed by an archaeologist or physical anthropologist, the field crew continues to survey and map the target area in great detail (Fig. 8-2). In addition, field crew members begin searching carefully for bones and artifacts eroding out of the soil, taking pollen and soil samples for ecological analysis, and carefully collecting rock samples for use in various dating techniques. If, in this early stage of exploration, members of the field crew find fossil hominin remains, they will feel very lucky indeed. The international press usually considers human fossils the most exciting kind of discovery, a situation that produces wide publicity and often ensures future financial support. More likely, the crew will accumulate much information on geological setting, ecological data (particularly faunal remains), and, with some luck, artifacts and other archaeological traces.

Although paleoanthropological fieldwork is typically a long and arduous process, the detailed analyses of collected samples and other data back in the laboratory are even more time-consuming. Archaeologists must clean, sort, label, and identify all artifacts, and

Figure **8-2**

A paleoanthropologist maps an area in Ethiopia where geological exposures, as well as specific areas containing archaeological, faunal, and other remains are carefully recorded.

Institute of Human Origins

paleontologists must do the same for all faunal remains. Knowing the kinds of animals represented—whether forest browsers, woodland species, or open-country forms—greatly helps in reconstructing the local *paleoecological* settings in which early hominins lived. Analyzing the fossil pollen collected from hominin sites by a palynologist further aids in developing a detailed environmental reconstruction. All these paleoecological analyses can assist in reconstructing the diet of early humans. Also, the **taphonomy** of the site must be worked out in order to understand its depositional history—that is, how the site formed over time and if its present state is in a *primary* or *secondary* **context**.

In the concluding stages of interpretation, the paleoanthropologist draws together the following essentials:

1. *Dating*
   geological
   paleontological
   geophysical
2. *Paleoecology*
   paleontology
   palynology
   geomorphology
   taphonomy
3. *Archaeological traces of behavior*
4. *Anatomical evidence from hominin remains*

taphonomy (*taphos*, meaning "grave") The study of how bones and other materials came to be buried in the earth and preserved as fossils. A taphonomist studies the processes of sedimentation, the action of streams, preservation properties of bone, and carnivore disturbance factors.

context The environmental setting where an archaeological trace is found. A *primary* context is the setting in which the archaeological trace was originally deposited. A *secondary* context is one to which it has been moved (e.g., by the action of a stream).

By analyzing all this information, scientists try to "flesh out" the kind of animal that may have been our direct ancestor, or at least a very close relative. Primatologists may assist here by showing the detailed relationships between the anatomical structure and behavior of humans and that of contemporary nonhuman primates (see Chapters 6 and 7). Cultural anthropologists and ethnoarchaeologists (see p. 186) may contribute ethnographic information concerning the varied nature of human behavior, particularly the cultural adaptations of those contemporary hunter-gatherer groups exploiting roughly similar environmental settings as those reconstructed for a hominin site.

The end result of years of research by dozens of scientists will (we hope) produce a more complete and accurate understanding of human evolution—how we came to be the way we are. Both biological and cultural aspects of our ancestors contribute to this investigation, each process developing in relation to the other.

Archaeology

As we noted in Chapter 1, archaeology is a body of methods designed to understand the human past through the examination and study of its material remains. Archaeologists use basically the same methods and techniques to research early hominin sites in the Old World as they do to study the prehistory of modern humans and their cultures. The big differences are, first, that the archaeological record holds much less material evidence of the lifeways of early hominins than of modern humans and, second, that the oldest archaeological data are difficult to interpret accurately because early hominins were physically and culturally quite different from modern humans. As we move closer in time to modern humans, the archaeological record becomes more extensive, more diverse, and more readily interpreted.

GOALS OF ARCHAEOLOGY

In its study of the human past, anthropological archaeology has at least four main goals, several of which play a role in virtually every research project. The first goal, a very basic one, is to reconstruct the chronicle of past human events as they were played out across space and through time. This goal is essentially that of providing order to the archaeological record, an order that implicitly answers the fundamental "when" and "where" questions. When did plant domestication arise in the Near East? What sustained contacts existed between the people of western Mexico and northern Peru in 800–400 B.C.? Does the distribution of hand axes (a type of stone tool discussed in Chapter 10) extend into Southeast Asia? Descriptive questions such as these, anchored as they are in time and space, are essential to the successful examination of more challenging questions about the human past.

Archaeology's second main goal is to reconstruct past human lifeways. Using clues from recovered artifacts, archaeological features, sites, and contexts, archaeologists try to understand how people actually created and used those cultural products to interact with each other and their surroundings. How did they use these tools? How were people treated in death? What did their huts or shelters look like? Think of this area of research as the archaeological equivalent of the ethnographies of cultural anthropology.

Third, archaeologists want to *explain* how and why the past happened as it did. Why does the earliest evidence of farming occur after the end of the last Ice Age and not before? Are social inequalities inevitable correlates of the development of the earliest civilizations? Such questions are tough to answer because of their general nature and because the answers can sometimes require that we come to understand more about the past than anyone has yet learned.

Theoretical changes in archaeology over the past two decades also yielded what many researchers now regard as a fourth main goal, which can be loosely described as interpreting the cognitive and symbolic aspects of past cultures. This research complements the search for general explanations of past cultural patterns and explores questions that reflect archaeology's roots in the humanities. What can changing representational conventions of clothing in medieval Hindu art tell us about changes in the nature of kingship and the relations between kings? To what extent is the current scientific understanding of Russian prehistory biased by the values, beliefs, and social history of past generations of archaeologists? Such questions defy *general* explanation but are just as important to our understanding of the human past.

ARCHAEOLOGICAL RESEARCH PROJECTS

Modern archaeology, like paleoanthropology, is a complex undertaking that often draws on the expertise of specialists from many fields. Field projects range in scale from relatively

Figure 8-3

Excavation of this "test pit" at a late prehistoric site in western Kentucky will enable archaeologists to assess the site's depositional history, its approximate age, how well preserved it is, and the diversity and kind of remains preserved there. Researchers will compare this information with the results of similar test pits at other sites in the same region and use it in deciding which sites should be excavated more extensively.

Figure 8-4

Excavation of this large, deeply stratified archaeological site in western Illinois took years of sustained effort by large field crews and support staff to complete. It yielded far greater contextual information than researchers would expect to find in something like a test pit (see Fig. 8-3).

simple tasks that can be completed in a few days (Fig. 8-3) to major undertakings that may take decades to complete (Fig. 8-4). The justification for allocating resources to such research also varies greatly, from cultural resource management (CRM) projects intended to meet legal guidelines for conserving historical sites and monuments to public or private agency-sponsored projects designed to answer specific questions about the past.

Given an important question or problem to motivate research, archaeological fieldwork assumes a fairly common pattern. First, an appropriate location is chosen for the research, and the archaeological resources of that region are identified and inventoried. Second, sites selected from the region's known sites are carefully examined, often using methods that cause minimal disturbance to the archaeological record. Finally, some sites may be wholly or partially excavated.

Modern archaeologists and other paleoanthropologists can (and do) turn to an extraordinary array of high-tech tools to help them discover the location of sites, including aerial and satellite imagery and remote sensing technologies with such obscure-sounding names as ground-penetrating radar, side-scan sonar, proton magnetometers, and subbottom profilers, to name only a few (Fig. 8-5). Even so, fieldworkers on foot who look for artifacts and other telltale material evidence on the ground surface probably still discover most sites.

As they identify sites in the field, archaeologists record information about the local terrain, including the kinds of artifacts and other cultural debris that may be present on the surface, the area covered by this scatter of debris, and other basic facts that become part of the permanent record of the site. Later, back in the lab, analyses of these data often

yield estimates of the approximate age of each site, what the prehistoric site inhabitants did there, how long they used the site, and sometimes even where they may have come from and the rough age and sex composition of the group (Fig. 8-6).

Information from this **site survey**, as it is often called, enables the project directors to make informed decisions about excavating the sites. They'll choose sites that are most likely to yield information necessary to solve the problem that motivated the research or, if it is a CRM project, to comply with relevant heritage management priorities, guidelines, and laws.

The popular stereotype of archaeology and archaeologists is that they spend most of their time digging square holes in the ground. Although this kind of activity will always be archaeology's defining characteristic, the professional attitude toward excavation changed during the twentieth century from a this-is-what-we-do attitude to a deep appreciation of the fact that the archaeological record is a finite resource, much like oil and gas deposits. We can be confident, for example, that all the 2,000-year-old sites that will ever exist were laid down 2,000 years ago. There aren't going to be any more of them, only fewer. And since excavation is obviously destructive, it's not like archaeologists do a site any favor by digging it up! Having come to this realization in the second half of the twentieth century, archaeologists have since tried to take a leadership role in promoting the adoption of national policies that conserve the world's remaining archaeological resources for the maximum public and scientific benefit. So yes, excavation will always be a distinctively archaeological activity. But such excavations should happen only in those situations where the data are needed to answer specific nontrivial questions about the human past or to collect basic archaeological information about sites that face imminent threat of destruction. Anything else simply vandalizes our collective heritage.

Figure 8-5

Dr. Michael L. Hargrave conducts an electrical resistance survey to locate archaeological features at a site in central Missouri. The electrical resistance is measured between two electrodes inserted in the earth. By systematically recording these measures across an archaeological site, researchers can plot the data to show soil disturbances such as ditches, walls, roads, and similar features that show no visible traces on the ground surface.

site survey The process of discovering the location of archaeological sites; sometimes called site reconnaissance.

5 Cm

Figure 8-6

By analyzing this collection of cultural debris from the surface of a prehistoric site in southeastern Missouri, the archaeologist can estimate the site age and the kinds of activities its inhabitants performed there. Other information about the site—including approximate site area, site preservation conditions, present land use, soil type, ground cover, and visible cultural features—was recorded when this surface collection was made.

Piecing Together the Past

Archaeology produces useful information only because we can reasonably assume that the organization and structure of the archaeological record reflects the behavior of humans in the past. Were this assumption to be false, archaeology would cease to exist. It's also undeniably true that it's easier to use archaeological data to examine some aspects of the past than others. Archaeologists, for example, seem to delight in telling us about what ancient people ate. They're typically far less prepared to tell us about such things as regional patterns of Neandertal ethnic identity in southwestern France or the social meaning of tattooed faces among the late prehistoric Native American villagers of the American Southeast.

It's not that no one cares about these things. It's just that it's far easier to talk about the archaeology of food than about the archaeology of identity and body art. After all, the archaeological record really is "other people's garbage"; it only becomes something more than garbage when we attempt to use it to inform ourselves about the past. Only then must we confront the possibility that what we wish to know may not be preserved in the archaeological record or be open to direct examination. If that's the case, then the researcher must explore ways to examine the phenomenon of interest indirectly. And if that doesn't work, the archaeologist smacks up against the state-of-the-art wall, something that exists in every field and beyond which the potentially knowable cannot yet be known until someone develops new technologies or theoretical approaches that make it possible.

ARTIFACTS, FEATURES, AND CONTEXTS

Four essential products—artifacts, **features**, **ecofacts**, and contexts—result from archaeological research. The relationships between these categories of remains are most often observed on *archaeological sites*, which are the locations of past human activity, such as the remains of a long-ago abandoned village or the place where an ancient hunter skinned and butchered a buffalo.

Figure **8-7**

The discovery of these sherds of decorated Native American pottery on the surface of a Mississippi Gulf Coast prehistoric site enables the archaeologist to estimate how old the site is and to determine regional ties between the group who lived at this site and groups who lived elsewhere on the Gulf Coast.

features Products of human activity that are usually integral to a site and therefore not portable. Examples include fire hearths and foundations.

ecofacts Natural materials that give environmental information about a site. Examples include plant and animal remains discarded as food waste and also pollen grains preserved in the soil.

Barry Lewis

Artifacts are tangible objects; in fact, anything that was made or modified by people in the past qualifies as an artifact (Fig. 8-7). It might be a stone tool or a sherd (fragment) of broken pottery or even a tin can. Artifacts differ from archaeological features because they can be removed as a single entity from the archaeological record. You can't do that with *features*, such as a medieval Hindu temple, a mud-lined hearth or fireplace, or a human burial, because none of them can be taken from the archaeological record in one piece (Fig. 8-8). *Ecofacts* are natural materials that are used mostly to reconstruct the local environment of a site (Fig. 8-9). Ecofacts can be found as both artifacts and features.

As noted, *context* describes the spatial and temporal associations existing in the archaeological record among artifacts and features (Fig. 8-10). What was the object's precise location, recorded from several coordinates so as to provide its three-dimensional position within the site? Was it associated somehow with any other artifact or feature? For example, was this projectile point found deep within a trash pit, on the floor of a hunter's shelter, or lodged between the ribs of a large animal? Can we be certain that this apparent association was really contemporaneous and not the result of natural processes of erosion or mixing (a key consideration of taphonomy; see p. 180)? Our point is that the context can be just as important as the artifact itself in understanding the past. With only artifacts, archaeology can give us a pretty limited understanding of the past, but with artifacts and their context, the limitations of what we can potentially know about the past probably rest more with archaeologists than with the archaeological record.

Figure **8-8**

Burials, such as the remains of this cow that were exposed during the excavation of a nineteenth-century Illinois farm, are classic examples of archaeological features. They can be exposed and studied in the archaeological record but cannot be removed without taking them apart.

Figure **8-9**

Thousands of land snails like the ones resting on this Lincoln penny were collected from a 4,000-year-old campsite in Illinois. These snails lived on the site location before, during, and after it was used by Native Americans; by analyzing them, archaeologists can reconstruct how the local site environment changed during that time.

Figure **8-10**

The large, dark wedge of soil is a partially excavated late prehistoric house in southeast Missouri. Preserved parts of the house wall are dotted along the upper edge of the feature in the upper half of the photo. The remains of this house provide archaeological context for the artifacts, ecofacts, and smaller features found within it.

Figure **8-11**

To learn about the pottery-making technology of prehistoric Native Americans in Iowa, archaeologist Colin Betts apprenticed himself to Afro-Caribbean potters who use similar methods on the island of Nevis in the West Indies. Here he stacks freshly made clay vessels so they can be fired, which is the final step that turns them into usable pots.

site survey The process of discovering the location of archaeological sites; sometimes called site reconnaissance.

ethnoarchaeology Approach used by archaeologists to gain insights into the past by studying contemporary people.

haft To equip a tool or implement with a handle or hilt.

ETHNOARCHAEOLOGY

In addition to **site surveys** and excavations, archaeologists sometimes seek to enhance their understanding and interpretations of the past by turning to **ethnoarchaeology**, which examines contemporary societies to gain insights into past human behavior (Fig. 8-11).

An ethnoarchaeologist personally conducts in-depth ethnographic research among a living group, such as the !Kung San in southern Africa (Yellen, 1980), the Australian aborigines (Gould, 1977; Meehan, 1982), the Nunamiut peoples of the Alaskan Arctic (Binford, 1978), or urban America. Such studies yield detailed information about hunting or gathering, toolmaking, discard of debris, residence data, and the like. By being "on the scene" as modern people literally create a site, the ethnoarchaeologist can better appreciate the comparable processes that formed the archaeological record (at the same time often becoming painfully aware of how much potential evidence simply decays and disappears between the time a site is created and the time an archaeologist may excavate it thousands or millions of years later).

So, how does ethnoarchaeological information get applied in archaeological research? It gives archaeologists testable ideas about the interpretation of archaeological patterns in much the same way that paleoanthropologists apply observation studies of modern living primates to their understanding of the behavior and biology of hominins known only from the fossil record. The researcher examines the modern information and asks the question, "If early hominins behaved like modern hunter-gatherer X or supermarket shopper Y or rodeo performer Z, what physical evidence and associations should I expect to find in the archaeological record only if this is true?" If the predicted evidence and associations are found, then the researcher reasons that the observed modern human behavior can't be excluded as a possible interpretation of comparable patterning in the archaeological record.

EXPERIMENTAL ARCHAEOLOGY

Yet another way to gain a closer understanding of our ancestors is by learning how they made their tools (Fig. 8-12), containers, houses (Fig. 8-13), and other artifacts and features and how they used and discarded them. After all, it's the artifactual traces of prehistoric tools of stone (and, to a lesser degree, of bone) that constitute our primary information about the earliest identified humanlike behavior. As we mentioned earlier, stone is by far the most common residue of prehistoric cultural behavior, and tons of stone tool debris litter archaeological sites worldwide. For example, if you were taking a casual walk along the bottom of Olduvai Gorge in Tanzania, you'd likely be interrupted every few seconds by tripping over prehistoric tools!

But what can these artifacts tell us about our ancestors? Quite a lot. Let's say your excavation reveals a bunch of stone axe heads from the remains of an ancient campsite. If you were to make copies of these axe heads using appropriate technology, **haft** them on wooden shafts in ways that replicate the wear patterns found on the ancient axe heads, and use them for a few hours in a set of experiments (say, cutting down a tree with one axe, clearing brush with another, and so on), you'd end up with a much better understanding of how the ancient axes were made and used and, very likely, why they tended to break in patterned ways. You would even be able to compare the wear patterns of modern stone axes used for different tasks with observable wear on the archaeological specimens and identify the tasks for which the ancient tools were used.

Figure **8-12**

Archaeologist Richard Vanderhoek taught himself how to make and use spear technology like that found in the earliest Alaskan sites so he could better understand and interpret the lifeways of the first inhabitants of the New World.

Figure **8-13**

Drawing upon archaeological research and tribal ingenuity, modern descendants of New England's aboriginal people construct a traditional-style round house, or wigwam, at Plimoth Plantation, Massachusetts. Saplings set into the ground, bent and lashed together, provide a framework for the house, which will be lined and covered with water-deflecting reed matting.

It's precisely this logic that drives **experimental archaeology**, which, like ethnoarchaeology, uses observations of modern behavior as testable ideas about the interpretation of archaeological patterning.

Dating Methods

An essential consideration of archaeology and, more generally, paleoanthropology is to establish the age of artifacts, fossils, features, and sites. Only after placing discoveries firmly in time and space can researchers accurately interpret the relationships of archaeological materials and sites to each other and construct a valid and reliable picture of human evolution. Because of the importance of dating in every chapter that follows, in this section we provide a basic introduction to the most widely used dating methods and how they work. Table 8-2 summarizes the main characteristics of each method.

The question of the age of archaeological and other paleoanthropological materials can be answered in two ways. First, we can say that the hominin that became fossil X lived before or after the hominin that became fossil Y. This is an example of *relative dating*, which establishes the relative order of events but does not scale the amount of time that separates them. Many questions can be answered by knowing only relative ages. Second, we can say that a particular village site is X number of years old. This is an example of *chronometric dating*, which establishes the age of events (and obviously their relative order too) according to some fixed time scale—often, as in this example, in calendar years. Chronometric dating is sometimes called *absolute dating* because the result is a measured quantity of time, not a relative order.

Both relative and chronometric dating are used daily in archaeological research. Because, like most instruments, every dating method has its strengths and limitations, researchers often employ multiple methods to estimate the age of a given artifact or context. This helps to ensure that their interpretations are based on the most valid and reliable age estimates.

experimental archaeology Research that attempts to replicate ancient technologies and construction procedures to test hypotheses about past activities.

Table **8-2   Summary of Dating Methods Described in This Chapter**

Method	Basis	Limitations	Comments
Relative dating methods establish the relative order of events			
Stratigraphy	Principle of superpositioning of strata	Most robust relative dating method	Geological stratigraphy and archaeological stratigraphy are created by different processes and must be interpreted separately
Biostratigraphy	Estimates of consistent modifications in evolving lineages of animals; presence/absence of species	Requires very well-documented sequences and somewhere must be correlated with chronometric results (e.g., with K/Ar)	Best estimates in East Africa using pigs, monkeys, antelope, and rodents; has been important dating method in South Africa
Cross-dating	Shared similarities of material remains found in an undated context with remains from a context of known age	Weak when used by itself; best applied in conjunction with other dating methods	Widely applied in archaeological research, the logic of cross-dating is similar to that of biostratigraphy
Seriation	Orders artifacts from different sites or contexts into series based on presence/absence or frequencies of shared attributes	There's no way to know which end of a seriated sequence of artifacts is the oldest unless it is determined by stratigraphic or chronometric methods	Gradually being replaced in archaeological research by a quantitative method called correspondence analysis, which achieves the same end
Fluorine analysis	Estimates the relative age of bones from a given site based on fluorine content	Applicable only to bones found in the same location	The key to exposing the Piltdown hoax in the early 1950s
Chronometric methods give absolute measures of age, often scaled in calendar years			
Potassium-argon (K/Ar)	Regular radioactive decay of potassium isotope	Contamination can occur; usually requires corroboration from other independent methods	Can be used only on sediments that have been superheated (usually volcanic deposits)
Argon-argon (^{40}Ar/^{39}Ar)	Works similar to potassium-argon technique	Same as above	Same as above; often used to check the validity and reliability of potassium-argon results
Fission-track dating	Regular fission of uranium atoms, leaving microscopic tracks	Usually derived from volcanic deposits; estimates generally less accurate than for K/Ar	Very important corroboratory method in East Africa
Paleomagnetism	Regular shifts in earth's geomagnetic pole; evidence preserved in magnetically charged sediments	Requires precise excavation techniques; both major and minor reversals occur and can easily confuse interpretation	Important corroboratory method in East and South Africa
Radiocarbon dating	Measures the ^{14}C/^{12}C ratio in samples of organic materials	Applications limited to roughly the past 50,000 years	Most widely used chronometric dating method
Thermoluminescence (TL)	Measures the accumulated radiation dose since the last heating or sunlight exposure of an object	Yields the estimated age of the *last* heating event	Widely used for dating ceramics, hearths, and other artifacts and features that were subjected to extremes of heat
Electron spin resonance (ESR)	Measurement (counting) of accumulated trapped electrons	Age estimates can be biased by tooth enamel uptake of uranium; best applied in conjunction with other dating methods	Widely applied in paleoanthropology to date fossil tooth enamel
Uranium series dating	Radioactive decay of short-lived uranium isotopes	Can yield high-precision age estimates; main limitation is the potential range of datable materials	Used to date limestone formations (e.g., stalagmites) and ancient ostrich eggshells
Dendrochronology	Tree-ring dating	Direct archaeological applications limited to temperate regions for which a master chart exists for tree species that were used by humans in the past	Although very important for archaeological dating in some parts of the world (e.g., the American Southwest), its greatest general application is to calibrate radiocarbon age estimates, which greatly enhances their accuracy and precision

At a Glance
Relative and Chronometric Dating

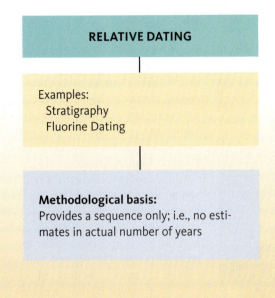

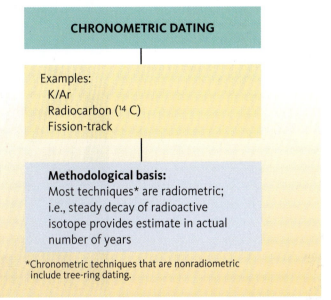

RELATIVE DATING	CHRONOMETRIC DATING
Examples: Stratigraphy Fluorine Dating	**Examples:** K/Ar Radiocarbon (^{14}C) Fission-track
Methodological basis: Provides a sequence only; i.e., no estimates in actual number of years	**Methodological basis:** Most techniques* are radiometric; i.e., steady decay of radioactive isotope provides estimate in actual number of years

*Chronometric techniques that are nonradiometric include tree-ring dating.

RELATIVE DATING

The oldest relative dating method is **stratigraphy**. A basic understanding of the nature of geological stratigraphy and the **principle of superpositioning** has been critical to the development of the scientific understanding of human evolution for at least the past 150 years. When you stand and look at the rock layers visible in the side of the Grand Canyon, the Rift Valley in East Africa, or even many interstate highway road cuts, there's nothing that cries out to you that the stuff on top must have been put there last and that, therefore, the stuff on the bottom is older than the stuff on the top. To make sense of it, you must, like James Hutton, Charles Lyell, and other nineteenth-century geologists, understand the processes by which sedimentary strata form and how they change. Once you grasp these concepts, then it's obvious that every stratigraphic exposure is a time-ordered record that if systematically studied can inform you about the past (Fig. 8-14).

Conveniently, the layer upon layer of sedimentary rock and other earth strata that compose much of the earth's near-surface geological record also contains most of the fossil evidence of our earliest ancestors and relatives. And even now, when so many chronometric dating methods exist, every researcher in the field knows that when he or she finds a fossil piece of an early hominin skull weathering out of an exposure in a geological **stratum**, then it must be more recent than skull fragments found in context in stratigraphic layers below it and older than fossils found in layers superimposed on it. The principle of superpositioning is therefore both robust, because only one sequence of events is possible, and useful, because this sequence establishes the order, or relative dating, of events.

It's appropriate to note here that geological stratigraphy and archaeological stratigraphy (in other words, the stratigraphy of an archaeological site) are not the same, nor are they created by precisely the same processes. As the archaeologist Edward Harris (1989) points out, geological stratigraphy is formed only by natural processes, whereas archaeological stratigraphy is formed by both cultural and natural processes. Geological strata are also typically sedimentary rocks that formed under water and that cover large areas, but archaeological strata are unconsolidated deposits that cover only small areas. The good news is that the principle of superpositioning applies both to geological

stratigraphy Study of the sequential layering of deposits.

principle of superpositioning In a stratigraphic sequence, the lower layers were deposited before the upper layers. Or, simply put, the stuff on top of a heap was put there last.

stratum (*pl.*, strata) A single layer of soil or rock; sometimes called a level.

Figure **8-14**

Archaeological stratigraphy of a pre-historic Native American site along the Susquehanna River in Pennsylvania. Spanning 6,000 years of prehistory, the strata bearing numbered tags represent periods during which people occupied the site. The intervening layers are natural flood deposits laid down by river overflows.

William Turnbaugh

and archaeological stratigraphy; the bad news is that these two kinds of stratigraphy differ enough in other ways that the interpretation of many early hominin sites requires stratigraphic interpretations from both perspectives.

Closely connected to geological stratigraphy is the method called **biostratigraphy**, or *faunal correlation*, a dating technique employed in the Early Pleistocene deposits at Olduvai and other African sites. This technique is based on the regular evolutionary changes in well-known groups of mammals. Animals that have been widely used in biostratigraphic analysis in East and South Africa are fossil pigs, elephants, antelopes, rodents, and carnivores. From areas where evolutionary sequences have been dated by chronometric means (such as potassium-argon dating, discussed shortly), approximate ages can be extrapolated to other lesser-known areas by noting which genera and species are present and treating them as **index fossils**.

In a similar manner, archaeologists use **cross-dating** to estimate the age of artifacts and features based on their similarities with comparable materials from contexts that have been dated by other means. The reasoning is simple. Suppose that you'd excavated the remains of an ancient burned hut and found several rusted iron hoes of a distinctive design in one corner of the building. If you were to turn to the archaeological literature for that region and research the evidence for similar hoes, you might find that other excavated sites had yielded hoes of the same shape in contexts dated by chronometric techniques to between A.D. 1450 and 1600. By applying the logic of cross-dating, you could tentatively infer that the hoes—and perhaps more important, the hut in which the hoes were found—cannot be older than A.D. 1450. The weakness of such reasoning is its assumption that close material similarities are a reliable measure of contemporaneity of contexts; although it's often true, this assumption is false enough of the time to warrant caution. Consequently, cross-dating is best applied as one of several independent methods of estimating the age of a given context.

Archaeologists also exploit the tendency for many items of material culture to change in patterned ways over time in another relative dating method called **seriation**, which simply orders artifacts into series based on their similar attributes or the frequency of these attributes. The familiar Stone–Bronze–Iron Age sequence long recognized by prehistorians is a good example of seriation: Sites containing metal tools are generally more recent than those where only stone was used, and since bronze technology is known to have developed before iron making, sites containing bronze but no iron occupy an intermediate chronological position. Likewise, the presence of clay vessels of a specific form in a given site may allow researchers to place that site in a sequence relative to others containing only pots known to be of earlier or later styles. Using this approach, archaeologists working in the southwestern United States determined the correct sequence of ancient Pueblo Indian sites based on the presence or absence of pottery and a comparison of stylistic traits. Later, radiocarbon dating—a chronometric technique—confirmed this sequence. Unless we have some independent means of actually assigning chronometric dates to some or all of the artifacts in the series, we know only that certain types (and, by extension, the sites where they occur) are relatively older or younger than others.

biostratigraphy A relative dating technique based on regular changes seen in evolving groups of animals as well as the presence or absence of particular species.

index fossils Fossil remains of known age, used to estimate the age of the geological stratum in which they are found. For example, extinct marine arthropods called trilobites can be used as an index fossil of Cambrian and Ordovician geological formations.

cross-dating Relative dating method that estimates the age of artifacts and features based on their similarities with comparable materials from dated contexts.

seriation Relative dating method that orders artifacts into a temporal series based on their similar attributes or the frequency of these attributes.

Another method of relative dating is **fluorine analysis**, which can be applied only to bones (Oakley, 1963). Bones in the earth are exposed to the seepage of groundwater that often contains fluorine. The longer a bone lies in the earth, the more fluorine it will incorporate during the fossilization process. This means that bones deposited at the same time in the same location should contain the same amount of fluorine. The use of this technique by Kenneth Oakley of the British Museum in the early 1950s exposed the famous Piltdown (England) hoax by demonstrating that a human skull was considerably older than the jaw (ostensibly also human) found with it (Weiner, 1955). A discrepancy in fluorine content led Oakley and others to more closely examine the bones, and they found that the jaw was not that of a hominin at all, but of a young adult orangutan!

Unfortunately, fluorine is useful only with bones found at the same location. Because the amount of fluorine in groundwater is based on local conditions, it varies from place to place. Also, some groundwater may not contain any fluorine. For these reasons, comparing bones from different localities by fluorine analysis is impossible.

CHRONOMETRIC DATING

It's impossible to calculate the age in calendar years of a site's geological stratum, and the objects in it, by using only relative dating techniques. To estimate absolute measures of age, scientists have developed a variety of chronometric techniques based on the phenomenon of **radiometric decay**. The theory is quite simple: Radioactive isotopes are unstable; over time, these isotopes decay and form an isotopic variation of another element. Since the rate of decay is known, the radioactive material can be used to measure past time in the geological and archaeological records. By measuring the amount of decay in a particular sample, scientists can calculate the number of years it took for the given radioactive isotope to decay to produce the measured level. The result is an age estimate that can be converted to calendar years. As with relative dating methods, chronometric methods have strengths and limitations. Some can be used to date the immense geological age of the earth; others may be limited to artifacts less than 1,000 years old. (For more on these techniques, see Lambert, 1997; Taylor and Aitken, 1997.)

The most important chronometric technique used to date early hominins involves potassium-40 (^{40}K), which has a **half-life** of 1.25 billion years and produces argon-40 (^{40}Ar). Known as the K/Ar or **potassium-argon method**, this procedure has been extensively used by paleoanthropologists in dating materials in the 1- to 5-million-year range, especially in East Africa. In addition, a variant of this technique, the $^{40}Ar/^{39}Ar$ or **argon-argon method**, has recently been used to date a number of hominin localities. The $^{40}Ar/^{39}Ar$ method allows analysis of smaller samples (even single crystals), reduces experimental error, and is more precise than standard K/Ar dating. Consequently, it can be used to date a wide chronological range—indeed, the entire hominin record, even up to modern times. Recent applications have provided excellent dates for several early hominin sites in East Africa (discussed in Chapter 9) as well as somewhat later sites in Java (discussed in Chapter 10). In fact, the technique was recently used to date the famous Mt. Vesuvius eruption of A.D. 79 (which destroyed the city of Pompeii). Remarkably, the midrange date obtained by the $^{40}Ar/^{39}Ar$ method was A.D. 73, just six years from the known date (Renne et al., 1997)! Organic material, such as bone, cannot be measured by these techniques, but the rock matrix in which the bone is found can be. K/Ar was used to provide a minimum date for the deposit containing the *Zinjanthropus* cranium by dating a volcanic layer above the fossil.

Rocks that provide the best samples for K/Ar and $^{40}Ar/^{39}Ar$ dating are those heated to extremely high temperatures, such as that generated by volcanic activity. When the rock is in a molten state, argon, a gas, is driven off. As the rock cools and solidifies, potassium-40 continues to break down to argon, but now the gas is physically trapped in the cooled rock. To obtain the date of the rock, it is reheated and the escaping gas measured.

fluorine analysis Relative dating method that measures and compares the amounts of fluorine that bones have absorbed from groundwater during burial.

radiometric decay A measure of the rate at which certain radioactive isotopes disintegrate.

half-life The time period in which one-half the amount of a radioactive isotope is chemically converted to a daughter product. For example, after 1.25 billion years, half the potassium-40 remains; after 2.5 billion years, one-fourth remains.

potassium-argon (K/Ar) method Dating technique based on accumulation of argon-40 gas as a by-product of the radiometric decay of potassium-40 in volcanic materials; used especially for dating early hominin sites in East Africa.

argon-argon ($^{40}Ar/^{39}Ar$) method Working on a similar basis as the potassium-argon method, this approach uses the ratio of argon-40 to argon-39 for dating igneous and metamorphic rocks; it offers precision and temporal range advantages for dating some early hominin sites.

When dating relatively recent samples (from the perspective of a half-life of 1.25 billion years for K/Ar, *all* paleoanthropological material is relatively recent), the amount of radiogenic argon (the argon produced by decay of a potassium isotope) is going to be exceedingly small. Experimental errors in measurement can therefore occur as well as the thorny problem of distinguishing the atmospheric argon normally clinging to the outside of the sample from the radiogenic argon. In addition, the initial sample may have been contaminated, or argon leakage may have occurred while it lay buried. Due to these potential sources of error, K/Ar dating must be cross-checked using other independent methods.

Fission-track dating is one of the most important techniques for cross-checking K/Ar determinations. The key to fission-track dating is that uranium-238 (^{238}U) decays regularly by spontaneous fission. By counting the fraction of uranium atoms that have fissioned (shown as microscopic tracks caused by explosive fission of ^{238}U nuclei), we can determine the age of a mineral or natural glass sample (Fleischer and Hart, 1972). One of the earliest applications of this technique was on volcanic pumice from Olduvai, giving a date of 2.30 ± 0.28 mya—in good accord with K/Ar dates.

Another important means of cross-checking dates is called **paleomagnetism**. This technique is based on the constantly shifting nature of the earth's magnetic pole. Of course, the earth's magnetic pole is now oriented in a northerly direction, but it hasn't always been. In fact, the orientation and intensity of the geomagnetic field have undergone numerous documented changes in the last few million years. From our present point of view, we call a northern orientation "normal" and a southern one "reversed." Here are the major epochs (also called chrons) of recent geomagnetic time:

0.7 mya–present	Normal
2.6–0.7 mya	Reversed
3.4–2.6 mya	Normal
?–3.4 mya	Reversed

Paleomagnetic dating is accomplished by carefully taking samples of sediments that contain magnetically charged particles. Since these particles maintain the magnetic orientation they had when they were consolidated into rock (many thousands or millions of years ago), they function as a kind of fossil compass. Then the paleomagnetic sequence is compared against the K/Ar dates to check if they agree. Some complications may arise, for during an epoch, a relatively long period of time can occur when the geomagnetic orientation is the opposite of what is expected. For example, during the reversed epoch from 2.6 to 0.7 mya (the Matuyama epoch), there was an *event* lasting about 210,000 years when orientations were normal (Fig. 8-15). (Because this phenomenon was first conclusively demonstrated at Olduvai, it is appropriately called the *Olduvai event*.) Once these oscillations in the geomagnetic pole are worked out, though, the sequence of paleomagnetic orientations can provide a valuable cross-check for K/Ar and fission-track age determinations.

The standard chronometric method for dating later prehistory is carbon-14 (^{14}C) dating, also known as **radiocarbon dating**. This technique has been used to date organic material ranging from less than 1,000 years old up to around 50,000 years old. The radiocarbon dating method is based on the following natural processes: Cosmic radiation enters the earth's atmosphere as nuclear particles, some of which react with nitrogen to produce small quantities of an unstable isotope of carbon, ^{14}C. This radioactive ^{14}C diffuses through the atmosphere, mixing with ordinary carbon-12 (^{12}C). Combined with oxygen (O_2) in the form of carbon dioxide (CO_2), carbon is taken up by plants during photosynthesis. Herbivorous animals absorb it by feeding on plants, and carnivores absorb it by feeding on herbivores. So ^{14}C and ^{12}C are found in all living forms at a ratio that reflects the atmospheric proportion. Once an organism dies, it absorbs no more ^{14}C, neither through photosynthesis nor through its diet. Without replacement, the ^{14}C atoms in the tissue continue decaying at a constant rate to nitrogen-14 (^{14}N) and a beta particle, while the

fission-track dating Dating technique based on the natural radiometric decay (fission) of uranium-238 atoms, which leaves traces in certain geological materials.

paleomagnetism Dating method based on the earth's shifting magnetic pole.

radiocarbon dating Method for determining the age of organic archaeological materials by measuring the decay of the radioactive isotope of carbon, carbon-14; also known as carbon-14 dating.

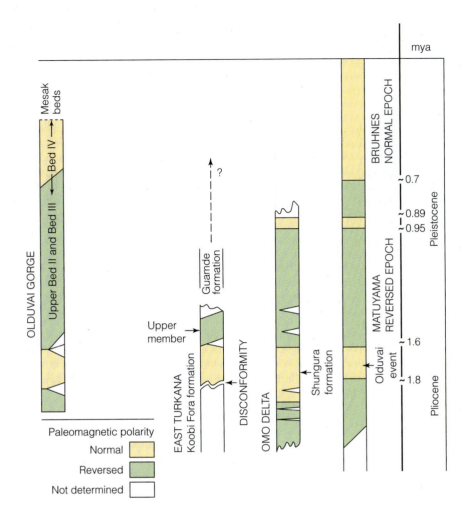

Figure **8-15**

Paleomagnetic sequences correlated for some East African sites—Olduvai, East Turkana, and Omo. (After Isaac, 1975.)

^{12}C remains unchanged. Thus, the ^{14}C/^{12}C ratio in the tissues of a dead plant or animal decreases steadily through time at a rate that can be precisely measured.

This method is limited primarily to dating organic materials that were once alive and part of the carbon cycle, but the constraint can be a somewhat loose one. For example, South African archaeologist Nikolaas van der Merwe (1969) successfully devised a technique to use radiocarbon dating for archaeological samples of iron alloy, a material that was obviously never alive itself but that does contain carbon from living things due to its manufacturing process. This alone is sufficient for it to be dated by the radiocarbon method.

Carbon-14 has a radiometric half-life of 5,730 years, meaning it takes 5,730 years for half the remaining ^{14}C to decay. Let's say that charred wood, the remains of a campfire, is found at an archaeological site and analyzed for its ^{14}C/^{12}C ratio. First, the sample is carefully collected to avoid contamination. It doesn't have to be a large sample, because even tiny quantities of carbon—just a few milligrams—can be analyzed. In the laboratory, radiation detectors measure the residual ^{14}C (Fig. 8-16). Suppose the findings show that only 25 percent of the original ^{14}C remains, as indicated by the ^{14}C/^{12}C ratio. Since we know that it takes 5,730 years for half the original number of ^{14}C atoms to become ^{14}N and another 5,730 years for half the remaining ^{14}C to decay, the sample must be about 11,460 years old. Half of the yet-remaining ^{14}C will disappear over the next 5,730 years (when the charcoal is 17,190 years old), leaving only 12.5 percent of the original amount. This process continues, and as you can estimate, there would be very little ^{14}C left after 40,000 years, when

Figure 8-16

Technician in a radiocarbon dating laboratory.

accurate measurement becomes difficult. Radiocarbon dates (and most other chronometric age determinations) are often reported as a mean age estimate and its associated standard error (1 standard deviation, by convention). So the age estimate of the campfire charcoal, as reported by the dating lab, might be expressed as 11,460 ± 200 radiocarbon years ago. Expressed in words, such an estimate states that the true age of the dated specimen will fall between 11,260 and 11,660 radiocarbon years ago about two times out of three, or roughly 68 percent of the time.

Some inorganic artifacts can be directly dated through the use of **thermoluminescence (TL)**. Used especially for dating ceramics, but also applied to clay cooking hearths and even burned flint tools and hearthstones on later hominin sites (see p. 307), this method, too, relies on the principle of radiometric decay. Clays used in making pottery invariably contain trace amounts of radioactive elements, such as uranium or thorium. As the potter fires the ware (or a campfire burns on a hearth), the rapid heating releases displaced beta particles trapped within the clay. As the particles escape, they emit a dull glow known as thermoluminescence. After that, radioactive decay resumes within the fired clay or stone, again building up electrons at a steady rate. To determine the age of an archaeological sample, the researcher must heat the sample to 500°C and measure its thermoluminescence; from that the date can be calculated. TL is routinely used to authenticate fine ceramic vessels prized by collectors and museums, and the technique has exposed many fake Greek and Maya vases displayed in prominent collections.

Like TL, two other techniques used to date sites from the latter phases of hominin evolution (where neither K/Ar nor radiocarbon dating is possible) are uranium series dating and electron spin resonance (ESR) dating. Uranium series dating relies on radioactive decay of short-lived uranium isotopes, and ESR is similar to TL because it's based on measuring trapped electrons. However, while TL is used on heated materials such as clay or stone tools, ESR is used on the dental enamel of animals. All three of these dating methods have been used to provide key dating controls for hominin sites discussed in Chapters 11 and 12.

An archaeologically important chronometric dating technique that does not involve radioactive elements is **dendrochronology**, or dating by tree rings. Its use is limited to contexts in temperate latitudes, where trees show pronounced seasonal growth rings and where ancient wood is commonly preserved. So far, the longest dendrochronological sequences have been developed in the arid American Southwest and the bogs of western Europe, especially Ireland and Germany.

Because tree rings represent seasonal growth layers, the amount of new wood added each year depends directly on rainfall and other factors. People have known for centuries, if not millennia, that the growth rings of an individual tree read like its biography. If we know when the tree was cut and then count from the outer rings inward toward the center, we can readily determine the year the tree began growing. The outstanding contribution of A. E. Douglass, an early twentieth-century astronomer, was to systematically exploit this idea. He reasoned that if we can tell how old a tree is by counting its seasonal growth rings, then we should be able to take a tree of known age and match its growth-ring pattern with the patterns compiled from older and older trees of the same species. The limit on how old this "master chart" of growth rings can extend into the past depends entirely on the extent to which old tree trunks are preserved, because they provide data from which the chart can be built.

By cutting or drawing core samples from living trees, recently dead trees, and successively older wood (including archaeological sources such as ancient house posts or beams), archaeologists obtain overlapping life histories of many trees. When compared, these life histories form an extensive record of tree-ring growth through many centuries. Remember,

thermoluminescence (TL) (ther-mo-loo-min-es´-ence) Technique for dating certain archaeological materials, such as ceramics, that release stored energy of radioactive decay as light upon reheating.

dendrochronology Archaeological dating method based on the study of yearly growth rings in ancient wood.

the archaeologist is mostly interested in determining precisely when a tree *stopped* growing and became part of a cultural process such as construction or cooking. As a result, a tree used as a beam in a prehistoric structure in the American Southwest may be dated to the very year in which it was felled (Fig. 8-17), since the distinctive pattern of its growth should exactly match some segment of the tree-ring record compiled for the region. Archaeologists studying the ceiling beams in the traditional homes still occupied by the Acoma people in northern New Mexico were able to precisely date construction undertaken in the mid-seventeenth century (Robinson, 1990). Wood from the commonly used pinyon pines and the long-lived Douglas fir trees, sequoia redwoods, and bristlecone pines of the American West, as well as preserved oak logs from western European bogs, afford archaeologists continuous regional tree-ring records extending back thousands of years.

But there is yet another dimension to tree-ring dating. By radiocarbon dating wood taken from individual growth rings of known age, researchers have used dendrochronology to fine-tune ^{14}C dating accuracy, factoring in past fluctuations in the atmospheric reservoir of ^{14}C over the past 9,800 years (the period for which tree-ring dates are available). They then use this factor to recalibrate the raw dates obtained by standard ^{14}C analyses, thereby enabling archaeologists to convert radiocarbon age estimates to calendar year ages. Recently, by comparing ^{14}C dates obtained from coral reefs with dates on the same samples obtained using a uranium-thorium ($^{234}U/^{230}Th$) dating method, technicians have been able to adjust the radiocarbon calibration curve back to 23,700 years ago (Fiedel, 1999b).

In some areas, including Egypt and Central America, the recorded calendar systems of ancient civilizations have also been cross-referenced to our own, resulting in direct dating of some sites and inferential or cross-dating of others shown to be contemporaneous with them by the presence of distinctive artifacts. For example, firmly dated artifacts originating in the Nile valley and traded into the Aegean allow us to assign dates to archaeological contexts of Bronze Age Greece. Obviously, this approach is of little use outside those regions having some connection with literate societies.

Since the advent of radiocarbon and other chronometric dating methods in the latter half of the twentieth century, the age of many archaeological and paleoanthropological finds has been precisely and accurately estimated. Although no other dating technique is as widely used as radiocarbon dating, each is an ingenious method with its own special applications. Still, as with any instrument, researchers must consider the strengths and limitations of each chronometric method, both when applying it in the field and when interpreting the lab results.

Figure **8-17**

Doorway in White House Ruin, Canyon de Chelly, Arizona. Wooden beams and supports can be dated by dendrochronology. Archaeologists have removed a core sample from the left end of the lintel (on the left at the top of the door) for dating.

Paleoanthropology and Archaeology at Olduvai Gorge

We conclude this methodological introduction to paleoanthropology and archaeology with a case study from East Africa—Olduvai Gorge (Fig. 8-18), a locality that has yielded the finest quality and greatest abundance of anthropological information concerning the behavior of early hominins and an extraordinarily informative sequence of excavated **Lower Paleolithic** sites. The object of this case study is to illustrate how paleoanthropological methods, including most especially archaeological approaches, work together to create the modern understanding of early hominin life in this part of East Africa. It also sets the stage for Chapter 9, in which we explore in detail the early hominin fossil record and the oldest Lower Paleolithic archaeological evidence.

Beginning in the 1930s, the pioneering team of Louis and Mary Leakey (Fig. 8-19) worked at Olduvai. Together, they made Olduvai Gorge one of the most widely known place names in Africa. It was, you might say, one of the best mom-and-pop shops in twentieth-century paleoanthropology.

Lower Paleolithic A unit of archaeological time that begins about 2.6 mya with the earliest identified tools made by hominins and ends around 200,000 years ago.

195

Figure **8-18**

Olduvai Gorge and the Rift Valley system in East Africa.

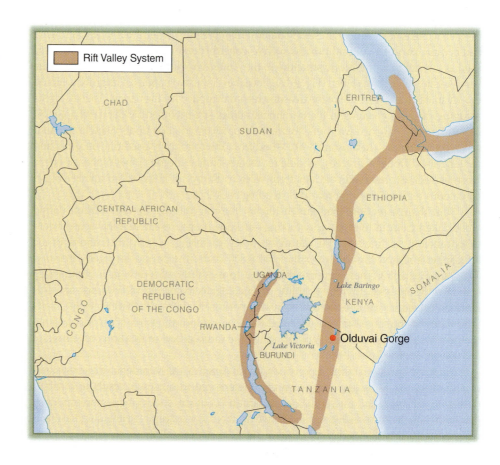

Figure **8-19**

Mary Leakey (1913–1996), a major figure in twentieth-century paleoanthropology, devoted most of her life to fieldwork in Olduvai Gorge, where she made many important discoveries, including the *Zinjanthropus* skull (see Fig. 8-21) in 1959.

L.S.B. Leakey Foundation

Located on the Serengeti Plain of northern Tanzania, Olduvai is a steep-sided valley resembling a miniature version of the Grand Canyon (Fig. 8-20). A massive ravine some 300 feet deep, Olduvai cuts for more than 25 miles across the grassy plateau of East Africa. The present semiarid climate of the Olduvai region is believed to be similar to what it has been for the last 2 million years. The surrounding countryside is a grassland savanna dotted with scrub bushes and acacia trees. Dry though it may be, this environment presently (as well as in the past) supports a vast number of mammals (such as zebra, wildebeest, and gazelle), representing an enormous supply of "meat on the hoof."

Geographically, Olduvai is located on the eastern branch of the Great Rift Valley, which stretches for 4,000 miles down the east side of Africa (see Fig. 8-18). The geological processes associated with forming the Rift Valley make Olduvai (and many other East African regions) extremely important because they created an environment that favored the preservation of hominin remains and make it easier for paleoanthropologists and archaeologists to discover these remains. Here are the four most significant results of geological rifting:

1. Faulting, or earth movement, exposes geological strata that are normally hidden deep in the earth.
2. Active volcanic processes cause rapid sedimentation, which often yields excellent preservation of bone and artifacts that normally would be scattered by carnivore activity and erosion forces.
3. Strata formed by rapid sedimentation and, more important, the hominin fossils and archaeological sites preserved within them, can be dated by relative methods such as stratigraphy and cross-dating.
4. Volcanic activity provides a wealth of materials datable by chronometric methods.

As a result, Olduvai offers researchers superb preservation of ancient hominins, good evidence of the environments in which these hominins lived, and archaeological sites containing the material remains of their existence in datable contexts, all of which are readily accessible. Such advantages cannot be ignored, and Olduvai continues to be the focus of considerable archaeological and other paleoanthropological research.

Over the decades of paleoanthropological fieldwork, partial remains of more than 40 fossilized hominins have been found at Olduvai. Many of these individuals are quite fragmentary, but a few are excellently preserved. Although the center of hominin discoveries has now shifted to other areas of East Africa, it was the initial discovery by Mary Leakey of the *Zinjanthropus* skull at Olduvai in July 1959 that focused the world's attention on this remarkably rich area (see Fig. 8-21). "Zinj" is an excellent example of how financial support can result directly from hominin fossil discoveries. Prior to 1959, the Leakeys had worked sporadically at Olduvai on a financial shoestring, making marvelous paleontological and archaeological discoveries but never attracting the financial assistance they needed for large-scale excavations. However, following the discovery of Zinj, the National Geographic Society funded the Leakeys' research, and within a year, more than twice as much dirt had been excavated than during the previous 30 years!

Olduvai's greatest contribution to paleoanthropological research in the twentieth century was the establishment of an extremely well-documented and correlated *sequence* of archaeological, geological, paleontological, and hominin remains over the last 2 million years. At the very foundation of all paleoanthropological research is a well-established geological context. At Olduvai, the geological and paleogeographical situation is now known in minute detail. It's been a great help that Olduvai is a geologist's delight, containing sediments in some places 350 feet thick, accumulated from lava flows (basalts), tuffs (windblown or waterborne fine deposits from nearby volcanoes), sandstones, claystones, and limestone conglomerates, all neatly stratified (see Fig. 8-20). A hominin site can therefore be accurately dated relative to other sites in the Olduvai Gorge by cross-correlating known stratigraphic marker beds.

Because the vertical cut of the Olduvai Gorge provides a ready cross section of 2 million years of earth history, sites can be excavated by digging "straight in" rather than first having to remove tons of overlying dirt (Fig. 8-22). In fact, sites are usually discovered in Olduvai Gorge by merely walking the stratigraphic exposures and observing what kinds of bones, stones, and so forth, are eroding out, just as archaeologists often do when discovering sites in other parts of the world.

At the most general geological level, the stratigraphic sequence at Olduvai is broken down into four major beds (Beds I–IV), each containing hominin and other animal fossils and sites with artifacts and features created by early hominin cultural behavior. These contexts are reasonably well dated by both relative and chronometric methods. The fossilized remains of more than 150 animal species, including fishes, turtles, crocodiles, pigs, giraffes, horses, and many birds, rodents, and antelopes, have been found throughout these Olduvai beds and provide much of the basis for reconstructing the environmental conditions that existed when the early hominin sites were deposited.

The earliest identified hominin site (circa 1.85 mya) at Olduvai Gorge contains a Lower Paleolithic stone tool assemblage that archaeologists named *Oldowan* (Leakey,

Robert Jurmain

Figure **8-20**

View of the main gorge at Olduvai. Note the clear sequence of geological beds. The discontinuity in the stratigraphic layers (to the right of the red arrow) is a major fault line.

© Jeffrey Schwartz

Figure **8-21**

Zinjanthropus skull, discovered by Mary Leakey at Olduvai Gorge in 1959. As we will see in Chapter 9, this fossil is now included as part of the genus *Australopithecus*.

Figure **8-22**

Excavations in progress at Olduvai. This site, more than 1 million years old, was located when a hominin ulna (arm bone) was found eroding out of the side of the gorge.

1971). For now, it is enough to know that Oldowan tools are simple and very crude to our eyes and that most were made by knocking small flakes off bigger rocks and by battering (Fig. 8-23). (We'll look at Oldowan tools in more detail in Chapter 9.) Considerable research continues to focus on understanding the nature of these tools, with archaeologists eager to know just why they were made and what they were used for. Many insights about Oldowan tool function and use come from the results of experimental archaeology projects in which researchers try to replicate the wear, breakage, and discard patterns of artifacts found in Lower Paleolithic sites.

For example, in the mid-twentieth century, many archaeologists described Oldowan as primarily a "chopping tool industry" because they concluded that the large, broken cobbles found in these assemblages were used as heavy chopper-like implements (see Fig. 8-23). They also inferred that many of the equally common stone flakes were simply debris from making these so-called "core tools." Over the decades, as archaeologists investigated more Oldowan sites and compared excavated artifacts with similar implements re-created by experimental archaeologists, these initial hypotheses came into question. Many of the choppers or core tools, while they were clearly artifacts, might not have actually been used as tools. In one such study, Richard Potts (1991, 1993), of the Smithsonian Institution, analyzed Olduvai Bed I artifacts and concluded that early hominins were deliberately producing flake tools, not heavy chopper-like core tools, and that the various stone nodule forms (discoids, polyhedrons, choppers, and so on) were simply "incidental stopping points in the process of removing flakes from cores" (Potts, 1993, p. 60).

To many students, the idea that one class of artifacts is not what we once assumed probably seems trivial, but it actually had important implications for how archaeologists view early hominins as cultural animals. If Oldowan tool use emphasized cutting (the flake tools), not chopping (the so-called core tools), then what were they cutting? What kinds of use wear are present on the flake tools, and what kinds of cutting scars are present on the animal bones found in Oldowan sites? And what are the lumps of rock once thought to be core tools? Just broken bits of raw material, or something else entirely? Researchers have paid a fair amount of attention to such questions over the past couple of decades, and their results continue to enhance our understanding of how early hominins, as creatures that were still learning to be tool-using animals, exploited the landscapes in which they lived.

The recognition that flake tools were a key part of the Oldowan tool industry forced paleoanthropologists and archaeologists to reassess their ideas about early human tool use. A comparable impact may be felt from recent research on rocks that early humans may not have used at all! The Oldowan industry traditionally includes *manuports*—unmodified rocks of types that are not present in the geology of the immediate vicinity of the Oldowan sites where they are found. In other words, they're just rocks, and the only reasons for not treating them as such are that they are geologically out of place and that they are found in archaeological contexts believed to be the product of hominin behavior.

For decades, archaeologists have believed that the best explanation for the presence of manuports in Oldowan sites was that early hominins picked up the stones where they naturally occurred and carried them to the site where they were much later excavated. If that's true, such an otherwise irrelevant artifact depends for its significance entirely on the assumption that an early human moved it from point A to point B. So long as we believe that the evidence supports only this interpretation, these rocks are artifacts; once we cannot believe this evidence, they're just rocks.

Although they don't seem important, manuports became key elements in some interpretations of the ecological niche of early hominins as tool-using animals on the arid savannas of East Africa. For example, among the several kinds of Oldowan sites excavated in Olduvai Gorge are those originally identified as "multipurpose localities," or campsites, which were interpreted as general-purpose areas where hominins possibly ate, slept, and put the finishing touches on tools. Mary Leakey and the archaeologist Glynn Isaac (1976) were strong proponents of this interpretation, which carried with it the necessary implication that early hominins were **home-based foragers**. Lewis Binford's (1983) comparisons of bone assemblages from early hominin contexts at Olduvai and similar assemblages drawn from his ethnoarchaeological research in Alaska on modern human and animal behavior led him to a different conclusion. He argued that much of the accumulated bone refuse on Oldowan sites can be explained as the result of nonhominin (that is, predator) activities and that early hominins were little more than passive scavengers of big game kills. This stance opened the door to a continuing debate about whether early hominins were primarily hunters or scavengers (e.g., Domínguez-Rodrigo, 2002; O'Connell et al., 2002; Domínguez-Rodrigo and Pickering, 2003).

One of the alternative interpretations put forth in the hunter versus scavenger debate came from Richard Potts (1988, 1991), who claimed that these sites served as stockpiles, or caches, for raw materials such as manuports in anticipation of future use. Potts' argument was especially important, partly because other researchers picked up the idea and incorporated it into their own models of early hominin behavior and partly because the argument implied a particular set of behaviors as part of the way early hominins used landscapes and interacted with technology. De la Torre and Mora (2005) recently reanalyzed the Olduvai manuport collections and concluded that it's unlikely that they are raw material caches in Potts' sense because (1) they share few characteristics with objects that were modified by early hominins and (2) natural geomorphological processes are sufficient to account for their presence at Olduvai sites. In other words, many, and perhaps most, manuports are just rocks and have nothing to do with the behavior of early hominins.

Research will undoubtedly continue to focus on Oldowan chopping tools as well as manuports, but their stories make good examples of how we learn about the human past. As in every scientific endeavor, archaeologists and other paleoanthropologists will never cease to question everything they may currently think is accurate, knowing full well that tomorrow, or the next day, or 10 years from now, someone will conduct the test, excavate the site, or simply ask a different question that opens the door to a fresh understanding about how and why we made it from the African savannas to exploring other planets. And that's how science is supposed to work!

Barry Lewis

Figure **8-23**

Oldowan core tools, such as this "chopper," were made by knocking flakes off a fist-size stone using another rock as a hammer.

home-based foragers Hominins that hunt, scavenge, or collect food and raw materials from the general locality where they habitually live and bring these materials back to some central or home base site to be shared with other members of their coresiding group.

Summary

In this chapter, we've seen that to achieve any meaningful understanding of human origins, the biocultural nature of human evolution requires us to examine both biological and cultural information. The multidisciplinary approach of paleoanthropology, including especially archaeology, brings together varied scientific specializations to reconstruct the anatomy, behavior, and environments of early hominins. Such a task centers on the knowledge, skills, and abilities of the archaeologist, geologist, paleontologist, paleoecologist, and physical anthropologist.

In a sense, our view of the human past is something like what we see out of the small passenger window of a jet cruising high above the continent. On the ground far below us, we can see evidence of human activity—in the net of roadways, plowed fields, towns, and other large constructions. But from our high altitude, we can't see the individuals who create these patterns on the landscape. The archaeologist's understanding of an ancient cultural landscape is much the same. It's usually difficult, if not impossible, to pick out the actions of individuals, but by systematically examining the archaeological record, even across the distance of hundreds of thousands (if not millions) of years, we can gain important insights into how they lived, what they achieved, and why the human past happened the way it did.

In paleoanthropology in general and archaeology in particular, *time* rather than space is the important dimension that separates us from those we study, and one of the main tasks of this chapter has been to describe the varied ways in which researchers estimate past time. We've also seen that archaeologists and other paleoanthropologists apply a battery of research methods to discover, excavate, and evaluate fossils, sites, features, and artifacts associated with the development and dispersion of hominins to all regions of the globe. Essentially, all of these techniques are attempts to close the distance between ourselves and our predecessors so that we might better understand their lives and our past.

The chapter closed with a quick look at Olduvai Gorge in East Africa, one of the best-known early hominin localities in the world. By reviewing the history of research at Olduvai, we've seen how scientists apply many of the methods described in the first part of the chapter, and we've noted the close collaboration of paleoanthropology and archaeology. And recalling some of the lessons learned in Chapter 1, we've seen how gaining scientific understanding of the past is a continuing process of learning, integrating, and reassessing the empirical basis of our knowledge.

Critical Thinking Questions

1. How are early hominin sites found, and what kinds of specialists are involved in excavating and analyzing such sites?
2. Why are cultural remains so important in interpreting human evolution? What do you think is the most important thing you can learn from cultural remains—say, from a site that is 2 million years old? What is the most important thing you *can't* learn?
3. Compare relative dating and chronometric dating. Name one or two examples of each, and briefly explain the principles used in determining the dates.
4. What kinds of cultural information may not be represented by artifacts alone? How do archaeologists attempt to compensate for these shortcomings through approaches such as ethnoarchaeology and ethnographic analogy?

Paleoanthropology/Fossil Hominins

CHAPTER

9

Hominin Origins

Focus Questions

Who are the oldest members of the human family, and how do these early hominins compare with modern humans? With modern apes? How do they fit within a biological continuum?

▶ Click!

Go to the following media for interactive activities and exercises on topics covered in this chapter:

- Online Virtual Laboratories for Physical Anthropology, Version 4.0
- Hominid Fossils: An Interactive Atlas CD-ROM

Introduction

Today our species dominates our planet; indeed, we use our brains and cultural inventions to invade every corner of the earth. Yet, 5 million years ago, our ancestors were little more than bipedal apes, confined to a few regions in Africa. What were these creatures like? When and how did they begin their evolutionary journey?

In Chapter 8, we discussed the techniques archaeologists use to locate and excavate sites as well as the multidisciplinary approaches used by paleoanthropologists to interpret discoveries. In this chapter, we turn first to the physical evidence of earlier primates and then to the hominin fossils themselves. The earliest fossils identifiable as hominins are all from Africa. They date from as early as 7 mya, and after 4 mya, varieties of these early hominins became more plentiful and widely distributed in Africa; this period of time is referred to as the **Plio-Pleistocene**. It's fascinating to think about all these quite primitive early members of our evolutionary tribe living side by side for millions of years, especially when we also try to figure out how these animals managed, with perhaps very different adaptations, to coexist with each other. Most of these species became extinct. But why? What's more, were some of these apelike animals possibly our direct ancestors?

Hominins, of course, evolved from earlier primates (dating back close to 50 mya), and we will briefly review this long and abundant prehominin fossil record to provide a better context for understanding the subsequent evolution of the human lineage. In recent years, paleoanthropologists from several countries have been excavating sites in Africa, and many exciting new finds have been uncovered. However, because many finds have been made so recently, detailed evaluations are still in progress, and conclusions must remain tentative.

One thing is certain, however. The earliest members of the human tribe were confined to Africa. Only much later did their descendants disperse from the African continent to other areas of the Old World. (This "out of Africa" saga will be the topic of the next chapter.)

Early Primate Evolution

Long before bipedal hominins first evolved in Africa, more primitive primates had diverged from even more distant mammalian ancestors. The roots of the primate order go back to the early stages of the placental mammal radiation as far back as 75–65 mya. Thus, the earliest primates were diverging from early and still primitive placental mammals. We've seen (in Chapter 6) that strictly defining living primates using clear-cut derived features is not an easy task. The further back we go in the fossil record, the more primitive and, in many cases, the more generalized the fossil primates become. Such a situation makes classifying them all the more difficult.

In fact, we only have scarce traces of the earliest primates. Some anthropologists have suggested that recently discovered bits and pieces from North Africa *may* be those of a very small primitive primate. But until more evidence is found, we will just have to wait and see.

Plio-Pleistocene Pertaining to the Pliocene and first half of the Pleistocene, a time range of 5–1 mya. For this time period, numerous fossil hominins have been found in Africa.

Fortunately, a vast number of fossil primates from the Eocene (55–34 mya) have been discovered and now total more than 200 recognized species (see Fig. 5-5, p. 110, for a geological chart). Unlike the available Paleocene forms, those from the Eocene display distinctive primate features. Indeed, primatologist Elwyn Simons (1972, p. 124) called them "the first primates of modern aspect." These animals have been found primarily in sites in North America and Europe (which for most of the Eocene were still connected). It's important to recall that the landmasses that connect continents, as well as the water boundaries that separate them, have obvious impact on the geographical distribution of such terrestrially bound animals as primates (see p. 111).

Some interesting late Eocene forms have also been found in Asia, which was joined to Europe by the end of the Eocene epoch. Looking at the whole array of Eocene primates, it is certain that they were (1) primates, (2) widely distributed, and (3) mostly extinct by the end of the Eocene. What is less certain is how any of them might be related to the living primates. Some of these forms are probably ancestors of the *prosimians*—the lemurs and lorises.* Others are probably related to the tarsier. New evidence of Eocene *anthropoid* origins has recently been discovered at a few sites in North Africa. The earliest of these African fossils go back to 50 mya, but the remains are very fragmentary. More conclusive evidence comes from Egypt and is well dated to 37 mya. At present, it looks likely that the earliest anthropoids first evolved in Africa.

The Oligocene (33–23 mya) has yielded numerous additional fossil remains of several different species of early anthropoids. Most of these forms are *Old World anthropoids*, all discovered at a single locality in Egypt, the Fayum (Fig. 9-1). In addition, there are a few known bits from North and South America that relate only to the ancestry of New World monkeys. By the early Oligocene, continental drift had separated the New World (that is, the Americas) from the Old World (Africa and Eurasia). Some of the earliest Fayum forms, nevertheless, may potentially be close to the ancestry of both Old and New World anthropoids. It has been suggested that late in the Eocene or very early in the Oligocene, the first anthropoids (primitive "monkeys") arose in Africa and later reached South America by "rafting" over the water separation on drifting chunks of vegetation. What we call "monkey," then, may have a common Old World origin, but the ancestry of New and Old World varieties remains separate after about 35 mya. The closest evolutionary affinities humans have after this time are with other Old World anthropoids, that is, with Old World monkeys and apes.

Figure **9-1**

(a) Fayum site in Egypt. (b) Excavations in progress at the Fayum, where dozens of fossil primates have been discovered.

(a)

(b)

---

*In strict classification terms, especially from a cladistic point of view, lemurs and lorises should be referred to as strepsirhines (see p. 130).

Table **9-1**   Inferred General Paleobiological Aspects of Oligocene Primates

	Weight Range	Substratum	Location	Diet
Apidium	750–1,600 g (2–3 lb)	Arboreal	Quadruped	Fruit, seeds
Aegyptopithecus	6,700 g (15 lb)	Arboreal	Quadruped	Fruit, some leaves?

Source: After Fleagle, 1999.

The possible roots of anthropoid evolution are illustrated by different forms from the Fayum; one is the genus *Apidium*. Well known at the Fayum, *Apidium* is represented by several dozen jaws or partial dentitions as well as many **postcranial** remains. Because of its primitive dental arrangement, some paleontologists have suggested that *Apidium* may lie near or even before the evolutionary divergence of Old and New World anthropoids. As so much fossil material of teeth and limb bones of *Apidium* has been found, some informed speculation regarding diet and locomotor behavior is possible. It is thought that this small, squirrel-sized primate ate mostly fruits and some seeds and was most likely an arboreal quadruped, adept at leaping and springing (Table 9-1).

The other genus of importance from the Fayum is *Aegyptopithecus*. This genus, also well known, is represented by several well-preserved crania and abundant jaws and teeth. The largest of the Fayum anthropoids, *Aegyptopithecus* is roughly the size of a modern howler monkey (13 to 20 pounds; Fleagle, 1983) and is thought to have been a short-limbed, slow-moving arboreal quadruped. *Aegyptopithecus* is important because, better than any other known form, it bridges the gap between the Eocene fossils and the succeeding Miocene hominoids.

Nevertheless, *Aegyptopithecus* is a very primitive Old World anthropoid, with a small brain and long snout and not showing any derived features of either Old World monkeys or hominoids. Thus, it may be close to the ancestry of *both* major groups of living Old World anthropoids. Found in geological beds dating to 35–33 mya, *Aegyptopithecus* further suggests that the crucial evolutionary divergence of hominoids from other Old World anthropoids occurred *after* this time (Fig. 9-2).

Miocene Fossil Hominoids

During the approximately 18 million years of the Miocene (23–5 mya), a great deal of evolutionary activity took place. In Africa, Asia, and Europe, a diverse and highly successful group of hominoids emerged (Fig. 9-3). Indeed, there were many more forms of hominoids

Figure 9-2

Major events in early primate evolution.

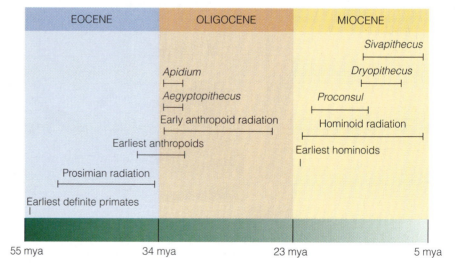

postcranial (*post*, meaning "after") In a quadruped, referring to that portion of the body behind the head; in a biped, referring to all parts of the body *beneath* the head (i.e., the neck down).

Figure **9-3**
Miocene hominoid distribution, from fossils thus far discovered.

from the Miocene than are found today (now represented by the highly restricted groups of apes and one species of humans). In fact, the Miocene could be called "the golden age of hominoids." Many thousands of fossils have been found from dozens of sites scattered in East Africa, southern Africa, southwest Asia, into western and southern Europe, and extending into southern Asia and China.

During the Miocene, significant transformations relating to climate and repositioning of landmasses took place. By 23 mya, major continental locations approximated those of today (except that North and South America were separate). Nevertheless, the movements of South America and Australia farther away from Antarctica significantly altered ocean currents. Likewise, the continued movement of the South Asian plate into Asia produced the Himalayan Plateau. Both of these paleogeographical modifications had significant impact on the climate, and the early Miocene was considerably warmer than the preceding Oligocene. Moreover, by 19 mya, the Arabian Plate (which had been separate) "docked" with northeastern Africa. As a result, migrations of animals from Africa directly into southwest Asia (and in the other direction as well) became possible. Among the earliest transcontinental migrants (around 16 mya) were African hominoids who colonized both Europe and Asia at this time.

A problem arises in any attempt to simplify the complex evolutionary situation regarding Miocene hominoids. For example, for many years, paleontologists tended to think of these fossil forms as either "apelike" or "humanlike" and used modern examples as models. But as we have just noted, very few hominoids remain. Therefore, we should not hastily generalize from the living forms to the much more diverse fossil forms; otherwise, we obscure the evolutionary uniqueness of these animals. In addition, we should not expect all fossil forms to be directly or even particularly closely related to living species. Indeed, we should expect the opposite; that is, most lines vanish without descendants.

Over the last three decades, the Miocene hominoid assemblage has been interpreted and reinterpreted. As more fossils are found, the evolutionary picture grows more complicated. The vast array of fossil forms has not yet been completely studied, so conclusions remain tenuous. Given this uncertainty, it's probably best, for the present, to group Miocene hominoids geographically:

1. *African forms (23–14 mya)* Known especially from western Kenya, these include quite generalized, and in many ways primitive, hominoids. The best-known genus

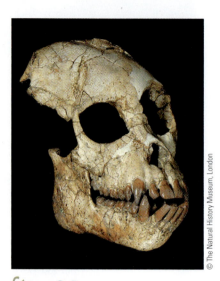

Figure **9-4**

Proconsul skull, an early Miocene hominoid.

large-bodied hominoids Those hominoids including the great apes (orangutans, chimpanzees, gorillas) and hominins, as well as all ancestral forms back to the time of divergence from small-bodied hominoids (i.e., the gibbon lineage).

hominins Colloquial term for members of the tribe Hominini, which includes all bipedal hominoids back to the divergence from African great apes.

Figure **9-5**

Comparison of a modern chimpanzee (left), *Sivapithecus* (middle), and a modern orangutan (right). Notice that both *Sivapithecus* and the orangutan exhibit a dished face, broad cheekbones, and projecting upper jaw and incisors.

is *Proconsul* (Fig. 9-4). In fact, *Proconsul* is mostly not like an ape, and postcranially it more closely resembles a monkey. It is only some features of the teeth that link these primitive early Miocene forms with hominoids at all.

2. *European forms (16–11 mya)* Known from widely scattered localities in France, Spain, Italy, Greece, Austria, Germany, and Hungary, most of these forms are quite derived. However, this is a varied and not well-understood group. The best known of the forms are placed in the genus *Dryopithecus*; the Hungarian and Greek fossils are usually assigned to other genera. The Greek fossils are called *Ouranopithecus*, and remains date to sites 9 to 10 million years of age. Evolutionary relationships are uncertain, but several researchers have suggested a link with the African ape-hominin group.

3. *Asian forms (15–7 mya)* The largest and most varied group from the Miocene fossil hominoid assemblage, geographically dispersed from Turkey through India/Pakistan and east to the highly prolific site Lufeng, in southern China, most of these forms are *highly* derived. The best-known genus is *Sivapithecus* (known from Turkey and Pakistan). The Lufeng material (now totaling more than 1,000 specimens) is usually placed in a separate genus from *Sivapithecus* (and is referred to as *Lufengpithecus*).

Four general points are certain concerning Miocene hominoid fossils: They are widespread geographically; they are numerous; they span a considerable portion of the Miocene, with *known* remains dated between 23 and 6 mya; and at present, they are poorly understood. However, we can reasonably draw the following conclusions:

1. These are hominoids—more closely related to the ape-human lineage than to Old World monkeys.

2. They are mostly **large-bodied hominoids**, that is, more akin to the lineages of orangutans, gorillas, chimpanzees, and humans than to smaller-bodied apes (that is, gibbons).

3. Most of the Miocene forms thus far discovered are so derived that they are probably not ancestral to *any* living form.

4. One lineage that appears well established relates to *Sivapithecus* from Turkey and Pakistan. This form shows some highly derived facial features similar to the modern orangutan, suggesting a fairly close evolutionary link (Fig. 9-5).

5. Evidence of *definite* **hominins** from the Miocene has not yet been indisputably confirmed. However, exciting new (and not fully studied) finds from Kenya, Ethiopia, and Chad (the latter dating as far back as 7 mya) strongly suggest that hominins diverged sometime in the latter Miocene (see pp. 211–216 for further discussion). As we shall see shortly, the most fundamental feature of the early hominins is the adaptation to bipedal locomotion. In addition, recently discovered Miocene remains

of the first fossils linked closely to gorillas (Suwa et al., 2007) provide further support for a late Miocene divergence (about 10–7 mya) of our closest ape cousins from the hominin line. The only fossil chimpanzee so far discovered is much later in time, and at close to 500,000 years ago (500 kya), is long after the time that hominins split from African apes (McBrearty and Jablonksi, 2005).

Definition of Hominin

The earliest evidence of hominins that has been found dates to the end of the Miocene and mainly includes dental and cranial pieces. But dental features alone don't describe the special features of hominins, and they certainly aren't distinctive of the later stages of human evolution. Modern humans, as well as our most immediate hominin ancestors, are distinguished from the great apes by more obvious features than tooth and jaw dimensions. For example, various scientists have pointed to such distinctive hominin characteristics as bipedal locomotion, large brain size, and toolmaking behavior as being significant (at some stage) in defining what makes a hominin a hominin.

It's important to recognize that not all these characteristics developed simultaneously or at the same pace. In fact, over the last several million years of hominin evolution, quite a different pattern has been evident, in which each of the components (dentition, locomotion, brain size, and toolmaking) have developed at quite different rates. This pattern, in which physiological and behavioral systems evolve at different rates, is called **mosaic evolution**. As we first pointed out in Chapter 1 and will emphasize in this chapter, the single most important defining characteristic for the full course of hominin evolution is **bipedal locomotion**. In the earliest stages of hominin emergence, skeletal evidence indicating bipedal locomotion is the only truly reliable indicator that these fossils were indeed hominins. But in later stages of hominin evolution, other features, especially those relating to brain development and behavior, become highly significant (Fig. 9-6).

WHAT'S IN A NAME?

Throughout this book, we refer to members of the human lineage as hominins (the technical name for members of the tribe Hominini). Most professional paleoanthropologists now prefer this terminology, since it more accurately reflects evolutionary relationships. As we mentioned briefly in Chapter 6, the more traditional classification of hominoids is not as accurate and actually misrepresents key evolutionary relationships.

In the last several years, detailed molecular evidence clearly shows that the great apes do not make up a coherent evolutionary group, sharing a single common ancestor (traditionally classified as pongids and including orangutans, gorillas, chimpanzees, and bonobos). Indeed, the molecular data indicate that the African great apes (gorillas, chimpanzees, and bonobos) are significantly more closely related to humans than is the orangutan. What's more, at an even closer evolutionary level, we now know that chimpanzees and bonobos are yet more closely linked to humans than is the gorilla. As a result of this crucial new information, hominoid classification has been significantly revised to show these more complete relationships, and two further taxonomic levels (subfamily and tribe) have been added (see Fig. 9-7).

We should mention a couple of important ramifications of this new classification. First, it further emphasizes the *very* close evolutionary relationship of humans with African apes and most especially that with chimpanzees and bonobos. Second, the term *hominid*, which has been used for decades to refer to our specific evolutionary lineage (that is, "us", the family of "hominids"), has a quite different meaning in the revised classification; now it refers to *all* great apes and humans together.

mosaic evolution A pattern of evolution in which the rate of evolution in one functional system varies from that in other systems. For example, in hominin evolution, the dental system, locomotor system, and neurological system (especially the brain) all evolved at markedly different rates.

bipedal locomotion Walking on two feet. Walking habitually on two legs is the single most distinctive feature of hominins.

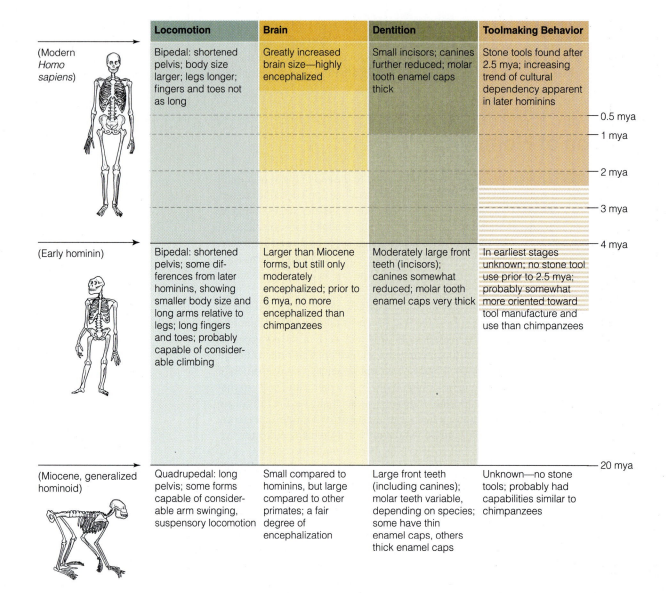

	Locomotion	Brain	Dentition	Toolmaking Behavior
(Modern *Homo sapiens*)	Bipedal: shortened pelvis; body size larger; legs longer; fingers and toes not as long	Greatly increased brain size—highly encephalized	Small incisors; canines further reduced; molar tooth enamel caps thick	Stone tools found after 2.5 mya; increasing trend of cultural dependency apparent in later hominins
(Early hominin)	Bipedal: shortened pelvis; some differences from later hominins, showing smaller body size and long arms relative to legs; long fingers and toes; probably capable of considerable climbing	Larger than Miocene forms, but still only moderately encephalized; prior to 6 mya, no more encephalized than chimpanzees	Moderately large front teeth (incisors); canines somewhat reduced; molar tooth enamel caps very thick	In earliest stages unknown; no stone tool use prior to 2.5 mya; probably somewhat more oriented toward tool manufacture and use than chimpanzees
(Miocene, generalized hominoid)	Quadrupedal: long pelvis; some forms capable of considerable arm swinging, suspensory locomotion	Small compared to hominins, but large compared to other primates; a fair degree of encephalization	Large front teeth (including canines); molar teeth variable, depending on species; some have thin enamel caps, others thick enamel caps	Unknown—no stone tools; probably had capabilities similar to chimpanzees

Time scale markers: 0.5 mya, 1 mya, 2 mya, 3 mya, 4 mya, 20 mya

Figure 9-6

Mosaic evolution of hominin characteristics: a postulated time line.

Unfortunately, during the period of transition to the newer classification scheme, confusion is bound to result. For this reason, we won't use the term *hominid* in this book except where absolutely necessary (for example, in a formal classification; see Fig. 6-9). To avoid confusion, we'll simply refer to the grouping of great apes and humans as "large-bodied hominoids." And when you see the term *hominid* in earlier publications (including earlier editions of this text), simply regard it as the prior term and one we now use synonymously with *hominin*.

The Bipedal Adaptation

In our discussion of primate anatomical trends in Chapter 6, we noted a general tendency in all primates for erect body posture and some bipedalism. Of all living primates, however, efficient bipedalism as the primary form of locomotion is seen *only* in hominins. Functionally, the human mode of locomotion is most clearly shown in our striding gait, where weight is alternately placed on a single fully extended lower limb. This specialized

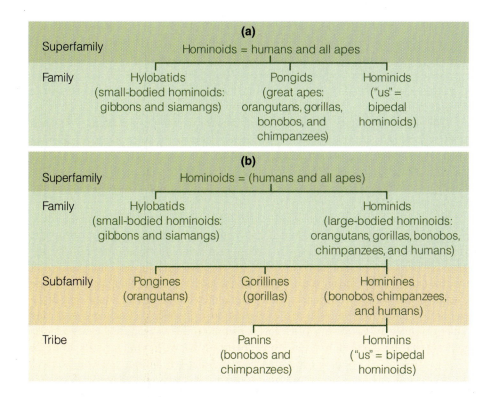

Figure **9-7**

(a) Traditional classification of hominoids. (b) Revised classification of hominoids. Note that two additional levels of classification are added (subfamily and tribe) to show more precisely and more accurately the evolutionary relationships among the apes and humans. In this classification, "hominin" is synonymous with the use of "hominid" in Figure 9-7a.

form of locomotion has developed to a point where energy levels are used to near peak efficiency. Such is not the case in nonhuman primates, who move bipedally with hips and knees bent and maintain balance in a clumsy and inefficient manner.

From a survey of our close primate relatives, it is apparent that while still in the trees, our ancestors were adapted to a fair amount of upper-body erectness. Prosimians, monkeys, and apes all spend considerable time sitting erect while feeding, grooming, or sleeping. Presumably, our early ancestors also displayed similar behavior. What caused these forms to come to the ground and embark on the unique way of life that would eventually lead to humans is still a mystery. Perhaps natural selection favored some Miocene hominoids coming occasionally to the ground to forage for food on the forest floor and forest fringe. In any case, once they were on the ground and away from the immediate safety offered by trees, bipedal locomotion could become a tremendous advantage.

First of all, bipedal locomotion freed the hands for carrying objects and for making and using tools. Such early cultural developments had an even more positive effect on speeding the development of yet more efficient bipedalism—once again emphasizing the dual role of *biocultural* evolution. In addition, in the bipedal stance, animals have a wider view of the surrounding countryside, and in open terrain, early spotting of predators (particularly the large cats, such as lions, leopards, and saber-tooths) would be of critical importance. We know that modern ground-living primates, such as savanna baboons and vervets, occasionally adopt this posture to "look around" when out in open country. It has also been hypothesized that a bipedal stance would more effectively have aided in cooling early hominins while out in the open. In bipeds, less of the body is exposed directly to the sun than in quadrupeds. Moreover, a greater portion of the body is farther from the ground and thus more removed from heat radiating from the ground surface. It would perhaps have been most adaptive to favor such cooling mechanisms if early hominins had adopted activity patterns exposing them in the open during midday. This last supposition is not really possible to test, but if hominins had ranged more freely at midday, they would have avoided competition from more nocturnal predators and scavengers (such as large cats and hyenas).

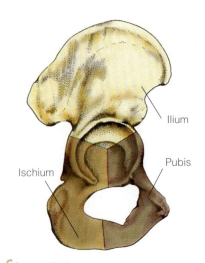

Figure 9-8

The human os coxae, composed of three bones (right side shown).

Ilium

Pubis

Ischium

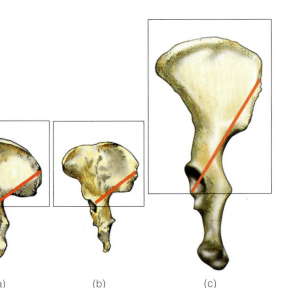

(a)   (b)   (c)

Figure 9-9

Ossa coxae. (a) *Homo sapiens*. (b) Early hominin (*Australopithecus*) from South Africa. (c) Great ape. Note especially the length and breadth of the iliac blade (boxed) and the line of weight transmission (shown in red).

Moreover, bipedal walking is an efficient means of covering long distances, and when large game hunting came into play (several million years after the initial adaptation to ground living), further refinements increasing the efficiency of bipedalism may have been favored. Exactly what initiated the process is difficult to say, but all these factors probably played a role in the adaptation of hominins to their special niche through a special form of locomotion.

Our mode of locomotion is indeed extraordinary, involving, as it does, a unique kind of activity in which "the body, step by step, teeters on the edge of catastrophe" (Napier, 1967, p. 56). The problem is to maintain balance on the "stance" leg while the "swing" leg is off the ground. In fact, during normal walking, both feet are simultaneously on the ground only about 25 percent of the time, and as speed of locomotion increases, this figure becomes even smaller.

Maintaining a stable center of balance in this complex form of locomotion necessitates many drastic structural and functional changes in the basic primate quadrupedal pattern. Functionally, the foot must be altered to act as a stable support instead of a grasping limb. When we walk, our foot is used like a prop, landing on the heel and pushing off on the toes, particularly the big toe. In addition, the leg has become elongated to increase the length of the stride. An efficient bipedal adaptation required further remodeling of the lower limb to allow full extension of the knee and to keep the legs close together during walking, in this way maintaining the center of support directly under the body. Finally, significant changes are seen in the pelvis that permit stable weight transmission from the upper body to the legs and that help further maintain balance.

These major structural changes that are essential for bipedalism are all seen in many of the earliest hominins from Africa (although, to date, no early hominin postcranial bones have been found in central Africa.) In the pelvis, the ilium (the upper bone of the pelvis, shaped like a blade) is shortened top to bottom, which permits more stable weight support in the erect position by lowering the center of gravity (Figs. 9-8 and 9-9). In addition, the ilium is bent backward and downward, thus altering the position of the muscles that attach along the bone. Most important, these muscles increase in size and act to stabilize the hip. One of these muscles (the *gluteus maximus*) also becomes important as an extensor, pulling the thigh back during running, jumping, and climbing.

Other structural changes shown by even the earliest definitively hominin postcranial evidence further confirm the morphological pattern seen in the pelvis. For example, the vertebral column, known from beautifully preserved specimens from South and East Africa, shows the same forward curvature as in modern hominins, bringing the center of support forward. In addition, the lower limb is elongated and is apparently proportionately about as long as in modern humans. Fossil evidence of a knee fragment from South Africa and pieces from East Africa also shows that full extension of this joint was possible, thus allowing the leg to be completely straightened, as when a field goal kicker follows through.

Fossil evidence of early hominin foot structure has come from two sites in South Africa, and especially important are some recently announced new fossils coming from the same individual as the mostly complete skeleton currently being excavated (see p. 223; Clarke and Tobias, 1995). These foot specimens, consisting of four articulating elements from the ankle and big toe, indicate that the heel and longitudinal arch were both well adapted for a bipedal gait. However, paleoanthropologists Ron Clarke and Phillip Tobias also suggest that the large toe was *divergent* and thus unlike the hominin pattern. If the large toe really did possess this (abducted) anatomical position, it most likely would have aided the foot in grasping. In turn, this grasping ability (as in other primates) would have enabled early hominins to more effectively exploit arboreal habitats. Finally, since anatomical remodeling is always constrained by a set of complex functional compromises, a foot highly capable of grasping and climbing is less capable as a stable platform during bipedal locomotion. Some researchers therefore see early hominins as perhaps not quite as fully committed to bipedal locomotion as are later hominins.

Further evidence for evolutionary changes in the foot comes from two sites in East Africa where numerous fossilized elements have been recovered. As in the remains from South Africa, the East African fossils suggest a well-adapted bipedal gait. The arches are developed, but some differences in the ankle also imply that considerable flexibility was possible (again, probably indicating some continued adaptation to climbing). From this evidence, some researchers have recently concluded that many forms of early hominins probably spent considerable time in the trees. What's more, they may not have been quite as efficient bipedally as has previously been suggested. Nevertheless, to this point, most researchers think that *all* the early hominins that have been identified from Africa displayed both **habitual** and **obligate bipedalism** (despite the new evidence from South Africa and the earliest traces from central and East Africa, all of which will require further study). For a review of the anatomical features associated with bipedal locomotion, see Figure 9-10.

Early Hominins from Africa

Now that we've reviewed the early primate fossil record and the basic bipedal anatomical adaptation that best defines hominins, it's time to turn to the fossil record of the earliest hominins themselves.

As you are now well aware, these early hominins come from Africa, and in this chapter we'll cover their comings and goings over a 6-million-year period, 7–1 mya. It's also important to appreciate that these hominins were geographically widely distributed, with fossil discoveries coming from central, East, and South Africa. Paleoanthropologists generally agree that among these early African hominins, there were at least six different genera, which in turn comprised upward of 12 different species. At no time, nor in any other place, were hominins ever as diverse as were these very ancient members of our lineage (Fig. 9-12 on page 214).

As you've already guessed, there are quite a few different hominins from many sites, and you'll find that their formal naming can be difficult to pronounce and not easy to remember. So we'll try to discuss these fossil groups in a way that's easy to understand. Our primary focus will be to organize them by time and by major evolutionary trends. In so doing, we recognize three major groups:

- Pre-australopiths— the earliest and most primitive hominins (7.0–4.4 mya)
- Australopiths—diverse forms, some more primitive, others highly derived (4.2–1.0 mya)
- Early *Homo*—the first members of our genus (2.4–1.4 mya)

PRE-AUSTRALOPITHS (7.0–4.4 MYA)

The oldest and most surprising of these earliest members of the hominin tribe is a cranium discovered at a central African site called Toros-Menalla in the modern nation of Chad (Brunet et al., 2002). Provisional dating using faunal correlation (biostratigraphy;

habitual bipedalism Bipedal locomotion as the form of locomotion shown by hominins most of the time.

obligate bipedalism Bipedalism as the *only* form of hominin terrestrial locomotion. Since major anatomical changes in the spine, pelvis, and lower limb are required for bipedal locomotion, once hominins adapted to this mode of locomotion, other forms of locomotion on the ground became impossible.

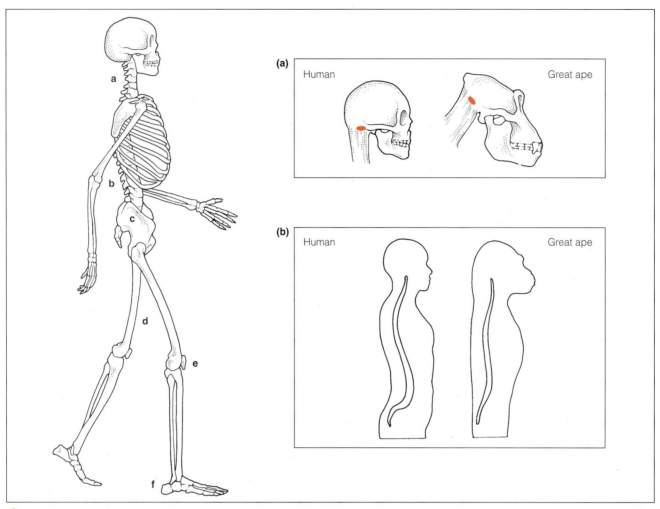

Figure 9-10

Major features of hominin bipedalism. During hominin evolution, several major structural features throughout the body have been reorganized (from that seen in other primates) to facilitate efficient bipedal locomotion. These are illustrated here, beginning with the head and progressing to the foot: (a) The *foramen magnum* (shown in red) is repositioned farther underneath the skull, so that the head is more or less balanced on the spine (and thus requires less robust neck muscles to hold the head upright). (b) The spine has two distinctive curves—a backward (thoracic) one and a forward (lumbar) one—that keep the trunk (and weight) centered above the pelvis. (c) The pelvis is shaped

© Mission Paléoanthropologique Franco-Tchadienne

Figure 9-11

A nearly complete cranium of *Sahelanthropus* from Chad, dating to 7 mya.

see p. 190) suggests a date of nearly 7 mya (Vignaud et al., 2002). Surprisingly, this proposed very early date for this fossil places it at almost 1 million years earlier than *any* of the other proposed early hominins (and close to 3 million years earlier than the oldest well-established hominin discoveries).

The morphology of the fossil is unusual, with a combination of characteristics unlike that found in other early hominins. The braincase is small, estimated at no larger than a modern chimpanzee's (preliminary estimate in the range of 320 to 380 cm^3), but it is massively built, with huge browridges in front, a crest on top, and large muscle attachments in the rear (Fig. 9-11). Yet, combined with these apelike features is a smallish vertical face containing front teeth very unlike an ape's. In fact, the lower face, being more tucked in under the brain vault (and not protruding, as in most other early hominins), is more of a *derived* feature more commonly expressed in much later hominins (especially members of genus *Homo*).

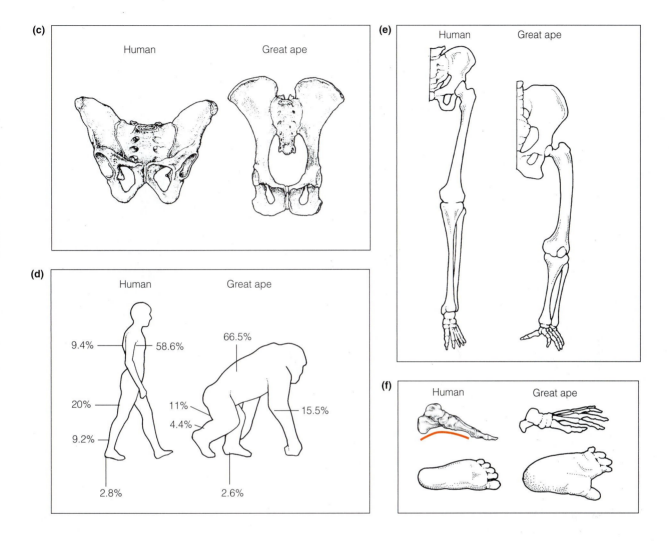

more in the form of a basin to support internal organs; moreover, the ossa coxae (specifically, iliac blades) are shorter and broader, thus stabilizing weight transmission. (d) Lower limbs are elongated, as shown by the proportional lengths of various body segments (e.g., in humans the thigh comprises 20 percent of body height, while in gorillas it comprises only 11 percent). (e) The femur is angled inward, keeping the legs more directly under the body; modified knee anatomy also permits full extension of this joint. (f) The big toe is enlarged and brought in line with the other toes; in addition, a distinctive longitudinal arch forms, helping absorb shock and adding propulsive spring.

In recognition of this unique combination of characteristics, paleoanthropologists have placed the Toros-Menalla remains into a new genus and species of hominin, *Sahelanthropus tchadensis* (Sahel being the region of the southern Sahara in North Africa).

These new finds from Chad have forced an immediate and significant reassessment of early hominin evolution. Two cautionary comments, however, are in order. First, the dating is only approximate, based, as it is, on biostratigraphic correlation with sites in Kenya (1,500 miles to the southeast). The faunal sequences, nevertheless, seem to be clearly bracketed by two very well-dated sequences in Kenya. Second, and perhaps more serious, is the hominin status of the Chad fossil. Given the facial structure and dentition, it is difficult to see how *Sahelanthropus* could be anything but a hominin. However, some researchers (Wolpoff et al., 2002) have raised questions regarding the evolutionary interpretation of *Sahelanthropus*, suggesting that this fossil may represent an ape rather than a hominin. As we have previously said, the best-defining anatomical characteristics of

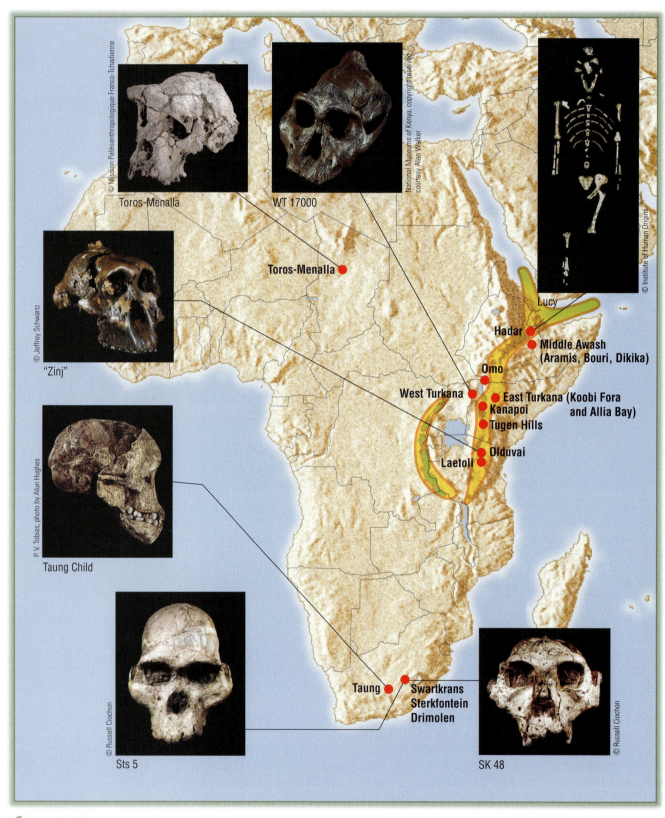

Figure **9-12**

Early hominin finds (pre-australopith, australopith localities).
The Rift Valley is shown in gold.

hominins relate to bipedal locomotion. Unfortunately, no postcranial elements have been recovered from Chad—at least not yet. Consequently, we do not yet know the locomotor behavior of *Sahelanthropus*, and this raises even more fundamental questions: What if further finds show this form not to be bipedal? Should we still consider it a hominin? What, then, are the defining characteristics of our lineage?

About a million years later than *Sahelanthropus*, two other very early hominins have been found at sites in central Kenya in the Tugen Hills and from the Middle Awash area of northeastern Ethiopia. The earlier of these finds (dated by radiometric methods to about 6 mya) comes from the Tugen Hills and includes mostly dental remains, but also some quite complete lower limb bones, the latter interpreted as clearly indicating bipedal locomotion (Senut et al., 2001; Galik et al., 2004; Richmond and Jungers, 2008). Following preliminary analysis of the fossils, the primary researchers have suggested placing these early hominins in a separate genus—*Orrorin*.

The last group of fossil hominins thought to date to the late Miocene (that is, earlier than 5 mya) comes from the Middle Awash in the Afar Triangle of Ethiopia. Radiometric dating places the age of these fossils in the very late Miocene, 5.8–5.2 mya. The fossil remains themselves are very fragmentary. Some of the dental remains resemble some later fossils from the Middle Awash (discussed shortly), and Yohannes Hailie-Selassie, the researcher who first found and described these earlier materials, has provisionally assigned them to the genus *Ardipithecus* (Haile-Selassie et al., 2004; see At a Glance). In addition, some postcranial elements have been preserved, most informatively a toe bone, a phalanx from the middle of the foot (see Appendix A, Fig. A–8). From clues in this bone, Hailie-Selassie concludes that this primate was a well-adapted biped (once again, the best-supporting evidence of hominin status).

From another million years or so later in the geological record in the Middle Awash region, along the banks of the Awash River, a very large and significant assemblage of fossil hominins has been discovered at the Aramis site. Radiometric calibration firmly dates this site at about 4.4 mya.

Fossil remains from Aramis include up to 50 different individuals, and this crucial and quite large fossil assortment includes several dental specimens as well as an upper arm bone (humerus) and some fragmentary cranial remains. Most exciting of all, in 1995, 40 percent of a skeleton was discovered; there are also reports of other partial skeletons from Aramis. However, in all cases, the bones are encased in limestone matrix, thus requiring a long and tedious process to remove the fossils intact from the cement-like material surrounding them. In fact, as of this writing, the Aramis remains (including the skeletons) have not yet been fully described. Nevertheless, details from initial reports are highly suggestive that these remains are, in fact, very early hominins.

First of all, in an Aramis partial cranium, the *foramen magnum* is positioned farther forward in the base of the skull than is the case in quadrupeds (Fig. 9-13). Second, features of the humerus also differ from those seen in quadrupeds, indicating that the Aramis humerus did not function in locomotion to support weight. From these two features, the primary researchers have concluded that the Aramis individuals were *bipedal*. Moreover, initial interpretation of the partial skeleton (while not yet fully cleaned and reported) also suggests obligate bipedalism (Wolpoff, 1999).

Nevertheless, these were clearly quite primitive hominins, displaying an array of characteristics quite distinct from other members of our lineage. These primitive characteristics include flattening of the cranial base and relatively thin enamel caps on the molar teeth. From measurements of the humerus, body weight for one of the individuals is estimated at 42 kg (93 pounds); if this bone comes from a male individual, this weight estimate is very similar to that hypothesized for other early hominins (Table 9-2).

Thus, current conclusions (which will be either unambiguously confirmed or falsified as the skeleton is fully cleaned and studied) interpret the Aramis remains as among the earliest hominins yet known. These individuals, while very primitive hominins, were apparently bipedal, although not necessarily in the same way that later hominins were.

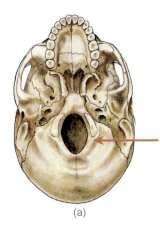

(a)

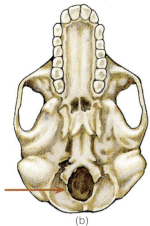

(b)

Figure **9-13**

Position of the *foramen magnum* in (a) a human and (b) a chimpanzee. Note the more forward position in the human cranium.

Table 9-2   Estimated Body Weights and Stature in Plio-Pleistocene Hominins

	Body Weight		Stature	
	Male	**Female**	**Male**	**Female**
A. afarensis	45 kg (99 lb)	29 kg (64 lb)	151 cm (59 in.)	105 cm (41 in.)
A. africanus	41 kg (90 lb)	30 kg (65 lb)	138 cm (54 in.)	115 cm (45 in.)
South African "robust"	40 kg (88 lb)	32 kg (70 lb)	132 cm (52 in.)	110 cm (43 in.)
East African "robust"	49 kg (108 lb)	34 kg (75 lb)	137 cm (54 in.)	124 cm (49 in.)
H. habilis	52 kg (114 lb)	32 kg (70 lb)	157 cm (62 in.)	125 cm (49 in.)

Source: After McHenry, 1992.

Tim White and colleagues (1995) have argued that the fossil hominins from Aramis are so primitive and so different from other early hominins that they should be assigned to a new genus (and, necessarily, a new species as well): *Ardipithecus ramidus*. Most especially, the thin enamel caps on the molars are in dramatic contrast to all other early hominins, who show quite thick enamel.

Another intriguing aspect of all these late Miocene/early Pliocene locales (that is, Tugen Hills, early Middle Awash sites, and Aramis) relates to the ancient environments associated with the suggested earliest of hominins. Rather than the more open grassland savanna habitats so characteristic of most later hominin sites, the environment at all these early locales is more heavily forested. Perhaps we are seeing at Aramis and these other ancient sites the very beginnings of hominin divergence, very soon after the division from the African apes!

EARLIER MORE PRIMITIVE AUSTRALOPITHS (4.2–3.0 MYA)

australopiths A colloquial name referring to a diverse group of Plio-Pleistocene African hominins. They are the most abundant and widely distributed of all early hominins and are also the most completely studied.

The best-known, most widely distributed, and most diverse of the early African hominins are colloquially called **australopiths**. In fact, this diverse and very successful group of hominins is made up of two closely related genera, *Australopithecus* and *Paranthropus*. These hominins have an established time range of over 3 million years, stretching back as

At a Glance
Key Pre-Australopith Discoveries

DATES	REGION	HOMININS	SITES	EVOLUTIONARY SIGNIFICANCE
4.4 mya	East Africa	*Ardipithecus ramidus*	Aramis	Large collection of fossils, including partial skeletons; bipedal, but derived
5.8–5.2 mya		*Ardipithecus*	Middle Awash	Fragmentary, but probably bipedal
~6.0 mya		*Orrorin tugenensis*	Tugen Hills	First hominin with postcranial remains; probably bipedal
~7.0 mya	Central Africa	*Sahelanthropus tchadensis*	Toros-Menalla	Oldest hominin; well-preserved cranium; very small-brained; bipedal?

early as 4.2 mya and not becoming extinct until apparently close to 1 mya—making them the longest-enduring hominin yet documented. In addition, these hominins have been found in all the major geographical areas of Africa that have, to date, produced early hominin finds—namely, South Africa, central Africa (Chad), and East Africa. From all these areas combined, there appears to have been considerable complexity in terms of evolutionary diversity, with numerous species now recognized by most paleoanthropologists.

There are two major subgroups of australopiths, with an earlier group (dated to 4.2–3 mya) composed of at least two different species. These earlier australopiths show several more primitive (ancestral) hominin characteristics than the later australopith group, whose members are more derived, some extremely so. These more derived hominins lived after 2.5 mya and are composed of two different genera, together represented by at least four different species (see Appendix B for a complete listing and more discussion of early hominin fossil finds).

Given the 3-million-year time range as well as quite varied ecological niches, there are numerous intriguing adaptive differences among these varied australopith species. We'll discuss the major adaptations of the various species in a moment. But let's begin by emphasizing those major features that all australopiths share:

1. They are all clearly bipedal (although not necessarily identical to *Homo* in this regard).
2. They all have relatively small brains (at least compared to *Homo*).
3. They all have large teeth, particularly the back teeth, with thick to very thick enamel on the molars.

In short, then, all these australopith species are relatively small-brained, big-toothed bipeds.

The earliest australopiths, dating to 4.2–3.9 mya, come from East Africa at a couple of sites in northern Kenya. Among the fossils finds of these earliest australopiths, a few postcranial pieces clearly indicate that locomotion was *bipedal*. There are, however, a few primitive features in the dentition, including a large canine and a **sectorial** lower first premolar (Fig. 9-14).

Since these particular fossils have initially been interpreted as more primitive than all the later members of the genus, paleoanthropologists have provisionally assigned them to a separate species of *Australopithecus*. This important fossil species is now called *Australopithecus anamensis*, and some researchers suggest that it is a potential ancestor for many later australopiths as well as perhaps early members of the genus *Homo* (White et al., 2006).

Australopithecus afarensis Slightly later and much more complete remains of *Australopithecus* have come from the sites of Hadar (in Ethiopia) and Laetoli (in Tanzania). Much of this material has been known for three decades, and the fossils have been very well studied; indeed, in certain instances, they are quite famous. For example, the Lucy skeleton was discovered at Hadar in 1974, and the Laetoli footprints were first found in 1978. These hominins are classified as members of the species *Australopithecus afarensis*.

Literally thousands of footprints have been found at Laetoli, representing more than 20 different kinds of animals (Pliocene elephants, horses, pigs, giraffes, antelopes, hyenas, and an abundance of hares). Several hominin footprints have also been found, including a trail more than 75 feet long made by at least two—and perhaps three—individuals (Leakey and Hay, 1979; Fig. 9-15). Such discoveries of well-preserved hominin footprints are extremely important in furthering our understanding of human evolution. For the first time, we can make *definite* statements regarding the locomotor pattern and stature of early hominins.

Studies of these impression patterns clearly show that the mode of locomotion of these hominins was bipedal (Day and Wickens, 1980). As we have emphasized, the development of bipedal locomotion is the most important defining characteristic of early

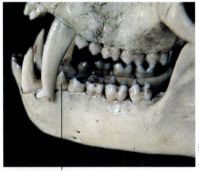

Sectorial lower first premolar

Figure **9-14**

Left lateral view of the teeth of a male patas monkey. Note how the large upper canine shears against the elongated surface of the *sectorial* lower first premolar.

sectorial Adapted for cutting or shearing; among primates, refers to the compressed (side-to-side) first lower premolar, which functions as a shearing surface with the upper canine.

Figure 9-15

Hominin footprint from Laetoli, Tanzania. Note the deep impression of the heel and the large toe (arrow) in line (adducted) with the other toes.

Peter Jones

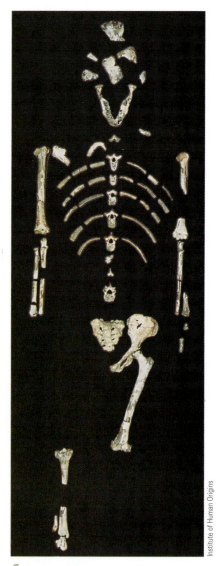

Institute of Human Origins

Figure 9-16

"Lucy," a partial hominin skeleton, discovered at Hadar in 1974. This individual is assigned to *Australopithecus afarensis*.

hominin evolution. Some researchers, however, have concluded that *A. afarensis* was not bipedal in quite the same way that modern humans are. From detailed comparisons with modern humans, estimates of stride length, cadence, and speed of walking have been ascertained, indicating that the Laetoli hominins moved in a slow-moving ("strolling") fashion with a rather short stride.

One extraordinary discovery at Hadar is the Lucy skeleton (Fig. 9-16), found by Don Johanson eroding out of a hillside. This fossil is scientifically designated as Afar Locality (AL) 288-1, but is usually just called Lucy (after the Beatles song "Lucy in the Sky with Diamonds"). Representing almost 40 percent of a skeleton, this is one of the most complete individuals from anywhere in the world for the entire period before about 100,000 years ago.

Because the Laetoli area was covered periodically by ashfalls from nearby volcanic eruptions, accurate dating is possible and has provided dates of 3.7–3.5 mya. Dating from the Hadar region has not proved as straightforward; however, more complete dating calibration using a variety of techniques has determined a range of 3.9–3.0 mya for the hominin discoveries from this area.

Several hundred *A. afarensis* specimens, representing a minimum of 60 individuals (and perhaps as many as 100), have been removed from Laetoli and Hadar. At present, these materials represent the largest *well-studied* collection of early hominins and as such are among the most significant of the hominins discussed in this chapter.

Without question, *A. afarensis* is more primitive than any of the other later australopith fossils from South or East Africa (discussed shortly). By "primitive" we mean that *A. afarensis* is less evolved in any particular direction than are later-occurring hominin species. That is, *A. afarensis* shares more primitive features with other early hominoids and with living great apes than do later hominins, who display more derived characteristics.

For example, the teeth of *A. afarensis* are quite primitive. The canines are often large, pointed teeth. Moreover, the lower first premolar is semisectorial (that is, it provides a shearing surface for the upper canine), and the tooth rows are parallel, even converging somewhat toward the back of the mouth (Fig. 9-17).

The cranial portions that are preserved also display several primitive hominoid characteristics, including a crest in the back as well as several primitive features of the cranial base. Cranial capacity estimates for *A. afarensis* show a mixed pattern when compared with later hominins. A provisional estimate for the one partially complete cranium—apparently a large individual—gives a figure of 500 cm³, but another, even more fragmentary cranium is apparently quite a bit smaller and has been estimated at about 375 cm³ (Holloway, 1983). Thus, for some individuals (males?), *A. afarensis* is well within the range of other australopith species, but others (females?) may have a significantly smaller cranial capacity. However, a detailed depiction of cranial size for *A. afarensis* is not possible at this time; this part of the skeleton is unfortunately too poorly represented. One thing is clear: *A. afarensis* had a small brain, probably averaging for the whole species not much over 420 cm³.

On the other hand, a large assortment of postcranial pieces representing almost all portions of the body of *A. afarenisis* have been found. Initial impressions suggest that relative to lower limbs, the upper limbs are longer than in modern humans (also a primitive hominoid condition). (This statement does not mean that the arms of *A. afarensis* were longer than the legs.) In addition, the wrist, hand, and foot bones show several differences from modern humans (Susman et al., 1985). From such excellent postcranial evidence, stature can now be confidently estimated: *A. afarensis* was a short hominin. From her partial skeleton, Lucy is estimated to be only 3 to 4 feet tall (see Fig. 9-16). However, Lucy—as demonstrated by her pelvis—was probably a female, and there is evidence of larger individuals as well. The most economical hypothesis explaining this variation is that *A. afarensis* was quite sexually dimorphic: The larger individuals are male, and the smaller ones, such as Lucy, are female. Estimates of male stature can be approximated from the larger footprints at Laetoli, inferring a height of not quite 5 feet. If we accept this interpretation, *A. afarensis* was a very sexually dimorphic form indeed. In fact, for overall body size, this species may have been as dimorphic as *any* living primate (that is, as much as gorillas, orangutans, or baboons).

An important new find of a mostly complete infant *A. afarensis* skeleton was announced in 2006 (Fig. 9-18). The discovery was made at the Dikika locale in northeastern Ethiopia, very near the Hadar sites mentioned earlier. What's more, the infant comes from the same geological horizon as Hadar, with the same dating (3.3 mya). Although the initial discovery of the fossil was back in 2000, it has taken several years and thousands of hours of preparation to remove portions of the skeleton from the surrounding cemented matrix (full preparation will likely take several more years; Alemseged et al., 2006).

What makes this find of a 3-year-old infant so remarkable is that for the first time in hominin evolution prior to about 100,000 years ago, we have a very well-preserved immature individual. From the infant's extremely well-preserved teeth, scientists hypothesize that she was female. A comprehensive study of her developmental biology has already begun, and many more revelations are surely in store as the Dikika infant is more completely cleaned and studied. For now, and accounting for her immature age, the skeletal pattern appears to be quite similar to adult *A. afarensis*. What's more, the limb proportions, anatomy of the hands and feet, and shape of the scapula (shoulder blade) reveal a similar "mixed" pattern of locomotion. The foot and lower limb indicate that this infant would have been a terrestrial biped; yet, the shoulder and (curved) fingers suggest that she was also capable of climbing about quite ably in the trees.

What makes *A. afarensis* a hominin? The answer is revealed by its manner of locomotion. From the abundant limb bones recovered from Hadar and those beautiful footprints from Laetoli, we know unequivocally that *A. afarensis* walked bipedally when on the ground. (At present, we do not have nearly such good evidence concerning locomotion for *any* of the earlier hominin finds.) Whether Lucy and her contemporaries still spent considerable time in the trees and just how efficiently they walked have become topics of some controversy. Most researchers, however, agree that *A. afarensis* was an efficient habitual biped while on the ground. These hominins were also clearly *obligate* bipeds, which would have hampered their climbing abilities but would not necessarily have precluded arboreal behavior altogether. As one physical anthropologist has surmised: "One could imagine these diminutive early hominids [called "hominins" in our terminology] making maximum use of *both* terrestrial and arboreal resources in spite of their commitment to exclusive bipedalism when on

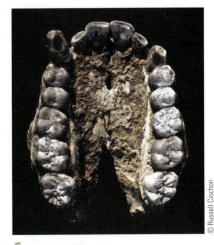

Figure **9-17**

Upper jaw of *Australopithecus afarensis* from Hadar, Ethiopia. (Note the parallel tooth rows and large canines.)

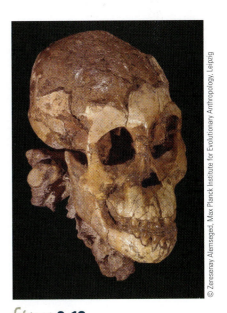

Figure **9-18**

Complete skull with attached vertebral column of the infant skeleton from Dikika, Ethiopia (estimated age, 3.3 mya).

the ground. The contention of a mixed arboreal and terrestrial behavioral repertoire would make adaptive sense of the Hadar australopithecine forelimb, hand, and foot morphology without contradicting the evidence of the pelvis" (Wolpoff, 1983, p. 451).

Australopithecus afarensis is a crucial hominin group. Since it comes after the earliest, poorly known group of pre-australopith hominins, but prior to all later australopiths as well as *Homo*, it is an evolutionary bridge, linking together much of what we assume are the major patterns of early hominin evolution. The fact that there are many well-preserved fossils and that they have been so well studied also adds to the paleoanthropological significance of *A. afarensis*. The consensus among most experts over the last several years has been that *A. afarensis* is a potentially strong candidate as the ancestor of *all* later hominins. Some ongoing analysis has recently challenged this hypothesis (Rak et al., 2007), but at least for the moment, this new major reinterpretation has not been widely accepted. Still, it reminds us that science is an intellectual pursuit that constantly reevaluates older views and seeks to provide more systematic explanations about the world around us. When it comes to understanding human evolution, we should always be aware that things might change. So stay tuned.

LATER MORE DERIVED AUSTRALOPITHS (2.5–1.0 MYA)

Following 2.5 mya, hominins became more diverse in Africa. As they adapted to varied niches, australopiths became considerably more derived. In other words, they show physical changes making them quite distinct from their immediate ancestors.

In fact, there were at least three separate lineages of hominins living (in some cases side by side) between 2.5 and 1 mya. One of these is a later form of *Australopithecus*; another is represented by the highly derived three species that belong to the genus *Paranthropus*; and the last consists of early members of the genus *Homo*. Here we'll discuss *Paranthropus* and *Australopithecus*. *Homo* will be discussed in the next section.

Paranthropus The most derived australopiths are the various members of *Paranthropus*. While all australopiths are big-toothed, *Paranthropus* has the biggest teeth of all, especially as seen in its huge premolars and molars. Along with these massive back teeth, these hominins show a variety of other specializations related to powerful chewing (Fig. 9-19). For example, they all have large, deep lower jaws and large attachments for muscles associated with chewing. In fact, these chewing muscles are so prominent that major anatomical alterations evolved in the architecture of their face and skull vault. In particular, the *Paranthropus* face is flatter than that of any other australopith; the broad cheekbones (to which the masseter muscle attaches) flare out; and a ridge develops on top of the skull (this is called a **sagittal crest**, and it's where the temporal muscle attaches).

All these morphological features suggest that *Paranthropus* was adapted for a diet emphasizing rough vegetable foods. However, this does not mean that these very big-toothed hominins did not also eat a variety of other foods, perhaps including some meat. In fact, sophisticated new chemical analyses of *Paranthropus* teeth suggest that their diet may have been quite varied (Sponheimer et al., 2006).

The first member of the *Paranthropus* evolutionary group (clade) comes from a site in northern Kenya on the west side of Lake Turkana. This key find is that of a nearly complete skull, called the "Black Skull" (owing to chemical staining during fossilization), and it dates to approximately 2.5 mya (Fig. 9-20). This skull, with a cranial capacity of only 410 cm³, is among the smallest for any hominin known, and it has other primitive traits reminiscent of *A. afarensis*. For example, there's a compound crest in the back of the skull, the upper face projects considerably, and the upper dental row converges in back (Kimbel et al., 1988).

But here's what makes the Black Skull so fascinating: Mixed into this array of distinctively primitive traits are a host of derived ones that link it to other members of the robust group (including a broad face, a very large palate, and a large area for the back teeth). This

sagittal crest A ridge of bone that runs down the middle of the cranium like a short Mohawk. This serves as the attachment for the large temporal muscles, indicating strong chewing.

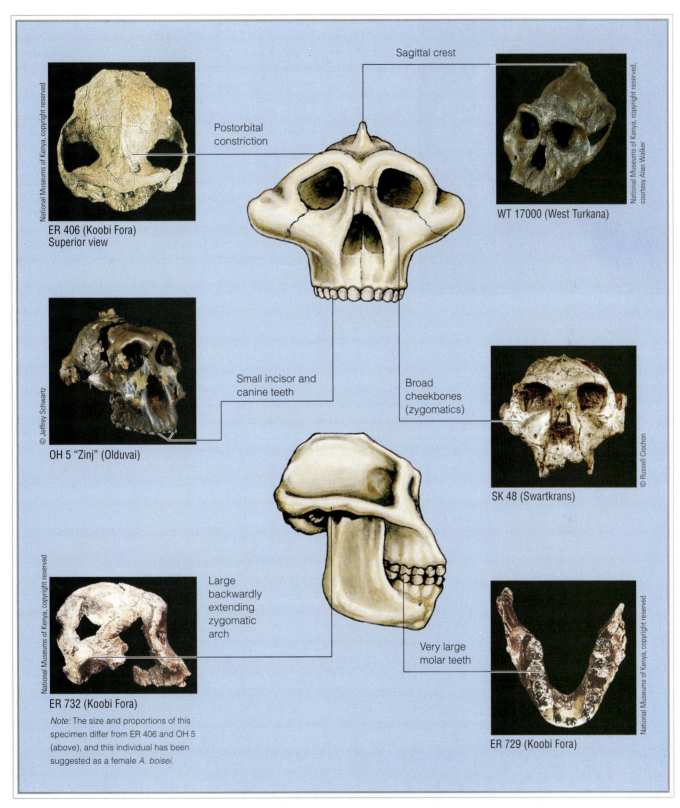

Sagittal crest

Postorbital constriction

ER 406 (Koobi Fora)
Superior view

WT 17000 (West Turkana)

Small incisor and canine teeth

OH 5 "Zinj" (Olduvai)

Broad cheekbones (zygomatics)

SK 48 (Swartkrans)

Large backwardly extending zygomatic arch

Very large molar teeth

ER 732 (Koobi Fora)

Note: The size and proportions of this specimen differ from ER 406 and OH 5 (above), and this individual has been suggested as a female *A. boisei.*

ER 729 (Koobi Fora)

Figure **9-19**

Morphology and variation of the robust australopiths (*Paranthropus*). (Note both typical features and range of variation as shown in different specimens.)

Figure 9-20

The "Black Skull," discovered at West Lake Turkana. This specimen is usually assigned to *Paranthropus aethiopicus*. It's called the Black Skull due to its dark color from the fossilization (mineralization) process.

© Russell Ciochon

mosaic of features seems to place this individual between earlier *A. afarensis* on the one hand and the later robust *Paranthropus* species on the other. Because of its unique position in hominin evolution, the Black Skull (and the population it represents) has been placed in a new species, *Paranthropus aethiopicus*.

Around 2 mya, different varieties of even more derived members of the *Paranthropus* lineage were on the scene in East Africa. As well documented by finds dated after 2 mya from Olduvai and East Turkana, *Paranthropus* continues to have relatively small cranial capacities (ranging from 510 to 530 cm^3) and very large, broad faces with massive back teeth and lower jaws. The larger (probably male) individuals also show that characteristic raised ridge (sagittal crest) along the midline of the cranium. Females are not as large or as robust as the males, indicating a fair degree of sexual dimorphism. In any case, the East African *Paranthropus* individuals are all extremely robust in terms of their teeth and jaws—although in overall body size they are much like other australoptiths (see Table 9-2). Since these somewhat later East African *Paranthropus** fossils are so robust, they are usually placed in their own separate species, *Paranthropus boisei*.

Paranthropus fossils have also been found at several sites in South Africa. However, in South Africa, owing to more complex geology, precise dating and determination of clear archaeological context are much more difficult than is the case in East Africa. Based on less precise dating methods (such as paleomagnetism; see p. 192), *Paranthropus* in South Africa existed about 2–1 mya.

Paranthropus in South Africa is very similar to its close cousin in East Africa, but its teeth and jaws were not as large. As a result, paleoanthropologists prefer to regard South African *Paranthropus* as a distinct species—one called *Paranthropus robustus*.

What became of *Paranthropus*? After 1 mya, these hominins seem to vanish without descendants. Nevertheless, we should be careful not to think of them as "failures." After all, they lasted for 1½ million years, during which time they expanded over a considerable area of sub-Saharan Africa. Moreover, while their extreme dental/chewing adaptations may seem peculiar to us, it was a fascinating "evolutionary experiment" in hominin evolution. And it was an innovation that worked for a long time. Still, these big-toothed cousins of ours did eventually die out. It remains to us, the descendants of another hominin lineage, to find their fossils, study them, and ponder what these creatures were like.

Later *Australopithecus* (*Australopithecus africanus*) No *Australopithecus* fossils have been found at East African sites more recent than 3 mya. As you know, their close *Paranthropus* kin were doing quite well during this time. Whether *Australopithecus* actually did become extinct in East Africa following 3 mya or whether we just haven't yet found their fossils is impossible to say.

South Africa, however, is another story. A very well-known *Australopithecus* species has been found at four sites in southernmost Africa, in a couple of cases in limestone caves very close to where *Paranthropus* fossils have also been found.

In fact, the very first early hominin discovery from Africa (indeed, from *anywhere*) came from the Taung site back in 1924. The story of the discovery of the beautifully preserved child's skull from Taung is a fascinating tale (Fig. 9-21). When first published in 1925 by a young anatomist named Raymond Dart (Fig. 9-22), most experts were unimpressed. They thought Africa to be an unlikely place for the origins of hominins. These skeptics, who had been long focused on European and Asian hominin finds, were initially unprepared to acknowledge Africa's central place in human evolution. Only years later, following many more African discoveries from other sites, did professional opinion shift.

---

*Note that these later East African *Paranthropus* finds are at least 500,000 years later than the earlier species (*P. aethiopicus*, exemplified by the Black Skull).

With this admittedly slow scientific awareness came the eventual consensus that Taung (which Dart classified as *Australopithecus africanus*) was indeed an ancient hominin.

Like other australopiths, the "Taung baby" and other *A. africanus* individuals (Fig 9-23) were small-brained, with an adult cranial capacity of about 440 cm³. They were also big-toothed, although not as extremely so as in *Paranthropus*. Moreover, from very well-preserved postcranial remains from Sterkfontein, we know that they also were well-adapted bipeds. The ongoing excavation of a remarkably complete skeleton at Sterkfontein (Fig. 9-24) should tell us about *A. africanus*' locomotion, body size and proportions, and much more.

The precise dating of *A. africanus*, as with other South African hominins, has been disputed. Over the last several years, it's been assumed that this species existed as far back as 3.3 mya. However, the most recent analysis suggests that *A. africanus* lived approximately between 2.5 and 2.0 mya (Walker et al., 2006). In other words, *A. africanus* overlapped in time considerably with both *Paranthropus* and with early members of the genus *Homo* (Fig. 9-25).

EARLY *HOMO* (2.4–1.4 MYA)

In addition to the australopith remains, there's another largely contemporaneous hominin that is quite distinctive. In fact, as best documented by fossil discoveries from Olduvai and East Turkana, these materials have been assigned to the genus *Homo*—and thus are different from all species assigned to either *Australopithecus* or *Paranthropus*.

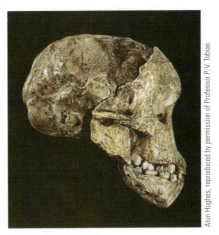

Figure 9-21

The Taung child's skull, discovered in 1924. There is a fossilized endocast of the brain in back, with the face and lower jaw in front.

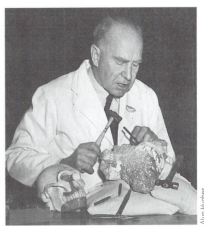

Figure 9-22

Raymond Dart, shown working in his laboratory.

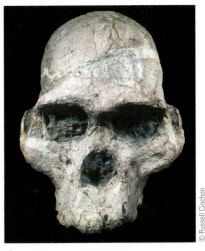

Figure 9-23

Australopithecus africanus adult cranium from Sterkfontein.

Figure 9-24

Paleoanthropologist Ronald Clarke carefully excavates a 2-million-year-old skeleton from the limestone matrix at Sterkfontein cave. Clearly seen are the cranium (with articulated mandible) and the upper arm bone.

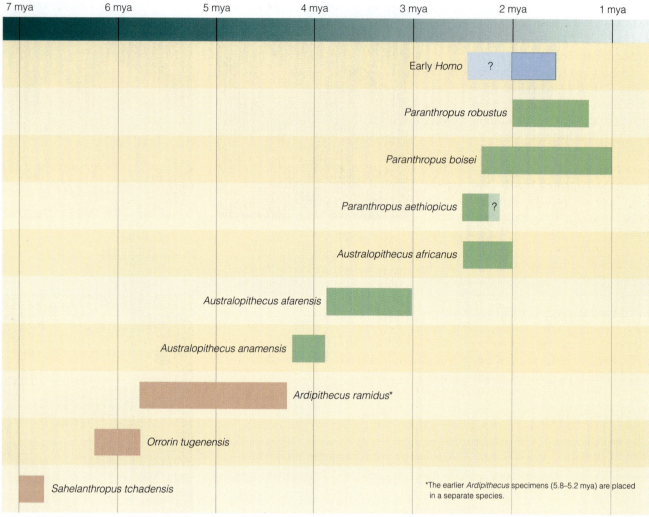

7 mya   6 mya   5 mya   4 mya   3 mya   2 mya   1 mya

Early *Homo*   ?

Paranthropus robustus

Paranthropus boisei

Paranthropus aethiopicus   ?

Australopithecus africanus

Australopithecus afarensis

Australopithecus anamensis

*Ardipithecus ramidus**

Orrorin tugenensis

Sahelanthropus tchadensis

*The earlier *Ardipithecus* specimens (5.8–5.2 mya) are placed in a separate species.

Figure 9-25

Time line of early African hominins. Note that most dates are approximations. Question marks indicate those estimates that are most tentative.

The earliest appearance of genus *Homo* in East Africa may be as ancient as that of the robust australopiths. (As we have discussed, the Black Skull from West Turkana has been dated to approximately 2.5 mya.) Discoveries in the 1990s from central Kenya and from the Hadar area of Ethiopia suggest that early *Homo* was present in East Africa by 2.4–2.3 mya.

The presence of a Plio-Pleistocene hominin with a significantly larger brain than seen in australopiths was first suggested by Louis Leakey in the early 1960s on the basis of fragmentary remains found at Olduvai Gorge. Leakey and his colleagues gave a new species designation to these fossil remains, naming them *Homo habilis*. There may, in fact, have been more than one species of *Homo* living in Africa during the Plio-Pleistocene. So, more generally, we'll refer to them all as "early *Homo*." The species *Homo habilis* refers particularly to those early *Homo* fossils from Olduvai.

The *Homo habilis* material at Olduvai dates to about 1.8 mya, but due to the fragmentary nature of the fossil remains, evolutionary interpretations have been difficult. The most immediately obvious feature distinguishing the *H. habilis* material from the australopiths is cranial size. For all the measurable early *Homo* skulls, the estimated average cranial capacity is 631 cm^3, compared to 520 cm^3 for all measurable robust australopiths and 442 cm^3 for the less robust species (McHenry, 1988; see Table 9-3). Early *Homo*, therefore, shows an increase in cranial size of about 20 percent over the larger of the australopiths and an even greater increase over some of the smaller-brained forms. In their initial description of *H. habilis*, Leakey and his associates also pointed to differences from australopiths in cranial shape and in tooth proportions (with early members of genus *Homo* showing larger front teeth relative to back teeth and narrower premolars).

The naming of this fossil material as *Homo habilis* ("handy man") was meaningful from two perspectives. First of all, Leakey argued that members of this group were the early Olduvai toolmakers; this view is still widely held, although it's difficult to prove. Second, and most significantly, by calling this group *Homo*, Leakey was arguing for at least *two separate branches* of hominin evolution in the Plio-Pleistocene. Clearly, only one could be on the main branch eventually leading to *Homo sapiens*. By labeling this new group *Homo* rather than *Australopithecus*, Leakey was guessing that he had found our ancestors.

Because the initial evidence was so fragmentary, most paleoanthropologists were reluctant to accept *H. habilis* as a valid species distinct from *all* australopiths. Later discoveries, especially those from Lake Turkana, of better-preserved fossils have shed further light on early *Homo* in the Plio-Pleistocene.[*] The most important of this additional material is a nearly complete cranium (Fig. 9-26). With a cranial capacity of 775 cm^3, this individual is well outside the known range for australopiths and actually overlaps the lower boundary for later species of *Homo* (that is, *Homo erectus*, discussed in the next chapter). In addition, the shape of the skull vault is in many respects unlike that of australopiths. However, the face is still quite robust (Walker, 1976), and the fragments of tooth crowns that are preserved indicate that the back teeth in this individual were quite large.[†] The East Turkana early *Homo* material is generally contemporaneous with the Olduvai remains. The oldest date back to about 1.8 mya, but a newly discovered specimen dates to as recently as 1.44 mya, making it by far the latest surviving early *Homo* fossil yet found (Spoor et al., 2007). In fact, this discovery indicates that a species of early *Homo* coexisted in East Africa for several hundred thousand years with *Homo erectus* (with both species living in the exact same area on the eastern side of Lake Turkana). This new evidence raises numerous fascinating questions regarding how two closely related species existed for so long in the same region.

Table 9-3 **Estimated Cranial Capacities in Early Hominins with Comparable Data for Modern Great Apes and Humans**

Hominin	Cranial Capacity Range (cm³)	Average(s) (cm³)
Early Hominins		
Sahelanthropus		~350
Ardipithecus	Not presently known	Not presently known
Australopithecus afarensis		420
Later australopiths		410–530
Early members of genus *Homo*		631
Contemporary Hominoids		
Human	1150–1750	1330
Chimpanzee	285–500	395
Gorilla	340–752	506
Orangutan	276–540	411
Bonobo		350

---

[*]Many of the early *Homo* fossils from East Turkana are classified by paleoanthropologists into a different species (here called *Homo rudolfensis*) from those found at Olduvai (see Appendix B).

[†]In fact, some researchers have suggested that all these "early *Homo*" fossils are better classified as *Australopithecus* (Wood and Collard, 1999a).

Figure **9-26**

A nearly complete early *Homo* cranium from East Lake Turkana (ER 1470), one of the most important single fossil hominin discoveries from East Africa. (a) Frontal view. (b) Lateral view.

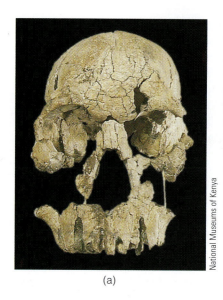

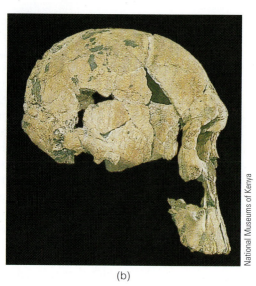

(a)   (b)

As in East Africa, early members of the genus *Homo* have also been found in South Africa, apparently living contemporaneously with australopiths. At both Sterkfontein and Swartkrans, fragmentary remains have been recognized as most likely belonging to *Homo* (Fig. 9-27).

On the basis of evidence from Olduvai and East Turkana, we can reasonably postulate that one or more species of early *Homo* were present in East Africa probably by 2.4 mya, developing in parallel with at least two different lines of australopiths. These three hominin lines lived contemporaneously for a minimum of 1 million years, after which both australopith lineages apparently disappeared forever. At the same time, the early *Homo* line was probably evolving into one or more species of later *Homo*.

The Lower Paleolithic Period: Emergence of Human Culture

As we've seen, the oldest identifiable stone tools date to 2.6 mya, and it is from this evidence that archaeologists determine the beginning of the Lower Paleolithic period. The two major Lower Paleolithic stone tool industries or tool complexes are the Oldowan, which spans roughly 2.6–1.4 mya, and the **Acheulian**, which dates to 1.4–0.2 mya. This section describes the Oldowan tool industry. We'll consider the Acheulian and the end of the Lower Paleolithic in Chapter 10.

The name Oldowan was coined decades ago by Louis and Mary Leakey to describe early stone tools and archaeological sites found at Olduvai Gorge, Tanzania (see Chapter 8, pp. 197-199). Subsequent research elsewhere in East Africa discovered Oldowan sites that are more than half a million years older than the oldest Olduvai Gorge locations. These Oldowan assemblages demonstrate that by 2.6 mya, hominins were already inventing and adopting cultural, rather than purely biological, means of dealing with the world around them.

The meager Oldowan archaeological evidence (Fig 9-28) may seem unremarkable, especially when you consider that the cultural changes it reflects occurred so slowly that they would have been virtually unnoticeable to the Oldowan tool users themselves. Nevertheless, this seemingly insignificant beginning was profoundly important to the development of humans. As Thomas Plummer (2004, p.118) recently observed: "The

Acheulian (ash´-oo-lay-en) Pertaining to a stone tool industry from the Lower and Middle Pleistocene; characterized by a large proportion of bifacial tools (flaked on both sides). Acheulian tool kits are common in Africa, southwest Asia, and western Europe, but they're thought to be less common elsewhere. Also spelled Acheulean.

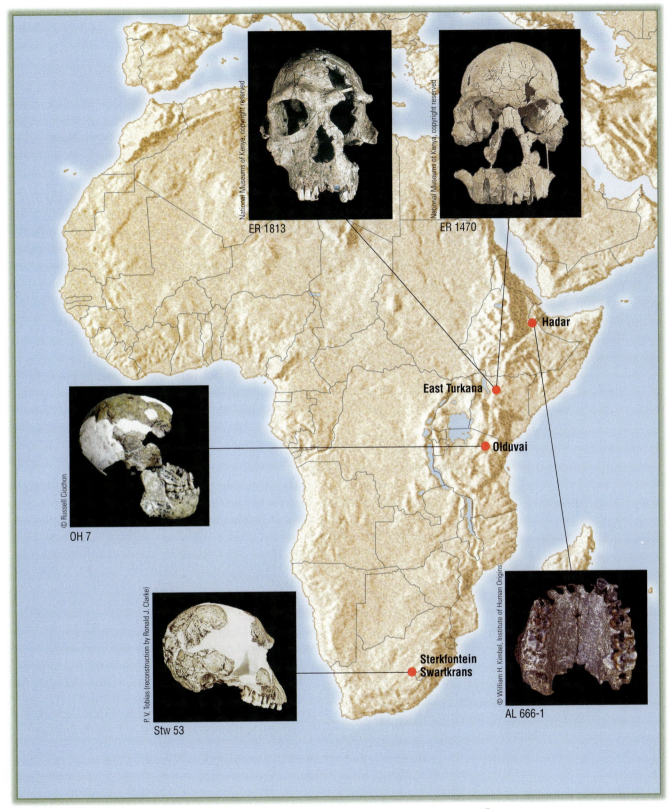

ER 1813

ER 1470

Hadar

East Turkana

OH 7

Olduvai

Stw 53

Sterkfontein
Swartkrans

AL 666-1

Figure 9-27

Early *Homo* fossil finds.

Barry Lewis

Figure **9-28**

The Oldowan assemblage consisted of a few simple stone tools, mostly flakes, choppers, cores, and hammerstones.

appearance of Oldowan sites ca. 2.6 million years ago . . . may reflect one of the most important adaptive shifts in human evolution. Stone artifact manufacture, large mammal butchery, and novel transport and discard behaviors led to the accumulation of the first recognized archaeological debris." These small steps also created a new phenomenon—the archaeological record, the source of the only direct evidence by which researchers can understand the cultural side of our biocultural evolution.

Oldowan tools (see Fig. 9-28) are extremely rudimentary compared with the simplest known modern human technology. Assemblages mostly consist of stone flakes, which were used for cutting; hammerstones, used as the name implies; core tools such as choppers, which show considerable battering on their edges; and stone cores, which were used only as a source of flakes. These early hominins may have also made bone and wooden tools, but such implements have not survived in the archaeological record.

Most Oldowan stone tools were made by the **"hard hammer" percussion** method (Fig. 9-29), which, as the name implies, means that these toolmakers simply took one rock and smashed it with another rock until they got the sharp flakes or cutting edge they wanted. The resulting tools typically owe most of their shape or form to that of the original pebble or cobble from which they were made. This pattern begins to change during the Acheulian, when we find tools that clearly are the result of the toolmakers sharing a common target design they wished to produce.

Compared with most hunter-gatherer tool kits from, say, 20,000 years ago, Oldowan tools were of a generalized nature— where any given tool might serve several tasks. They were also relatively expedient tools, which means that they tended to be made when they were needed, used, and then discarded. Expedient tools are the opposite of curated tools, which are made, used, and kept ("curated") in anticipation of future use. The overall trend, as we shall see in later chapters, is for human tools to become both more specialized and more curated, but it took a long time for this trend to be measurable in the archaeological record. An important exception can be found in areas where suitable stones for tools do not occur naturally. In these cases, the available archaeological evidence suggests that Early Pleistocene hominins carried stones as much as 6 miles from their source areas.

Oldowan tools are properly viewed as the oldest tools that archaeologists can reliably *identify*. Our knowledge of the beginnings of human toolmaking is complicated greatly by the rudimentary nature of the earliest tools and by factors of preservation that removed wooden and other organic tools from the archaeological record. It is reasonable to anticipate that early hominins were tool users for thousands, if not hundreds of thousands, of years before the oldest identified Oldowan stone tools were made and used (see Harris and Capaldo, 1993).

The earliest hominin fossils that are directly associated with Oldowan stone tools are those of early *Homo*. Although it is possible that *Australopithecus* or *Paranthropus* may have been tool users, no Oldowan artifacts are, as yet, definitely associated solely with their remains. Even at Bouri, Ethiopia, the evidence of *Australopithecus* tool use is thus far only circumstantial.

So what did Lower Paleolithic hominins use Oldowan tools to do? They are best described as "tool-assisted" gatherers and meat scavengers. We can be reasonably certain

"hard hammer" percussion A direct percussion method of making stone tools that uses one rock as a hammer to knock flakes from another rock that serves as a core.

that they were not hunters of big game, nor did their technology confer more than a minor competitive advantage over bigger, more aggressive savanna animals. If anything, these hominins were more equipped physically to be prey rather than hunter. Our earliest direct ancestors may have been inching their way up the food chain, but to get there, thousands of generations spent time waiting to pick over what was left after the real predators and scavengers ate their fill.

The Oldowan archaeological record is a controversial area of anthropological research. We are confident that early hominins created the earliest archaeological evidence of human cultural behavior. But which hominins and why? How did they use the tools they made? Were they hunter, prey, or both? We have answers to these questions, but all too often, they are slippery, chameleon-like ones that can change dramatically with the next fossil find or archaeological site excavation. It is a frustrating but fascinating area of science.

Figure **9-29**
Hard hammer percussion.

Interpretations: What Does It All Mean?

By this time, you may think that anthropologists are obsessed with finding small scraps buried in the ground and then assigning them confusing taxonomic labels impossible to remember. But it's important to realize that the collection of all the basic fossil data is the foundation of human evolutionary research. Without fossils and artifacts, our speculations would be largely hollow—and most certainly not scientifically testable. Several large, ongoing paleoanthropological projects are now collecting additional data in an attempt to answer more of the perplexing questions about our evolutionary history.

Following the discovery of fossil hominins, the fossils must be cleaned and usually substantially reconstructed—a process that can take several years. From their first discovery, the individual specimens are given numbers (see Fig. 9-19) to keep the designations neutral and to make reference to each individual fossil as clear as possible. The formal naming of finds as *Australopithecus*, *Paranthropus*, or *Homo habilis* should come much later, since it involves a lengthy series of complex interpretations. Assigning generic and specific names to fossil finds is more than just a convenience; when we attach a particular label, such as *A. africanus*, to a particular fossil, we should be fully aware of the biological implications of such an interpretation.

From the time that early hominin sites are first located until the eventual interpretation of evolutionary patterns, several steps take place. Ideally, they should follow a logical order, for if interpretations are made too hastily, they confuse important issues for many years. Here's a reasonable sequence:

1. Selecting and surveying sites
2. Excavating sites and recovering fossil hominins and artifacts
3. Designating individual finds with specimen numbers for clear reference
4. Cleaning, preparing, studying, and describing fossils and artifacts
5. Comparing with other fossil and archaeological material—in a chronological framework if possible
6. Comparing fossil variation with known ranges of variation in closely related groups of living primates and analyzing ancestral and derived characteristics
7. Comparing archaeological evidence with that of contemporary hominin sites in other regions and interpreting cultural similarities and differences
8. Assigning taxonomic names to fossil material

But the task of interpretation still isn't complete, for what we really want to know in the long run is what happened to the populations represented by the fossil remains. In looking at the fossil hominin record, we're actually looking for our ancestors. In the process of eventually determining those populations that are our most likely antecedents, we may conclude that some hominins are on evolutionary side branches. If this conclusion is

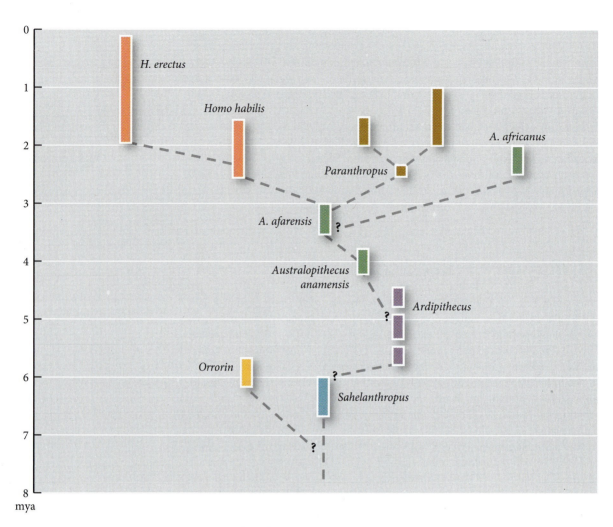

Figure 9-30

A tentative early hominin phylogeny. Note the numerous question marks, which indicate continuing uncertainty regarding evolutionary relationships.

accurate, those hominins necessarily must have become extinct. It's both interesting and relevant to us as hominins to try to find out what influenced some earlier members of our lineage to continue evolving while others died out.

Although a clear evolutionary picture is not yet possible for organizing all the early hominins discussed in this chapter, there are some general patterns that for now make good sense (Fig 9-30). New finds may of course require serious alterations to this scheme. Science can be exciting but can also be frustrating to many in the general public looking for simple answers to complex questions. For well-informed students of human evolution, it's most important to grasp the basic principles of paleoanthropology and *how* interpretations are made and *why* they sometimes must be revised. This way you'll be prepared for whatever shows up tomorrow.

Seeing the Big Picture: Adaptive Patterns of Early African Hominins

As you are by now aware, there are several different African hominin genera and certainly lots of species. This in itself is interesting. Speciation was occurring quite frequently among the various lineages of early hominins—more frequently, in fact, than among later hominins. What explains this pattern?

Evidence has been accumulating at a furious pace in the last decade, but it's still far from complete. What's clear is that we'll never have anything approaching a complete record of early hominin evolution, so significant gaps will remain. After all, we're able to discover hominins only in those special environmental contexts where fossilization was likely. All the other potential habitats they might have exploited are now invisible to us.

Still, patterns are emerging from the fascinating data we do have. First, it appears that early hominin species (pre-australopiths, *Australopithecus*, *Paranthropus*, and early *Homo*) all had restricted ranges. It's therefore likely that each hominin species exploited a relatively small area and could easily have become separated from other populations of its own species. So genetic drift (and to some extent natural selection) could have led to rapid genetic divergence and eventual speciation.

Second, most of these species appear to be at least partially tied to arboreal habitats, although there's disagreement on this point regarding early *Homo* (see Wood and Collard, 1999b; Foley 2002). Also, robust forms (*Paranthropus*) were probably somewhat less arboreal than pre-australopiths or *Australopithecus*. These very big-toothed hominins apparently concentrated at least in part on a diet of coarse, fibrous plant foods, such as roots. Exploiting such resources may have routinely taken these hominins farther away from the trees than their dentally smaller—and perhaps more omnivorous—cousins.

Third, except for some early *Homo* individuals, there's very little in the way of an evolutionary trend of increased body size or of markedly greater encephalization. Beginning with *Sahelanthropus*, brain size was no more than that in chimpanzees—although when controlling for body size, this earliest of all known hominins may have had a proportionately larger brain than any living ape. Close to 6 million years later (that is, the time of the last surviving australopith species), relative brain size increased by no more than 10 to 15 percent. Perhaps tied to this relative stasis in brain capacity, there's no absolute association of any of these hominins with patterned stone tool manufacture.

Although conclusions are becoming increasingly controversial, for the moment, early *Homo* appears to be a partial exception. This group shows both increased encephalization and numerous occurrences of likely association with stone tools (though at many of the sites, australopith fossils were *also* found).

Lastly, all of these early African hominins show an accelerated developmental pattern (similar to that seen in African apes), one quite different from the *delayed* developmental pattern characteristic of *Homo sapiens* (and our immediate precursors). This apelike development is also seen in some early *Homo* individuals (Wood and Collard, 1999a). Rates of development can be accurately reconstructed by examining dental growth markers (Bromage and Dean, 1985), and these data may provide a crucial window into understanding this early stage of hominin evolution.

These African hominin predecessors were rather small, able bipeds, but still closely tied to arboreal and climbing niches. They had fairly small brains and, compared to later *Homo*, matured rapidly. Some of them were the earliest known hominin tool users. It would take a major biocultural evolutionary jump to push one of their descendants in a more human direction. For the next chapter in this more human saga, read on.

Summary

Our earliest primate relatives probably diverged from other mammals prior to 65 mya. The first good evidence of prosimian forebears comes much later, from geological beds dating to the Eocene, or about 50 mya. The earliest well-dated anthropoid evidence discovered to this point comes from about 37 mya.

Our closest primate ancestors, early hominoids, had a highly successful adaptive radiation during most of the Miocene (23–7 mya), and it was to this time that we can trace the origins of all apes as well as our own hominin lineage.

As a text about human evolution, we naturally concentrate most on the hominin fossil record. The earliest members of our evolutionary group date as far back as 7 mya. For the next 5 million years, at least six different hominin genera and upward of 12 species have been identified from the fossil record. At least one of these hominins became a tool user between 2.5 and 3.0 mya. This change was so fundamental that our subsequent evolution turned in a completely new direction, to one that is both biological and cultural.

We can organize these fascinating early African hominins into three major groupings:

Pre-australopiths (7.0–4.4 mya)
>   Including three genera of very early, and still primitive, hominins (*Sahelanthropus*, *Orrorin*, and *Ardipithecus*)

Australopiths (4.2–1.0 mya)
>   Early, more primitive australopith species (4.2–3.0 mya), including *Australopithecus anamensis* and *Australopithecus afarenisis*

>   Later, more derived australopith species (2.5–1.0 mya), including two genera (*Paranthropus* and a later species of *Australopithecus*)

Early *Homo* (2.4–1.4 mya)
>   The first members of our genus, who around 2 mya likely diverged into more than one species; at least one of these species is considered the most likely early hominin tool user

What's Important   Key Early Hominin Fossil Discoveries from Africa

Dates	Hominins	Sites/Regions	The Big Picture
1.8–1.4 mya	Early *Homo*	Olduvai; E. Turkana (E. Africa)	Bigger-brained; possible ancestor of later *Homo*
2.5–2.0 mya	Later *Australopithecus* (*A. africanus*)	Taung; Sterkfontein (S. Africa)	Quite derived; likely evolutionary dead end
2.0–1.0 mya	Later *Paranthropus*	Several sites (E. and S. Africa)	Highly derived; very likely evolutionary dead end
2.4 mya	*Paranthropus aethiopicus*	W. Turkana (E. Africa)	Earliest robust australopith; likely ancestor of later *Paranthropus*
3.6–3.0 mya	*Australopithecus afarensis*	Laetoli; Hadar (E. Africa)	Many fossils; very well studied; earliest well-documented biped; possible ancestor of all later hominins
4.4 mya	*Ardipithecus ramidus*	Aramis (E. Africa)	Many fossils; not yet well studied; bipedal, but likely quite derived; any likely ancestral relationship to later hominins not yet possible to say
~7.0 mya	*Sahelanthropus*	Toros-Menalla (Central Africa)	The earliest hominin; bipedal?

Critical Thinking Questions

1. In what ways are the remains of *Sahelanthropus* and *Ardipithecus* primitive? How do we know that these forms are hominins? How sure are we?
2. Assume that you are in the laboratory analyzing the "Lucy" *A. afarensis* skeleton. You also have complete skeletons from a chimpanzee and a modern human. (a) Which parts of the Lucy skeleton are more similar to the chimpanzee? Which are more similar to the human? (b) Which parts of the Lucy skeleton are most informative?
3. Discuss the first thing you would do if you found an early hominin fossil and were responsible for its formal description and publication. What would you include in your publication?
4. Discuss two current disputes regarding taxonomic issues concerning early hominins. Try to give support for alternative positions.
5. What is a phylogeny? Construct one for early hominins (7.0–1.0 mya). Make sure you can describe what conclusions your scheme makes. Also, try to defend it.
6. The oldest identified hominin tools are roughly 2.6 million years old. Why didn't Plio-Pleistocene hominins become toolmakers before, say, 3 mya? Why did they become toolmakers at all?

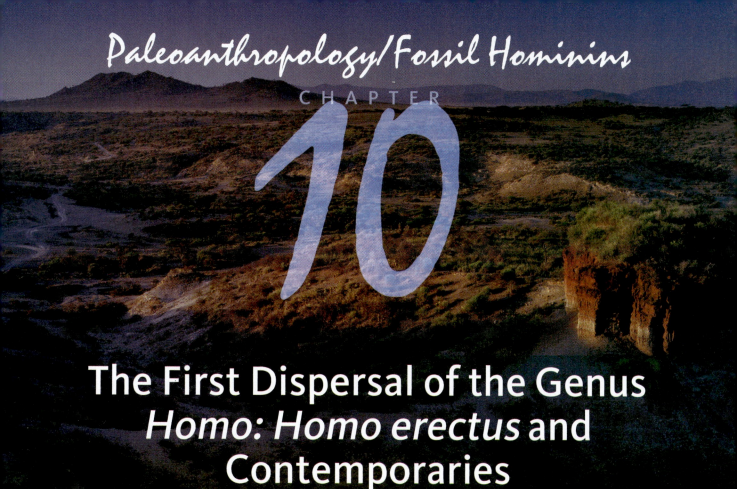

Paleoanthropology/Fossil Hominins

CHAPTER

10

The First Dispersal of the Genus *Homo: Homo erectus* and Contemporaries

O U T L I N E

Focus Question

Who were the first members of the human family to disperse out of Africa, and what were they like (behaviorally and anatomically)?

 Click!

Go to the following media for interactive activities and exercises on topics covered in this chapter:

- Online Virtual Laboratories for Physical Anthropology, Version 4.0
- Hominid Fossils: An Interactive Atlas CD-ROM

Introduction

Today it's estimated that upward of 1 million people daily cross national borders. Some individuals travel for business, others for pleasure, and others to find new homes. Regardless, it seems that modern humans have wanderlust—a desire to see distant places. Our most distant hominin ancestors were essentially homebodies, staying in fairly restricted areas, exploiting the local resources, and trying to stay out of harm's way. In this respect, they were much like other primate species.

One thing's for sure: All these early hominins were restricted to Africa. When did the first hominins leave Africa? What were they like, and why might they have left their ancient homeland? Did they differ physically from their australopith and early *Homo* forebears, and did they have new behavioral and cultural capabilities that helped them successfully exploit new environments?

It would be a romantic misconception to think of these first hominin transcontinental emigrants as "brave pioneers, boldly going where no one had gone before." They weren't deliberately striking out to go someplace in particular. It's not as though they had a map! Still, for what they did, deliberate or not, we owe them a lot.

Sometime, close to 2 mya, something decisive occurred in human evolution. As the title of this chapter suggests, for the first time, hominins expanded widely out of Africa into other areas of the Old World. Since all the early hominin fossils have been found *only* in Africa, it seems that hominins were restricted to this continent for perhaps as long as 5 million years. Later on, the more widely dispersed hominins were quite different both anatomically and behaviorally from their African ancestors. They were much larger, were more committed to a completely terrestrial habitat, used more elaborate stone tools, and were capable of adapting culturally to the demands of the new environments into which they spread.

Anthropologists continue to debate how to classify biological variations among the different geographical groups of these highly successful hominins. Moreover, discoveries of hominin fossils and artifacts are ongoing. New fossil finds from Europe are forcing a major reevaluation of exactly which kind of hominin was the first to leave Africa (Fig. 10-1). And recent artifact and fossil discoveries in Asia are also greatly expanding our understanding of the earliest hominin inhabitants and questioning conventional thinking that Asia was a "passive recipient" rather than an active donor in the earliest transcontinental hominin dispersals (e.g., see Dennell and Roebroeks, 2005).

Nevertheless, after 2 mya, there's less biological diversity in these hominins than is apparent in their pre-australopith and australopith predecessors. Consequently, there is universal agreement that the hominins found outside of Africa are all members of genus *Homo*. Thus, taxonomic debates focus solely on how many species are represented. The species for which there is the most evidence is called *Homo erectus*. Furthermore, this is the one group that most paleoanthropologists have recognized for decades and still agree on. Thus, in this chapter we will concentrate our discussion on *Homo erectus*. We will, however, also discuss alternative interpretations that "split" the fossil sample into more species.

On the cultural side, the archaeological evidence of the earliest hominins in Europe and Asia is more diverse than that of their African ancestors but generally reflects African roots. While much of the diversity of Lower Paleolithic tool assemblages and sites can be explained as cultural adaptations to the new habitats into which these hominins spread, these early humans were not yet cultural beings in the same sense as modern humans.

Around 1.4 mya, well after the initial dispersal of hominins, the Lower Paleolithic stone tool industry called **Acheulian** developed across parts of Africa, western Asia, and eventually Europe. Technologically more advanced than Oldowan (see p. 226), the Acheulian tool kit provides us with convincing evidence of increasing tool dependence by hominins, who by this time inhabited several tropical and temperate regions of the Old World.

Throughout this part of the Lower Paleolithic, whether viewed in Africa or beyond, the archaeological record shows that hominins were slowly constructing the basic elements of human culture. And as with the study of the hominin fossils, the archaeology of this dispersal outside of Africa is a quickly changing area of research, about which archaeologists still have much to learn.

A New Kind of Hominin

The discoveries of fossils now referred to as *Homo erectus* began in the nineteenth century. Later in this chapter, we will discuss in some detail the historical background of these earliest discoveries in Java and the somewhat later discoveries in China. From this work, as well as presumably related finds in Europe and North Africa, a variety of taxonomic names were suggested.

It's important to realize that such taxonomic *splitting* was quite common in the early years of paleoanthropology. More systematic biological thinking came to the fore only after World War II and with the incorporation of the Modern Synthesis into paleontology (see p. 62). Most of the fossils that were given these varied names are now placed in the species *Homo erectus*—or at least they've all been lumped into one genus (*Homo*).

In the last few decades, discoveries from East Africa of firmly dated finds have established the clear presence of *Homo erectus* by 1.8 mya. Some researchers see several anatomical differences between these African hominins and their Asian cousins (the latter recognized by almost everybody as *Homo erectus*). Thus, they place the African fossils into a separate species, one they call *Homo ergaster* (Andrews, 1984; Wood, 1991).

While there are some anatomical differences between the African specimens and those from Asia, they are all clearly *closely* related and quite possibly represent geographical varieties of a single species. We'll thus refer to all these hominins as *Homo erectus*.

All analyses have shown that *H. erectus* represents a different **grade** of evolution than their more ancient African predecessors. A grade is an evolutionary grouping of organisms showing a similar adaptive pattern. Increase in body size and robustness, changes in limb proportions, and greater encephalization all indicate that these hominins were more like modern humans in their adaptive pattern than their African ancestors were.* We should point out that a grade only implies general adaptive aspects of a group of animals; it implies nothing directly about shared ancestry (organisms that share common ancestry are said to be in the same *clade*; see p. 104). For example, orangutans and African great apes could be said to be in the same grade, but they are not in the same clade (see p. 209).

The hominins discussed in this chapter are not only members of a new and distinct grade of human evolution; they're also closely related to each other. Whether they all belong to the same clade is debatable. Nevertheless, a major adaptive shift had taken place—one setting hominin evolution in a distinctly more human direction.

Acheulian (ash´-oo-lay-en) A Lower Paleolithic stone tool industry that includes bifacially worked hand axes and cleavers and many kinds of flake tools. It began as early as 1.4 mya in Africa, spread across many parts of the temperate to tropical parts of Europe and Asia, and ended roughly 200,000 ya. Also spelled Acheulean.

grade A grouping of organisms sharing a similar adaptive pattern. Grade isn't necessarily based on closeness of evolutionary relationship, but it does contrast organisms in a useful way (e.g., *Homo erectus* with *Homo sapiens*).

---

*We did note in Chapter 9 that early *Homo* is a partial exception, being transitional in some respects.

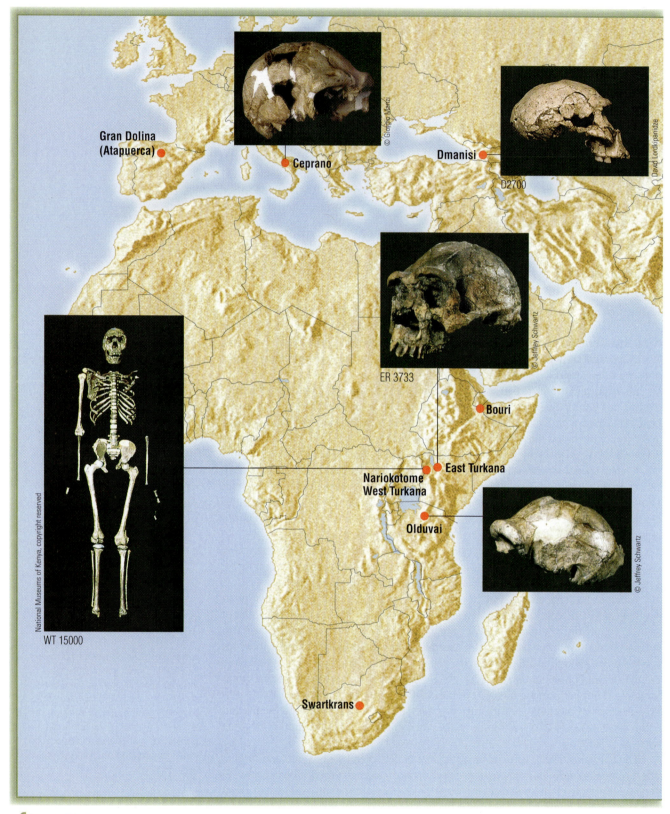

Gran Dolina
(Atapuerca)

Ceprano

© Giorgio Manzi

Dmanisi

D2700

David Lordkipanidze

ER 3733

© Jeffrey Schwartz

Bouri

East Turkana

Nariokotome
West Turkana

Olduvai

© Jeffrey Schwartz

National Museums of Kenya, copyright reserved

WT 15000

Swartkrans

Figure **10-1**

Major *Homo erectus* sites and localities of
other contemporaneous hominins.

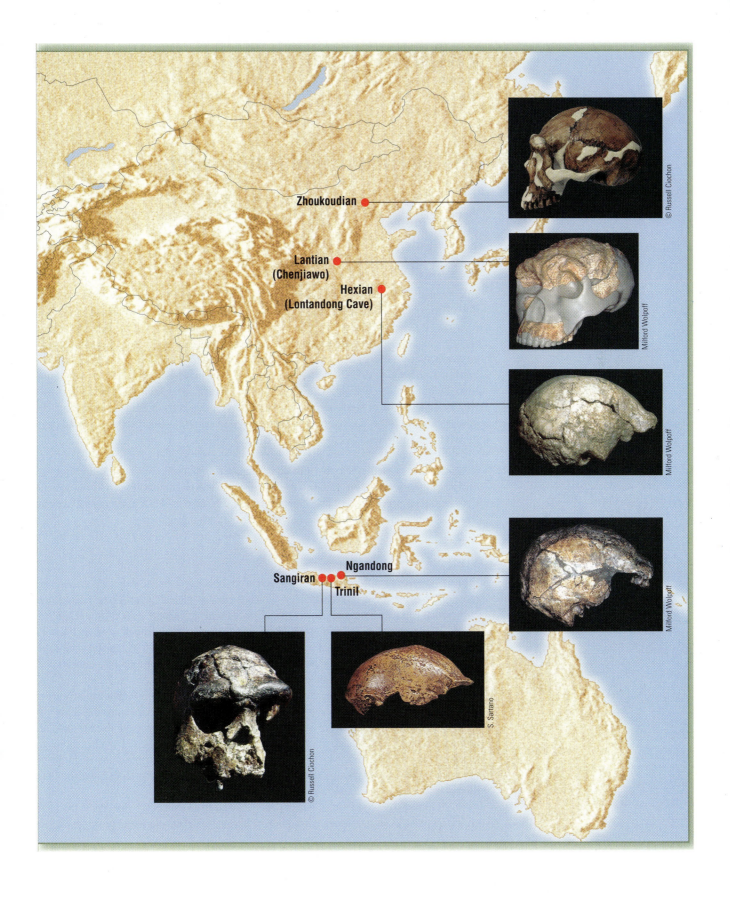

Zhoukoudian

Lantian
(Chenjiawo)

Hexian
(Lontandong Cave)

Ngandong

Sangiran

Trinil

© Russell Ciochon

Milford Wolpoff

Milford Wolpoff

Milford Wolpoff

S. Sartono

© Russell Ciochon

We mentioned that there is considerable variation in different regional populations of hominins broadly defined as *Homo erectus*. New discoveries are showing even more dramatic variation, suggesting that some of these hominins may not fit closely at all with this general adaptive pattern (more on this presently). For the moment, however, let's review what *most* of these fossils look like.

The Morphology of *Homo erectus*

Homo erectus populations lived in very different environments over much of the Old World. They all, however, shared several common physical traits that we'll now summarize briefly.

BODY SIZE

As conclusively shown by the discovery of the nearly complete skeleton of "Nariokotome Boy" (from **Nariokotome**, on the west side of Lake Turkana in Kenya), we know that *H. erectus* was larger than earlier hominins. From this and other less-complete specimens, anthropologists estimate that some *H. erectus* adults weighed well over 100 pounds, with an average adult height of about 5 feet 6 inches (McHenry, 1992; Ruff and Walker, 1993; Walker and Leakey, 1993). Another point to keep in mind is that *H. erectus* was quite sexually dimorphic—at least as indicated by the East African specimens. For adult males, weight and height in some individuals may have been considerably greater than 100 pounds. In fact, if the Nariokotome Boy had lived to adulthood, he probably would have grown to an adult height of over 6 feet (Walker, 1993).

Increased height and weight in *H. erectus* are also associated with a dramatic increase in robusticity. In fact, a heavily built body was to dominate hominin evolution not just during *H. erectus* times, but through the long transitional era of premodern forms as well. Only with the appearance of anatomically modern *H. sapiens* did a more gracile skeletal structure emerge, and it still characterizes most modern populations.

BRAIN SIZE

While *Homo erectus* differs in several respects from both early *Homo* and *Homo sapiens*, the most obvious feature is its cranial size—which is closely related to brain size. Early *Homo* had cranial capacities ranging from as small as 500 cm^3 to as large as 800 cm^3. *H. erectus*, on the other hand, shows considerable brain enlargement, with a cranial capacity of about 700* to 1,250 cm^3 (and a mean of approximately 900 cm^3). However, in making such comparisons, we must bear in mind two key questions: What is the comparative sample, and what were the overall body sizes of the species being compared?

As for the first question, you may recall that many anthropologists are now convinced that more than one species of early *Homo* existed in East Africa around 2 mya. If so, only one of them could have been the ancestor of *H. erectus*. If we choose the smaller-bodied sample of early *Homo* as our presumed ancestral group, then *H. erectus* shows as much as a 40 percent increase in average cranial capacity. But if the comparative sample we use is the larger-bodied group of early *Homo* (for example, skull 1470, from East Turkana), then *H. erectus* shows a 25 percent increase in cranial capacity.

As we've discussed, brain size is closely linked to overall body size. We've focused on the increase in *H. erectus* brain size, but *H. erectus* was also considerably larger overall

---

*Even smaller cranial capacities are seen in recently discovered fossils from the Caucasus region of southeastern Europe.

Nariokotome (nar´-ee-oh-koh´-tow-may)

than earlier members of the genus *Homo*. In fact, when we compare *H. erectus* with the larger-bodied early *Homo* sample, their *relative* brain size is about the same (Walker, 1991). What's more, when we compare the relative brain size of *H. erectus* with that of *H. sapiens*, we see that *H. erectus* was considerably less encephalized than later members of the genus *Homo*.

CRANIAL SHAPE

Homo erectus crania display a highly distinctive shape, partly because of increased brain size, but probably more correlated with increased body size. The ramifications of this heavily built cranium are reflected in thick cranial bone, large browridges above the eyes, and a projecting **nuchal torus** at the rear of the skull (Fig. 10-2).

The braincase is long and low, receding from the large browridges with little forehead development. Also, the cranium is wider at the base compared with earlier *and* later species of genus *Homo*. The maximum cranial breadth is below the ear opening, giving the cranium a pentagonal shape (when viewed from behind). In contrast, the skulls of early *Homo* and *H. sapiens* have more vertical sides, and the maximum width is *above* the ear openings.

Most specimens also have a sagittal ridge (also called a sagittal keel) running along the midline of the skull. Very different from a sagittal crest, the keel is a small ridge that runs front to back along the sagittal suture. The sagittal keel, along with the browridges and the nuchal torus, don't seem to have served an obvious function in the life of *H. erectus*, but most likely reflect bone buttressing in a very robust skull.

The First *Homo erectus: Homo erectus* from Africa

Where did *Homo erectus* first appear? The answer seems fairly simple: Most likely, this species initially evolved in Africa, probably in East Africa, where its remains are associated with artifacts of the Oldowan stone tool industry (see p. 226). Two important pieces of evidence help confirm this hypothesis. First, *all* the earlier hominins prior to the appearance of *H. erectus* come from Africa. What's more, by 1.8 mya, there are well-dated fossils of this species at East Turkana, in Kenya, and not long after at other sites in East Africa.

Still, there's a small wrinkle in this neat view. Around 1.8 mya, in addition to *H. erectus* in East Africa, similar populations were already living far away in both southeastern Asia and in southeastern Europe. Nevertheless, it is very likely that *H. erectus* first arose in East Africa but very quickly migrated to other continents far away from their African homeland. So let's begin at the beginning.

Fossils identified as *H. erectus* have been found at several locales in East Africa. As mentioned, the earliest *H. erectus* fossils come from East Turkana, from the same area where earlier australopith and early *Homo* fossils have been found (see Chapter 9). Indeed, it seems likely that in East Africa around 2–1.8 mya, some form of early *Homo* evolved into *H. erectus*.

The most significant *H. erectus* discovery from East Turkana is a nearly complete skull (Fig. 10-3). Dated at 1.8 mya, this specimen is the oldest *H. erectus* ever found. The cranial capacity is estimated at 848 cm^3, in the lower range for *H. erectus* (700 to 1,250 cm^3), which isn't surprising considering its early date. A second very significant new find from East Turkana is notable because it has the smallest cranium of any *H. erectus* from anywhere in Africa. Dated to around 1.5 mya, the skull has a cranial capacity of only 691 cm^3. As we'll see shortly, there are a couple of crania from southeastern Europe that are even smaller. The small skull from East Turkana also shows more gracile features (such as

nuchal torus (nuke´-ul) (*nuchal*, meaning "pertaining to the neck") A projection of bone in the back of the cranium where neck muscles attach; used to hold up the head.

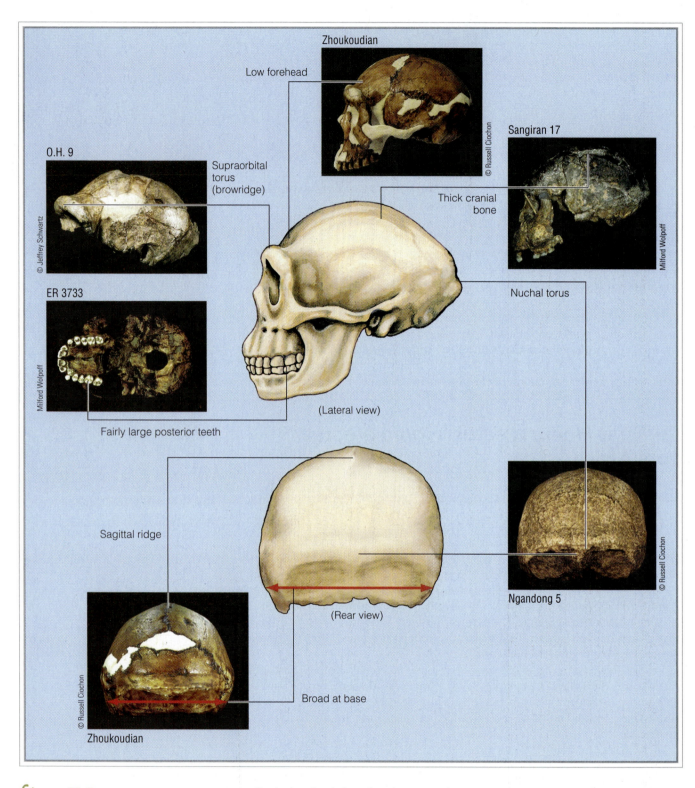

Low forehead

Zhoukoudian

© Russell Ciochon

Sangiran 17

Milford Wolpoff

O.H. 9

© Jeffrey Schwartz

Supraorbital torus (browridge)

Thick cranial bone

ER 3733

Milford Wolpoff

Nuchal torus

(Lateral view)

Fairly large posterior teeth

Sagittal ridge

Ngandong 5

© Russell Ciochon

(Rear view)

© Russell Ciochon

Zhoukoudian

Broad at base

Figure 10-2

Morphology and variation in *Homo erectus*.

smaller browridges) than do other East African *H. erectus* individuals. It's been proposed that perhaps this new find is a female and that the variation shown indicates a very high degree of sexual dimorphism in this species (Spoor et al., 2007).

Other important *H. erectus* finds have come from Olduvai Gorge, including a very robust skull discovered there by Louis Leakey back in 1960. The skull is dated at 1.4 mya and has a well-preserved cranial vault with just a small part of the upper face. Estimated at 1,067 cm³, the cranial capacity of the Olduvai *H. erectus* skull is the largest of all the African *H. erectus* specimens. The browridge is huge, the largest known for any hominin, but the walls of the braincase are thin. This latter characteristic is seen in most East African *H. erectus* specimens; in this respect, they differ from Asian *H. erectus*, in which cranial bones are thick.

Another remarkable discovery was made in 1984 by Kamoya Kimeu, a member of Richard Leakey's team known widely as an outstanding fossil hunter. Kimeu discovered a small piece of skull on the west side of Lake Turkana at the site known as Nariokotome. The careful excavations that took place there were a resounding success. In fact, the work produced the most complete *H. erectus* skeleton ever found (Fig. 10-4). Known properly as WT 15000, the almost complete skeleton includes facial bones, a pelvis, and most of the limb bones, ribs, and vertebrae. Such well-preserved postcranial elements make for a very unusual and highly useful discovery, because these elements are scarce at other *H. erectus* sites. The Nariokotome skeleton is quite ancient, dated chronometrically to about 1.6 mya. The skeleton is that of a boy about 12 years of age with an estimated height of about 5 feet 3 inches. Had he grown to maturity, it's estimated that his height would have been more than 6 feet—taller than *H. erectus* was previously thought to have been. The postcranial bones look very similar, though not quite identical, to those of modern humans. The cranial capacity of WT 15000 is estimated at 880 cm³; brain growth was nearly complete, and the boy's adult cranial capacity would have been approximately 909 cm³ (Begun and Walker, 1993).

Two other sites, both from Ethiopia, have yielded *H. erectus* fossils, the most noteworthy coming from the Bouri locale in the Middle Awash region. As you've seen, numerous remains of earlier hominins have come from this area (see Chapter 9 and Appendix B). The recent discovery of a mostly complete cranium from Bouri is important because this individual (dated at approximately 1 mya) is more like Asian *H. erectus* than are most of the earlier East African remains we've discussed (Asfaw et al., 2002). Consequently, the suggestion by several researchers that East African fossils are a different species from (Asian) *H. erectus* isn't supported by the morphology of the Bouri cranium.

Figure **10-3**

Nearly complete skull of *Homo erectus* from East Lake Turkana, Kenya, dated to approximately 1.8 mya.

© Jeffrey Schwartz

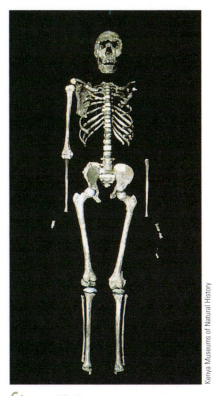

Kenya Museums of Natural History

Figure **10-4**

WT 15000 from Nariokotome, Kenya: the most complete *H. erectus* specimen yet found.

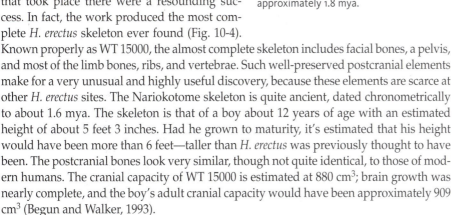

At a Glance

Key *Homo erectus* Discoveries from Africa

DATES	SITE	EVOLUTIONARY SIGNIFICANCE
1.4 mya	**Olduvai**	Large individual, very robust (male?) *H. erectus*
1.6 mya	**Nariokotome W. Turkana**	Nearly complete skeleton; young male
1.8 mya	**E. Turkana**	Oldest well-dated *H. erectus*; great amount of variation seen among individuals, possibly due to sexual dimorphism

Who Were the Earliest African Emigrants?

The fossils from East Africa imply that a new grade of human evolution appeared in Africa not long after 2 mya. Thus, the hominins who migrated to Asia and Europe are generally assumed to be their immediate descendants. This conclusion makes good sense on at least three levels: geography, anatomy, and behavior. As noted, geographically, Africa is where *all* the earlier hominins lived, so *H. erectus* would probably have first appeared there (and East Africa especially would have been a likely locality). Moreover, these were now bigger, brainier hominins capable of traveling longer distances. Finally, these tool-assisted hominins were culturally capable of exploiting a wider range of resources.

Consider the following reasonable hypothesis: *Homo erectus* first evolved in East Africa close to 2 mya and with its new physical and behavioral capacities soon emigrated to other areas of the Old World. This hypothesis helps pull together several aspects of hominin evolution, and much of the fossil evidence after 2 mya supports it. Nevertheless, recently discovered evidence seriously challenges this tidy view.

First, while 1.8 mya is a well-established date for the appearance of *H. erectus* in East Africa, similar hominins also appear at about the same time in southeastern Europe and in Indonesia (see Fig. 10-1).

Radiometric dates of sediments on the island of Java have recently placed *H. erectus* there at 1.6 mya. No stone tools or other artifacts can yet be definitely linked to the earliest Indonesian fossils. It's possible for us to explain these hominins in Asia at this early date *if* we assume that *H. erectus* evolved in East Africa by 1.8 mya (or slightly earlier) and, in just a few thousand years, expanded rapidly to other regions.

Elsewhere in Asia, the earliest evidence, all of which remains controversial and the object of continuing research, comes from the discovery of stone artifacts, not hominin fossils. For example, several excavated sites in northern China have yielded modified flakes, cores, and other artifacts. Goudi, a recently excavated site, is estimated by paleomagnetic methods and stratigraphic analysis to date to 1.66–1.36 mya (Gao et al., 2005). Claims of even older stone tools, found in contexts dated as early as 1.9 mya by paleomagnetic and other methods, have also been made for sites in northern Pakistan (Dennell et al., 2004).

Far to the west and at an even earlier date than the Asian sites, hominins associated with Oldowan-like stone tools were present in the Caucasus region of easternmost Europe. Newly discovered fossils and artifacts from the **Dmanisi** site in the Republic of Georgia (see Fig. 10-1) have been radiometrically dated to 1.75 mya. Not only do the Dmanisi hominins show up early, but they also look different from the usual *H. erectus* we've just briefly described.

In some respects, the Dmanisi crania are similar to those of *H. erectus* (for example, the long, low braincase, wide base, and sagittal keeling; see especially Fig. 10-5b, and compare with Fig. 10-2). However, other characteristics of the Dmanisi individuals are

Dmanisi (dim´-an-eese´-ee)

Figure **10-5**

Dmanisi crania discovered in 1999 and 2001 and dated to 1.8–1.7 mya.
(a) Specimen 2282.
(b) Specimen 2280.
(c) Specimen 2700.

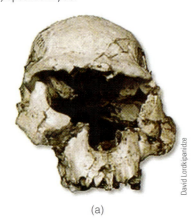

(a)

(b)

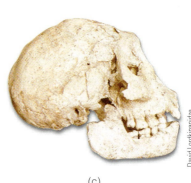

(c)

different from other hominin finds outside of Africa. In particular, the most complete specimen (Fig. 10-5c) has a less-robust and thinner browridge, a projecting lower face, and a relatively large upper canine. At least when viewed from the front, this skull is more reminiscent of the smaller early *Homo* specimens from East Africa than it is of *Homo erectus*. Also, this individual's cranial capacity is very small—estimated at only 600 cm³, well within the range of early *Homo*. In fact, the four Dmanisi crania so far described have relatively small cranial capacities—the other three were estimated at 630 cm³, 650 cm³, and 775 cm³.

Probably the most remarkable discovery yet from Dmanisi is a fourth skull that researchers excavated in 2002 (and published in 2005). This nearly complete cranium is of an older adult male; and surprisingly for such an ancient find, he died with only one tooth remaining in his jaws (Lordkipanidze et al., 2006). Because his jawbones show advanced resorption of bone, it seems that he lived for several years without being able to chew his food (Fig. 10-6). David Lordkipanidze, who leads the excavations at Dmanisi, and his colleagues have suggested that this individual required a fair amount of assistance to survive in an era when the only way to process food was to use your teeth (Lordkipanidze et al., 2005, 2006). However, this contention requires more detailed investigation before it can be confirmed.

The newest evidence from Dmanisi includes several postcranial bones, coming from at least four individuals (Lordkipanidze et al., 2007). This new evidence is especially important because it allows us to make comparisons with what is known of *Homo erectus* from other areas. The Dmanisi fossils have an unusual combination of traits. These hominins were not especially tall, with an estimated height ranging from about 4 feet 9 inches to 5 feet 5 inches. Certainly, based on this evidence, they seem much smaller than the full *H. erectus* from East Africa or from Asia. Yet, although very short in stature, they still show body proportions (such as leg length) like that of *H. erectus* (and *H. sapiens*) and quite different from that seen in earlier hominins.

Based on these recent, startling revelations from Dmanisi, we can ask several questions:

1. Was *Homo erectus* the first hominin to leave Africa—or did an earlier form of *Homo* migrate even earlier?
2. Did hominins require a large brain and sophisticated stone tool culture to disperse out of Africa?
3. Was the large, robust body build of *H. erectus* a necessary adaptation for the initial occupation of Eurasia?

Of course, since the Dmanisi discoveries are very new, it's important to view any conclusions as highly tentative. But in any case, the recent evidence raises important and exciting possibilities. The Dmanisi findings suggest that the first hominins to leave Africa were quite possibly a very early form of *H. erectus*, possessing smaller brains than later *H. erectus* and carrying with them a typical African Oldowan stone tool culture. As we mentioned, newly discovered remains of the postcranial skeleton show that the Dmanisi individuals were quite small. In fact, they average not much more than five feet in height. Certainly, based on this evidence, they seem much smaller than the full *H. erectus* from East Africa or from Asia.

What we do have so far shows that the Dmanisi hominins were generally very short and small-brained hominins, having none of the adaptations many researchers thought to be essential to hominin migration—that is, being tall and having relatively large brains. It's possible we may find that there were *two* migrations out of Africa at this time: one consisting of the small-brained, diminutive Dmanisi hominins and an almost immediate second one that founded the well-recognized *H. erectus* populations of Java and China. All this evidence is so new, however, that it's too soon even to predict what further revisions may be required.

David Lordkipanidze

Figure 10-6

Most recently discovered cranium from Dmanisi, almost totally lacking in teeth (with both upper and lower jaws showing advanced bone resorption).

Figure **10-7**

The famous Trinil skullcap found by Eugene Dubois in Java.

S. Sartano

Homo erectus from Indonesia

After Charles Darwin published *On the Origin of Species* in 1859, debates about evolution were prevalent throughout Europe. While many theorists simply stayed home and debated the merits of natural selection and the likely course of human evolution, one young Dutch anatomist decided to go find evidence of it. Eugene Dubois (1858–1940) enlisted in the Dutch East Indian Army and was shipped to the island of Sumatra, Indonesia, providing him his chance to look for what he called "the missing link."

In October 1891, after moving his search to the neighboring island of Java, Dubois' field crew unearthed the upper portion of a skull (called a "skullcap") along the Solo River near the town of Trinil—a fossil that was to become internationally famous (Fig. 10-7). The following year, a human femur was recovered about 15 yards upstream in what Dubois claimed was the same level as the skullcap, and he assumed that the skullcap (with a cranial capacity of slightly over 900 cm^3) and the femur belonged to the same individual.

H. erectus fossil remains have thus far been found at six sites in Java. The most precise chronometric dating estimates suggest that the earliest fossils are close to 1.6 million years old, and very late *H. erectus* survivors from Ngandong, Java, may be as young as 27,000 years old. The earliest *H. erectus* fossils from Java come from the central part of the island. Beginning with Dubois' famous discovery at Trinil, over 80 fossil specimens have been located, with many coming from an area called the Sangiran Dome, located just west of Trinil. Several crania have been found, although only one preserves the face. Cranial capacities range between 813 cm^3 and 1,059 cm^3.

By far, the most recent group of *H. erectus* fossils from Java come from Ngandong, in an area to the east of the other finds already mentioned. At Ngandong, an excavation along an ancient river terrace produced 11 mostly complete hominin crania. Two specialized dating techniques, discussed in Chapter 8, have determined that animal bones found at the site—and presumably associated with the hominins—are only about 50,000–25,000 years old (Swisher et al., 1996). These dates are controversial, but further evidence is now establishing a *very* late survival of *Homo erectus* in Java, long after the species had disappeared elsewhere. So these individuals would be contemporary with *H. sapiens*—which, by this time, had expanded widely throughout the Old World, even into Australia around 60,000–40,000 years ago (ya). As we'll see in Chapter 12, even later—and very unusual—hominins have been found elsewhere, apparently evolving while isolated on another Indonesian island.

We can't say much about the *H. erectus* way of life in Java. Few artifacts have been found, and none of them are directly associated with the earliest Javanese fossils (Corvinus, 2004). Later *H. erectus* fossils are possibly associated with a tool industry based on small flakes. This industry lacks large stone tools and differs greatly from the Oldowan and Acheulian tool assemblages of Africa and western Asia.

Homo erectus from China

The story of the first discoveries of Chinese *H. erectus* is another saga filled with excitement, hard work, luck, and misfortune. Europeans had known for a long time that "dragon bones," used by the Chinese as medicine and aphrodisiacs, were actually ancient mammal bones. Scientists eventually located one of the sources of these bones near Beijing at a site called **Zhoukoudian**, which would go on to become the most intensively investigated Chinese Paleolithic site. Serious excavations were begun there in the 1920s, and in 1929, a fossil skull was discovered. The skull turned out to be a juvenile's, and although it was thick, low, and relatively small, there was no doubt that it belonged to an early hominin.

Zhoukoudian (Zhoh´-koh-dee´-en)

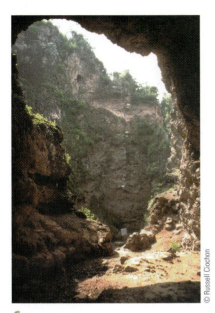

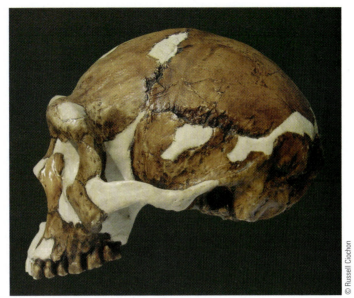

Figure **10-8**
Zhoukoudian cave.

Figure **10-9**
Composite cranium of Zhoukoudian *Homo erectus*, reconstructed by
Ian Tattersall and Gary Sawyer, of the American Museum of Natural
History in New York.

ZHOUKOUDIAN *HOMO ERECTUS*

The fossil remains of *H. erectus* discovered in the 1920s and 1930s, as well as some more
recent excavations at Zhoukoudian (Fig. 10-8), are by far the largest collection of *H. erectus*
material found anywhere. This excellent sample includes 14 skullcaps (Fig. 10-9), other
cranial pieces, and more than 100 isolated teeth, but only a scattering of postcranial elements (Jia and Huang, 1990). Various interpretations to account for this unusual pattern
of preservation have been offered, ranging from ritualistic treatment or cannibalism by
the hominins themselves to the more mundane suggestion that the *H. erectus* remains are
simply the leftovers of the meals of giant hyenas (the fossil remains of which have also
been found at Zhoukoudian).

At a Glance

Key *Homo erectus* Discoveries from Asia

DATES	SITE	EVOLUTIONARY SIGNIFICANCE
50,000–25,000 ya	**Ngandong** (Java)	Very late survival of *H. erectus* in Java
670,000–410,000 ya	**Zhoukoudian** (China)	Large sample; most famous *H. erectus* site; shows some *H. erectus* populations well adapted to temperate (cold) environments
1.6 mya	**Sangiran**	First discovery of *H. erectus* from anywhere; shows dispersal out of Africa by 1.6 mya

At any rate, the hominin remains belong to upward of 40 adults and children and together provide much evidence. Because of meticulous analysis done on the original fossils (before they were lost), the Zhoukoudian fossils have led to a good overall picture of Chinese *H. erectus*. Like the materials from Java, they have typical *H. erectus* features, including a large browridge in front and a nuchal torus behind. Also, the skull has thick bones, a sagittal keel, and a protruding face and, like the Javanese forms, is broadest near the bottom. These specimens have been dated at various times to between 670,000 and 410,000 years old.

Cultural Remains More than 100,000 artifacts have been recovered from this vast site, which was intermittently used by hominins and other animals for many thousands of years. Common tools include choppers and chopping tools, as well as small quartz flakes that were fashioned into scrapers, points, burins, and awls (Fig. 10-10).

In the mid-twentieth century, paleoanthropologists believed that Zhoukoudian's *H. erectus* inhabitants were hunter-gatherers who killed deer, horses, and other animals and gathered fruits, berries, tubers, and ostrich eggs. This site was also widely recognized at the time as one of the earliest examples of the controlled use of fire. (Other even older potential instances of hominin fire use were subsequently discovered at sites in Africa and the Near East.) A tremendously important innovation in human prehistory, the controlled use of fire provided warmth, protection from other animals, a means of cooking, and an aid to the toolmaking process.

Further research, including new excavations in the 1990s and the reanalysis of older excavations, refuted or cast considerable doubt on many of these inferences. The current view is that much of the Zhoukoudian material likely accumulated from the activities of now-extinct giant hyenas that used the cave as a den and less from early hominin use of the site. Boaz and Ciochon (2004) also hypothesize that most of the *H. erectus* remains found at Zhoukoudian were deposited as hyena food refuse. Stone tools and the discovery of cut-marked bones demonstrate that *H. erectus* frequented the site and likely did occasionally use fire in it, but the evidence points more to a scavenger than a hunter mode of existence in which *H. erectus* competed with giant hyenas and other large predators and scavengers for meat from their kills (Binford and Ho, 1985; Binford and Stone, 1986a, 1986b).

Evidence for the controlled use of fire at Zhoukoudian continues to be controversial. Recent investigations of the cave deposits found that burnt bone was only rarely found in association with tools, and in most cases the burning appeared to have taken place *after* fossilization—that is, the bones were not cooked (Weiner et al., 1998). Chemical analyses of "ash" layers identified by earlier researchers as evidence of hominin use of fire at the site proved not to be ash, but naturally accumulated organic sediments. Other studies also showed no sign of wood having been burnt inside the cave and revealed that features

Figure **10-10**

Chinese tools likely made by *Homo erectus*.

Quartzite chopper

Flint point

Flint awl

Graver, or burin

earlier identified as hearths or fireplaces contained no evidence of burning and were of natural origin. Nevertheless, the cave does contain evidence, such as burned bones and fire-cracked rocks, that cannot be easily explained except as the result of hominin use of fire inside the cave (Boaz and Ciochon, 2004).

OTHER CHINESE SITES

While Zhoukoudian will continue to be viewed as an important Chinese *H. erectus* site, research conducted over the past half century has revealed older examples of *H. erectus* fossils at other Chinese sites, from Lantian County (including two sites, often simply referred to as Lantian), Yunxian County, and Hexian County (with several discoveries, usually referred to as the Hexian finds).

Before the excavation of two sites in Lantian County, Shaanxi Province, in the mid-1960s, Zhoukoudian was widely believed to be the oldest hominin fossil site in China. Dated to 1.15 mya, Lantian is older than Zhoukoudian (Zhu et al., 2003). From the Lantian sites, the cranial remains of two adult *H. erectus* females have been found in association with fire-treated pebbles and flakes as well as ash (Woo, 1966; Fig. 10-11a). One of the specimens, an almost complete mandible containing several teeth, is quite similar to those from Zhoukoudian.

Two badly distorted crania were discovered in Yunxian County, Hubei Province, in 1989 and 1990 (Li and Etler, 1992). A combination of ESR and paleomagnetism dating methods gives us an average dating estimate of 800,000–580,000 ya. If the dates are correct, this would place Yunxian between Lantian and Zhoukoudian in the Chinese sequence. Due to extensive distortion of the crania from ground pressure, it was very difficult to compare these crania with other *H. erectus* fossils; recently, however, French paleoanthropologist Amélie Vialet has restored the crania using sophisticated imaging techniques (Vialet et al., 2005). And from a recent analysis of the fauna and paleoenvironment at Yunxian, the *H. erectus* inhabitants are thought to have had limited hunting capabilities, since they appear to have been restricted to the most vulnerable prey, namely, the young and old animals. This interpretation agrees with the recent reinterpretation of Zhoukoutian *H. erectus* as more a scavenger-gatherer than a hunter-gatherer.

In 1980 and 1981, the remains of several individuals, all bearing some resemblance to similar fossils from Zhoukoudian, were recovered from Hexian County, in southern China (Wu and Poirier, 1995) (Fig. 10-11b). A close relationship has been postulated between

Figure **10-11**

(a) Reconstructed cranium of *Homo erectus* from Lantian, China, dated to approximately 1.15 mya. (b) Hexian cranium.

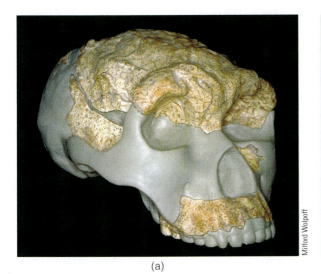

(a)

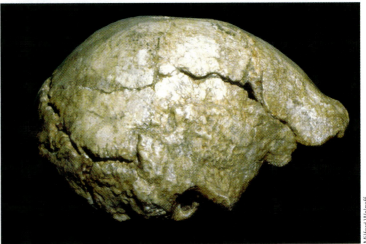

(b)

247

the *H. erectus* specimens from the Hexian finds and from Zhoukoudian (Wu and Dong, 1985). Indeed, some date the Hexian remains to 400,000 ya (Wu et al., 2006), making it contemporaneous with Zhoukoudian; these dates are disputed, and others experts place the age at only 190,000 ya.

The Asian crania from both Java and China share many similar features, which may be explained by *H. erectus* migration from Java to China perhaps around 1 mya. African *H. erectus* forms are generally older than most Asian forms, and they're different from them in several ways.

Asian and African *Homo erectus*: A Comparison

The *Homo erectus* remains from East Africa show several differences from the Javanese and Chinese fossils. Some African cranial specimens—particularly the skull from East Turkana (ER 3733), presumably a female, and WT 15000, presumably a male—aren't as strongly buttressed at the browridge and nuchal torus, and their cranial bones aren't as thick. Indeed, some researchers are so impressed by these differences, as well as others in the postcranial skeleton, that they're arguing for a *separate* species status for the African material, to distinguish it from the Asian samples. Bernard Wood, the leading proponent of this view, has suggested that the name *Homo ergaster* be used for the African remains and that *H. erectus* be reserved solely for the Asian material (Wood, 1991). In addition, the very early dates now postulated for the dispersal of *H. erectus* into Asia (Java) would argue for a more than 1-million-year separate history for Asian and African populations.

In any case, this species division has not been fully accepted, and the current consensus (and the one we prefer) is to continue referring to all these hominins as *Homo erectus* (Kramer, 1993; Conroy, 1997; Rightmire, 1998; Asfaw et al., 2002). So, as with some earlier hominins, we'll have to accommodate a considerable degree of intraspecific variation within this species. Wood has concluded, regarding variation within such a broadly defined *H. erectus* species, that "it is a species which manifestly embraces an unusually wide degree of variation in both the cranium and postcranial skeleton" (Wood, 1992, p. 329).

Later Hominins from Europe

Because of the recent discoveries from Dmanisi (see p. 242), the time frame for the earliest hominin occupation of Europe is being dramatically pushed back. For several decades, researchers assumed that hominins didn't reach Europe until late in the Middle **Pleistocene** (after 400,000 ya) and were already identifiable as a form very similar to *Homo sapiens*. So they concluded that *H. erectus* (and contemporaries) never got there. But as the new discoveries are evaluated, these assumptions are being discarded, and radical revisions concerning hominin evolution in Europe are becoming necessary.

While not as old as the Dmanisi material, fossils from the Atapuerca region in northern Spain are significantly extending the antiquity of hominins in western Europe. There are several caves in the Atapuerca region, two of which (Sima del Elefante and Gran Dolina) have yielded hominin fossils contemporaneous with *H. erectus*; another cave has somewhat later remains, similar in many ways to Neandertals (and will be discussed in Chapter 11).

The earliest finds from Atapuerca (from Sima del Elefante) have been recently discovered and date to 1.2 mya, making these clearly the oldest hominins yet found in

Pleistocene The epoch of the Cenozoic from 1.8 mya until 10,000 ya. Frequently referred to as the Ice Age, this epoch is associated with continental glaciations in northern latitudes.

western Europe (Carbonell et al, 2008). So far, just one specimen has been found here, a partial jaw with a few teeth. Very provisional analysis suggests that its closest resemblances are with the Dmanisi fossils. There are also tools and animal bones from the site. Like Dmanisi, the implements are simple flake tools similar to what we've called Oldowan. Some of the animal bones also bear the scars of hominin activity with cut marks indicating butchering (similar to what we discussed in Chapter 9 for Olduvai). Gran Dolina is a later site; based on specialized techniques discussed in Chapter 8 (see p. 194), it is dated to approximately 850,000–780,000 ya (Parés and Pérez-González, 1995; Falguéres et al., 1999). Because all the remains so far identified from both these caves at Atapuerca are fragmentary, assigning these fossils to particular species poses something of a problem. Spanish paleoanthropologists who have studied the Atapuerca fossils have decided to place these hominins into another (separate) species, one they call *Homo antecessor* (Bermúdez de Castro et al., 1997; Arsuaga et al., 1999). However, it remains to be seen whether this newly proposed species will prove to be distinct from other species of *Homo* (see p. 252 for further discussion).

Finally, the southern European discovery of a well-preserved cranium from the Ceprano site in central Italy may be the best evidence yet of *H. erectus* in Europe (Ascenzi et al., 1996). Provisional dating of a partial cranium from this important site suggests a date of 900,000–800,000 ya (Fig. 10-12). Phillip Rightmire (1998) has concluded that cranial morphology places this specimen quite close to *H. erectus*. Italian researchers have proposed other views. The exact relationship of the Ceprano fossil to *H. erectus* remains to be fully determined.

After about 400,000 ya, the European fossil hominin record becomes increasingly abundant. More fossils mean more variation, so it's not surprising that interpretations regarding the proper taxonomic assessment of many of these remains have been debated, in some cases for decades. In recent years, several of these somewhat later "premodern" specimens have been considered either as early representatives of *H. sapiens* or as a separate species, one immediately preceding *H. sapiens*. These enigmatic premodern humans are discussed in Chapter 11. A time line for the *H. erectus* discoveries discussed in this chapter as well as other finds of more uncertain status is shown in Figure 10-13.

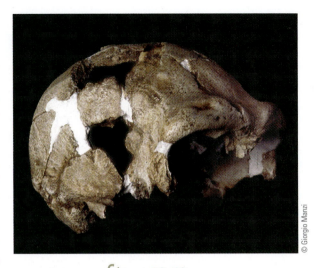
© Giorgio Manzi

Figure **10-12**

The Ceprano *Homo erectus* cranium from central Italy, provisionally dated to 800,000–900,000 ya. This is the best evidence for *Homo erectus* in Europe.

At a Glance

Key *Homo erectus* and Contemporaneous Discoveries from Europe

DATES	SITE	EVOLUTIONARY SIGNIFICANCE
900,000–800,000 ya	**Ceprano** (Italy)	Well-preserved cranium; best evidence of full *H. erectus* morphology from any site in Europe
850,000–780,000 ya	**Gran Dolina** (Atapuerca, Spain)	Oldest evidence of hominins in western Europe; likely not *H. erectus*
1.75 mya	**Dmanisi** (Republic of Georgia)	Oldest well-dated hominins outside of Africa; not like full *H. erectus* morphology, but are small-bodied and small-brained

Figure **10-13**

Time line for *Homo erectus* discoveries and other contemporary hominins.

Archaeology of Early Hominin Dispersal

The first hominins to leave Africa were tool-assisted scavenger-gatherers who carried with them the basic concepts and technological capabilities of the Oldowan tool industry. As such, they differed greatly from modern humans. They began their extraordinary journey without the benefit of language, the controlled use of fire, or projectile weapons and other killing tools. They were also culturally ill equipped, at least in the beginning, to cope with the climatic seasonal extremes of life outside the tropics and southern temperate regions. Nevertheless, archaeological and fossil evidence offers convincing proof of their extraordinary success in invading new habitats across the Old World, from the Atlantic to the Pacific.

Evidence of butchering is widespread in early *H. erectus* sites, and in the past, such evidence has been cited in arguments for consistent hunting. Researchers formerly interpreted any association of bones and tools as evidence of hunting, but many studies now suggest that cut marks on bones from this period often overlay carnivore tooth marks. This means that hominins were gaining access to the carcasses after the carnivores and were therefore scavenging the meat, not hunting the animals. It's also crucial to mention that these hominins gained most of their daily calories from gathering wild plants, tubers, and fruits.

Just as with the fossil evidence of their dispersal, the stone tools and other artifacts found in the earliest sites are not the same everywhere. While the stone tool assemblages of Oldowan sites in East Africa and such early sites as Dmanisi in Georgia and Atapuerca in Spain reflect a similar grasp of technology, some of the early Southeast and East Asian sites contain small flake tool assemblages that do not appear to have their roots in the Oldowan stone tool industry. The problem, of course, is how to explain the differences. Did stone tool industries other than Oldowan leave Africa with the earliest emigrants? Or did new industries develop in Southeast and East Asia as early hominins adapted to new habitats and resources? We have the questions, but finding the answers requires more research.

By 1.4 mya, a new stone tool industry called Acheulian is found in Africa and, soon after, at sites in the Near East and even farther east on the Indian subcontinent, if not also into parts of East Asia (Corvinus, 2004). The Acheulian tool kit was both more diverse and more complex than the Oldowan. It represented several new concepts about making stone tools. First, Acheulian toolmakers invented the idea of a *bifacial* stone tool—one that has been worked to create two opposing faces. A notable example of an Acheulian bifacial tool is the hand axe (Fig. 10-14), thousands of which have been found at Lower Paleolithic sites from Africa to Europe and eastward to India.

Second, Acheulian toolmakers developed a new way to knock flakes from stone cores, which gave more predictable results than the *"hard hammer" percussion* method (see p. 229) used by their Oldowan predecessors. **"Soft hammer" percussion** employs a hammer made of a somewhat flexible material, such as wood, bone, or antler. When struck against a core, the soft hammer absorbs some of the striking force, giving an experienced stone toolmaker greater control over the length, width, and thickness of the resulting flakes (Fig. 10-15). While this may sound like a small change, it was an era during which such small technological changes could make big differences in how stone tools were made and how they looked when finished.

Finally, some kinds of Acheulian tools tend to reflect shared notions of form, or what they should look like. In other words, not only did Acheulian toolmakers create new stone

© Barry Lewis

Figure **10-14**

Hand axe (left) and cleaver (right), both of which were basic tools of the Acheulian tradition.

Figure **10-15**

Soft hammer percussion. Here the stone tool maker uses a more flexible (bone) hammer which allows more precise removal of flakes of the desired size and shape.

"Soft hammer" percussion A direct percussion method of making stone tools that uses a resilient hammer or billet to gain greater control over the length, width, and thickness of flakes driven from a core.

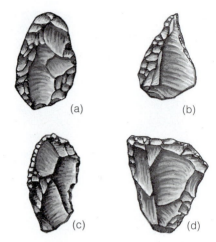

(a)

(b)

(c)

(d)

Figure **10-16**

Small tools of the Acheulian industry.
(a) Side scraper.
(b) Point. (c) End scraper. (d) Burin.

tools and ways to make them; they were also capable of developing *and communicating to each other* ideas of form and design. For example, pretty much everything was a "Swiss Army knife" to an Oldowan toolmaker; but when an Acheulian toolmaker sat down to make, say, a hand axe, he or she clearly expected to end up with a stone tool that was bifacially worked, often about 6 to 8 inches long, and possessing a pear or teardrop shape with a point at one end and a rounded base at the other (see Fig. 10-14). Conceptualizing tools in this way was something new.

The most distinctive Acheulian artifacts were hand axes, which we just described, and cleavers, which are much like hand axes except that they end in a broad straight edge rather than a point. While we still don't have a clear idea what cleavers were used for, hand axes show wear patterns and other evidence of having been used for many different kinds of tasks, especially cutting and chopping.

The Acheulian tool kit was not just hand axes and cleavers. It also included many kinds of flake tools (Fig. 10-16), which were used for cutting, abrading, scraping, piercing, and other tasks, as well as hammerstones, cores, and other artifacts, many of which would also have been familiar to an Oldowan toolmaker.

Seeing the Big Picture: Interpretations of *Homo erectus*

Several aspects of the geographical, physical, and behavioral patterns shown by *H. erectus* (broadly defined) seem clear. But new discoveries and more in-depth analyses are helping us to reevaluate our prior ideas. The fascinating fossil hominins discovered at Dmanisi are perhaps the most challenging piece of this puzzle.

Past theories suggest that *Homo erectus* was able to emigrate from Africa owing to more advanced culture and a more modern anatomy as compared to earlier African predecessors. Yet, the Dmanisi cranial remains show that these very early Europeans still had small brains; what's more, *H. erectus* has been found in Java at 1.6 mya.

So it seems that some key parts of earlier hypotheses are not fully accurate. At least some of the earliest emigrants from Africa didn't yet show the entire suite of *H. erectus* physical and behavioral traits. How different the Dmanisi hominins are from the full *H. erectus* pattern remains to be seen, and the discovery of more complete postcranial remains will be most illuminating.

Going a step further, the four crania from Dmanisi are extremely variable; one of them, in fact, does look more like *H. erectus*. It would be tempting to conclude that more than one type of hominin is represented here, but they're all found in the same geological context. The archaeologists who excavated the site conclude that all the fossils are closely associated with each other. The simplest hypothesis is that they all are members of the *same* species. This degree of apparent intraspecific variation is biologically noteworthy, and it's influencing how paleoanthropologists interpret all of these fossil samples.

This growing awareness of the broad limits of intraspecific variation among some hominins brings us to our second consideration: Is *Homo ergaster* in Africa a separate species from *Homo erectus*, as strictly defined in Asia? While this interpretation was popular in the last decade, it now is losing support. The finds from Dmanisi raise fundamental issues of interpretation. Among these four crania from one locality (see Fig. 10-5), we see more variation than between the African and Asian forms, which many researchers have interpreted as different species. Also, the new discovery from Bouri (Ethiopia) of a more *erectus*-looking cranium further weakens the separate-species interpretation of *H. ergaster*.

The separate-species status of the early European fossils from Atapuerca in Spain is also not yet clearly established. We still don't have much good fossil evidence from this site; but an early date of 1.2 mya is well confirmed. Recall also that no other hominin fossils from the southern or western part of Europe are known until at least 300,000 years later (Bischoff et al., 2007). It's quite apparent that later in the Pleistocene, the possible descendants of these hominins are well established both in Africa and in Europe. These later premodern humans are the topic of the next chapter.

When looking back at the evolution of *H. erectus*, we realize how significant this early human's achievements were. It was *H. erectus* who increased in body size with more efficient bipedalism; who embraced culture wholeheartedly as an adaptive strategy; whose brain was reshaped and increased in size to within the range of *H. sapiens*; and who became a more efficient scavenger. In short, it was *H. erectus*, committed to a cultural way of life, who transformed hominin evolution to human evolution. As Richard Foley states, "The appearance and expansion of *H. erectus* represented a major change in adaptive strategy that influenced the subsequent process and pattern of human evolution" (1991, p. 425).

Summary

Homo erectus remains are found in geological contexts dating from about 1.8 mya to at least 200,000 ya—and probably much later—and spanning a period of more than 1.5 million years. While the nature and timing of migrations are uncertain, it's likely that *H. erectus* first appeared in East Africa and quickly migrated to other areas. This widespread and highly successful hominin defines a new and more modern grade of human evolution.

Historically, the first fossil finds were made by Dubois in Java, and later fossil and artifact discoveries came from China and Africa. Differences from early *Homo* are notable in *H. erectus'* larger brain, taller stature, robust build, and changes in facial structure and cranial buttressing.

The long period of *H. erectus* existence was marked by a remarkably slow rate of technological change, certainly compared to modern human culture. Even so, *H. erectus* and contemporaries developed new tools and new ways of making tools. Given these achievements, along with the controlled use of fire and the growing cultural capacity to adapt to new habitats and environments, they spread quickly across much of the Old World.

It's generally assumed that certain *H. erectus* populations evolved into later premodern humans, some of which, in turn, evolved into *Homo sapiens*. Evidence supporting such a series of transitions is seen in the Ngandong fossils (and others discussed in Chapter 11), which display both *H. erectus* and *H. sapiens* features.

There are still many questions about *H. erectus* behavior. For example, did they hunt? What was their relationship to later hominins? Was the mode of evolution gradual or rapid, and which *H. erectus* populations contributed genes? The search for answers continues.

In the What's Important feature on page 254, you'll find a useful summary of the most significant hominin fossils discussed in this chapter.

Critical Thinking Questions

1. Why is the nearly complete skeleton from Nariokotome so important? What kinds of evidence does it provide?
2. Assume that you're in the laboratory and you're going to compare the Nariokotome skeleton with a skeleton of a modern human. First, given a choice, what age and sex would you choose for the human skeleton, and why? Second, what similarities and differences do the two skeletons show?

3. What fundamental questions of interpretation do the fossil hominins from Dmanisi raise? Does this evidence completely overturn the hypothesis concerning *H. erectus* dispersal from Africa? Explain why or why not.

4. What are the main differences between Acheulian and Oldowan tool industries? What do these differences tell us about the evolution of human culture? Why did Lower Paleolithic culture change so slowly?

5. You're interpreting the hominin fossils from three sites in East Africa (Nariokotome, Olduvai, and Bouri)—all considered possible members of *H. erectus*. What sorts of evidence would lead you to conclude that there was more than one species? What would convince you that there was just one species? Why do you think some paleoanthropologists (splitters) would tend to see more than one species, while others (lumpers) would generally not? What kind of approach would you take, and why?

What's Important Key Fossil Discoveries of *Homo Erectus*

Dates	Region	Site	The Big Picture
1.6 mya–25,000 ya	**Asia** (Indonesia)	Java (Sangiran and other sites)	Shows *H. erectus* early on (by 1.6 mya) in tropical areas of Southeast Asia; *H. erectus* persisted here for more than 1 million years
600,000–400,000 ya	China	Zhoukoudian	Largest, most famous sample of *H. erectus*; shows adaptation to colder environments; conclusions regarding behavior at this site have been exaggerated and are now questioned
900,000–800,000 ya	**Europe** (Italy)	Ceprano	Likely best evidence of full-blown *H. erectus* morphology in Europe
1.8–1.7 mya	(Republic of Georgia)	Dmanisi	Very early dispersal to southeastern Europe (by 1.8 mya) of small-bodied, small-brained H. erectus population; may represent an earlier dispersal from Africa than one that led to wider occupation of Eurasia
1.6 mya	**Africa** (Kenya)	Nariokotome	Beautifully preserved nearly complete skeleton; best postcranial evidence of *H. erectus* from anywhere
1.8 mya		East Turkana	Earliest *H. erectus* from Africa; some individuals more robust, others smaller and more gracile; variation suggested to represent sexual dimorphism

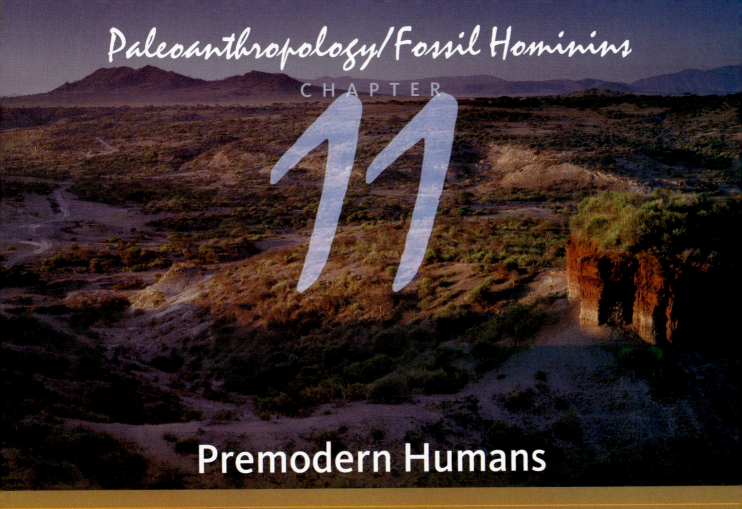

Paleoanthropology/Fossil Hominins

Premodern Humans

Focus Question

Who were the immediate precursors to modern *Homo sapiens*, and how do they compare with modern humans?

 Click!

Go to the following media for interactive activities and exercises on topics covered in this chapter:

- Online Virtual Laboratories for Physical Anthropology, Version 4.0

- Hominid Fossils: An Interactive Atlas CD-ROM

Middle Pleistocene The Pleistocene stage beginning 780,000 ya and ending 125,000 ya.

Late Pleistocene The Pleistocene stage beginning 125,000 ya and ending approximately 10,000 ya.

Middle Paleolithic Cultural period that began about 200,000 ya and ended around 30,000–40,000 years ago. Roughly the same period in sub-Saharan Africa is called the Middle Stone Age.

Upper Paleolithic Cultural period beginning roughly 30,000–40,000 ya and ending about 10,000 ya and distinguished by major technological innovations, the creation of the earliest human art widely recognized as such, and many other accomplishments. Best known from western Europe, similar industries are also known from central and eastern Europe and Africa.

glaciations Climatic intervals when continental ice sheets cover much of the northern continents. Glaciations are associated with colder temperatures in northern latitudes and more arid conditions closer to the equator, most notably in Africa.

Introduction

What do you think of when you hear the term *Neandertal*? Most people think of imbecilic, bent-over brutes. Yet, Neandertals were quite advanced; they had brains at least as large as ours, and they showed many sophisticated cultural capabilities. What's more, they definitely weren't bent over, but fully erect (as hominins had been for millions of years previously). In fact, Neandertals and their immediate predecessors could easily be called human.

That brings us to possibly the most basic of all questions: What does it mean to be human? The meaning of this term is highly varied, encompassing religious, philosophical, and biological considerations. As you know, physical anthropologists primarily concentrate on the biological aspects of the human organism, while archaeologists focus on behavioral clues revealed by archaeological traces. All living people today are members of one species, sharing a common anatomical pattern and similar behavioral potentials. We call hominins like us "modern *Homo sapiens*," and in the next chapter we'll discuss the origin of forms that were essentially identical to living people.

When in our evolutionary past can we say that our predecessors were obviously human? Certainly, the further back we go in time, the less hominins look like modern *Homo sapiens*. This is, of course, exactly what we'd expect in an evolutionary sequence.

We saw in Chapter 10 that *Homo erectus* took crucial steps in the human direction and defined a new *grade* of human evolution. In this chapter, we'll discuss the hominins who continued this journey. Both physically and behaviorally, they're much like modern *Homo sapiens*, though they still show several significant differences. So, while most paleoanthropologists are comfortable referring to these hominins as "human," we need to qualify this recognition a bit to set them apart from fully modern people. Thus, in this text, we'll refer to these fascinating immediate predecessors as "premodern humans."

When, Where, and What

Most of the hominins discussed in this chapter lived during the Pleistocene epoch, a unit of geological time that is often called the Ice Age. The **Middle Pleistocene** stage began 780,000 ya and ended 125,000 ya. Some of the later premodern humans, especially the Neandertals, lived well into the **Late Pleistocene** (125,000–10,000 ya).

Viewed archaeologically, this chapter addresses significant cultural changes of the late Lower Paleolithic period and all of the **Middle Paleolithic**, which began about 200,000 ya and ended around 40,000–30,000 years ago. Chapter 12 focuses on the **Upper Paleolithic** period, addressing the archaeology of fully modern humans to the end of the Ice Age.

THE PLEISTOCENE

The Pleistocene was marked by periodic continental **glaciations** that had global climatic effects. During glacial periods, when temperatures dropped dramatically, ice accumulated as a result of more snow falling each year than melting, sea levels dropped hundreds

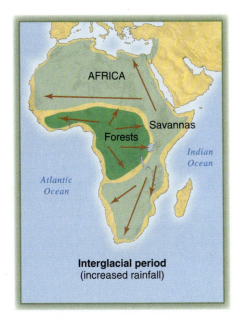 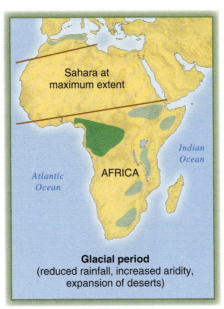

Interglacial period
(increased rainfall)

Glacial period
(reduced rainfall, increased aridity,
expansion of deserts)

Figure **11-1**

Changing Pleistocene environments in Africa.

of feet, and massive glaciers measuring nearly a mile thick covered much of the earth's landmass. As the climate fluctuated, at times it became much warmer. During these **interglacials**, the ice that had built up during the glacial periods melted, sea levels rose, and the glaciers retreated back toward the earth's polar regions. The Pleistocene was characterized by numerous advances and retreats of ice, with at least 15 major and 50 minor glacial advances documented in Europe alone (Tattersall et al., 1988).

These glaciations, which enveloped huge swaths of Europe, Asia, and North America as well as Antarctica, were mostly confined to northern latitudes. Hominins living at this time—all still restricted to the Old World until sometime after 30,000 ya, when they began to populate the New World—were severely affected as the climate, flora, and animal life shifted during these Pleistocene oscillations. The most dramatic of these effects were in Europe and northern Asia—less so in southern Asia and in Africa. Still, the climate also fluctuated in the south. In Africa, the main effects were related to changing rainfall patterns. During glacial periods, the climate in Africa became more arid, while during interglacials, rainfall increased. The changing availability of food resources certainly affected hominins in Africa; but probably even more importantly, migration routes also swung back and forth. For example, during glacial periods (Fig. 11-1), the Sahara Desert expanded, blocking migration in and out of sub-Saharan Africa (Lahr and Foley, 1998).

In Eurasia, glacial advances also greatly affected migration routes. As the ice sheets expanded, sea levels dropped nearly 500 feet (150 m) below modern levels, more northern regions became uninhabitable, and some key passages between areas became blocked by glaciers. For example, during glacial peaks, much of western Europe would have been cut off from the rest of Eurasia (Fig. 11-2).

During the warmer—and, in the south, wetter—interglacials, the ice sheets shrank, sea levels rose, and certain migration routes reopened (for example, from central into western Europe). Clearly, to understand Middle Pleistocene hominins, it's crucial to view them within their shifting Pleistocene world.

DISPERSAL OF MIDDLE PLEISTOCENE HOMININS

Like their *Homo erectus* predecessors, later hominins were widely distributed in the Old World, with discoveries coming from three continents—Africa, Asia, and Europe. For the first time, Europe became more permanently and densely occupied, as Middle Pleistocene

interglacials Climatic intervals when continental ice sheets are retreating, eventually becoming much reduced in size. Interglacials in northern latitudes are associated with warmer temperatures, while in southern latitudes the climate becomes wetter.

Figure **11-2**

Changing Pleistocene environments in Eurasia. Green areas show regions of likely hominin occupation. White areas are major glaciers. Arrows indicate likely migration routes.

Interglacial period

Scandinavian continental glacier

Glacial period
(near maximum of glaciations)

hominins have been discovered widely from England, France, Spain, Germany, Italy, Hungary, and Greece. Africa, as well, probably continued as a central area of hominin occupation, and finds have come from North, East, and South Africa. Finally, Asia has yielded several important finds, most especially from China (see Fig. 11-7, pp. 262–263). We should point out, though, that these Middle Pleistocene premodern humans didn't vastly extend the geographical range of *Homo erectus*, but largely replaced the earlier hominins in previously exploited habitats. One exception appears to be the more successful occupation of Europe, a region where earlier hominins have only sporadically been found.

MIDDLE PLEISTOCENE HOMININS: TERMINOLOGY

The premodern humans of the Middle Pleistocene (that is, after 780,000 ya) generally succeeded *H. erectus*. Still, in some areas—especially in Asia—there apparently was a long period of coexistence, lasting 300,000 years or longer; you'll recall the very late dates for the Javanese Ngandong *H. erectus* (see p. 244).

The earliest premodern humans exhibit several *H. erectus* characteristics: The face is large, the brows are projected, the forehead is low, and in some cases the cranial vault is still thick. Even so, some of their other features show that they were more derived toward the modern condition than were their *Homo erectus* predecessors. Compared to *H. erectus*, these premodern humans possessed an increased brain size, a more rounded braincase (that is, maximum breadth is higher up on the sides), a more vertical nose, and a less-angled back of the skull (occipital). We should note that the maximum span of time encompassed by Middle Pleistocene premodern humans is at least 500,000 years, so it's no surprise that over time, we can observe certain trends. Later Middle Pleistocene hominins, for example, show even more brain expansion and an even less-angled occipital than do earlier forms.

We know that premodern humans were a diverse group dispersed over three continents. Deciding how to classify them has been in dispute for decades, and anthropologists still have disagreements. However, a growing consensus has recently emerged. Beginning perhaps as early as 850,000 ya and extending to about 200,000 ya, the fossils from Africa and Europe are placed within *Homo heidelbergensis*, named after a fossil found in Germany in 1907. What's more, some Asian specimens possibly represent a regional variant of *H. heidelbergensis*.

Until recently, many researchers regarded these fossils as early, but more primitive, members of *Homo sapiens*. In recognition of this somewhat transitional status, the fossils were called "archaic *Homo sapiens*," with all later humans also belonging to the species *Homo sapiens*. However, most paleoanthropologists now find this terminology unsatisfactory. For example, Phillip Rightmire concludes that "simply lumping diverse ancient groups with living populations obscures their differences" (1998, p. 226). In our own discussion, we recognize *Homo heidelbergensis* as a transitional species between *Homo erectus* and later hominins (that is, primarily *Homo sapiens*). Keep in mind, however, that this species was probably an ancestor of both modern humans and Neandertals. It's debatable whether *H. heidelbergensis* actually represents a fully separate species in the biological sense, that is, following the biological species concept (see p. 106). Still, it's useful to give this group of premodern humans a separate name to make this important stage of human evolution more easily identifiable. (We'll return to this issue later in the chapter, when we discuss the theoretical implications in more detail.)

Premodern Humans of the Middle Pleistocene

AFRICA

In Africa, premodern fossils have been found at several sites (Figs. 11-3 and 11-4). One of the best known is Kabwe (Broken Hill). At this site in Zambia, fieldworkers discovered a complete cranium, together with other cranial and postcranial elements belonging to several individuals. In this and other African premodern specimens, we can see a mixture of older and more recent traits. The skull's massive browridge (one of the largest of any hominin), low vault, and prominent occipital torus recall those of *H. erectus*. On the other hand, the occipital region is less angulated, the cranial vault bones are thinner, and the cranial base is essentially modern. Dating estimates of Kabwe and most of the other premodern fossils from Africa have ranged throughout the Middle and Late Pleistocene, but recent estimates have given dates for most of the sites in the range of 600,000–125,000 ya.

A total of eight other crania from South and East Africa also show a combination of retained ancestral with more derived (modern) characteristics, and they're all mentioned in the literature as being similar to Kabwe. The most important of these African finds come from the sites of Florisbad and Elandsfontein in South Africa, Laetoli in Tanzania, and Bodo in Ethiopia (see Fig. 11-7, pp. 262–263).

Bodo is one of the most significant of these other African fossils. A nearly complete cranium, Bodo has been dated to relatively early in the Middle Pleistocene (estimated at 600,000 ya), making it one of the oldest specimens of *Homo heidelbergensis* from the African continent. The Bodo cranium is particularly interesting because it shows a distinctive pattern of cut marks, similar to modifications seen in butchered animal bones. Researchers have thus hypothesized that the Bodo individual was defleshed by other hominins, but for what purpose is not clear. The defleshing may have been related to cannibalism, though it also may have been for some other purpose, such as ritual. In any case, this is the earliest evidence of deliberate bone processing of hominins *by* hominins (White, 1986).

The general similarities in all these African premodern fossils indicate a close relationship between them, almost certainly representing a single species (most commonly referred to as *H. heidelbergensis*). These African premodern humans also are quite similar to those found in Europe.

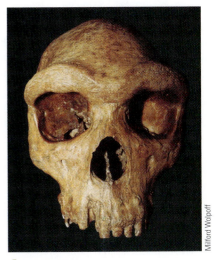

Milford Wolpoff

Figure **11-3**

The Kabwe (Broken Hill) *Homo heidelbergensis* skull from Zambia. Note the very robust browridges.

Figure **11-4**

The Bodo cranium, the earliest evidence of *Homo heidelbergensis* in Africa.

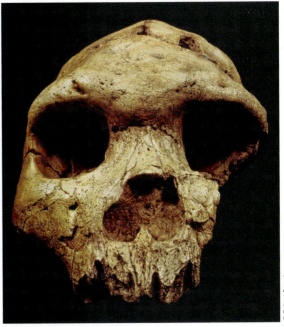

© Robert Franciscus

At a Glance

Key Premodern Human (*H. heidelbergensis*) Fossils from Africa

DATE	SITE	EVOLUTIONARY SIGNIFICANCE
130,000+ ya	**Kabwe Broken Hill** (Zambia)	Nearly complete skull; mosaic of features (brow-ridge very robust, but brain case expanded)
600,000 ya	**Bodo** (Ethiopia)	Earliest example of African *H. heidelbergensis*; likely evidence of butchering

EUROPE

More fossil hominins of Middle Pleistocene age have been found in Europe than in any other region. Maybe it's because more archaeologists have been searching longer in Europe than elsewhere. In any case, during the Middle Pleistocene, Europe was more widely and consistently occupied than it was earlier in human evolution.

The time range of European premodern humans extends the full length of the Middle Pleistocene and beyond. At the earlier end, the Gran Dolina finds from northern Spain (discussed in Chapter 10; see p. 248) are definitely not *Homo erectus*. The Gran Dolina remains may, as proposed by Spanish researchers, be members of a new hominin species. However, Rightmire (1998) has suggested that the Gran Dolina hominins may simply represent the earliest well-dated occurrence of *H. heidelbergensis*, possibly dating as early as 850,000 ya.

More recent and more completely studied *H. heidelbergensis* fossils have been found throughout much of Europe. Examples of these finds come from Steinheim (Germany), Petralona (Greece), Swanscombe (England), Arago (France), and another cave at Atapuerca (Spain). Like their African counterparts, these European premoderns have retained certain *H. erectus* traits, but they're mixed with more derived ones—for example, increased cranial capacity, more rounded occiput, parietal expansion, and reduced tooth size (Fig. 11-5).

The hominins from Atapuerca are especially interesting. These finds come from another cave in the same area as the Gran Dolina and Sima del Elefante discoveries. Dated to between 600,000 and 530,000 ya (Bischoff et al., 2007), a total of at least 28 individuals have been recovered from a site called Sima de los Huesos, literally meaning "pit of bones." In fact, with more than 4,000 fossil fragments recovered, Sima de los Huesos contains more than 80 percent of all Middle Pleistocene hominin remains in the world (Bermudez de Castro et al., 2004). Excavations continue at this remarkable site, where bones have somehow accumulated within a deep chamber inside a cave. From initial descriptions, paleoanthropologists interpret the hominin morphology as showing several indications of an early Neandertal-like pattern, with arching browridges, projecting midface, and other features (Rightmire, 1998).

ASIA

Like their contemporaries in Europe and Africa, Asian premodern specimens discovered in China also display both earlier and later characteristics. Chinese paleoanthropologists suggest that the more ancestral traits, such as a sagit-

Figure **11-5**

Steinheim cranium, a representative of *H. heidelbergensis* from Germany.

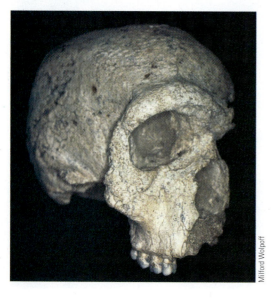

Milford Wolpoff

At a Glance

Key Premodern Human (*H. heidelbergensis*) Fossils from Europe

DATES	SITE	EVOLUTIONARY SIGNIFICANCE
300,000?–259,000? ya	**Swanscombe** (England)	Partial skull, but shows considerable brain expansion
600,000–530,000 ya	**Atapuerca** (Sima de los Huesos, northern Spain)	Large sample; very early evidence of Neandertal ancestry (>500,000 ya); earliest evidence of deliberate disposal anywhere

tal ridge (see p. 240) and flattened nasal bones, are shared with *H. erectus* fossils from Zhoukoudian. They also point out that some of these features can be found in modern *H. sapiens* in China today, indicating substantial genetic continuity. That is, some Chinese researchers have argued that anatomically modern Chinese didn't evolve from *H. sapiens* in either Europe or Africa; instead, they evolved specifically in China from a separate *H. erectus* lineage. Whether such regional evolution occurred or whether anatomically modern migrants from Africa displaced local populations is the subject of a major ongoing debate in paleoanthropology. This important controversy will be the central focus of the next chapter.

Dali, the most complete skull of the later Middle or early Late Pleistocene fossils in China, displays *H. erectus* and *H. sapiens* traits, with a cranial capacity of 1,120 cm^3 (Fig. 11-6a). Like Dali, several other Chinese specimens combine both earlier and later traits. In addition, a partial skeleton from Jinniushan, in northeast China (Fig. 11-6b), has been given a provisional date of 200,000 ya (Tiemel et al., 1994). The cranial capacity is fairly large (approximately 1,260 cm3), and the walls of the braincase are thin. These are both modern features, and they're somewhat unexpected in an individual this ancient—if the dating estimate is indeed correct. Just how to classify these Chinese Middle Pleistocene hominins has been a subject of debate and controversy. Recently, though, a leading paleoanthropologist has concluded that they're regional variants of *H. heidelbergensis* (Rightmire, 2004).

Figure **11-6**

(a) Dali skull and (b) Jinniushan skull, both from China. These two crania are considered by some to be Asian representatives of *Homo heidelbergensis*.

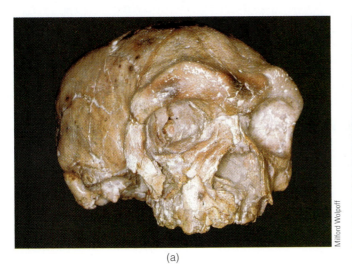

(a)

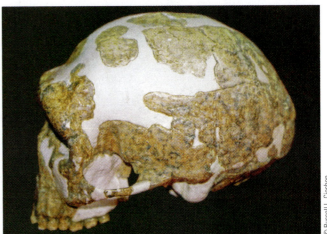

(b)

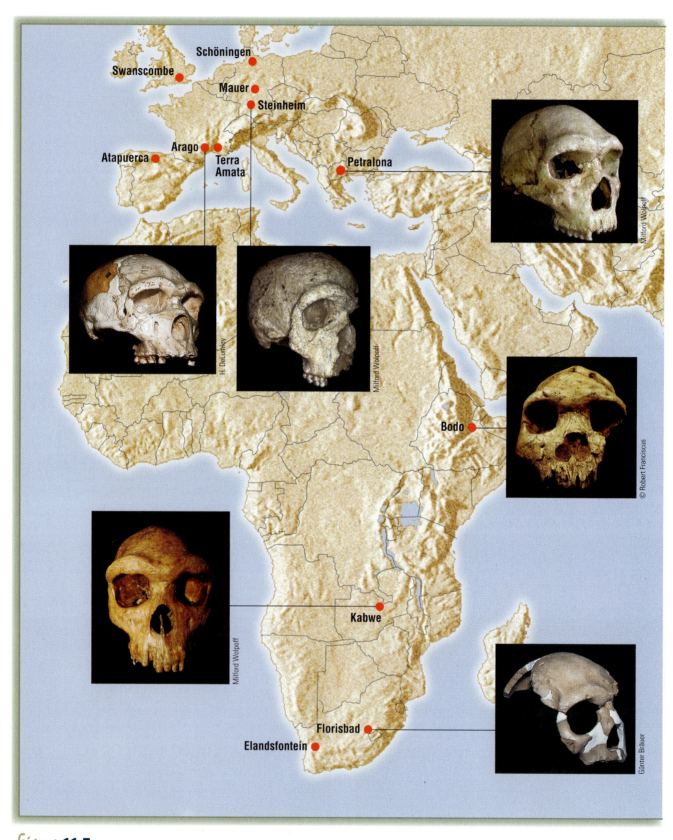

Schöningen

Swanscombe

Mauer

Steinheim

Arago

Atapuerca

Terra
Amata

Petralona

Bodo

Kabwe

Florisbad

Elandsfontein

Milford Wolpoff

H. DeLumley

Milford Wolpoff

© Robert Franciscus

Milford Wolpoff

Günter Bräuer

Figure **11-7**

Fossil discoveries and archaeological localities of
Middle Pleistocene premodern hominins.

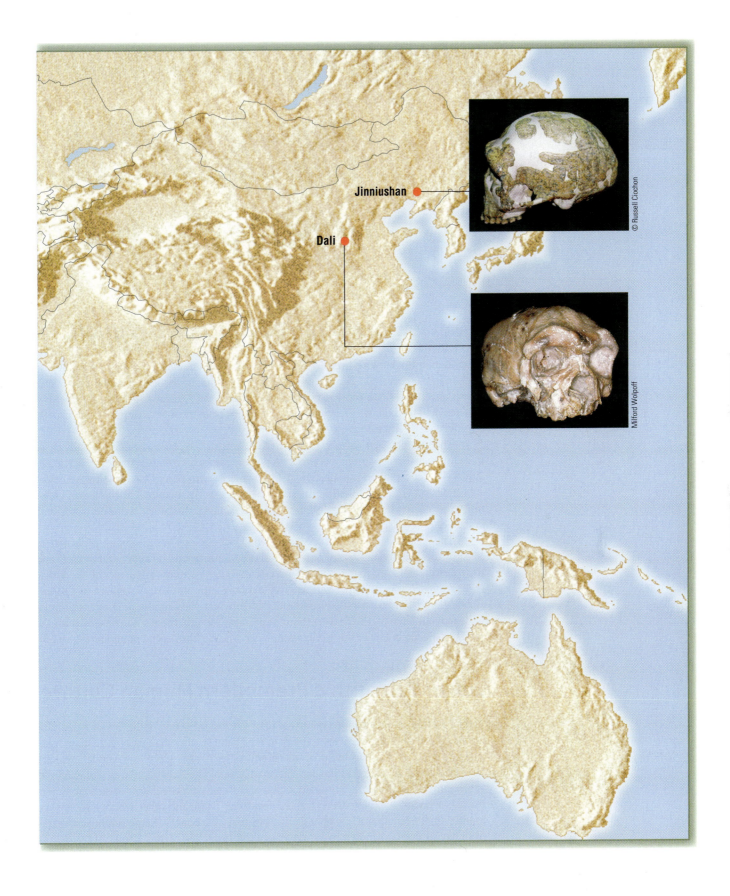

Jinniushan

Dali

© Russell Ciochon

Milford Wolpoff

At a Glance

Key Premodern Human (*H. heidelbergensis*)
Fossils from Asia

DATES	SITE	EVOLUTIONARY SIGNIFICANCE
180,000–230,000 ya	**Dali** China	Nearly complete skull; best evidence of *H. heidelbergensis* in Asia
200,000 ya	**Jinniushan** China	Partial skeleton with cranium showing relatively large brain size; some Chinese scholars suggest it as possible ancestor of early Chinese *H. sapiens*

A Review of Middle Pleistocene Evolution

Premodern human fossils from Africa and Europe resemble each other more than they do the hominins from Asia. The mix of some ancestral characteristics—retained from *Homo erectus* ancestors—with more derived features gives the African and European fossils a distinctive look; thus, Middle Pleistocene hominins from these two continents are usually referred to as *H. heidelbergensis*.

The situation in Asia isn't so tidy. To some researchers, the remains, especially those from Jinniushan, seem more modern than do contemporary fossils from either Europe or Africa. This observation explains why Chinese paleoanthropologists and some American colleagues conclude that the Jinniushan remains are early members of *H. sapiens*. Other researchers (for example, Rightmire, 1998, 2004) suggest that they represent a regional branch of *H. heidelbergensis*.

The Pleistocene world forced many small populations into geographical isolation. Most of these regional populations no doubt died out. Some, however, did evolve, and their descendants are likely a major part of the later hominin fossil record. In Africa, *H. heidelbergensis* is hypothesized to have evolved into modern *H. sapiens*. In Europe, *H. heidelbergensis* evolved into Neandertals. Meanwhile, the Chinese premodern populations may all have met with extinction. Right now, though, there's no consensus on the status or the likely fate of these enigmatic Asian Middle Pleistocene hominins (Fig. 11-8).

Lower Paleolithic Premodern Human Culture

Acheulian technology changed relatively little until near the end of the Lower Paleolithic period. Flake tools and hand axes, many of which are smaller than early Acheulian hand axes, are commonly found in European assemblages. Amazingly, a few wooden artifacts have also been uncovered in the excavation of several late Acheulian sites. For example, at Schöningen, in the Harz Mountain region of Germany, archaeologists discovered more than six wooden spears between 6 and 8 feet long. These and other wooden tools were found with the remains of horses and other big game, the bones of some bearing cut marks from having been butchered by Lower Paleolithic hunters (Thieme, 2005).

Toolmakers made little use of bone, antler, and ivory, all of which would become common raw materials for Upper Paleolithic hunter-gatherers. Among their technological accomplishments, about 300,000 ya, later premodern humans in Africa and Europe

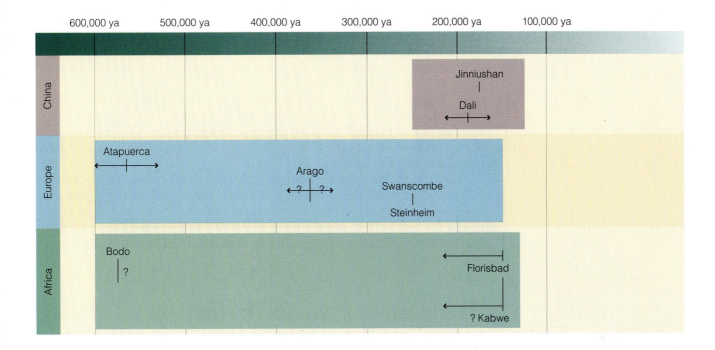

Figure 11-8

Time line of Middle Pleistocene hominins. Note that most dates are approximations. Question marks indicate those estimates that are most tentative.

invented the **prepared-core method** for striking flakes from stone cores (Klein, 1999). Requiring several coordinated steps, a prepared-core method called the Levallois technique required a toolmaker to work each stone core into a preplanned shape before beginning to detach flakes from it (Fig. 11-9). While this may sound like more trouble than it was worth, the prepared-core method enabled toolmakers to strike off flakes of predictable shape and get more usable flakes from each core.

Hominin populations adapted to the seasonal climatic extremes of life outside the tropics in many ways, including the controlled use of fire and the construction of shelters. The most convincing archaeological evidence of the earliest controlled use of fire in Eurasia comes from Gesher Benot Ya'aqov, Israel, where researchers report burned wood, seeds, and flint flakes from contexts dated stratigraphically to nearly 790,000 ya (Goren-Inbar et al., 2004). Klein (1999) reports similar but younger archaeological evidence from France, Germany, and Hungary. What's more, Chinese archaeologists insist that many Middle Pleistocene sites in China contain evidence of human-controlled fire.

A few sites have also contained patches of artifacts, food waste, stones, and other debris interpreted as the remains of temporary shelters, as well as burned areas interpreted as the remains of hearths or fireplaces. At Terra Amata, a French site on the Mediterranean coast near Nice, excavators uncovered fascinating evidence relating to short-term, seasonal

prepared-core method Pertaining to stone cores that a toolmaker shapes into a pre-planned form before striking flakes from it; enables predictable flake shape and thickness; can be efficient in the use of raw materials.

Figure 11-9

The Levallois technique

Nodule

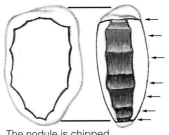

The nodule is chipped on the perimeter.

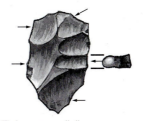

Flakes are radially removed from top surface.

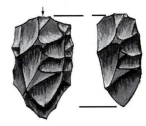

A final blow struck at one end removes a large flake. The flake on the right is the goal of the whole process and is the completed tool.

visits by hominin groups, who built flimsy shelters, gathered plants, ate food from the ocean, and possibly hunted medium- to large-sized mammals (de Lumley and de Lumley, 1973; Villa, 1983).

Archaeologists continue to debate the extent to which later Lower Paleolithic hominins were hunters in the same sense as modern hunter-gatherers. With the notable exception of the Schöningen spears mentioned earlier, late Lower Paleolithic sites include few artifacts that could have been true weapons or killing tools. Meat was apparently an important part of the diet for at least some populations, and plant foods were undoubtedly so, but archaeologists are generally skeptical that these hominins were true hunter-gatherers in the modern sense.

The Middle Paleolithic period began about 200,000 ya in western Europe. Roughly the same period in sub-Saharan Africa is called the Middle Stone Age. As documented by the fossil remains and Middle Paleolithic artifactual evidence, the long period of transitional hominins in Europe continued well into the Late Pleistocene (after 125,000 ya). But with the appearance and expansion of the Neandertals, the evolution of premodern humans took a unique turn.

Neandertals: Premodern Humans of the Late Pleistocene

Since their discovery more than a century ago, the Neandertals have haunted the minds and foiled the best-laid theories of paleoanthropologists. They fit into the general scheme of human evolution, and yet they're misfits. Classified variously either as *H. sapiens* or as belonging to a separate species, they are like us and yet different. It's not easy to put them in their place. Many anthropologists classify Neandertals within *H. sapiens* but as a distinctive subspecies, *Homo sapiens neanderthalensis*,* with modern *H. sapiens* designated as *Homo sapiens sapiens*. However, not all experts agree with this interpretation. The wide consensus that *Homo heidelbergensis* was a likely ancestor of both Neandertals and modern *Homo sapiens* as well as new archaeological and crucial genetic data have all led to the increasingly common placement of Neandertals into a separate species: *Homo neanderthalensis*.

Neandertal fossil remains have been found at dates approaching 130,000 ya; but in the following discussion of Neandertals, we'll focus on those populations that lived especially during the last major glaciation, which began about 75,000 ya and ended about 10,000 ya (Fig. 11-10). We should also note that the evolutionary roots of Neandertals apparently reach quite far back in western Europe, as evidenced by the 500,000+-year-old remains from Sima de los Huesos, Atapuerca, in northern Spain. The majority of fossils have been found in Europe, where they've been most studied. Our description of Neandertals is based primarily on those specimens, usually called *classic* Neandertals, from western Europe. Not all Neandertals—including others from eastern Europe and western Asia and those from the interglacial period just before the last glacial one—exactly fit our description of the classic morphology. They tend to be less robust, possibly because the climate in which they lived was not as cold as in western Europe during the last glaciation.

One striking feature of Neandertals is brain size, which in these hominins actually was larger than that of *H. sapiens* today. The average for contemporary *H. sapiens* is between 1,300 and 1,400 cm³, while for Neandertals it was 1,520 cm³. The larger size may be associated with the metabolic efficiency of a larger brain in cold weather. The Inuit (Eskimo), also

---

Thal, meaning "valley," is the old spelling; but due to rules of taxonomic naming, this spelling is retained in the formal species designation *Homo neanderthalensis* (although the *h* was *never* pronounced). The spelling now in modern German is *tal*; we follow this contemporary usage in the text with the spelling of the colloquial *Neandertal*.

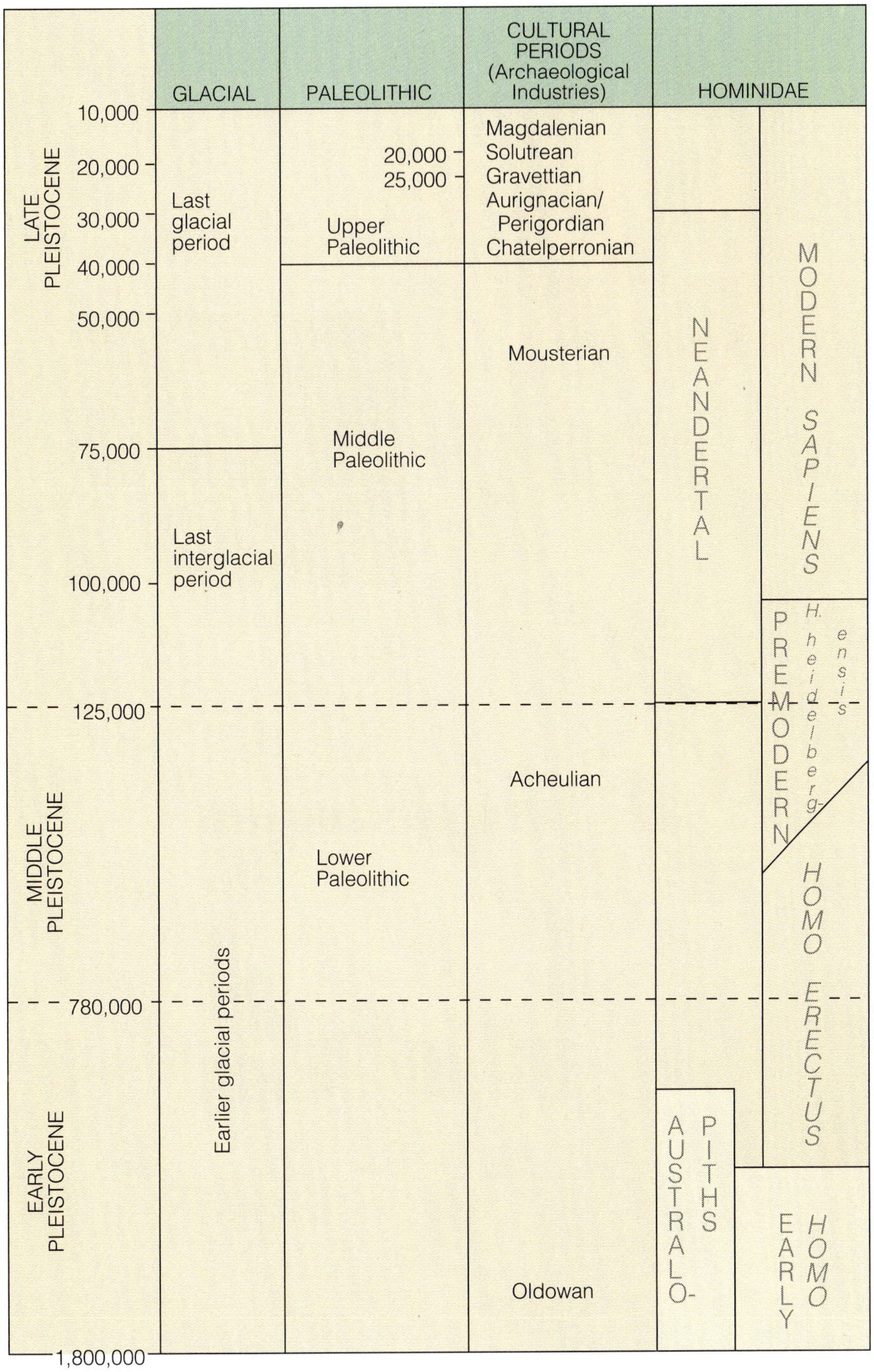

	GLACIAL	PALEOLITHIC	CULTURAL PERIODS (Archaeological Industries)	HOMINIDAE	
LATE PLEISTOCENE 10,000 / 20,000 / 30,000 / 40,000 / 50,000 / 75,000 / 100,000	Last glacial period / Last interglacial period	Upper Paleolithic / Middle Paleolithic	20,000 / 25,000 Magdalenian Solutrean Gravettian Aurignacian/ Perigordian Chatelperronian / Mousterian	N E A N D E R T A L	M O D E R N S A P I E N S
MIDDLE PLEISTOCENE 125,000 / 780,000	Earlier glacial periods	Lower Paleolithic	Acheulian	P R E M O D E R N	H. h e i d e l b e r g- e n s i s / H O M O E R E C T U S
EARLY PLEISTOCENE 1,800,000			Oldowan	A U S T R A L O- P I T H S	E A R L Y H O M O

figure **11-10**
Correlation of Pleistocene subdivisions with archaeological industries and hominins. Note that the geological divisions are separate and different from the archaeological stages (e.g., Late Pleistocene is *not* synonymous with Upper Paleolithic).

living in very cold areas, have a larger average brain size than most other modern human populations. We should also point out that the larger brain size in both premodern and contemporary human populations adapted to cold climates is partially correlated with larger body size, which has also evolved among these groups (see Chapter 4).

The classic Neandertal cranium is large, long, low, and bulging at the sides. Viewed from the side, the occipital bone is somewhat bun-shaped, but the marked occipital angle typical of many *H. erectus* crania is absent. The forehead rises more vertically than that of *H. erectus*, and the browridges arch over the orbits instead of forming a straight bar (Fig. 11-11).

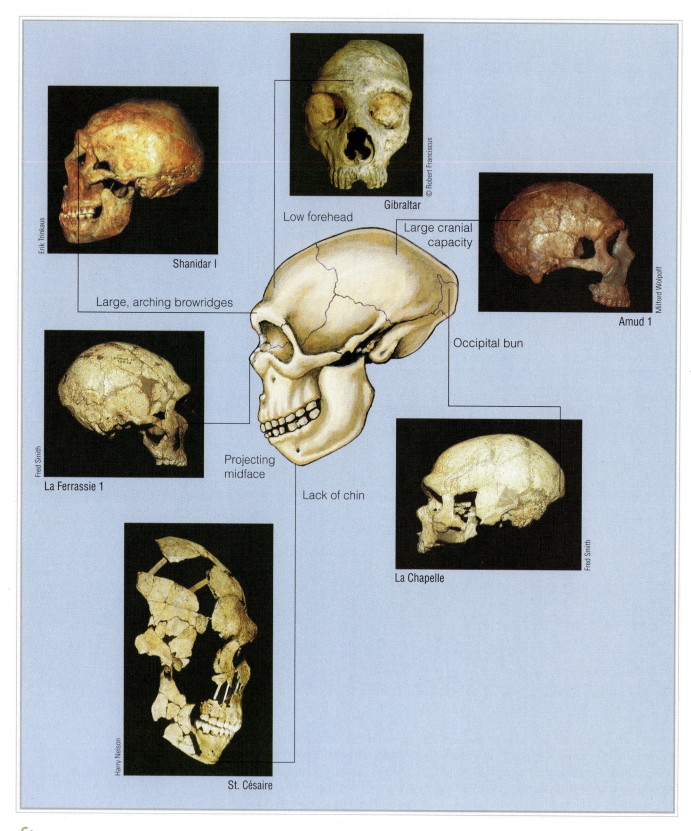

Figure **11-11**

Morphology and variation in Neandertal crania.

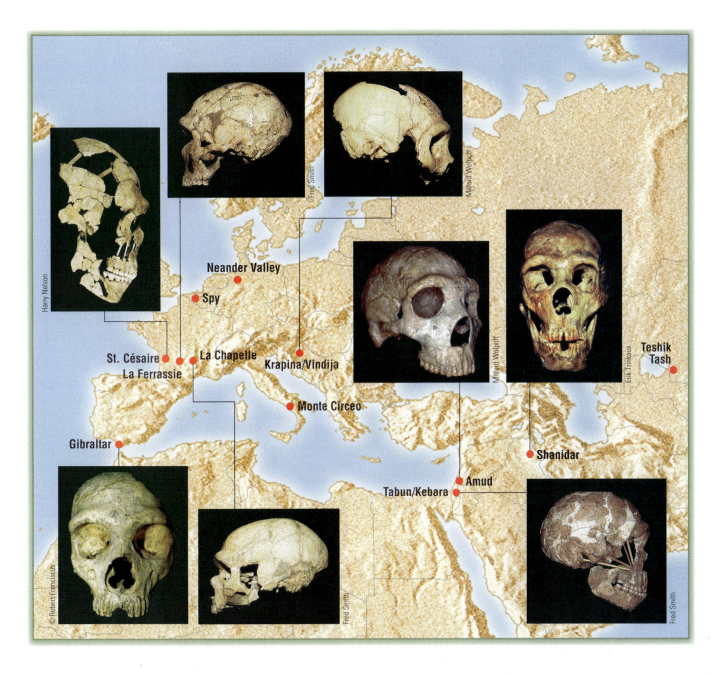

Neander Valley

Spy

St. Césaire

La Chapelle

La Ferrassie

Krapina/Vindija

Monte Circeo

Gibraltar

Teshik
Tash

Shanidar

Amud

Tabun/Kebara

Harry Nelson

Fred Smith

Milford Wolpoff

Milford Wolpoff

Erik Trinkaus

© Robert Franciscus

Fred Smith

Fred Smith

Figure **11-12**

Fossil discoveries of Neandertals.

Compared with anatomically modern humans, the Neandertal face stands out. It projects almost as if it were pulled forward. Postcranially, Neandertals were very robust, barrel-chested, and powerfully muscled. This robust skeletal structure, in fact, dominates hominin evolution from *H. erectus* through all premodern forms. Still, the Neandertals appear particularly robust, with shorter limbs than seen in most modern *H. sapiens* populations. Both the facial anatomy and the robust postcranial structure of Neandertals have been interpreted by Erik Trinkaus, of Washington University in St. Louis, as adaptations to rigorous living in a cold climate.

For about 100,000 years, Neandertals lived in Europe and western Asia (Fig. 11-12), and their coming and going have raised more questions and controversies than for any other hominin group. As we've noted, Neandertal forebears were transitional forms dating to the later Middle Pleistocene. However, it's not until the Late Pleistocene that Neandertals become fully recognizable.

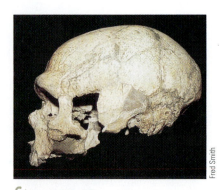

Figure **11-13**

La Chapelle-aux-Saints. Note the occipital bun, projecting face, and low vault.

Fred Smith

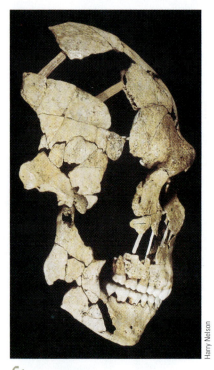

Figure **11-14**

St. Césaire, among the "last" Neandertals.

Harry Nelson

flexed The position of the body in a bent orientation, with arms and legs drawn up to the chest.

Chatelperronian Pertaining to an Upper Paleolithic industry found in France and Spain.

Mousterian A Middle Paleolithic stone tool industry associated with Neandertals and some modern *H. sapiens* groups.

Aurignacian An early Upper Paleolithic stone tool industry found across southern Europe and the Near East.

WESTERN EUROPE

One of the most important Neandertal discoveries was made in 1908 at La Chapelle-aux-Saints, in southwestern France. A nearly complete skeleton was found buried in a shallow grave in a **flexed** position. Several fragments of nonhuman long bones had been placed over the head, and over them, a bison leg. Around the body were flint tools and broken animal bones.

The skeleton was turned over for study to a well-known French paleontologist, Marcellin Boule, who depicted the La Chapelle Neandertal as a brutish, bent-kneed, not fully erect biped. Because of this exaggerated interpretation, some scholars, and certainly the general public, concluded that all Neandertals were highly primitive creatures.

Why did Boule draw these conclusions from the La Chapelle skeleton? Today, we think he misjudged the Neandertal posture because this adult male skeleton had osteoarthritis of the spine. Also, and probably more important, Boule and his contemporaries found it difficult to fully accept as a human ancestor an individual who appeared in any way to depart from the modern pattern.

The skull of this male, who was possibly at least 40 years of age when he died, is very large, with a cranial capacity of 1,620 cm^3. Typical of western European classic forms, the vault is low and long; the browridges are immense, with the typical Neandertal arched shape; the forehead is low and retreating; and the face is long and projecting. The back of the skull is protuberant and bun-shaped (Figs. 11-11 and 11-13).

The La Chapelle skeleton isn't a typical Neandertal, but an unusually robust male who "evidently represents an extreme in the Neandertal range of variation" (Brace et al., 1979, p. 117). Unfortunately, this skeleton, which Boule claimed didn't even walk completely erect, was widely accepted as "Mr. Neandertal." But not all Neandertal individuals express the suite of classic Neandertal traits to the degree seen in this one (see Fig. 11-11).

Some of the most recent of the western European Neandertals come from St. Césaire in southwestern France and are dated at about 35,000 ya (Fig. 11-14). The bones were found in association with scrapers, points, and other stone tools of the **Chatelperronian**, an Upper Paleolithic tool industry that shows similarities to the Middle Paleolithic **Mousterian** industry. And at another late site in central Europe, radiocarbon dating points to the most recent Neandertal remains at Vindija, in Croatia (discussed shortly), at about 32,000 to 33,000 years old (Janković et al., 2006).

The St. Césaire and Vindija sites are important for several reasons. Anatomically modern humans were living in central and western Europe by about 35,000 ya or a bit earlier. So it's possible that Neandertals and modern *H. sapiens* were living quite close to each other for several thousand years (Fig. 11-15). How did these two groups interact? The possible answers continue to be hotly debated among paleoanthropologists, but the archaeological evidence suggests that while they may have led quite different lives, the two groups probably did interact. For example, as previously noted, Chatelperronian tools and other artifacts are similar to those of the Mousterian, which has been found in association with modern *H. sapiens* and Neandertals. And chronometric dates for the **Aurignacian**, another early Upper Paleolithic industry, show that it was contemporaneous with the most recent Neandertal fossils and the oldest remains of modern *H. sapiens* in western Europe. Unfortunately, paleoanthropologists have yet to find a clear instance that links Aurignacian assemblages to any diagnostic hominin fossil remains (Janković et al., 2006). The nature, timing, and duration of interaction between Neandertals and modern *H. sapiens* remain open research questions.

CENTRAL EUROPE

There are quite a few other European classic Neandertals, including significant finds in central Europe (see Fig. 10-12). At Krapina, Croatia, researchers have recovered an abundance of bones—1,000 fragments representing up to 70 individuals—and 1,000 stone

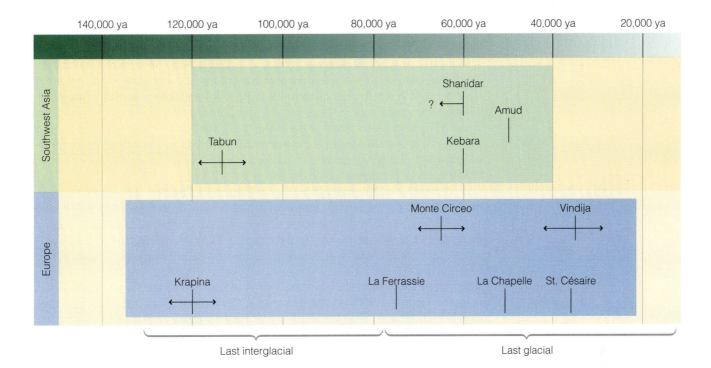

Figure **11-15**

Time line for Neandertal fossil discoveries.

tools or flakes (Trinkaus and Shipman, 1992). Krapina is an old site, possibly the earliest showing the full classic Neandertal morphology, dating back to the beginning of the Late Pleistocene (estimated at 130,000–110,000 ya). And despite the relatively early date, the characteristic Neandertal features of the Krapina specimens, although less robust, are similar to the western European finds (Fig. 11-16). Krapina is also important as an intentional burial site—one of the oldest on record.

About 30 miles from Krapina, Neandertal fossils have also been discovered at Vindija. The site is an excellent source of faunal, cultural, and hominin materials stratified in *sequence* throughout much of the Late Pleistocene. Neandertal fossils consisting of some 35 specimens are dated between about 42,000 and 32,000 ya. (The latter date would be the best verified of the more recent Neandertal discoveries; Higham et al., 2006.) While the overall anatomical pattern is definitely Neandertal, some features of the Vindija individuals, such as smaller browridges and slight chin development, approach the morphology seen in early modern south-central European *H. sapiens*. These similarities have led some researchers to suggest a possible evolutionary link between the late Vindija Neandertals and modern *H. sapiens*.

(a)   (b)

Fred Smith

Figure **11-16**

Krapina partial cranium. (a) Lateral view showing characteristic Neandertal traits. (b) Three-quarters view.

WESTERN ASIA

Israel In addition to European Neandertals, many important discoveries have been made in southwest Asia. Several specimens from Israel display some modern features and are less robust than the classic Neandertals of Europe, though again, the overall pattern is Neandertal. The best known of these discoveries is from Tabun—short for Mugharet-et-Tabun, meaning "cave of the oven"—at Mt. Carmel, a short drive south from Haifa (Fig. 11-17). Tabun, excavated in the early 1930s, yielded a female skeleton, recently dated by thermoluminescence (TL) at about 120,000–110,000 ya. If this dating is accurate, Neandertals at Tabun were generally contemporary with early modern *H. sapiens* found in nearby caves. (TL dating is discussed on p. 194.)

A more recent Neandertal burial, a male discovered in 1983, comes from Kebara, a neighboring cave of Tabun at Mt. Carmel. A partial skeleton, dated to 60,000 ya, contains the most complete Neandertal pelvis so far recovered. Also recovered at Kebara is a hyoid—a small bone located in the throat, and the first ever found from a Neandertal; this bone is especially important because of its usefulness in reconstructing language capabilities.*

Iraq A most remarkable site is Shanidar cave, in the Zagros Mountains of northeastern Iraq, where fieldworkers found partial skeletons of nine individuals, four of them deliberately buried. Among these individuals is a particularly interesting one called Shanidar 1. This is a skeleton of a male who lived to be approximately 30 to 45 years old, a considerable age for a prehistoric human (Fig. 11-18). His height is estimated at 5 feet 7 inches, and his cranial capacity is 1,600 cm³. Shanidar 1 also exhibits several other fascinating features:

> There had been a crushing blow to the left side of the head, fracturing the eye socket, displacing the left eye, and probably causing blindness on that side. He also sustained a massive blow to the right side of the body that so badly damaged the right arm that it became withered and useless; the bones of the shoulder blade,

Figure **11-17**

Excavation of the Tabun Cave, Mt. Carmel, Israel.

Harry Nelson

---

*The Kebara hyoid is identical to that of modern humans, suggesting that Neandertals did not differ from modern *H. sapiens sapiens* in this key element.

collar bone, and upper arm are much smaller and thinner than those on the left. The right lower arm and hand are missing, probably not because of poor preservation . . . but because they either atrophied and dropped off or because they were amputated. (Trinkaus and Shipman, 1992, p. 340)

Besides these injuries, the man had further trauma to both legs, and he probably limped. It's hard to imagine how he could have performed day-to-day activities. This is why Erik Trinkaus, who has studied the Shanidar remains, suggests that to survive, Shanidar 1 must have been helped by others: "A one-armed, partially blind, crippled man could have made no pretense of hunting or gathering his own food. That he survived for years after his trauma was a testament to Neandertal compassion and humanity" (Trinkaus and Shipman, 1992, p. 341).

CENTRAL ASIA

Neandertals extended their range even farther to the east, far into central Asia. A discovery made in the 1930s at the Teshik-Tash site in Uzbekistan of a Neandertal child associated with tools of the Mousterian industry suggested that this species had dispersed a long way into Asia. However, owing to poor archaeological control during excavation and the young age of the individual, the find was not considered by many paleoanthropolgists as clearly that of a Neandertal. New finds and molecular evaluation have provided crucial evidence that Neandertals did in fact extend their geographical range far into central Asia and perhaps even farther east.

DNA analysis of the Teshik-Tash remains shows that they are clearly Neandertal. What's more, other fragments from southern Siberia also show a distinctively Neandertal genetic pattern (Krause et al., 2007). As we'll see shortly (see p. 276), researchers have recently been able to identify and analyze DNA from several Neandertal specimens. It's been shown that Neandertals and modern humans differ in both their mitochondrial DNA (mtDNA) and nuclear DNA, and these results are extremely significant in determining the evolutionary uniqueness of the Neandertal lineage. Moreover, in the case of the fragmentary remains from southern Siberia, it was the DNA findings that provided the key evidence to determine whether the hominin was even a Neandertal. In a sense, this is analogous to doing forensic analysis on our ancient hominin predecessors.

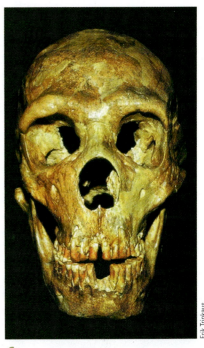

Erik Trinkaus

Figure **11-18**

Shanidar 1. Does he represent Neandertal compassion for the disabled?

At a Glance
Key Neandertal Fossil Discoveries

DATES	SITE	EVOLUTIONARY SIGNIFICANCE
42,000–28,000 ya	**Vindija** (Croatia)	Large sample (best evidence of Neandertals in eastern Europe); latest well-dated Neandertal site
50,000 ya	**La Chapelle** (France)	Most famous Neandertal site; historically provided early, but distorted, interpretation of Neandertals
70,000–60,000 ya	**Shanidar** (Iraq)	Several well-preserved skeletons; good example of Neandertals from southwestern Asia; one individual with multiple injuries
110,000 ya; date uncertain	**Tabun** (Israel)	Well-preserved and very well-studied fossils showing early evidence of Neandertals in southwestern Asia

Middle Paleolithic Culture

The best-known Middle Paleolithic tool industry is the Mousterian, which many anthropologists closely associate with the Neandertals. Nevertheless, Mousterian artifacts have occasionally been also found with the remains of early modern *H. sapiens* (although *H. sapiens* remains are more frequently found associated with Upper Paleolithic tool industries). It is because of this archaeological overlap that it wasn't entirely clear until the DNA evidence came in whether the central Asian remains were actually Neandertal. Early in the last glacial episode, Mousterian culture extended across Europe and North Africa into the former Soviet Union, Israel, Iran, and as far east as central Asia and possibly even China. Also, in sub-Saharan Africa, the contemporaneous Middle Stone Age industry is broadly similar to the Mousterian.

TECHNOLOGY

One of the most significant Middle Paleolithic technological innovations was the **composite tool** (Fig. 11-19), which was developed in Africa as early as the Lower-to-Middle Paleolithic transition, 300,000–200,000 ya. Modern kitchens and garage workshops are stuffed with composite tools—knives, spatulas, hammers, hatchets, pizza cutters, and the like. We take such tools for granted, but somewhere along the line, a long, long time ago, some smart hominin first figured out that you can make many tools more effective if you first attach them to a handle, or shaft. When a Lower Paleolithic hominin used a hand axe, cleaver, or flake tool, it was entirely handheld (now you can see where we get the name "hand axe"); but when a Middle Paleolithic toolmaker picked up a tool, chances are the business end of that implement was embedded in a handle and held in place by glue, leather bindings, or friction.

Some researchers hypothesize that composite tools marked a significant step forward in other ways too; their existence clearly implies that hominins had begun to master and communicate complex behavioral sequences. Archaeologist Stanley Ambrose (2001) argues that these complex toolmaking abilities may have coevolved with grammatical language. Both require fine motor skills and the ability to solve problems and plan complex tasks, and both are controlled by adjacent areas of the human brain. Viewed from this perspective, it is no accident that subsequent to the invention of composite tools, the pace of cultural change began to accelerate.

Most Middle Paleolithic stone tools were based on flakes that had been struck from cores and chipped into their final form. Common flake tools include several kinds of scrapers; points for making composite tools such as thrusting spears and knives; and denticulates, which are deeply notched flakes that have a serrated appearance (Fig. 11-20). Middle Paleolithic stone toolmakers also developed the **discoid** prepared-core technique, which enabled a more efficient use of raw material than the Levallois. They trimmed a flint nodule around the edges to form a disk-shaped core. Each time they struck the edge, they drove off a flake toward the center of the core. The flake struck by the discoid technique wasn't preshaped like a Levallois flake, but this technique did make it easier for the toolmaker to get more usable flakes from a given core.

While Middle Paleolithic peoples developed many specialized tools for skinning and preparing meat, hunting, woodworking, and hafting, they made little use of bone, antler, and ivory as raw materials. This resource use pattern is in striking contrast to that of the Upper Paleolithic, in which these and other materials were commonly used. Nevertheless, Middle Paleolithic technological advances undoubtedly contributed significantly to the remarkable cultural changes of the Upper Paleolithic, which we'll discuss in the next chapter.

Veerle Rots, KULeuven

Figure **11-19**

A hafted scraper. Composite tools consist of a haft or handle, the working part of the tool (here, a stone scraper), and binding or glue to hold it firmly in place.

composite tool Minimally, a tool made of several pieces. For example, a prehistoric knife typically included a handle or shaft, a chipped stone blade, and binding materials such as glue or sinew to hold the blade firmly in place.

discoid technique A prepared-core technique in which flakes are struck toward the center of the stone core; greater efficiency of raw material use than Levallois; also called "radial core" technique.

Figure **11-20**

Examples of the Mousterian tool kit, including (from left to right), a Levallois point, a perforator, and a side scraper.

SUBSISTENCE

We know, from the abundant remains of animal bones at their sites, that Neandertals and other Middle Paleolithic premodern humans were successful hunters, but many archaeologists characterize them as "generalized" hunter-gatherers, which means that they ate many different kinds of animals and plant foods and didn't specialize on just a few species as staple foods. Researchers question if they were hunter-gatherers in the same sense as some Upper Paleolithic groups, who focused much of their hunting on a few big game species.

These are reasonable questions because it wasn't until the beginning of the Upper Paleolithic that such long-distance weaponry as the spear-thrower, or atlatl, came into use (see p. 302), followed later by the bow and arrow. Middle Paleolithic hunting technology was mostly limited to thrusting spears. Consequently, hunters may have been more prone to serious injury—a hypothesis supported by paleoanthropologists Thomas Berger and Erik Trinkaus. Berger and Trinkaus (1995) analyzed the pattern of trauma, particularly fractures, in Neandertals and compared it with that seen in modern human samples. Interestingly, the Neandertal pattern, which included a relatively high proportion of head and neck injuries, was most similar to that seen in contemporary rodeo performers. Berger and Trinkaus concluded that "the similarity to the rodeo distribution suggests frequent close encounters with large ungulates unkindly disposed to the humans involved" (Berger and Trinkaus, 1995, p. 841).

We know much more about European Middle Paleolithic culture than any earlier period because it's been studied longer and by more scholars. Recently, however, Africa has been a target not only of physical anthropologists but also of archaeologists, who have added considerably to our knowledge of African Pleistocene hominin history. In many cases, the technology and assumed cultural adaptations in Africa were similar to those in Europe and southwest Asia. We'll see in the next chapter that the African technological achievements also kept pace with, or even preceded, those in western Europe.

SPEECH AND SYMBOLIC BEHAVIOR

There are a variety of hypotheses concerning the speech capacities of Middle Paleolithic premodern humans, and many of these views are contradictory. Some researchers argue that Neandertals were incapable of human speech. But the prevailing consensus has been that they *were* capable of articulate speech and likely fully competent in producing the full range of sounds used by modern humans.

However, recent genetic evidence may call for a reassessment of just when fully human language first emerged (Enard et al., 2002). In humans today, mutations in a particular gene (locus) are known to produce serious language impairments. From an evolutionary perspective, what's perhaps most significant concerns the greater variability seen in the alleles at this locus in modern humans as compared to other primates. One explanation for this increased variation is intensified selection acting on human populations, and as we'll see shortly, DNA evidence from Neandertal fossils shows that they had already made this transformation.

But even if we conclude that Neandertals *could* speak, it doesn't necessarily mean that their abilities were at the level of modern *Homo sapiens*. Today, paleoanthropologists are quite interested in the apparently sudden expansion of modern *H. sapiens* (discussed in Chapter 12), and they've proposed various explanations for this group's rapid success. Also, as we attempt to explain how and why modern *H. sapiens* expanded its geographical range, we're left with the problem of explaining what happened to the Neandertals. In making these types of interpretations, a growing number of paleoanthropologists suggest that *behavioral* differences are the key.

Researchers believe that Upper Paleolithic *H. sapiens* had some significant behavioral advantages over Neandertals and other premodern humans. Was it some kind of new and expanded ability to symbolize, communicate, organize social activities, elaborate technology, obtain a wider range of food resources, or care for the sick or injured—or was it some other factor? Were the Neandertals limited by neurological differences that may have contributed to their demise?

The direct anatomical evidence derived from Neandertal fossils isn't much help in answering these questions. Ralph Holloway (1985) has maintained that Neandertal brains—at least as far as the fossil evidence suggests—aren't significantly different from those of modern *H. sapiens*. What's more, as we've seen, Neandertal vocal tracts (as well as other morphological features), compared with our own, don't appear to have seriously limited them.

From this type of behavioral and anatomical evidence, Neandertals in recent years have increasingly been viewed as an evolutionary dead end. Right now, we can't say whether their disappearance and ultimate replacement by anatomically modern Upper Paleolithic peoples—with their presumably "superior" culture—was the result of cultural differences alone or whether it was also influenced by biological variation.

BURIALS

Anthropologists have known for some time that Neandertals deliberately buried their dead. Undeniably, the spectacular discoveries at La Chapelle, Shanidar, and elsewhere were the direct results of ancient burial, which permits preservation that's much more complete. Such deliberate burial treatment goes back at least 90,000 years at Tabun. From a much older site, some form of consistent "disposal" of the dead—not necessarily belowground burial—is evidenced: At Atapuerca, Spain, more than 700 fossilized elements (representing at least 28 different individuals) were found in a cave at the end of a deep vertical shaft. From the nature of the site and the accumulation of hominin remains, Spanish researchers are convinced that the site demonstrates some form of human activity involving deliberate disposal of the dead (Arsuaga et al., 1997).

The recent redating of Atapuerca to more than 500,000 ya suggests that Neandertals—more precisely, their immediate precursors—were, by quite early in the Middle Pleistocene, handling their dead in special ways. Such behavior was previously thought to have emerged only much later, in the Late Pleistocene. As far as current data indicate, this practice is seen in western European contexts well before it appears in Africa or eastern Asia. For example, in the premodern sites at Kabwe and Florisbad (discussed earlier), deliberate disposal of the dead is not documented. Nor is it seen in African early modern sites—for example, the Klasies River Mouth, dated at 120,000–100,000 ya (see p. 289).

Lest too much be read into such acts, it's important to remember that humans have lots of reasons to bury their dead. The act of burial and the meaning assigned to it are entirely cultural. Humans invented the concept of burying the dead (along with many other ways of getting rid of bodies), just as they invented all the different ways that we think about the dead. Our point is that sometimes the act of burial, even in the Middle Paleolithic, may have reflected shared beliefs, symbolic behavior, compassion, or status, and sometimes it was just a quick and easy way to dispose of a smelly corpse. Since these two extremes represent very different acts, the problem that nags archaeologists is to identify accurately when it's one thing and not the other.

In later contexts (after 35,000 ya), where modern *H. sapiens* remains are found in clear burial contexts, their treatment is considerably more complex than in Neandertal burials. In these later (Upper Paleolithic) sites, grave goods, including bone and stone tools as well as animal bones, are found more consistently and in greater concentrations. Because many Neandertal sites were excavated in the nineteenth or early twentieth century, before more rigorous archaeological methods had been developed, many of these supposed Neandertal burials are now in question. Still, the evidence seems quite clear that deliberate burial was practiced at several localities. In many cases, the body's position was deliberately modified and placed in the grave in a flexed posture (see p. 270).

Finally, as further evidence of Neandertal symbolic behavior, researchers point to the placement of supposed grave goods in burials, including stone tools, animal bones (such as cave bear), and even arrangements of flowers, together with stone slabs on top of the burials. Unfortunately, in many instances, again due to poorly documented excavation, these finds are questionable. Placement of stone tools, for example, is occasionally seen, but it apparently wasn't done consistently. In those 33 Neandertal burials for which we have adequate data, only 14 show definite association of stone tools and/or animal bones with the deceased (Klein, 1989). It's not until the Upper Paleolithic period that we see a major behavioral shift, as demonstrated in more elaborate burials and development of art.

Genetic Evidence

With the revolutionary advances in molecular biology (discussed in Chapter 3), fascinating new avenues of research have become possible in the study of earlier hominins. It's becoming fairly commonplace to extract, amplify, and sequence ancient DNA from contexts spanning the last 10,000 years or so. For example, researchers have analyzed DNA from the 5,000-year-old "Iceman" found in the Italian Alps.

It's much harder to find usable DNA in even more ancient remains, since the organic components, often including the DNA, have been destroyed during the mineralization process. Still, in the past few years, exciting results have been announced about DNA found in more than a dozen different Neandertal fossils dated between 100,000 and 32,000 ya. These fossils come from sites in France (including La Chapelle), Germany (from the original Neander Valley locality), Belgium, Italy, Spain, Croatia, Russia, and Uzbekistan (Krings et al., 1997, 2000; Ovchinnikov et al., 2000; Schmitz et al., 2002; Serre et al., 2004; Green et al., 2006; Krause et al., 2007).

The technique most often used in studying the Neandertal fossils involves extracting mtDNA, amplifying it through polymerase chain reaction (PCR; see p. 60), and sequencing nucleotides in parts of the molecule. Results from the Neandertal specimens show that these individuals are genetically more different from contemporary *H. sapiens* populations than modern human populations are from each other—in fact, about three times as much. Consequently, Krings and colleagues (1997) have hypothesized that the Neandertal lineage separated from that of our modern *H. sapiens* ancestors sometime between 690,000 and 550,000 ya.

Major advances in molecular biology have allowed much more of the Neandertal genetic pattern to be determined with the ability to now sequence big chunks of the *nuclear* DNA (which, as you may recall, contains more than 99 percent of the human genome). In fact, one group of researchers in Germany has already sequenced more than 1 million bases and will likely complete the sequencing for the entire Neandertal genome within the next few years (Green et al., 2006)! Just a couple of years ago, this sort of enterprise would have seemed like science fiction.

One immediate application of these remarkable new data is further confirmation of the suggested divergence dates derived from mitochondrial DNA. From the studies reported in 2006 and 2007 (Green et al. 2006; Noonan et al., 2006; Pennisi, 2007), the origins of the Neandertals have been traced to approximately 800,000–500,000 ya. Moreover, the early date (more than 500,000 ya) of the transitional Neandertal fossils at Atapuerca, Spain (Bischoff et al., 2007), further confirms this early divergence date. Lastly, the much more extensive Neandertal nuclear DNA patterns are as distinct from those of modern humans as are the differences seen in mtDNA. Considering the length of time that Neandertals were likely separate from the lineage of modern humans as well as their distinct genetic patterning, it seems reasonable that they should be considered a separate species—or at least a population well on its way to becoming separate (see p. 280).

Trends in Human Evolution: Understanding Premodern Humans

As you can see, the Middle Pleistocene hominins are a very diverse group, broadly dispersed through time and space. There is considerable variation among them, and it's not easy to get a clear evolutionary picture. Because we know that regional populations were small and frequently isolated, many of them probably died out and left no descendants. So it's a mistake to see an "ancestor" in every fossil find.

Still, as a group, these Middle Pleistocene premoderns do reveal some general trends. In many ways, for example, it seems that they were *transitional* between the hominin grade that came before them (*H. erectus*) and the one that followed them (modern *H. sapiens*). It's not a stretch to say that all the Middle Pleistocene premoderns derived from *H. erectus* forebears and that some of them, in turn, were probably ancestors of the earliest fully modern humans.

Paleoanthropologists are certainly concerned with such broad generalities as these, but they also want to focus on meaningful anatomical, environmental, and behavioral details as well as underlying processes. So they consider the regional variability displayed by particular fossil samples as significant—but just *how* significant is up for debate. In addition, increasingly sophisticated theoretical approaches are being used to better understand the processes that shaped the evolution of later *Homo*, at both macroevolutionary and microevolutionary levels.

Scientists, like all humans, assign names or labels to phenomena, a point we addressed in discussing classification in Chapter 5. Paleoanthropologists are certainly no exception. Yet, working from a common evolutionary foundation, paleoanthropologists still come to different conclusions about the most appropriate way to interpret the Middle/Late Pleistocene hominins. Consequently, a variety of species names have been proposed in recent years.

Paleoanthropologists who advocate an extreme lumping approach recognize only one species for all the premodern humans discussed in this chapter. These premoderns are classified as *Homo sapiens* and are thus lumped together with modern humans, although they're partly distinguished by such terminology as "archaic *H. sapiens*." As we've noted, this degree of lumping is no longer supported by most researchers. Alternatively, a second, less extreme view postulates modest species diversity and labels the earlier premoderns as *H. heidelbergensis* (Fig. 11-21).

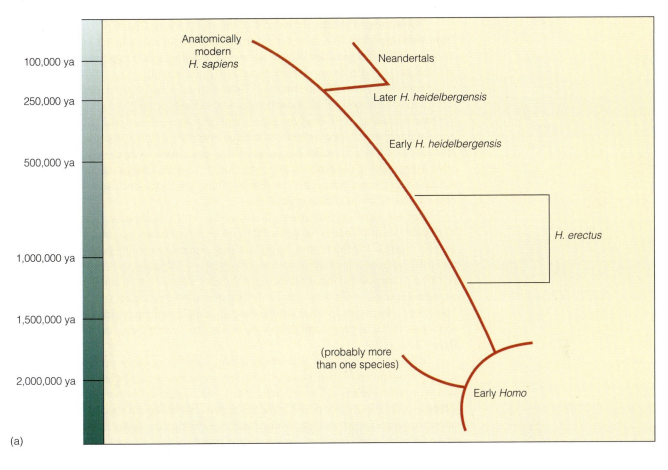

(a)

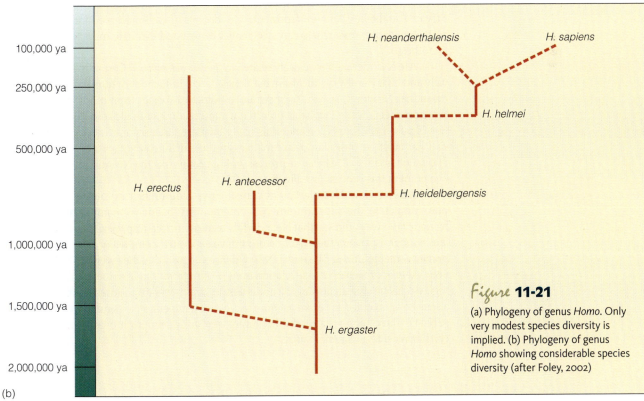

(b)

Figure **11-21**

(a) Phylogeny of genus *Homo*. Only very modest species diversity is implied. (b) Phylogeny of genus *Homo* showing considerable species diversity (after Foley, 2002)

We addressed similar differences of interpretation in Chapters 9 and 10, and we know that disparities like these can be frustrating to students who are new to paleoanthropology. The proliferation of new names is confusing, and it might seem that experts in the field are endlessly arguing about what to call the fossils.

Fortunately, it's not quite that bad. There's actually more agreement than you might think. No one doubts that all these hominins are closely related to each other as well as to modern humans. And everyone agrees that only some of the fossil samples represent populations that left descendants. Where paleoanthropologists disagree is when they start discussing which earlier hominins are the most likely to be closely related to later ones. The grouping of hominins into evolutionary clusters (clades) and assigning different names to them is a reflection of differing interpretations—and, more fundamentally, of somewhat differing philosophies.

But we shouldn't emphasize these naming and classification debates too much. Most paleoanthropologists recognize that a great deal of these disagreements result from simple, practical considerations. Even the most enthusiastic splitters acknowledge that the fossil "species" are not true species as defined by the biological species concept (see p. 106). As prominent paleoanthropologist Robert Foley puts it, "It is unlikely they are all biological species. . . . These are probably a mixture of real biological species and evolving lineages of subspecies. In other words, they could potentially have interbred, but owing to allopatry [that is, geographical separation] were unlikely to have had the opportunity" (Foley, 2002, p. 33).

Even so, Foley, along with an increasing number of other professionals, distinguishes these different fossil samples with species names to highlight their distinct position in hominin evolution. That is, each of these hominin groups is more loosely defined as a type of paleospecies (see p. 109) rather than as a fully biological species. Giving distinct hominin samples separate (species) names makes them more easily identifiable to other researchers and makes various cladistic hypotheses more explicit—and equally important, more directly testable.

The hominins that best illustrate these issues are the Neandertals. Fortunately, they're also the best known, represented by dozens of well-preserved individuals. With all this evidence, researchers can systematically test and evaluate many of the differing hypotheses.

Are Neandertals very closely related to modern *H. sapiens*? Certainly. Are they physically and behaviorally distinct from both ancient and fully modern humans? Yes. Does this mean that Neandertals are a fully separate biological species from modern humans and therefore theoretically incapable of fertilely interbreeding with modern people? Probably not. Finally, then, should Neandertals really be placed in a separate species from *H. sapiens*? For most purposes, it doesn't matter, since the distinction at some point is arbitrary. Speciation is, after all, a *dynamic* process. Fossil groups like the Neandertals represent just one point in this process (see Fig. 5-4, p. 107).

We can view Neandertals as a distinctive side branch of later hominin evolution. Similar to the situation among contemporary baboons—comparing savanna to hamadryas—we could say that Neandertals were an incipient species. Given enough time and enough isolation, they likely would have separated completely from their modern human contemporaries. The new DNA evidence suggests that they were well on their way, very likely approaching full speciation from *Homo sapiens*. But as some fossil and archaeological data are still suggesting, Neandertals perhaps never quite got that far. Their fate, in a sense, was decided for them as more successful competitors expanded into Neandertal habitats. These highly successful hominins were fully modern humans, and in the next chapter we'll focus on their story.

Summary

The Middle Pleistocene (780,000–125,000 ya) was a time of transition in human evolution. Archaeological evidence encompassing this same time span (and including the later part of the Lower Paleolithic and early portion of the Middle Paleolithic) also shows a slow but steady change in human biocultural evolutionary capabilities. Fossil hominins from this period show similarities both with their predecessors (*H. erectus*) and with their successors (*H. sapiens*). They've also been found in many areas of the Old World, in Africa, Asia, and Europe—in the latter case, being the first truly successful occupants of that continent. Because these transitional hominins are more derived and more advanced in the human direction than *H. erectus*, we can refer to them as premodern humans. With this terminology, we also recognize that these hominins display several significant anatomical and behavioral differences from modern humans.

Although there's some dispute about the best way to formally classify the majority of Middle Pleistocene hominins, most paleoanthropologists now prefer to call them *H. heidelbergensis*. Similarities between the African and European Middle Pleistocene hominin samples suggest that they all can be reasonably seen as part of this same species. Further support for this view comes from the Middle Paleolithic archaeological record, which doesn't vary consistently across premodern human species. The contemporaneous Asian fossils, however, don't fit as neatly into this model, and conclusions regarding these premodern humans remain less definite.

Some of the later *H. heidelbergensis* populations in Europe likely evolved into Neandertals. Abundant Neandertal fossil and archaeological evidence has been collected from the Late Pleistocene time span of Neandertal existence, about 130,000–30,000 ya. But unlike their Middle Pleistocene (*H. heidelbergensis*) predecessors, Neandertals are more geographically restricted; they're found only in Europe and some parts of Asia (and not in eastern Asia and nowhere in Africa). Anatomical and genetic evidence also suggest that they were isolated and distinct from other hominins.

These observations have led to a growing consensus among paleoanthropologists that the Neandertals were largely a side branch of later hominin evolution. Still, there remain significant differences in theoretical approaches regarding how best to deal with the Neandertals; that is, should they be considered as a separate species or as a subspecies of *H. sapiens*? We suggest that the best way to view the Neandertals is within a dynamic process of speciation. Neandertals can thus be interpreted as an incipient species—one in the process of splitting from early *H. sapiens* populations.

In the What's Important feature on page 282, you'll find a useful summary of the most significant premodern human fossils discussed in this chapter.

Critical Thinking Questions

1. Why are the Middle Pleistocene hominins called premodern humans? In what ways are they human?
2. What is the general popular conception of Neandertals? Do you agree with this view? (Cite both anatomical and genetic evidence to support your conclusion.)
3. Compare the skeleton of a Neandertal with that of a modern human. In which ways are they most alike? In which ways are they most different?
4. What evidence suggests that Neandertals deliberately buried their dead? Do you think the fact that they buried their dead is important? Why? How would you interpret this behavior (remembering that Neandertals were not identical to us)?
5. How are species defined, both for living animals and for extinct ones? Use the Neandertals to illustrate the problems encountered in distinguishing species among extinct hominins. Contrast specifically the interpretation of Neandertals as a distinct species with the interpretation of Neandertals as a subspecies of *H. sapiens*.

What's Important   **Key Fossil Discoveries of Premodern Humans**

Dates	Region	Site	Hominin	The Big Picture
50,000 ya	Western Europe	La Chapelle (France)	Neandertal	Most famous Neandertal discovery; led to false interpretation of primitive, bent-over creature
110,000 ya	Southwestern Asia	Tabun (Israel)	Neandertal	Best evidence of early Neandertal morphology in S. W. Asia
130,000 ya	South Africa	Kabwe (Broken Hill, Zambia)	*H. heidelbergensis*	Transitional-looking fossil; perhaps a close ancestor of early *H. sapiens* in Africa
600,000–530,000 ya	Western Europe	Atapuerca (Sima de los Huesos)	*H. heidelbergensis* (early Neandertal)	Very early evidence of Neandertal ancestry; suggests Neandertals likely are a different species from *H. sapiens*
600,000 ya	East Africa	Bodo (Ethiopia)	*H. heidelbergensis*	Earliest evidencce of *H. heidelbergensis* in Africa—and possibly ancestral to later *H. sapiens*

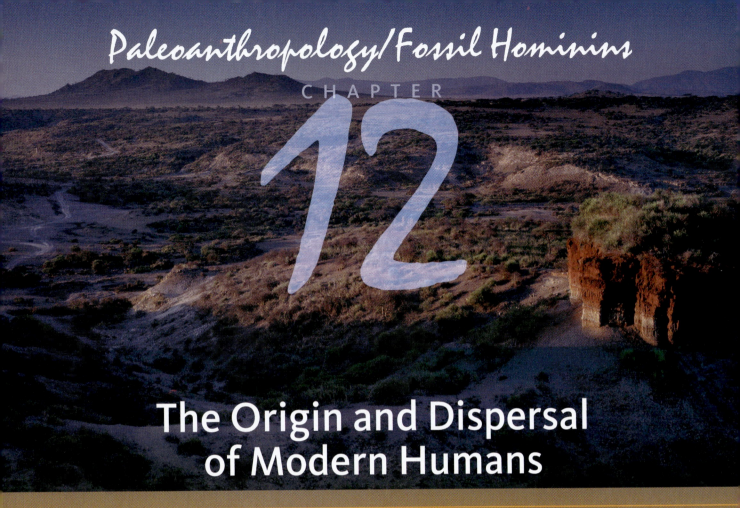

Paleoanthropology/Fossil Hominins

CHAPTER

12

The Origin and Dispersal of Modern Humans

Focus Questions

Is it possible to determine when and where modern humans first appeared?

Can the rapid dispersal of modern humans from Africa be explained in terms of biological and/or cultural adaptations?

 Click!

Go to the following media for interactive activities and exercises on topics covered in this chapter:

- Online Virtual Laboratories for Physical Anthropology, Version 4.0

- Hominid Fossils: An Interactive Atlas CD-ROM

Introduction

Today, our species numbers more than 6 billion individuals, scattered all over the globe, but there are no other living hominins but us. The last really close cousin of ours disappeared several thousand years ago. But about 40,000 years ago, modern peoples moving into Europe may have encountered beings that walked on two legs, hunted large animals, made fire, lived in caves, and fashioned complex tools. These beings were the Neandertals, and imagine what it would have been like to be among a band of modern humans following game into what is now Croatia and coming across these *other* humans, so like yourself in some ways, so disturbingly odd in others. It's almost certain that such encounters took place, perhaps many times. How strange would it have been to look into the face of a being who shared so much with you, yet was a total stranger both culturally and, to some degree, biologically as well? What would you think seeing a Neandertal for the first time? What do you imagine they would think seeing you?

Sometime, probably close to 200,000 ya, the first modern *Homo sapiens* evolved in Africa. Within 150,000 years or so, their descendants had spread across most of the Old World, even expanding as far as Australia (and somewhat later to the Americas).

Who were they, and why were these early modern people so successful? What was the fate of the other hominins, such as the Neandertals, who were already long established in areas outside Africa? Did they evolve as well, leaving descendants among some living human populations? Or were they completely swept aside and replaced by African emigrants?

In this chapter, we'll discuss the origin and dispersal of modern *H. sapiens*. All contemporary populations are placed within this species (and the same subspecies as well). Most paleoanthropologists agree that several fossil forms, dating back as far as 100,000 ya, should also be included in the same fully modern group as us. In addition, some recently discovered fossils from Africa also are clearly *H. sapiens*, but they show some (minor) differences from living people and could thus be described as near-modern. Still, we can think of these early African humans as well as their somewhat later relatives as "us."

These first modern humans, who evolved by 195,000 ya, are probably descendants of some of the premodern humans we discussed in Chapter 11. In particular, African populations of *H. heidelbergensis* are the most likely ancestors of the earliest modern *H. sapiens*. The evolutionary events that took place as modern humans made the transition from more ancient premodern forms and then dispersed throughout most of the Old World were relatively rapid, and they raise several basic questions:

1. When (approximately) did modern humans first appear?
2. Where did the transition take place? Did it occur in just one region or in several?
3. What was the pace of evolutionary change? How quickly did the transition occur?
4. How did the dispersal of modern humans to other areas of the Old World (outside their area of origin) take place?
5. What does archaeological evidence tell us about important cultural characteristics of early modern people that allowed them to so quickly and successfully disperse throughout the Old World?

These questions concerning the origins and early dispersal of modern *Homo sapiens* continue to fuel much controversy among paleoanthropologists. And it's no wonder, for members of early *H. sapiens* are our direct ancestors, which makes them close relatives of all contemporary humans. They were much like us skeletally, genetically, and behaviorally, too. In fact, it's the various hypotheses regarding the behaviors and abilities of our most immediate predecessors that have most fired the imaginations of scientists and laypeople alike. In every major respect, these are the first hominins that we can confidently refer to as *fully* human.

This chapter also examines archaeological evidence that helps to place Late Pleistocene human biological changes into cultural context. The Upper Paleolithic period begins around 40,000 ya and ends roughly 10,000 ya. Unlike the extraordinarily slow rates of cultural change that marked the Lower and Middle Paleolithic periods, the Upper Paleolithic witnessed profound changes in human culture. By 12,000–10,000 ya, the technology of Upper Paleolithic hunter-gatherers was as diverse and effective as that of (very recent) historically documented hunter-gatherers.

The evolutionary story of *Homo sapiens* is really the biocultural autobiography of all of us. It's a story that still has many unanswered questions; but several theories can help us organize the diverse information that's now available.

Approaches to Understanding Modern Human Origins

In attempting to organize and explain modern human origins, paleoanthropologists have developed two major theories: the complete replacement model and the regional continuity model. These two views are quite distinct, and in some ways they're completely opposed to each other. What's more, the popular press has further contributed to a wide and incorrect perception of irreconcilable argument on these points by "opposing" scientists. In fact, there's a third theory, which we call the partial replacement model, that's a kind of compromise, incorporating some aspects of the two major theories. Since so much of our contemporary view of modern human origins is influenced by the debates linked to these differing theories, let's start by briefly reviewing each one. Then we'll turn to the fossil and archaeological evidence to see what answers it can contribute to the five questions we've posed.

THE COMPLETE REPLACEMENT MODEL: RECENT AFRICAN EVOLUTION

The *complete replacement model* was developed by British paleoanthropologists Christopher Stringer and Peter Andrews (1988). It's based on the origin of modern humans in Africa and later replacement of populations in Europe and Asia (Fig. 12-1). This theory proposes that anatomically modern populations arose in Africa within the last 200,000 years and then migrated from Africa, *completely replacing* populations in Europe and Asia. It's important to note that this model doesn't account for a transition from premodern forms to modern *H. sapiens* anywhere in the world except Africa. A critical initial deduction of the Stringer and Andrews theory was that anatomically modern humans appeared as the result of a biological speciation event. So in this view, migrating African modern *H. sapiens* could not have interbred with local non-African populations, because the African modern humans were a biologically different species. Taxonomically, all of the premodern populations outside Africa would necessarily be classified as belonging to different species of *Homo*. For example, the Neandertals would be classified as *H. neanderthalensis* (see p. 280 for further discussion). This speciation explanation fits nicely with, and in fact helps

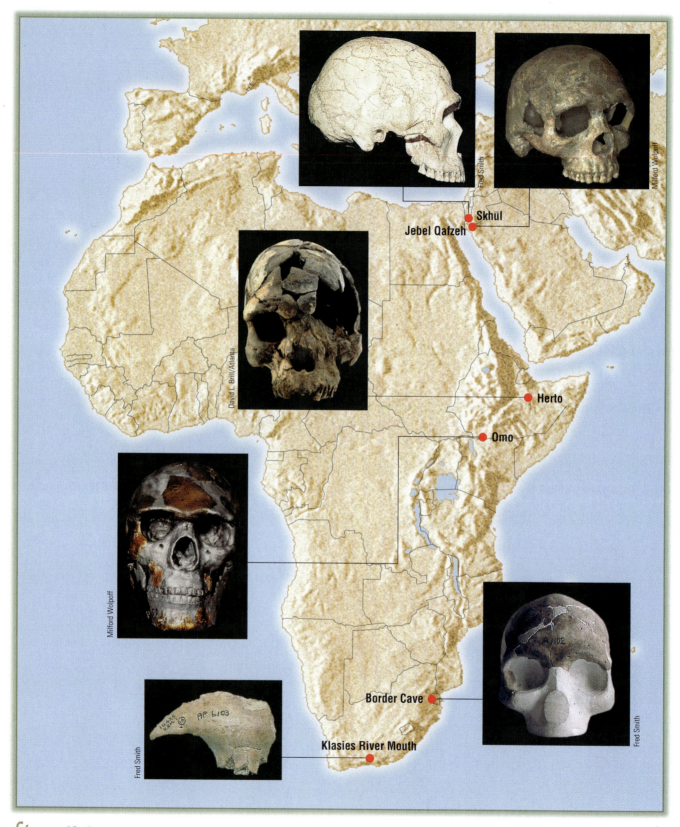

Figure **12-1**

Modern humans from Africa and the Near East.

explain, *complete* replacement; but Stringer has more recently stated that he isn't dogmatic on this issue. He does suggest that even though there may have been potential for interbreeding, apparently very little actually took place.

Interpretations of the latter phases of human evolution have recently been greatly extended by newly available genetic techniques. As we emphasized elsewhere, advances in molecular biology have revolutionized the biological sciences, including physical anthropology, and they've recently been applied to the question of modern human origins. Using numerous modern human populations as a data source, geneticists have precisely determined and compared a wide variety of DNA sequences. The theoretical basis of this approach assumes that at least some of the genetic patterning seen today can act as a kind of window on the past. In particular, the contemporary genetic patterns observed between geographically widely dispersed humans are thought to partly reflect migrations occurring in the Late Pleistocene. This hypothesis has been further tested and well substantiated as various types of contemporary population genetic patterning have been better documented.

To get a clearer picture of these genetic patterns, geneticists have studied both nuclear and mitochondrial DNA (mtDNA; see p. 60). They consider Y chromosome and mtDNA patterns particularly informative, since neither is significantly recombined during sexual reproduction. As a result, mitochondrial inheritance follows a strictly maternal pattern (inherited through females), while the Y chromosome follows a paternal pattern (transmitted only from father to son). In addition, much more complete data on human population patterning are now being obtained from large-scale genomic scans of nuclear DNA (see Chapter 4, p. 79).

As these new data have accumulated, consistent relationships are emerging, especially in showing that indigenous African populations have far greater diversity than do populations from elsewhere in the world. The consistency of the results is highly significant, because it strongly supports an African origin for modern humans and some mode of replacement elsewhere.

Certainly, most molecular data come from contemporary species, since DNA is not *usually* preserved in long-dead individuals. Even so, exceptions do occur, and these cases open another genetic window—one that can directly illuminate the past. As discussed in Chapter 11 (see p. 277), Neandertal DNA has been recovered from more than a dozen Neandertal fossils.

In addition, nine ancient fully modern *H. sapiens* skeletons from sites in Italy, France, the Czech Republic, and Russia have recently had their mtDNA sequenced (Caramelli et al., 2003, 2006; Kulikov et al., 2004; Serre et al., 2004). The results show mtDNA sequence patterns very similar to the patterns seen in living humans—and thus significantly different from the DNA patterns found in all the Neandertals so far analyzed.

If these results are further confirmed, they provide strong *direct* evidence of a genetic discontinuity between Neandertals and these early fully modern humans. In other words, these data suggest that no—or very little—interbreeding took place between Neandertals and anatomically modern humans.

PARTIAL REPLACEMENT MODELS

Various alternative perspectives also suggest that modern humans originated in Africa and then, when their population increased, expanded out of Africa into other areas of the Old World. But unlike those who subscribe to the complete replacement hypothesis, supporters of these partial replacement models claim that some interbreeding occurred between emigrating Africans and resident premodern populations elsewhere. So, partial replacement assumes that no speciation event occurred, and all these hominins should be considered members of *H. sapiens*. Günter Bräuer, of the University of Hamburg, suggests that very little interbreeding occurred—a view supported more recently by John

Relethford (2001) in what he describes as "mostly out of Africa." Fred Smith, of Loyola University, also favors an African origin of modern humans; but his "assimilation" model hypothesizes that in some regions, more interbreeding took place (Smith, 2002).

THE REGIONAL CONTINUITY MODEL: MULTIREGIONAL EVOLUTION

The regional continuity model is most closely associated with paleoanthropologist Milford Wolpoff, of the University of Michigan, and his associates (Wolpoff et al., 1994, 2001). They suggest that local populations—not all, of course—in Europe, Asia, and Africa continued their indigenous evolutionary development from premodern Middle Pleistocene forms to anatomically modern humans. But if that's true, then we have to ask how so many different local populations around the globe happened to evolve with such similar morphology. In other words, how could anatomically modern humans arise separately in different continents and end up so much alike, both physically and genetically? The multiregional model answers this question by (1) denying that the earliest modern *H. sapiens* populations originated *exclusively* in Africa, challenging the notion of complete replacement, and (2) asserting that significant levels of gene flow (migration) between premodern populations was extremely likely.

Through gene flow and natural selection, according to the multiregional hypothesis, local populations would *not* have evolved totally independently from one another, and such mixing would have "prevented speciation between the regional lineages and thus maintained human beings as a single, although obviously *polytypic* [see p. 74], species throughout the Pleistocene" (Smith et al., 1989). Thus, under a multiregional model, there are no taxonomic distinctions between modern and premodern hominins. That is, all hominins following *H. erectus* through modern humans are classified as *H. sapiens*.

Advocates of the multiregional model aren't dogmatic about the degree of regional continuity. They recognize that a likely strong influence of African migrants existed throughout the world and is still detectable today. Agreeing with Smith's assimilation model, this modified multiregionalism suggests that perhaps only minimal gene continuity existed in several regions (for example, western Europe) and that most modern genes are the result of large African migrations and/or more incremental gene flow (Relethford, 2001; Wolpoff et al., 2001).

SEEING THE BIG PICTURE

Looking beyond the arguments concerning modern human origins—which the popular media often overstates and overdramatizes—most paleoanthropologists now recognize an emerging consensus view. In fact, new evidence from fossils and especially from molecular comparisons is providing even more clarity. Data from sequenced ancient DNA, various patterns of contemporary human DNA, and the newest fossil finds from Ethiopia all suggest that a "strong" multiregional model is extremely unlikely. Supporters of this more extreme form of multiregionalism claim that modern human populations in Asia and Europe evolved *mostly* from local premodern ancestors—with only minor influence coming from African population expansion. But with the breadth and consistency of the latest research, this strong version of multiregionalism is falsified.

Also, as various investigators integrate these new data, views are beginning to converge even more. Several researchers suggest an out-of-Africa model that leads to virtually complete replacement elsewhere. At the moment, this complete replacement rendition can't be falsified. Still, even devoted advocates of this strong replacement version recognize the potential for at least *some* interbreeding, although they believe it was likely very minor. For their part, some archaeologists point to a growing body of cultural similarities between the Middle and Upper Paleolithic, which implies at least some degree of cultural continuity and not the sort of break in archaeological sequences that might signal sudden population "replacements." We can conclude, then, that during the later Pleistocene, one or more major migrations from Africa fueled the worldwide dispersal of modern humans. However, the African migrants might have occasionally interbred with resident populations outside Africa. In a sense, it's all the same, whether we see this process either as very minimal multiregional continuity or as not quite complete replacement.

The Earliest Discoveries of Modern Humans

AFRICA

In Africa, several early fossil finds have been interpreted as fully anatomically modern forms (see Fig. 12-1). The earliest of these specimens comes from Omo Kibish, in southernmost Ethiopia. Using radiometric techniques, recent redating of a fragmentary skull (Omo 1) demonstrates that, coming from 195,000 ya, this is the earliest modern human yet found in Africa—or, for that matter, anywhere (McDougall et al., 2005). An interesting aspect of fossil finds at this site concerns the variation shown between the two individuals discovered there. Omo 1 (Fig. 12-2) is essentially modern in most respects (note the presence of a chin; Fig. 12-3), but another ostensibly contemporary cranium (Omo 2) is much more robust and less modern in morphology.

Somewhat later African modern human fossils come from the Klasies River Mouth on the south coast and Border Cave, just slightly to the north. Using relatively new techniques, paleoanthropologists have dated both sites to about 120,000–80,000 ya. The original geological context at Border Cave is uncertain, and the fossils may be younger than those at Klasies River Mouth. Although recent reevaluation of the Omo site has provided much more dependable dating, there are still questions remaining about some of the other early African modern fossils. Nevertheless, it now seems very likely that early modern humans appeared in East Africa by shortly after 200,000 ya and had migrated to southern Africa prior to 100,000 ya. In southern Africa, there are no well-dated modern humans until after 100,000 ya, but as early as 160,000 ya, there are intriguing archaeological signs of modern-like behavior from South Africa (see p. 306). Further fossil evidence as well as more detailed archaeological evaluations will help confirm this hypothesis.

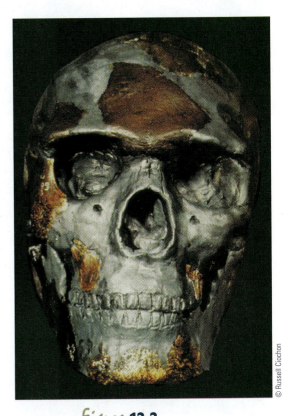

© Russell Ciochon

Figure 12-2

Reconstructed skull of Omo 1, an early modern human from Ethiopia, dated to 195,000 ya. Note the clear presence of a chin.

Herto The announcement in 2003 of well-preserved *and* well-dated *H. sapiens* fossils from Ethiopia has now gone a long way toward filling gaps in the African fossil record. As a result, these fossils are helping to resolve key issues regarding modern human origins. Tim White, of the University of California, Berkeley, and his colleagues have been working for over a decade in the Middle Awash area of Ethiopia. They've discovered a remarkable array of early fossil hominins (*Ardipithecus* and *Australopithecus anamensis*) as well as somewhat later forms (*H. erectus*). From this same area in the Middle Awash—in the Herto member of the Bouri formation—highly significant new discoveries came to light in 1997. For simplicity, these new hominins are referred to as the Herto remains.

These exciting new Herto fossils include a mostly complete adult cranium and several other fragmentary remains. Well-controlled radiometric dating securely places the remains at between 160,000 and 154,000 ya, making these the best-dated hominin fossils from this time period from anywhere in the world. And note, especially, that this date is clearly *older* than for any other equally modern *H. sapiens* from anywhere else in the world. Moreover, the preservation and morphology of the remains leave little doubt about

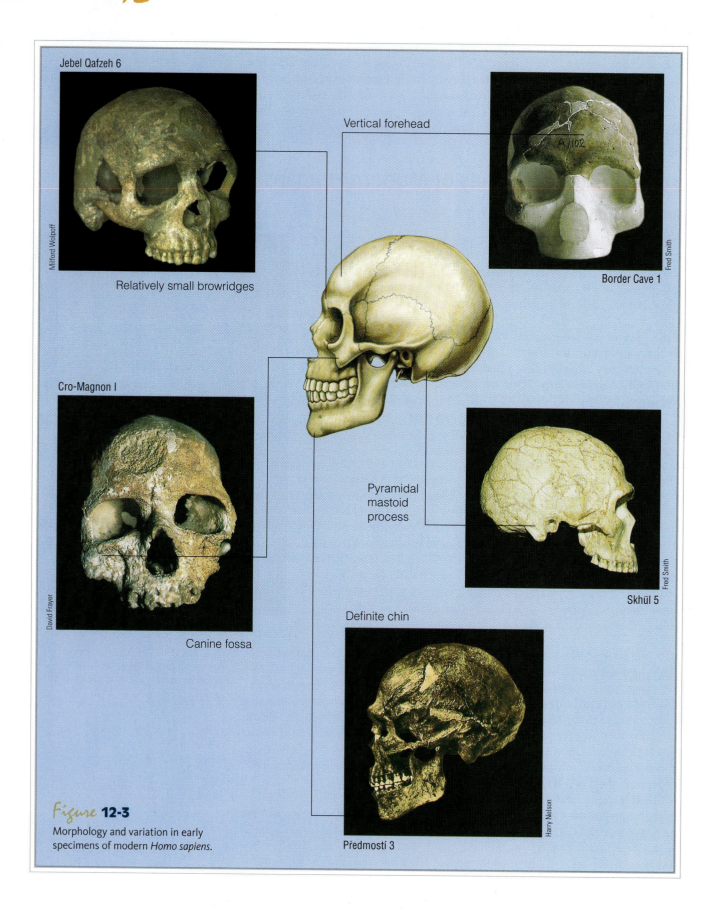

Jebel Qafzeh 6

Vertical forehead

Border Cave 1

Relatively small browridges

Cro-Magnon I

Pyramidal mastoid process

Skhūl 5

Canine fossa

Definite chin

Předmostí 3

Figure **12-3**

Morphology and variation in early specimens of modern *Homo sapiens*.

Milford Wolpoff

Fred Smith

David Frayer

Fred Smith

Harry Nelson

their relationship to modern humans. The cranium (Fig. 12-4) is very large, with an extremely long cranial vault. The cranial capacity is 1,450 cm^3, well within the range of contemporary *H. sapiens* populations.

White and his team performed comprehensive statistical studies, comparing these fossils with other early *H. sapiens* remains as well as with a large series from modern populations. They concluded that while not identical to modern people, the Herto fossils are near-modern (White et al., 2003). To distinguish these individuals from fully modern humans (*H. sapiens sapiens*), the researchers have placed them in a newly defined subspecies: *Homo sapiens idaltu*. The word *idaltu*, from the Afar language, means "elder."

The Herto fossils are the right age, and they come from the right place. Besides that, they look much like what we might have predicted. These new Herto finds are the most conclusive fossil evidence yet supporting an African origin of modern humans. They're thus compatible with an array of genetic data indicating some form of replacement model for human origins.

THE NEAR EAST

In Israel, researchers found early modern *H. sapiens* fossils, including the remains of at least 10 individuals, in the Skhūl Cave at Mt. Carmel (Figs. 12-5 and 12-6a). This is very near the Neandertal site of Tabun, also located at Mt. Carmel. Nearby, the Qafzeh Cave has yielded the remains of at least 20 individuals (Fig. 12-6b). Although their overall configuration

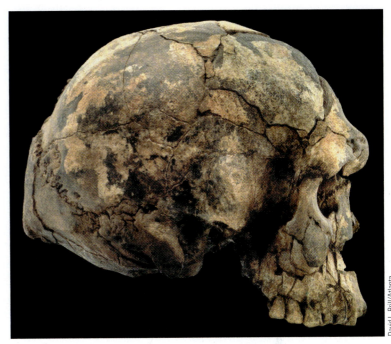

David L. Brill/Atlanta

Figure **12-4**

Herto cranium from Ethiopia, dated 160,000–154,000 ya. This is the best-preserved early modern *H. sapiens* cranium yet found.

At a Glance

Key Early Modern *Homo sapiens* Discoveries from Africa and the Near East

DATES	SITE	HOMININ	EVOLUTIONARY SIGNIFICANCE
110,000 ya	**Qafzeh** (Israel)	*H. sapiens sapiens*	Large sample (at least 20 individuals); definitely modern, but some individuals fairly robust; early date (> 100,000 ya)
115,000 ya	**Skhūl**	*H. sapiens sapiens*	Minimum of 10 individuals; like Qafzeh modern morphology, but slightly earlier date (and earliest modern humans known outside of Africa)
160,000–154,000 ya	**Herto** (Ethiopia)	*H. sapiens idaltu*	Very well-preserved cranium; dated > 150,000 ya, the best-preserved early modern human found anywhere
195,000 ya	**Omo** (Ethiopia)	*H. sapiens*	Dated almost 200,000 ya and the oldest modern human found anywhere; two crania found, one more modern looking than the other

Figure **12-5**

Mt. Carmel, studded with caves, was home to *H. sapiens sapiens* at Skhūl (and to Neandertals at Tabun and Kebara).

David Frayer

is definitely modern, some specimens show certain premodern features. Skhūl has been dated to between 130,000 and 100,000 ya (Grün et al., 2005), while Qafzeh has been dated to around 120,000–92,000 ya (Grün and Stringer, 1991). The time line for these fossil discoveries is shown in Figure 12-7.

Such early dates for modern specimens pose some problems for those advocating the influence of local evolution, as proposed by the multiregional model. How early do the premodern *H. sapiens* populations—that is, Neandertals—appear in the Near East? A recent chronometric calibration for the Tabun Cave suggests a date as early as 120,000 ya. This date for Tabun indicates that there's considerable chronological overlap in the occupation of the Near East by Neandertals and modern humans.

ASIA

There are six early anatomically modern human localities in China, the two most significant of which come from the area near the village of Zhoukoudian (Fig. 12-8). The fossils from these Chinese sites are all fully modern, and all are considered to be from

Figure **12-6**

(a) Skhūl 5. (b) Qafzeh 6. These specimens from Israel are thought to be representatives of early modern *Homo sapiens*. The vault height, forehead, and lack of prognathism are modern traits.

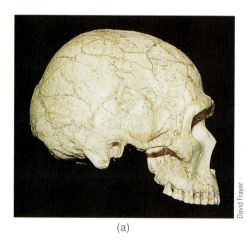

David Frayer

Milford Wolpoff

(a)   (b)

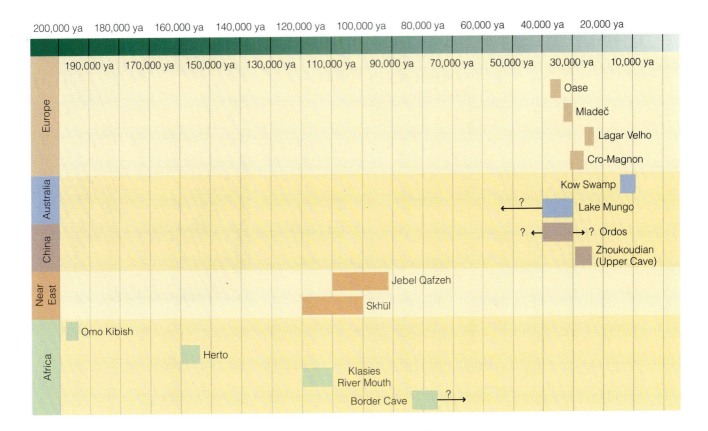

Figure **12-7**

Time line of modern *Homo sapiens* discoveries. Note that some dates are approximations. Question marks indicate those estimates that are most tentative.

the Late Pleistocene, with dates likely less than 40,000 ya. Upper Cave at Zhoukoudian, from later strata in the same locale as the famous *H. erectus* finds, has been dated to 27,000 ya.

Just 4 miles down the road from the famous Zhoukoudian Cave is another cave called Tianyuan, from where an important find came in 2003. Consisting of a fragmentary skull, a few teeth, and several postcranial bones, this fossil is accurately dated by radiocarbon at close to 40,000 ya (Shang et al., 2007). The individual shows mostly modern skeletal features, but has a few archaic characteristics as well. The Chinese and American team of researchers who have analyzed the remains from Tianyuan suggest that these remains indicate an African origin of modern humans but also show a good possibility of at least some interbreeding in China with resident archaic populations. More complete analysis and (with some luck) further finds at this new site will help provide a better picture of early modern *H. sapiens* in China. For the moment, this is the best-dated early modern *H. sapiens* from China and one of the two earliest from anywhere in Asia.

The other early modern Asian find is a partial skull from Niah Cave, on the north coast of the Indonesian island of Borneo (see Fig. 12-8). This is actually not a new find, but was, in fact, first excavated 50 years ago. However, until recent more extensive analysis, this find had been relegated to the paleoanthropological back shelf due to uncertainties regarding its archaeological context and dating. Now all this has changed with a better understanding of the geology of the site and new dates strongly supporting an age of more than 35,000 ya and most likely as old as 45,000–40,000 ya, making it perhaps older than Tianyuan (Barker et al., 2007). Like its Chinese counterparts, the Niah skull is also modern in morphology. It is hypothesized that some population contemporaneous with Niah or somewhat earlier inhabitants of Indonesia was perhaps the first group to colonize Australia.

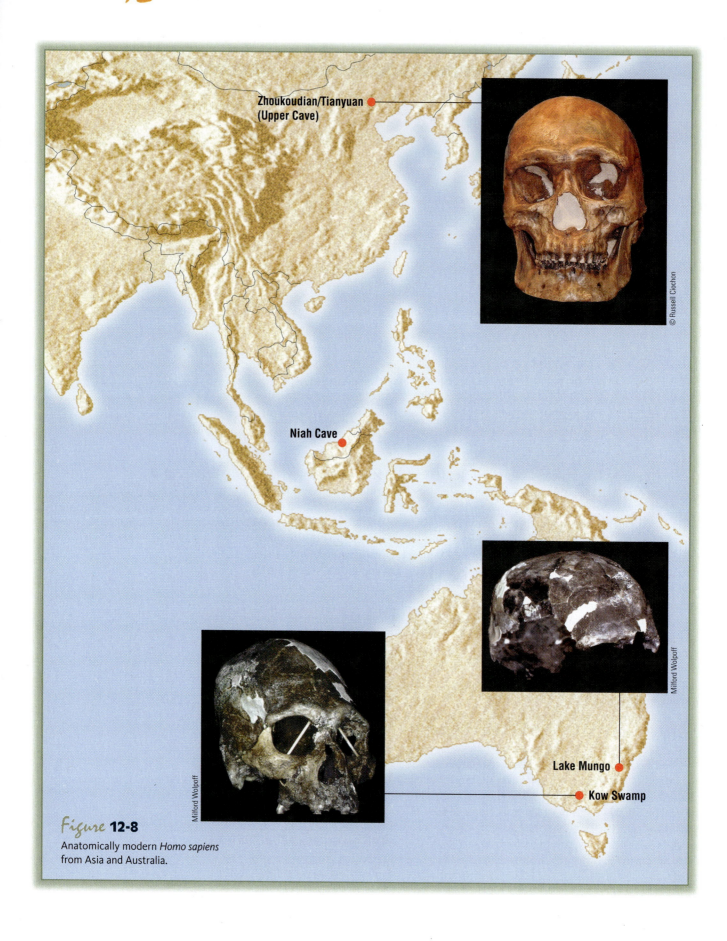

Zhoukoudian/Tianyuan
(Upper Cave)

© Russell Ciochon

Niah Cave

Milford Wolpoff

Lake Mungo

Kow Swamp

Milford Wolpoff

Figure **12-8**

Anatomically modern *Homo sapiens*
from Asia and Australia.

AUSTRALIA

During glacial times, the Indonesian islands were joined to the Asian mainland, but Australia was not. It's likely that by 50,000 ya, modern humans inhabited Sahul—the area including New Guinea and Australia. Bamboo rafts may have been the means of crossing the sea between islands, and doing so would have been dangerous and difficult. It's not known just where the future Australians came from, but as noted, Indonesia has been suggested.

Human occupation of Australia appears to have occurred quite early, with some archaeological sites dating to 55,000 ya. There's some controversy about dating of the earliest Australian human remains, which are all modern *H. sapiens*. The earliest finds so far discovered have come from Lake Mungo, in southeastern Australia (see Fig. 12-8). In agreement with archaeological context and radiocarbon dates, the hominins from this site have been dated at approximately 30,000–25,000 ya. Newly determined age estimates, using electron spin resonance (ESR) and uranium series dating (see p. 194), have dramatically extended the suggested time depth to about 60,000 ya (Thorne et al., 1999). The lack of correlation of these more ancient age estimates with other data, however, has some researchers seriously concerned (Gillespie and Roberts, 2000).

Unlike the more gracile early Australian forms from Lake Mungo are the Kow Swamp people, who are thought to have lived between about 14,000 and 9,000 ya (see Fig. 12-8). These fossils display certain archaic traits—such as receding foreheads, heavy supraorbital tori, and thick cranial bones—that are difficult to explain, since these features contrast with the postcranial anatomy, which matches that of recent native Australians. Regardless of the differing morphology of these later Australians, new genetic evidence indicates that all native Australians are descendants of a *single* migration dating back to about 50,000 ya (Hudjashov et al., 2007).

CENTRAL EUROPE

Central Europe has been a source of many fossil finds, including the earliest anatomically modern *H. sapiens* yet discovered anywhere in Europe. Dated to 35,000 ya, the best dated of these early *H. sapiens* fossils come from recent discoveries at the Oase Cave in Romania (Fig 12-9). Here, cranial remains of three individuals were recovered, including a complete mandible and a partial skull (Fig. 12-10). While quite robust, these individuals are quite similar to later modern specimens, as seen in the clear presence of both a chin and a canine fossa (see Fig. 12-3; Trinkaus et al., 2003).

Another early modern human site in central Europe is Mladeč, in the Czech Republic. Several individuals have been excavated here and are dated to approximately 31,000 ya. While there's some variation among the crania, including some with big browridges, Fred Smith (1984) is confident that they're all best classified as modern *H. sapiens* (Fig 12-11). It's clear that by 28,000 ya, modern humans are widely dispersed in central Europe and into western Europe (Trinkaus, 2005).

WESTERN EUROPE

For several reasons, one of them probably serendipity, the fossils and archaeology of western Europe have received the most attention. Over the last 150

Figure **12-9**

Excavators at work within the spectacular cave at Oase, in Romania. The floor is littered with the remains of fossil animals, including the earliest-dated cranial remains of *Homo sapiens* in Europe.

© Mircea Gerhase

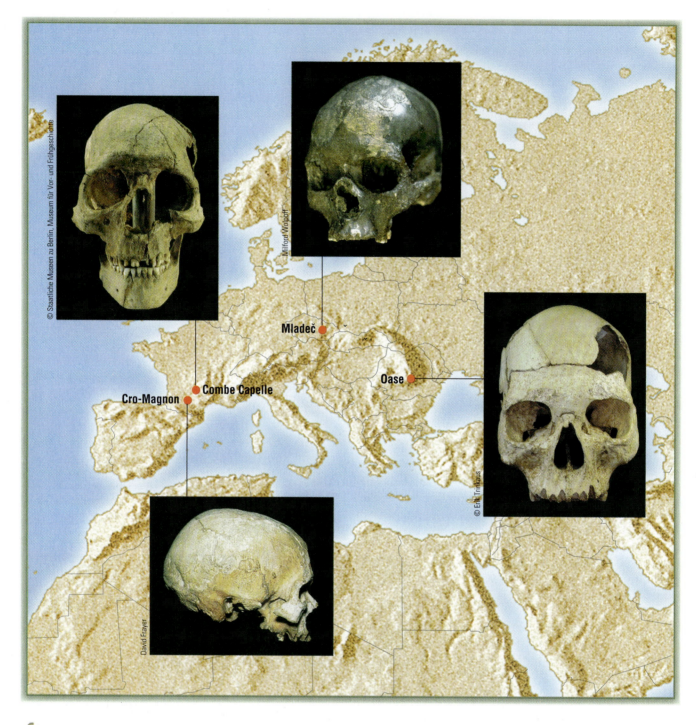

Mladeč

Oase

Cro-Magnon   Combe Capelle

Figure **12-10**

Anatomically modern humans from Europe.

years, many of the scholars interested in this kind of research happened to live in western Europe, and the southern region of France proved to be a fossil treasure trove. Also, early on, discovering and learning about human ancestors caught the curiosity and pride of the local population.

As a result of this scholarly interest, beginning back in the nineteenth century, a great deal of data accumulated, and little reliable comparative information was available from elsewhere in the world. Consequently, theories of human evolution were based almost exclusively on the western European material. It's only been in recent years, with growing evidence from other areas of the world and with the application of new dating techniques, that recent human evolutionary dynamics are being seriously considered from a worldwide perspective.

Western Europe has yielded many anatomically modern human fossils, but by far the best-known sample of western European *H. sapiens* is from the **Cro-Magnon** site. From a rock shelter in southern France, remains of eight individuals were discovered here in 1868.

The Cro-Magnon materials are associated with a late Aurignacian tool assemblage, an Upper Paleolithic industry. Dated at about 28,000 ya, these individuals represent the earliest of France's currently known well-dated anatomically modern humans. The so-called Old Man (Cro-Magnon 1) became the original model for what was once termed the Cro-Magnon, or Upper Paleolithic, "race" of Europe (Fig. 12-12). Actually, of course, there's no such valid biological category, and Cro-Magnon 1 is not typical of Upper Paleolithic western Europeans—and not even all that similar to the other two male skulls found at the site.

Most of the genetic evidence, as well as the newest fossil evidence, from Africa argue against continuous local evolution producing modern groups directly from any Eurasian premodern population (in Europe, these would be Neandertals). Still, for some researchers, the issue isn't completely settled. With all the latest evidence, there's no longer much debate that a *large* genetic contribution from migrating early modern Africans influenced other groups throughout the Old World. What's being debated is just how much admixture might have occurred between these migrating Africans and the resident premodern groups. One group of researchers that has evaluated genetic evidence from living populations (Eswaran et al., 2005) suggests that significant admixture occurred in much of the Old World. What's more, for those paleoanthropologists who also hypothesize that significant admixture (assimilation) occurred in western Europe as well as elsewhere (e.g., Trinkaus, 2005), a recently discovered child's skeleton from Portugal provides some of the best evidence of ostensible interbreeding between Neandertals and anatomically modern *H. sapiens*. This important discovery from the Abrigo do Lagar Velho site (Fig. 12-13) was excavated in late 1998 and is dated to 24,500 ya—that's at least 5,000 years later than the last clearly Neandertal find. Associated with an Upper Paleolithic industry and buried with red ocher and pierced shell is a fairly complete skeleton of a 4-year-old child (Duarte et al., 1999). In studying the remains, Cidália Duarte, Erik Trinkaus, and colleagues found a highly mixed set of anatomical features. Many characteristics, especially of the teeth, lower jaw, and pelvis, were like those seen in anatomically modern humans. Yet, several other features—including lack of chin, limb

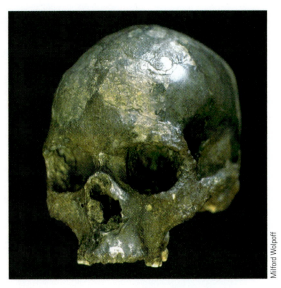

Milford Wolpoff

Figure **12-11**

The Mladeč cranium, from the Czech Republic, is a good example of early modern *Homo sapiens* in central Europe. Along with Oase in Romania, the evidence for early modern *H. sapiens* appears first in central Europe, then later in western Europe.

David Frayer

(a)

(b)

Milford Wolpoff

Figure **12-12**

Cro-Magnon 1 (France). In this specimen, modern traits are quite clear. (a) Lateral view. (b) Frontal view.

Cro-Magnon (crow-man´-yon)

At a Glance

Key Early Modern *Homo sapiens* Discoveries from Europe and Asia

DATES	SITE	HOMININ	EVOLUTIONARY SIGNIFICANCE
24,500 ya	**Abrigo do Lagar Velho** (Portugal)	*H. sapiens sapiens*	Child's skeleton; some suggestion of possible hybrid between Neandertal and modern human—but is controversial
30,000 ya	**Cro-Magnon** (France)	*H. sapiens sapiens*	Most famous early modern human find in world; earliest evidence of modern humans in France
40,000 ya	**Tianyuan Cave** (China)	*H. sapiens sapiens*	Partial skull and a few postcranial bones; oldest modern human find from China
45,000– 40,000 ya	**Niah Cave** (Borneo, Indonesia)	*H. sapiens sapiens*	Partial skull recently redated more accurately; oldest modern human find from Asia

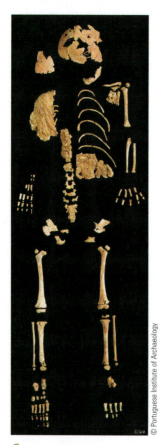

© Portuguese Institute of Archaeology

Figure **12-13**

The skeleton of the Lagar Velho child thought by some to be a Neandertal–modern human hybrid.

proportions, and muscle insertions—were more similar to Neandertal traits. The authors thus conclude that "the presence of such admixture suggests the hypothesis of variable admixture between early modern humans dispersing into Europe and local Neandertal populations" (Duarte et al., 1999, p. 7608). They suggest that this new evidence strongly supports the partial replacement model while seriously weakening the complete replacement model. Of course, the evidence from one child's skeleton—while intriguing— certainly isn't going to convince everyone.

Something New and Different

As we've seen, by 25,000 ya, modern humans had dispersed to all major areas of the Old World, and they would soon journey to the New World as well. But at about the same time, remnant populations of earlier hominins still survived in a few remote and isolated corners. We mentioned in Chapter 10 that populations of *Homo erectus* in Java managed to survive on this island long after their cousins had disappeared from other areas, for example, China and East Africa. What's more, even though they persisted well into the Late Pleistocene, physically these Javanese hominins were still very similar to other *H. erectus* individuals (see p. 244).

Even more surprising, it seems that other populations branched off from some of these early inhabitants of Indonesia and either intentionally or accidentally found their way to other, smaller islands to the east. There, under even more extreme isolation pressures, they evolved in an astonishing direction. In late 2004, the world awoke to the startling announcement that an extremely small-bodied, small-brained hominin had been discovered in Liang Bua Cave, on the island of Flores, east of Java (Fig. 12-14). These remains consist of an incomplete skeleton of an adult female (LB1) as well as additional pieces from nine other individuals, which the press have collectively nicknamed "hobbits." The female skeleton is remarkable in several ways (Fig. 12-15), though surprisingly similar to the Dmanisi hominins (from which she and her cohorts may have derived; see p. 242). First, she stood barely 3 feet tall—as short as the small-

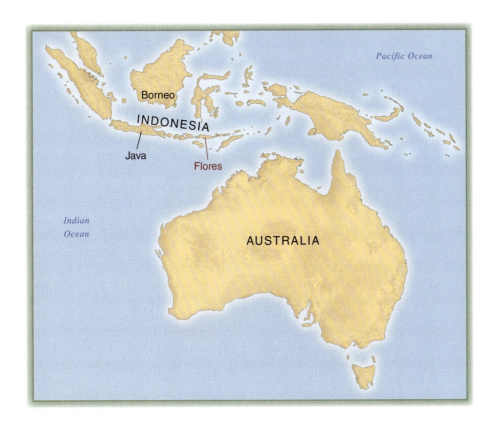

Figure **12-14**

Location of the Flores site, in Indonesia.

est australopith—and her brain, estimated at a mere 417 cm³ (Falk et al., 2005), was no larger than that of a chimpanzee (Brown et al., 2004). Possibly most startling of all, these extraordinary hominins were still living on Flores just 13,000 ya (Morwood et al., 2004; 2005)!

Where did they come from? As we said, their predecessors were probably *H. erectus* populations like those found on Java. How they got to Flores—some 400 miles away, partly over open ocean—is a mystery. There are several connecting islands, and to get between them, these hominins may have drifted across on rafts; but there's no way to be sure of this.

How did they get to be so physically different from all other known hominins? Here we're a little more certain of the answer. Isolated island populations can quite rapidly diverge from their relatives elsewhere. Among such isolated animals, natural selection frequently favors reduced body size. For example, populations of dwarf elephants are found on islands in the Mediterranean as well as on some channel islands off the coast of southern California. And perhaps most interesting of all, dwarf elephants *also* evolved on Flores; they were found in the same geological beds with the little hominins. The evolutionary mechanism (called "insular dwarfing") thought to explain such extreme body size reduction in both the elephants and the hominins is an adaptation to a reduced amount of resources, leading through selection to smaller size.

Other than short stature, what did the Flores hominins look like? In their cranial shape, thickness of cranial bone, and dentition, they most resemble *H. erectus*, specifically those specimens from Dmanisi. Still, they have some derived features that also set them apart from all other hominins. For that reason, many researchers have placed them in a separate species, *Homo floresiensis*.

Some stone tools have also been found at Liang Bua, and they're technologically similar to much earlier Paleolithic assemblages excavated elsewhere in Indonesia. At these other earlier sites, it's assumed that these artifacts were used by *H. erectus*; but on Flores they were made and used by *H. floresiensis* (Brumm et al., 2006).

Figure **12-15**

Cranium of adult female *Homo floresiensis* from Flores, Indonesia, dated 18,000 ya.

Immediately following the first publication of the Flores remains, considerable controversy arose regarding their interpretation (Jacob et al., 2006; Martin et al., 2006). Some researchers have argued that the small-brained find (LB1) is actually a pathological modern *H. sapiens* afflicted with a severe growth disorder called microcephaly. The researchers who did most of the initial work reject this conclusion and provide some further details to support their original interpretation (for example, Dean Falk's further analysis of microcephalic endocasts, as reported in Bower, 2006).

The conclusion that among this already small-bodied island population the one individual found with a preserved cranium happened to be afflicted with a severe (and rare) growth defect is highly unlikely. Yet, it must also be recognized that long-term, extreme isolation of hominins on Flores leading to a new species showing dramatic body size dwarfing and even more dramatic brain size reduction is also quite unusual.

A third possibility has been suggested by anthropologist Gary Richards, of the University of California, Berkeley. He argues that LB1 (and the other little Flores hominins) are normal *H. sapiens* individuals, but ones that have undergone a microevolutionary change leading to unusually small body and brain size (Richards, 2006).

So where does this leave us? Because a particular interpretation is unlikely, it is not necessarily incorrect. We do know, for example, that such "insular dwarfing" has occurred in other mammals. For the moment, the most comprehensive analyses indicate that a new hominin species (*H. floresiensis*) did, in fact, evolve on Flores (Nevell et al., 2007; Tocheri et al., 2007). For several researchers, this conclusion still requires more detailed and more convincing evidence. Although considered a long shot due to poor bone preservation, there is only a slight possibility that DNA can be retrieved from the Flores bones and sequenced. If such analysis could ever be done, it would go a long way to solving the mystery.

tundra Treeless plains characterized by permafrost conditions that support the growth of shallow-rooted vegetation such as grasses and mosses.

Upper Paleolithic Technology and Art

SOUTHWEST ASIA AND EUROPE

In Eurasia, cultural changes viewed as part of the Upper Paleolithic period spread rapidly, with early sites in southwest Asia (Israel/Lebanon) dated at 47,000 ya. Soon after, Upper Paleolithic culture expanded throughout Europe, and several sites dated to approximately 41,000 ya located from southeastern Russia all the way to southern France and northern Spain have been excavated (Fig. 12-16; Mellars, 2006; Anikovich et al., 2007).

The European climate was quite different than it is today. At the beginning of the Upper Paleolithic, glacial ice covered land and sea in northern Europe. Where the glaciers stopped, ice desert and **tundra** began. The tundra gradually merged into vast grasslands that stretched as far south as the northern Mediterranean region. The overall climatic trend was one of gradually cooler average annual temperature, which reached its coldest with the last major glacial advance of the Ice Age between 20,000 and 12,000 ya.

Figure **12-16**

Cultural periods of the European Upper Paleolithic and their approximate beginning dates.

GLACIAL	UPPER PALEOLITHIC (beginnings)	CULTURAL PERIODS
W Ü R M	17,000 –	Magdalenian
	21,000 –	Solutrean
	27,000 –	Gravettian
	40,000 –	Aurignacian Chatelperronian
	Middle Paleolithic	Mousterian

The tundra and grasslands created an enormous pasture for herbivorous animals, large and small, and a rich hunting ground for the predators that ate them. This hunter's paradise stretched from Spain through Europe and across the Russian steppes. Reindeer herds roamed its vast expanse, along with mammoths, bison, horses, and other animals, many of which were staple foods of Upper Paleolithic hunters. It is also during this period that archaeologists find the earliest evidence of the extensive exploitation of birds and fish as game animals. Bear in mind, however, that our understanding of the human use of marine resources is undoubtedly distorted somewhat by how little is known archaeologically of the thousands of square miles of coastal plains, hills, and valleys that were buried by rising sea levels at the end of the Ice Age.

Upper Paleolithic hunters focused most of their efforts on the immense herds of reindeer, horses, and a few other big game species that seasonally migrated across the European grasslands. Such specialized hunting is viewed by many researchers as a key aspect of the cultural transition from the Middle to the Upper Paleolithic (Mellars, 1989). While the technology of Middle and Upper Paleolithic hunters did indeed differ greatly, recent research shows that the focus of their hunting may have been more similar than once believed possible. Analysis of well-documented faunal remains from the Dordogne region of southern France reveals that the frequency of ungulates (in other words, reindeer, roe deer, and the like) shows little change between late Middle and early Upper Paleolithic strata (Grayson and Delpech, 2003). Farther south, archaeologists also found evidence of similar Middle and Upper Paleolithic land use patterns in three valleys of eastern Spain (Miller and Barton, 2008). Had the way of life of Upper Paleolithic hunters differed greatly from that of their Middle Paleolithic predecessors, more obvious differences should be seen both in the type and amount of game that was hunted and in overall land use patterns.

Many archaeologists now conclude that "Middle and Upper Palaeolithic hunting and gathering was largely determined by what was available seasonally in the local environment" (Bar-Yosef, 2004, p. 333). While acknowledging the similarities, other researchers remind us that the material culture differences between these two periods are such that cultural continuity cannot simply be assumed (Adler et al., 2006). Our understanding of Upper Paleolithic subsistence also suffers from how little we know about the economic importance of plant foods and other gathered resources.

A potentially important contrast between the Middle and Upper Paleolithic is seen by archaeologists when they examine the remains of Upper Paleolithic sites. They find that these settlements were often larger and used longer than Middle Paleolithic sites in the same regions. These encampments were home to around 25 to 50 people and perhaps even more during the fall and spring, when game herds made their seasonal migrations in search of fresh pasture. Remnants of Upper Paleolithic huts, some of which measure 15 to 20 feet in diameter, have been uncovered at several sites in the grasslands of Ukraine. Similar structures undoubtedly dotted camps across Europe.

Upper Paleolithic human burials provide additional insight into the nature of these communities. The graves sometimes include ornaments, tools, and other artifacts that were deliberately placed with corpses. Such grave goods may indicate possible status differences among community members, the existence of burial rituals, and possibly even fundamental notions of an afterlife. For example, burials uncovered at the 24,000-year-old Sungir site near Moscow (Fig. 12-17) include adults and adolescents dressed in beaded clothing, with grave inclusions of red ocher, thousands of ivory beads, long spears made of straightened mammoth tusks, ivory engravings, and jewelry (Formicola and Buzhilova, 2004). Although child burials are rarely discovered, far to the west at the 27,000-year-old Krems-Wachtberg site in Austria, two newborn infants have been found that were covered in red ocher and buried with scores of ivory beads (Einwögerer et al., 2006).

While Upper Paleolithic groups shared many similarities with their Middle Paleolithic predecessors, there were also many important differences. The Upper Paleolithic was an age of technological innovation that can be compared in its impact on society to the past few hundred years of our own history of amazing technological advances. Modern humans of the Upper Paleolithic not only invented new and specialized tools, but, as we've seen, also turned to new materials, such as bone, ivory, and antler.

Consider, for example, the changes in hunting technology. We noted in Chapter 11 that Neandertals relied on close-encounter weapons, and while these weapons and the tactics that went with them were clearly effective, they placed hunters at great risk of serious injury (see p. 275). Even such seemingly formidable weapons as the Middle Paleolithic wooden spears from Schöningen (see p. 264) may have had an effective range of only 25 feet or less (Shea, 2006). Hunting practices must have changed considerably with the advent of projectile weaponry such as spear-thrower darts around 40,000 ya (Shea, 2006), which had much greater effective ranges. The spear-thrower, or atlatl, was a wooden or bone hooked rod that acted to extend the hunter's arm, thus enhancing the force and

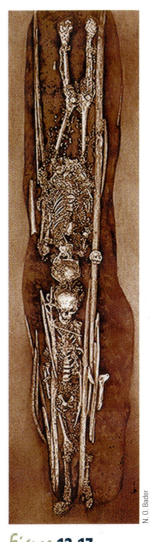

N. O. Bader

Figure **12-17**

Skeletons of two teenagers, a male and a female, from Sungir, Russia. Dated 24,000 ya, this is the richest find of any Upper Paleolithic grave.

Figure **12-18**

(a) Spear-thrower (atlatl). Note the carving.
(b) A modern example of an ancient idea.

(a)

(b)

Lynn Kilgore

distance of a stone projectile-tipped dart or short spear (Fig. 12-18). Spear-thrower technology and, much later in the period, the bow and arrow undoubtedly had a big impact on hunting, on hunters, and on the game animals they pursued.

Archaeologists have long recognized five major Upper Paleolithic industries in western Europe: Chatelperronian, Aurignacian, Gravettian, Solutrean, and **Magdalenian**. These industries differ by age, distribution, and the style and type of artifacts. Important among their shared features is the use of **blade technology** for making most stone tools. A chipped stone blade is a flake that is more than twice as long as it is wide. The technology for making ribbonlike blades of predictable length, width, and thickness was invented in Africa more than 100,000 ya, but it wasn't widely adopted until the Upper Paleolithic.

Blades were struck from stone cores using an **indirect percussion** method, the most common of which was the *punch technique*, in which a toolmaker positioned a bone or antler "punch" on a prepared core and then either hit the punch with a billet or applied pressure with a crutch to drive a blade off the core. Given a properly prepared core, blades with razor-like edges could be quickly struck until the core was used up (Fig. 12-19).

While blades could be (and were) used without further modification, they were often just the first step in making dart points, knives, scrapers, and other tools. For example, a **burin** could be made by snapping off bits of a blade to create a chisel-like working end (Fig. 12-20), which was then mounted in a handle and used to cut bone, antler, ivory, and wood. As anyone who has tried to cut through a big deer bone with a stone flake could tell you, a burin can make the difference between success and failure.

Another technique, called *pressure flaking*, was often used to finish a chipped stone tool. By pressing the tip of a deer antler or similarly shaped piece of bone or wood against the edge of a core, toolmakers found that they could precisely remove small, thin flakes (Fig. 12-21). Applied by skilled hands, pressure flaking was used to fashion stone tools, such as **Solutrean** laurel leaf points (Fig. 12-22), that reflect an expert command of the technology and are aesthetically pleasing even by modern standards.

Along with the everyday tools of Upper Paleolithic life, archaeologists also find evidence of clothing and personal ornaments, both of which are rarely found in Middle Paleolithic sites and are unknown from Lower Paleolithic contexts. Tanned hides and fur were the basis for much Upper Paleolithic clothing, but twined and simply woven fabrics are also known from as early as 27,000 ya (Soffer et al., 2000). Personal ornaments, including such things as bone necklaces, shell beads, drilled bear canines, and bone and ivory bracelets, were probably more than just trinkets. Like clothing, they could also express the status of individuals, their roles within society, and even group identity.

Magdalenian A late Upper Paleolithic stone tool industry in Europe that dates to 17,000–11,000 ya.

blade technology Chipped stone toolmaking approach in which blades struck from prepared cores are the main raw material from which tools are made. A blade is a chipped stone flake that is at least twice as long as it is wide.

indirect percussion The method of driving off blades and flakes from a prepared core using a bone or antler punch to press off a thin flake.

burin A small flake tool with a chisel-like end, used to cut bone, antler, and ivory.

Solutrean An Upper Paleolithic stone tool industry in southwestern France and Spain that dates to 21,000–18,000 ya.

(a) A large core is selected and the top portion removed by use of a hammerstone.

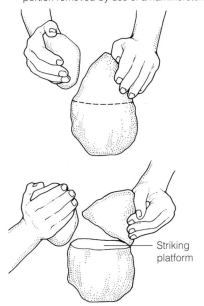

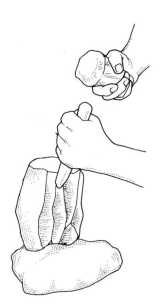

Striking platform

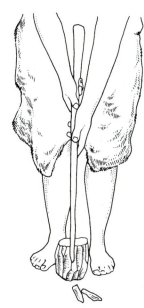

(b) The objective is to create a flat surface called a striking platform.

(c) Next, the core is struck by use of a hammer and punch (made of bone or antler) to remove the long narrow flakes (called blades).

(d) Or the blades can be removed by pressure flaking. (See Fig. 12-21 for another example of pressure flaking.)

(e) The result is the production of highly consistent sharp blades, which can be used, as is, as knives; or they can be further modified (retouched) to make a variety of other tools (such as burins, scrapers, and awls).

Figure 12-19

The punch blade technique.

Personal ornaments can be thought of as a form of art. Indeed, the period between 35,000 and 10,000 ya was an era of "unparalleled creativity and symbolic expression" (Nowell, 2006, p. 240). Best known from sites in Europe, Upper Paleolithic art is now also well documented from Siberia, Africa, and Australia. It found expression in a variety of ways, from painted cave walls to everyday tools that show engraved and carved decorations. New methods of mixing pigments and applying them were important in rendering painted or drawn images. Bone and ivory carving and engraving were made easier with the use of burins (see Fig. 12-20) and other stone tools. Once believed to have originated toward the end of the Upper Paleolithic, recent cave art discoveries demonstrate that it was already well developed by 35,000–32,000 ya (see p. 305).

Upper Paleolithic art divides readily into two broad categories—*portable art*, or that which can be removed from the archaeological record in its entirety, and *cave art*, or that which cannot be so removed. Portable art includes everything from decorated everyday objects to artifacts interpreted as instances of symbolic or artistic expression. For example, many small bone, stone, and ivory sculptures collectively

Figure 12-20

The thick tip of this blade was flaked into a burin (indicated by the red arrow), a chisel-like tool used to cut such dense material as bone and ivory.

Figure 12-21

Pressure flaking.

Figure 12-22

Solutrean laurel leaf points, France. Left specimen length 38 cm.

Figure 12-23

Venus of Brassempouy, France. Height 3.6 cm.

called "Venus figurines" have been excavated at sites from westernmost Europe to western Russia. Some figures were realistically carved, and the faces appear to be modeled after actual women (Fig. 12-23). Other female figures are more stylized representations, often with exaggerated sexual characteristics, and they sometimes depict body decoration, clothing, and headgear (Fig. 12-24). Although Venus figurines have often been narrowly viewed as objects created for fertility or other ritual purposes, these objects actually represent women in diverse statuses and roles in Upper Paleolithic society (Soffer et al., 2000).

At two sites in the Czech Republic, Dolní Věstonice and Předmostí (both dated at approximately 27,000–26,000 ya), archaeologists have also found small animal figures of fired clay. This is the first documented use of ceramic technology anywhere; in fact, it precedes the earliest documented examples of fired clay pottery by more than 15,000 years.

Upper Paleolithic cave art—material symbolic expressions that can't be removed from the archaeological record without destroying them—comprises what are probably the most widely recognized images of human prehistory in the world. It began during the Aurignacian and continued to the end of the Ice Age. It is beautiful, exotic, rare, old, and only partly understood.

Most cave art depicts common food animals, such as reindeer, bison, mammoths, and horses, and occasionally even fish, but there are also many pictures of dangerous animals, such as cave bears, rhinos, and lions (Fig. 12-25). Many of these animals went extinct at the end of the Ice Age. Other representations include hand stencils (an outline created by blowing pigment over a hand held against a cave wall) and patterns of dots and lines. Images of people are uncommon by comparison with those of other animals.

The importance of cave art ultimately rests in it being far more than just a bunch of pretty pictures executed in strange places. When the first site was discovered in the late 1800s, it caused an immediate sensation because it was either an elaborate hoax, which seemed likely at first, or it truly was old. If the latter, then there was a problem: Its execution defied the then dominant view of cultural "progress" as something that gradually proceeded from a "savage" ancient past to the "civilization" of the present. Since cave art

did prove to be quite old, we can reasonably claim that these Upper Paleolithic sites played a role in encouraging a reevaluation of basic notions about the nature of culture change and the course of biocultural evolution.

Cave art is now known from more than 200 sites, many of which are in southwestern France and northern Spain. The most famous of these sites are Altamira, in Spain, and Lascaux and Grotte Chauvet, in France (Fig. 12-26). Altamira was discovered by a hunter in 1869. The walls and ceiling of this immense cave are filled with superb portrayals of bison in red and black pigments. The artist even took advantage of bulges in the walls to create the visual illusion of depth in the paintings. Nearly 70 years after the discovery of Altamira, Lascaux Cave came to light and soon attracted worldwide attention for its huge paintings of bulls that dominate the long passage now called the Great Hall of Bulls. Here and elsewhere in the cave, painting after painting of horses, deer, wild bulls, ibex, and other animals were drawn with remarkable skill in black, red, and yellow pigments.

Chauvet is one of the most recently discovered art caves, having been found by cave explorers in December 1994. It contains more than 200 paintings and engravings of animals, including cave bears, horses, rhinos, lions, and mammoths, as well as stone tools, torches, and fireplaces left by Upper Paleolithic visitors to the cave. Radiocarbon dating of pigments sampled from the paintings shows that they were executed during the Aurignacian, around 35,000–32,000 ya (Balter, 2006; Cuzange, 2007), making Grotte Chauvet considerably earlier than the Magdalenian sites of Lascaux and Altamira.

A recent comparative analysis of art cave hand stencils from four French caves has concluded that both men and women participated in cave art (Snow, 2006). And their art was not limited to caves. Evidence discovered during the past 15 years shows that they also painted and engraved images on cliff faces and rocks outside of caves (Bicho et al., 2007), but very little of this art has survived thousands of years of weathering in the open air.

The big question, of course, is why did they paint? There is probably no single reason that explains all Upper Paleolithic art. Certainly, many ideas have been suggested over the decades—for example, that the art represents early religious beliefs, hunting magic (perhaps I can capture the animal if I capture its essence in an image), a visual representation of cosmology or world view, and group identity or boundaries. It is a question for which archaeologists still have much to learn before they can answer it convincingly.

Figure **12-24**

Venus of Willendorf, Austria.
Height 11.1 cm.

Figure **12-25**

Cave art from Grotte Chauvet, France.
(a) Bear. (b) Aurochs and rhinoceros.

(a)

(b)

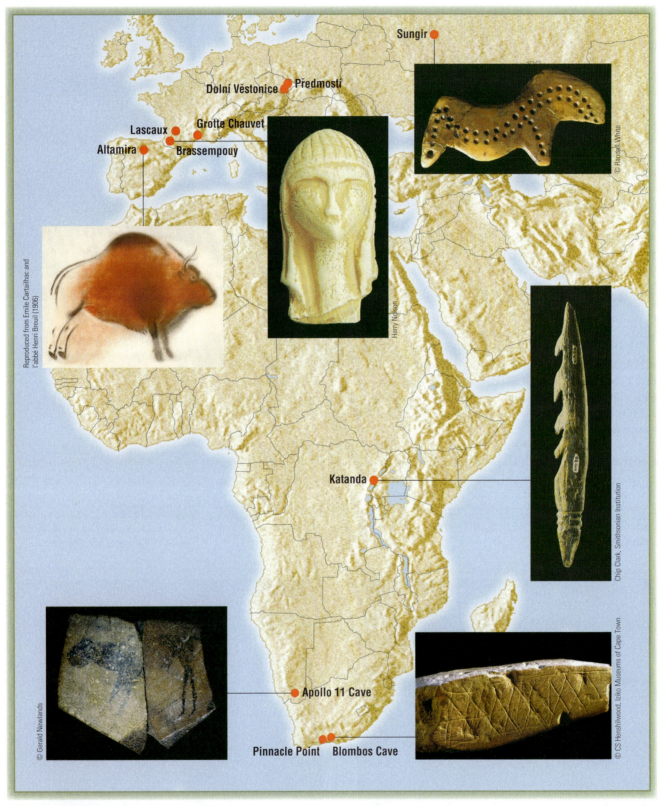

Figure 12-26

Symbolic artifacts from the Middle Stone Age of Africa and the Upper Paleolithic in Europe. It is notable that evidence of symbolism is found in Blombos Cave (77,000 ya) and Katanda (80,000 ya), both in Africa, a full 50,000 years *before* any comparable evidence is known from Europe. Moreover, the ochre found at Pinnacle Point is yet another 80,000 years older, dating to more than 160,000 ya.

AFRICA

Many significant innovations and cultural changes that have traditionally been cited as markers for the earliest modern human behavior in the Upper Paleolithic of Europe had their beginnings in Africa (Zilhão, 2007). Early accomplishments in rock art, as early as in Europe, are seen in southern Africa (Namibia) at the Apollo 11 rock shelter site, where painted slabs have been dated to between 28,000 and 26,000 ya (Freundlich et al., 1980; Vogelsang, 1998). At Blombos Cave, farther to the south, remarkable bone tools, beads, and decorated ocher fragments are all dated to 73,000 ya (Henshilwood et al., 2004; Jacobs et al., 2006). The most recent and highly significant discovery from South Africa comes from another cave located at Pinnacle Point, not far from Blombos. At Pinnacle Point, ocher has been found (perhaps used for personal adornment) as well as clear evidence of systematic exploitation of shellfish and use of very small stone blades (microliths, thumbnail-sized stone flakes hafted to make knives and saws, for example). What is both important and surprising is that the site is dated to approximately 165,000 ya, providing the earliest evidence from anywhere of these behaviors thought by many as characteristic of modern humans (Marean et al., 2007). Indeed, all these discoveries at Pinnacle Point are remarkably early: The use of microliths is almost 100,000 years earlier than anywhere else, while the exploitation of marine resources as well as the ochre from here come 40,000 years prior to systematic evidence from any other site.

Throughout Africa, stone tool technology is characterized by wide use of microliths and blades during what is called the Late Stone Age.* In central Africa, there was also considerable use of bone and antler, some of it possibly quite early. Excavations in the Katanda area of the eastern portion of the Democratic Republic of the Congo (Fig. 12-26) have shown remarkable development of bone craftwork. In fact, preliminary reports by Alison Brooks, of George Washington University, and John Yellen, of the National Science Foundation, have demonstrated that these technological achievements rival those of the more renowned European Upper Paleolithic (Yellen et al., 1995).

The most important artifacts discovered in the Katanda area are a dozen intricately made bone tools excavated from three sites. These tools, made from the bones of large mammals, apparently were first ground to flatten and sharpen them. Some of them were then precisely pressure-flaked to produce a row of barbs. In form, these tools are similar to what have been called harpoons from the later Upper Paleolithic of Europe (Magdalenian, about 15,000 ya).

The dating of the Katanda sites is crucial for drawing useful comparisons with the European Upper Paleolithic. Unfortunately, the bone used for the tools was unsuitable for radiocarbon dating (it may have been too old and beyond the range of this technique). As a result, the other techniques now used for this time range—thermoluminescence (TL), electron spin resonance (ESR), and uranium series dating (see p. 194)—were all applied. The results proved consistent, indicating dates between 180,000 and 75,000 ya.†

However, there are still some problems in clearly associating the bone implements with the materials that have supplied the chronometric age estimates. In fact, Richard Klein, a coauthor of one of the initial reports (Brooks et al., 1995), doesn't accept the suggested great antiquity for these finds; he believes they may be much younger. Even so, if the early age estimates should hold up, once again we'll look *first* to Africa as the crucial source for human origins—not just for biological aspects, but for cultural aspects as well.

---

*The Late Stone Age in Africa is equivalent to the Upper Paleolithic in Eurasia.
†If these dates prove accurate, Katanda would actually be earlier than Late Stone Age and thus be considered Middle Stone Age and thus equivalent to the Middle Paleolithic in Eurasia.

Summary of Upper Paleolithic Culture

In looking back at the Upper Paleolithic, we can see it as the culmination of 2 million years of cultural development. Change proceeded incredibly slowly for most of the Pleistocene; but as cultural traditions and materials accumulated, and the brain—and, we assume, intelligence—expanded and reorganized, the rate of change quickened.

Cultural evolution continued with the appearance of early premodern humans and moved a bit faster with later premoderns. Neandertals in Eurasia and their contemporaries elsewhere added deliberate burials, technological innovations, and much more.

Building on existing cultures, late Pleistocene populations attained sophisticated cultural and material heights in a seemingly short—by previous standards—burst of exciting activity. In Europe as well as in southern and central Africa particularly, there seem to have been dramatic cultural innovations, among them big game hunting with powerful new weapons, such as spear-throwers, harpoons, and the bow and arrow. Other innovations included personal ornaments, needles, "tailored" clothing, and burials with elaborate grave goods—a practice that may indicate some sort of status hierarchy.

The last Ice Age ended about 10,000 ya, and the retreat of glacial ice affected global climate, plants, and animals, including humans. As average annual temperatures slowly increased, coastlines were drowned by rising sea levels, and the vast grasslands of western Europe were replaced by hardwood forests. Many traditional food animals either went extinct or migrated to find better range, and much the same happened to important plant foods. Chapter 13 continues our story of human biocultural evolution by first considering how and when the first humans arrived in the Americas and then exploring how humans everywhere adjusted to the rapidly changing post-Pleistocene world.

Summary

For the past two decades, and there's no end in sight, researchers have fiercely debated the date and location of the origin of anatomically modern human beings. One hypothesis (complete replacement) claims that anatomically modern forms first evolved in Africa close to 200,000 ya and then, migrating out of Africa, completely replaced premodern *H. sapiens* in the rest of the world. Another school (regional continuity) takes a completely opposite view and maintains that in various geographical regions of the world, local groups of premodern *H. sapiens* evolved directly to anatomically modern humans. A third hypothesis (partial replacement) takes a somewhat middle position, suggesting an African origin but also accepting some later hybridization outside of Africa.

Recent research coming from several sources is beginning to clarify the origins of modern humans. Molecular evidence, the dramatic new fossil finds from Herto (in Ethiopia), and the early cultural innovations seen archaeologically at Pinnacle Point (in South Africa) all suggest that a multiregional origin of modern humans is unlikely. Sometime, soon after 150,000 ya, complete replacement of all hominins outside Africa may have occurred when migrating Africans displaced the populations in other regions. However, such absolutely *complete* replacement will be very difficult to prove, and it's not really what we'd expect. More than likely, at least some interbreeding took place. Still, from the increasing and highly informative genetic data, it's looking more and more like there wasn't very much intermixing of migrating African populations with other Old World groups. And yet, there is still some dispute about this conclusion. A few physical anthropologists suggest more intermixing could have occurred, as shown, for example, by the child's skeleton from Abrigo do Largar Velho. And finally, some archaeological data from Europe show more cultural continuity between the Middle and Upper Paleolithic than can be easily explained by rapid population replacement.

Archaeological evidence of early modern humans also paints a fascinating picture of our most immediate ancestors. The Upper Paleolithic was an age of extraordinary innovation and achievement in technology and art. Many new and complex tools were introduced, and their production indicates fine skill in working wood, bone, and antler. Cave art in western Europe displays the masterful ability of Upper Paleolithic painters, and beautiful sculptures have been found at many European sites. Sophisticated symbolic representations have also been found in Africa and elsewhere. Upper Paleolithic *H. sapiens* displayed amazing cultural development in a relatively short period of time.

In the What's Important feature, you'll find a useful summary of the most significant fossil discoveries discussed in this chapter.

What's Important Key Fossil Discoveries of Early Modern Humans and *Homo floresiensis*

Dates	Region	Site	Hominin	The Big Picture
95,000–13,000 ya	Southeast Asia	Flores (Indonesia)	*H. floresiensis*	Late survival of very small-bodied and small-brained hominin on island of Flores; designated as different species (*H. floresiensis*) from modern humans
30,000 ya	Europe	Cro-Magnon(France)	*H. sapiens sapiens*	Famous site historically; good example of early modern humans from France
35,000 ya	Europe	Oase Cave(Romania)	*H. sapiens sapiens*	Earliest well-dated modern human from Europe
110,000 ya	Southwest Asia	Qafzeh (Israel)	*H. sapiens sapiens*	Early site; shows considerable variation
115,000 ya	Southwest Asia	Skhūl (Israel)	*H. sapiens sapiens*	Earliest well-dated modern human outside of Africa; perhaps contemporaneous with neighboring Tabun Neandertal site
160,000–154,000 ya	Africa	Herto (Ethiopia)	*H. sapiens idaltu*	Best-preserved and best-dated early modern human from anywhere; placed in separate subspecies from living *H. sapiens*

Critical Thinking Questions

1. What anatomical characteristics define *modern* as compared to *premodern* humans? Assume that you're analyzing an incomplete skeleton that may be early modern *H. sapiens*. Which portions of the skeleton would be most informative, and why?

2. Go through the chapter and list all the forms of evidence that you think support the complete replacement model. Now, do the same for the regional continuity model. What evidence do you find most convincing, and why?

3. Why are the fossils recently discovered from Herto so important? How does this evidence influence your conclusions in question 2?

4. What archaeological evidence shows that modern human behavior during the Upper Paleolithic was significantly different from that of earlier hominins? Do you think that early modern *H. sapiens* populations were behaviorally superior to the Neandertals? Be careful to define what you mean by "superior."

5. Why do you think some Upper Paleolithic people painted in caves? Why don't we find such evidence of cave painting from a wider geographical area?

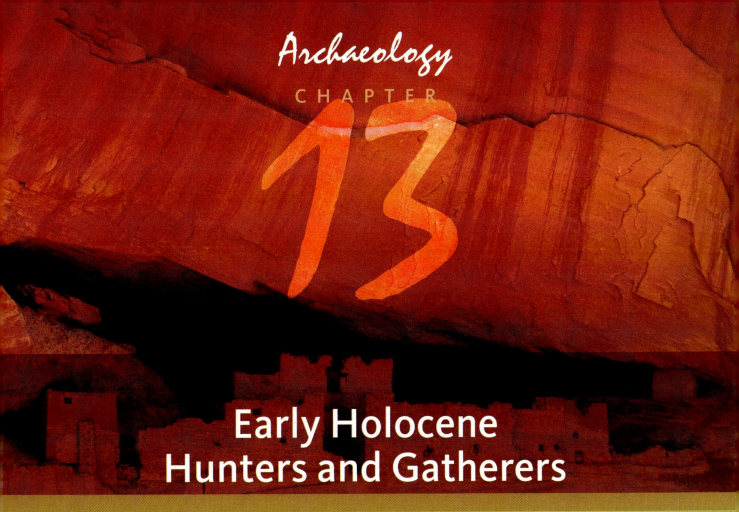

Archaeology

Early Holocene Hunters and Gatherers

Focus Questions

Where did the first inhabitants of the New World come from, and when did they arrive?

What major cultural changes accompanied the end of the last Ice Age in the Americas and the Old World?

 Click!

Introduction

During the summer of 1996, two men found a human skull and other bones along the muddy shore of the Columbia River near Kennewick, Washington. They reported the discovery to the police and coroner, who in turn asked James Chatters, a forensic anthropologist and archaeologist, to examine the remains and provide an initial assessment. The results suggested that they were probably dealing with a Caucasian male in his mid-40s, but one who looked thousands of years old. When a CAT scan also showed a large stone spear point embedded in the man's hip, Chatters and others understandably wondered just how old this skeleton was (Chatters, 2001). Bone samples sent for radiocarbon dating returned an early **Holocene** age estimate of roughly 9,300 ya.* Instead of explaining this man's past, the analyses just added to the mystery. Who was this guy?

"Kennewick Man," as he was soon called, became the center of an extraordinary controversy, one that was more legal than scientific; it took nine years and more than $8.5 million of taxpayers' money to sort out the case in federal courts (Dalton, 2005). It involved a swarm of attorneys, the U.S. Army Corps of Engineers, the U.S. Department of the Interior, several Native American tribal groups, a handful of internationally known anthropologists, a Polynesian chief, and several federal judges, decisions, and appeals. Several important legal questions were ultimately at issue, not the least of which was the right of the American public to information about the distant past (Bruning, 2006; Malik, 2007). At stake on the scientific side of the picture was what could be learned from the physical remains of a person who lived during the early days of the human presence in North America, when few people were spread over this huge continent. So few human skeletons (currently less than 10 individuals) are known in North America from this period that each new one, like Kennewick Man, is a major discovery that potentially opens a fresh window on the prehistory of the continent.

As we noted in Chapter 12, men, women, and children made the first footprints in New World mud sometime between 30,000 and 13,500 ya. The genetic evidence suggests that this most likely happened after about 16,500 ya (Goebel et al., 2008). With their first steps, they expanded the potential range of our species by more than 16 million square miles, spanning two continents and countless islands, or roughly 30 percent of the earth's land surface. It was a big deal, comparable in scope and significance to the dispersal of the first hominins into Europe and Asia from Africa during the Lower Paleolithic.

In this chapter, we'll consider the story of these first New World inhabitants and also begin to look at the major cultural developments of roughly the past 10,000 years (Fig. 13-1), during which world cultural changes increased at a dramatic rate. Following the end of the last Ice Age, the world's modest human population of perhaps a few tens of

Holocene The geological epoch during which we now live. The Holocene follows the Pleistocene epoch and began roughly 11,000–10,000 ya.

---

*Dates cited in the early American prehistory sections of this chapter have been adjusted to reflect calendar years before the present.

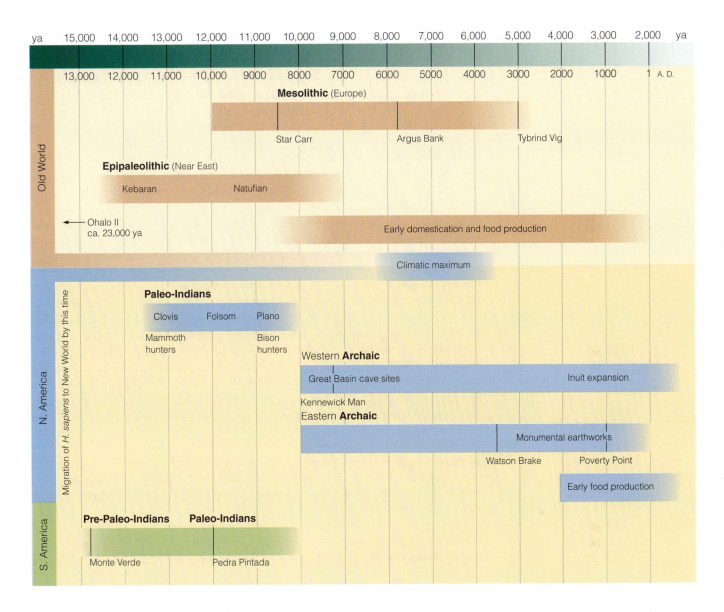

millions sustained itself by hunting and gathering food, living in small groups, constructing humble shelters, and making use of effective but simple equipment crafted from basic natural materials. Obviously, quite a lot has happened since then! What *is* important to note is that these changes are not primarily the result of human physical evolution, which has played a decreasing role in human changes during the short span since the last Ice Age (see Chapters 4 and 5). Rather, the most radical developments affecting the human condition continue to be the consequences of our uniquely human *biocultural evolution*, mostly stimulated by cultural innovations and the inescapable effects of our ever-growing population.

Let's begin our look at human communities at the end of the Ice Age by examining the archaeological and biological clues relating to the origins of the first Americans and review the evidence indicating not only when they first arrived but also what cultural adjustments they made in their new homeland. We'll then explore how lifeways changed for many human groups both in the New and Old Worlds as the glaciers retreated, average sea levels rose, plant and animal communities migrated, and even such seemingly permanent entities as rivers and lakes became transformed in a postglacial world.

Figure **13-1**

Time line for Chapter 13.

Entering the New World

Major archaeological problems, such as the entry of the first humans into the New World, inevitably attract a lot of research interest, not to mention a little contentious debate (e.g., Waguespack, 2007). When did the first humans arrive in the Americas? Where did they come from? How did they get here? How did they make a living after they arrived? We want firm answers to these questions, but, as with all research that centers on "first" events, finding the answers is never easy. Consider, for example, the crucial question of *when* the first humans arrived in the New World. Strictly speaking, to answer this question you need to identify the locality—somewhere in the 16 million square miles of two continents—where the oldest material evidence of the presence of humans is preserved in well-dated archaeological contexts. It's as though you're trying to find a particular sand grain that may or may not be on a beach. Once you understand the difficulty of finding "the" answer, it's easy to see why the question is likely to remain with us for a while.

When people arrived is necessarily tied up with *where* they came from because the two, taken together, tell us where to search in the archaeological record for these first New World immigrants. There's general consensus that the late Pleistocene marked something of a watershed in human prehistory. For millions of years, continental glaciers waxed and waned while humans evolved from ancestral primates. This activity meant little to our remote ancestors because glaciation primarily affected the higher latitudes, and early hominins ranged the tropics, where relatively few effects of such climatic changes reached them. But by late Pleistocene times, during the Upper Paleolithic of Europe and the Late Stone Age of Africa, modern humans had long ago pushed well into the temperate latitudes and even into regions just exposed by glacial meltwaters (see Chapter 12). These humans were capable of culturally adapting to changing natural and social environments and could do so at a pace that would have been unthinkable to their Lower Paleolithic ancestors. Members of these human groups became the first New World immigrants.

Archaeologists depend on geographical, biological, archaeological, and linguistic evidence to trace the earliest Americans back to their Old World origins and construct today's answers to the when and where questions. Right now, there are three major competing hypotheses to explain the route of entry of humans into the New World: by way of the Bering land bridge that connected Asia and North America several times during the late Pleistocene (Fig. 13-2); along the coast of the northern Pacific Rim (Fig. 13-3); and

 13-2

The earliest inhabitants of North America may have entered the continent during the late Pleistocene epoch by way of the Bering land bridge, which was exposed during periods of maximum glaciation. These groups may have passed southward into what is now the United States by following the ice-free corridor that periodically emerged between the Cordilleran and Laurentide ice sheets in western Canada.

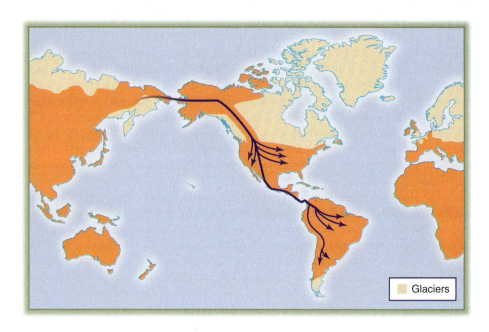

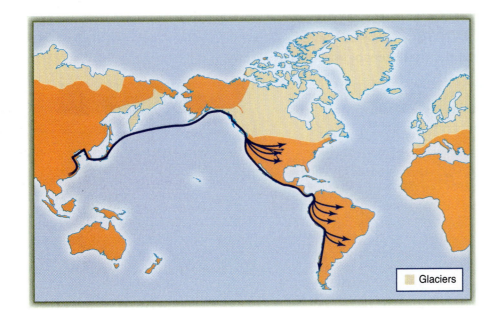

<figure>Figure 13-3

The Pacific coastal route hypothesis asserts that the earliest immigrants into the Americas may have traveled by boat along the islands and environmental refugia that dotted the Pacific coast during the late Pleistocene.</figure>

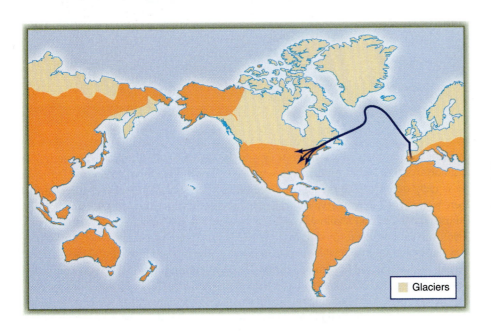

Figure 13-4

The North Atlantic ice-edge corridor hypothesis argues that the earliest arrivals in the New World may have come not from Asia, but from the Solutrean culture of western Europe, which was technologically similar to the Clovis Paleo-Indian culture in North America. These groups would have traveled north up the coast of Europe and across to North America by following the edge of the ice sheet that stretched between the two continents in late Pleistocene times.

by following the ice edge across the northern Atlantic from western Europe (Fig. 13-4). Although more than one scenario could be true, they're not equally likely. Let's consider the evidence for each in turn.

BERING LAND BRIDGE

As long ago as the late sixteenth century, José de Acosta, a Jesuit priest with extensive experience in Mexico and Andean South America, examined the geographical and other information available to him and argued that humans must have entered the New World from Asia (Acosta, 2002). Until recently, few practicing archaeologists questioned this interpretation of events.

A lot of evidence favors this idea. First, there's the basic geography of the situation. If you cast around for a feasible, low-tech way to get people into the Americas, a quick

At a Glance
Entry of the First Humans into the New World

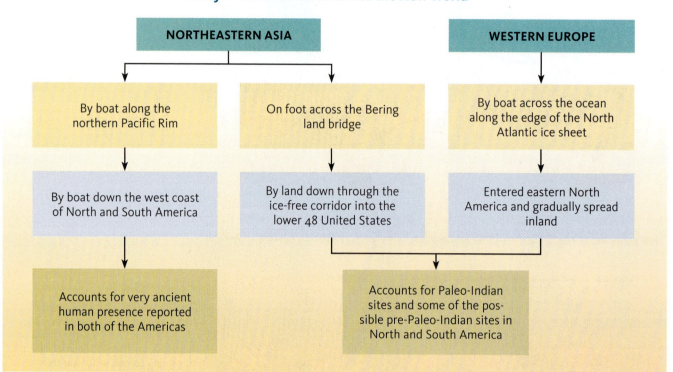

NORTHEASTERN ASIA		WESTERN EUROPE
By boat along the northern Pacific Rim	On foot across the Bering land bridge	By boat across the ocean along the edge of the North Atlantic ice sheet
By boat down the west coast of North and South America	By land down through the ice-free corridor into the lower 48 United States	Entered eastern North America and gradually spread inland
Accounts for very ancient human presence reported in both of the Americas	Accounts for Paleo-Indian sites and some of the possible pre-Paleo-Indian sites in North and South America	

check of a world map will draw your eyes to the Bering Strait, where northeastern Asia and northwestern North America are separated by only 50 miles of ocean (see Fig 13-2). An equally quick visit to the geology section of your local library will also reveal that there were several long intervals during the Pleistocene when lowered sea levels actually exposed the floor of the shallow Bering Sea, creating a wide "land bridge"(West and West, 1996). The land bridge formed during periods of maximum glaciation, when the volume of water locked up in glacial ice sheets reduced worldwide sea levels by 300 to 400 feet.* During the Last Glacial Maximum (28,000–15,000 ya), **Beringia**, as it is known, comprised a broad plain up to 1,300 miles wide from north to south (see Fig. 13-2). Ironically, the cold, dry arctic climate kept Beringia relatively ice-free. The primary plant cover of this low-lying windswept area included mostly mosses and lichens, but patches or *refugia* of boreal trees and shrubs also managed to preserve a toehold in the region (Brubaker et al., 2005).

Beringia's dry steppes and tundra supported herds of grazing animals and could just as easily have supported human hunters who preyed on them. The region was, after all, an extension of the familiar landscape of northern Asia. Archaeology confirms that during the later phases of the Pleistocene, Upper Paleolithic hunters pursuing large herbivores with efficient stone- and bone-tipped weapons, and probably with the aid of domesticated dogs, drifted into the farthest reaches of Eurasia (Soffer and Praslov, 1993). The earliest evidence of their presence in northern Siberia is the recently reported Yana RHS site in the Yana River region (Fig. 13-5), where archaeologists have found rhinoceros horn and mammoth ivory spear foreshafts as well as stone tools and other artifacts in

Beringia (bare-in´-jya) The dry-land connection between Asia and America that existed periodically during the Pleistocene epoch.

*To put these glaciers in perspective, visualize a mile-high ice sheet where Chicago is now—not a film of ice on your car's windshield in the winter.

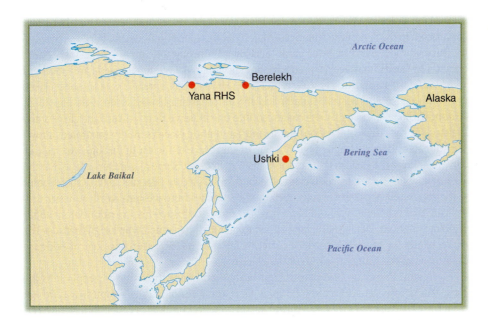

Figure **13-5**
Late Pleistocene sites in Siberia and Beringia mentioned in the text.

contexts dated to about 30,000 ya (Pitulko et al., 2004). Yana RHS is at least twice as old as the western Beringia site of Berelekh (see Fig. 13-5), the next oldest candidate for a possible Arctic Circle campsite, and it demonstrates that at a very early date, people were successfully adapted to high-latitude conditions similar to what hunters would have encountered in crossing Beringia. Culturally and geographically, these Asian hunters were capable of becoming the first Americans (Goebel et al., 2008).

Geologists have determined that except for short spans, the Bering passage was dry land between about 25,000 and 11,000 ya and for other extended periods even before then (especially between 75,000 and 45,000 ya). If the first humans entered the New World by traveling on foot across Beringia, they probably made their trips during the later episode. As yet, there's no generally accepted evidence of humans in the Americas before that time.

At a Glance

Important Northeastern Asia Sites and Regions

SITE	DATES (YA)	SIGNIFICANCE
Yana RHS (Russia)	30,000	Earliest evidence of late Pleistocene hunters beyond the Arctic Circle in northern Siberia; stone tools and horn and ivory spear foreshafts similar to that found much later on North American Paleo-Indian sites
Berelekh (Russia)	ca. 14,000–13,000	Archaeological evidence of Arctic human adaptations
Bering land bridge (Russia & USA)	ca. 75,000–45,000 and 25,000–11,000	Also called "Beringia"; a Pleistocene land bridge that formed between northeastern Asia and northwestern North America during periods of maximum glaciation

After entering Alaska by way of Beringia, early immigrants would not have had easy access to the rest of the Americas. Major glaciers to the southeast of Beringia blocked the further movement of both game and people throughout most of the Pleistocene epoch. The **Cordilleran** ice mass covered the mountains of western Canada and southern Alaska, and the **Laurentide** glacier, centered on Hudson Bay, spread a vast ice sheet across much of eastern and central Canada and the northeastern United States (see Fig. 13-2). Around 20,000 ya, these glaciers coalesced into one massive flow. Toward the close of the Pleistocene, the edges of the Cordilleran and Laurentide glaciers finally separated, allowing animals and, in principle, their hunters to gain entry to the south through an "ice-free corridor" along the eastern flank of the Canadian Rockies. Some researchers argue that the ice-free corridor became passable as early as 13,700–13,400 ya (Haynes, 2005). Others point to the geographical pattern of radiocarbon age estimates from western North America that indicate that humans could not have traveled through this ice-free corridor before about 13,400 ya (Arnold, 2006). In the long run, it may not matter much who's right because the earliest dates for an ice-free corridor currently fall *after* the earliest archaeological evidence of humans in the Americas south of the glaciers.

To sum things up, the Bering land bridge model for the entry of people into the New World rests on several key notions. First, the technologically simplest way to get from the Old World to the New World was on foot. Second, lots of other animals arrived by this route during the Pleistocene, so, archaeologists have long reasoned, it was feasible for people to do the same. Third, as we discuss in a later section, the skeletal and genetic evidence clearly favor an Asian origin for Native Americans. On all these points, at least, there's little debate. The main problem with the Bering land bridge explanation is that the age estimates for the earliest humans in North and South America are hard to reconcile with the age estimates for the most favorable intervals during which humans could have crossed Beringia, walked through the ice-free corridor, and populated the Americas. The archaeological evidence currently supports the inference that humans passed the glaciers and established themselves on both continents before 13,500 ya.

PACIFIC COASTAL ROUTE

The second scenario also envisions the earliest New World inhabitants coming from Asia. But it has them moving along the coast, where climatic conditions were generally not as harsh as those of the interior and where they could simply go around the North American glaciers. Looking again at the northern Pacific Rim between Asia and North America (see Fig. 13-3), we can see that given canoes, rafts, or other forms of water transport, it was geographically possible for humans to enter the New World by traveling along the coast. Unlike the Bering land bridge, this route would have been less dependent on the waxing and waning of glaciers. In principle, therefore, humans traveling by this route could have arrived in the New World tens of thousands of years ago (Dixon, 1999; Erlandson, 2002).

But why should we assume that the late Pleistocene inhabitants of East Asia had water transport capable of making this trip? Here, sound archaeological evidence comes to our rescue. As discussed in Chapter 12, humans colonized Australia roughly 50,000 ya, and it could only be reached by water. So, the rafts or boats necessary to carry humans successfully along the Pacific coast—but not, apparently, across the Pacific Ocean—from Asia to the New World must have existed and been used by at least some late Pleistocene populations before the first people began to settle in the Americas.

Passage along the Pacific Rim may have been eased by the kelp forest ecosystems that line much of the Pacific coast of the Americas outside of the tropics (Erlandson et al., 2007). Kelp is a seaweed that grows in dense stands in shallow water. Kelp "forests" provide a rich and diverse ecosystem of fish, mammals, and birds that were exploited by Native Americans well into the twentieth century. These forests lined much of the Pacific Rim by 16,000 ya (Erlandson et al., 2007) and would have provided an important resource for human migrants along the coast.

Cordilleran (cor-dee-yair´-an) Pleistocene ice sheet originating in mountains of western North America.

Laurentide (lah-ren´-tid) Pleistocene ice sheet centered in the Hudson Bay region and extending across much of eastern Canada and the northern United States.

Many archaeologists find the possibility that people used a coastal route to enter the New World an attractive idea, partly because it avoids the time constraints on the availability of the Bering land bridge and ice-free corridor and partly because migrants traveling by boat along the northern Pacific coast need not have abandoned their boats once they got around the glaciers. They could just as easily have kept going down the west coast of the Americas, following the "kelp highway" (Erlandson et al., 2007). Had they done so, it would help to explain why there are a lot of apparently very early South America sites, but few in the interior of North America (Kelly, 2003).

Still, the coastal route has several possible shortcomings. An often cited problem, one even noted by its proponents, is that the archaeological evidence that could be used to test this hypothesis rests at the bottom of the Pacific Ocean, having likely been covered, if not destroyed, by rising sea levels as the glaciers melted. Fortunately, coastlines react locally, not globally, to such changes. Paleogeographical researchers are beginning to identify specific parts of the modern coasts and offshore islands of Canada that would have been exposed land where human migrants may have traveled (Hetherington et al., 2003). Farther to the south, off the California coast, 13,000-year-old human skeletal remains were recently found in excavations on Santa Rosa Island (Johnson et al., 2007). What makes the Santa Rosa remains particularly relevant is that humans could not have reached this island without some form of water transport. Taken together, these examples show that relevant archaeological evidence is indeed discoverable, even if we cannot (as yet) adequately explore the ocean floor.

Another problem, possibly related to the preceding one, is that we currently have little archaeological evidence of marine-adapted human populations along the coast of northeastern Asia—from which the earliest immigrants into the New World would have been drawn—until *after* the end of the last Ice Age. As on the other side of the Pacific, much of the archaeological evidence of marine adaptations may have been buried by rising sea levels at the end of the Pleistocene. Most archaeologists with firsthand experience in the region feel that if immigrants to the New World had arrived by the coastal route, they must have had the necessary technology and arctic marine experience needed to survive in this harsh, quickly changing environment.

So to sum things up, the Pacific coastal route was feasible in principle. Considering the generally milder climate and rich resources of the coast relative to the interior, the presence of natural refugia, the resource-rich kelp forest highway, and the apparent technological capabilities of late Pleistocene populations, the earliest migrants could have pulled it off. Factoring the Bering land bridge and the glaciers out of the equation also removes the temporal bottlenecks on migration that haunt the land bridge hypothesis. These are definitely marks in its favor. The main problem is that if the earliest people came by this route, then much—but fortunately not all—of the most relevant archaeological evidence is buried in the muck on the floor of the Pacific from northeastern Asia to the Americas. Even with this drawback, the coastal route hypothesis is perhaps the most promising explanation of how the first inhabitants arrived in the New World.

NORTH ATLANTIC ICE-EDGE CORRIDOR

The third and final scenario in our lineup of possible migration hypotheses seeks to explain the entry of the earliest humans into the Americas as well as the origins of the **Clovis** complex (13,200–12,800 ya), which, until recently, was widely believed to be the earliest archaeological evidence of humans in North America. Although Clovis itself is reasonably well known, archaeologists have yet to find any clear antecedents for its sophisticated stone tool technology in the Upper Paleolithic sites of Siberia. Given the lack of identified Asian precursors and the problems of getting the earliest inhabitants south of the Canadian glaciers before the oldest Clovis sites were being deposited, Bradley and Stanford (2004, 2006) suggest that it's time to look elsewhere. Rather than continuing to focus on the possible Asia–North America link, they argue that we should be trying to

Clovis North American archaeological complex characterized by distinctive fluted projectile points, dating roughly 13,500–13,000 ya; once widely believed to be representative of specialized big game hunters, who may have driven many late Pleistocene species into extinction.

identify the most similar technology that could be ancestral to Clovis and then exploring how it may have reached the shores of North America.

According to Bradley and Stanford's North Atlantic ice-edge corridor hypothesis, the Upper Paleolithic *Solutrean* culture of southwestern France and northern Spain is technologically very similar to Clovis and old enough to be its original source. The technological similarities are so close, they argue, that if a Solutrean site were found in Siberia, it would immediately answer the question of Clovis origins. Since that hasn't happened after decades of fieldwork, they argue that Solutrean peoples may have entered North America by following the edge of the North Atlantic sea-ice bridge that linked Europe and North America during the Last Glacial Maximum (see Fig. 13-4). Eventually, having traversed the southwestern edge of the glacial ice to eastern North America, these groups dispersed inland, became North America's earliest human inhabitants, and laid the foundation for the distinctive stone, bone, and ivory tool assemblages that archaeologists call Clovis.

To sum up the case for the Solutrean-Clovis connection, the two strengths of the hypothesis are that first, it clearly identifies a similar technology that is older than Clovis, and second, it describes a process by which people who made and used this technology could have crossed the Atlantic and entered North America. The idea also has many shortcomings, not the least of which is that—as Lawrence Straus, a Solutrean specialist, and his colleagues point out—the Solutrean ended about 5,000 years, or roughly 250 generations, before the earliest-dated Clovis material in North America; the archaeological evidence that might link Solutrean with the precursors of Clovis simply isn't there; and the genetic evidence all points to northeastern Asia, not Europe (Straus et al., 2005). These are not mere quibbles that can be easily brushed aside, and the Solutrean-Clovis scenario looks unlikely at best. In the long run, the main contribution of the North Atlantic ice-edge corridor hypothesis may well be that it encourages archaeologists to break away from the centuries-long obsession with the Bering Strait and Asia and consider other possible routes by which the earliest inhabitants arrived in the Americas. To the extent that Bradley and Stanford are successful in doing this, the results may benefit the scientific understanding of the human colonization of both North and South America.

The Earliest Americans

We'll now leave behind the question of how the first people arrived in North America and explore some ideas about who they were.

PHYSICAL AND GENETIC EVIDENCE

Biological data bearing directly on the earliest people to reach the New World are frustratingly scarce. Well-documented skeletons are especially rare. The physical remains of fewer than two dozen North American individuals appear to date much before 9,500 ya, by which time humans had certainly been present in the New World for millennia (Fig. 13-6). The tremendous information value of well-preserved and documented early skeletons is the reason archaeologists spent nine years in federal courts contesting what they believed to be the government's well-intentioned but misguided decision to turn over the remains of Kennewick Man to Native American tribal groups for reburial before the remains could be studied.

The rare early finds provide valuable insights on ancient life and death. What little we currently know about Kennewick Man (Fig. 13-7), for example, is that he suffered multiple violent trauma and other health problems during his 40 to 50 years of life. His most intriguing injury is an old wound in his pelvis that had healed around a still-embedded stone spear point. To this we can add the largely healed effects of massive blunt trauma to

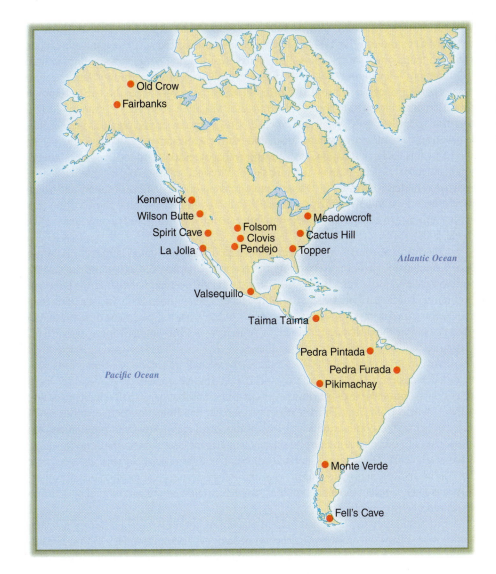

Figure **13-6**

Location of some early New World sites. The dates for many of these sites are still disputed as archaeologists grapple with mounting evidence that the earliest evidence of humans in the New World is older than the 13,500– 13,000 ya Paleo-Indian Clovis culture of North America.

the chest, a depressed skull fracture, and a fracture of the left arm. He also had an infected head injury and a fractured shoulder blade (scapula), neither of which shows the effects of healing, as well as osteoarthritis (Chatters, 2004). What's more, the list is probably incomplete because it was compiled from a preliminary examination of the remains. But by any measure, this man had a pretty hard life. Just how hard it was will become evident in a couple of years, after researchers complete the scientific analysis of his remains.

Anthropologists are also analyzing other cases, all from the American West. The 12,800-year-old partial skeleton of a young woman, discovered in a cave above the Snake River near Buhl, Idaho, reveals signs of interrupted growth in both her long bones and her teeth; this evidence suggests that the woman experienced some metabolic stress in childhood, possibly because of disease or seasonal food shortages (Green et al., 1998). At Spirit Cave, Nevada, researchers discovered the partially desiccated body of a man, wrapped in fine matting, who was in his early 40s when he died some 10,600 years ago; his skeleton exhibits a fractured skull and tooth abscesses as well as signs of back problems (Winslow and Wedding, 1997). Near Grimes Point rock-shelter, another Nevada site, researchers found a teenager from about the same period who died of his wounds after being stabbed in the chest with an obsidian blade that left slash marks and stone flakes embedded in one of his ribs (Owsley and Jantz, 2000).

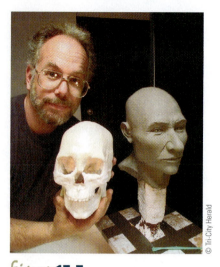

Figure **13-7**

Reconstruction of the facial features of Kennewick Man (right), based on a cast of the skull (left) found by two young men in the Columbia River, Washington, in 1996. The reconstruction was the collaborative effort of Tom McClelland (holding the skull) and James Chatters.

Physical anthropologists who made the preliminary studies of Kennewick Man, the Spirit Cave mummy, and other early specimens announced surprising interpretations based on this modest sample. Statistical analyses comparing a series of standard cranial measurements—including those that define overall skull size and proportion, shape of nasal opening, face width, and distance between the eyes—place the earliest-known American remains outside the normal range of variation observed in modern Native American populations (Owsley and Jantz, 2000). The more derived craniofacial morphological traits seen in most modern Asian and Native American populations appear to be absent in this early population. Instead, the archaeological examples display relatively small, narrow faces combined with long skulls. Physical anthropologists note these generalized (nonderived) traits in living populations among the Ainu of Japan and some Pacific Islanders and Australians. Crania that more closely resemble those of modern Native Americans became prevalent only after about 7,000 ya (Owsley and Jantz, 2000; Steele, 2000).

There are, of course, no uniform biological "types" of human beings in the sense once assumed by traditional classifiers of race (see Chapter 4). Generalities regarding human variation must, considering the nature of genetic recombination and the effects of environment and nutrition, be taken simply as that—generalities. Still, the lack of distinctive Native American physical markers on the oldest skeletal specimens has stimulated research on how the early population of the Americas, as represented by these individuals, may be related to contemporary populations.

Neves and colleagues (2004) compared the cranial morphology of nine individuals dated to around 10,200 ya from central Brazil. The researchers concluded that these individuals represent one of possibly several populations that participated in the peopling of the Americas from Asia. The researchers argue that the differences between the cranial morphology of these individuals and that of modern Native American populations are consistent with those seen in morphological comparisons elsewhere in the Americas (e.g., Brace et al., 2001; Owsley and Jantz, 2000). Similar differences also exist between late Pleistocene and recent populations in Asia, and the modern typical morphological pattern of Asia is likely a recent development that may have followed the adoption of agriculture (Jantz and Owsley, 2001).

Studies like these are a great help in placing recent finds such as Kennewick Man into context. When the facial reconstruction of Kennewick Man (see Fig. 13-7) was completed in 1997, more than a few people wondered why it looked more like the British actor Patrick Stewart of *Star Trek* fame than the popular stereotype of Native Americans (think of the man's profile on the old U.S. buffalo nickel). Quite a lot was read into that reconstruction, but all it really showed was what researchers like Neves, Jantz, Owsley, and others already knew: We don't have much data to work from, but what we do have shows similar morphological variation in Asia and the Americas among late Pleistocene–early Holocene skeletons. The data support Steele and Powell's (1999) conclusions that there seems to have been more than one prehistoric migration from Asia into the New World. The argument has intuitive appeal. After all, why would the supply of immigrants dry up after the first humans arrived in the New World?

Looking at the entire span of the human presence in the New World, it seems evident that the flow of people to the New World has roughly kept pace with the development of technology to bring them here. In this view, at least, the peopling of the New World can best be viewed as a continuing process, not as a one-time event.

The particular physical traits shared by modern Native Americans are almost surely derived from a small founding gene pool and thus a product of founder effect. (For a discussion of founder effect, an example of genetic drift, see p. 64). As in virtually all other areas of biological anthropology, molecular research is shedding new light on where the earliest Americans came from. Recent analyses of mitochondrial DNA among contemporary Native American populations suggest that just four or five genetically related lineages contributed to the early peopling of the Americas and that these groups came from Asia

(Tamm et al., 2007). Far more detailed molecular evidence showing geographical patterns in nuclear DNA support this view (Jacobsson et al., 2008; Li et al., 2008). While these molecular data show very clearly that early Americans share their closest genetic links with East Asian populations, particularly those from Siberia, it remains less certain what route early immigrants took once they reached North America. More detailed analysis using nuclear DNA, which already has provided data on hundreds of thousands of genetic loci, may well provide more complete answers.

Another intriguing source of genetic data that may provide insights has recently come from the Paisley Caves site in Oregon, where 14,000-year-old feces, or **coprolites**, yielded human hair and human DNA (Gilbert et al., 2008). These new data support the coastal route hypothesis for the entry of humans into the continental United States well before the development of the Clovis complex and before the ice-free corridor opened up.

CULTURAL TRACES OF THE EARLIEST AMERICANS

Much of the cultural evidence documenting the presence of the earliest Americans is no less controversial than that gained from analyses of the skeletal data. Nearly all archaeologists agree that Native Americans originated in Asia; yet they have varying opinions about when people first arrived in the New World and the routes by which they traveled (Madsen, 2004; Bonnichsen et al., 2005). Most of the controversy focuses on the span between 30,000 and 13,200 ya. The earlier date represents the time by which modern people first began to appear in those parts of Asia closest to North America—for example, the Yana RHS site in Siberia (see p. 316). And everyone agrees that the **Paleo-Indian** Clovis complex was present in North America by the later date.

Like the biological anthropologists, archaeologists have a tough time reaching consensus on such basic questions as: What are the material remains of the earliest inhabitants of the New World? When did they arrive? and Where did they come from? That robust answers are not forthcoming isn't for want of research; it is simply the case that the evidence is sparsely scattered over millions of square miles and is not necessarily very distinctive. As the biological anthropologists and archaeologists have learned, answering these questions takes decades of hard work—and more than a little luck.

What kind of archaeological evidence can we point to that *has* survived from this early period of American prehistory? The answer depends largely on how one evaluates the "evidence." For example, isolated artifacts, including stone choppers and large flake tools of simple form, are at times recovered from exposed ground surfaces and other undatable contexts in the Americas. They are sometimes proposed as evidence of a period predating the use of bifacial projectile points, which were common in North America by 13,200 ya. If typologically primitive-looking finds cannot be securely dated, most (but not all) archaeologists regard them with justifiable caution. The appearance of great age or crude condition may be misleading and is all but impossible to verify without corroborating evidence. To be properly evaluated, an artifact must be unquestionably the product of human handiwork and must have been recovered from a geologically sealed and undisturbed context that can be dated reliably.

Sounds pretty straightforward, right? The reality of the situation is not necessarily that easy. Take, for example, the projectile points. Alan Bryan and Ruth Gruhn (2003) point out that North American archaeologists' obsession with bifacially flaked stone points may ultimately do more harm than good to research, because we have no basis for believing that such tools were a consistent part of prehistoric assemblages everywhere in the Americas. They note, for example, that bifacially flaked projectile points are far less common in Central and South America than they are in the continental United States and southern Canada. In fact, in some parts of lowland South America, Native American groups never did use bifacially worked stone tool technology (Bryan and Gruhn, 2003, p. 175). The implication is obvious: The criteria that work for identifying the earliest Americans in one part of the two continents may not apply to other parts.

coprolites Preserved fecal material, which can be studied for what the contents reveal about diet and health.

Paleo-Indian (*paleo*, meaning "ancient") Referring to early hunter-gatherers who occupied the Americas from about 13,500 to 10,000 ya.

Most difficult to assess are some atypical sites that have been carefully excavated by researchers who sincerely believe that their work offers proof of great human antiquity in the New World. Currently, several sites fall into this disputed category (see Fig. 13-6). Pedra Furada is a rock-shelter in northeastern Brazil where excavators found what they claim to be simple stone tools in association with charcoal hearths dating back 40,000 years (Guidon et al., 1996). Others who have examined these materials remain convinced that natural, rather than cultural, factors account for them (Lynch, 1990; Meltzer et al., 1994). The dating of this and other sites in the same general region also continue to be reexamined. Additional radiocarbon age estimates on samples from hearths in the lowest levels of Pedra Furada recently yielded dates in excess of 50,000 ya (Santos et al., 2003). However, fresh radiocarbon dates on Pedra Furada pigments and rock paintings, both of which are thought by their excavators to be nearly 30,000 years old, yielded estimates of only 3,500–2,000 ya (Rowe and Steelman, 2003). So, it could be the oldest site in South America—or it could be so recent as to be irrelevant. Pedra Furada joins several other Central and South American locations that in recent decades have been proposed as extremely early cultural sites (Lynch, 1990; Parfit, 2000). Archaeologists have been uncertain how to evaluate most of them because the associated cultural materials are so typologically diverse and their contexts are frequently secondary, or mixed, geological deposits.

The United States, too, has its share of sites that defy easy explanation. At Pendejo Cave in southern New Mexico, excavators have discovered 16 friction skin prints impressed on fire-hardened clay nodules in three stratigraphic zones dated from 37,000 to 12,000 ya (Chrisman et al., 1996, 2003). Clear impressions of ridge patterns and even of sweat pores, visible under magnification, seem to confirm the palm prints and fingerprints as primate, and most likely human; but their origin and significance remain uncertain (Dincauze, 1997; Shaffer and Baker, 1997). Possible cultural materials from the same levels include charred wood, crude stone tools, and the toe bone of an extinct horse with what may be an embedded bone tool possibly used to extract marrow (MacNeish and Libby, 2003). Far to the east, at the Cactus Hill site along the Nottoway River in southern Virginia and at the Topper site in Allendale County, South Carolina, archaeologists have retrieved unusual assemblages of stone cores, flakes, and tools from strata lying well beneath more

At a Glance

Important Pre–Paleo-Indian Sites in the New World

SITE	DATES (YA)	SIGNIFICANCE
Pedra Furada (Brazil)	?50,000–?40,000	One of several South American sites for which great antiquity is claimed, but not yet convincingly proved
Pendejo Cave (New Mexico)	37,000–12,000	Controversial claim of great antiquity for the human presence in the American Southwest
Meadowcroft (Pennsylvania)	19,000–14,000	Often cited as evidence of pre-Clovis presence of humans in eastern North America
Monte Verde (Chile)	14,500	Pre-Clovis campsite in southern South America; one of the first sites to be widely accepted as evidence of pre-Clovis human presence in the New World

typical Paleo-Indian components (Dixon, 1999). The unusually early radiocarbon dates (18,000–15,000 ya) associated with these materials are consistent with their stratigraphic position (e.g., Wagner and McAvoy, 2004), but the evidence will require cautious review before these sites are generally accepted.

The scientific method is not a democratic process; we can't simply dismiss (or side with) unpopular positions without assessing the evidence as it is presented. The method is, however, a skeptical one; and the burden of proof to substantiate claims of great antiquity falls upon those who make them. Each allegation requires critical evaluation, a process that the general public sometimes perceives as unnecessarily conservative or obstructive. Information regarding dating results, archaeological contexts, and whether or not materials are of cultural origin must all be scrutinized and accepted before intense debate can resolve into consensus.

This evaluation process may take years. Consider, for example, the case of the Meadowcroft rock-shelter, near Pittsburgh, Pennsylvania. In a meticulous excavation over 25 years ago, archaeologists explored a deeply stratified site containing cultural levels dated between 19,000 and 14,000 ya by standard radiocarbon methods (Adovasio et al., 1990). Stratum IIa, from which the earliest dates derive, contained several prismatic blades, a retouched flake, a biface, and a knifelike implement (Fig. 13-8). None of the tools from this deep stratum are particularly distinctive, so it's hard to assess technological relationships with other known assemblages. Despite lingering concern over the possibility that fossil carbon from nearby coal seams may have contaminated the carbon-dated samples, more archaeologists are coming to accept the Meadowcroft evidence because of the excavators' careful documentation and the coherence of the dated strata with one another.

Excavations at Monte Verde in southern Chile revealed another remarkable site of apparent pre–Paleo-Indian age (Dillehay, 1989, 1997). Here, remnants of the wooden foundations of a dozen rectangular huts were arranged back to back in a parallel row. The structures measured between 10 and 15 feet on a side, and animal hides may have covered their sapling frameworks. Apart from the main cluster, a separate wishbone-shaped building contained stone tools and animal bones (Fig. 13-9). The cultural equipment comprised spheroids (possibly sling stones), flaked stone points, perforating tools, a wooden lance, digging sticks, mortars, and fire pits. Mastodon bones represented at least seven individuals, and remains of some 100 species of nuts, fruits, berries, wild tubers, and firewood testify to the major role of plants in subsistence activities at this site.

Monte Verde's greatest significance, however, was simply its age, which its excavator claimed to be about 14,500 years old, with a few features possibly much older. These claims were contested until 1997, when a "jury" of archaeological specialists reviewed the findings, visited the site, and finally agreed that the excavator's claims for the pre-Clovis age of Monte Verde were substantiated. This was important because it meant that the mainstream of archaeological thought accepted that Monte Verde contained material evidence of a human presence in the New World more than a thousand years before the beginning of the Clovis complex around 13,200 ya in North America. And, more generally, the acceptance of Monte Verde's great antiquity implied that archaeologists had a lot to learn about the colonization of the New World because it had just gotten a lot older (Grayson, 2004; Meltzer, 2004).

Figure 13-8

Knifelike implement from Stratum IIa at the Meadowcroft rock-shelter in Pennsylvania.

Figure 13-9

The semicircular ridge of soil at lower right in the photograph marks the remains of a 14,800-year-old hut at Monte Verde, Chile. Mastodon bones, hide, and flesh were preserved in association with this feature, along with 26 species of medicinal plants.

Tom Dillehay

Paleo-Indians in the Americas

For much of the twentieth century, most archaeologists held the view that the Clovis complex marked the earliest materials evidence for the entry of people into the Americas below the Canadian glaciers about 13,200 ya. These highly mobile Paleo-Indian hunters and, to a much lesser extent, gatherers spread rapidly across the United States (Hamilton and Buchanan, 2007; Fig. 13-10).

The distinctive **fluted point** became the Paleo-Indian period's hallmark artifact, at least in North America. Each face of a fluted point typically displays a groove (or "flute") resulting from the removal of a long channel flake, possibly to make it easier to use a special hafting technique for mounting the point on a shaft (Fig. 13-11). Other typical Paleo-Indian artifacts include a variety of stone cutting and scraping tools and, less commonly, preserved bone rods and points (Gramly, 1992).

While the general Paleo-Indian tool kit from North America probably would have been familiar to Upper Paleolithic groups in northeastern Asia, no clear technological predecessors of fluted points have yet been identified in Asia. As you may recall, this was one of the main motivations for Bradley and Stanford's (2004) decision to look elsewhere for the entry of people into North America, a search that culminated with their argument for a northern Atlantic crossing from western Europe. It's entirely possible that fluted point technology is an American invention and there are no ancestral forms to find elsewhere, whether it be in Spain, Siberia, or Mongolia. Sites such as Yana RHS in Siberia demonstrate

fluted point A biface or projectile point having had long, thin flakes removed from each face to prepare the base for hafting, or attachment to a shaft.

Figure **13-10**

North American Paleo-Indian and Archaic sites.

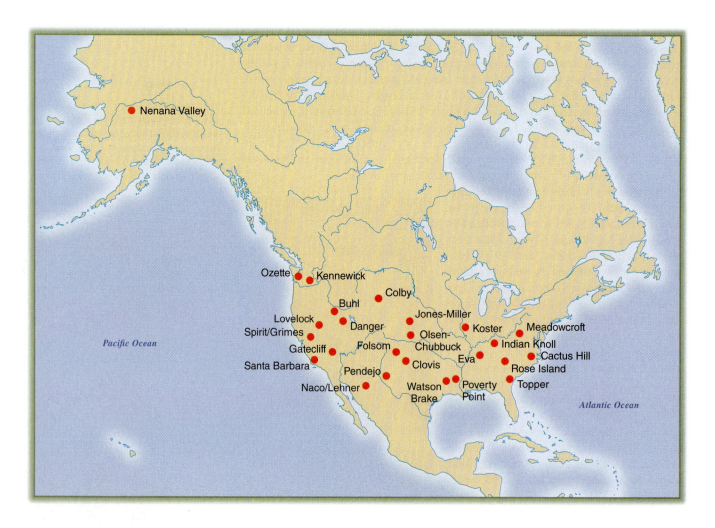

that Upper Paleolithic hunter-gatherers, like Paleo-Indians, made bifacially worked stone tools and tipped their spears with projectile points—but not *fluted* projectile points. These Siberian hunters set projectile points in bone or ivory foreshafts and were living in the general region of Beringia more than 15,000 years before the earliest evidence of human presence appears in the New World. Bifacial points and knives are also part of the Nenana complex sites of central Alaska and the lower levels of Ushki Lake in Siberia's Kamchatka peninsula. All of these sites are currently believed to date to around 13,400–13,000 ya (Goebel et al., 2003), which is too late for their inhabitants to have been the ancestors of the people who developed Paleo-Indian fluted point technology, but the sites do demonstrate that generally similar tool industries *were* moving into the New World at an early date.

PALEO-INDIAN LIFEWAYS

Current research is chiseling away at the long-standing image of Paleo-Indian uniformity in weaponry and hunting behavior and the rapid spread of Paleo-Indian populations across the Americas about 13,200 ya to reach as far south as Fell's Cave in Patagonia (see Fig. 13-6) by some 11,000 ya. It was also long felt that these rapidly moving Paleo-Indian hunters quickly made cultural adjustments as they dispersed through the varied environments of the New World during the terminal Pleistocene and early Holocene.

The recent acceptance of Monte Verde and other sites as evidence of a human presence in the Americas *before* Clovis is stimulating a major reexamination of these and other interpretations of Paleo-Indian lifeways. One of the main shortcomings of these interpretations is the assumption that the fluted point technology was a consistent part of prehistoric assemblages across the Americas and that people everywhere were using the technology to do the same things. As Bryan and Gruhn (2003) point out, there are certainly parts of the Americas in which these assumptions aren't warranted. To the extent that this is true, the uniformity of Paleo-Indian tool kits may often be more the creation of archaeologists than of the archaeology.

The same appears to be true of the long-held view of Paleo-Indians as specialized hunters of Pleistocene **megafauna**—animals over 100 pounds, including the mammoth, mastodon, giant bison, horse, camel, and ground sloth (Fig. 13-12). Of the sites associated with Paleo-Indians, the most impressive are undoubtedly the places where ancient hunters actually killed and butchered such megafauna as mammoth and giant bison (Figs. 13-13 and 13-14). At many of these kill sites, knives, scrapers, and finely flaked and fluted projectile points are directly associated with the animal bones, all of which are convincing evidence that the megafauna were human prey. Even so, as Cannon and Meltzer (2004) recently discovered in a review of the faunal remains, taphonomy, excavation procedures, and archaeological features of 62 excavated early Paleo-Indian sites in the United States, the data "provide little support for the idea that all, or even any, Early Paleo-Indian hunter-gatherers were megafaunal specialists" (Cannon and Meltzer, 2004, p. 1955). The kinds of game they hunted and other foodstuffs they collected varied with the environmental diversity of the continent (Walker and Driskell, 2007), which, when you think about it, isn't that surprising. So, in the end, yes, Paleo-Indian hunters killed megafauna, but was it an everyday event? Should we view the fortunate

Figure **13-11**

Clovis fluted points in simulated mountings.

megafauna Literally, "large animals," those weighing over 100 pounds.

Figure **13-12**

Molar teeth of mastodon (left) and mammoth (right). Mastodons browsed on evergreen branches; mammoths grazed on low vegetation. Paleo-Indian hunters may have contributed to their extinction.

Figure **13-13**

The largest American woolly mammoths were over 13 feet high at the shoulder, with long, downward-curving tusks.

Figure **13-14**

Giant Pleistocene long-horned bison were hunted by Paleo-Indians.

hunter as a rugged Terminator-like man who gnaws another notch in his trusty spear and then strides off into the sunset looking for the rest of the herd? Probably not.

North American archaeologists have identified a sequence of Paleo-Indian cultures in the western Plains and Southwest based on changing tool technology, chronology, and the biggest game species thought to be typical of each period. From about 13,200 to 12,800 ya, hunters employed Clovis-type fluted points (see Fig. 13-11; also see Fig. 13-15a). On at least 20 western sites, including Colby in Wyoming and Naco and Lehner in southern Arizona, their spear tips lie embedded in mammoth remains (Fig. 13-16). Similar points from northern Alaska retain residues that have been biochemically identified as mammoth red blood cells and hemoglobin crystals (Loy and Dixon, 1998). Meat—but not all of it from mammoths—was part of the diet of these early Americans. Isotopic analysis of Buhl Woman's (see p. 321) bone collagen indicates that her diet was largely game and fish, much of it probably preserved by sun-drying or smoking. The heavy wear on her teeth suggests that she regularly ingested grit in her food, probably the residue of grinding stones used to pulverize the dried meat (Green et al., 1998).

Figure **13-15**

North American Paleo-Indian projectile points. (a) Clovis. (b) Folsom. (c) Plano. (d) Dalton (length 2.4 inches).

(a)   (b)   (c)   (d)

Fluted projectile points are also found throughout eastern North America. In fact, more fluted projectile points are found in the East than in the West, yet more kill sites associated with late Pleistocene megafauna are found in the West than in the East. Here, too, the evidence indicates a varied Paleo-Indian diet; they were also eating caribou, deer, and smaller game (Cannon and Meltzer, 2004). Early Paleo-Indian sites in New Hampshire, Massachusetts, and New York appear to be the remains of caribou-hunting camps (Cannon and Meltzer, 2004, p. 1971). A mixed subsistence of smaller game, fish, and gathered plants supplied Paleo-Indians at a site in eastern Pennsylvania (McNett, 1985). In Florida, another site also yielded a bison skull that has what looks like part of a Paleo-Indian projectile point embedded in it. The age of this specimen, however, is uncertain (Mihlbachler et al., 2000). Acquiring such resources surely involved the use of a variety of equipment made from perishable materials, such as nets and baskets, but only the stone spear tips survive at most Paleo-Indian sites.

Excavations along the lower Amazon in northern Brazil provide further evidence for other kinds of Paleo-Indian food-getting practices (Roosevelt et al., 1996). Carbonized seeds, nuts, and faunal remains at Pedra Pintada Cave in the Amazon basin indicate a broad-based food-collecting, fishing, and small game hunting way of life in the tropical rain forest around 12,000 ya. In other sites along the Pacific slope of the Andes, mastodons, horses, sloths, deer, camelids, and smaller animals were consumed, along with tuberous roots (Lynch, 1983).

During later Paleo-Indian times on the Great Plains of North America, the Clovis fluted spear points gave way to another fluted point style that archaeologists call **Folsom**

Reproduced with permission from George C. Frison, Prehistoric Hunters of the High Plains, New York: Academic Press, Copyright 1978

Figure 13-16

Partially articulated remains of three mammoths, one of several bone piles that probably represent Paleo-Indian meat caches at the Colby site in Wyoming.

Folsom Paleo-Indian archaeological complex of the southern Great Plains, around 12,500 ya, during which long-fluted projectile points were used for bison hunting.

At a Glance
Important Paleo-Indian Sites in the New World

SITE	DATES (YA)	SIGNIFICANCE
Colby (Wyoming) and **Naco/Lehner** (Arizona)	13,500–13,000	Paleo-Indian sites where tools and other artifacts are found associated with the remains of mammoths
Pedra Pintada Cave (Brazil)	ca. 12,000	Early site with evidence of a broad-spectrum hunter-gatherer way of life in the tropical rain forest
Olsen-Chubbuck (Colorado)	9,400	Bison kill site, created when a herd was stampeded across a narrow gully in eastern Colorado
Kennewick (Washington)	9,300	One of the few early North American human skeletons; object of a nine-year court battle to decide if scientists would be permitted to study his remains

At a Glance

North American Paleo-Indian Cultures

SITE	DATES (YA)	SIGNIFICANCE
Clovis	13,200–12,800	Earliest universally acknowledged Late Pleistocene hunter-gatherers who occupied much of North America below the glacial ice masses of the northern latitudes; used distinctive fluted spear or dart projectile points
Folsom	ca. 12,500	Late Pleistocene hunter-gatherers who hunted now-extinct giant long-horned bison in the American Southwest
Plano	11,000–9,000	Hunter-gatherers of the Great Plains; their unfluted spear or dart points are associated only with modern fauna

(Meltzer, 2006) (Fig. 13-15b). Smaller and thinner than Clovis points, but with a proportionally larger central flute, Folsom points are associated exclusively with the bones of the now-extinct giant long-horned bison (see Fig. 13-14).

In turn, Folsom points soon gave way to a long sequence of new point forms—a variety of unfluted but slender and finely parallel-flaked projectile points collectively called **Plano** (Fig. 13-15c), which came into general use throughout the West even as modern-day *Bison bison* was supplanting its larger Pleistocene relatives. At some Great Plains sites, like Olsen-Chubbuck and Jones-Miller in Colorado, an effective technique of bison hunting was for hunters to stampede the animals into dry streambeds or over cliffs and then quickly dispatch those that survived the fall (Wheat, 1972; Frison, 1978). Remember, the horse had not yet been reintroduced onto the Plains (the Spanish brought them in the sixteenth century), so these early bison hunters were strictly pedestrians.

Again, there was regional variation, not only in how different groups of hunter-gatherers made a living in the diverse environments of North America but also in their technology. The temporal pattern of changing point styles found in the western United States does not hold in the East, where later Paleo-Indians employed other types of projectile points, such as the **Dalton** variety (Fig. 13-15d). Poor bone preservation generally leaves us with little direct information about these groups' hunting techniques or favored prey in this region, though deer probably extended their range at the expense of caribou as oak forests expanded over much of the eastern United States.

PLEISTOCENE EXTINCTIONS

Evidence like that found mainly in the American West, where bones of mammoths and other large herbivores have been excavated in undeniable association with the weapons used to kill them, leads some researchers to blame Paleo-Indian hunters for the extinction of North American Pleistocene megafauna. Archaeologist Paul S. Martin (1967, 2005), who viewed Clovis sites as evidence of the first people in North America, argued for decades that overhunting by the newly arrived and rapidly expanding human population caused the swift extermination, around 13,000 ya, of these animals throughout the New World. He pointed out that over half of the large mammal species found in the Americas when humans first arrived were gone within just a few centuries, especially those whose habits and habitats would have made them most vulnerable to hunters. Martin recognized a

Plano Great Plains bison-hunting culture of 11,000–9,000 ya, which employed narrow, unfluted points.

Dalton Late or transitional Paleo-Indian projectile point type that dates between 10,000 and 8,000 ya in the eastern United States.

comparable extinction event with the peopling of Australia tens of thousands of years earlier, when most of that continent's native fauna died off. African and Eurasian species were less affected, he argued, due to the long coexistence of humans and their prey and the prey's conditioning to human hunting behaviors.

Paleo-Indian **hunter-gatherers** certainly hunted Pleistocene megafauna. As we noted earlier, archaeologists have excavated several sites where such game was killed and butchered. But evidence that these animals were human prey doesn't also prove that humans hunted them to extinction. The problem is complex for reasons that are still hotly contested (Haynes, 2006). First, it has yet to be convincingly demonstrated that Paleo-Indian hunter-gatherers anywhere focused most of their food-getting effort on Pleistocene megafauna (Meltzer, 1993a; Cannon and Meltzer, 2004). What we're finding instead is that Paleo-Indian groups hunted and collected a range of animals and plants, the mix of which varied regionally (Walker and Driskell, 2007).

Second, species extinction is a natural process, and it's no less common than the emergence of new species. It happens for various reasons, and at least until modern times, these reasons seldom had anything to do with human agency. Yes, many North American megafaunal species went extinct toward the end of the Pleistocene. But if you look at the North American geological record, you'll find that many species also became extinct in the Pliocene, Miocene, and so on. Our point is that the geological record provides abundant evidence that natural processes are sufficient to account for species extinctions in the absence of humans. The presence of Paleo-Indian hunters may also be sufficient, but it hasn't yet been convincingly demonstrated that these hunters are *necessary* to explain Pleistocene extinctions.

One possible exception appears to be the extinction of proboscideans—mammoths, mastodons, elephants, and their relatives. Surovell and colleagues (2005) took a long-term view of the problem and examined the global archaeological record of human exploitation of proboscideans in 41 sites that span roughly the past 1.8 million years. They conclude that local extinctions of proboscideans on five continents correlate well with the global colonization patterns of humans, not climatic changes or other natural factors. This finding suggests that we can't entirely dismiss the possibility that humans played an important role in the late Pleistocene extinctions of some species.

The end of the Pleistocene marked an interval of profound climatic and geographical changes (for example, the creation of the Great Lakes) in North America and elsewhere. Geoarchaeologists also recognize that late Pleistocene extinctions and the expansion of Paleo-Indian hunters coincided with a time of widespread drought that was immediately followed by rapidly plunging temperatures. The latter climatic event, called the **Younger Dryas**, marked a return to near-glacial conditions and persisted for 1,500 years, from roughly 13,000 to 11,500 ya (Fiedel, 1999). And in an extraordinary twist to the story, Firestone and colleagues (2007) recently argued that the explosion of a meteor or other large extraterrestrial object over North America about 12,900 ya contributed directly to the Pleistocene megafaunal extinctions and the onset of the Younger Dryas and, ultimately, to the end of the Paleo-Indian period! While their hypothesis has attracted considerable attention, especially by the edutainment television networks, the scientific community has expressed considerable skepticism (Kerr, 2008).

The degree of human involvement in these New World extinctions will continue to be a controversial issue in American archaeology. Grayson and Meltzer (2002, 2003, 2004) maintain that no archaeological evidence supports the idea that humans caused the mass extinction of Pleistocene megafauna in North America. They further argue that Paul S. Martin's original hypothesis has been altered into something that is no longer testable and that persists partly because it feeds contemporary political views concerning human effects on the environment. Others take issue with such views, both directly (e.g., Fiedel and Haynes, 2003) and indirectly (Barnosky et al., 2004), and argue for a possible human role.

hunter-gatherers People who make their living by hunting, fishing, and gathering their food and not by producing it.

Younger Dryas A stadial, or colder stage, between roughly 13,000 and 11,500 ya. The climate became colder and drier but did not return to full glacial conditions in higher latitudes.

Early Holocene Hunter-Gatherers

Across North America and Eurasia, gradual warming conditions during the transition from the late Pleistocene to the mid-Holocene had profound ecological effects that extended well beyond the waning glaciers. Much of the Northern Hemisphere experienced radical environmental change, leaving only the polar regions and Greenland with permanent ice caps. Climatic fluctuations, the redistribution or even extinction of many plant and animal species, and the reshaping of coastlines as glacial meltwaters flowed to the sea all affected many of the world's human inhabitants. When we examine the archaeological record, we can see that people devised new technologies and economic patterns to adjust to their changing world.

ENVIRONMENTAL CHANGES

In the Old World, much as in the Americas, major changes in climate, landscapes, plants, and animals accompanied the end of the Ice Age. Dramatically higher temperatures— for example, an increase of average July temperature by perhaps 20°F—rapidly melted the glaciers. As they receded to higher latitudes, these great ice sheets left behind thick mantles of silt, mud, rocks, and boulders in **till plains**. Rivers and streams cut fresh channels and deposited new terraces with the ebb and flow of meltwater runoff. Tons upon tons of fine silt were lifted by winds across the newly exposed plains and redeposited as *loess*. In North America, the Great Lakes gradually formed as the glaciers retreated. Eventually, by 5,000 ya, sea levels had risen as much as 400 feet in some parts of the world, drowning the broad coastal plains and flooding into inlets to shape the continental margins we recognize today. By then, overflow from the rising Mediterranean had spilled into a low-lying basin to create the Black Sea, and the North and Baltic seas finally separated England and Scandinavia from the rest of Europe.

As deglaciation proceeded, the major biotic zones expanded northward, so that areas once covered by ice were clothed successively in tundra, grassland, fir and spruce forests, pine, and then mixed deciduous forests (Delcourt and Delcourt, 1991). Likewise, animals that thrived in temperate environments displaced their arctic counterparts. Grazers like the musk ox and caribou, or reindeer, which had ranged over open tundra or grasslands, gave way to browsing species, such as moose and deer, which fed on leaves and the tender twigs of forest plants. Meanwhile, the annual mean summer temperatures continued to climb toward the local **climatic maximum**, attained between 8,000 and 6,000 ya in many areas. By then, July temperatures averaged as much as 5°F higher than at present. Lakes that had formed during the Ice Age as a result of increased precipitation in nonglaciated areas of the American West, southwest Asia (the Near East), and Africa now evaporated under more arid conditions, bringing great ecological changes to those regions, too.

These geoclimatic transformations most directly affected the temperate latitudes, including northern and central Europe and the northern parts of America. They were sufficient to alter conditions of life for plants and animals by creating new niches for some species and pushing others toward extinction. We can't measure precisely how these shifting natural conditions may have affected human populations, although they surely did.

CULTURAL ADJUSTMENTS

Environmental readjustments were the natural consequences of climatic change. Although many such changes happened at rates that were slow enough that they passed largely unnoticed by individuals, much depended on the terrain where the changes occurred. For example, on the low-lying coast of Denmark, where sea level rose 1.5 to 2 inches per year during the early Holocene, "during his lifetime many a Stone Age man must have seen his childhood home swallowed up by the sea" (Fischer, 1995, p. 380). The environmental

till plains Accumulations of stones, boulders, mud, sand, and silt deposited by glaciers as they melt; ground moraines.

climatic maximum Episode of higher average annual temperatures that affected much of the globe for several millennia after the end of the last ice age; also known as the *altithermal* in the western United States or *hypsithermal* in the East.

impacts were cumulative, and in time the redistribution of living plant and animal species, plus variations in local topography, drainage, and exposure, resulted in a mosaic of new habitats, some of which invited human exploitation and settlement.

Cultures in both hemispheres kept pace with these changes by adjusting their ways of coping with local conditions. Distinctive climatic and cultural circumstances prevailed in different regions. Recognizing this variability (and acknowledging regional differences in the history of archaeologists' reconstruction of the past), archaeologists have devised specific terms to designate the early and middle Holocene cultures that turned to intensive hunting, fishing, and gathering lifeways in response to post-Pleistocene conditions. In Europe, this period is called the **Mesolithic**. In the Near East and eastward into parts of Asia, the **Epipaleolithic** period spans much the same interval. And in the New World, the **Archaic** period broadly applies to post-Pleistocene hunter-gatherers.

Holocene hunter-gatherers in temperate latitudes extracted their livelihood from a range of local resources by hunting, fishing, and gathering. The relative economic importance of each of these subsistence activities varied from region to region, and even from season to season within a given area. In some places, the focus on different food sources, particularly more plants, fish, shellfish, birds, and smaller mammals, corresponded to a lesser emphasis on hunting big game. What accounts for this shift? First, many former prey animals were by then extinct or—like the reindeer—locally unobtainable, having followed their receding habitat north with the waning ice sheets. Additionally, one way to accommodate both the environmental changes and human population growth was to broaden the definition of *food* by exploiting more species.

New habitats and prey species presented both challenges and opportunities. Among the important archaeological reflections of the cultural adjustments to the changing natural and social environments of the postglacial world were new tools and ways of making tools that can be found in the sites of these periods. Important raw materials for tools and other implements included stone, bone, antler, and leather, as well as bark and other plant materials (Clark, 1967; Bordaz, 1970). With the spread of forests, ground stone axes, adzes, and other tools became important items in tool kits (Fig. 13-17). Wood tended to replace animal bones, tallow, and herbivore dung as the primary fuel and served well for house posts, spear shafts, bowls, and countless smaller items. Wooden dugout canoes and skin-covered boats aided in navigating streams and crossing larger bodies of water. Hunter-gatherers caught large quantities of fish in nets, woven basketry traps, and brushwood or stone fish dams designed to block the mouths of small tidal streams. With the aid of axes and containers, the people extracted the honey of wild bees from hollow trees (Fig. 13-18).

Hunter-Gatherer Lifeways

Under the general category of *hunting and gathering*, researchers recognize a range of subsistence strategies used by early Holocene people as well as their more recent counterparts (Kelly, 1995).

These strategies often vary with the relative mobility of such groups. At one end of the spectrum are **foragers**, who tend to live in small groups that move camp frequently as

Barry Lewis

Figure **13-17**

Mesolithic ground stone axes. Fitted into the socket of a wooden haft or handle, such axes were effective woodworking tools and weapons.

Figure **13-18**

A Mesolithic forager uses a basket or bag to collect honey from a nest of wild bees in this ancient painting on a rock-shelter wall in southeastern Spain.

Mesolithic (*meso*, meaning "middle," and *lith*, meaning "stone") Middle Stone Age; period of hunter-gatherers, especially in northwestern Europe.

Epipaleolithic (*epi*, meaning "after") Late Pleistocene and early Holocene period of foragers and collectors in the Near East and adjacent parts of Asia.

Archaic North American archaeological period that follows the end of the Ice Age and traditionally ends with the beginning of the use of ceramics; equivalent to the Mesolithic in the Old World.

foragers Hunter-gatherers who live in small groups that move camp frequently to take advantage of fresh resources as they come into season, with few resources stored in anticipation of future use.

valued food resources come into season across their home range. Viewed archaeologically, forager campsites often show little investment in substantial shelters, storage facilities, and other features that reflect a long-term commitment to that site. At the other end are **collectors**, who are typically less mobile, staying in some camps for long periods and drawing on a wide range of locally available plant and animal foods that they bring back to camp for consumption. Collector campsites tend to show evidence of long-term occupation, including **middens**, storage facilities, cemeteries, and mounds. As Conneller (2004, p. 920) simply puts it, "foragers can be characterised as people moving to resources, while collectors move resources to people." Most hunter-gatherers lived somewhere between these extremes and emphasized more of one or the other food-getting approaches as the changing natural and social conditions warranted.

Considering the environmental complexity of the temperate regions in the Holocene, including a diverse array of potentially exploitable plants and animals, the food-getting methods that worked well in one region were not always effective in another. Holocene hunter-gatherers invented specialized equipment to help them take advantage of local resources, and we can reasonably assume that they approached cultural solutions to such problems with detailed practical knowledge and understanding of the local environment and its assets.

In foraging, anyone—young or old, male or female—might contribute to the general food supply by taking up whatever resources are at hand. But this isn't the same as saying that foragers eat whatever comes to hand. Human food-getting is selective, whether it's based on what you encounter in the forest that day or find on sale in the local supermarket. Preferred foods are usually those that are most readily available, easily collected and processed, tasty, and nutritious. So, while the San people of the Kalahari Desert in southwestern Africa regard about 80 local plants as edible, they rely mostly on about a dozen of them as primary foods (A. Smith et al., 2000). They use the rest of the foods less often, but know they could eat them when times are tough.

Particularly in regions with only minor seasonal fluctuations in wild food supplies, foraging held prospects for good returns. Jochim (1976, 1998) estimated that foraging activities could maintain a stable population density of about one person per 4 square miles in some regions. More territory might be required to sustain people in less-favorable situations or where continuing environmental fluctuations influenced the composition and predictability of animal and plant communities or the stability of estuaries and coastlines.

In areas where dramatic seasonal variations in rainfall or temperature affected resource availability, day-to-day foraging might not always yield a stable diet. Human population density and equilibrium could be maintained only if the group adopted an alternative strategy. Familiarity with their environment enabled people to predict when specific resources should reach peak productivity or desirability. By making well-informed decisions, hunters and gatherers scheduled their movements so they would arrive on the scene at the optimum time for obtaining a particularly important food. Seasonality and resource scheduling are familiar issues for most, if not all, foragers.

Compared with foragers, food collectors relied much more on a few seasonally abundant resources, and their camps often show evidence of specialized processing and storage technologies that allowed them to balance out fluctuations and remain longer in one place. For example, migratory fish might be split and cured; and nuts or seeds could be parched and stored away in baskets or bags until needed.

Case Studies of Early Holocene Cultures

Now that we've looked at some general hunting and gathering strategies, we can get down to specifics. In this section, we'll consider how the foragers and collectors from various regions found food and adjusted to changes in their environment.

collectors Hunter-gatherers who tend to stay in one place for a long time. A task group may range far afield to hunt and collect food and other resources that are brought back to camp and shared among its inhabitants. Valued food resources are commonly stored in anticipation of future use.

middens Archaeological sites or features within sites formed largely by the accumulation of domestic waste.

ARCHAIC HUNTER-GATHERERS OF NORTH AMERICA

With the retreat of the North American glacial ice sheets, the environments, plants, animals, and people of the temperate and boreal latitudes changed significantly. *Archaic* hunter-gatherers exploited new options in their much-altered environments, which no longer included megafauna (see Fig. 13-10). In eastern North America, dense forests of edible nut-bearing trees spread across the midcontinent and offered rich resources that attracted humans and other animals alike. Along the coasts, rising sea levels submerged tens of thousands of square miles of low-lying coastlines, creating rich new estuarine and marine environments that Archaic people exploited with a broad array of gear, including fishing equipment, dugout boats, traps, weirs, and nets. The main killing weapon used by these hunter-gatherers was the spear and spear-thrower, or *atlatl* (see pp. 301–302); the earliest archaeological evidence of the bow and arrow dates to 1,800–1,500 ya in much of the continental United States.

In many parts of North America, hunter-gatherer lifeways were more the collector than the forager type common among their Paleo-Indian ancestors. These collectors scheduled subsistence activities to coincide with the annual availability of particularly productive resources at specific locations within their territories. They lived in smaller and more circumscribed territories and acquired, through exchange with neighbors or more distant groups, whatever might be lacking locally. Especially in temperate regions, efficient exploitation of edible nuts, deer, fish, shellfish, and other forest and riverine products was enhanced by new tools, storage techniques, and regional exchange networks. The density of sites and their average size and permanence increased in many localities. Toward the end of the Archaic period, the archaeological remains of some sites exhibit signs of more complex sociopolitical organization, religious ceremonialism, and economic interdependence than had ever existed before.

Archaic Cultures of Western North America Arid rock-shelters in the **Great Basin**, a harsh expanse between the Rocky Mountains and the Sierra Nevadas, preserve material evidence of desert Archaic lifeways (D'Azevedo, 1986). Hunting weapons, milling stones, twined and coiled basketry, nets, mats, feather robe fragments, fiber sandals and hide moccasins, bone tools, and even gaming pieces are sealed in deeply stratified sites, such as Gatecliff Shelter (Thomas et al., 1983) and Lovelock Cave in Nevada and Danger

Great Basin Rugged, dry plateau between the mountains of California and Utah, comprising Nevada, western Utah, southern Oregon, and Idaho.

At a Glance
Important Archaic Sites in the New World

SITE	DATES (YA)	SIGNIFICANCE
Danger Cave (Utah)	ca. 10,000–historic times	Deeply stratified site that contains rich evidence of Desert Archaic lifeways in the American Southwest
Koster (Illinois)	9,000–4,000	Important stratified sequence of camp sites that document the changing lifeways of prehistoric Native Americans in the Midwest during the Archaic period
Poverty Point (Louisiana)	3,500	A large series of earthworks that covers nearly 1 square mile; the most elaborate example of planned communities that were built in the Southeast in late Archaic times

Figure **13-19**

The arid Great Basin of the American West supported hunter-gatherer cultures for thousands of years.

William Turnbaugh

Cave in Utah, and illuminate nearly 10 millennia of hunting and gathering. Coprolites occasionally found in these deposits contain seeds, insect exoskeletons, and often the tiny scales and bones of fish, rodents, and amphibians, all of which provide direct evidence of diet and health (Reinhard and Bryant, 1992). Freshwater and brackish marshes were focal points for many subsistence activities—sources of fish, migratory fowl, plant foods, and raw materials during half the year—but upland resources such as pine nuts and game were important, too. Larger animals might be taken occasionally, though smaller prey, such as jackrabbits and ducks, and the seasonal medley of seed-bearing plants afforded these foragers their most reliable diet. Success in this environment was a direct measure of cultural flexibility (Fig. 13-19).

Prehistoric societies throughout California's varied environments likewise sustained themselves without agriculture. Rich oak forests fed much of the region's human and animal population. Hunter-gatherers routinely ranged across several productive resource zones, from seacoast to interior valleys. Typical California societies, such as the Chumash of the Santa Barbara coast and Channel Islands, obtained substantial harvests of acorns and deer in the fall, supplemented by migratory fish, small game, and plants throughout the year (Glassow, 1996). Collected wild resources sustained permanent villages of up to 1,000 inhabitants. The Chumash were the latest descendants of a long sequence of southern California hunter-gatherers that archaeologists have traced back more than 8,000 years (Moratto, 1984). As environmental fluctuations and population changes necessitated adjustments in coastal and terrestrial resources, Archaic Californians at times ate more fish and shellfish, then more sea mammals or deer, and later more acorns and smaller animal species.

Archaeological and cultural anthropological studies along the northwestern coast of the United States and Canada have delineated other impressive nonfarming societies whose economies also centered around collecting rich and diverse sea and forest resources. Inhabitants of this region caught, dried, and stored salmon as the fish passed upriver from the sea to spawn each spring or fall. Berries and wild game such as bear and deer were locally plentiful; oily candlefish, halibut, and whales could be captured with the aid of nets, traps, large seaworthy canoes, and other well-crafted gear. Excavations at Ozette, on Washington's Olympic Peninsula, revealed a prosperous Nootka whaling community buried in a mud slide 250 years ago (Samuels, 1991).

By historical times along the northwestern coast, clan-based lineages resided in permanent coastal communities of sturdy plank-built cedar houses, guarded by carved cedar **totem** poles proclaiming their owners' genealogical heritage. They vied with one

totem An animal or being associated with a kin-group and used for social identification; also, a carved pole representing these beings.

another for social status by staging elaborate public functions (now generally known as the **potlatch**) in which quantities of smoked salmon, fish or whale oil, dried berries, cedar-bark blankets, and other valuables were bestowed upon guests (Jonaitas, 1988). There are archaeological signs that these practices may be quite ancient, with substantial houses, status artifacts, and evidence of warfare dating back some 2,500 years (Ames and Maschner, 1999).While a successful potlatch earned prestige for the hosts and incurred obligations to be repaid in the future, it also served larger purposes. By fostering a network of mutual reciprocity that created both sociopolitical and economic alliances, this ritualized redistribution system ensured a wider availability of the region's dispersed resources. As a result, highly organized sedentary communities prospered without relying on domesticated crops.

Farther to the north, western Arctic Archaic bands pursued coastal sea mammals or combined inland caribou hunting with fishing; however, their diet included virtually no plant foods (McGhee, 1996). Beginning about 2,500 ya, Thule (Inuit/Eskimo) hunters expanded eastward across the Arctic with the aid of a highly specialized tool kit that included effective toggling harpoons for securing sea mammals; blubber lamps for light, cooking, and warmth; and sledges and kayaks (skin boats) for transportation on frozen land or sea.

Archaic Cultures of Eastern North America Locally varied environments across eastern North America supported a range of Archaic cultures after about 10,000 ya. A general warming and drying trend lasting several thousand years promoted deciduous forest growth as far north as the Great Lakes. Archaic societies exploited the temperate oak-hickory forests of the Midwest and the oak-chestnut forests and rivers of the Northeast and Appalachians. Nuts of many kinds were an important staple for these forest groups. Acorn, chestnut, black walnut, butternut, hickory, and beechnut represent plentiful foods that are both nutritious and palatable, rich in fats and oils, and above all easily stored. Some nuts were prepared by parching or roasting, others by crushing and boiling into soups; leaching in hot water neutralized the toxic tannic acids found in acorns. Whitetail deer and black bear provided meat, hides for clothing, and bone and antler for toolmaking. Other important food items included migratory fowl, wild turkey, fish, turtles, and small mammals such as raccoons, as well as berries and seeds.

In New England, some coastal Archaic groups from Massachusetts to Labrador used canoes to hunt sea mammals and swordfish with bone-bladed harpoons in summer, then relied on caribou and salmon the rest of the year (Snow, 1980). North of the St. Lawrence river, other Archaic bands dispersed widely through the sparse boreal forests, hunting caribou or moose, fishing, and trapping.

In the Midwest around the Great Lakes, seasonally mobile collectors employed an extensive array of equipment to fish, hunt, and gather. The productive valleys of the midcontinent, where a nexus of great rivers join the Mississippi, supported a riverine focus. Favored sites in this region attained substantial size and were occupied for many generations, some—such as Eva and Rose Island, in Tennessee, and Koster, in southern Illinois—for thousands of years. Trade networks moved valued raw materials and finished goods hundreds, and in some cases thousands, of miles; tools of soft native copper from northern Minnesota and Wisconsin have been found in Archaic sites as far away as Georgia and Mississippi, and marine shells from the Gulf Coast have been uncovered in western Great Lakes sites.

Eastern Archaic groups at times reinforced their claims to homelands by laying out cemeteries for their dead or by erecting earthwork mounds. These activities imply an emerging social differentiation within some of the preagricultural Archaic societies as well as a degree of **sedentism**. Archaeologists studying more than 1,000 Archaic burials at Indian Knoll, in Kentucky (Webb, 1974), found possible status indicators reflected in the distribution of grave goods. Though two-thirds of the graves contained no offerings at all, certain females and children had been given disproportionate shares; only a few males were buried with tools and weapons (Rothschild, 1979).

potlatch Ceremonial feasting and gift-giving event among Northwest Coast Indians.

sedentism The practice of residing in a single location for most or all of the year.

Figure **13-20**

The Late Archaic Poverty Point site in northeastern Louisiana.

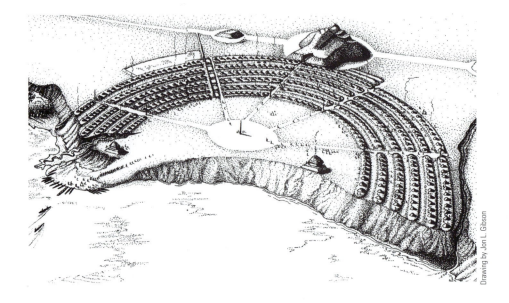

Drawing by Jon L. Gibson

Archaic people in the Lower Mississippi Valley began raising monumental earthworks beginning as early as 5,500 ya. Mound building required communal effort and planning. Near Monroe, Louisiana, Watson Brake is a roughly oval embankment enclosing a space averaging 750 feet across and capped by about a dozen individual mounds up to 24 feet in height (Saunders et al., 2005). Not far to the east, Poverty Point's elaborate 3,500-year-old complex of six concentric semicircular ridges is flanked by a large platform mound on its west side (Fig. 13-20), plus several nearby mounds, and covers a full square mile (Gibson, 2001). That hunter-gatherers chose to invest their energies in creating these planned earthworks with public spaces and dozens of other impressive structures suggests highly developed Archaic social organization and ritualism, though their precise meaning remains unclear.

MESOLITHIC OF NORTHERN EUROPE

As in North America, people colonized Europe's northern reaches as the glacial ice retreated (Jochim, 1998). Rising waters began to reclaim low-lying coastlines, flooding the North and Baltic seas and the English Channel and burying Paleolithic and Mesolithic sites in the process (Fischer, 1995). On land, temperate plant and animal species succeeded their Ice Age counterparts. Across northwestern Europe, as grasses and then forests invaded the open landscape, red deer, elk, and **aurochs** replaced the reindeer, horse, and bison of Pleistocene times. Human hunters, armed with efficient weapons, accommodated themselves to the relatively low **carrying capacity** of the northern regions (where plant foods, at least, were seasonally scarce) by eating more meat and fish.

Star Carr, near the North Sea coast in east-central England (Fig. 13-21), provides clues to the early ecology and foraging economy practiced by northern Mesolithic peoples some 10,500 ya. Periodically over several centuries, this lakeshore site served as a temporary hunting camp, where the people regularly pursued aurochs, deer, elk, and wild pigs (Clark, 1972, 1979). Because deer grow and shed their antlers annually on a species-specific cycle, the discovery of deer skulls with antlers in different development stages indicated that Mesolithic hunters visited Star Carr throughout the year, though they used it much more in spring and summer (Mellars and Dark, 1999).

Again, as in the New World, Mesolithic hunter-gatherers modified the environment for their own purposes. At Star Carr, people used stone axes and adzes to fell birch trees with which they built platforms and trackways over the marshy ground. In spring, they burned off the reeds along the lake margin to open the view and probably also to

aurochs European wild oxen, ancestral to domesticated cattle.

carrying capacity In an environment, the maximum population of a specific organism that can be maintained at a steady state.

induce new growth that would attract game. Hunters employed long wooden or bone arrows, knives, and spear points tipped by *microliths*—small flint blades of geometric shape—set into slots along the shaft and held in place by resin. Another extremely effective weapon, the bow and arrow was used in Europe even before the end of the last Ice Age—that is, considerably earlier than in the New World. Domesticated dogs probably aided in the hunt at Star Carr as well. Barbed bone and antler spear points, butchering implements, and burins (see p. 303) for working bone and antler were common artifacts.

Along the coasts of northern Europe, the British Isles, and even the Mediterranean, Mesolithic groups came to rely on coastal resources (Smith, 1998). At the 8,000–7,500-year-old Mesolithic settlement on the Argus Bank, which today lies in 15 to 20 feet of water off the coast of Denmark, preserved food waste and the stable isotopic analysis of human skeletal remains show that fish were the mainstay of the diet, followed by game animals, nuts, and fruits (Fischer et al., 2007). Such favored site locations, sometimes marked by great shell middens, offered a combination of land and sea resources that encouraged year-round residence based on food collecting. The

Figure **13-21**

Mesolithic sites of northern Europe mentioned in the text.

At a Glance

Important Mesolithic and Epipaleolithic Sites in the Old World

SITE	DATES (YA)	SIGNIFICANCE
Star Carr (England)	10,500	Mesolithic campsite excavated by Grahame Clark; greatly influenced how archaeologists still view the Mesolithic in Europe
Tybrind Vig (Denmark)	ca. 7,500–6,000	Mesolithic village submerged by rising sea levels off the coast of Denmark; excellent preservation of organic remains including such things as dugout canoes, paddles, fishing gear, and fabric
Ohalo II (Israel)	23,000	Kebaran or pre-Kebaran campsite; extraordinary preservation of huts, living floors, grass bedding, and plant remains, especially of small-grained grass seeds, which appear to have been a staple food
Abu Hureyra (Syria)	13,000–7,800	Natufian and Neolithic site; the Natufian occupation was a sedentary hunter-gatherer village whose members, unlike their predecessors at Ohalo II, harvested mostly wild cereal grasses

impressive size of some middens—the countless shells of oysters, mussels, periwinkles, and scallops piled along the shore—should not disguise the fact that one red deer carcass may represent the caloric equivalent of 50,000 oysters (Bailey, 1975). Still, for at least some Mesolithic foragers, shellfish provided a readily available alternative source of protein, probably exploited primarily in the spring when their normal fare of fish, sea mammals, and birds was in shortest supply (Erlandson, 1988). This supplement could have encouraged people to remain longer in one location.

Since many of these coastal sites were later covered by rising sea level, they can sometimes show extraordinary preservation of organic remains. For example, underwater excavations at Tybrind Vig, a late Mesolithic site that lies in 6 to 9 feet of water about 270 yards off the coast of Denmark, have recovered dugout canoes and paddles, fishing line, fishhooks, and even pieces of fabric, along with plant and animal remains and several human burials (Malm, 1995).

EPIPALEOLITHIC OF THE NEAR EAST

Star Carr and other sites of northwestern Europe represent one end of a spectrum of early Holocene lifeways in the Old World. In those regions, plant foods were scarce for much of each year, and hunter-gatherers often relied mostly on hunting or fishing. Farther south, in central and southern Europe and the Near East—regions that were never covered by ice sheets, even during maximum glacial periods—late Pleistocene and early Holocene environmental and cultural changes proceeded along different lines. People in these regions tended to rely more heavily on wild plant resources, supplemented by animal protein. These distinctions in climate and culture justify the use of the separate term *Epipaleolithic* to distinguish late Pleistocene and early Holocene cultural changes of the Near East and adjacent parts of southwest Asia (Fig. 13-22) from their contemporaries in northern Europe. For the most part, Epipaleolithic subsistence strategies resulted merely in more efficient hunting and gathering. But in some locations, food-collecting strategies were already taking people quite perceptibly toward an entirely new way of making a living—the development of food production (see Chapter 14).

For the moment, let's consider the transition of hunter-gatherers from small-scale, mobile groups to what were essentially permanent communities in the Levant region, in what is today Israel and Lebanon. A late Pleistocene foraging culture known to archaeologists as the **Kebaran** occupied this region for millennia. Our understanding of Kebaran subsistence has until recently been based mostly on the analysis of faunal remains and tools used in plant food processing, because the direct evidence of plant remains was rarely found in excavations. Ohalo II, a very early Kebaran or pre-Kebaran (23,000 ya) site in the Sea of Galilee, recently demonstrated that archaeologists still have much to learn about late Pleistocene plant use in the Levant. The Ohalo II excavations revealed a camp comprising several huts, including some with the grass bedding still intact, hearths, tools, and an outstanding collection of more than 90,000 plant remains, representing 142 genera and species (Nadel, 2004; Weiss et al., 2004a). Small-grained grass seeds, including brome, foxtail, and alkali grass, were gathered for consumption as staple foods (Weiss et al., 2004b), as were seeds of wild cereals such as barley and wheat. Analysis of starch grains from a grinding slab found in one of the

Kebaran Late Pleistocene hunter-gatherers of the eastern Mediterranean region and Levant.

Figure **13-22**

Epipaleolithic sites in the Levant region of the Near East.

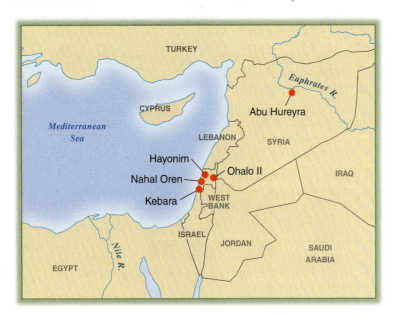

huts revealed that the small-grained grasses and the wild cereal grasses were processed for consumption (Piperno et al., 2004). The Ohalo II remains demonstrate that early Kebaran groups in the Levant were collector-type hunter-gatherers more than 10,000 years farther into the past than we once believed and that the beginnings of agriculture can be traced at least to Epipaleolithic times.

Viewed generally, many Kebaran groups adopted a strategy of **transhumance**, a specific seasonality and scheduling technique by which people divided their activities between resource zones at different elevations. We know from later Kebaran sites that they harvested seeds of wild cereal grasses in the lowlands from fall through springtime (Henry, 1989). In summer, they made extended forays into the sparsely wooded uplands to hunt and to gather nuts. Gazelles and fallow deer were the primary sources of meat, with smaller game becoming more common than deer in site assemblages toward the end of the Epipaleolithic (Bar-Oz, 2004), possibly as deer became scarce.

Between 12,000 and 11,000 ya, a moderating climate associated with the waning Pleistocene took effect in the arid lands bordering the eastern Mediterranean. As both temperatures and precipitation increased, the range of native lowland cereal grasses expanded into the higher forested zones (Henry, 1989). Sites were more permanent than the early Epipaleolithic camps such as Ohalo II, and the newer sites contain house remains, heavy seed-processing equipment and other nonportable items, art objects, and cemeteries; they're also larger, with a five- or tenfold increase in population, accompanied by signs of social ranking (Henry, 1989).

Because the sites of these more sedentary collectors are so dramatically different from earlier camps, archaeologists gave their culture a new label, identifying it as **Natufian** (Belfer-Cohen, 1991). Natufian subsistence depended heavily on diverse resources, including large-seeded legumes, the seeds of wild cereal grasses—but not the small-grained grass seeds that were so common at Ohalo II—and the gazelle, a kind of antelope (Bar-Yosef, 1987; Savard et al., 2006). Ancient gazelle-hunting practices are revealed through a study of tooth eruption and wear patterns on animal teeth recovered from Natufian sites (Legge and Rowley-Conwy, 1987). After analyzing a nonselective population structure of newborns, yearlings, and adults, these researchers suggested that the dominant hunting method was to surround or ambush an entire herd soon after the females gave birth to their young, probably in late April or early May.

Gazelle horn sickles with inset flint blades frequently appear on Natufian sites, along with an abundance of grinding stones and mortars (Fig. 13-23). Small clusters of semipermanent pit houses with stone foundations, often in close association with cemeteries, such as those excavated at several sites in Israel and Syria (Moore et al., 2000), confirm the Natufians' reliance on local species without moving from place to place. These finds, as well as an increase in human **dental caries** (tooth decay), *hypoplasias* (interrupted enamel formation), periodontal disease, and an overall reduction in tooth size in Natufian skeletons, all testify to the fact that starchy cereal grains figured prominently in this group's diet (P. Smith et al., 1984).

Viewed across the span of the Epipaleolithic, hunter-gatherer groups took a more active role in manipulating the landscape to enhance the productivity or yield of favored species. Whether intentionally or not, they may have created forest clearings or eliminated competing animals or "weed" plants; or, as their camps expanded into fresh regions, they might have introduced wild food species into new habitats. At times, as among the Natufians in the Near East, these intensive exploitation patterns greatly altered the overall relationship between people and their environment, promoting further changes in their society as well as in the resources on which they depended. So, we see larger populations drawn to certain prime areas, where intergroup competition would be inevitable and where selection pressures on resources could become significant. In some cases, the changes brought about by collector-type hunter-gatherers were actually a prelude to food production, which we'll focus on in the next chapter.

© Dorling Kindersley

Figure **13-23**

Sickles were useful tools for harvesting wild cereal grasses. An embedded row of small flint blades formed the working edge of the sickle, the handle of which could be wood, bone, or horn.

transhumance Seasonal migration from one resource zone to another, especially between highlands and lowlands.

Natufian Referring to collector-type hunter-gatherers who established sedentary settlements in parts of the Near East after 12,000 ya.

dental caries Erosions in teeth caused by decay; cavities.

Summary

By the early to middle Holocene, modern humans had expanded into all the inhabitable regions of the globe. Current evidence suggests that people initially arrived in the New World between 30,000 and 13,500 ya. Learning where they came from and how they entered the New World is an active area of research that continues to be hotly debated, but at least for now, the evidence most strongly supports some combination of entry from northeastern Asia by way of the Bering land bridge and the Pacific coastal route sometime after 16,500 ya.

The scarce skeletal evidence that survives from the earliest era of New World prehistory shows considerable morphological diversity, and it has encouraged much speculation about Native American origins. Even so, available cultural and biological traces clearly link the first Americans with their Asian roots. The similarities of material culture between the earliest sites in the Americas and northeastern Asia are more general than archaeologists would like, but Siberian sites such as Yana RHS do offer encouraging evidence that researchers are on the right track.

By about 12,000 ya, after the end of the Pleistocene Ice Age, significant climatic changes altered the weather, seasonal variations, average temperatures, topography, sea levels, and animal and plant communities across much of the Northern Hemisphere, including North America and Eurasia. The general warming trend in temperate latitudes promoted the expansion of grasslands and the reforestation of formerly glaciated areas. At the same time, many megafaunal species became extinct, particularly in North America, where human hunters may have contributed to the demise of mammoths and a few other species.

Early Holocene foragers in Europe, the Near East, and North America adapted readily to the ongoing environmental changes. Generalized food-getting economies promoted long-term cultural stability for many hunter-gatherers, such as the Mesolithic hunters of Star Carr and the Archaic peoples of California, the Great Basin, and the eastern American woodlands, who exploited their environments' varied resources at relatively low levels of intensity. Especially in regions with great seasonal resource fluctuations, experiencing intensely dry or cold months, people tended to concentrate on a few more productive species, which they collected in quantity and stored. Long-term, and in some cases permanent, settlements became part of hunter-gatherer lifeways in many regions.

As sites like Ohalo II demonstrate, some food-collecting communities experienced economic changes, as long ago as the Last Glacial Maximum, that led to the use of a wide range of wild plants and animals as food. Such changes fostered the development of food production in some regions. Since we are looking back in time at these events, it's tempting, but misleading, to view them as conscious steps toward the invention of agriculture. There's no reason to think that Early Holocene foragers had the slightest inkling about how the eventual domestication of plants and animals would also fundamentally change humans.

We've organized the remaining two chapters of this text around two primary cultural developments associated with humans in the later Holocene epoch: first, the process of food production, and second, the rise of civilizations. Much of what we associate with modern humanity is linked to these central driving forces.

In the What's Important feature, you'll find a useful summary of the most important archaeological sites discussed in this chapter.

What's Important The Most Significant Archaeological Sites Discussed in This Chapter

Location	Site	Dates (ya)	The Big Picture
North America	Poverty Point (Louisiana)	3,500	A large series of earthworks that covers nearly 1 square mile; the most elaborate example of planned communities built in the Southeast in late Archaic times
	Koster (Illinois)	9,000–4,000	Important stratified sequence of camp sites that document the changing lifeways of prehistoric Native Americans in the Midwest during the Archaic period
	Kennewick (Washington)	9,300	One of the few early North American human skeletons; object of a nine-year court battle to decide if scientists would be permitted to study his remains
	Danger Cave (Utah)	~10,000–historic times	Deeply stratified site that contains rich evidence of Desert Archaic lifeways in the American Southwest
	Meadowcroft (Pennsylvania)	19,000–14,000	Often cited as evidence of pre-Clovis presence of humans in eastern North America
	Pendejo Cave (New Mexico)	37,000–12,000	Controversial claim of great antiquity for the human presence in the American Southwest
South America	Monte Verde (Chile)	14,500	Pre-Clovis campsite in southern South America; one of the first sites to be widely accepted as evidence of pre-Clovis human presence in the New World
	Pedra Furada (Brazil)	?50,000–?40,000	One of several South American sites for which great antiquity is claimed, but not yet convincingly proved
Old World	Star Carr (England)	10,500	Mesolithic campsite excavated by Grahame Clark; greatly influenced how archaeologists still view the Mesolithic in Europe
	Abu Hureyra	13,000–7,800	Natufian and Neolithic site; the Natufian occupation was a sedentary hunter-gatherer village whose members, unlike their predecessors at Ohalo II, harvested mostly wild cereal grasses
	Ohalo II (Israel)	23,000	Kebaran or pre-Kebaran campsite; extraordinary preservation of huts, living floors, grass bedding, and plant remains, especially of small-grained grass seeds, which appear to have been a staple food
	Yana RHS (Russia)	30,000	Earliest evidence of late Pleistocene hunters beyond the Arctic Circle in northern Siberia; stone tools and horn and ivory spear foreshafts similar to those found much later on North American Paleo-Indian sites

Critical Thinking Questions

1. What are the specific biological and cultural clues that point to an Asian ancestry for the *earliest* American populations? How convincing do you find the evidence?
2. What are some of the significant environmental changes associated with the end of the Pleistocene? Which of these changes would have most affected humans? Do you see parallels with climate changes today?
3. Is there enough archaeological evidence to prove that Paleo-Indians were primarily responsible for the extinction of Pleistocene animals? Discuss.
4. Contrast Mesolithic cultural adaptations of northern Europe, as represented at Star Carr and Argus Bank, with those of the Near East, as represented by the Kebarans and Natufians in the Levant.
5. What are the differences between forager and collector types of hunter-gatherers? What are some of the economic and biocultural implications of each of these subsistence strategies?

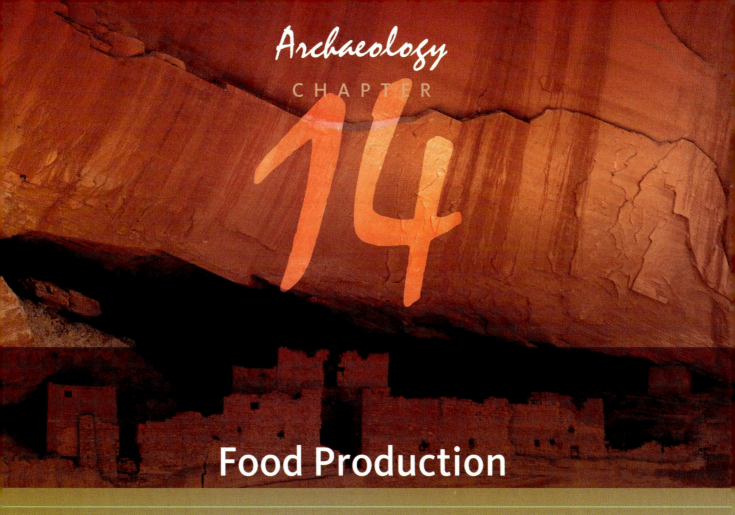

Archaeology

CHAPTER

14

Food Production

Click!

Go to the following media for interactive activities and exercises on topics covered in this chapter:

- Online Virtual Laboratories for Physical Anthropology, Version 4.0
- Genetics in Anthropology: Principles and Applications CD-ROM, Version 2.0
- Hominid Fossils: An Interactive Atlas CD-ROM

Introduction

By the end of the last Ice Age, humans were living in most of the world's inhabitable places. They achieved a global distribution without becoming multiple species in the process, which isn't the way things usually happen in nature. They were able to do this because they possessed extraordinary adaptive flexibility as biocultural organisms. Without such flexibility, humans might still be restricted to the tropical and subtropical regions of the Old World.

The archaeological record provides abundant evidence that the rate of change in human lifeways accelerated markedly during the past 10,000 years or so. Throughout this long period, human culture accounted for more and more of the changes in how and where our ancestors lived. By making cultural choices and devising new cultural solutions to age-old problems, human groups succeeded in mitigating some of the processes that operate in the natural world (for example, starvation due to seasonal food shortages), and either turned them to their advantage or at least tried to minimize their negative effects. However, humans also discovered that part of the cost of such cultural solutions were consequences that interacted with and affected the natural world and human biology as well. Some of the consequences were fantastically good; some weren't.

Two of the most profound and far-reaching developments of later prehistory were the shift from hunting and gathering to food production and the emergence of the early civilizations. This chapter deals with plant and animal domestication and the associated spread of farming, both of them integral to the development of the first civilizations, which we will examine in Chapter 15. We'll start by examining competing explanations for the origins of food production. This will give you a sense of the diverse perspectives from which researchers investigate how and why farming developed after the end of the last Ice Age. From there, we'll discuss the archaeological evidence for the origins of food production in several regions around the world (Fig. 14-1). Finally, we'll wrap things up by reviewing some of the most important biocultural consequences of this fundamental change in lifeways, to which our species and the world continue to adjust.

The Neolithic Revolution

The change from hunting and gathering to agriculture is often called the **Neolithic revolution**, a name coined decades ago by archaeologist V. Gordon Childe (1951) to acknowledge the fundamental changes brought about by the beginnings of food production. While hunter-gatherers collected whatever foods nature made available, farmers employed nature to produce only those crops and animals that humans selected for their own exclusive purposes.

Beyond domestication and farming, **Neolithic** activities had other far-reaching consequences, including new settlement patterns, new technologies, and significant biocultural effects. The emergence of food production eventually transformed most human societies either directly or indirectly and, in the process, brought about dramatic changes

Neolithic revolution Childe's term for the far-reaching consequences of food production.

Neolithic (*neo*, meaning "new," and *lith*, meaning "stone") New Stone Age; period of farmers.

predominant economic basis of human communities because it offered so many obvious advantages? Because it offered the fewest disadvantages? Or because there just weren't a lot of alternatives?

Ironically, although farming didn't get started in a big way until later, it was the hunter-gatherers of the Mesolithic/Epipaleolithic and Archaic periods who actually initiated the critical processes and even developed many of the innovations we usually credit to the Neolithic. Essentially, the lifestyles of some early Holocene hunter-gatherers anticipated many of the developments we associate with agriculture. Neolithic farmers were mostly the *recipients* of the domesticated species and agricultural ways from their predecessors.

DEFINING AGRICULTURE AND DOMESTICATION

To avoid confusion later on, it's useful to consider the difference between **domestication** and **agriculture**. These terms are often found together in discussions of the beginnings of food production, but they mean different things (Rindos, 1984).

Domestication is an *evolutionary process*. When we say that a certain plant or animal is domesticated, we mean that there's interdependency between this organism and humans, such that part of its life history depends on human intervention. To achieve and maintain this relationship requires the *genetic* transformation of a wild species by selective breeding or other ways of interfering, intentionally or not, with a species' natural life processes.

Agriculture differs from domestication because it's a *cultural activity*, not an evolutionary process. It involves the propagation and exploitation of domesticated plants and animals by humans. Agriculture in its broad sense includes all the activities associated with both farming and animal herding. Although domestication and agriculture are typically examined together in archaeological discussions of Neolithic lifeways, domestication isn't inevitably associated with an economic emphasis on food production. Plant and animal domestication can take place for purposes other than to improve the utility of a given organism as human food. For example, some cultures have raised birds and animals solely for ritual offerings or ornamental use. Native Americans of Mexico and the American Southwest reared colorful macaw parrots for their bright plumage, and Peruvian natives herded alpaca camelids primarily for their wool. Many domesticated medicinal herbs, attractive flowers, and fibrous plants have also served nonfood uses.

True agriculture, on the other hand, would be unthinkable without domesticated plants and animals. Domestication makes agriculture possible, especially when we consider how humans have manipulated the life history strategies of other organisms to maximize particular qualities, such as yield per unit area, growth rate to maturity, ease of processing, seed color, average seed size, and flavor.. The cultural activity we call agriculture ensures that the plants and animals with these desirable qualities are predictably available as human food and raw materials. One useful way to view this fundamental change in the relationships between humans and other animals and plants is as **symbiosis**, a mutually beneficial association between members of different species (Rindos, 1984).

In the next two sections, we'll give a brief but important overview of some of the major competing explanations for the beginnings of agriculture. Although most of these approaches address the problem of explaining the development of farming in the Near East, it's important to note that their proponents tend to view them as generally applicable to agricultural origins everywhere. The Near East dominates the discussion mostly because it received the lion's share of research on this problem over the past century, not because it was some sort of primal hearth for the development of agriculture. Also, as you review these competing explanations, bear in mind that the central questions at issue are open areas of research. Right now, no single approach is both sufficient and necessary to explain all known cases.

domestication A state of interdependence between humans and selected plant or animal species. Intense selection activity induces permanent genetic change, enhancing a species' value to humans.

agriculture Cultural activities associated with planting, herding, and processing domesticated species; farming.

symbiosis (*syn*, meaning "together," and *bios*, meaning "life") Mutually advantageous association of two different organisms; also known as *mutualism*.

Loosely following Verhoeven (2004), we present our overview of approaches in two groups, those that primarily invoke natural or environmental factors to explain the development of agriculture and those largely based on cultural (including cognitive) factors.

ENVIRONMENTAL APPROACHES

Most approaches to explain the origins of domesticated plants and animals and the beginnings of agriculture identify one or more natural mechanisms, such as climate change or human population growth, that may have promoted the biocultural changes documented in the late Pleistocene and early Holocene archaeological record of many parts of the world. The reasoning behind such hypotheses is that if some change limits a society's ability to feed its people, there typically are several options. The least disruption to everyday life can be achieved by reducing the population, extending the territory, or making more intensive use of the environment. Farming, of course, represents a more intensive use of the environment. Through their efforts, farmers attempt to increase the land's carrying capacity by harnessing more of its energy for the production of crops or animals that will feed people (Fig. 14-2).

In their most extreme form, environmental approaches smack of *environmental determinism*, the notion that certain cultural outcomes can be predicted from—or are determined by—a combination of purely environmental causes. For example, V. Gordon Childe himself conjectured that climate changes at the end of the Pleistocene increased Europe's rainfall while making southwestern Asia and North Africa much more arid (Childe, 1928, 1934). Humans, animals, and vegetation in the drought areas concentrated into shrinking zones around a few permanent water sources. At these **oases**, Childe hypothesized, the interaction between humans and certain plants and animals resulted in domestication of some species, including wheat, barley, sheep, and goats, which people then began to use to their advantage. The eventual result was the spread of sedentary village communities across the Near East.

Hypotheses based on any form of determinism tend to be relatively straightforward, which is both their strength and their weakness. Because they hold so many factors constant, it's easy to see how such approaches should work and why certain important outcomes should arise. The main drawback of such ideas is that their focus is typically too general to explain a given case because they omit the key contextual factors that are unique to a real event. In environmental approaches, such factors are often history and culture. What people are already familiar with and what they and their ancestors did in the past often, if not always, play a big role in their decisions. So, for example, a desert region might simultaneously sustain opportunistic hunter-gatherers, nomadic pastoralists, farmers using special deep-planting procedures, or even lawn-mowing suburbanites willing to pay for piped-in water, not because these groups are unaware of the possibilities posed by alternative ways of living, but because they are living their traditional ways of life and they prefer them.

To return to what has come to be called Childe's oasis theory, its simplicity quickly enabled archaeologist Robert Braidwood to demonstrate that the predicted outcomes didn't exist in the archaeological record (see p. 353 for details). Pollen and sediment profiles now confirm that at least some of the climatic changes hypothesized by Childe did occur in parts of the Near East prior to Neolithic times, and so they

oases (*sing.*, oasis) Permanent springs or water holes in an arid region.

Figure **14-2**

Through a symbiotic relationship with humans, domesticated plants such as lettuce and tomatoes have even spread to Antarctica. There, they are grown by hydroponic farming techniques without the benefits of soil or sunlight in New Zealand's Scott Base greenhouse, which consists of two 20-foot shipping containers in which the staff grows vegetables, herbs, and flowers.

© D. Rich, Scott Base Greenhouse

may have had a role in fostering new relationships between humans and other species in this marginal environment (Henry, 1989; Wright, 1993). Even so, both the causes and the apparent effects were complex. In places like the Near East, climate change that resulted in diminished or redistributed resources didn't directly induce people to become farmers (Munro, 2004), though it may have made farming one of the more reasonable options. On the other hand, the arid conditions familiar to us today in some parts of the Near East may be as much a *result* as a cause of Neolithic activities in the region. That is, the ecologically disruptive activities of farmers and herd animals during the Neolithic period may have contributed to the destructive process of **desertification**. Their plowed fields exposed soil to wind erosion and evaporation, while the irrigation demands of their crops lowered the water table. And overgrazing herbivores rapidly reduced the vegetation that holds moisture and binds soil, thus destroying the fragile margin between grassland and desert.

One large group of environmental hypotheses that, unlike Childe's, continues to be examined by researchers looks to increased competition for resources. Whether the competition resulted from natural increases in population density or from climatic changes, such as rising sea levels, increased rainfall, or lower average seasonal temperatures, they're seen as major factors that encouraged the domestication of plants and animals and, ultimately, the beginnings of agriculture (e.g., Boserup, 1965; Binford, 1968; Flannery, 1973; Cohen, 1977). These explanations share the view that agriculture developed in societies where competition for the resources necessary to sustain life favored increasing the diversity of staple foods in the diet. For one reason or another, population control or territorial expansion may not have been feasible or desirable choices in these societies. For example, competition may have arisen from decreased human mortality rates rather than increased fertility or possibly even been driven by the increasing proportion of people living to an old age. The point is that people faced a "prehistoric food crisis"(Cohen, 1977) unlike most modern cases because it was a chronic problem that worsened over decades and showed no sign of ever getting any better. Concentrated in a restricted territory or faced with the dwindling reliability of once-favored resources, such hunter-gatherers might have taken up **horticulture** or herding to enhance the productivity or distribution of one or more particularly useful species. It was this economic commitment that eventually led to the emergence of true farmers.

Binford's (1968) "packing model" develops one such hypothesis involving **demographic** stresses. As modern climatic conditions became established in the early Holocene, people resided in every prime habitat in the temperate regions of Eurasia. Foraging areas became confined as territories filled, leading to increased competition for resources and a more varied diet. Forced to make more intensive use of smaller segments of habitat, hunter-gatherers applied their Mesolithic technology to a broader range of plant and animal species. A few of these resources proved more reliable, easier to catch or process, tastier, or even faster to reproduce than others, so they soon received greater attention. Archaeological evidence of such changes can be found on many Mesolithic/ Epipaleolithic sites in the form of sickles, baskets and other containers, grinding slabs, and other processing tools.

As local populations continued to grow and other groups tried to expand their territory, their only choice would be to move into the marginal habitats that lay at the edges of the optimal, resource-rich parts of their territory (Binford, 1968). Because population stress would quickly reach critical levels in these marginal environments, where resources were already sparse, it was here that domesticated plants were first developed. To feed itself, the expanding population might have tried to expand the native ranges of some of the resources they knew from their homeland by sowing seeds of the wild plants. Over time, this activity resulted in domestication of those species and fundamental changes in the relationship between them and the people who by then depended on them.

Aspects of Binford's approach appealed to many archaeologists, who agreed that the wild ancestors of some of the world's most important domesticates originally held a low status in the diet. Many were small, hard seeds that were once seldom used except

desertification Any process resulting in the formation or growth of deserts.

horticulture Farming method in which only hand tools are used; typical of most early Neolithic societies.

demographic Pertaining to the size or rate of increase of human populations.

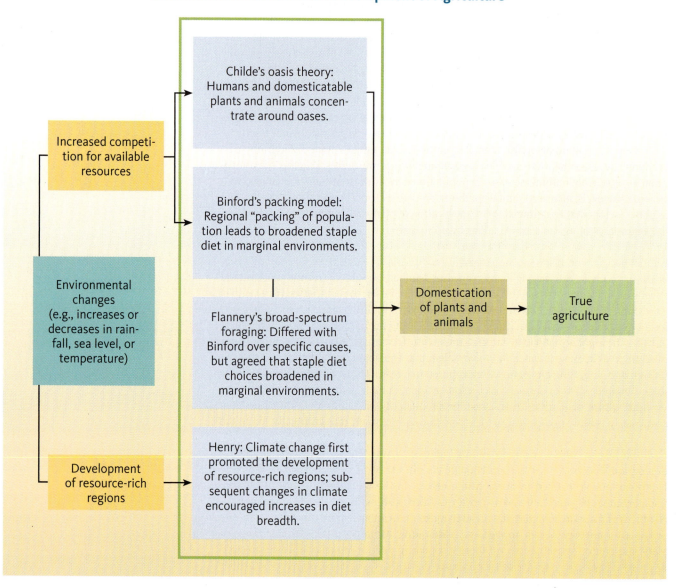

At a Glance

Environmental Factors in the Development of Agriculture

as secondary or emergency foods. Ethnographic research had also shown that, given their choice, hunter-gatherers everywhere prefer to eat fruit and meat (Yudkin, 1969). Still, grains and roots became increasingly important in the Mesolithic/Epipaleolithic diet—supplemented whenever possible by available animal or fish protein—and not only when the more desirable foods were in short supply. An interpretation based on increased competition for resources offered a testable explanation for why this happened.

Although he took issue with certain aspects of Binford's approach, Flannery (1973) agreed with the basic thesis because it explained why the earliest archaeological evidence of plant domestication should be found in what would have been marginal environments. Flannery described the increasing breadth of the Epipaleolithic diet as a "broad spectrum revolution" in which hunter-gatherers turned to many kinds of food resources in order to make up for local shortfalls. Especially in marginal environments, this activity promoted the development of domesticates and, ultimately, the origins of true agriculture.

Henry (1989) built on somewhat similar ground because he assumed that climatic change was an important factor motivating the development of domestication and agriculture, specifically in the Levant. In Henry's view, the colder and drier climate of the Younger Dryas (13,000–11,500 ya) created relatively resource-rich regions of the Levant that attracted human hunter-gatherers. As the climate shifted again at the end of the Younger Dryas, descendants of these populations experienced essentially the same stresses envisioned in other environmental approaches. The primary cause of these stresses, in Henry's view, was not so much the climatic changes after the Younger Dryas as it was the flexibility of human populations—living in what had been resource-rich regions during the Younger Dryas—in dealing with the changes. The outcomes, however, would be the same.

In short, environmental approaches identify forces external to humans as the active ingredients in the development of agriculture. In these hypotheses, human agency is primarily reactive. Something in the natural environment changes, and it makes life increasingly hard for hunter-gatherers. They react culturally to changed circumstances in various ways, some of which include incorporating a wider range of less-preferred foods in their staple diet and colonizing marginal environments. At some point, they take up the alternative of applying cultural means to increase the production of one or more food species. So basically, these approaches envision the development of agriculture more as something that humans backed into from a lack of better alternatives rather than something they enthusiastically embraced.

CULTURAL APPROACHES

Not everyone agrees that the roots of domestication and agriculture are to be explained by the operation of external environmental factors, all of which, by design, place human culture and agency in a passive role. Instead, some archaeologists contend, social and ideological factors, such as enhancing group or individual status through competitive feasting, tribute payments, or offerings to the deities (Price, 1995), may have pushed societies to come up with more food than could be readily obtained on a regular basis from natural sources. The reasoning behind these hypotheses is that human agency and culture alone may be sufficient and necessary to explain many of the fundamental changes documented in the archaeological record.

As you may suspect from your reading of the previous section, these approaches are also not immune to extreme positions. Just as we can identify some environmental approaches as teetering on the brink of determinism, we can find some cultural and cognitive approaches that seek to emphasize the role of human culture to the near, or certain, exclusion of noncultural factors. In these approaches, such natural phenomena as climatic changes are either irrelevant to the explanation of cultural outcomes or were consciously exploited by people to further cultural objectives, so they weren't merely phenomena to which people reacted.

Robert Braidwood's (Braidwood and Howe, 1960) "nuclear zone" or "hilly flanks" hypothesis is a good mid-twentieth-century example to start with in looking at cultural approaches. Braidwood built on V. Gordon Childe's earlier work (see p. 350) and pointed out that subsequent research didn't find evidence of the environmental changes on which Childe based his oasis theory. What's more, the wild ancestors of common domesticated plants and animals in the Near East were in the foothills of the mountains, not around the oases, which is where they should be if Childe's oasis theory is correct. Without a clear environmental trigger or cause for the origins of domestication and agriculture, Braidwood and Howe (1960) reasoned that domestication and, ultimately, agriculture came about as early Holocene hunter-gatherers gradually became familiar with local plant and animal resources and grew increasingly inclined to the notion of domestication. In other words, domestication and agriculture happened when "culture was ready." But Braidwood never adequately addressed the compelling questions that such an argument stimulates: Why was culture "ready"? Why then and not, say, 30,000 years ago? Or 100,000 years ago? Or never?

In his examination of the beginnings of agriculture in Europe, Ian Hodder (1990) took a more evenhanded approach than Braidwood. Building on the symbolic meaning assigned to houses and household activities, Hodder developed an argument in which the process of domestication and the activities of agriculture were properly viewed as the human "transformation of nature into culture, with an expansion of cultural control and a domination of nature" (Verhoeven, 2004, p. 210). He identified both social and natural factors as possible pressures in bringing about the transition from foraging to agriculture at the end of the Pleistocene. The strength of Hodder's approach rests in his assignment of considerable weight both to human agency and culture and to the widely accepted effects of environmental factors.

Recently, Jacques Cauvin (2000) offered an ambitious interpretation of the Neolithic revolution, which he views as a "revolution of symbols," not a revolution of economic arrangements. He feels that there isn't enough evidence to support such approaches as Binford's packing model, but he does see value in Braidwood's argument that domestication and agriculture didn't happen until culture was ready to receive it. To Cauvin, the Neolithic represents a fundamental transformation of worldviews that took place before the emergence of agricultural economies in the Near East. The primary symbols are the Goddess and the Bull, which represent the cultural creation of the divine and a fundamental symbolic transformation of the pre-Neolithic world. Cauvin's claim that the birth of the gods created a sense of self and, in turn, promoted the development of human agency and agriculture (Cauvin, 2000, p. 209) is reflected in his book's title, *The Birth of the Gods and the Origins of Agriculture*. Even though Cauvin asserts that domestication was the product of both cultural and natural factors, he devotes considerable attention to arguing against the possible role played by natural and some cultural factors, which, as Hodder (2001, p. 109) notes, leaves him "backed into the corner of arguing for a causal and chronological primacy for the psychocultural." Regrettably, Cauvin doesn't devote enough attention to explaining why these symbols were created, what caused them, and why they became particularly powerful during the Neolithic. As one archaeologist remarked (Rollefson, 2001, p. 102), in Cauvin's treatment they remain as mysterious and unexplained as the black monolith in Stanley Kubrick's film *2001: A Space Odyssey*.

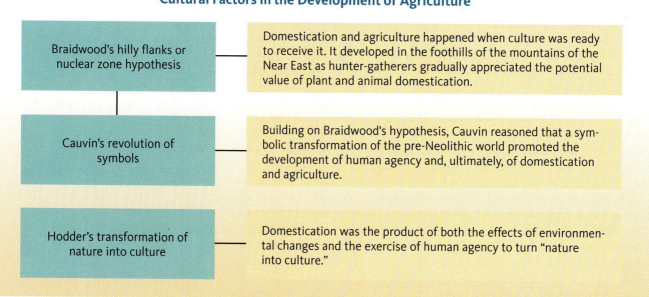

At a Glance

Cultural Factors in the Development of Agriculture

Braidwood's hilly flanks or nuclear zone hypothesis	Domestication and agriculture happened when culture was ready to receive it. It developed in the foothills of the mountains of the Near East as hunter-gatherers gradually appreciated the potential value of plant and animal domestication.
Cauvin's revolution of symbols	Building on Braidwood's hypothesis, Cauvin reasoned that a symbolic transformation of the pre-Neolithic world promoted the development of human agency and, ultimately, of domestication and agriculture.
Hodder's transformation of nature into culture	Domestication was the product of both the effects of environmental changes and the exercise of human agency to turn "nature into culture."

So, to sum things up, cultural approaches to explain the origins of domestication and agriculture assume an active role for human agency and tend to discount, if not deny completely, the importance of natural or environmental factors. In these approaches, cultural changes, such as a transformation of the human relationship with the divine or of the conceptualization of self, can be enough in some cases to account for the changes we see in the archaeological record. The main drawback with these hypotheses is that sometimes it's not immediately clear why such transformations would occur. Such answers as Braidwood's "when culture was ready" were unacceptable even in 1960, and they're no less so now. These approaches envision the development of agriculture as something humans achieved through cultural means, and not necessarily from a lack of alternatives.

FROM COLLECTING TO CULTIVATING

If today we had to choose an explanation for the origins of domestication and agriculture (and we should at least suggest a preference, since this is an introductory college textbook), we would adopt one of the moderate environmental approaches as the most robust because it explains the most real cases. Most such approaches also consider cultural factors, but they assign the greatest weight to the forces of nature. For us, that's their greatest appeal. They don't require researchers to assume that just because we're biocultural animals, humans are somehow exempt from natural factors that affect all living things. Disasters such as the devastating Southeast Asian tsunami of December 2004 and Hurricane Katrina in August 2005 are eloquent testimony that, for all our human posturing to the contrary, nature often has the final word.

Ultimately, we have no reason to believe that the origins of domestication and agriculture can be explained *only* by natural forces or *only* by cultural factors. These are complex problems for which there may even be multiple valid explanations. It could easily be the case that approaches such as those recently proposed by Barker (2006) and Verhoeven (2004), which seek explanations in the interaction of both natural and cultural forces, will prove to be the most productive route to follow.

So, working within our admitted preference for environmental approaches, let's now consider why and how hunter-gatherers became farmers in a real example drawn from the Near East. As Epipaleolithic gatherers in the Levant region harvested natural stands of wild cereal grasses such as wheat or barley, their movements would cause many of the ripened seed heads to shatter spontaneously, with considerable loss of grain. Each time someone used a gazelle-horn sickle to cut through a stalk, some of the seeds would fall to the ground. This normal process of seed dispersal is a function of the **rachis**, a short connector linking each seed to the primary stalk (Fig. 14-3). While the embryonic seed develops, the rachis serves as an umbilical that conveys the nutrients to be stored and later used by the germinating seed. Once the seed reaches its full development on the stalk, the rachis normally becomes dry and brittle, enabling the seed to break away easily.

Even without human interference, wild cereal grasses tended to be particularly susceptible to natural genetic modification (much more so than, say, nut-bearing trees), since the plants grew together in dense patches, were highly polytypic, and were quick to reproduce. In fact, a stand of wild grasses was like an enormous genetic laboratory. The normal range of genetic variability among the grasses included some plants with slightly larger seeds and others with tougher or more flexible rachis segments, meaning that their seed heads would be slightly less prone to shattering. As people worked through the stands, seeds from these genetic variants would end up in the gathering baskets slightly more often. Later, as the gatherers carried their baskets to camp, stored or processed the grain, or moved from place to place, a disproportionate number of the seeds they dropped, defecated, or perhaps even scattered purposely in likely growing areas would carry the flexible-rachis allele. (The same thing happened with the larger seeds preferred by the collectors.) As these genetic variants became isolated from the

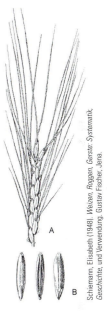

Schiemann, Elisabeth (1948). *Weizen, Roggen, Gerste: Systematik, Geschichte, und Verwendung.* Gustav Fischer, Jena.

Figure **14-3**

In seed heads of wild cereal grasses, individual grains are linked together by a flexible jointed stem, or rachis, as they develop. At maturity, the rachis breaks apart and the seeds scatter. In domesticated forms, the rachis remains supple, keeping the seed head intact until harvested. A, ear of wild einkorn wheat (1:1); B, grains of wild einkorn wheat (3:1).

rachis The short stem by which an individual seed attaches to the main stalk of a plant as it develops.

general wild population, each subsequent harvest advanced the "selection" process in favor of the same desirable traits.

So, human manipulation became an evolutionary force in modifying the species, a process Darwin labeled unconscious selection. People didn't have to be aware of genetic principles to act as effective agents of evolution. And where desirable traits could be readily discerned— larger grain size, plumper seed heads, earlier maturity, and so forth—human choice would even more predictably and consistently favor the preferred characteristics. The result within just a few seasons might be a significant shift in allele frequencies— that is, evolution— resulting from classic Darwinian selection processes, in this case the result of long-term pressure by gatherers, who consistently selected for those traits that improved the plant's productivity and quality (Rindos, 1984).

Of course, the rate of divergent evolution away from the wild ancestral forms of a plant (or animal) species accelerates as people continue to exercise control by selecting for genetically based characteristics they find desirable. With the cereal grasses such as barley and wheat, the human-influenced varieties typically came to average more grains per seed head than their wild relatives had. The rachis became less brittle in domesticated forms, making it easier for people to harvest the grain with less loss because the seed head no longer shattered to disperse its own seed. At the same time, individual seed coats or husks (glumes) became less tough, making them easier for humans to process or digest. Many of these changes obviously would have been harmful to the plant under natural conditions. Frequently, a consequence of domestication is that the plant species becomes dependent on humans to disperse its seeds. After all, symbiosis is a mutual, two-way relationship.

Whenever favorable plant traits developed, hunter-gatherers could be expected to respond to these improvements by quickly adjusting their collecting behavior to take the greatest advantage, in turn stimulating further genetic changes in the subject plants and eventually producing a **cultigen**, or domesticate, under human control. Again, these unconscious, or artificial (as opposed to *natural*, in Darwin's terminology) selection pressures constitute an evolutionary force in their own right. As continuous selection and isolation from other plants of the same species continued to favor desirable genetic variants, the steps to full domestication would have been small ones.

Likewise, the distances that separated hunter-gatherers from early farmers were also small ones. It's usually impossible to determine archaeologically when harvesting activities may have expanded to include the deliberate scattering of selected wild seeds in new environments or the elimination of competing plants by "weeding" or even burning over a forest clearing. As they intensified their focus on wheat and barley in the Near East—or on species such as maize or runner beans in Mexico—hunter-gatherers finally abandoned the rhythm of their traditional food-collecting schedules and further committed themselves to increasing the productivity of these plants through cultivation.

Archaeological Evidence for Domestication and Agriculture

Archaeologist Graeme Barker (2006, p. 414) argues that the change from hunting and gathering to agriculture "was the most profound revolution in human history." It also profoundly affected other species and continues to do so. The accumulated archaeological evidence reveals that humans *independently* domesticated local species and developed agriculture in several geographically separate regions relatively soon after the Ice Age ended. From recent applications of molecular genetics research and other methodological advances in archaeology, it's also clear that more independent instances of prehistoric domestication are likely to be identified, some locations currently identified as possible independent centers of domestication may be deleted from the list, and some plants and

cultigen A plant that is wholly dependent on humans; a domesticate.

animals were probably domesticated multiple times in various places (Armelagos and Harper, 2005).

Archaeologists have yet to fully explain how and why agriculture spread and eventually dominated economic life in many parts of the world. Peter Bellwood's (2005) recent "early farming dispersal hypothesis" integrates archaeology, genetics, and historical linguistics in a highly original argument that early farming grew out of the Mesolithic/Epipaleolithic and spread into new lands with the movement or dispersal of farmers from agricultural "homelands." Working within what is essentially an environmental approach that identifies human population growth as the main driving factor of farmer dispersal, or "demic diffusion," this hypothesis offers a highly controversial explanation for the spread of agriculture, human populations, and languages, as well as major spatial patterns in human genetics (Bellwood, 2005; Bellwood et al., 2007). Building on much the same archaeological and genetic data, Graeme Barker (2006) reached very different conclusions. He essentially questions the existence of such primal hearths or homelands and traces the roots of this revolution back to early Upper Paleolithic hunter-gatherers. It is too soon to tell which, if any, of these interpretations offer a more accurate picture of the spread of prehistoric agriculture.

In examining independent centers of domestication around the world, it's important to realize that the domestication of a local species or two would not necessarily trigger the enormous biocultural consequences we usually associate with the Neolithic period in the Near East. In fact, most altered species retained only local significance. For example, in the Eastern Woodlands of the United States, hunter-gatherers domesticated several small-seeded species very early; still, the wild forest products obtained by hunting and gathering retained their primary importance until relatively late prehistoric times, when true farming developed in the East. The prehistoric yam cultivators of sub-Saharan Africa serve as a similar example.

In most regions, agriculture didn't develop fully until people were exploiting a mosaic of plants—and sometimes animals, too—from different locations, brought together in various combinations to meet such cultural requirements as nutrition, palatability, hardiness, yield, processing ease, and storage. In the Near East, this threshold was reached around 11,000 ya, when an agricultural complex consisting of wheat, barley, sheep, and goats was widely and rapidly adopted.

PLANTS

In most areas where agriculture emerged, early farmers relied on local plant species whose wild relatives grew close by. Old World cereal grasses, including barley and some wheat varieties, were native throughout the Near East and perhaps into southeastern Europe (Dennell, 1983). Wild varieties of these plants still flourish today over parts of this range. Therefore, barley or wheat domestication could have occurred anywhere in this region, possibly more than once. The same is true for maize and beans in Mexico. So, as we noted earlier, domestication and agriculture were "invented" independently in different regions around the world.

It's best to explain these separate but parallel processes from a cultural and ecological perspective. We've already seen that certain kinds of wild plants were more likely than others to become domesticated. Many of these species tend to grow in regions where a very long dry season follows a short wet period (Harlan, 1992). After the last Ice Age, around 10,000 ya, these conditions existed around the Mediterranean basin and the hilly areas of the Near East and in the dry forests and savanna grasslands of portions of sub-Saharan Africa, India, southern California, southern Mexico, and eastern and western South America.

Most scientific understanding of ancient human plant use has come from the **archaeobotanical** study of preserved seeds, fruits, nutshell fragments, and other **plant macrofossils**

archaeobotanical Referring to the analysis and interpretation of the remains of ancient plants recovered from the archaeological record.

plant macrofossils Plant parts such as seeds, nutshells, and stems, preserved in the archaeological record and large enough to be clearly visible to the naked eye.

Figure 14-4

Plant remains from a pit feature in an Illinois archaeological site. Clockwise from top are pieces of charred wood, nutshell fragments, and seeds.

plant microfossils Small to microscopic plant remains, most falling in a range of 10 to 100 micrometers (μm), or roughly the size of individual grains of wheat flour in the bag from your grocer's shelf.

pollen Microscopic grains containing the male gametes of seed-producing plants.

phytoliths (*phyto*, meaning "plant," and *lith*, meaning "stone") Microscopic silica structures formed in the cells of many plants.

starch grains Subcellular structures that form in all plant parts and are classifiable by family or genus; particularly abundant in seeds and tubers.

like those shown in Figure 14-4 (Pearsall, 2000). It isn't easy to preserve seeds, tubers, leaves, and other delicate organic materials for thousands of years. Archaeologists recover some macrofossils from depositional environments that are always dry, wet, or frozen, because all of these conditions slow down or halt the process of decomposition. Most, however, are preserved because the way they were harvested, threshed, processed for consumption, or discarded brought them into contact with enough fire to char them, but not enough heat to reduce them to ash. Once charred, macrofossils preserve well in many kinds of archaeological sites and can often be classified to genus, if not to species.

Macrofossils offer direct evidence for important archaeological research such as reconstructing hunter-gatherer plant use patterns, identifying farming locations, and determining the precise nature of harvested crops. They also provide insights of other kinds. The presence of perennial and biennial weed seeds in an ancient agricultural context may suggest that each year's farming activities only minimally disturbed the soil; the seed planter may have used a digging stick, hoe, or simple scratch plow. If, on the other hand, seeds of annual weeds predominate, the farmer may have used a moldboard plow—one that turns over the soil as it cuts through.

Right now, the best archaeological data on the shift toward food production come from sites located in arid regions of both hemispheres, where ancient organic remains are best preserved. Were the first steps toward farming really taken in such seemingly marginal agricultural situations, or are dry areas just better environments for preservation? Many researchers are still convinced that most of our significant food plants originated in the dry temperate environments and that they were probably domesticated there, too. But not all archaeobotanists agree; some argue instead that early domesticated forms may have been introduced from other, more humid environments, where preservation is poor and research has been limited.

The major shortcomings of macrofossil-based interpretations of past human plant use are due to potential preservation biases. Plant macrofossils tend to be preserved because they were charred before entering the archaeological record (see Fig. 14-4 for examples). But not all plant parts char easily, and many don't char at all. For example, it's pretty easy to char a bean, but you'll be disappointed if you try the same thing with a leaf of lettuce. Because the necessary conditions could only be met sometimes in prehistory and by some plants and plant parts, archaeologists are understandably concerned about the validity and reliability of many reconstructions of human plant use that are based only on macrofossils.

Fortunately, modern archaeologists can turn to several other important sources in their research on prehistoric human plant use. **Plant microfossils**, such as **pollen**, **phytoliths**, and **starch grains**, often survive even where macrofossils can't—for example, as residues on the cutting edges of ancient stone tools, inside pottery containers, and embedded in the pores of grinding stones (Bryant, 2003). Unlike many macrofossils, these remains preserve readily in a wide range of archaeological contexts; they can be classified as to the kind of plant they represent, if not also to the plant part they represent; and they can be archaeologically present even in sites where macrofossils were destroyed or never deposited.

Pollen grains (Fig. 14-5) have been a valuable source of environmental and subsistence data for decades (Traverse, 2007). Their strengths are that they're abundant (as any hay fever sufferer can tell you); the grains are taxonomically distinctive and often can be classified to genus, if not to species; the outer shell of each grain is tough; and the wind-

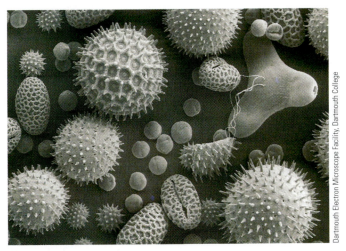

Figure 14-5

Pollen grains from common flowering plants. The spiked ball in the lower left of the photograph is roughly 75 micrometers (µm), or three-thousandths of an inch, in diameter.

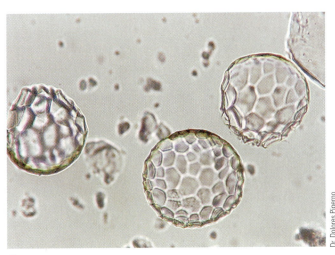

Figure 14-6

Squash (*Cucurbita ficifolia*) phytoliths. The large one in the lower center of the photo measures about 120 µm across.

borne dispersal of pollen from seed-producing plants continues before, during, and after humans occupy a particular archaeological site. The main shortcoming of pollen grains is that they tend to preserve poorly in many kinds of open sites, depending on soil acidity, moisture, drainage, and weathering.

Phytoliths (Fig. 14-6) are less familiar, but potentially even more valuable than many macrofossils (Piperno, 2006). They're microscopic, inorganic structures that form in many seed-producing plants as well as other plants. Like pollen, phytoliths are taxonomically distinctive. They even vary according to where they form in the plant, so phytoliths from leaves can be distinguished from those that formed in the stems and seeds of the same plant. Importantly, they don't suffer from the same preservation biases that macrofossils do. Are the plant remains at your site unidentifiable, reduced to a powdery ash, or simply not preserved? Not a problem. Chances are the phytoliths from these plants are not only present in the archaeological deposit but also recoverable and identifiable.

Starch grains (Fig. 14-7) are subcellular particles that form in all plant parts. They are particularly abundant in such economically important portions as seeds and tubers (Coil et al., 2003). They are a useful complement to phytoliths as a data source and are a major tool in archaeological investigations of root crops (Piperno, 2008). Like pollen and phytoliths, starch grains can be taxonomically classified, currently mostly to family or genus. A good example of the archaeological application of starch grain analysis is the recent examination of the surface of a grinding stone found on the floor of one of the 23,000-year-old huts at Ohalo II in Israel. This study, which was based on carefully sampled residues from cracks and pits in the working surface of the grinding stone, enabled archaeobotanists to identify that it was a specialized implement used to grind wild cereal grasses, including barley (Piperno et al., 2004).

As we saw in Chapter 8, some plant species also leave biochemical traces in those who consume them. Because temperate and tropical region plants evolved with slightly different processes for photosynthesis, their chemical compositions vary in the ratio of carbon-13 to carbon-12. This distinctive chemical profile gets passed along the food chain, and the bones of the human skeleton may provide evidence of dietary change. For example,

Figure 14-7

Wild emmer wheat (*Triticum dicoccoides*) starch grains, which show distinctive craterlike surface impressions. The largest starch grain (top center) is about 30 µm in diameter.

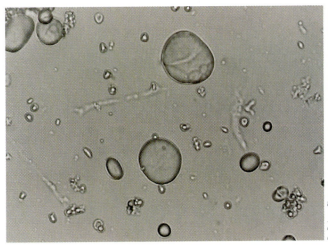

their lower ^{13}C levels reveal that females at Grasshopper Pueblo, in east-central Arizona, consumed mostly the local plants they gathered, while their male relatives at first enjoyed more maize, a plant higher in ^{13}C. Later, maize became a staple in everyone's diet at Grasshopper, resulting in equivalent carbon isotopes in males and females (Ezzo, 1993).

Other biochemical analyses, using different isotopes, have been devised to assess overall diet—not necessarily just the domesticated portions—from individual skeletons. A higher ratio of nitrogen-15 to nitrogen-14 (^{15}N/^{14}N), for instance, corresponds to a greater seafood component to the diet (Schoeninger et al., 1983), while a higher strontium-to-calcium (Sr/Ca) ratio indicates that plant foods were of greater dietary importance than meat (Schoeninger, 1981). Other chemicals taken up by bones may inform us about ancient lifeways. For example, lead (Pb) is a trace element found in unusually high concentration in the bones of Romans who drank wine stored in the lead containers typical of that period. The interplay among culture, diet, and biology is, of course, a prime example of biocultural evolution. But to put it more simply, "You are what you eat," and the odds are increasingly good that archaeologists can measure it.

Microfossil analyses complement and greatly extend the valuable insights that archaeobotanists have achieved through the study of macrofossils. Recent key advances include the growing field of *archaeogenetics*, which applies the methods of molecular genetics to archaeological problems, as well as improvements in radiocarbon dating, which can yield accurate age estimates from samples as small as 100 micrograms (μg)—that's one ten-thousandth of a gram, or roughly one-fifth the weight of a grain of rice (Armelagos and Harper, 2005). As a result, researchers are now able to more completely understand the prehistory of the human use of plants and the beginnings of agriculture.

ANIMALS

To some extent, the process of animal domestication differed from plant domestication, and it probably varied even from one animal species to another. For example, the dog was one of the first domesticated animals; mtDNA evidence suggests an origin between 40,000 and 15,000 ya (Savolainen, 2002), and dogs may even have accompanied late Ice Age hunter-gatherers (Olsen, 1985). The dog's relationship with humans was different (and it still is) from that of most subsequently domesticated animals. Often valued less for its meat or hide, a dog's primary role was most likely as a ferocious hunting weapon under at least a bit of human control and direction. As people domesticated other animals, they changed the dog's behavior even more for service as a herder and later, in the Arctic and among the Native Americans of the Great Plains, as an occasional transporter of possessions. But the burial of a puppy with a Natufian person who died some 12,000 ya in the Near East suggests that dogs may have earned a role as pets very early (Davis and Valla, 1978).

Most other domesticated animals were maintained solely for their meat at first. Richard J. Harrison's (1985) insightful analysis of faunal collections from Neolithic sites in Spain and Portugal concluded that meat remained the primary product up until about 4,000 ya, when subsequent changes in herd composition (age and sex ratios), slaughter patterns, and popularity of certain breeds all point to new uses for some livestock. Oxen pulled plows, horses carried people and things, cattle and goats contributed milk products, and sheep were raised for wool. Animal waste became fertilizer in agricultural areas. Leather, horn, and bone—and even social status for the animals' owners—were other valued byproducts. (In much the same way, recent East African cattle herders appreciate their animals as much more than packages of beefsteak, for a sizable herd testifies to a man's standing and may be used to fulfill social obligations such as bridewealth payments.)

Of course, animals are more mobile than plants, and most of them are no less mobile than the early people pursuing them. So it's unlikely that hunters could have promoted useful genetic changes in wild animals just by trying to restrict their movements or by selective hunting alone. Possibly, by simultaneously destroying wild predators and reducing the number of competing herbivores, humans became surrogate protectors of the herds, though this arrangement would not have had the genetic impact of actual domestication.

Animals such as gazelle or reindeer might be managed to a degree in the wild state, possibly by establishing a "rapport" with the herds and encouraging them to graze in cleared areas in the winter or by restricting hunting activities to a few quick raids, during which the herd might be selectively harvested or thinned. Culling out all nonbreeding males, for example, wouldn't limit the potential for herd expansion, and it wouldn't have much effect on the population genetics. Epipaleolithic Natufians in the Near East were once thought to have managed wild gazelle in this way (Legge, 1972); but reexamination of the faunal remains casts these peoples' gazelle hunting in a very different light, implying the use of large-scale surrounds or ambush techniques to nonselectively kill entire herds at once (Legge and Rowley-Conwy, 1987). This drastic approach would suppress the animal population for years. Obviously, true domestication, involving further genetic changes, must have been reached by other steps.

Since domestication is a process, not an event, it's nearly impossible to say precisely when a plant or animal species has been domesticated. The process involves much more than an indication of "tameness" in the presence of humans. More significant are the changes in allele frequencies that result from selective breeding and isolation from wild relatives. People may have started with young animals spared by hunters for that purpose or, in the case of large and dangerous species such as the auroch (the wild ancestor of domesticated cattle), with individuals that were exceptionally docile or small (Fagan, 1993). Maintained in captivity, these animals could be selectively bred for desirable traits, such as more meat, fat, wool, or strength. Once early farmers were consistently selecting breeding stock according to some criteria and succeeding in perpetuating those characteristics through subsequent generations, then domestication—that is, evolution—clearly had occurred.

Overall, not many mammal species were ever domesticated. Those most amenable to domestication are animals that form hierarchical herds, are not likely to flee when frightened, and are not strongly territorial (Diamond, 1989). In other words, animals that will tolerate and transfer their allegiance to human surrogates make the best potential domesticates. Several large Eurasian mammals met these specifications, so that cultures of Asia, Europe, and Africa came to rely on sheep and goats, pigs, cattle, and horses (listed here in approximately their order of domestication) as well as water buffalo, camels, reindeer, and a few other regionally significant species.

Even fewer New World herd animals were capable of being domesticated. Aside from two South American camelids—the llama and the alpaca—no large American mammal was brought fully under human control (Fig. 14-8). Dogs had probably accompanied the first people into the New World. None of these animals were suitable for transporting or pulling heavy loads—llamas balk at carrying more than about 100 pounds, and Plains Indian dogs dragged only small bundles—so the people of the New World continued to bear their own burdens, till their fields by hand, and hunt and fight on foot until the introduction of the Old World's livestock in the 1500s.

Archaeological evidence of nonhuman animal domestication is subtle and difficult to assess from the bones themselves (Fig. 14-9). For most species, no significant increase in body size occurred, and early domesticated cattle, sheep, and goats are actually smaller than their wild relatives. Comparisons of the bones of wild and domestic members of the same species disclose only relatively minor differences in skeletal form (Herre, 1969). For example, the bony horn cores of domestic goats display a

Figure **14-8**

Peoples of highland South America bred the llama primarily as a source of wool and, to a limited extent, to transport loads.

William Turnbaugh

Figure 14-9

A typical collection of faunal remains from an excavation level in an Illinois archaeological site.

somewhat flattened cross section when compared with their wild antecedents, and domesticated pigs exhibit a shortening of the upper jaw (maxilla) in relation to the lower jaw (mandible).

Archaeozoologists also examine changes in prehistoric herd demography to document domestication. The population curve for animals randomly hunted from a wild herd tends to reflect a normal distribution that approximates the overall age and sex ratio of the herd. On the other hand, a notable increase in the number of skeletal elements of, say, young adult rams found in kitchen refuse may indicate that humans were selecting those particular animals for slaughter while reserving most females and lambs for breeding purposes (Bokonyi, 1969). Such indicators are seldom definitive, however, unless very large samples of faunal remains confirm domestication.

Old World Farmers

As we've noted, independent invention accounts best for the diversity of domesticates and the distinctiveness of Neolithic lifeways in the Far East, Southeast Asia, India, sub-Saharan Africa, the Near East, and the Americas. What's more, many wild species, such as wheat and sheep, probably occupied more extensive natural ranges in the early Holocene and may in fact have undergone local domestication more than a few times (Armelagos and Harper, 2005).

But as Bellwood (2005) reminds us, we can't entirely discount the spread of Neolithic lifeways or people from place to place. As we'll see, in at least some areas—southeastern Europe, for example—colonizing farmers appear to have brought their domesticates and their culture with them as they migrated into new territories in search of suitable farmland. Neolithic practices also spread through secondary contact as people on the margins of established farming societies acquired certain tools, seeds, and ideas and passed them along to cultures still further removed. Seeds and animals often must have become commodities in prehistoric exchange networks, just like the Spanish horses obtained by Native Americans did in the sixteenth century. Maybe marriage partners from other groups introduced their in-laws to the new ways. It's important to bear in mind that each archaeological event is unique in its own way. "One-size-fits-all" explanations are rarely adequate, even if the results are the same—in this case, the expansion of Neolithic lifeways. With that in mind, let's consider a sampling of Neolithic societies from around the world to get some idea of the variations on this common theme.

THE NEAR EAST

Neolithic lifeways and their consequences appeared throughout the Near East and adjacent areas, but not necessarily because farming was a superior way of life. As we saw in Chapter 13, Epipaleolithic foraging cultures such as Kebaran and Natufian apparently took the first steps, though perhaps inadvertently, toward agriculture in the Near East (Fig. 14-10). As discussed in Chapter 13, the extraordinary preservation of plant remains at Ohalo II, an early Epipaleolithic campsite in northern Israel, shows that small-grained grass and wild cereal seeds were important in hunter-gatherer diets in the Levant by 23,000 ya (see p. 000; Piperno et al., 2004; Weiss et al., 2004a, 2004b). The diverse staple diet of these early Epipaleolithic hunter-gatherers also offers important support for Flannery's (1973) conception of a broad-spectrum revolution that preceded the development of domestication and agriculture.

Between 11,500 and 11,000 ya, at the site of Abu Hureyra in the upper Euphrates of Syria, hunter-gatherers consumed more than 250 plant species, only a few of which were staple foods (Moore et al., 2000, p. 397). With the beginning of the cooler and drier conditions of the Younger Dryas, many of these species vanish from the Abu Hureyra archaeological record, to be replaced by increased frequencies of weed seeds and the earliest evidence of domesticated rye, specimens of which date to roughly 11,200–10,600 ya (Moore et al., 2000). These changes point to two important inferences: First, environmental conditions were sufficient to account for these shifts in Abu Hureyra's subsistence economy, and second, at least part of the economy of this settlement was based on the cultivation of domesticated plants (rye, in this case) by around 11,000 ya.

A similar story was played out at Kebara and El Wad, which are in Israel to the southwest of Abu Hureyra, where stone-bladed sickles aided in harvesting the ancestral varieties of wheat and barley by 10,000 ya (Henry, 1989). This technique, more efficient than plucking seeds by hand, netted greater yields during a short harvest period. The process of genetic selection that we've considered as the basis for plant domestication must have been well under way by this time. That we don't yet know the whole story about the selective forces acting on these species is evident from recent field research that demonstrated that there is no reason Epipaleolithic hunter-gatherers couldn't also have harvested fallen grain. Kislev and colleagues (2004) collected spikelets of wild barley and wild wheat that had fallen to the ground at stands chosen from three areas of Israel and found that such harvesting methods would have yielded a reliable summer food supply. The Natufians adopted farming to augment food supplies for their rapidly growing population at a time when natural subsistence resources were again in decline. The warming trends that first had created optimal conditions for upland cereal and nut crops continued for several more centuries, leaving much of the Levant parched (Henry, 1989). Natufians then abandoned many upland sites, retreating to the lower stream valleys. There, in an effort to duplicate the once-productive natural environments of the highlands, some groups established new stands of cereal grasses by dispersing seeds in favorable areas along the streams near their villages (Bar-Yosef, 1998). It seems that, at least in this case, the stresses associated with a destabilized population/resource balance stimulated the agricultural response.

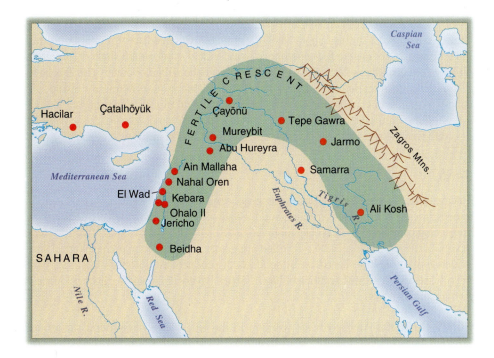

Figure **14-10**

Early Neolithic sites of the Fertile Crescent.

At a Glance

Important Near Eastern Sites and Regions

SITE	DATES (YA)	SIGNIFICANCE
Abu Hureyra (Syria)	11,500–11,000	Hunter-gatherer settlement that also depended on a few domesticated plants; earliest evidence of domesticated rye
Kebara and **El Wad** (Israel)	ca. 10,000	Sites where hunter-gatherers supplemented their diet by harvesting the wild ancestral varieties of wheat and barley
Jericho (West Bank)	<11,000–3,500	One of the early sedentary communities founded in the Levant; Jericho began in Natufian times and was occupied throughout the Neolithic

These food collectors and earliest farmers established the first permanent sedentary communities in the Near East. Drawn by an ever-flowing spring in an otherwise arid region, settlers at the site of Jericho (or Tell es-Sultan), in the West Bank, and at other Natufian sites in Israel built their round stone or mud-brick houses some 11,500 ya. Though they were made of more substantial materials, in form these structures closely resembled the temporary huts of the region's earlier hunters and gatherers. Numerous grinding stones and clay-lined storage pits found in these communities testify to the economic importance of cereal grains (Moore, 1985; Bar-Yosef, 1987).

Foraging for the seeds of wild cereals, fruits, nuts, and the meat of wild game long remained an important, but slowly declining, component of the diet. At Abu Hureyra, villagers were cultivating wheat, rye, and lentils by 9,800 ya, but wild plant food staples were still a part of the diet (Moore et al., 2000). By 9,000 ya, sedentary villagers across a broad arc from the Red Sea to western Iran—also known as the Fertile Crescent (see Fig. 14-10)—engaged in wheat and barley agriculture and sheep and goat herding. As demonstrated at many sites in this region, Neolithic families lived in adjacent multiroom rectangular houses, in contrast to the compounds of individual small, round shelters commonly built by Epipaleolithic collectors as well as the early Jericho settlers. Flannery (1972) believes that this change in residence pattern signals a shift toward more economically and socially cohesive communities. Comprised of extended-family and multifamily groups, these villagers differed radically in outlook and actions from their predecessors. These were the beginnings of the region's later urbanism, which we'll look at in the next chapter.

AFRICA

Tracing Africa's Neolithic past is challenging, considering the continent's vast size, its varied climates and vegetation zones, and the extent to which many of its regions are still archaeologically unknown. What's more, because many tropical foods lack woody stems or durable seeds, plant macrofossils often are poorly represented at archaeological sites; evidence of agriculture based on these kinds of products awaits more intensive plant microfossil research. Arid sections of North Africa have yielded some direct evidence of farming and herding.

Northern Africa Archaeologists working in the Nile Valley have found sickles and milling stones relating to early wild grain harvesting (Wendorf and Schild, 1989). The so-called Qadan culture, whose sites are found near present-day Aswan (Fig. 14-11), probably typified the Epipaleolithic food collectors who occupied the valley around 8,000 ya (Hoffman, 1991). Qadan people employed spears or nets for taking large Nile perch and catfish. Along the riverbanks they hunted wildfowl and gathered wild produce, processing starchy aquatic tubers on their milling stones. They also stalked the adjacent grasslands for gazelle and other game and may have begun the process of domesticating the local wild cattle (Wendorf and Schild, 1994). Considering the wealth of naturally occurring resources along the Nile, this foraging and collecting way of life might have continued indefinitely. So why did farming develop there at all?

Geologists and paleoecologists recognize that shifting rainfall patterns have affected North Africa since the late Pleistocene. Long-term cycles brought increased precipitation, which broadened the Nile and its valley and gave the river a predictable seasonal rhythm. Rains falling on its tropical headwaters, thousands of miles to the south, caused the river to overflow its downstream channels by late summer, flooding the low-lying basins of northern Egypt for about three months of the year. Although desiccation followed, the flood-deposited silt grew lush with wild grasses through the following season. Periodically, however, extended drought episodes intervened to narrow the river's life-giving flow.

The expansive area west of the Nile, known today as the Sahara, was particularly susceptible to these fluctuations. The Sahara was a fragile environment, always marginal for humans. Down to 11,000 ya, this arid region was uninviting even to hunter-gatherers. Then a period of increased rainfall created shallow lakes and streams that nurtured the grasslands, attracting game animals and humans. Around 7,000 ya, people in the Sahara devised a strategy of nomadic pastoralism, allowing their herds of sheep, goats, and possibly cattle to act as ecological intermediaries by converting tough grasses to meat and by-products useful to humans (Wendorf and Schild, 1994). Soon after, around 6,000 ya, further deterioration of the region's climate—and possibly overgrazing—forced the herders and their animals to seek greener pastures closer to the Nile (Williams, 1984; Harlan, 1992; A. Smith, 1992).

As drought parched the adjacent areas, the narrowing Nile Valley attracted more settlers. Wild resources were then insufficient to feed the growing sedentary population, and even the local domesticates that had been casually cultivated on the floodplain gave way to more productive cereals—the domesticated wheat and barley that had been brought under human control elsewhere by people like the Natufians.

Farmers gradually made the river's rhythm their own. Communities of reed-mat or mud-brick houses appeared across the Nile delta and along its banks. Basket-lined storage pits or granaries, milling stones, and sickles indicate a heavy reliance on grain. Pottery vessels of river clay, linen woven from flax fibers, flint tools, and occasional hammered copper items were produced locally. These ordinary Neolithic beginnings laid the foundation for the remarkable Egyptian civilization, which we'll explore in Chapter 15.

Outside the Nile Valley, cattle herding took priority over farming in much of East Africa, where conditions were generally not suitable for cultivation.

Sub-Saharan Africa In West Africa along the southern edge of the Sahara, where little is currently known about the early Holocene human presence, the pattern appears similar to that described for the Sahara. At **Ounjougou**, in the Dogon Plateau region of central Mali, erosional gullies cut through a long sequence of Pleistocene and early Holocene sites, some of which were recently excavated (Huysecom, 2004). Hunter-gatherers appear to have been in the region from the earliest Holocene, around 12,000–11,000 ya. By 10,000–9,000 ya, such groups were harvesting wild cereal grasses and making and using ceramics.

The limited evidence available from archaeology and linguistic studies hints that hunters and gatherers in several other parts of Africa also experimented with local **cultivars**. For example, mobile foragers and semisedentary fishers of tropical Africa practiced yam horticulture in clearings and along riverbanks by at least 5,000 ya (Clark, 1976; Ehret, 1984).With digging sticks, they pried out the starchy wild yam tubers and carried them

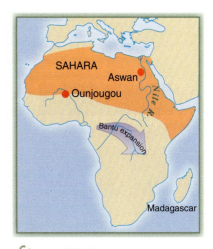

Figure **14-11**

Early farming in Africa and Bantu expansion.

Ounjougou A site populated by African hunter-gatherers who made early use of wild cereal grasses on the southern edge of the Sahara between 12,000 and 9,000 ya.

cultivars Wild plants fostered by human efforts to make them more productive.

At a Glance
Important African Sites and Regions

SITE	DATES (YA)	SIGNIFICANCE
Qadan culture (Egypt)	ca. 8,000	Epipaleolithic hunter-gatherers who harvested the rich wild plant and animal resources of the Nile region upriver from modern Aswan
Ounjougou (Mali)	12,000–9,000	African hunter-gatherers who made early use of wild cereal grasses on the southern edge of the Sahara

Don Farall, Getty Images

Figure **14-12**

A stand of sorghum, which, along with rice and millet, is an important starch grain crop in many parts of Africa and Asia.

millet Small-grained cereal grasses native to Asia and Africa.

sorghum A cereal grass. Some subspecies are grown for food grains, others for their sweet, juicy stalk.

taros Species of a tropical plant with an edible starchy root.

away for cooking. As an added bonus, the people discovered that if they pressed the leafy tops or cuttings of the largest roots into the soil at the edge of the camp clearing, the yams would regenerate into an informal garden.

In these tropical regions, the standard Near Eastern cereals tended to rot. So between 5,000 and 3,000 ya, African farmers developed comparable domesticates from local cereal grasses, including local varieties of **millet** and **sorghum** (Fig. 14-12), which they successfully grew along the edges of the rain forest and the savanna grasslands (Smith, 1999).

More dramatic shifts in sub-Saharan subsistence followed the introduction and spread of different Neolithic crops. Tropical plants from Southeast Asia reached Africa when Asian traders crossed the Indian Ocean to Madagascar about 2,000 ya (Murdock, 1959; Harlan, 1992). These new products spread quickly to the interior, where people throughout the rain forest zone adopted bananas, **taros**, and Asian yams. Bantu-speaking peoples, native to west-central Africa, relied on these productive new crops to support their rapid expansion through central and southern Africa (Phillipson, 1984). Driving herds of domestic goats and cattle and acquiring the technology of ironworking as they moved southeastward through central Africa (Van Noten and Raymaekers, 1987), the Bantu easily overwhelmed most hunting and gathering groups. The conventional view is that with iron tools and weapons, they carved out gardens and maintained large semipermanent villages, and today, their numerous descendants live in eastern, southern, and southwestern Africa (see Fig. 14-11). There's at least some evidence that food-producing methods spread into parts of southern Africa before the Bantu. The bones of domesticated sheep found in Late Stone Age sites in South Africa may not be the result of the spread of pastoralists, as once widely believed, but the remains of the camps of Bushmen (also called the San), whom Karim Sadr (2003) describes as "hunters-with-sheep."

ASIA

Several centers of domestication in southern and eastern Asia gave rise to separate Neolithic traditions based on the propagation of productive local plant and animal species. The exploitation of these resources spread widely and in turn heralded further economic and social changes associated with the rise of early civilizations in these regions (see Chapter 15).

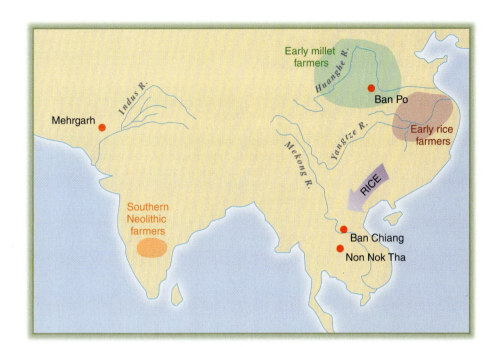

Figure **14-13**
Early Farming in Asia.

South Asia Excavations at Mehrgarh, in central Pakistan, have illuminated Neolithic beginnings on the Indian subcontinent (Fuller, 2006; Jarrige and Meadow, 1980). Located at the edge of a high plain west of the broad Indus Valley (Fig. 14-13), the site's lower levels, dating between 8,000 and 6,000 ya, reveal the trend toward dietary specialization that accompanied the domestication of local plant and animal species. Early on, the people harvested both wild and domesticated varieties of barley and wheat, among other native plants. Mehrgarh's archaeological deposits also include bones of many local herbivores: water buffalo, gazelle, swamp deer, goats, sheep, pigs, cattle, and even elephants. By 6,000 ya, the cultivated cereals prevailed, along with just three animal species— domestic sheep, goats, and cattle. Researchers believe that this early Neolithic phase at Mehrgarh represents a transition from seminomadic herding to a more sedentary existence that became the basis for later urban development in the Indus Valley. Other planned settlements boasting multiroom mud-brick dwellings and granaries soon appeared in the region, supported by a productive agriculture and bustling trade in copper, turquoise, shells, and cotton.

Archaeologists know much less about the origins of agriculture in South India. Recent archaeobotanical analyses of samples taken from Southern Neolithic, or Ash Mound Tradition, sites in Karnataka and Andhra Pradesh suggest that the earliest agriculture in these regions dates between 5,000 and 4,000 ya and was based on several native domesticated species, principally two lentils (horsegram and mung bean) and two species of millet (browntop millet and bristly foxtail grass), along with nonnative crops including wheat and barley (Fuller et al., 2004). The high frequencies of native domesticates in these samples lend support to Vavilov's (1992) identification of India as a possible independent center of domestication.

China Far to the east, village farmers of the Peiligang culture in northern China's central Yellow River basin were already cultivating local varieties of millet by perhaps 9,000 ya (Chang, 1986; Barnes, 1992). River terrace deposits of deep **loess** soil ensured large yields and undoubtedly contributed to the growth of populous settlements during this and the next Yangshao farming period around 2,000 years later (7,000 ya). Millet was a staple of both humans and their domesticated animals, which included pigs, chickens, and dogs; foraging continued to provide wild plants, fish, and animals. Wines and other fermented

loess (luss) Fine-grained soil composed of glacially pulverized rock, deposited by the wind.

At a Glance
Important Asian Sites and Regions

SITE	DATES (YA)	SIGNIFICANCE
Mehrgarh (Pakistan)	8,000–6,000	Early Neolithic community in South Asia that depended on domesticated plants and animals; represents a transition from semi-nomadic herding to sedentary villages and towns
Southern Neolithic, or **Ash Mound** (India)	5,000–4,000	Early evidence of South Indian agriculture based on native crops of lentils and millet, plus introduced domesticates such as wheat and barley
Peiligang culture (China)	ca. 9,000	Early Yellow River basin farmers who cultivated local millet varieties
Ban Po (or **Banpo**) (China)	ca. 7,000–6,000	Yangshao period (Neolithic) site near Xi'an, northern China; extensive excavations have exposed about 100 houses that formed a sedentary community

beverages, which have a long history in Chinese ceremonies, ritual feasting, and everyday life, were made from millet, rice, fruit, and other plant products as much as 9,000 ya (McGovern, 2004). At the site of Ban Po (see Fig. 14-13), more than 100 pit houses were placed around a plaza and its communal house. Cemeteries and pottery kilns typically were located near the residential parts of Yangshao villages. Jade carving, painted ceramics of tripod form, silkworm cultivation, and elite burials anticipated some of the hallmarks of the later Neolithic, or Longshan, period beginning 4,700 ya.

In warmer and wetter central and southern China, rice agriculture supported substantial permanent villages, especially along the Yangtze River. Researchers now believe that food collectors were gathering this productive grain in southern China more than 11,000 ya and that cultivators were growing it in the Yangtze delta by 8,500 ya (Normille, 1997; Crawford and Shen, 1998). Farmers introduced rice into Southeast Asia over the next several thousand years, bringing settled village life and domesticated cattle, pigs, and dogs to locations such as Ban Chiang and Non Nok Tha. High yields and the varied conditions under which rice could be grown made it the basis for sustained population growth in many parts of this region (Higham and Lu, 1998; Kharakwal et al., 2004).

EUROPE

Farmers in southeastern Europe already were tilling the Balkan Peninsula by about 9,000 ya at such sites as Argissa and Franchthi Cave, in Greece (Fig. 14-14; Perlès, 2001). Researchers continue to debate whether the spread of farming into southeastern Europe was caused by the movement of people, ideas, or some combination of the two (Bellwood, 2005; Barker, 2006; Colledge and Conolly, 2007). The current consensus, as far as we can speak of one, suggests that the earliest farming cultures of Europe were products of both the spread of farmers and cultural diffusion from the Near East. This view accounts for the seemingly sudden appearance of fully domesticated sheep, goats, wheat, and barley in southeastern Europe, along with a host of specific Near Eastern cultural traits, includ-

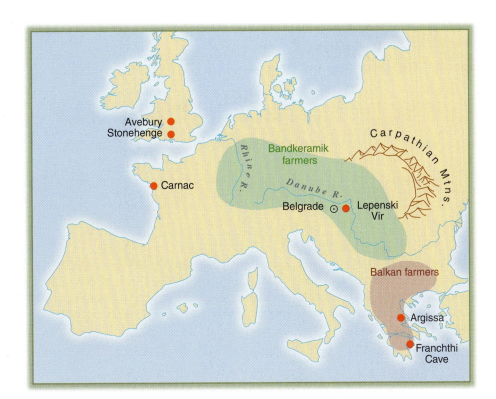

Figure **14-14**

Early Neolithic sites of Europe.

ing structured settlements, burial practices, clay figurines, painted pottery, and specific flaked stone forms (Tringham, 1971). Cultivated cereals and domesticated animals were in use from Turkey to Iraq several millennia earlier than in Europe, and compact clusters of houses were typical features of Near Eastern agricultural communities long before similar settlements showed up in southeastern Europe alongside the other traits associated with early farming. In short, many southeastern European cultural elements can be interpreted as extensions of Near Eastern Neolithic culture.

Neolithic lifeways transformed other parts of Europe somewhat later than in the Balkans, and the source of these changes has also generated debate. Beginning around 7,000 ya, farming village sites littered with linear-decorated pottery, or **Bandkeramik** (Fig. 14-15), appeared across central and (still later) northern regions of the continent (Bogucki, 1988). Bandkeramik culture farmers sought deep, well-drained **alluvial** and loess soils located along the Danube, the Rhine, and their tributaries. There they cultivated cereals and legumes, raised cattle and pigs, and collected wild hazelnuts (Whittle, 1985; Howell, 1987). Their settlements consisted of sturdy timber-framed structures averaging 100 feet long, with some up to 150 feet. These longhouses sheltered extended families and possibly served as barns for storing harvested crops or for harboring animals. Wooden fences barred livestock from planted fields during the growing season and then, following the harvest, confined them in the field so that their manure could restore soil nutrients. The fertility of loess soils could be maintained for relatively long periods with simple manuring and crop rotation, and fixed-plot farming on rich alluvium could sustain permanent settlements for up to 500 years (Whittle, 1985; Howell, 1987).

In Britain, archaeologists have tried to view Neolithic ideology and subsistence as somewhat independent phenomena and explain the transition to agriculture in largely ideological terms (e.g., Thomas, 1988; Edmonds, 1999). In this view, the fundamental shift in the subsistence economy from foraging to food production *followed* rather than preceded the kinds of ideological changes that archaeologists see reflected in Neolithic material culture and monuments. If supported by data, this argument would have considerable implications for our general understanding of the Neolithic, because it would explain the

Helmut Voss

Figure **14-15**

Bandkeramik vessel from Motzenstein, near Wattendorf, Germany.

Bandkeramik Literally, "lined pottery"; refers to a Neolithic ceramic ware widely encountered in central Europe and to the culture that produced it.

alluvial Deposited by streams, usually during flood stages.

Important European Sites and Regions

SITE	DATES (YA)	SIGNIFICANCE
Argissa and **Franchthi Cave** (Greece)	9,000	Early Neolithic farming settlements in Greece
Bandkeramik culture (central Europe)	ca. 7,000	Archaeological culture that contains the earliest Neolithic farming communities in central Europe

development of the British Neolithic as resulting more from cultural than natural factors. Regrettably, data for the Mesolithic-Neolithic transition in Britain, Ireland, and southern Scandinavia support the possibly less-surprising inference that while the transition to the Neolithic was rapid and probably traumatic, it was not primarily driven by ideological changes (Rowley-Conwy, 2004).

New World Farmers

While Old World Neolithic cultures generally relied on agricultural practices that linked domesticated cereal grasses together with herd animals, the farmers of the Americas focused almost exclusively on plant resources. Most of these plants had very limited ranges, but one important cereal grass—maize, or corn—came to dominate prehistoric Native American agriculture nearly everywhere it could be grown (Fig. 14-16).

Cereal grasses suitable for domestication were abundant on several continents, but the people of the Old World brought more of those species under control. Except for maize, whose wild ancestor may at first have been used in a different way, human cultural behavior in the New World did not induce the same genetic transformations in American grasses as it had in the Old World.

NEW WORLD DOMESTICATES

Considered together, the products of New World farmers make up a remarkable catalog of familiar plants. Besides maize, the list includes important staple foods like white potatoes, sweet potatoes, yams, **manioc**, many varieties of beans, peanuts, sunflowers, and **quinoa** (*Chenopodium* sp.). Nearly as important, but not staples, are domesticated vegetables and fruits including sweet peppers, chili peppers, tomatoes, squashes, and pumpkins, along with pineapples, papayas, avocados, guavas, and passion fruit. Vanilla and chocolate* came from American tree beans. Tobacco, coca, and peyote were major stimulants, and a host of other American plant domesticates had medicinal, utilitarian, or ornamental uses long before the arrival of the Europeans. The principal New World domesticates were developed in several locations in Mexico and in South America, but the use of a few of these plants eventually spread well beyond those regional centers of domestication.

Figure **14-16**

A sample of modern maize diversity. Maize benefits from a very large gene pool, which was by no means ignored by early Native American farmers.

manioc Cassava, a starchy edible root crop of the tropics.

quinoa (keen-wah´) Seed-bearing member of the genus *Chenopodium*, cultivated by early Peruvians.

---

*Although chocolate, or cacao, was not a major prehistoric food crop, it did play important social and ritual roles in Mesoamerica, both as a beverage and in solid form. Cacao use began in the Maya lowlands between 3,900 and 3,700 ya (Powis et al., 2007).

One domesticated plant, the bottle gourd (*Lagenaria siceraria*), appears to have had a much different origin than other New World domesticates. It was long suspected that the bottle gourd reached the New World by floating across the Atlantic Ocean from Africa, where it occurs in the wild, but genetic research shows that the closest relatives of the oldest New World specimens were from northeastern Asia. Based on AMS radiocarbon dates of gourd samples and analyses of DNA markers, the domesticated bottle gourd was present in the Americas by 10,000 ya and may have been carried from Asia by Paleo-Indian colonists (Erickson et al., 2005)!

Aside from the dog, which also accompanied the first humans into the New World, domesticated animals had a relatively minor role in the Americas, as we noted earlier (see p. 361). The llama and alpaca, both of which are long-haired relatives of the camel found in highland South America, were the only large domesticated species (Kent, 1987). Other domesticates—the guinea pig (raised for its meat, not as a pet) and Muscovy duck in western South America, turkeys in Mexico—were small in size and not very important beyond their localized distribution areas.

MEXICO

Of the more than 100 plant species fully domesticated by Native Americans, maize (a grass), beans (legumes), and squashes (cucurbits) ultimately attained the widest prehistoric significance for food purposes. Ancient use of this important set of crops has been documented in the states of **Oaxaca** and **Tamaulipas**, and especially in the **Tehuacán Valley** of Puebla, southeast of Mexico City. In the 1960s, archaeologist Richard MacNeish led an exemplary interdisciplinary study in this arid highland valley, where archaeology, botany, and paleoecology shed light on early phases of New World agriculture (Byers, 1967; MacNeish et al., 1972; MacNeish 1978).

The Tehuacán archaeological sites are especially important not because they could be a center of New World plant domestication, but because MacNeish's research yielded an excellent stratigraphic record of early human settlements in this dry valley. The early maize cobs and kernels excavated from Tehuacán sites represent an intermediate variety of maize that had developed elsewhere. In fact, the Tehuacán sites lie somewhat beyond the natural range of the variety of wild grass, **teosinte** (*Zea* sp.), that most archaeobotanists consider ancestral to maize (Beadle, 1980; Benz and Iltis, 1990; Piperno and Pearsall, 1998). Maize probably originated somewhere in the humid lowlands of southern or western Mexico. For example, researchers who analyzed soil cores pulled from the site of San Andrés, in the Gulf Coast state of Tabasco, recovered maize pollen dated to 7,100 ya in contexts that suggest that farmers were cultivating fields in the lowland rain forest more than a millennium before the earliest evidence of maize in the Mexican highlands (Pope et al., 2001).

Teosinte, which bears a few hard seed kernels on tiny spikelets growing from its multiple stalks, was probably just one of many wild plants that attracted local food collectors. Its young green seeds were sweet and edible, as were the tender stems; mature seeds could either be ground or popped like popcorn and eaten. To promote the growth of teosinte, people may have scattered its seeds, transplanted young stalks to favorable locations, or reduced competition from other less-desirable plants by burning or weeding. Doing so may have inadvertently altered the genetic makeup of the plants by allowing them to cross-pollinate with other varieties.

DNA studies suggest that very few genetic loci control the features that distinguish teosinte from domestic maize (Doebley, 1994). Mutation of teosinte produced a variant having softer, naked kernels arranged around a spike or cob and encased in a single papery husk. Further artificial (human-induced) selection favored these heritable genetic changes, which became "fixed" when people carried the new varieties beyond teosinte's natural range, possibly to regions like the Tehuacán Valley. So, in this way, New World farmers

Oaxaca (wah-ha´-kah) A southern Mexican state bordering the Pacific Ocean.

Tamaulipas (tah-mah-leep´-ahs) A Mexican state located on the Gulf Coast south of Texas.

Tehuacán Valley (tay-wah-kahn´) A dry highland region on the boundary of the states of Puebla and Oaxaca in southern Mexico.

teosinte (taeo-sin´-tae) A native grass of southern Mexico, believed to be ancestral to maize.

produced the first in a series of domesticated forms of maize, a cultigen having much larger, more numerous, and more easily collected and processed kernels; the plant also became dependent on human assistance for detaching and dispersing its seeds. Today's many varieties of maize make it one of the world's primary staples (see Fig. 14-16).

Other plants were coming under cultivation in southern Mexico around the same time, including several kinds of beans, squashes, gourds, chili peppers, avocados, and cactus fruit (Flannery, 1986; Smith, 1997). At least some of these plants also originated in the lowlands at some earlier time and at a considerable distance from their first recognized use at Tehuacán (Piperno and Pearsall, 1998). For example, domesticated seeds of pumpkin-like squashes excavated at Guilá Naquitz Cave in Oaxaca proved to be nearly 10,000 years old.

Modern nutritionists recognize that maize and beans contain complementary amino acids that, when eaten together, form a complete protein that can be synthesized effectively by the body, thereby reducing the nutritional need for meat. Eating only one or the other type of seed doesn't have this beneficial effect. In any case, these two American plants, in tandem, became more nutritionally important than others and may have encouraged some groups to take further steps toward full agriculture.

How quickly did people in places like Tehuacán come to rely on food production? Based on the archaeobotanical fragments preserved in the excavated caves, MacNeish (1964, 1967) concluded that even with the availability of domesticated maize, beans, and other plants, agricultural products only gradually came to contribute even one-third of the diet. By getting involved in horticulture, these food collectors at first probably reaped no significant increases in *productivity*. Still, they may have benefited from greater *predictability* by using the stored seeds or dried flesh of domesticates as nutrition sources in leaner times (Wills, 1989).

At a Glance

Important Mexican and South American Sites and Regions

SITE	DATES (YA)	SIGNIFICANCE
Tehuacán Valley (Mexico)	12,000–historic times	Valley in the state of Puebla, Mexico, that was the focus of a major 1960s archaeological field investigation of the origins of agriculture; project results include an excellent stratigraphic sequence of excavated early sites
San Andrés (Mexico)	7,100	Soil cores extracted from this site yielded maize pollen, which suggests that lowland farmers were cultivating fields in the rain forest more than 1,000 years before maize evidence is known from the highlands of Mexico
Guilá Naquitz (Mexico)	10,200–9,200	Small cave in Oaxaca occupied by 4–6 persons; early dated contexts for pumpkin-like squashes and maize cobs
Guitarrero Cave (Peru)	11,500–10,700?	Early evidence of cultivated plants in Andean South America
Paloma (Peru)	7,900–5,000	Coastal preceramic village mostly dependent on marine resources; planting of some crops, such as bottle gourds, squashes, and beans

The tiny maize cobs from Tehuacán, recently submitted to an improved ^{14}C technique, yield dates of only 4,700–4,500 ya, much later than the 7,000 years at first indicated by standard carbon dating (Fritz, 1994). Currently, the oldest-known maize cobs date to about 6,250 ya and are from Guilá Naquitz Cave in Oaxaca.

SOUTH AMERICA

Research into the history of domestication and agriculture in South America is in progress, with several major issues at question. First, what were the relative roles of marine resources and agricultural products throughout prehistory on the continent's west coast? Second, to what extent did Mexican crops, particularly maize, contribute to South American agriculture? Finally, what was the nature of Amazonian agriculture in eastern South America?

Sites in southwestern Ecuador have yielded squash and gourd (cucurbit) phytoliths that date to 12,000–10,000 ya. Their large size suggests they're from domesticated plants; if this is true, it means that the beginnings of food production in lowland South America began about the same time as in Mesoamerica, and maybe even earlier (Piperno and Stothert, 2003).

Sediment cores and other geomorphological evidence indicate that the periodic climatic phenomenon known as **El Niño** became established between 7,000 and 5,000 ya in the Pacific (Sandweiss et al., 1996). El Niño events are triggered when a persistent trough of atmospheric low pressure forces warm equatorial waters southward along South America's west coast, partially displacing the northward flow of deep cold currents. El Niño typically disrupts the maritime food chain and dramatically disturbs precipitation patterns over land, bringing excess rainfall and flooding to some areas, drought to others. El Niño returns every four years or so, on average, and some episodes are more severe or last longer than others.

Early farming in coastal Peru seems somewhat related to the El Niño pattern (Piperno and Pearsall, 1998). At Paloma (Fig. 14-17), a short distance south of present-day Lima, summer fishing expeditions had extended into year-round reliance on large and small fish species, shellfish, sea mammals, turtles, and seabirds. Midden contents, analyses of coprolites, and high strontium levels in human skeletons confirm the nearly exclusive role of sea resources by 5,000 ya (Moseley, 1992). The fishers also began experimenting with nonlocal plant crops, using bottle gourds for carrying water and adding several kinds of squashes and beans to their diet. By about 4,500 ya, they had taken up small-scale horticulture in nearby river valleys, growing cotton for nets and cloth and, significantly, supplementing their predominantly seafood diet with at least 10 more edible plants. While they maintained their basic maritime focus for centuries to come, coastal Peruvians may have decided that a greater variety of foods helped to minimize the periodic shortfalls in sea resources that they could expect with most El Niño events every few years.

The intercontinental dispersal or exchange of American cultigens is a topic of active archaeobotanical research and debate (Piperno and Pearsall, 1998; Smith, 1999). Maize may have reached coastal South America not long after being domesticated in southern Mexico (see Fig. 14-17). Preserved botanical elements, maize motifs on pottery, and even the impression of a kernel in the wall of a fired clay vessel, as well as an increase in grinding stones and human dental caries, attest to the early presence of maize in this region. Maize eventually became a significant food source for all the native cultures of western South America. Sixteenth-century Spanish chroniclers noted that many different varieties of maize accommodated Peru's demanding climatic and topographical diversity from sea level to 6,500 feet, with potatoes taking over at higher elevations. Each of these varieties, developed through careful selection and hybridization, probably derived from a common ancestral form of Mexican maize.

Plant cultivation was under way in a few highland areas of South America before 8,500 ya. Nonfood species useful for fiber, containers, tool shafts, bedding, and medicines were tended even more often than edible plants around Guitarrero Cave (see Fig. 14-17)

El Niño Periodic climatic instability, related to temporary warming of Pacific Ocean waters, which may influence storm patterns and precipitation for several years.

Figure **14-17**

Early farming in the Americas.

in the Andes Mountains (Lynch, 1980). Native tree fruits, broad lima beans, small-seeded quinoa, and several starchy tubers were among the local food crops grown there (Lynch, 1980, 1983). One of these ancient root crops was the white potato, and when eventually adopted into Old World agriculture and cuisine, it became today's familiar baked potato, Dutch *frites met*, and Indian *alu masala*.

Other native South American cultigens were developed in the tropical forests on the eastern slopes of the Andes or in the humid Amazon basin to the east. Roots of manioc shrubs and sweet potatoes became dietary staples in the eastern lowlands, supplying abundant carbohydrate energy, but little else. Peanuts added some protein and fats to the starchy diet, but fish and insects remained essential food resources for most of the natives of Amazonia, since their small gardens alone generally couldn't sustain them entirely.

SOUTHWESTERN UNITED STATES

Maize, beans, and squash seeds up to 3,000 years old are preserved on several Archaic sites in the southwestern United States (Simmons, 1986; Tagg, 1996). Introduced to the region possibly much earlier by farmers expanding northward in search of suitable planting areas, these domesticates came under increasing selection pressure as societies ever farther from the southern Mexican source area adopted them. Climatic conditions associated with higher latitudes and elevations shortened the growing season for these Mexican imports and thus slowed or limited agricultural expansion in some regions.

The maize-beans-squash crop complex gradually gained precedence over hunting and gathering in the American Southwest. Between 2,300 and 1,300 ya, reliance on these domesticated products promoted increased population density and overall cultural elaboration, resulting in the emergence of several distinctive prehistoric cultural traditions in the Southwest (Fig. 14-18). Archaeologists distinguish each of these regional traditions based on such features as pottery styles, architecture, religious ideas, and sociopolitical organization (Plog, 1997).

The **Hohokam** of southern Arizona were growing both food and cotton by 1,500 ya and possibly much earlier, irrigating their gardens through an extensive system of hand-dug channels that conveyed water from the Gila River or its tributaries. By around 1,000 ya, architecture and artifacts on large Hohokam sites, such as Las Colinas and Snaketown, near Phoenix, reveal links to Mexican centers of domestication and culture. They include ball courts and platform mounds as well as copper bells, parrot feathers, and other Mesoamerican products (Haury, 1976). The Hohokam crafted human figurines and shell and turquoise ornaments in sufficient quantities for trade (Crown, 1991). The Casas Grandes district of northern Chihuahua, Mexico, may have served as a major exchange corridor between Mesoamerica and the Southwest (DiPeso, 1974). But whether the Hohokam maintained direct contact with Mexican civilizations or simply participated in the diffusion of ideas and products passed along trade routes is a matter for debate.

The **Mogollon**, whose prehistoric culture straddled southern New Mexico and Arizona, lived in pit houses until about A.D.1000. Around that time, they began constructing aboveground room blocks and—in imitation of their northern neighbors—creating

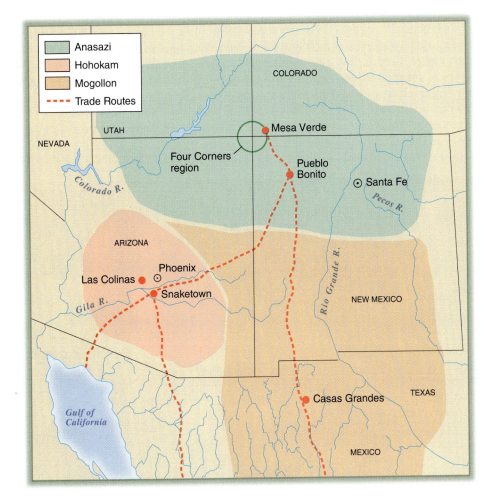

Figure 14-18

Village farming cultures of the American Southwest, showing trade routes (red) and sites mentioned in the text.

Hohokam (ho-ho-kahm´) Prehistoric farming culture of southern Arizona.

Mogollon (mo-go-yohn´) Prehistoric village culture of northern Mexico and southern Arizona/New Mexico.

U.S. National Park Service

Figure 14-19

Pueblo Bonito is the largest prehistoric structure in Chaco Canyon National Historic Park, New Mexico. Its 650 rooms cover nearly 2 acres.

boldly painted black-on-white pottery. Archaeological traces of the Mogollon faded a century or more before Europeans arrived in the mid-1500s, possibly as its people drifted southward into Mexico.

In the Four Corners region to the north, prehistoric farmers known to archaeologists as the **Anasazi** built impressive prehistoric masonry villages and towns, called **pueblos**, beginning around A.D. 900. With their large scale, picturesque settings, and excellent preservation, some Anasazi sites—including Chaco Canyon (Fig. 14-19), New Mexico, and the so-called cliff dwellings of Mesa Verde (Fig. 14-20), Colorado—are among the most famous archaeological locations in the United States. Anasazi towns consisted of multiroom, multistory residential and storage structures and usually included underground ceremonial chambers, called **kivas**. Their compact sites were situated with good access to the limited agricultural lands and scarce water supply of this high and arid region.

The rise of the Chaco Canyon towns and related villages was probably stimulated by a brief period of increased rainfall and sustained by social factors such as political or religious ideology, trade, and regional strife. A growing body of evidence also points to Chaco-era warfare and terrorism among the Anasazi, extending even to cannibalism (White, 1992; Turner and Turner, 1999). Beginning in the mid-1100s, the Anasazi abandoned Chaco and, eventually, most of the region's other large pueblos. By then, shifting precipitation patterns associated with a general warming period were leaving marginal zones of the Southwest, especially the Colorado Plateau, without adequate rainfall to grow maize (Cordell, 1998). As the drought worsened through the late 1200s, Anasazi townspeople persisted in a few places like Mesa Verde (see Fig. 14-20), where they built their communities into easily defended niches in the steep cliffs and tilled their fields on the canyon rim by day. By A.D. 1300, even Mesa Verde stood empty; the Anasazi of the Four Corners had dispersed toward the south and southeast to become the people known today as Hopi, Zuni, and the Rio Grande Puebloans.

Figure 14-20

Cliff Palace was the largest of the pueblos built by Anasazi farmers living at Mesa Verde, Colorado, about 800 ya.

Anasazi (an-ah-saw´-zee) Ancient culture of the southwestern United States, associated with preserved cliff dwellings and masonry pueblo sites.

pueblos Spanish for "town"; multiroom residence structures built by village farmers in the American Southwest; when spelled with an uppercase P, the several cultures that built and lived in such villages.

kivas Underground chambers or rooms used for gatherings and ceremonies by pueblo dwellers.

William Turnbaugh

At a Glance

Important North American Sites and Regions

SITE	DATES (YA)	SIGNIFICANCE
Las Colinas and **Snaketown** (Arizona)	1,000	Hohokam sites in the American Southwest that show ties to Mexican civilizations and centers of domestication
Chaco Canyon (New Mexico)	1,150–750	Region that contains several important Anasazi sites, many of which are characterized by monumental public and ceremonial architecture; now part of the Chaco Culture National Historical Park
Pueblo Bonito (New Mexico)	1050–825	This multistory building comprised approximately 600 rooms and was the primary town of Chaco Canyon
Mesa Verde (Colorado)	1,400–700	Anasazi sites, most widely known for their well-preserved "cliff dwellings"; forms Mesa Verde National Park
Cahokia (Illinois)	1,200–600	Large Mississippian town in the American Bottom region of west-central Illinois; Monks Mound is the largest prehistoric earthwork in the United States and Canada

EASTERN NORTH AMERICA

In eastern North America, aboriginal peoples developed an independent center of domestication and cultivation. Small gourds, apparently native to the region and not derived from Mesoamerican species, were widely cultivated by Archaic hunter-gatherers more than 5,000 ya, probably for use as containers and fishing-net floats rather than food (Fritz, 1999). Several other local plants—marsh elder (sumpweed), sunflower, and goosefoot— are associated with ancient campsites and shell heaps along major river valleys, where, about 3,000 ya, people maintained "incidental gardens" of plants selected to complement rather than replace foraging activities (Smith, 1992, 1999). In the next millennium, several more native species, such as knotweed, maygrass, and little barley, were added to the inventory. Stone hoes also began to appear on sites in the Illinois River valley at about the same time (Odell, 1998).

It wasn't easy to harvest and process these weedy, small-seeded species, so they probably weren't much more than supplements to a diet of wild foods. Still, the river valleys of the Southeast and the Midwest as well as the rich forests covering much of the Northeast clearly supported large, successful communities even without maize agriculture. For example, the widespread practice of mound building and associated death and burial rituals began long before any reliance on maize. As we've seen, Late Archaic hunter-gatherers constructed mounds that, like those at Poverty Point, Louisiana (see Chapter 13), were considerably more than mere stacks of dirt.

It's not until after 1,200 ya in the Southeast and around 800 ya in the Northeast that we begin to see archaeological evidence of a widespread economic commitment to agriculture, possibly brought about by new varieties of maize and the introduction of domesticated beans (Smith, 1992; Hart and Scarry, 1999). Even then, wild nuts, seeds, fish, and game were staples in the diets of many groups. In the broad river valleys of the Southeast, maize farming was the economic mainstay of **Mississippian** chiefdoms (Fig. 14-21). Mississippian

Mississippian Referring to late prehistoric chiefdoms of the southeastern United States and southern Midwest between roughly 1,100 and 300 ya.

Figure **14-21**

Flint hoe blade used by Mississippian farmers.

elites relied on elaborate rituals and displays of valued symbols to enhance their privileged positions. Populations and ceremonial centers throughout the region were linked by exchanges of symbolic copper, shell, pottery, and stone items, as well as a common focus on the construction of towns centered on impressive earthen-mound groups that flanked public spaces or plazas (Lewis and Stout, 1998; Emerson and Lewis, 2000). Most buildings that flanked the plazas were erected on substructure or platform mounds. Some of these buildings were dwellings; others were **charnel houses** and other community structures. The houses and workplaces of the town's rank and file clustered around these mound-and-plaza complexes (Fig. 14-22).

The Mississippian site of Cahokia, located below the junction of the Missouri and Mississippi rivers near St. Louis, once boasted some 120 mounds (Milner, 1998; Pauketat and Wright, 2004). The primary earthwork was Monks Mound (Fig. 14-23), as long as three football fields and as high as a six-story building—the largest prehistoric structure north of Mexico. Cahokia's homes and garden plots spread over 6 square miles beyond the log stockade that enclosed the central mounds and elite living area. Fields of maize, squash, and pumpkins extending along the river floodplain provided the harvest sheltered in many storage pits and granaries (Iseminger, 1996).

OTHER NEW WORLD REGIONS

Elsewhere in the Americas, farming hadn't gained much importance even by the time Europeans were arriving with their own ways of life and their Old World domesticates (Brown, 1994). In fact, throughout much of the far West, the far North, and most of South America, hunting, fishing, and gathering were still the principal ways of making a living. These lifeways persisted in part because the more productive American domesticates, those native to warm temperate zones, couldn't be introduced and maintained in other geographical settings without sustained effort. Even so, it wasn't always a question of whether farming was possible; it was often a matter of choice. Maize was far from an ideal crop, even where it could be grown most readily. Old World domesticated cereal grasses, including wheat, barley, oat, rye, millet, and rice, grew in dense stands that farmers could harvest readily with a sickle and clean by threshing and winnowing. Maize, the primary New World cereal grass, required more space per plant and more moisture during its long growing season, and it was much harder to harvest and process by hand.

Figure **14-22**

Reconstructed Mississippian village huts at Angel Mounds State Historic Site, near Evansville, Indiana.

charnel houses Buildings that hold the bones or bodies of the dead.

Hannah Lewis

Figure **14-23**

Monks Mound at Cahokia Mounds State Historic Site, near Collinsville, Illinois. Built in late prehistoric times, it is about 1,000 feet long and 100 feet high.

What's more, these agricultural products could seldom beat the nutritional value of a mixed diet obtained through foraging. Maize itself is deficient in lysine (an amino acid) and niacin and contains a chemical that may promote iron-deficiency anemia. Similarly, in the Amazon basin in South America, the peoples who domesticated manioc, sweet potatoes, and other starchy root crops before 1,500 ya found that these foods supplied bulk and carbohydrates, but little protein—a deficiency the people of the Amazon overcame by continuing to rely on hunting, fishing, and gathering.

Biocultural Consequences of Food Production

Domestication and agriculture were the driving forces of the Neolithic revolution, but we've seen that the impact of Neolithic lifeways went far beyond subsistence. Looking back, we can see that humans have reaped tremendous benefits and paid significant costs for the spread of food production; opinions differ regarding which is greater. The physiologist and popular writer Jared Diamond (1987) bluntly refers to agriculture as "the worst mistake in the history of the human race." At the other extreme, Paul Colinvaux (1979), an eminent ecologist, expresses the same glowing perspective as the archaeologist Graeme Barker (see p. 356) and calls it the "most momentous event in the history of life." In the following sections, we'll examine some of the reasoning behind such statements.

POPULATION DENSITY AND PERMANENT SETTLEMENTS

Some researchers theorize that population growth initiated the agricultural response; others see it happening the other way around. But there's no question that population size and density both tended to increase as farming activities produced larger and more predictable yields. People clustered into permanent villages and towns surrounded by fields and pastures. Sedentary living (which in many cases began *before* agriculture) permitted closer birth spacing, since mothers no longer carried infants from site to site, and the availability of soft cereals for infant food allowed for earlier weaning. Potentially, therefore, a woman might bear more children. It's not surprising that even very early

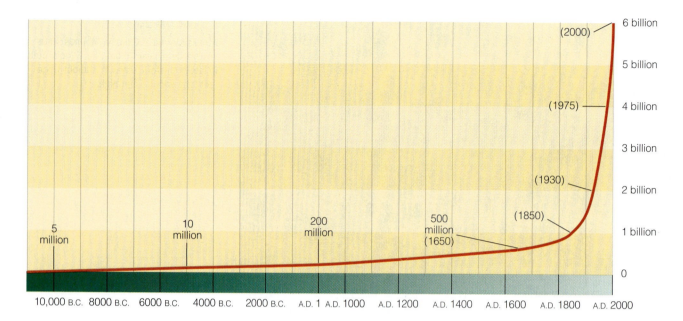

6 billion (2000)
5 billion
4 billion (1975)
3 billion
2 billion (1930)
1 billion (1850)
0

5 million
10 million
200 million
500 million (1650)
(1850)
(1930)

10,000 B.C. 8000 B.C. 6000 B.C. 4000 B.C. 2000 B.C. A.D. 1 A.D. 1000 A.D. 1200 A.D. 1400 A.D. 1600 A.D. 1800 A.D. 2000

Figure **14-24**

World population growth.

Neolithic settlements—such as Jericho in the Jordan River valley and Çatalhöyük in Turkey—quickly reached considerable size. Today's world population, sustained largely by the same set of Neolithic domesticates, has attained 6 billion people and shows no signs of slowing (Fig. 14-24). Such an extraordinary growth in human population would have been impossible without agriculture. But from a quick glance at Figure 14-24, it's clear that population growth rates of this magnitude are not sustainable over the long run.

TECHNOLOGIES

Changes in material culture accompanied food production and the development of permanent settlements. For example, farmers everywhere soon replaced most of their basketry and skin containers with bulkier but more versatile ceramic vessels. Their pottery (see Fig. 14-15) made simmering and boiling more practical, more easily converting grains to digestible foods. They used looms to weave cloth from the wool and plant fibers that replaced wild animal skins; still, where durability was required, as in grinding slabs and axe heads, stone persisted for a time as the material of choice.

The traditional view is that as harvests increased, some food-producing communities could support and in turn benefit from nonfarmers who engaged in specialized crafts, exchanging the products of their skill for food grown by others. So, for example, the use of copper in the Near East expanded once people could devote the necessary effort to refining and processing the ore into various metal implements and ornaments. While we've learned that it's quite a bit more complicated than that, it's still true that specialization encouraged a proliferation of new inventions that simply wouldn't have been sustainable in most hunter-gatherer communities.

ECONOMIC AND SOCIAL RELATIONS

Now and then, whether intentionally, by chance, or through coercion, farmers had surpluses in the form of stored grain or herds of animals at the end of the year. They could use these products to level out shortages in following seasons. Often, excess production served as a kind of capital, or wealth, that fostered new socioeconomic transactions. Thus, in Mesopotamia, barter and exchange flourished, as did credit, or lending against future productivity. (A need for accurate accounts also inspired early Mesopotamian writing in the form of symbols pressed into clay tablets.)

As agricultural techniques and resulting harvests improved, other segments of the population were relieved of the obligation of producing food and came to fill specialized roles as priests, merchants, crafters, administrators, and the like. A social and economic hierarchy of productive peasants, nonfarming specialists of many kinds, and a tiny but dominant elite emerged in a few Neolithic state societies, or civilizations (see Chapter 15).

ENVIRONMENTAL CHANGES

Unlike hunter-gatherers, who extracted their livelihood from the available natural resources, Neolithic farmers altered the environment by substituting their own domesticated plants and animals for native species. We aren't implying that all hunter-gatherers had been conservationists; many clearly weren't, but their numbers were few, their tools simple, and their needs relatively modest. On the other hand, Neolithic plowing, terracing, cutting of forests, draining of wetlands, and animal grazing contributed to severe soil erosion and the decline of many natural species (Fig. 14-25). Moreover, many of these practices encouraged the growth of weeds and created fresh habitats for crop-damaging insects, malaria-bearing mosquitoes, and other pests.

Intensive agriculture depletes soil nutrients, especially potassium. In the lower Tigris-Euphrates Valley, high levels of soluble salts carried by irrigation waters slowly poisoned the fields once farmed by Ubaidians and Sumerians. In North Africa, Neolithic herders allowed their animals to overgraze the fragile Sahara grasslands, furthering the development of the world's largest desert. These early farming practices left many areas so damaged that they remained unproductive for thousands of years, until they could begin to be reclaimed with the aid of modern technology. Unfortunately, comparable processes—such as burning forests for grazing lands—continue at an accelerated pace today.

ENVIRONMENTAL DIVERSITY

Some hunter-gatherers selected from hundreds of wild species for food and other purposes as they moved from camp to camp throughout the year. The strategy of most Neolithic societies was different, emphasizing only a few domesticated crops and animal species. Through selective breeding practices, people tried to enhance the traits they valued—thicker wool or body fat, greater milk production, more and larger seeds, and so

Figure 14-25

The Inka terraces, in Peru, required intensive effort to modify mountain land for farming.

Katherine Pomonis

forth—while strictly limiting random variability. These experiments resulted in genetically similar strains.

Today, the earth's human population still relies for food primarily on the seeds of just a half dozen grasses (wheat, barley, oats, rice, millet, maize), several root crops (potatoes, yams, manioc), and a few domesticated fowl and mammals (in addition to fish). Because of their relative genetic similarity, these domesticated species are susceptible to disease, drought, and pests. Agricultural scientists are trying to prevent potential disaster by reestablishing some genetic diversity in these plants and animals through the controlled introduction of heterogeneous (usually "wild") strains. A few farmers have realized the benefits of multicropping—interspersing different kinds of crops in a single agricultural plot. Combining grains, root crops, fruit trees, herbs, and plants used for fiber or tools mimics the natural species diversity and reduces soil depletion and insect infestation.

SCIENCE AND RELIGION

Prescribed rites, sanctions, and shrines ensured bountiful harvests and other supernatural blessings for Neolithic farmers. Hunter-gatherers certainly did not ignore the supernatural realm, but because of differences in population size and organization, farmers tended to make more impressive, permanent monuments to their beliefs and sometimes gave practitioners the opportunity to engage full-time in religious specialties. In some cultures, sciences such as astronomy, mathematics, and metallurgy developed early because they had many ritual and practical applications.

CULTURAL COMPETITION AND CHANGE

Neolithic societies were often on a collision course with their nonfarming neighbors. Expanding agriculturalists displaced hunter-gatherers or even eradicated them altogether because of direct competition for suitable land or due to habitat changes brought on by farming activities. Some food producers involved their nonfarming neighbors in exchange networks, trading surplus products of agriculture, animal husbandry, or new technology for raw materials, wild produce, and even slaves (Gregg, 1988). In time, farmers came to prevail almost everywhere, except in those marginal areas where agriculture or herding was impractical. And even those regions came under siege as modern food-producing and industrialized societies competed for land and other resources in the diminished domains left to hunter-gatherers. Today, few groups survive primarily by hunting and gathering. For others, fishing remains a viable option to farming.

HEALTH CONSEQUENCES

As with other biocultural aspects relating to the development of food production, the effects on human health were a mixed bag of benefits and costs. Working closely with archaeologists, physical anthropologists who study human skeletal remains have been particularly interested in evaluating how patterns of health and disease changed among early agriculturalists as compared to hunter-gatherers. These researchers who specialize in the closely related subfields of paleopathology and bioarchaeology (see Chapter 1, pp. 9–10, 13) have had much to say about this topic (Cohen and Armelagos, 1984; Cohen, 1989; Larsen, 1995, 1997).

It's easy to see why. First, as early agricultural groups became more sedentary and larger in size, they buried their dead in increasingly larger cemeteries than was generally the case for hunter-gatherers. Paleopathologists thus have many more skeletons from agricultural populations to study than they have for the vast majority of hunter-gatherer groups; and with more skeletons to analyze, they obviously have more opportunity to find some individuals with evidence of disease. Second, as farming villages and towns grew larger, *infectious disease* became a much more serious factor (see Chapter 4, pp. 94–97).

As you know, infectious diseases can cause epidemics, some small, some catastrophic—for example, the Black Death of the Middle Ages or the worldwide influenza epidemic of 1918. They can potentially kill thousands or even millions of people. Because hunter-gatherer populations generally were small and not sedentary, the "reservoir" of human hosts for harmful viruses and bacteria wasn't sufficient to sustain itself in such groups long-term.

Using skeletal indicators of health, such as stature, tooth enamel defects, and bone changes resulting from anemia, many bioarchaeological studies have shown that general health quality declined for many people with the development of agriculture (Cohen and Armelagos, 1984; Steckel and Rose, 2002). Nevertheless, even with greater exposure to disease pathogens and other health risks associated with living in denser populations, the health picture for early farmers wasn't entirely bleak. After all, it's ultimately our success as a species (that is, more people) that helped infectious pathogens to be more successful. The advent of farming was just one component of humankind's success.

We must also acknowledge that the lives of hunter-gatherers weren't easy or disease-free by any means. Hunter-gatherers suffered periodic food shortages that could end in starvation, traumatic injuries, and certainly some infectious diseases (even if there were no major epidemics). New mothers could die from bacterial infections following childbirth. The infections that accompanied cuts or broken bones that penetrated the skin also killed many people. And both farmers and hunter-gatherers suffered high infant mortality rates (Acsadi and Nemeskeri, 1970). Regrettably, many still do.

If many new mothers and infants died so often both before and after the agricultural transition, then how is it that population size grew among early food producers? The answer is simple: With more predictable food sources, women could wean their children earlier and reduce the amount of time between births. A woman could thus bear more offspring, and this fact alone meant that overall, more children survived to adulthood. For most of hominin history, our ancestors' reproductive capacity wasn't much different from that of our ape cousins. A woman who gave birth every three or four years was probably typical of hominins up to just a few thousand years ago. With food production and the ability to stay in one place, human populations began to expand—a trend that continues today in most of the world.

If it seems paradoxical that average health was declining among food producers at the same time that populations were expanding, that's because it is. As one researcher has commented, "Yet, although humans became physically worse-off in marked respects, they also became more numerous. The agricultural age made possible far denser populations, but less healthy ones than ever before. Historians, anthropologists, and others concerned with this apparent paradox are still exploring its implications in detail" (Curtin, 2002, p. 606).

As we mentioned earlier, probably the greatest new challenge faced by sedentary food producers came from increased risk of infectious disease. One major contributor to heightened disease exposure came from close proximity of humans to domestic animals. Many pathogens—including viruses, bacteria, and intestinal parasites—can be transferred from nonhuman animals to humans. Diseases that can be transmitted to humans by other vertebrates, particularly mammals and birds, are called **zoonoses**. For example, influenza can be transmitted to humans by pigs or poultry.

Early farmers who grew crops and tended herds in ancient Mesopotamia, China, the Indus Valley, and elsewhere in the Old World (but not to the same degree in the New World, where animal domestication was little practiced) faced many dangerous health challenges. We noted in Chapter 3 how human cultural modifications with slash-and-burn agriculture produced a more conducive environment for the spread of malaria.

zoonoses (*sing.*, zoonosis) Diseases that can be transmitted to humans from other vertebrates.

Another major human disease likely stimulated by the activities of food producers is tuberculosis. The origin of tuberculosis in humans isn't completely understood, but we do know that several wild animals harbor a form of the disease; it's seen in bison, moose, elk, deer, and domestic cattle. The tuberculosis variant called *bovine tuberculosis* can be transmitted from the animal host to a human through ingestion of infected meat or milk. Clearly, with the domestication of cattle—which, as we've shown, occurred in the Middle East by 8,000 ya— humans had much greater exposure to bovine tuberculosis, and their exposure increased even more with the development of dairying (Sherratt, 1981). In its later stages, tuberculosis can produce distinctive skeletal changes, especially of the spine (see Figure 1-8b, p. 9). The earliest evidence of such skeletal involvement comes from Italy and is dated to nearly 7,500 ya (Roberts and Buikstra, 2003).

Tuberculosis in humans has evolved over the last six millennia; in fact, today most infected humans carry a related variety of pulmonary tuberculosis that can spread from person to person. The relationship of bovine tuberculosis to pulmonary tuberculosis isn't clearly understood, but the pulmonary form may have evolved from the bovine one. What's more, this transformation seems to have occurred only *after* humans became agriculturalists.

Several other significant human diseases are associated with sedentism and increasing population size and density. Measles, for example, has been shown to require a very large population pool—in the thousands—to sustain itself long-term (Cohen, 1989). So, measles can be viewed as a condition that became prevalent only with the emergence of larger urban centers, making it a "disease of civilization." Likewise, cholera is most commonly found in urban contexts, where large numbers of people share a common (and contaminated) water source.

LOOKING AT THE BIG PICTURE

In this chapter, we've reviewed what may be the most important cultural and ecological transition the human species ever experienced. In those areas where food production was adopted, it transformed human subsistence, technology, society, habitation patterns, relationships with other species, and much more. Eventually, these changes spread to the entire inhabitable portion of the world, and the effects have been momentous. In fact, there's basically nothing recognizable in our cultural world today that would exist without the transformation to food production just a few thousand years ago. Keep in mind that in the larger picture of human prehistory—and even more so, considering the immense span of hominin evolution—this is but a flicker of time.

Some people, even some scientists, claim that the costs of these changes outweigh the benefits. Others feel just as strongly that the opposite is true. We've discussed some of the costs and benefits, especially those relating to overall human health. However, regardless of the perspective you take, there's no going back; the world we live in would be impossible without the remarkable contributions first made possible by the adoption of agriculture. Obviously, without efficient and widespread food production, most of us wouldn't be here at all. There would be no cities, no art, no educational institutions, no writing, no books—meaning, of course, no textbooks and exams either. And there are all the amazing innovations from the last few centuries from which many people have benefited, including a doubling of average life span, mass transportation, high-tech communication and entertainment, and a diverse and easily obtainable assortment of foods, clothing, and shelter.

Our point is simply that there's little to be gained by taking extreme views regarding what costs our ancestors paid to produce the modern world we have inherited. It would seem a more useful goal to discuss where we choose to go. While the benefits we've been provided are undeniable, our species' remarkable success now is at a point where many people think that continuing down the same road will prove catastrophic.

Summary

In this chapter, we've examined the record of plant and animal domestication and the origin of early agricultural societies. Archaeological excavations, along with refined dating methods and the analytical techniques of archaeobotany and archaeozoology, have yielded a wealth of comparative data on Neolithic cultures in several regions of the globe. Even so, the answers to ultimate questions about how and why domestication and agriculture developed remain elusive.

The invention and widespread adoption of agriculture occurred within the past 12,000 years, during the early to middle Holocene. This so-called Neolithic revolution represents a major force in human biocultural evolution. As a species, our biology and our cultural behavior are inextricably linked. For example, many of the cultural activities associated with agriculture have actually stimulated further biological changes, such as the spread of the sickle-cell allele as an adaptive response to malaria, a disease harbored in tropical environments disturbed by farmers (see pp. 77–78).

With the ability to produce food and support larger populations, the pace of human affairs dramatically quickened in the social, political, and economic realms as well. One consequence of relying on agriculture was a society's basic need for large tracts of productive cropland and adequate water supplies. Maintaining access to these essential resources was critical to a farming culture's survival. Certainly, the primary functions of any Neolithic society, large or small, were securing land and water and supporting the vital agricultural process itself.

In a few areas of the world, the emergence of large-scale, complex societies followed quickly on the heels of the Neolithic revolution. In Chapter 15, we'll consider the development and course of early civilizations founded on Neolithic food-producing economies in the Old World and in the Americas.

In the What's Important feature on page 386, you'll find a useful summary of the most important archaeological sites discussed in this chapter.

Critical Thinking Questions

1. What are the most important differences between the environmental and cultural approaches to explaining why farming began? Your answer should include the basic assumptions, strengths, and weaknesses of each approach.
2. Based on your reading of this chapter as well as other materials outside of class, what are the three most important consequences, both good and bad, of the shift from foraging to food production for our species? Why are these consequences important? Compare your list with that of your classmates and discuss the differences.
3. What kinds of evidence from the archaeological record do researchers use as indicators or measures of the extent of plant or animal domestication?

What's Important The Most Significant Archaeological Sites Discussed in This Chapter

Location	Site	Dates (ya)	The Big Picture
Old World	**Mehrgarh** (Pakistan)	8,000–6,000	Early Neolithic community in South Asia that depended on domesticated plants and animals; represents a transition from seminomadic herding to sedentary villages and towns
	Jericho (West Bank)	<11,000–3,500	One of the early sedentary communities founded in the Levant; Jericho began in Natufian times and was occupied throughout the Neolithic
New World	**Las Colinas** and **Snaketown** (Arizona)	1,000	Hohokam sites in the American Southwest that show ties to Mexican civilizations and centers of domestication
	Chaco Canyon (New Mexico)	1,150–750	Region that contains several important Anasazi sites, many of them characterized by monumental public and ceremonial architecture; now part of the Chaco Culture National Historical Park
	Cahokia (Illinois)	1,200–600	Large Mississippian town in the American Bottom region of west-central Illinois; Monks Mound is the largest prehistoric earthwork in the United States and Canada
	Mesa Verde (Colorado)	1,400–700	Anasazi sites, most widely known for their well-preserved "cliff dwellings"; forms Mesa Verde National Park
	San Andrés (Mexico)	7,100	Soil cores extracted from this site yielded maize pollen, which suggests that lowland farmers were cultivating fields in the rain forest more than 1,000 years before maize evidence is known from the highlands of Mexico
	Paloma (Peru)	7,900–5,000	Coastal preceramic village mostly dependent on marine resources; planting of some crops, such as bottle gourds, squashes, and beans
	Guilá Naquitz (Mexico)	10,200–9,200	Small cave in Oaxaca occupied by 4–6 persons; early dated contexts for pumpkin-like squashes and maize cobs
	Guitarrero Cave (Peru)	10,200–9,200	Early evidence of cultivated plants in Andean South America
	Tehuacán Valley (Mexico)	12,000–historic times	Valley in the state of Puebla, Mexico, that was the focus of a major 1960s archaeological field investigation of the origins of agriculture; project results include an excellent stratigraphic sequence of excavated early sites

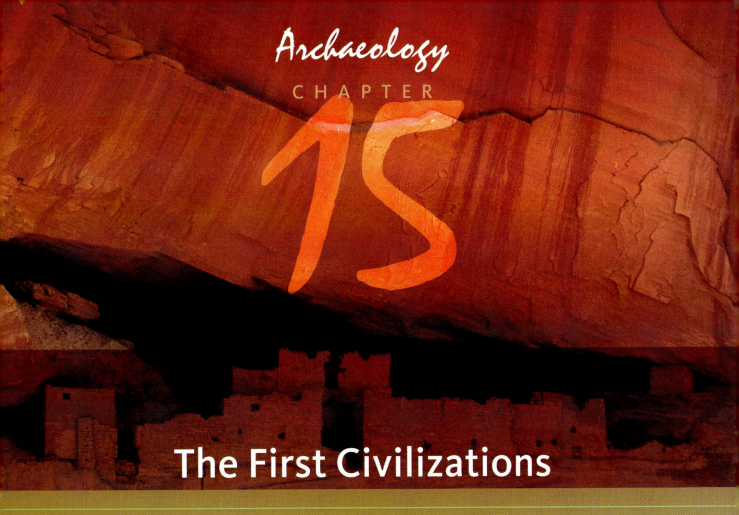

Archaeology

The First Civilizations

OUTLINE

Focus Questions

Why did the earliest civilizations develop?

What roles did cities play in these developments? Were cities essential to the emergence of all early civilizations?

 Click!

Go to the following media for interactive activities and exercises on topics covered in this chapter:

- Online Virtual Laboratories for Physical Anthropology, Version 4.0
- Genetics in Anthropology: Principles and Applications CD-ROM, Version 2.0
- Hominid Fossils: An Interactive Atlas CD-ROM

Introduction

The ruins of the city of Vijayanagara lie strewn along the banks of the Tungabhadra River in South India (Fig. 15-1). As you walk south from the river, you're seldom out of sight of broken granite pillars and the shattered foundations of palaces, temples, and courtyards in fertile valleys surrounded by hills that look like great jumbles of boulders. Founded in the early fourteenth century and destroyed about two centuries later, Vijayanagara had a fairly short life as cities go, but by all accounts, it was an extraordinary place (Fritz and Michell, 2003). With a sixteenth-century population estimated at 500,000 (or about 2½ times the estimated population of London in 1600), the city covered roughly 10.5 square miles. It was the capital of an empire that included other states, both large and small, across South India. Following the defeat of its armies in A.D. 1565, Vijayanagara was destroyed, its buildings burned, blown apart, or pulled down with the aid of elephants; its citizens were scattered, its riches looted. The remnants of the empire limped along for another century or so, but never recovered their former strength (Stein, 1994).

The Vijayanagara ruins are now a UNESCO World Heritage site. Where once there were picturesque buildings, crowded markets, busy city streets, royal pageantry, and the scent of roses, there are now tour buses, shepherds, security guards, thorn bushes, and the occasional leopard that snatches puppies for late-night snacks. Vijayanagara lives mostly in stories told to small children in villages across South India about such rulers as Krishnadevaraya and their dynasties, their might, and the great events they caused.

Vijayanagara exemplifies three interrelated concepts that are central to this chapter—cities, states, and civilizations, the earliest instances of which can be identified

Figure **15-1**

Ruins of royal buildings in the urban core of the late medieval city of Vijayanagara, in Karnataka, India.

Barry Lewis

in the archaeological record after the emergence of true agriculture thousands of years ago. Such developments marked the beginning of history in many parts of the world and laid the foundation for the modern era. By about 5,500 ya, several agricultural societies in both the Old and New Worlds were transforming themselves into states and civilizations.

Civilizations in Perspective

The term **civilization** is not, as many people think, just another word for culture or society, nor is it the same thing as a city or a state. In this section, we'll clarify our use of the terms *city, state*, and *civilization* before discussing theoretical perspectives on their origins and describing some archaeological examples.

CITIES

Most of us take **cities** for granted. It just seems natural that they exist, they're big, and they're the social, political, and economic centers we often turn to. We even treat some cities, such as London, Paris, and New York, as icons for entire civilizations. Six or seven thousand years ago, the complete absence of cities also seemed just as natural to our ancestors. Most settled communities were small hamlets, villages, or towns, and that's the way communities had been for thousands of years.

Cities, when they developed in prehistory, were often at the center of ancient states. Commonly, one or more prominent cities dominated smaller, dependent towns and villages in a region that also supported tiny farming hamlets. Cities are also characterized by social complexity, formal (nonkin) organization, and the concentration of specialized, nonagricultural roles (Redman, 1978). The city is the nucleus where production, trade, religion, and administrative activities converge (Cowgill, 2004). These central places usually proclaimed their own importance in prehistory by erecting prominent structures for ceremonial or other civic purposes.

The roots of cities or urbanism are currently best known archaeologically in the Near East, where settled communities existed in some regions before the beginning of the Neolithic and true agriculture (Fig. 15-2). In Chapter 14, for example, we saw that Natufians or their contemporaries in the lower Jordan River valley had established a permanent community of dome-shaped dwellings at Jericho centuries before its residents became fully reliant on farming (Kenyon, 1981). Although it never attained the size or status of a true city, early Jericho anticipated some of the characteristics of later urban centers, including evidence of social complexity. Before 10,000 ya, Jericho traders also participated in the regional exchange of such commodities as salt, sulfur, shells, obsidian, and turquoise. Some of these products ended up as offerings in the graves of individuals buried at Jericho. More impressive were Jericho's remarkable construction features, clearly the products of organized communal effort. A massive stone wall 6 feet thick, incorporating a 28-foot stone tower with interior stairs, enclosed the settlement of several hundred modest houses. A deep trench, cut into the bedrock beyond the wall, afforded even greater security, but against whom or what is uncertain. Viewed initially as fortifications against unknown human enemies, Jericho's wall and ditch may have been intended instead to divert mud flows brought on by severe erosion due to deforestation and poor farming practices in the vicinity (Bar-Yosef, 1986). The tower could have functioned either for defense or as a community shrine.

A 32-acre site in south-central Turkey, **Çatalhöyük** was both larger and somewhat later than Jericho (Hodder, 1996; Balter 2005). Çatalhöyük served as a trade and religious center some 9,000 ya, during early Neolithic times. Its densely packed houses of timber and mud brick had only rooftop entrances; their painted plaster interiors included living

civilization The larger social order that includes states related by language, traditions, history, economic ties, and other shared cultural aspects.

cities Urban centers that both support and are supported by a hinterland of lesser communities.

Çatalhöyük (chaetal´-hae-yook´) A large early Neolithic site in southern Turkey. The name is Turkish for "forked mound."

Figure **15-2**

Sites associated with early civilizations in
Mesopotamia and the Nile Valley.

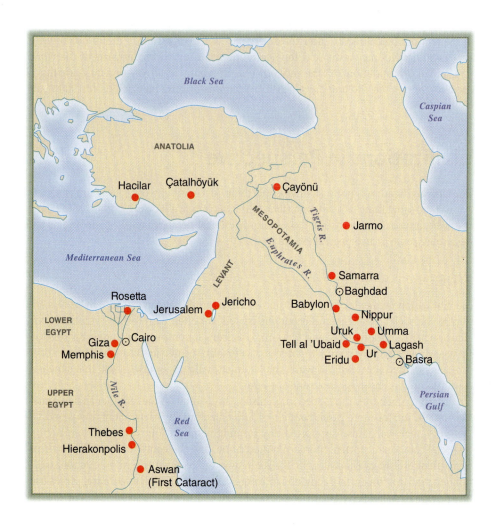

and storage space, sleeping platforms, and hearths. The community's several thousand inhabitants farmed outside its walls or engaged in craft production within. Some residents exploited nearby sources of obsidian or volcanic glass to make beads, mirrors, and blades to be exported in exchange for raw materials and finished goods. The wealth that this trade generated may have supported religious activities in elaborately decorated shrines uncovered in the site. Many of these shrines held representations of cattle, then only recently domesticated, as focal points for the worshipers.

Jericho and Çatalhöyük may be somewhat exceptional because specialized trade or religious activities promoted their early development into relatively large and complex Neolithic communities. Even so, they were not truly cities, nor did they pertain to any larger cultural entity that could be described as a state. They simply surpassed in size and sophistication such contemporary settlements as Jarmo (Iraq), **Çayönü** (Turkey), and **Hacilar** (Turkey), which remained modest villages. Despite their size and local prominence, they did not evolve into real urban centers of the kind associated with most ancient civilizations.

The earliest true city yet discovered is Uruk, in southern Iraq. Associated with the Sumerian civilization of the southern Tigris-Euphrates Valley, Uruk boasts remnants of massive mud-brick temples and residential areas that housed tens of thousands of people after 5,500 ya. Several other contemporary sites in northern Iraq and Syria, not yet excavated, indicate that urbanism was getting under way throughout that region in the late fourth millennium B.C. (about 5,200 ya).

Çayönü (chayu´-noo)

Hacilar (ha-ji-lar´)

STATES

If you were to examine the anthropological literature of the past century, you'd find many different perspectives on the concept of the **state**, some of which had considerable impact on archaeological research. Morton Fried (1967),* for example, described the evolution of political society as one that in its simplest form is "egalitarian." As the name implies, there's no social differentiation in egalitarian societies; leadership is informal, and "the best idea leads." Examples are most Paleolithic hunter-gatherer bands. Ranked societies are more complicated, particularly because some forms of social differentiation are present; a few people are "chiefs," but most are "Indians." These socially differentiated statuses and roles can be inherited, but there are no true social classes. Examples include Neolithic farming villages in the Near East and Mississippian chiefdoms in eastern North America. In stratified societies, we see significant differentiation, and true social classes do exist. An example is the Natchez, an early historic-period Native American group of west-central Mississippi, whose society was rigidly hierarchical by comparison with Mississippian societies, which it resembled in other ways. Finally, in the state we find social classes, as well as the concept of citizenship, true administrative bureaucracies, the monopoly of the use of force, and the other types of governing and administrative institutions that are typical of the states in which most of us live today.

The main interpretive drawback of such typologies is that they promote a progressive or evolutionary view of past political institutions—even where there's little empirical evidence to suggest that such a view is warranted. In Fried's typology, for example, ranked societies followed egalitarian societies and preceded stratified societies, and so on. Through frequent application in research, the built-in sequence of cultural evolutionary "stages" represented by such schemes can begin to seem both real and discoverable in the empirical world. Even so, through archaeological research on such important questions as how to explain the rise of the first states, we often discover that the changes identifiable in the archaeological record don't match these typologies very closely. Instead, researchers find that it's also useful to examine cultural differences, whether viewed through time or across space, as well as the similarities implied by such typologies in understanding the development of the earliest states (Trigger, 2003, p. 42). The result is still an evolutionary picture of the development of cities, states, and civilizations, but one that examines such changes within a web of possibilities rather than as the outcome of a succession of stages.

For our purposes, the state can be defined as a governmental entity that persists by politically controlling a territory and "by acting through a generalized structure of authority, making certain decisions in disputes between members of different groups, maintaining the central symbols of society, and undertaking the defense and expansion of the society"(Yoffee, 2005, p. 17). Examples include most modern nations.

With the emergence of the earliest states in antiquity, we also tend to see archaeological evidence of other important changes, among them **social stratification**, typically in the form of true social classes (recalling Fried, 1967). This is so consistent a feature of states that in his recent comparative analysis of early civilizations, archaeologist Bruce Trigger (2003) describes them categorically as "class-based" societies. In ancient states, most people worked the land, while a smaller number performed essential specialized tasks of craft production, military service, trade, and religion. At the top of this social heap were a few elite individuals who closely controlled access to goods and services produced by others, information, the means of force, and symbols of valued status; these individuals also made most essential decisions that affected the working of society—usually with the

---

*Another developmental typology of political complexity commonly applied by archaeologists in the late twentieth century is that of Elman Service (1962). The criticisms that we level against Fried apply equally to Service.

state A governmental entity that persists by politically controlling a territory; examples include most modern nations.

social stratification Class structure or hierarchy, usually based on political, economic, or social standing.

proclaimed sanction of gods and the assistance of a bureaucracy of lesser officials. Such decisions covered many critical functions, including the capacity to create and enforce laws, levy and collect taxes, store and redistribute food and other basic goods, and defend or expand the state's boundaries.

The development of true social classes implies another important aspect of states: Their main social institutions are commonly organized on the basis of criteria other than that of kinship. This doesn't mean that families and kinship cease to be important at every level of society, from the greatest of rulers to the person who hauls out the garbage at the end of the day. Kin relations continue to be important on the individual level. What changes is that some of the roles and duties that were once handled by your kin are now decided by the state. For example, states tend to appropriate the right to decide which acts of murder committed by its citizens will be punished as crimes and which will be rewarded with medals and marching bands. They also may take over the authority to pass judgment on local civil disputes, such as village squabbles over property boundaries, contract breaches, and the like. In nonstates, such as the kinds of communities we described in Chapter 14, these decisions were usually decided in kin-centered institutions such as families and lineages.

CIVILIZATIONS

Civilizations comprise "the larger social order and set of shared values in which states are culturally embedded" (Yoffee, 2005, p. 17). And while cities and states are building blocks of civilizations, the civilizations of which they are a part may show considerable diversity. Unlike what archaeologists believed half a century ago, we can't trace a simple developmental sequence in the archaeological record from villages to cities and then to states. For example, the Vijayanagara empire (roughly A.D. 1300–1650) appears to have been more unified and more urban than Maya civilization during the Classic period (A.D. 250–900). To understand why, you must consider differences of culture, technology, history, external relations, and even terrain, because they all played important roles, as shown in the archaeological records of these regions.

Why Did Civilizations Form?

Archaeological understanding of the development of the earliest civilizations has increased considerably over the past 50 years. Among the many things archaeologists have learned from this research is that answers to such questions as Why did civilizations form? tend to become more complex as our excavations teach us more about the past.

A half century ago, V. Gordon Childe specified the traits that he believed contributed to the evolution of early civilizations. His long list reflects his view of civilization as an outgrowth of increasing productivity, social complexity, and economic advantage (Childe, 1951, 1957). The use of writing, mathematics, animal-powered traction, wheeled carts, plows, irrigation, sailing boats, standard units of weight and measure, metallurgy, surplus production, and craft specialization, Childe argued, all had a stimulating effect and were themselves products of changes initiated by earlier Neolithic activities. But Childe's catalog of inventions and new social institutions failed to capture the central reality that a civilization is more than the sum of its parts.

What's more, it was evident even in the 1950s that Childe's trait list was not universally applicable. Although it characterized the Near Eastern civilizations that he was most familiar with, parts of it didn't fit New World societies such as the Maya and Inka.*

---

*Both Inka and Inca are accepted spellings; we've used Inka for the sake of consistency with other terms in the Quechua language spoken by the descendants of the native peoples of Peru.

These were clearly civilizations, even though they didn't use sailing boats, animal traction, wheeled carts, and so on.

Archaeologists tried to refine Childe's approach by singling out just the basic qualities shared by all civilizations. Clyde Kluckhohn proposed that civilizations are societies having (1) permanent towns with at least 5,000 residents, (2) record keeping, and (3) monumental ceremonial architecture (Kraeling and Adams, 1960). Notice that each of these criteria is an outward indicator of a society's underlying complexity. So, if a culture is able to maintain thousands of people in a permanent town, then surely it's exercising some form of governance or administrative control based on something other than kinship—possibly through the redistribution of goods and services. Record keeping (usually writing) manifests a need to maintain accurate accounts, ranging from inventories, economic reports, and tax tallies to law codes, histories, and literature. Large-scale construction activities for temples, pyramids, and other ceremonial architecture represent a society's surplus production capabilities, since such projects may not contribute to immediate and basic needs, like food, in the direct way that digging an irrigation canal would. A culture that can afford the luxury of monumental structures demonstrates that it has attained a measure of success in supplying the needs of its population and in maintaining some control over it.

At a Glance

Environmental Factors in the Development of Early Civilizations

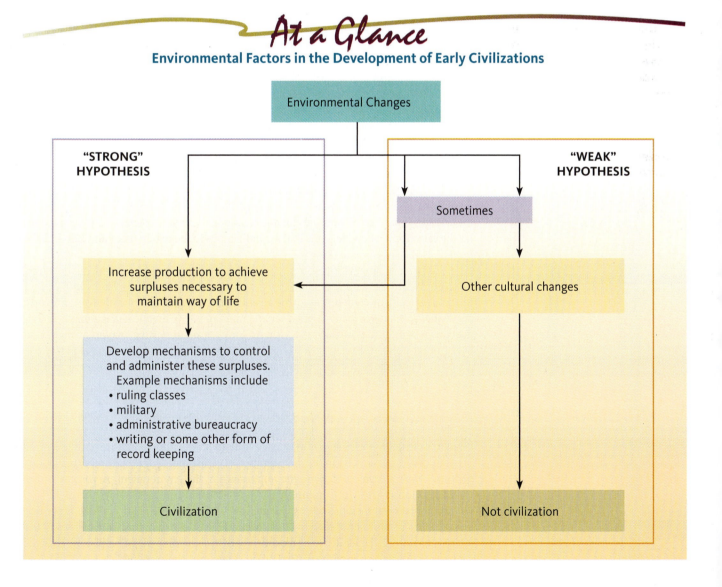

Still, descriptive approaches such as those of Childe and Kluckhohn remain inadequate because such trait lists ultimately fail to account for why and how the earliest civilizations emerged. The search for answers to such questions continues to be one of the most important objectives of archaeological research on complex societies. Let's now consider several recent competing explanations, with emphasis on Near Eastern civilizations, which offer the advantage of being among the most studied of the world's earliest civilizations. Bear in mind, however, that a good general explanation should also apply just as effectively to *all* civilizations, including those in the New World.

ENVIRONMENTAL EXPLANATIONS

At first glance, it may seem unlikely that the rise of civilizations could be the product of purely natural causes, independent of the actions of humans. Nevertheless, researchers have weighed the merits of these and many other possible factors over the past century. Theories that account for the origins of civilization tend to take a position between the extremes of environmental determinism, in which people, culture, and everything else obey the same laws of nature, and cultural determinism, the cultural relativist position that maintains that human behavior can be explained only in cultural and historical terms (Trigger, 2003, pp. 653–655).

Let's look briefly at an example of a strong environmental hypothesis. Arie Issar, a geologist, and his colleague Mattanyah Zohar, an archaeologist, argue that the fluctuating availability of water resources with major climatic changes was a key factor in the development of civilization in the Near East (Issar and Zohar, 2004). Based on their time series analyses of isotopes from lake sediments and cave stalagmites, these researchers identify several major periods between 6,000 and 5,000 ya during which the Near East was drier than present and periods during which it was colder than present. When correlated with major cultural changes documented in the archaeological record of the region, climatic conditions, they argue, are sufficient to account both for production surpluses and for the concentration of the control of these surpluses in the hands of ruling classes. This control gradually became more successful as administrative institutions and such inventions as writing developed in Mesopotamian society. Interregional commerce, the military, administrative bureaucracies, and local ruling dynasties, they argue, emerged because of the changes promoted by optimal climatic conditions. Climatic changes may also account for the catastrophic flood legends that are indigenous to the region (Issar and Zohar, 2004, pp. 112–113).

Elsewhere, however, research has shown that the possible causal relationships between environmental factors and early civilizations are much less likely. In fact, in a recent international conference on the relationship between climatic change and early civilizations, the participants agreed on one main point: "Climatic change for each civilization or community can act as a driving force, or a supporting player, or merely as background noise"(Catto and Catto, 2004). In other words, environmental explanations generally and climatic change in particular can't, by themselves, explain the rise and fall of all early civilizations.

CULTURAL EXPLANATIONS

If environmental theories sometimes leave little room for human culture and agency to play important causal roles in the development of civilization, some cultural explanations go to the other extreme and deny the importance of the environment. According to the views of cultural relativists, culture plays the significant role in shaping human behavior, not noncultural factors such as climate, population growth, and the like. From this perspective, culture cannot merely be reduced to the category of human reactions to the whims of nature, but is a force to be reckoned with in explaining major prehistoric changes such as the development of the earliest cities, states, and civilizations.

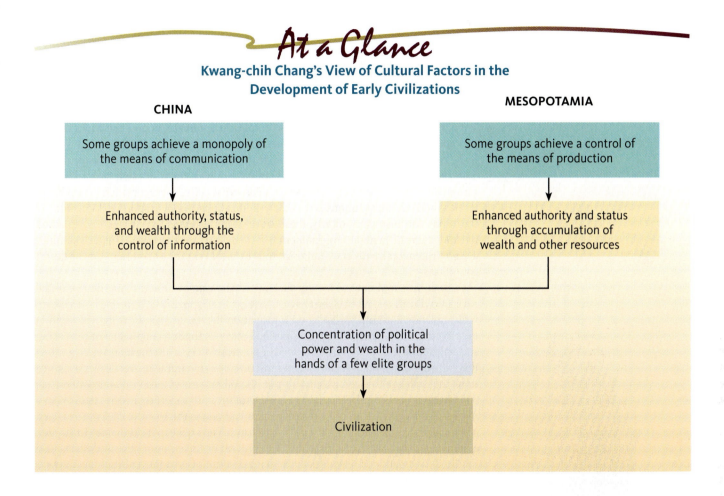

At a Glance

Kwang-chih Chang's View of Cultural Factors in the Development of Early Civilizations

CHINA

Some groups achieve a monopoly of the means of communication

↓

Enhanced authority, status, and wealth through the control of information

MESOPOTAMIA

Some groups achieve a control of the means of production

↓

Enhanced authority and status through accumulation of wealth and other resources

Concentration of political power and wealth in the hands of a few elite groups

↓

Civilization

For example, the archaeologist Kwang-chih Chang argued that the rise of the earliest civilizations in China may have owed more to the differential access by some groups to the means of communication within Chinese society than to the means of production (Chang, 2000). In short, Chang (2000, p. 2) asserted that "the wealth that produced the civilization was itself the product of concentrated political power, and the acquisition of that power was accomplished through the accumulation of wealth. The key to this circular working of the ancient Chinese society was the monopoly of high **shamanism**, which enabled the rulers to gain critical access to divine and ancestral wisdom, the basis of their political authority. Most of the markers of the ancient civilization were in fact related centrally to this shamanism." Chang's hypothesis is particularly interesting because it depends entirely on cultural factors as the active ingredients in developing early Chinese civilization. He pointedly denies the importance of technological advances and increasing control of the means of production, factors that are often mentioned as key aspects in general theories of the development of the early civilizations.

Although it's contested by many specialists on Chinese civilization, Chang's hypothesis has a novel twist in that he also argues that all early civilizations, with the notable exception of Mesopotamia in the Near East, controlled the means of communication (Chang, 2000, pp. 7–10). It was only in Mesopotamia, Chang reasons, that controlling the means of production was a key factor in developing the region's earliest civilizations. This difference, he conjectures, led to the creation of states that were fundamentally different from those of China and greatly influenced the development of much of Western civilization.

In his recent monumental worldwide comparative analysis of early civilizations, Bruce Trigger (2003) identifies several important uniformities that cast doubt on

shamanism Traditional practices that mediate between the world of humans and the world of spirits.

civilization theories that adopt extreme positions, whether they're in the direction of cultural relativism or environmental forces. To take only a few sociopolitical examples, Trigger found no evidence of Chang's control of the means of communication; but in the cases he examined, he did encounter relatively uniform conceptions of kingship, class systems, support of the upper classes through the controlled use of force, and control of the means of production (Trigger, 2003, pp. 272–273, 663). Significantly, Trigger also found that only two types of political organization and two types of general administrative institutions are present in early civilizations. What's striking about these and the many other cultural similarities he identifies is that it's not the sort of picture you would expect to see if human culture was unconstrained by noncultural forces. If culture were a free agent, so to speak, we would expect considerable diversity in these and other institutions across early civilizations as they respond to local cultural traditions and history. Similarly, these cultural uniformities can't be easily explained by the action of general environmental factors, because the cases Trigger examines are environmentally diverse, ranging from tropical rain forest settings to near-desert conditions.

If culture and natural factors such as climate cannot fully explain the rise of the earliest civilizations, what is the answer? Trigger (2003, pp. 272–274) proposes an essentially functional argument based on information theory. At its root is the observation that the transition from villages to cities and states is fundamentally one of increasing societal complexity, driven by economic or political forces. With the increased complexity of the organization of society, there must also be comparable increases in the institutions that manage this complexity. To put it another way, you can't manage a Fortune 500 multinational corporation from a small storefront in a suburban strip mall. What's missing from that picture is the massive organizational infrastructure necessary to keep a major corporation running on a daily basis, much less to keep it profitable. To Trigger, a state faces the same basic problem. The growth of the earliest cities and states also required the creation of new decision-making institutions and the distribution of power and authority. This is effectively what's seen archaeologically with increased material evidence for the emergence of social classes, ruling elites, administrative bureaucracies, settlement hierarchies, and the like. But Trigger's most important point may be that for all the ways in which early civilizations differed around the world— and there were many—"for societies to grow more complex they may have to evolve specific forms of organization." And as Trigger also observed, humans found only a limited number of ways to do this!

Old World Civilizations

So seemingly familiar are the ancient Near Eastern civilizations—Egypt and Mesopotamia— that we instinctively use them as a standard against which to measure all others. Still, it's inappropriate to do so, for as Bruce Trigger (2003) stresses, it's essential to understand both the differences and the similarities between early civilizations if we are to explain how and why such entities developed. This section is a selective glimpse of the development of the earliest Old World cities, states, and civilizations in several geographical regions: Mesopotamia, Egypt, the Indus Valley in South Asia, and northern China (Fig. 15-3). In the next section, we will take a similar look at the rise of several of the earliest New World civilizations. Each civilization devised ways of grappling with the challenges presented by entirely new social, political, and economic circumstances. Their legacies have survived for millennia, and we can often still recognize them within the framework of our modern civilizations.

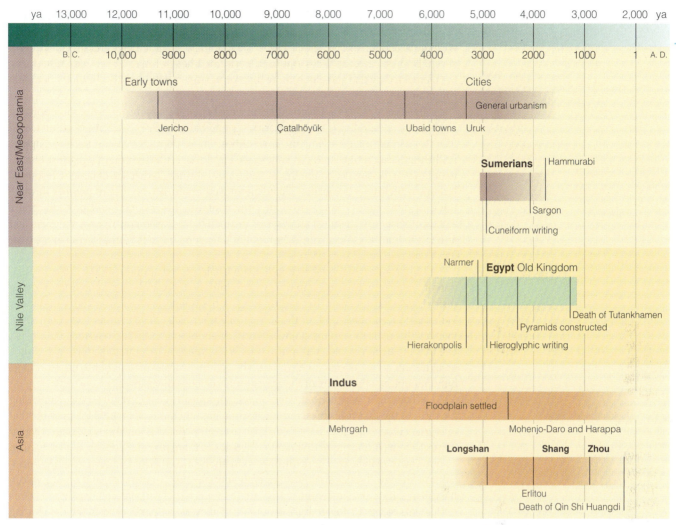

| ya | 13,000 | 12,000 | 11,000 | 10,000 | 9,000 | 8,000 | 7,000 | 6,000 | 5,000 | 4,000 | 3,000 | 2,000 | ya |

| | B.C. | 10,000 | 9000 | 8000 | 7000 | 6000 | 5000 | 4000 | 3000 | 2000 | 1000 | 1 | A.D. |

Near East/Mesopotamia

Early towns — Cities

General urbanism

Jericho — Çatalhöyük — Ubaid towns — Uruk

Sumerians | Hammurabi

| Sargon

| Cuneiform writing

Nile Valley

Narmer | **Egypt** Old Kingdom

| Death of Tutankhamen

| Pyramids constructed

Hierakonpolis | | Hieroglyphic writing

Asia

Indus

Floodplain settled

Mehrgarh — Mohenjo-Daro and Harappa

Longshan — **Shang** — **Zhou**

Erlitou
Death of Qin Shi Huangdi

Figure **15-3**
Time line for Old World civilizations.

MESOPOTAMIA

During the centuries after 8,000 ya, pioneering farmers settled the vast alluvial plains bordering the lower Tigris-Euphrates river system, an area called **Mesopotamia** (Fig. 15-2). These agriculturists shared the heritage of such early Neolithic communities as Jarmo, in the Zagros foothills to the east, and Çayönü, at the edge of the Anatolian plateau (Nissen, 1988). In fact, they were probably direct descendants of Samarran farmers, who had practiced small-scale irrigation agriculture along the edges of the central Tigris Valley and obtained painted pottery and obsidian through trade with upland communities. Now advancing onto the southern plains, possibly in search of vacant or more productive lands, these **Ubaid** farmers (as archaeologists call them) encountered great flood-prone streams bound only by immense mudflats and marshes.

The annual floods in this region began soon after the spring planting season, when young crops were particularly vulnerable. These seasonal overflows deposited rich layers of alluvium, and fifth-millennium B.C. sites have been found buried at depths of up to 16 feet below the modern ground surface (Crawford, 2004). When the waters receded, a long, dry summer followed. At first, farmers cultivated only the well-drained slopes above the river. But eventually they began the arduous task of redirecting the river's flow, even cutting through its banks to channel floodwater onto low-lying fields. Irrigation unlocked

Mesopotamia (*meso*, meaning "middle," and *potamos*, meaning "river") Land between the Tigris and Euphrates rivers, mostly included in modern-day Iraq.

Ubaid (oo-bide´) Early formative culture of Mesopotamia, 7,500–6,200 ya; predecessor to Sumerian civilization.

the fertility of the deep, stone-free silt that had accumulated on the floodplain for millennia. Barley was the Ubaidians' primary grain, but wheat and millet grew well too, along with the date palm and vegetable crops. Their animals included pigs and several kinds of sheep. Domesticated donkeys and oxen performed heavy tasks. The abundant harvests, supplemented by fish and game, more than kept pace with the rapidly growing floodplain communities.

By around 6,500 ya, Ubaid villagers were beginning to prosper in the southernmost Tigris-Euphrates Valley (Lamberg-Karlovsky and Sabloff, 1995). A degree of cultural uniformity marked their settlements. Each of their more populous towns, such as Nippur, Eridu, and Uruk in the southern valley (see Fig. 15-2), centered around a platform-based temple; even the smaller communities had central shrines. Perhaps to obtain the resources lacking in their new homeland, Ubaidians stayed in touch with distant peoples through trade in decorated pottery, obsidian, ornamental stones, copper, and possibly grain. Archaeologists use chemical analyses of distinctive trace elements in raw materials and artifacts to track these exchanges throughout the region, from the Persian Gulf to the eastern Mediterranean (Roaf, 1996).

Important changes ushered in the late Ubaid period, around 5,500 ya. The population of certain communities rapidly swelled into the thousands as people from outlying districts massed together. Expanding irrigation systems in the lower Tigris-Euphrates Valley produced more food for the concentrated populace. Altering the riverine environment on this scale by digging drainage and irrigation channels was a daunting enterprise, one that the people could accomplish only with organized communal effort, including a great deal of cooperation and direction. The activity transformed not only the landscape but undoubtedly the nature of the agricultural societies themselves.

What might these concentrated populations mean to us? Certainly, we're witnessing the birth of the first true cities. But what stimulated their development? It's possible that intensified economic or military rivalries in the region forced populations to come together for protection (Adams, 1981). Or maybe there was a more peaceful genesis, with urbanism an outgrowth of increased agricultural productivity and efficiency, in turn fostering sociocultural changes (social stratification, craft specialization, commerce, and so on) within the urban setting. Whatever the reason, these trends happened simultaneously at various settlements along the lower Tigris-Euphrates Valley as people flocked to the developing cities. These cities seem to have provided the social environments needed for the earliest Mesopotamian states to emerge (Yoffee, 2005).

Sumerians Over several centuries, Uruk's population expanded to possibly as many as 20,000 people. Today, the ruins of Uruk's mud-brick buildings cover nearly 1 square mile in southern Mesopotamia, 150 miles southeast of modern Baghdad (Nissen, 2001). The most ancient parts of Uruk reveal some features of the earliest city. Two massive temple complexes, built in stages and dedicated to the sun and to the goddess of love, probably served as focal points of political, religious, economic, and cultural activities. Inscribed clay tablets associated with these structures record that the temples distributed food to the populace and controlled nearby croplands. Growing social and religious complexity, including the rise of powerful kings and priests, kept pace with the city's physical growth.

The developments associated with Uruk and the other urban centers were an immediate prelude and stimulus to a new order in southern Mesopotamia around 5,000 ya. The inscribed tablets, teeming populations, and large-scale religious structures indicate that the essential elements of civilization had come together. Uruk marked the beginning of the **Sumerians**, the first complex urban civilization.

The region known as Sumer encompassed about a dozen largely autonomous political units, called **city-states**, in the southernmost Tigris-Euphrates Valley. About the same number of Akkadian city-states hugged the river to the north, near present-day Baghdad. The Sumerians and their neighbors shared the world's first modern society between

Sumerians Earliest civilization of Mesopotamia.

city-states Urban centers that form autonomous sociopolitical units.

At a Glance

Important Near Eastern Sites and Regions

SITE	DATES (YA)	SIGNIFICANCE
Uruk (Iraq)	ca. 5,500–1,800	Earliest true city; associated with the Sumerian civilization of the southern Tigris-Euphrates Valley
Ur (Iraq)	ca. 4,600–2,500	City in southern Iraq; its cemetery of >1,800 graves includes 16 "royal" tombs

4,900 and 4,350 ya. Each Sumerian city-state incorporated a major population center—Ur, Lagash, Umma, Nippur, Eridu, and Uruk are examples—as well as some smaller satellite communities and, of course, a great deal of irrigated cropland. These city-states were controlled by hereditary kings, who often fought for dominance with their counterparts in neighboring cities.

The Sumerians had an urbanized and technologically accomplished culture, economically dependent on large-scale irrigation agriculture and specialized craft production (Kramer, 1963; Roaf, 1996). They were among the first to refine metals such as gold, silver, and copper and to make bronze alloys. Sophisticated architecture incorporated the true arch and the dome. Other practical innovations included wheeled carts, draft animals, the plow, and sailing boats. Skilled crafters produced fine jewelry and textiles, while artists created sculpture and music. Sumerian merchants and administrators relied on written records and a counting system based on multiples of 6, which they also applied to measuring time and devising calendars. (Buying a dozen doughnuts, counting minutes in our 24-hour day, and measuring degrees in a circle are modern reminders of ancient Sumerian numeration.) Their system of law became a basis for later legal codes, and Sumerian contributions to literature included many of the traditions subsequently reflected in the Old Testament.

The influence of these cities reached beyond Mesopotamia through exchange and possibly even colonization. Excavations in northern Iraq, Turkey, and the Nile Valley of Egypt have revealed connections with Uruk through trade in prestige goods such as pottery, carved ivory, and lapis (Roaf, 1996). These valued products furnished the tombs of Sumerian elites in a society where social differentiation was becoming more pronounced.

Among the prerogatives of elite members of society was the right to burial in a lavish tomb. Sir Leonard Woolley's excavations of the 4,500-year-old "royal" tombs at Ur in the 1920s revealed that King Abargi and Queen Puabi were each accompanied in death by rich offerings—ceremonial vessels, tools, musical instruments, and even chariots complete with their animals and, apparently, also their human attendants—arranged within the burial pits (Woolley, 1929). Woolley interpreted other human remains found in association with these elite individuals as the men and women of their court, who were bedecked with precious jewelry, drugged, and then sealed into the tombs.

Mesopotamian citizens constructed brick walls around their city perimeters for security. The heart of each urban center was its sacred district, dominated by a grand temple and flanked by noble houses. In addition to a patron deity associated with each city, citizens worshipped many other gods. Chief among them was Enlil, the air god. Like most Mesopotamian gods, Enlil exhibited remarkably human characteristics, taking a fatherly concern for mortals and their daily affairs but also meting out punishment and

Figure **15-4**

Reconstructed lower stage of the late Sumerian ziggurat at Ur, Iraq.

Figure **15-5**

This small Sumerian clay tablet (actual size) is a 4,000-year-old tax receipt with cuneiform impressions on both sides.

ziggurat Late Sumerian mud-brick temple-pyramid.

cuneiform (*cuneus*, meaning "wedge") Wedge-shaped writing of ancient Mesopotamia.

Gilgamesh Semilegendary king and culture hero of early Uruk; reputed to have had many marvelous adventures.

misfortune. Some cities, like Ur, regularly augmented their shrines and eventually created an impressive artificial mountain called a **ziggurat** (Fig. 15-4). Rising from an elevated platform roughly the size of a football field, these stepped temples were solidly built of millions of molded and baked mud bricks.

Outside the ceremonial district, narrow unpaved alleyways twisted through crowded residential precincts. Much like city dwellers everywhere, Sumerians endured social problems and pollution in their urban environment. The size and location of individual homes correlated with family wealth and position. Contemporary written accounts indicate that the populace comprised three general classes: nobility, commoners, and slaves. Some slaves were formerly free citizens who had fallen on hard times and sold themselves into bondage; others were captives taken in conflicts with neighboring city-states. Some of the commoners specialized in craft or merchant activities, but many were farmers with fields and herds just beyond the surrounding walls. The houses of all but the nobility were generally one story, with several rooms opening onto a central courtyard. Wall and floor coverings brightened the interiors, which were furnished with wooden tables, chairs, and beds and an assortment of household equipment for cooking and storage.

From our perspective, their writing system was perhaps the Sumerians' most significant invention, enabling us to discover more about them than their other artifacts and monuments could ever reveal. Literacy was a hard-won accomplishment. By about 5,000 ya, the original pictographic form of Sumerian writing was evolving into a more flexible writing system using hundreds of standardized signs. Highly trained scribes formed the characteristic wedge-shaped, or **cuneiform**, script by pressing a reed stylus onto damp clay pads; these tablets were then baked to preserve them (Fig. 15-5). Ninety percent of early Sumerian writing concerned economic, legal, and administrative matters; like us, the Sumerians belonged to a complex and bureaucratic society. Later scribes recorded more historical and literary works, including several epic accounts featuring the adventures of **Gilgamesh**, an early Uruk king and culture hero reputed to have performed many amazing deeds in the face of overwhelming odds.

The loose conglomeration of Mesopotamian city-states faced hard times after around 4,500 ya. At least part of the problem may have been their long dependence on irrigation agriculture, which was slowly destroying the fertility of their fields because the irrigation water deposited soluble mineral salts on the soil. Other researchers (e.g., Powell, 1985) question the hard evidence on which these inferences are based, and this area needs more research. Another part of the problem was that this early civilization spent much of its energy in fruitless internal competition. Clustered together in an area about the size of Vermont, the city-states of Sumer and neighboring Akkad, to the north, vied with one another for supremacy in commerce, prestige, and religion.

Finally, around 2334 B.C., a minor Akkadian official assumed the name Sargon of Agade and led armies from the north to victory in the Sumerian lands and united what had been a collection of city-states into a **territorial state**. Military expansion led to economic, political, and linguistic dominance over a broad area. Under Sargon, his sons, and grandsons, the Akkadian state endured only a century before dissolving. But once it began, the unification process continued on and off for many centuries in Mesopotamia—next under the kings of Ur and later (about 3,800 ya) under **Hammurabi** of Babylon, famed for his "eye for an eye" code of law, among other accomplishments. Soon after the reign of Hammurabi, the ancient lands were incorporated into the realm of the Assyrians until 2,600 ya, when a new Babylonian empire reclaimed dominance under King **Nebuchadnezzar**.

EGYPT

The pyramids of Egypt remain unrivaled as the ancient world's most imposing monuments. They have adorned the banks of the Nile for so long that they seem timeless. Even so, as we saw in Chapter 14, Egyptian culture was rooted in the Nile Valley long before the pyramids.

Archaeological evidence of these most ancient Nile cultures is rarely preserved in the unstable river floodplain (Trigger et al., 1983; Hays, 1984). Still, excavations reveal that the early farmers grew Near Eastern varieties of wheat and barley as well as raising sheep and goats first domesticated in the same region. Neolithic villages lined the great river's banks by 6,000 ya. Even at this early stage, settlements in the section of the valley known as Upper Egypt—just north of Aswan, the "First Cataract" of ancient times—contrasted somewhat with those in the delta region, called Lower Egypt, close to the river's mouth. Archaeologists recognize a Mesopotamian influence at work among the Upper Egypt villagers, possibly introduced through direct contact or by way of Palestinian traders (Hoffman, 1991). Mineral resources, especially gold, apparently drew outsiders to the region.

Around 5,300 ya, increasing political and social cohesion brought some of these Upper Egypt settlements together as local chiefdoms. Walls protected the towns of Naqada and Hierakonpolis, and well-stocked stone and brick tombs marked the social status enjoyed by important individuals (Wenke, 1990). Pottery making and trading became specialized economic enterprises (Fig. 15-6). Continuing contact with Mesopotamian cultures may have stimulated these developments, although researchers do not yet have evidence of comparable Egyptian influence in the other direction.

In any event, during the next few centuries, this part of the Nile Valley transformed rapidly into a strong territorial state. Historical tradition and written evidence, including the Narmer Palette (Fig. 15-7), a relief-carved stone plaque from Hierakonpolis, record that one of Upper Egypt's early chiefs took the name Narmer and seized other communities of that region, successfully exerting his control over the delta villages in the north as well. This unification of Upper and Lower Egypt under Narmer, the traditional beginning of the First Dynasty of Egyptian civilization, dates to around 5,000 ya (3000 B.C.). The merger of Nile Valley societies under one king marked an important milestone in the development of ancient Egypt by creating the world's first nation-state.

After the first unification period, a 425-year span known as Old Kingdom times (4,575–4,150 ya) represented the first full flowering of Nile Valley civilization. Most of the estimated population of 1 to 3 million people lived in the far south (Trigger, 2003). The ruler, or **pharaoh**, was the supreme power of the society. Under his direction, Egypt

Brooklyn Museum

Figure **15-6**

The design on this pot from Adaima, a Predynastic period center near Hierakonpolis, shows a boat and its passengers; the vessel is about 7 inches tall.

territorial state A form of state political organization with multiple administrative centers and one or more capitals. The cities tended to house the elite and administrative classes, and food producers usually lived and worked in the surrounding hinterland.

Hammurabi (ham-oo-rah´-bee) Early Babylonian king, ca. 1800–1750 B.C.

Nebuchadnezzar (neh-boo-kud-neh´-zer) Late Babylonian king, ca. 605–562 B.C.

pharaoh Title of the ruler of ancient Egypt.

Figure **15-7**

The Narmer Palette, commemorating the unification of Upper and Lower Egypt under Pharaoh Narmer. The palette measures about 25 inches high.

Figure **15-8**

Egyptian Old Kingdom pyramid and Sphinx at Giza.

hieroglyphics (*hiero*, meaning "sacred," and *glyphein*, meaning "carving") The picture-writing of ancient Egypt.

faience (fay-ahnz´) Glassy material, usually of blue-green color, shaped into beads, amulets, and figurines by ancient Egyptians.

became a wonder of the ancient world and a source of endless fascination for millennia to follow.

Egyptians soon adopted a complex pictographic script called **hieroglyphics**, a writing system that is Egyptian in form but possibly Mesopotamian in inspiration. The earliest inscriptions are associated exclusively with the Egyptian royal court, as are other high-status products, such as cylinder seals, certain types of pottery, and specific artistic motifs and architectural techniques that also seem to be derived from beyond the Nile Valley. Advanced methods of copper working came into use as well, including ore refining and alloying, casting, and hammering techniques. Some of these processes likewise were invented elsewhere. An important by-product of copper metallurgy was **faience**, an Egyptian innovation produced by fusing powdered quartz, soda ash, and copper ore in a kiln. The blue-green glassy substance, molded into beads or statuettes, became a popular trade item throughout the region (Friedman, 1998).

Early pharaohs were godlike kings who ruled with divine authority through a bureaucracy of priests and public officials assigned to provinces throughout the kingdom. The pharaoh's power depended to a large degree on his assumed control over the annual Nile flood (Butzer, 1984), and throughout the course of Egypt's long history, pharaonic fortunes tended to fluctuate with the river's flow. Most Old Kingdom pharaohs maintained their royal courts at Memphis, about 15 miles south of present-day Cairo (see Fig. 15-2). In contrast to Mesopotamia, few urban centers emerged in the ancient Nile Valley, and even the capital was of modest size. Egypt remained almost entirely an agrarian and rural culture, the vast majority of its citizenry comprising farmers and a few traders engaged in their timeless routines (Aldred, 1998). Only in the immediate vicinity of Memphis and the sacred mortuary complexes along the Nile's west bank was Egypt's grandeur clearly evident.

The familiar Old Kingdom pyramids on the Nile's west bank at Giza evolved out of a tradition of royal tomb building that began at Hierakonpolis. In that early community, brick-lined burial pits were dug with adjoining chambers to stock the offerings for a deceased king's afterlife, and these rooms were then capped with a low, rectangular brick tomb (Lehner, 1997). The scale of these structures increased as successive rulers outdid their predecessors. The monumental pyramids are the best example of the pharaoh's

At a Glance

Important Egyptian Sites and Regions

SITE	DATES (YA)	SIGNIFICANCE
Hierakonpolis	ca. 5,300	Early Nile Valley urban center located about 45 miles to the south of Thebes; associated with the development of the unification of Egypt as one polity; home to the Narmer Palette
Memphis	ca. 5,100–3,300	Old Kingdom capital city located about 10 miles south of Cairo; abandoned after A.D. 641
Giza	ca. 4,500	Old Kingdom pyramid complex and Great Sphinx; located just to the southwest of Cairo
Valley of the Kings	ca. 3,500–3,000	Desert valley near Thebes (modern Luxor), where more than 50 New Kingdom subterranean tombs of pharaohs (including Tutankhamen) and other elites were found

absolute authority over the people and resources of his domain (Fig. 15-8). In a sense, these constructions were immense public works projects that helped to solidify the power of the state while also glorifying the memory of individual rulers. Contrary to popular view, they weren't built by slave labor, but by thousands of Egyptian farmers, put to work during the several months each year when the Nile floodwaters covered their fields.

In all, some 25 pyramids honored the Old Kingdom's elite (Lehner, 1997). The first stepped pyramids of stone were raised after 2630 B.C. (4,630 ya), and little more than a century later, the imposing tombs of Khufu and Khafra, Fourth Dynasty rulers, were among the last built in true pyramid form. Khufu's Great Pyramid is 765 feet square at its base and 479 feet in height, with 2.3 million massive limestone blocks required in its construction. Although Khafra's tomb is about 20 percent smaller, he compensated by having a nearby rock outcrop carved with the likeness of his face on the body of a lion, today called the Great Sphinx (Hawass and Lehner, 1994). Pyramid building ceased soon after, during a time of political decentralization and greater local control over such practical programs as state irrigation works.

The Old Kingdom pyramids represented a remarkable engineering triumph and an enormous cultural achievement that inspired the civilizations that followed. Bear in mind that the stark structures we see along the Nile today were adjoined by extensive complexes of connecting causeways, shrines, altars, and storerooms filled with statuary and furnishings and ornamented with colorful friezes and carved stonework. The pyramids' slanting sides signified pathways to the sacred Sun. Worshipers flocked to them, paying reverence to the memory of the dead kings. The mortuary cult of the pharaohs absorbed a large share of the work and wealth of Egyptian society.

Later kings contented themselves with being buried in smaller, but still lavishly furnished tombs in the Valley of the Kings, a cramped desert valley below a natural pyramid-shaped mountain near Thebes. Discovered in the 1920s, the treasure-choked burial chamber of the young pharaoh **Tutankhamen**, who died more than 3,300 ya (about 1323 B.C.) during New Kingdom times, is convincing evidence that dead royalty were not neglected even after the era of pyramids had passed (Carter and Mace, 1923). Near the same location,

Tutankhamen (toot-en-cahm´-en) Egyptian pharaoh of the New Kingdom period, who died at age 19 in 1323 B.C.; informally known today as King Tut.

in 1995, archaeologist Kent Weeks discovered another impressive New Kingdom tomb. Although looted long ago, rock-cut chambers prepared for many of the sons of Ramses II ("the Great") formed a vast underground mausoleum containing more than 130 rooms. The tomb, now called KV5, currently is being systematically explored and conserved (Weeks, 2001).

Much of what we know of ancient Egypt's religion and rulers is due to the translation of countless hieroglyphic inscriptions (Fig. 15-9). In 1799 at Rosetta, a small Nile delta town, French soldiers discovered a 2½-by-2½-foot stone bearing an identical decree engraved in three scripts, including Greek and hieroglyphics. Twenty years later, Jean-François Champollion finally succeeded in deciphering Egyptian hieroglyphic writing by using the Rosetta stone as a guide.

Egyptian hieroglyphics are a combination of signs that represent ideas with others indicating sounds. Because hieroglyphics were used primarily in formal contexts by members of the elite classes and bureaucrats (much like Latin in more recent times), their translation tells us much about pharaohs and their concerns, revealing less about the commonplace events and people of the era. In fact, archaeologists can read disappointingly little about daily life in Egypt's Old Kingdom period outside the major administrative and mortuary centers, where tomb scenes occasionally portray peasants at work in their fields or winnowing or grinding grain. Happily, later periods of Egyptian society are more fully documented (Montet, 1981; Casson, 2001).

Although nothing surpassed the original glory of the Old Kingdom period, Egypt proved remarkably resilient through the centuries, surviving foreign invaders such as the Hyksos and Hittites of southwest Asia, as well as frequent episodes of internal misrule and rebellion. Its pharaohs enjoyed periods of resurgence and revival until, in a state of decline and defeated by the Persians (about 2,500 ya), Egypt fell into the Greek sphere under Alexander the Great and eventually came under the rule of Rome.

Figure **15-9**

Egyptian hieroglyphic inscriptions on a pillar in the Karnak Temple complex at Thebes (modern Luxor).

INDUS

As the first great pyramids rose beside the Nile, a collection of urban settlements that dotted a broad floodplain far to the east was forming into the Harappan, or Indus, civilization (Fig. 15-10). For seven centuries, between about 4,600 and 3,900 ya, the banks of the Indus River and its tributaries in what is now Pakistan and India supported at least five primary urban centers, each with a population numbering in the tens of thousands (Kenoyer, 1998; Possehl, 1999, 2002). Many hundreds of smaller farming villages were socially and economically, if not politically, linked to these central places.

The people of the Indus were relative newcomers to the Indus Valley. As we saw in Chapter 14, their ancestors cultivated the higher valley margins to the west at sites like Mehrgarh by 8,000 ya. Farming and herding, along with regional trade, sustained village life from an early period in these uplands (Jarrige and Meadow, 1980). Around 5,300 ya, farmers began to populate the Indus floodplain itself, possibly seeking more productive cropland or better access to potential trade routes for valued copper, shell, and colorful stones. Occupying slight natural rises on the flat landscape at places like Kot Diji (see Fig. 15-10), they laid out fields for their vegetables, cereals, and cotton on the deep alluvium. As the new settlements grew, farmers diverted part of the river's flow into canals to irrigate their fields. They also constructed massive retaining walls or elevated platforms to protect their homes from the devastating effects of seasonal floods.

Some of these settlements prospered and grew. By 4,600 ya, several large urban centers hugged the river. Why had people accustomed to living in small farming communities congregated in these cities? Possibly an increased threat of flooding along the river—brought on by extensive deforestation and other poor farming practices—simply

Figure **15-10**

Location of the Indus civilization in Pakistan and India.

Figure **15-11**

An excavated section of Mohenjo-Daro, Pakistan.

James P. Blair/National Geographic Image Collection

forced people to come together in building and maintaining more levees and irrigation canals. An alternative hypothesis proposes that trade was the "integrative force" behind Indus urbanization (Possehl, 1990). A few entrepreneurs may have fostered exchange between the valley settlements and the uplands, promoting resource development, craft specialization, and product distribution to stimulate and reap the economic benefits. As commerce began to pay off, other changes, including urbanism and social stratification, attracted craftspeople, shopkeepers, and foreign traders, all of whom transformed Indus society even more.

As busy centers of craft production and trade, the cities prospered along the great river. Workshops in different neighborhoods turned out large quantities of wheel-thrown pottery, millions of burnt bricks, cut and polished stone beads and stamp seals, molded figurines, and work in copper, tin, silver, gold, and other metals. Merchants' scales used standardized stone cubes of precise weight to facilitate exchange transactions. The Indus itself became a commercial highway for boats loaded with goods moving up and down the river or destined for Persian Gulf ports. Carts, too, carried the colorfully dyed cotton cloth, pottery, shell, and precious metal goods overland to Mesopotamia. For a while, a distant Harappan trade outpost was even established near Sumerian Ur.

So far, archaeologists have carried out extensive excavations at several of the major cities and a few of the smaller contemporary agricultural and pastoral villages (Fig. 15-11). The largest Indus sites excavated so far are **Mohenjo-Daro** and **Harappa**, which flourished between about 4,600 and 3,900 ya in present-day Pakistan. Raised on massive brick terraces above the river's flow, these cities were carefully planned, using grids of approximately 1,300 by 650 feet for the residential blocks. Although these large sites certainly reveal social complexity and a certain degree of central control, the Indus civilization lacks grand picturesque ruins of the type found in Egypt and Sumer. You won't find sumptuous palaces or monumental religious structures here. Their absence may suggest a basic feature of Harappan society, whose people were less focused on glorifying their individual rulers. Richard H. Meadow, who has been excavating at Harappa since 1987, describes this civilization as "an elaborate middle-class society" (Edwards, 2000, p. 116). Gregory L. Possehl (2002), another archaeologist with decades of Indus civilization research experience, draws a similar conclusion and describes it as a socioculturally complex civilization that lacks evidence of the state form of political organization. Possehl (2002, pp. 5–6, 56–57) argues that the criteria by which the state is archaeologically identified—a hierarchy of social classes, kingship, state bureaucracies and the monopolization of power, state religions, and so forth—aren't readily identifiable in the archaeological remains of the Indus

Mohenjo-Daro (mo-henjo-dar´-o) An early Indus Valley city in south-central Pakistan.

Harappa (ha-rap´-pa) A fortified city in the Indus Valley of northeastern Pakistan.

civilization. This difference—that of a highly successful, complex society based on a form of political organization other than the state—sets the Indus civilization apart and makes it clear that we still have a lot to learn about this extraordinary development in South Asian prehistory.

Both Mohenjo-Daro and Harappa encompassed a public district and several residential areas. Mohenjo-Daro's "great bath" lies near what has been interpreted as that city's government center—a complex that also included elite residences and a large assembly hall, all of which were set on massive mud-brick and burnt-brick platforms. Water was ideologically important to Indus peoples (Possehl, 2002), and they may have used features like the great bath for ritual cleansing as a part of worship. Nearly 700 brick-lined wells have been recorded by archaeologists at Mohenjo-Daro, and similar features are found at other Indus sites.

In both cities, homes range from modest brick-walled dwellings that bordered unpaved streets and alleys to spacious multistoried houses with interior courtyards. What has been proclaimed as the world's first efficient sewer system carried waste away from these densely packed dwellings, many of them equipped with indoor toilets and baths.

What might this culture have to say for itself? Unfortunately, the writing system, consisting of brief pictographic notations commonly found on seal stones and pottery, remains undeciphered (Parpola, 1994; Possehl, 1996).

The Indus civilization's decline seems to have been as rapid as its ascent. After little more than half a millennium, its major sites were virtually abandoned, although hundreds of smaller towns and villages outlasted them. Without written records or any archaeological evidence of invasion or revolution, we can only guess what caused its demise. Did competing trade routes bypass the Indus? Did the irrigation system fail, or did the river shift in its channel, either flooding the fields or leaving them parched? Was the society simply unable to maintain its urban centers? Floodwaters were a frequent threat; Mohenjo-Daro had been rebuilt perhaps 10 times before being given up to the Indus floodwaters. All we know for sure is that in the end, the river that spawned the principal urban centers gradually reclaimed the surrounding fields and eventually the city sites themselves.

At a Glance
Important Asian Sites and Regions

SITE	DATES (YA)	SIGNIFICANCE
Mohenjo-Daro (Pakistan)	ca. 4,600–3,900	Most extensively excavated Indus civilization city, located in the Indus Valley of south-central Pakistan
Harappa (Pakistan)	ca. 4,600–3,900	Indus civilization city in northeastern Pakistan
Erlitou (China)	ca. 4,000	Elaborate site associated with the earliest phase of civilization in northern China
Shixianggou, Zhengzhou (China)	3,600–3,046	Early Shang capital cities
Shi Huangdi Tomb (China)	2,200	Tomb of the first emperor of China; his mausoleum at Mount Li, near the modern city of Xian, includes an entire terracotta army

NORTHERN CHINA

As we saw in Chapter 14 (see pp. 367–370), the deep roots of China's early civilization were nurtured in the loess uplands and stark alluvial plains bordering the great rivers of the north. Specialized production and exchange of valued ritual goods came to characterize the prosperous farming societies along the central and lower Huang He (Yellow River) Valley and brought about increased contact and conflict among them. This phase of regional development and interaction continued during the Longshan period beginning about 4,800 ya and culminated in the formation of a distinctive Chinese culture that emphasized social ranking and ritualism accompanied by persistent warfare (Chang, 1986).

During the Longshan period, the circulation of luxury products contributed to the concentration of wealth and the emergence of social hierarchies. Elite consumers supported craft specialties including fine wheel-thrown pottery, jade carving, and a developing metal industry based on copper and (later) bronze production. Status differences are reflected in the range of burial treatments—from unusually lavish to mostly austere—given to individuals in the large Longshan cemeteries. Walled towns, which were up to 1 mile in circumference, dominated the region's villages and hamlets (Yan, 1999). Some of the town walls were made of stamped earth, compacted to the hardness of cement, more than 20 feet high and 30 feet thick. These enormous constructions obviously required a large supervised labor force. Numerous arrowheads testify to the prevalence of warfare, but no clear explanations for these developments are yet possible.

Perhaps because of the differential access by some individuals and groups to the means of communication within Chinese society (as Chang suggests; see p. 395), their success in organizing and controlling communal agricultural efforts, or conceivably more directly through violence and coercion, local leaders who emerged in northern China over the next few centuries commanded the allegiance of ever-larger regions. The rising nobility played an increasingly prominent role in the next era of Chinese civilization.

Many Chinese archaeologists believe that Erlitou (Fig. 15-12), in Henan province, confirms the existence of the legendary **Xia** dynasty, proclaimed in myth as the dawn of Chinese civilization (Chang, 1980, 1986). The site displays evidence of increasing social complexity around 4,000 ya. It's here, for the first time, that walled palaces set onto stamped-earth foundations literally raised members of the royal household above all others. Valuable stone carvings and bronze and ceramic vessels figured in elaborate court ceremonies and rituals. Royal burials contrasted sharply with those of commoners, who were sometimes disposed of in rubbish pits.

Shang The following **Shang** dynasty, beginning in the eighteenth century B.C. (3,600 ya), attained a level of sophistication in material culture, architecture, art styles, and writing that only a highly structured society could achieve. Enduring for some six centuries, Shang is generally acknowledged as China's first civilization. While the large population of peasant farmers lived and labored as they always had, an elite and powerful ruling class, supported by slaves, specialized crafters, scribes, and other functionaries, topped the rigid social hierarchy. Unlike the Indus civilization, the Shang territorial state covered multiple cities and a large territory of roughly 8,900 square miles.

The power and actions of Shang rulers were sometimes directed through the rite of **divination**, or prophecy. This practice was one of the original purposes for which writing was used in ancient China. Divination was performed by first inscribing a question on a specially prepared bone, such as the shoulder blade of an ox or deer, or on turtle shells. Applying heat to the thin bones made them crack, and then the answer to the question could be "read" from the patterns formed by the cracks. Divination was a vital activity to the Shang, and thousands of the marked bones survive as a unique historical archive offering insights to early Chinese politics and society (Fitzgerald, 1978).

Many scholars identify the two capital cities of the initial Shang period as Shixianggou and Zhengzhou, both of which are in Henan Province (Maisels 1999). At Zhengzhou,

Figure 15-12

Centers of early civilization in Northern China.

Xia (shah) Semilegendary kingdom, or dynasty, of early China.

Shang The first historic civilization in northern China; also called the Yin dynasty.

divination Foretelling the future.

Figure **15-13**

Bronze ritual vessel of the Shang dynasty.

Figure **15-14**

Section of the Great Wall, erected by Qin Shi Huangdi.

Photo Archive Submitter/National Geographic Image Collection

Sue Lewis

archaeologists revealed portions of a large walled precinct encompassing the residences of nobles and rulers as well as their temples and other ceremonial structures. Within sight of the high enclosure, extending in all directions for more than a mile, were clustered homes and specialized production areas, including several bronze foundries, pottery kilns, and bone workshops.

Shang artisans created remarkable bronze work, particularly elaborate cauldrons cast in sectional molds (Fig. 15-13). Decorated with stylized animal motifs and worshipful inscriptions, the massive metal vessels were designed to hold ritual offerings of wine and food dedicated to ancestors and deities. They also served as prominent funerary items in the royal tombs, about a dozen of which were in the vicinity of the later Shang capital at Anyang (Chang, 1986). Digging each of these grave pits and its four ramped entryways probably kept about 1,000 laborers occupied for a week. In addition to the bronzes, lavish offerings of carved jade, horse-drawn chariots, and scores of human sacrificial victims accompanied the rulers in death. In much later times, as in the tomb of emperor **Qin Shi Huangdi** (died 2,200 ya) at Xian, life-size clay sculptures of warriors and horses sometimes substituted for their living counterparts.

It seems that the Shang kingdom was only one of several contentious feudal states in northern China. Despite their political competition, all shared a common culture, one that served as a foundation for most future developments in China. After the eclipse of the Shang state, successive **Zhou** rulers (1122–221 B.C.) adopted and extended the social and cultural innovations introduced by their Shang predecessors. Much of China remained apportioned among competitive warlords until the Qin and Han dynasties (221 B.C.–A.D. 220), when this huge region was at last politically unified into a cohesive Chinese empire. Consolidated by Shi Huangdi and protected from the outer world behind his 3,000-mile Great Wall (Fig. 15-14), China in later times maintained many of the cultural traditions linking it to an ancient past.

Qin Shi Huangdi (chin-shee-huangdee) First emperor of a unified China.

Zhou (chew) Chinese dynasty that followed Shang and ruled between 1122 and 221 B.C.

New World Civilizations

The rise of the earliest civilizations in the Americas was closely intertwined with the development of agriculture. In many regions where early farming prevailed, the combination of maize, beans, and plants such as squash came to substitute for diets rich in animal protein. In time, these primary domesticates supported large populations and established the economic basis for the development of states and civilizations in several New World areas.

Superficially, we can say that early New World cities, states, and civilizations are broadly comparable to those of the Old World. All shared some basic similarities: state economies based on agriculture and long-distance trade; powerful leaders and social stratification; human labor invested in large-scale constructions; public art styles; state religions; record keeping; and the prominent role of warfare. Still, there are significant points of contrast as well. For example, domesticated animals played only a small part in New World agriculture; the technological role of metal was limited; and the wheel had no important function, nor did watercraft. These differences reflect the unique historical traditions, resources, and geography of the continents upon which the earliest civilizations developed. This section examines three New World civilizations that developed in very different regions—lowland **Mesoamerica**, highland Mexico, and Peru Fig. 15-15).

Mesoamerica (*meso*, meaning "middle") Geographical and cultural region from central Mexico to northwestern Costa Rica; formerly called "Middle America" in the archaeological literature.

LOWLAND MESOAMERICA

Olmec By roughly 3,500 ya, farming villages dotted the lowlands of Mesoamerica. Local chiefdoms arose, and their archaeological hallmarks included prominent house

Figure **15-15**

Time line for New World civilizations.

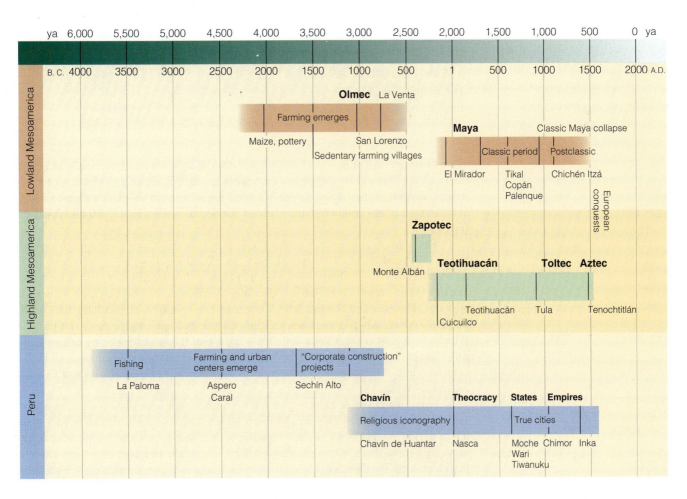

Mesoamerican archaeological sites mentioned in the text.

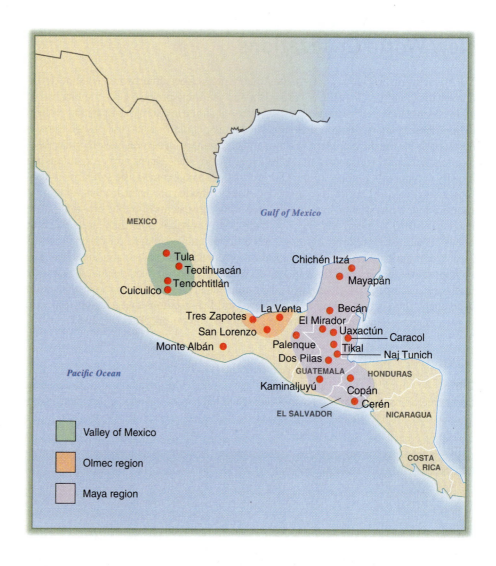

sites, status or ritual objects, and other signs of social differentiation, especially in burial offerings. For many years, archaeologists have been particularly interested in one of these groups, known as the **Olmec**, which achieved prominence in the river valleys, forests, and swamps of the southern Gulf Coast of Mexico between about 3,200 and 2,400 ya (Fig. 15-16).

The political organization of the Olmec is controversial, and there's no consensus in sight. Richard Diehl (2004) and Michael Coe (Diehl and Coe, 1996), who have both worked extensively on Olmec sites, identify Olmec as "America's first civilization" and one that exerted considerable influence on later Mesoamerican cultures. Other archaeologists (e.g., Flannery and Marcus, 2000; Spencer and Redmond, 2004) conclude that Olmec **polities** were chiefdoms, not states, and that they do not represent an early civilization. What's more, Spencer and Redmond (2004) argue that the most convincing archaeological evidence for the emergence of the earliest Mesoamerican state can be found not in the lowlands, but at the large Zapotec center of Monte Albán in the highlands of Oaxaca around 2,300 ya.

From an archaeological standpoint, it's probably more important to determine how extensively the Olmec affected contemporary societies in other parts of Mesoamerica than it is to decide in which sociopolitical pigeonhole their society belongs. Diehl and Coe, for example, believe that the Olmec anticipated, and may have inspired, important features that characterized subsequent Mesoamerican civilizations. Other archaeologists reject such

Olmec Prehistoric chiefdom in the Gulf Coast lowlands of Veracruz and Tabasco, Mexico, between 3,200 and 2,400 ya.

polities The political organizations of societies or groups.

arguments and feel that they were simply part of a web of interacting chiefdoms and early states (Grove 1989, 1996; Flannery and Marcus 2000).

The two best-known Olmec sites are San Lorenzo and La Venta (see Fig. 15-16), which Diehl (2004) identifies as the region's first cities. At both sites, people extensively modified the natural landscapes—without the aid of domestic animals or machinery—to convert them to proper settings for impressive constructions and sculptures of ritual significance (Coe, 1994; Diehl, 2004). Earthen-mound alignments enclose the wide courtyards, plazas, and artificial ponds at San Lorenzo. A 100-foot-high cone-shaped earthen pyramid dominates La Venta. Within and nearby the sites themselves, there are hundreds of smaller earthen platform mounds that once supported homes and workshops.

In addition to building ceremonial architecture, the Olmec produced remarkable monumental sculptures and smaller, well-crafted carvings of jade and other attractive stones. **Anthropomorphic** forms predominate, including some figurines and bas-reliefs that combine the features of humans with those of felines, probably jaguars. Olmec art and iconography are fascinating but poorly understood. Who or what did these anthropomorphic beings represent? Equally intriguing are the colossal Olmec heads, each of which seems to be an individualized portrait of a ruler in helmet-like headgear, carved from massive boulders of basalt weighing up to 20 tons (Fig. 15-17). Archaeologists estimate that the sustained effort of 1,000-member crews were needed to drag and raft the boulders from the distant source area, some 60 miles from the site (Lowe, 1989). Nine of these huge likenesses have been found at San Lorenzo itself.

Curiously, the Olmec intentionally buried caches of beads, as well as carved figurines and implements made from their highly valued jade. One pit offering at La Venta consisted of 460 green stone blocks, arranged into a giant mosaic design and then buried at a depth of more than 20 feet. Another held an assemblage of small jade figures set into place so that they all seem to be confronting one individual. Then, still in position, the group was buried (Fig. 15-18).

The latest Olmec controversy concerns the origins of writing in Mesoamerica. Several artifacts bearing signs reputed to be **glyphs** that could be part of an Olmec writing

Barry Lewis

Figure **15-17**

Monumental Olmec head excavated at La Venta, Mexico.

Philip Drucker, Robert Squier, "Excavations at La Venta, Tabasco, 1955." *Smithsonian Institution, Bureau of American Ethnology Bulletin 170*, plate 20. Washington, DC: Government Printing Office, 1969.

Figure **15-18**

Buried cache of small Olmec jade figurines found at La Venta, Mexico.

anthropomorphic (*anthro*, meaning "man," and *morph*, meaning "shape") Having or being given humanlike characteristics.

glyphs Carved or incised symbolic figures.

At a Glance

Important Lowland Mesoamerican Sites and Regions

SITE	DATES (YA)	SIGNIFICANCE
San Lorenzo (Mexico)	3,150–2,900	Olmec civic-ceremonial center in southern Veracruz
La Venta (Mexico)	ca. 2,800–2,400	Large Olmec civic-ceremonial center in the coastal lowlands of Tabasco
San Andrés (Mexico)	2,650	Olmec site near La Venta that recently yielded a cylinder seal with early evidence of writing in the Gulf Coast lowlands; San Andrés also cited in Chapter 14 for the discovery of ancient maize pollen in a soil core pulled from pre-Olmec contexts
Cerén (El Salvador)	ca. 1,400	Maya village buried by the eruption of a volcano; provides a Pompeii-like snapshot of Classic period Maya life
Copán (Honduras)	ca. 1,600–1,200	Major Maya city in western Honduras with an estimated population of around 27,000 at its peak
Naj Tunich (Guatemala)	ca. 1,750–1,450	A sacred cave in the Petén region that has furnished invaluable new information about Maya art, writing, and religious life

system have recently been reported from sites in the coastal states of Veracruz and Tabasco (Pohl et al., 2002; del Carmen Rodríguez Martínez et al., 2006). One of these artifacts, a serpentine block that bears 62 signs, or glyphs, could be as old as 900 B.C. Critics argue that these discoveries aren't sufficient evidence of a fully developed system of writing (Stokstad, 2004; see also Bruhns and Kelker, 2007).

To sum things up, the Olmec represent a fascinating early development of complex society in the lowlands of the Mexican Gulf Coast, but one about which archaeologists have considerably more questions than answers. The view supported by the most evidence is that the Olmec chiefdoms of southern Veracruz and Tabasco were similar in many respects to their neighbors in the highlands to the south and west and to those throughout central Mexico. The archaeological evidence may or may not eventually live up to Diehl's claim that they were America's first civilization (Lawler, 2007).

Classic Maya As we noted earlier, some suggest that Classic **Maya*** civilization originated in part with the Olmec, whose art, architecture, and rituals are reflected in some early Maya sites. Others suggest that Maya civilization resulted from an internal reorganization of Maya society itself; or that it reflects the regional impact of the developing states of central Mexico; or, more generally, that it came from the competitive interaction between contemporary Mesoamerican chiefdoms, which ultimately resulted in some of them becoming true states and civilizations. Right now, the third explanation appears to be the most likely (Flannery and Marcus, 2000; Braswell, 2003).

Maya Mesoamerican culture consisting of regional kingdoms and known for its art and architectural accomplishments; also, Native American ethnic group of southern Mexico, Guatemala, and Belize.

---

*The word *Classic* refers here to the archaeological period of the same name, which was roughly between A.D. 200 and 900.

By roughly 2,100 ya, the elements of Maya civilization were coming together. Crucial materials that were lacking in most of the Maya lowlands, especially suitable stone for making tools and milling slabs, were acquired in exchange for commodities such as salt or the feathers of colorful jungle birds, both of which the highland groups desired. Control of trade routes or strategic waterways may have promoted the growth of the Late Preclassic* center at El Mirador, where archaeologists have found the earliest evidence of Maya palaces, and following that at Uaxactún and Tikal, all of which are in northern Guatemala (see Fig. 15-16).

At these sites and others, Maya society came to be dominated increasingly by an elite social class. A host of Maya kings, each claiming descent through royal lineages back to the gods themselves, held sway over independent city-states centered on elaborate ceremonial precincts. Under the patronage of these kings, writing, fine arts, and architecture flourished in the Maya lowlands, as did chronic warfare among rival kingdoms (Sharer, 1996; Coe, 1999). Lisa Lucero (2003) argues that successful Maya rulers acquired and maintained their political power by skillfully manipulating domestic rituals, which in turn promoted political cohesion.

The Maya are best known for their impressive Classic period urban centers, with Tikal, Copán (Honduras), and Palenque (Mexico) among them (Fig. 15-19). These centers served essentially as capitals of regional Maya city-states, despite their somewhat dispersed populace. Including the ruling elite and their retainers, crafters, other specialists, and farmers, some 27,000 people were attached to the important city of Copán (Webster et al., 2000), although two-thirds of them actually lived in farming compounds scattered through the Copán Valley, within walking distance of Copán.

Formal, large-scale architecture dominated the largest cities. Tikal, with over 50,000 residents, boasted more than 3,000 structures in its core precinct alone. Most impressive were the stepped, limestone-sided pyramids capped with temples. Facing across the broad stuccoed plazas were multiroom palaces (presumably elite residences), generally a ritual

Barry Lewis

Figure **15-19**

The Temple of the Inscriptions at Palenque, Mexico, served as the tomb of the important Maya ruler Pacal, who died in A.D. 683.

---

*The Late Preclassic is a Mesoamerican archaeological period that dates roughly from 300 B.C. to A.D. 200.

Figure **15-20**

The ball court at Monte Albán, one of several types built by nearly all the major cultures of Mesoamerica.

Mark A. Gutchen

ball court or two (Fig. 15-20), and always elaborately carved **stelae** (Fig. 15-21). Other features might include graded causeways leading into the complex masonry reservoirs for storing crucial runoff from tropical cloudbursts. The Maya preferred to paint their structures in bold colors, so the overall effect must have been stunning.

Maya writing was well developed by 300–200 B.C. (Houston, 2006), and scholars have made significant progress in deciphering the complex inscriptions found on Maya stelae, temples, and other monuments. Many stelae proclaim the ancestry and noble deeds of actual Maya rulers and provide a precise chronology of major events in lowland Mesoamerica (Schele and Miller, 1986). These inscriptions offer direct insights to Classic Maya sociopolitical organization, including the uneasy and frequently embattled relationships among leading ceremonial centers and their rival aristocracies (Schele and Freidel, 1990; Coe, 1992).

Religion was a key component of Maya society, just as it was in all early civilizations. Architecture and art were dedicated to the veneration of divine kings and the worship of perhaps hundreds of major and minor deities. The nobility included a priestly caste who carefully observed the sun, moon, and planet Venus; predicted the rains; prescribed the rituals; and performed the sacrifices. Most of the priestly lore and learning faithfully recorded in the Maya **codices**, or books, was lost when the Spanish burned the ancient texts during the conquest. But a number of sacred caves, like **Naj Tunich** in Guatemala, preserve some forgotten aspects of Maya religion. Within these dusky chambers, archaeologists have come upon Classic period offerings, paintings that graphically depict ritual intercourse and self-mutilation, and the remains of young sacrificial victims (Brady and Stone, 1986).

Archaeologists historically have devoted much of their attention to the most spectacular Maya sites, but the importance of these sites is gradually being put into perspective as research also focuses on the entire range of Classic Maya lifeways. For example, extraordinary discoveries, such as the buried Maya community at Cerén, in El Salvador, give us detailed glimpses of village life (Sheets, 2002, 2006). Cerén—once a hamlet of mud-walled, thatched huts—lay entombed for 1,400 years beneath 18 feet of ash from the eruption of a nearby volcano. The inhabitants fled their homes, which were quickly buried by the volcanic ash. Remarkable traces of Maya peasant life survived, including a plentiful

stelae (*sing.*, stela) (stee´-lee) Upright posts or stones, often bearing inscriptions.

codices (*sing.*, codex) Illustrated books.

Naj Tunich (nah toon´-eesh) Maya sacred cave in Guatemala.

harvest of maize, beans, squash, tomatoes, and chilies stored in baskets and pots, arranged as if they had just been gathered from nearby garden plots.

The rise and fall of Maya city-states continued for centuries, and we now know a great deal about the historical events that figured in the changing fortunes of Maya kings. For example, the city of Tikal, one of the largest Maya cities, fell on hard times for more than a century after A.D. 562, when it was defeated by Caracol, a smaller city-state in modern-day Belize. Later, during A.D. 738, Copán's vigorous king, 18 Rabbit, lost his life at the hands of a neighboring ruler. These events reflect a common pattern of intrigue and competition between neighboring polities. Things came to a head around A.D. 900. Maya artisans no longer turned out their distinctive decorated ceramics, nor did they carve and erect inscribed stelae. The construction of palaces, temples, and other major works ceased altogether, and nearly all major sites were abandoned.

The remarkable Maya collapse has intrigued scholars for decades. Archaeologists are not yet quite sure what happened, let alone why. Proposed single-cause explanations, each of them inadequate, include devastation by hurricanes or earthquakes, extreme climatic fluctuations, insect infestations, epidemic diseases, malnutrition, overpopulation, an unbalanced male/female sex ratio, peasant revolts against the elite, and mass migrations. Some scholars have also cited external factors, such as the breakdown of trade relations with the areas that supplied the resource-poor Maya or invasion by peoples from highland Mexico.

Other scholars claim that political instability brought about the collapse (Rice et al., 2001). Cioffi-Revilla and Landman (1999) argue that the Classic Maya city-states collapsed primarily because they failed to integrate into a single unified political system, such as that achieved by the Aztecs in central Mexico and the Inka in highland South America. Unlike the people of Egypt or Mesopotamia, the Maya had no Narmer or Sargon to bring unity to their city-states—and those who tried met their match in the insurmountable logistical obstacles presented by the tropical jungles of the lowlands (Cioffi-Revilla and Landman, 1999, pp. 586–588).

HIGHLAND MEXICO

In central Mexico, far to the northwest of the Maya area, the convergence of two mountain ranges forms a great highland of some 3,000 square miles, commonly called the Valley of Mexico (see Fig. 15-16). An elevated plateau rimmed by mountains and volcanic peaks to the west, south, and east, the rich agricultural soils of the Valley of Mexico were watered by several rivers and with large lakes at its center. This broad semiarid basin, which is today dominated by Mexico City, was the stage on which several important prehistoric states and civilizations developed. The earliest city-state to dominate the Valley, **Teotihuacán**, became one of the largest urban centers in the New World up to the nineteenth century (Cowgill, 2000).

Teotihuacán With its fields nourished by a system of irrigation canals, Teotihuacán was a successful, growing community around 2,200 ya. Its closest competitor, Cuicuilco (see Fig. 15-16), had a population of around 20,000 at its peak but vanished from the scene around 2,000 ya, when it was buried by a lava flow. This unfortunate event worked to Teotihuacán's advantage, and it soon dominated the Valley of Mexico. After 1,700 ya, its presence can be archaeologically recognized in many parts of Mesoamerica, as far away as Guatemala (Spencer and Redmond, 2004).

At its height between 1,700 and 1,400 ya, Teotihuacán (Fig. 15-22) had more than 100,000 residents and covered 7.7 square miles. Somewhat in contrast to the Maya centers, Teotihuacán's layout was more orderly and its population more highly concentrated. Built on a grid pattern with a primary north-south axis, its avenues, plazas, major monuments, and homes alike—and even the San Juan River— were aligned to a master plan.

Mark A. Gutchen

Figure 15-21

Maya hieroglyphs on a stela at Copán record the date and purpose of its dedication.

Teotihuacán (tay-oh-tee-wah-cahn´) Earliest city-state to dominate the Valley of Mexico. It became one of the largest urban centers in the New World up to the nineteenth century.

Figure **15-22**

Feathered serpent figure on a temple façade at Teotihuacán, Mexico.

Mark A. Gutchen

The city's inhabitants lived in some 2,000 apartment compounds, arranged into formal neighborhoods based on occupation or social class and ranging from tradespeople to merchants, military officers, and even foreigners. Civic and religious leaders enjoyed more luxurious facilities in the central district (Millon, 1988). Artisans laboring in hundreds of individual household workshops produced ceramic vessels, obsidian blades, shell and jade carvings, fabrics, leather goods, and other practical or luxury items.

An impressive civic-ceremonial precinct covered nearly 1 square mile in the heart of the city. Imaginative Spanish explorers assigned the name Avenida de los Muertos (literally, "Avenue of the Dead") to the main thoroughfare, which extends northward 2.8 miles to a massive structure, the Pyramid of the Moon. An even greater Pyramid of the Sun, its base equal to that of Khufu's pyramid in Egypt (though it rises only half as high), occupies a central position along the same avenue. Archaeologists have come to recognize that the Teotihuacán rulers built this immense structure to resemble a sacred mountain, and they raised it directly over a natural cave that symbolized the entry to the underworld. Flanking the south end of the Avenida de los Muertos, the Ciudadela was the administrative complex, and the Great Compound served as Teotihuacán's central marketplace.

Unlike Maya art, that of Teotihuacán doesn't show identifiable rulers or personalized representations. There also are no Teotihuacán counterparts of Maya stelae commemorating the conquests and lineages of a given king. Artistic expression is both impersonal and repetitive, the same elements or motifs appearing again and again; this pattern is particularly evident in Teotihuacán architecture, the repetitive nature of which was relieved mostly by the use of bright colors. Although social differentiation clearly existed in Teotihuacán society, it is evident in art mostly in differences of costume, not in representations of the human body (Cowgill, 2000).

Warfare appears to have been common among Mesoamerican states, but cultural differences determined how war was expressed artistically (Brown and Stanton, 2003). These differences went unappreciated by archaeologists for a long time, and they believed that Teotihuacán was a relatively peaceful state. Now that researchers better understand Teotihuacán culture, we can see that warfare also was an important part of this early state.

Mention of warfare leads us logically to examine the possible influence that Teotihuacán wielded throughout Mexico's central region and beyond. The society's fine orange-slipped ceramics, architectural and artistic styles, and obsidian products are said to be present at distant contemporary centers such as Monte Albán in Oaxaca; the Maya site of **Kaminaljuyú** in the Guatemalan highlands; and Tikal, Uaxactún, and Becán in the Maya lowlands (Berlo, 1992). Some also argue that Teotihuacán played a large role in the development of Maya states (e.g., Sanders and Michels, 1977; Sanders et al., 1979).

As with many—if not most—archaeological generalizations like these, the more we learn, the more complex the picture gets. And while no one doubts that Teotihuacán interacted with other regions, the precise nature of this interaction is still being explored (Braswell, 2003). Some scholars point to the Escuintla region on the Pacific coast of Guatemala, where evidence was recently found of a Teotihuacán colony that established itself at several sites and soon made itself felt throughout this region as well as in southern Chiapas and western El Salvador (Bove and Busto, 2003). But other scholars, many of them Maya specialists, view the whole notion of Teotihuacán "influence" as greatly exaggerated; in cases where there is indisputable material evidence of contact, they argue that it hasn't yet been proved that Teotihuacán had a significant local impact or that it changed anything (e.g., Iglesias Ponce de Léon, 2003). It's more than likely that the truth lies somewhere in between these opposed views, but precisely where we've yet to discover.

Teotihuacán's demise also remains an archaeological mystery. After six remarkable centuries, the city was not doing well. Physical anthropologists who have examined human remains excavated from the site's later features identify among these bones common skeletal indicators of nutritional stress and disease as well as high infant mortality rates. Still, population levels remained stable for another century or so before declining rapidly.

The end came in flames and havoc about 1,350 ya (Cowgill, 2000). The entire ceremonial precinct blazed as temples were thrown down and their icons smashed, though

Kaminaljuyú (cam-en-awl-hoo-yoo´) Major prehistoric Maya site located at Guatemala City.

At a Glance
Important Highland Mesoamerican Sites and Regions

SITE	DATES (YA)	SIGNIFICANCE
Teotihuacán (Mexico)	ca. 2,200–1,350	Earliest city-state to dominate the Valley of Mexico, one of the largest urban centers in the New World up to the nineteenth century
Cuicuilco (Mexico)	ca. 2,300–2,000	Important early center in the Valley of Mexico; its destruction by a lava flow made it easier for Teotihuacán to take control of the valley
Kaminaljuyú (Guatemala)	ca. 3,000–1,100	Major Maya site located on the outskirts of Guatemala City; similarities of its elaborate tombs and architecture are often cited as evidence of the far-flung influence of Teotihuacán
Tula (Mexico)	ca. 1,200–850	Toltec capital in the Valley of Mexico

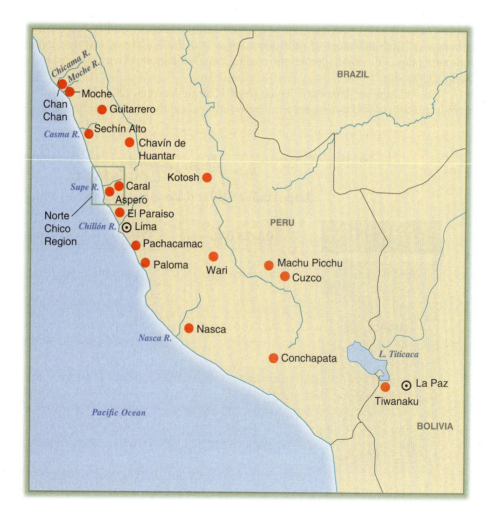

residential areas remained unscathed. In the frenzy, some of the nobility were seized and dismembered, apparently by their own people. As archaeologist George L. Cowgill (2000, p. 290) puts it, "What ended was not just a dynasty, it was the belief system that had supported the state." The city may even have been abandoned, or nearly so, for a brief period, but researchers still have much to learn about this period of the city's past. Regardless, the destruction ended Teotihuacán's political and religious preeminence, and many of its residents scattered to other communities. We have yet to determine the factors—whether internal or external—that brought this extraordinary city to its knees.

Toltecs Teotihuacán's collapse did not leave a political, economic, or religious vacuum in highland Mesoamerica. Of the many groups contending for control over the region during the next several centuries, the **Toltecs** eventually emerged as the most powerful. They established a capital at **Tula**, in the northern region of the Valley of Mexico some 40 miles northwest of Teotihuacán. By 1,200–1,100 ya, the city may have had as many as 50,000 to 60,000 residents. This city-state covered some 4.5 to 5 square miles and included several pyramids and ball courts in two ceremonial precincts (Healan and Stoutamire, 1989).

Although its more modest ceremonial precincts scarcely rivaled those of Classic period times, Tula does show some artistic and architectural continuities with Teotihuacán (Cowgill, 2000). The Toltecs also briefly guided a commercial and military enterprise that expanded through trade and tribute networks, colonization efforts, and probably conquest (Davies, 1983; Healan, 1989). Toltec prestige reached in several directions. We even recog-

Figure **15-23**

Peruvian sites and locations mentioned in the text.

Toltecs Central Mexican highlands people who created a pre-Aztec empire with its capital at Tula in the Valley of Mexico.

Tula (too´-la) Toltec capital in the Valley of Mexico; sometimes known as Tollan.

nize their influence in the copper bells, ceremonial ball courts, and other exotic products found on Hohokam sites in the American Southwest, from which the Toltecs acquired their valued blue turquoise stone, probably by making long-distance exchanges (see p. 375).

As Toltec power declined around 850 ya, a prolonged drought was withering many of the farming communities in northern Mexico and the American Southwest, bringing streams of refugees into the Valley of Mexico and throwing the region into chaos once more. One of the groups that appeared on the scene at this point was the **Mexica**, better known historically as the **Aztecs** (Smith, 2003). They dominated the Valley of Mexico from their capital at **Tenochtitlán** until the Spanish conquered the city in 1519.

PERU

Another New World civilization that fell to Old World invaders in the early 1500s had developed over several millennia along the western coast of South America. At first glance, Peru seems an unlikely region for nurturing early civilizations (Fig. 15-23). Its coast is a narrow desert, a dry fringe of land broken at intervals by deeply entrenched river valleys that slice down from the mountains to the sea. The Andes Mountains rise abruptly and dramatically behind the coastal plain, forming a rugged, snowcapped continental divide (Fig. 15-24). These geographical contrasts figured prominently in Peru's prehistory (Bruhns, 1994). In fact, the dynamic tension between coast and highlands—between fishers and farmers—provides a key to understanding the region's cultural past.

Fishing, Farming, and the Rise of Civilization Most of the world's early civilizations were built on the shoulders of farmers. However, in the central Andes region—that is, in Peru and parts of Bolivia and Ecuador—things played out a little differently, and archaeologists continue to explore the relative contributions of both fishing and farming to the development of Peruvian civilization (Moseley, 1975; Wilson, 1981; Bruhns, 1994). Archaeologist Michael Moseley points out that the deep, cold Pacific currents off the Peruvian coast that create the richest fishing waters in the Western Hemisphere are also responsible for the climatic conditions that make the central Andes coastal plain one of the world's driest deserts (Moseley, 1992, p. 102). Marine resources surely supported people in this region from the earliest period of human settlement.

Between 6,000 and 4,500 ya, when farming was already under way in a few highland areas, coastal fishing groups settled as permanent residents at sites such as La Paloma (see p. 373). The productive fisheries may have delayed farming in this dry coastal region for some time, until the long-term effects of a stronger, recurring El Niño pattern and other factors promoted the development of a simple form of agriculture. In early farming efforts near the coast, people planted squash, gourds, and beans in the damp beds of seasonal streams flowing down from the Andes.

Evidence of social differentiation and the intensification of agriculture spread widely in western South America between 5,500 and 3,800 ya and can be found at coastal sites in Ecuador and Peru. For example, the coastal site of Aspero, located in the Norte Chico region to the north of Lima and dated to 5,000–4,500 ya (see Fig. 15-23), covers roughly 37 acres and includes six platform mounds. This community depended on marine resources as well as several domesticated food crops plus cotton. A bit farther to the south, in the Chillón Valley, the preagricultural, marine-resources-focused El Paraiso site had a large population who lived in a community built around an impressive U-shaped ceremonial complex of enormous masonry structures (Haas and Creamer, 2004). Creating this complex may have required as many as 1 million person-days of labor. Both Aspero and El Paraiso are evidence of social differentiation and a certain amount of centralized power in some coastal centers at a very early date.

Recent surveys and excavations at inland sites in the Norte Chico region revealed more than 20 major preceramic sites with monumental architecture and large residential

Helaine Silverman

Figure **15-24**
The arid western flank of the Andes Mountains in Peru. Snow-covered and cloud-wrapped peaks can be seen in the distance.

Mexica (meh-shee´-ka) Original name by which the Aztecs were known before their rise to power.

Aztecs Militaristic people who dominated the Valley of Mexico and surrounding area at the time of the European conquest.

Tenochtitlán (tay-nosh-teet-lahn´) Aztec capital, built on the future site of Mexico City.

areas that existed between 5,000 and 3,800 ya (Haas et al., 2004). The large urban center of Caral in the Supe Valley covers roughly 270 acres and includes sunken circular plazas, large and small platform mounds, and many residential and other building complexes. Although Caral lies 14 miles inland, the faunal remains found in excavations of this site are all marine animals, principally small fishes such as anchovies and sardines (Haas and Creamer, 2004).

Haas and Creamer (2004) argue that when you consider Norte Chico sites such as Caral and Aspero together, it's evident that a sort of symbiotic economic relationship existed between inland and coastal sites. Coastal sites like Aspero provided the region's main source of animal protein, mostly in the form of anchovies and sardines, and the inland sites like Caral provided the main source of plant resources, including cotton for fishnets and gourds for net floats. The inland sites also appear to have had the upper hand in the emergence of leadership and political power in the region. At the inland sites we find archaeologically identifiable status differences, larger monumental architecture, motifs and features such as sunken circular plazas that appear to be pecursors of pan-Andean patterns, control over agricultural resources, and evidence of agricultural intensification (Haas and Creamer, 2004, pp. 46–47).

Peru's coastal regions were wholeheartedly committed to subsistence agriculture after about 3,800 ya. Farming communities are found in river valleys such as the Moche, where irrigation was feasible (see Fig. 15-23). There, local communities excavated canals to irrigate crops of maize, peanuts, and potatoes, plants originally domesticated in Mexico and the Andean highlands. Such staple crops made farming a worthwhile endeavor, especially considering the periodic unreliability of coastal resources due to El Niño. The success of these lowland communities may be measured by the imposing size of ceremonial complexes, such as Sechín Alto on the Casma River, that are found in more than two dozen coastal valleys and several upland sites in central and northern Peru.

Sechín Alto and other such sites are early examples of the "corporate construction" projects that became common in Peru. These huge U-shaped arrangements of temples, platforms, and courtyards—as well as irrigation networks, in many instances—must represent the labors of a large force of people drawn from resident populations as well as the general vicinity. Clearly, sites of this kind were important ceremonial and possibly market centers for several neighboring valleys (Pozorski and Pozorski, 1988).

What inspired the collective efforts that produced the civic architecture and the defined art styles in Peru? Most archaeologists interpret these developments as evidence of greater social complexity and greater authority invested in civil or religious leaders. Under their direction, public energies were applied to large-scale projects. But what motivated individuals to participate in these collective enterprises? And what guided their leaders? What was the source of their persuasive or coercive powers? In Peru, as elsewhere, archaeologists have considered militarism, religion, and control of resources, among other motivating forces, in explaining the rise of civilizations; still, they haven't yet come to many definite conclusions (e.g., Haas et al., 1987).

Chavín Around 3,200–2,850 ya, the peoples of the northern Peruvian highlands and coast came together in a religious fervor that brought some degree of cultural unity to this broad region. Underlying their unity was some form of centralized authority (Kembel and Rick, 2004), with a shared ideology that the people expressed especially through their ritual art. **Chavín de Huantar**, an intriguing civic-ceremonial center set in a high Andean valley, is the best-known archaeological example of this iconography (Pozorski and Pozorski, 1987; Burger, 1992). There, raised stone tiers flank sunken courtyards where ceremonies took place near a temple riddled by underground chambers and passageways. Anthropomorphic stone sculptures and other art at the site combined human characteristics with the features of jaguars, snakes, birds of prey, and mythological beings.

While Chavín de Huantar itself may have served as a religious pilgrimage center—possibly the seat of a respected oracle, or fortune-teller—and training center for initiates,

Chavín de Huantar Chavín civic-ceremonial center in the northern highlands of Peru.

At a Glance
Important Peruvian Sites and Regions

SITE	DATES (YA)	SIGNIFICANCE
Caral	ca. 5,200–4,500	Large preceramic urban center in the Supe Valley
Chavín de Huantar	ca. 2,900–2,500	Civic-ceremonial center in the northern highlands
Nasca	ca. 2,000–1,600	Nonstate theocracy in south-central Peru near the coast
Moche	ca. 1,900–1,300	Early state on Peru's north coast; its capital city (also called Moche) was possibly the earliest true city in the Andes
Wari	ca. 1,460–1,100	Early state in the central highlands
Tiwanaku	ca. 2,400–1,000	Early state in the southern highlands near Lake Titicaca
Chan Chan	ca. 1,000–600	Capital city of the Chimor (Chimú) state

the Chavín art style was influenced by earlier art and architecture (Kembel and Rick, 2004). Chavín motifs were reproduced most frequently on cotton and camelid wool textiles, but they also appeared on pottery, marine shell, and metal objects. The symbolism and artifacts bestowed prestige upon those who were privileged to acquire them. Although Chavín may have been an agent of widespread cultural change in the region, at least on a stylistic and ideological level, its influence had faded considerably by about 2,500 ya.

Early States Several Peruvian kingdoms, or states, including the **Moche** culture of Peru's north coast, formed between 1,900 and 1,300 ya (Stanish, 2001). Consistent with their identification as complex societies, these states soon had specialized craftsmen, pyramids, irrigation canals, and public buildings. The Moche rulers consolidated their hold over neighboring valleys initially through warfare and then by greatly expanding irrigated agricultural lands in the conquered areas. The archaeologist Charles Stanish (2001, p. 53) suggests that the Moche capital (of the same name) may have been "the first true city in the Andes." Among this city's monumental works, the **Huaca del Sol**, or Pyramid of the Sun, incorporated some 100 million hand-formed bricks and was one of the largest prehistoric structures in the Americas.

Artistic specialists created remarkable objects that served the elite as status symbols in life and in death. Unique **polychrome** ceramic vessels modeled to represent portraits, buildings, everyday scenes, or imaginative fantasies were a Moche specialty (Fig. 15-25). Metalsmiths also hammered, alloyed, and cast beautiful ornaments, ceremonial weapons, and religious paraphernalia from precious gold, silver, and copper. Unlike Old World societies, those in the Americas seldom employed metal for technological purposes, generally reserving it for ornamental use as a badge of social standing.

The contents of excavated tombs of Moche warrior-priests rival those of the rulers of Egypt or Mesopotamia (Alva and Donnan, 1993). These high officials, both male and female, officiated over the human sacrifice ceremony that was an important component of Moche state religion. Upon their own deaths, these officials were dressed in the elaborate and distinctive regalia of their elevated position. Protected by dead attendants, llamas, and dogs, their tombs have yielded ceremonial headdresses, earrings, necklaces, and goblets.

William Turnbaugh

Figure **15-25**

Moche portrait jar from northern Peru.

Moche (moh´-chay) Regional state, city, and valley of the same name in northern Peru.

Huaca del Sol (wah´-ka dell sole) Massive adobe pyramid built at Moche, in northern Peru.

polychrome Many-colored.

As Moche influences faded around 1,400 ya, the **Wari** and **Tiwanaku** states emerged in the central and southern highlands. The name Wari (also spelled Huari) derives from the capital city of Wari, the urban core of which covered roughly 2 square miles in an architectural plan that was repeated in other Wari centers (Stanish, 2001).

Like Wari, Tiwanaku, which was situated near Lake Titicaca, in Bolivia (see Figs. 15-23 and 15-26), used trade, control of food and labor resources, religion, and military conquest to extend its interests from the Andes to the coast (Isbell and Vranich, 2004). Wari and Tiwanaku shared similar expressions of religious art, including the prominent Staff God deity (Fig. 15-27), the origins of which can be traced back before Chavín to early representations known from the Norte Chico region around 3,250 ya (Haas and Creamer, 2004, pp. 48–49). Beneath these similarities, however, their architecture, lifeways, and cultural landscapes appear to have been fundamentally different (Isbell and Vranich, 2004).

The rise and fall of highland states was not limited to Moche, Wari, and Tiwanaku. Peru's north coast, for example, became the center of yet another episode of expansion beginning around 1,100–1,000 ya. This **Chimor** (archaeologically called Chimú) kingdom of the north was centered in the Moche Valley. The eroded mud-brick architecture of its capital, Chan Chan (Fig. 15-28), still blankets several square miles of coastal desert there. Among the ruins are nearly a dozen walled compounds, each of which served as a grand and secluded palace, storehouse, and tomb for the successive monarchs of ruling lineages. At the end of each reign, the ruler was interred in a burial platform amid prodigious wealth—and sometimes amid his harem of young women—and the compound was sealed. By contrast, the insubstantial quarters of tens of thousands of urban peasants once crammed the spaces below the massive compound walls (Moseley and Day, 1982).

The pattern of conquest and control set by Chimor was seen again in their successors—the **Inka**, the last native empire builders of ancient Peru. From its beginnings in the **Cuzco** area around 1,000 ya, this highland society used bold military initiatives and strategic alliances to dominate the southern highlands by 550 ya. The aging Chimor kingdom itself was conquered by the Inka about A.D. 1470. The Inka soon controlled all of modern Peru and the neighboring region (Lanning, 1967; Mason, 1968), briefly becoming the largest empire in the pre-Hispanic Americas (Covey, 2003), only to succumb in the 1500s, like Tenochtitlán in the Valley of Mexico, to the invasion of the New World by the Old.

Wari (wah´-ree) Regional state and city of the same name in southern Peru.

Tiwanaku (tee-wahn-ah´-koo) Regional state, city, and valley of the same name near Lake Titicaca, in Bolivia.

Chimor A powerful culture that dominated the northern Peruvian coast between about 1,000 and 500 ya.

Inka People whose sophisticated culture dominated Peru at the time of the European arrival; also, the term for that people's highest ruler; also spelled Inca.

Cuzco (coos'-koh)

Figure **15-26**
Ruins of the Kalasasaya Temple at Tiwanaku in Bolivia.

D. Donne Bryant Stock

Figure **15-27**

Staff God, Tiwanaku, Bolivia.

Paul G. Richmond

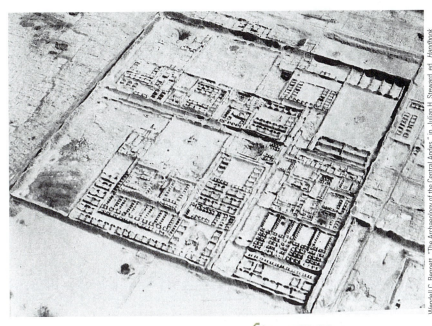

Wendell C. Bennett, "The Archaeology of the Central Andes," in, Julian H. Steward, ed., *Handbook of South American Indians*, Vol. 2, plate 51. Washington, DC: Government Printing Office, 1947.

Figure **15-28**

Aerial view of one of the royal enclosures at Chan Chan, the Chimor capital, Peru.

Summary

The pace of cultural change accelerated during the mid-Holocene. It's noteworthy that the emergence of early civilizations came directly after people achieved sustainable food production in several regions. The primary civilizations of the Old World thrived particularly well on the alluvial plains of several major rivers. The earliest, the Sumerian civilization, emerged as a collection of city-states in the valley of the Tigris-Euphrates after 5,500 ya. A unified Egyptian state was formed around 5,000 ya along the banks of the Nile, and the impressive cultural and architectural achievements of the Old Kingdom began several centuries later. Far to the east, urban commercial centers of the Harappan civilization dominated the Indus Valley by about 4,600 ya, and the Shang was one of a series of strongly hierarchical societies to emerge by 3,600 ya from the advanced Neolithic farming cultures on the Huang He floodplain of northern China.

A similar developmental pattern can be traced in the New World. In Mesoamerica, cultivated crops—among which maize was primary—supported stable populations in some parts of the central highlands and along the southern Gulf of Mexico by about 4,000 ya. In western South America, an area characterized by great topographical extremes, the first farming activities were complemented near the coast by fishing and in the highlands by maintaining flocks of camelids. These varied and productive resources served as the economic bases for a series of increasingly complex and sophisticated cultures in each of the regions we considered in this chapter. In time, some of these societies became states and civilizations. We have focused primarily on the Olmec and Maya in lowland Mesoamerica; Teotihuacán, Toltec, and Aztec in highland Mexico; and a 5,000-year sequence of increasingly integrated and expansive cultures in Peru, culminating in the Inka empire.

While there are some broad similarities in the major features of Old and New World development, especially regarding the connections between agriculture and civilization, we shouldn't overlook the subtle but significant distinctions between these regions. To mention only a few, American civilizations emerged in more ecologically diverse locations; they relied very little on domesticated animals, wheels, or metal for technological purposes; and they tended to move more rapidly from rise to decline. But again, keep in mind that these similarities are broad.

In the What's Important feature on page 424, you'll find a useful summary of the most important archaeological sites discussed in this chapter.

What's Important **The Most Significant Archaeological Sites Discussed in This Chapter**

Site	Dates (ya)	Comments
Uruk (Iraq)	ca. 5,500–1,800	Earliest true city; associated with the Sumerian civilization of the southern Tigris-Euphrates Valley
Ur (Iraq)	ca. 4,600–2,500	City in southern Iraq; its cemetery of >1,800 graves includes 16 "royal" tombs
Giza (Egypt)	ca. 4,500	Old Kingdom pyramid complex and Great Sphinx; located just to the south-west of Cairo
Mohenjo-Daro (Pakistan)	ca. 4,600–3,900	Most extensively excavated Indus civilization city; located in the Indus Valley of south-central Pakistan
Harappa (Pakistan)	ca. 4,600–3,900	Indus civilization city in northeastern Pakistan
Erlitou (China)	ca. 4,000	Elaborate site associated with the earliest phase of civilization in northern China
Shixianggou, Zhengzhou (China)	3,600–3,046	Early Shang capital cities
San Lorenzo (Mexico)	3,150–2,900	Olmec civic-ceremonial center in southern Veracruz
Teotihuacán (Mexico)	ca. 2,200–1,350	Earliest city-state to dominate the Valley of Mexico, one of the largest urban centers in the New World up to the nineteenth century
Tula (Mexico)	ca. 1,200–850	Toltec capital in the Valley of Mexico
Chavín de Huantar (Peru)	ca. 2,900–2,500	Chavín civic-ceremonial center in the northern highlands of Peru

Critical Thinking Questions

1. List some of the basic differences between the lifeways of ancient village farmers and the residents of early cities. What are the social, economic, and political implications of city life?
2. Why were major river valleys the primary setting for so many early civilizations?
3. In what ways did Old World and New World civilizations develop along similar lines? In what ways were they fundamentally different? How can we account for the similarities and differences?

Appendix A

Atlas of Primate Skeletal Anatomy

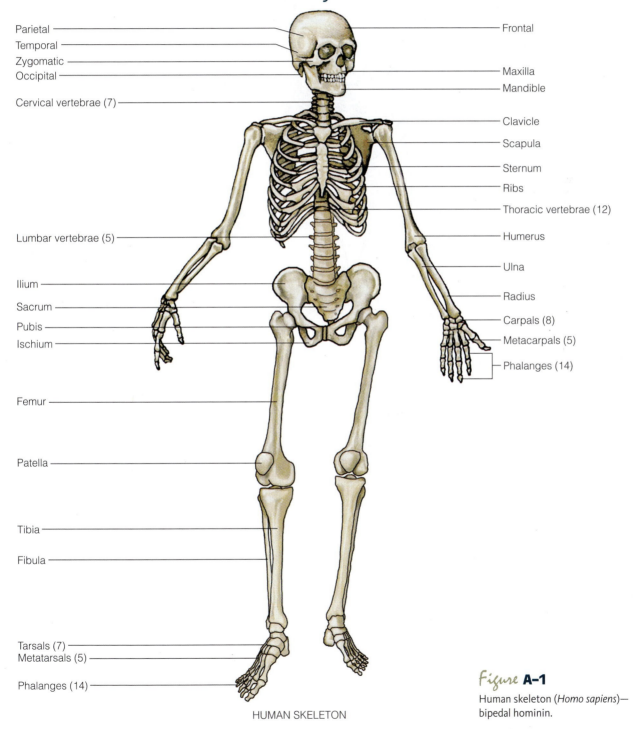

Parietal
Temporal
Zygomatic
Occipital
Cervical vertebrae (7)
Lumbar vertebrae (5)
Ilium
Sacrum
Pubis
Ischium
Femur
Patella
Tibia
Fibula
Tarsals (7)
Metatarsals (5)
Phalanges (14)

Frontal
Maxilla
Mandible
Clavicle
Scapula
Sternum
Ribs
Thoracic vertebrae (12)
Humerus
Ulna
Radius
Carpals (8)
Metacarpals (5)
Phalanges (14)

HUMAN SKELETON

Figure **A-1**

Human skeleton (*Homo sapiens*)—bipedal hominin.

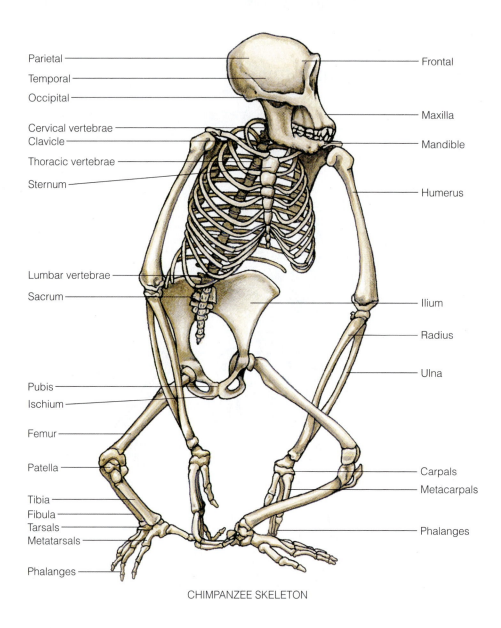

Parietal

Temporal

Occipital

Cervical vertebrae

Clavicle

Thoracic vertebrae

Sternum

Lumbar vertebrae

Sacrum

Pubis

Ischium

Femur

Patella

Tibia

Fibula

Tarsals

Metatarsals

Phalanges

Frontal

Maxilla

Mandible

Humerus

Ilium

Radius

Ulna

Carpals

Metacarpals

Phalanges

CHIMPANZEE SKELETON

Figure **A-2**

Chimpanzee skeleton (*Pan troglodytes*)—
knuckle-walking ape.

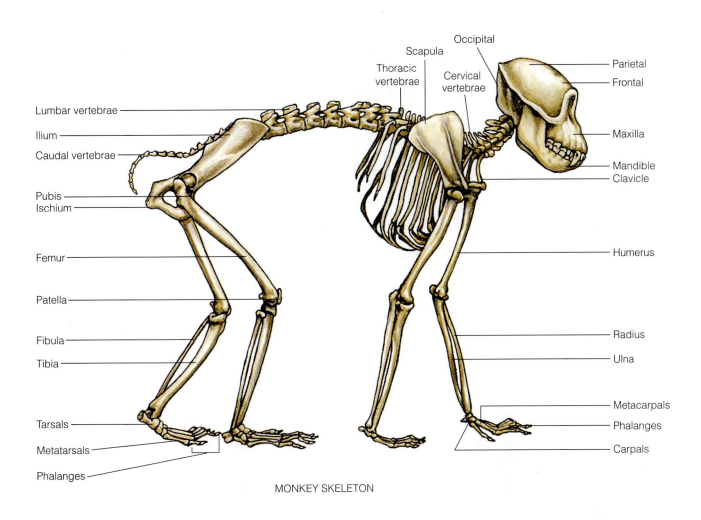

MONKEY SKELETON

Labels: Occipital · Scapula · Thoracic vertebrae · Cervical vertebrae · Parietal · Frontal · Lumbar vertebrae · Ilium · Caudal vertebrae · Maxilla · Mandible · Clavicle · Pubis · Ischium · Femur · Humerus · Patella · Fibula · Tibia · Radius · Ulna · Tarsals · Metatarsals · Phalanges · Metacarpals · Phalanges · Carpals

Figure **A-3**

Monkey skeleton (rhesus macaque; *Macaca mulatta*)—a typical quadrupedal primate.

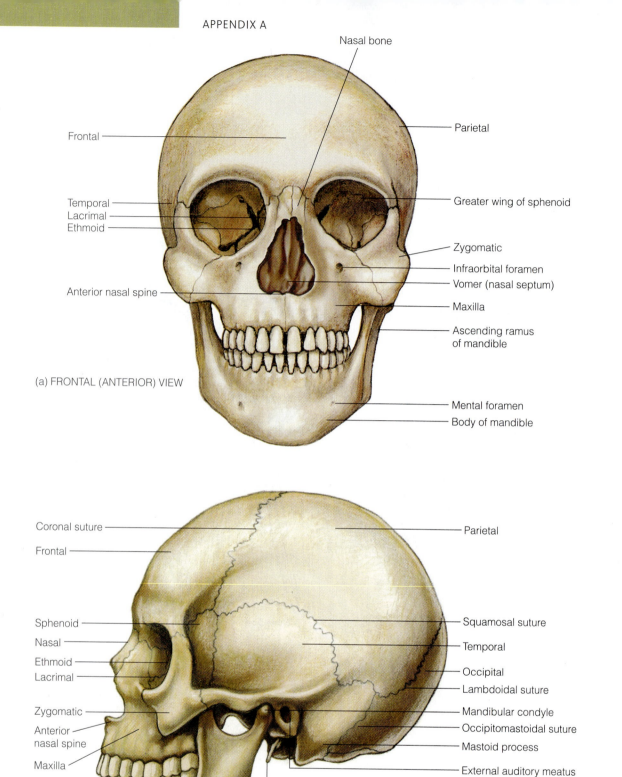

Nasal bone

Frontal

Parietal

Temporal
Lacrimal
Ethmoid

Greater wing of sphenoid

Zygomatic

Infraorbital foramen

Vomer (nasal septum)

Anterior nasal spine

Maxilla

Ascending ramus
of mandible

(a) FRONTAL (ANTERIOR) VIEW

Mental foramen

Body of mandible

Coronal suture

Parietal

Frontal

Sphenoid

Squamosal suture

Nasal

Temporal

Ethmoid

Occipital

Lacrimal

Lambdoidal suture

Zygomatic

Mandibular condyle

Anterior
nasal spine

Occipitomastoidal suture

Mastoid process

Maxilla

External auditory meatus

Incisors

Styloid process

Canine

Ascending ramus of mandible

Mental
foramen

Body of mandible

(b) LATERAL VIEW

Molars

Premolars

Figure **A-4**

Human cranium.
(continued on next page)

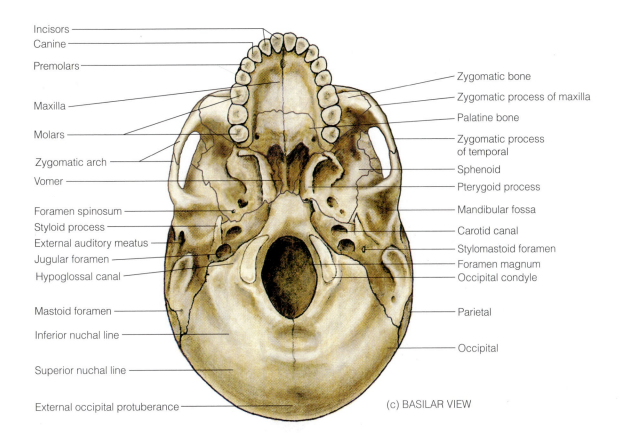

Incisors
Canine
Premolars
Maxilla
Molars
Zygomatic arch
Vomer
Foramen spinosum
Styloid process
External auditory meatus
Jugular foramen
Hypoglossal canal
Mastoid foramen
Inferior nuchal line
Superior nuchal line
External occipital protuberance

Zygomatic bone
Zygomatic process of maxilla
Palatine bone
Zygomatic process of temporal
Sphenoid
Pterygoid process
Mandibular fossa
Carotid canal
Stylomastoid foramen
Foramen magnum
Occipital condyle
Parietal
Occipital

(c) BASILAR VIEW

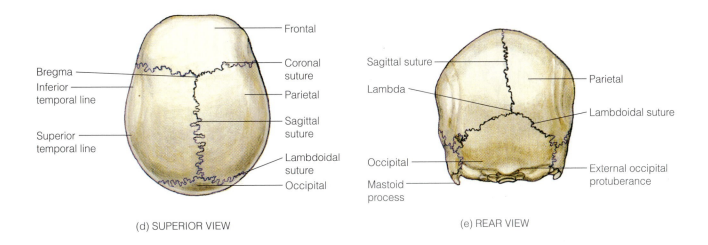

Frontal
Coronal suture
Bregma
Inferior temporal line
Parietal
Superior temporal line
Sagittal suture
Lambdoidal suture
Occipital

(d) SUPERIOR VIEW

Sagittal suture
Lambda
Parietal
Lambdoidal suture
Occipital
Mastoid process
External occipital protuberance

(e) REAR VIEW

Figure A-4
Human cranium.
(continued)

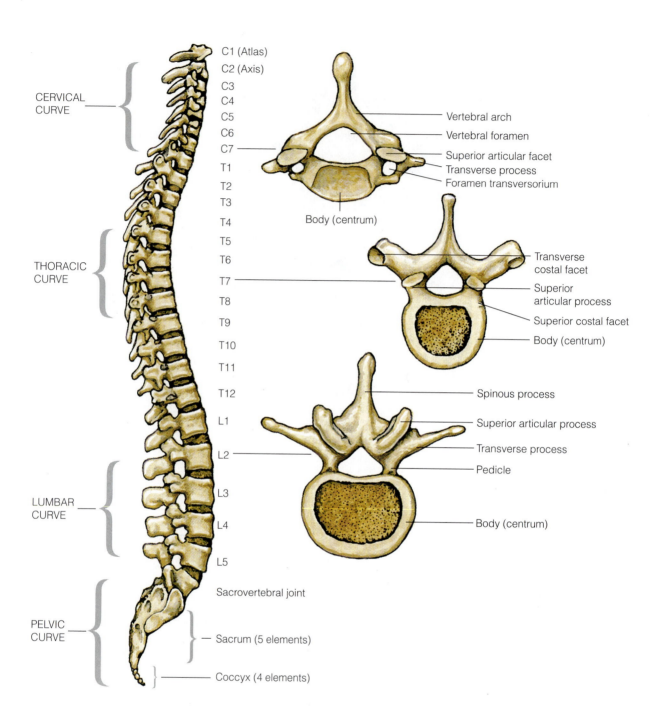

C1 (Atlas)
C2 (Axis)
C3
C4
C5
C6
C7
T1
T2
T3
T4
T5
T6
T7
T8
T9
T10
T11
T12
L1
L2
L3
L4
L5

CERVICAL
CURVE

THORACIC
CURVE

LUMBAR
CURVE

PELVIC
CURVE

Sacrovertebral joint

Sacrum (5 elements)

Coccyx (4 elements)

Vertebral arch
Vertebral foramen
Superior articular facet
Transverse process
Foramen transversorium
Body (centrum)

Transverse
costal facet
Superior
articular process
Superior costal facet
Body (centrum)

Spinous process
Superior articular process
Transverse process
Pedicle
Body (centrum)

Figure **A-5**

Human vertebral column (lateral view)
and representative cervical, thoracic, and
lumbar vertebrae (superior views).

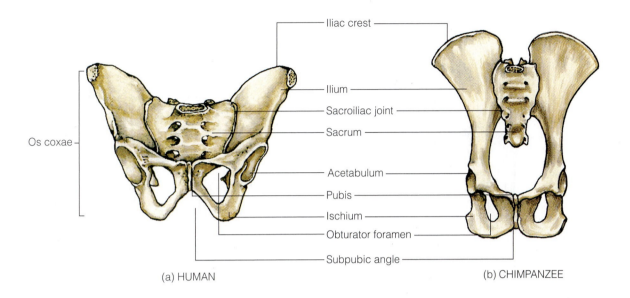

(a) HUMAN

(b) CHIMPANZEE

Iliac crest

Ilium

Sacroiliac joint

Sacrum

Acetabulum

Pubis

Ischium

Obturator foramen

Subpubic angle

Os coxae

Figure **A-6**

Pelvic girdles.

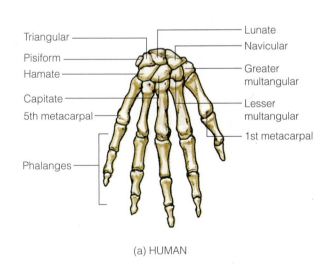

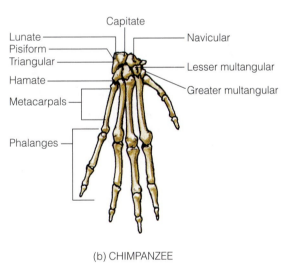

(a) HUMAN

(b) CHIMPANZEE

Triangular

Pisiform

Hamate

Capitate

5th metacarpal

Phalanges

Lunate

Navicular

Greater multangular

Lesser multangular

1st metacarpal

Lunate

Pisiform

Triangular

Hamate

Metacarpals

Phalanges

Capitate

Navicular

Lesser multangular

Greater multangular

Figure **A-7**

Hand anatomy.

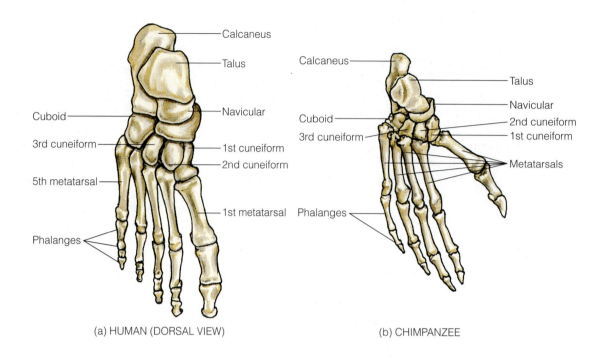

(a) HUMAN (DORSAL VIEW)

(b) CHIMPANZEE

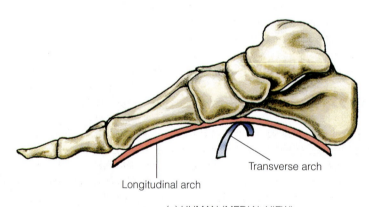

(c) HUMAN (MEDIAL VIEW)

Figure **A-8**

Foot (pedal) anatomy.

Appendix B

Summary of Early Hominin Fossil Finds from Africa

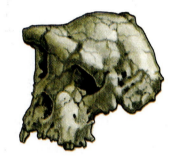

SAHELANTHROPUS

Taxonomic designation:
Sahelanthropus tchadensis

Year of first discovery: 2001

Dating: ~7 mya

Fossil material: Nearly complete cranium, 2 jaw fragments, 3 isolated teeth

ARDIPITHECUS

Taxonomic designation:
Ardipithecus ramidus

Year of first discovery: 1992

Dating: Earlier sites, 5.8–5.6 mya; Aramis, 4.4 mya

Fossil material: Earlier materials: 1 jaw fragment, 4 isolated teeth, postcranial remains (foot phalanx, 2 hand phalanges, 2 humerus fragments, ulna). Later sample (Aramis) represented by many fossils, including up to 50 individuals (many postcranial elements, including at least 1 partial skeleton). Considerable fossil material retrieved from Aramis but not yet published; no reasonably complete cranial remains yet published.

Location of finds: Toros-Menalla, Chad, central Africa

Location of finds: Middle Awash region, including Aramis (as well as earlier localities), Ethiopia, East Africa

ORRORIN

Taxonomic designation:
Orrorin tugenensis

Year of first discovery: 2000

Dating: ~6 mya

Fossil material: 2 jaw fragments, 6 isolated teeth, postcranial remains (femoral pieces, partial humerus, hand phalanx). No reasonably complete cranial remains yet discovered.

Location of finds: Lukeino Formation, Tugen Hills, Baringo District, Kenya, East Africa

AUSTRALOPITHECUS ANAMENSIS

Taxonomic designation:
Australopithecus anamensis

Year of first discovery: 1965 (but not recognized as separate species at that time); more remains found in 1994 and 1995

Dating: 4.2–3.9 mya

Fossil material: Total of 22 specimens, including cranial fragments, jaw fragments, and postcranial pieces (humerus, tibia, radius). No reasonably complete cranial remains yet discovered.

Location of finds: Kanapoi, Allia Bay, Kenya, East Africa

AUSTRALOPITHECUS AFARENSIS

Taxonomic designation:
Australopithecus afarensis

Year of first discovery: 1973

Dating: 3.6–3.0 mya

Fossil material: Large sample, with up to 65 individuals represented: 1 partial cranium, numerous cranial pieces and jaws, many teeth, numerous postcranial remains, including partial skeletons. Fossil finds from Laetoli also include dozens of fossilized footprints.

Location of finds: Laetoli (Tanzania), Hadar/Dikika (Ethiopia), also likely found at East Turkana (Kenya) and Omo (Ethiopia), East Africa

KENYANTHROPUS

Taxonomic designation:
  Kenyanthropus platyops
Year of first discovery: 1999
Dating: 3.5 mya
Fossil material: Partial cranium, temporal fragment, partial maxilla, 2 partial mandibles

AUSTRALOPITHECUS GARHI

Taxonomic designation:
  Australopithecus garhi
Year of first discovery: 1997
Dating: 2.5 mya
Fossil material: Partial cranium, numerous limb bones

PARANTHROPUS AETHIOPICUS

Taxonomic designation:
  Paranthropus aethiopicus
  (also called *Australopithecus aethiopicus*)
Year of first discovery: 1985
Dating: 2.4 mya
Fossil material: Nearly complete cranium

Location of finds: Lomekwi, West Lake Turkana, Kenya, East Africa

Location of finds: Bouri, Middle Awash, Ethiopia, East Africa

Location of finds: West Lake Turkana, Kenya

PARANTHROPUS BOISEI

Taxonomic designation:
Paranthropus boisei (also called *Australopithecus boisei*)

Year of first discovery: 1959

Dating: 2.2–1.0 mya

Fossil material: 2 nearly complete crania, several partial crania, many jaw fragments, dozens of teeth. Postcrania less represented, but parts of several long bones recovered.

AUSTRALOPITHECUS AFRICANUS

Taxonomic designation:
Australopithecus africanus

Year of first discovery: 1924

Dating: ~3.0?–2.0 mya

Fossil material: 1 mostly complete cranium, several partial crania, dozens of jaws/partial jaws, hundreds of teeth, 4 partial skeletons representing significant parts of the postcranium

PARANTHROPUS ROBUSTUS

Taxonomic designation:
Paranthropus robustus (also called *Australopithecus robustus*)

Year of first discovery: 1938

Dating: ~2–1 mya

Fossil material: 1 complete cranium, several partial crania, many jaw fragments, hundreds of teeth, numerous postcranial elements

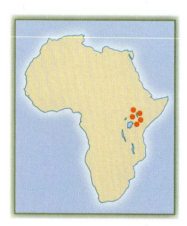

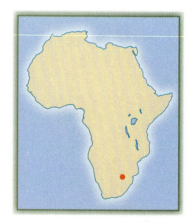

Location of finds: Olduvai Gorge and Peninj (Tanzania), East Lake Turkana (Koobi Fora), Chesowanja (Kenya), Omo (Ethiopia)

Location of finds: Taung, Sterkfontein, Makapansgat, Gladysvale (all from South Africa)

Location of finds: Kromdraai, Swartkrans, Drimolen, Cooper's Cave, possibly Gondolin (all from South Africa)

EARLY *HOMO*

Taxonomic designation:
Homo habilis

Year of first discovery: 1959/1960

Dating: 2.4–1.8 mya

Fossil material: 2 partial crania, other cranial pieces, jaw fragments, several limb bones, partial hand, partial foot, partial skeleton

EARLY *HOMO*

Taxonomic designation:
Homo rudolfensis

Year of first discovery: 1972

Dating: 1.8 mya–1.4 mya

Fossil material: 4 partial crania, 1 mostly complete mandible, other jaw pieces, numerous teeth, a few postcranial elements (none directly associated with crania)

Location of finds: Olduvai Gorge (Tanzania), Lake Baringo (Kenya), Omo (Ethiopia), Sterkfontein (?) (South Africa)

Location of finds: East Lake Turkana (Koobi Fora), Kenya, East Africa

Appendix C

Population Genetics

As noted in Chapter 4, the basic approach in population genetics makes use of a mathematical model called the Hardy-Weinberg equilibrium equation. The Hardy-Weinberg theory of genetic equilibrium postulates a set of conditions in a population where *no* evolution occurs. In other words, none of the forces of evolution are acting, and all genes have an equal chance of recombining in each generation (that is, there is random mating of individuals). More precisely, the hypothetical conditions that such a population would be *assumed* to meet are as follows:

1. The population is infinitely large. This condition eliminates the possibility of random genetic drift or changes in allele frequencies due to chance.
2. There is no mutation. Thus, no new alleles are being added by molecular changes in gametes.
3. There is no gene flow. There is no exchange of genes with other populations that can alter allele frequencies.
4. Natural selection is not operating. Specific alleles confer no advantage over others that might influence reproductive success.
5. Mating is random. There are no factors that influence who mates with whom. Thus, any female is assumed to have an equal chance of mating with any male.

If all these conditions are satisfied, allele frequencies will not change from one generation to the next (that is, no evolution will take place), and a permanent equilibrium will be maintained as long as these conditions prevail. An evolutionary "barometer" is thus provided that may be used as a standard against which actual circumstances are compared. Similar to the way a typical barometer is standardized under known temperature and altitude conditions, the Hardy-Weinberg equilibrium is standardized under known evolutionary conditions.

Note that the idealized conditions that define the Hardy-Weinberg equilibrium are just that: an idealized, *hypothetical* state. In the real world, no actual population would fully meet any of these conditions. But do not be confused by this distinction. By explicitly defining the genetic distribution that would be *expected* if *no* evolutionary change were occurring (that is, in equilibrium), we can compare the *observed* genetic distribution obtained from actual human populations. The evolutionary barometer is thus evaluated through comparison of these observed allele and genotype frequencies with those expected in the predefined equilibrium situation.

If the observed frequencies differ from those of the expected model, then we can say that evolution is taking place at the locus in question. The alternative, of course, is that the observed and expected frequencies do not differ sufficiently to state unambiguously that evolution is occurring at a locus in a population. Indeed, frequently this is the result that is obtained, and in such cases, population geneticists are unable to delineate evolutionary changes at the particular locus under study. Put another way, geneticists are unable to reject what statisticians call the *null hypothesis* (where "null" means nothing, a statistical condition of randomness).

The simplest situation applicable to a microevolutionary study is a genetic trait that follows a simple Mendelian pattern and has only two alleles (*A, a*). As you recall from earlier discussions, there are then only three possible genotypes: *AA, Aa, aa*. Proportions of these genotypes (*AA:Aa:aa*) are a function of the *allele frequencies* themselves (percentage of *A* and percentage of *a*). To provide uniformity for all genetic loci, a standard notation is employed to refer to these frequencies:

Frequency of dominant allele (*A*) = *p*
Frequency of recessive allele (*a*) = *q*

Since in this case there are only two alleles, their combined total frequency must represent all possibilities. In other words, the sum of their separate frequencies must be 1:

$$p \quad + \quad q \quad = \quad 1$$

| (frequency | (frequency | (100% of alleles |
| of *A* alleles) | of *a* alleles) | at that locus) |

To ascertain the expected proportions of genotypes, we compute the chances of the alleles combining with one another into all possible combinations. Remember, they all have an equal chance of combining, and no new alleles are being added.

These probabilities are a direct function of the frequency of the two alleles. The chances of all possible combinations occurring randomly can be simply shown as

$$
\begin{array}{r}
p + q \\
\times \quad p + q \\
\hline
pq + q^2 \\
p^2 + pq \\
\hline
p^2 + 2pq + q^2
\end{array}
$$

Mathematically, this is known as a binomial expansion and can also be shown as

$$(p + q)(p + q) = p^2 + 2pq + q^2$$

What we have just calculated is simply:

Allele Combination	Genotype Produced	Expected Proportion in Population
Chances of *A* combining with *A*	*AA*	$p \times p = p^2$
Chances of *A* combining with *a*;	*Aa*	$p \times q$
a combining with *A*	*aA*	$p \times q$ = 2*pq*
Chances of *a* combining with *a*	*aa*	$q \times q = q^2$

Thus, p^2 is the frequency of the *AA* genotype, *2pq* is the frequency of the *Aa* genotype, and *q2* is the frequency of the *aa* genotype, where *p* is the frequency of the dominant allele and *q* is the frequency of the recessive allele in a population.

Calculating Allele Frequencies: An Example

How geneticists use the Hardy-Weinberg formula is best demonstrated through an example. Let us assume that a population contains 200 individuals, and we will use the MN blood group locus as the gene to be measured. This gene produces a blood group antigen—similar to ABO—located on red blood cells. Because the *M* and *N* alleles are codominant, we can ascertain everyone's phenotype by taking blood samples and observing reactions with specially prepared antisera. From the phenotypes, we can then directly calculate the *observed* allele frequencies. So let us proceed.

All 200 individuals are tested, and the results are shown in Table C-1. Although the match between observed and expected frequencies is not perfect, it is close enough statistically to satisfy equilibrium conditions. Since our population is not a large one, sampling may easily account for the small observed deviations. Our population is therefore probably in equilibrium (that is, at this locus, it is not evolving). At the minimum, what we can say scientifically is that we cannot reject the *null hypothesis*.

Table C–1 Calculating Allele Frequencies in a Hypothetical Population

Observed Data

Genotype	Number of Individuals	Present	Number of Alleles M	N
MM	80	40%	160	0
MN	80	40%	80	80
NN	40	20%	0	80
Totals	200	100%	240 +	160 = 400
		Proportion:	.6 +	.4 = 1

*Each individual has two alleles. Thus, a person who is *MM* contributes two *M* alleles to the total gene pool. A person who is *MN* contributes one *M* and one *N*. Two hundred individuals, then, have 400 alleles for the *MN* locus.

Observed Allele Frequencies

$M = .6 (p)$

$N = .4 (q)$ ($p + q$ should equal 1, and they do)

Expected Frequencies

What are the predicted genotypic proportions if genetic equilibrium (no evolution) applies to our population? We simply apply the Hardy-Weinberg formula: $p^2 + 2pq + q^2$.

p^2	=	(.6)(.6)	=	.36
$2pq$	=	2(.6)(.4)	=	.48
q^2	=	(.4)(.4)	=	.16
Total				1.00

There are only three possible genotypes (*MM:MN:NN*), so the total of the relative proportions should equal 1; as you can see, they do.

Comparing Frequencies

How do the expected frequencies compare with the observed frequencies in our population?

	Expected Frequency	Expected Number of Individuals	Observed Frequency	Actual Number of Individuals with Each Genotype
MM	.36	72	.40	80
MN	.48	96	.40	80
NN	.16	32	.20	40

Glossary

acclimatization Physiological responses to changes in the environment that occur during an individual's lifetime. Such responses may be temporary or permanent, depending on the duration of the environmental change and when in the individual's life it occurs. The capacity for acclimatization may typify an entire species or population, and because it's under genetic influence, it's subject to evolutionary factors such as natural selection or genetic drift.

Acheulian (ash´-oo-lay-en) A Lower Paleolithic stone tool industry that includes bifacially worked hand axes and cleavers and many kinds of flake tools. It began as early as 1.4 mya in Africa, spread across many parts of the temperate to tropical parts of Europe and Asia, and ended roughly 200,000 ya. Also spelled Acheulean.

adaptation Functional response of organisms or populations to the environment. Adaptation results from evolutionary change (specifically, as a result of natural selection).

adaptive niche The entire way of life of an organism: where it lives, what it eats, how it gets food, how it avoids predators, etc.

adaptive radiation The relatively rapid expansion and diversification of life-forms into new ecological niches.

affectional A term used in psychology that refers to bonding or attachments between individuals, especially mothers and their infants.

affiliative Pertaining to amicable associations between individuals. Affiliative behaviors, such as grooming, reinforce social bonds and promote group cohesion.

agriculture Cultural activities associated with planting, herding, and processing domesticated species; farming.

allele frequency In a population, the percentage of all the alleles at a locus accounted for by one specific allele.

alleles Alternate forms of a gene. Alleles occur at the same locus on paired chromosomes and thus govern the same trait. However, because they are different, their action may result in different expressions of that trait. The term *allele* is often used synonymously with *gene*.

alluvial Deposited by streams, usually during flood stages.

altruism Behavior that benefits another individual but at some potential risk or cost to oneself.

amino acids Small molecules that are the components of proteins.

analogies Similarities between organisms based strictly on common function, with no assumed common evolutionary descent.

Anasazi (an-ah-saw´-zee) Ancient culture of the southwestern United States, associated with preserved cliff dwellings and masonry pueblo sites.

ancestral (primitive) Referring to characters inherited by a group of organisms from a remote ancestor and thus not diagnostic of groups (lineages) that diverged after the character first appeared.

anthropocentric Viewing nonhuman animals in terms of human motives, experiences, and capabilities, emphasizing the importance of humans over everything else.

anthropoids Members of a suborder of Primates, the suborder Anthropoidea (pronounced "ann-throw-poid´-ee-uh"). Traditionally, the suborder includes monkeys, apes, and humans.

anthropology The field of inquiry that studies human culture and evolutionary aspects of human biology; includes cultural anthropology, archaeology, linguistics, and physical anthropology.

anthropometry Measurement of human body parts. When osteologists measure skeletal elements, the term *osteometry* is often used.

anthropomorphic (*anthro*, meaning "man," and *morph*, meaning "shape") Having or being given humanlike characteristics.

antigens Large molecules found on the surface of cells. Several different loci governing antigens on red and white blood cells are known. (Foreign antigens provoke an immune response in individuals.)

antiquarian Relating to an interest in things and texts of the past.

arboreal Tree-living; adapted to life in the trees.

archaeobotanical Referring to the analysis and interpretation of the remains of ancient plants recovered from the archaeological record.

archaeological record The material remains of the human past and the physical contexts of these remains (e.g., stratigraphic relationships, association with other remains).

archaeological sites Locations of past human activity, often associated with artifacts and features.

archaeometry Application of the methods of the natural and physical sciences to the investigation of archaeological materials.

Archaic North American archaeological period that follows the end of the Ice Age and traditionally ends with the beginning of the use of ceramics; equivalent to the Mesolithic in the Old World.

argon-argon (^{40}Ar/^{39}Ar) method Working on a similar basis as the potassium-argon method, this approach uses the ratio of argon-40 to argon-39 for dating igneous and metamorphic rocks; it offers precision and temporal range advantages for dating some early hominin sites.

artifacts Objects or materials made or modified for use by hominins. The earliest artifacts are usually made of stone or, occasionally, bone.

Aurignacian An early Upper Paleolithic stone tool industry found across southern Europe and the Near East.

aurochs European wild oxen, ancestral to domesticated cattle.

australopiths A colloquial name referring to a diverse group of Plio-Pleistocene African hominins. They are the most abundant and widely distributed of all early hominins and are also the most completely studied.

autonomic Pertaining to physiological responses not under voluntary control. A chimpanzee example is erect body hair when an animal is excited. Blushing is a human example. Both convey information regarding emotional state, but neither is deliberate, and communication isn't intended.

autosomes All chromosomes except the sex chromosomes.

Aztecs Militaristic people who dominated the Valley of Mexico and surrounding area at the time of the European conquest.

Bandkeramik Literally, "lined pottery"; refers to a Neolithic ceramic ware widely encountered in central Europe and to the culture that produced it.

behavior Anything organisms do that involves action in response to internal or external stimuli; the response of an individual, group, or species to its environment. Such responses may or may not be deliberate, and they aren't necessarily the result of conscious decision making

behavioral ecology The study of the evolution of behavior, emphasizing the role of ecological factors as agents of natural selection. Behaviors and behavioral patterns have been favored because they increase the reproductive fitness of individuals (i.e., they are adaptive) in specific environmental contexts.

Beringia (bare-in´-jya) The dry-land connection between Asia and America that existed periodically during the Pleistocene epoch.

binocular vision Vision characterized by overlapping visual fields provided for by forward-facing eyes. Binocular vision is essential to depth perception.

binomial nomenclature (*binomial*, meaning "two names") In taxonomy, the convention established by Carolus Linnaeus whereby genus and species names are used to refer to species. For example, *Homo sapiens* refers to human beings.

bioarchaeologists Physical anthropologists who specialize in the analysis and interpretation of human skeletal remains that are discovered at archaeological sites.

biocultural Pertaining to the concept that biology makes culture possible and that culture influences biology.

biocultural evolution The mutual, interactive evolution of human biology and culture; the concept that biology makes culture possible and that developing culture further influences the direction of biological evolution; a basic concept in understanding the unique components of human evolution.

biological continuity Refers to a biological continuum—the idea that organisms are related through common ancestry and that traits present in one species are also seen to varying degrees in others. When expressions of a phenomenon continuously grade into one another so that there are no discrete categories, they exist on a continuum. Color is one such phenomenon, and life-forms are another.

biological continuum Refers to the fact that organisms are related through common ancestry and that behaviors and traits seen in one species are also seen in others to varying degrees. (When expressions of a phenomenon continuously grade into one another so that there are no discrete categories, they are said to exist on a continuum. Color is such a phenomenon.)

biological determinism The concept that phenomena, including various aspects of behavior (e.g., intelligence, values, morals), are governed by biological (genetic) factors; the inaccurate association of various behavioral attributes with certain biological traits, such as skin color.

biological species concept A depiction of species as groups of individuals capable of fertile interbreeding but reproductively isolated from other such groups.

biostratigraphy A relative dating technique based on regular changes seen in evolving groups of animals as well as the presence or absence of particular species.

bipedal locomotion Walking on two feet. Walking habitually on two legs is the single most distinctive feature of hominins.

blade technology Chipped stone toolmaking approach in which blades struck from prepared cores are the main raw material from which tools are made. A blade is a chipped stone flake that is at least twice as long as it is wide.

brachiation A form of locomotion in which the body is suspended beneath the hands and support is alternated from one forelimb to the other; arm swinging.

breeding isolates Populations that are clearly isolated geographically or socially from other breeding groups.

burin A small flake tool with a chisel-like end, used to cut bone, antler, and ivory.

carrying capacity In an environment, the maximum population of a specific organism that can be maintained at a steady state.

Çatalhöyük (chaetal´-hae-yook´) A large early Neolithic site in southern Turkey. The name is Turkish for "forked mound."

catastrophism The view that the earth's geological landscape is the result of violent cataclysmic events. This view was promoted by Cuvier, especially in opposition to Lamarck.

centromere The constricted portion of a chromosome. After replication, the two strands of a double-stranded chromosome are joined at the centromere.

cercopithecines (serk-oh-pith´-eh-seens) The subfamily of Old World monkeys that includes baboons, macaques, and guenons.

charnel houses Buildings that hold the bones or bodies of the dead.

Chatelperronian Pertaining to an Upper Paleolithic industry found in France and Spain.

Chavín de Huantar Chavín civic-ceremonial center in the northern highlands of Peru.

Chimor A powerful culture that dominated the northern Peruvian coast between about 1,000 and 500 ya.

Chordata The phylum of the animal kingdom that includes vertebrates.

chromosomes Discrete structures, composed of DNA and protein, found only in the nuclei of cells. Chromosomes are visible only under magnification during certain stages of cell division.

cities Urban centers that both support and are supported by a hinterland of lesser communities.

city-states Urban centers that form autonomous sociopolitical units.

civilization The larger social order that includes states related by language, traditions, history, economic ties, and other shared cultural aspects.

clade A group of organisms sharing a common ancestor. The group includes the common ancestor and all descendants.

cladistics An approach to classification that attempts to make rigorous evolutionary interpretations based solely on analysis of certain types of homologous characters (those considered to be derived characters).

cladogram A chart showing evolutionary relationships as determined by cladistic analysis. It's based solely on interpretation of derived characters. It contains no time component and does not imply ancestor-descendant relationships.

classification In biology, the ordering of organisms into categories, such as orders, families, and genera, to show evolutionary relationships.

climatic maximum Episode of higher average annual temperatures that affected much of the globe for several millennia after the end of the last ice age; also known as the *altithermal* in the western United States or *hypsithermal* in the East.

cline A gradual change in the frequency of genotypes and phenotypes from one geographical region to another.

clones A clone is an organism that is genetically identical to another organism. In addition to entire organisms, the term may also be used to refer to genetically identical DNA segments and molecules.

Clovis North American archaeological complex characterized by distinctive fluted projectile points, dating roughly 13,500–13,000 ya; once widely believed to be representative of specialized big game hunters, who may have driven many late Pleistocene species into extinction.

codices (*sing.*, codex) Illustrated books.

coding DNA sequences DNA sequences that code for the production of a protein.

codominance The expression of two alleles in heterozygotes. In this situation, neither is dominant or recessive; thus, both influence the phenotype.

collectors Hunter-gatherers who tend to stay in one place for a long time. A task group may range far afield to hunt and collect food and other resources that are brought back to camp and shared among its inhabitants. Valued food resources are commonly stored in anticipation of future use.

colobines (kole´-uh-beans) The subfamily of Old World monkeys that includes the African colobus monkeys and Asian langurs.

communication Any act that conveys information, in the form of a message, to another individual. Frequently, the result of communication is a change in the behavior of the recipient. Communication may not be deliberate but may instead be the result of involuntary processes or a secondary consequence of an intentional action.

complementary Referring to the fact that DNA bases form base pairs in a precise manner. For example, adenine can bond only to thymine. These two bases are said to be complementary because one requires the other to form a complete DNA base pair.

composite tool Minimally, a tool made of several pieces. For example, a prehistoric knife typically included a handle or shaft, a chipped stone blade, and binding materials such as glue or sinew to hold the blade firmly in place.

context The environmental setting where an archaeological trace is found. A *primary* context is the setting in which the archaeological trace was originally deposited. A *secondary* context is one to which it has been moved (e.g., by the action of a stream).

continental drift The movement of continents on sliding plates of the earth's surface. As a result, the positions of large landmasses have shifted drastically during the earth's history.

coprolites Preserved fecal material, which can be studied for what the contents reveal about diet and health.

Cordilleran (cor-dee-yair´-en) Pleistocene ice sheet originating in mountains of western North America.

core area The portion of a home range containing the highest concentration and most reliable supplies of food and water. The core area is defended.

craft specialization An economic system in which some individuals do not engage in food getting, but devote their labor to the production of other goods and services. Examples include potters, carpenters, smiths, shamen, oracles, and teachers.

cross-dating Relative dating method that estimates the age of artifacts and features based on their similarities with comparable materials from dated contexts.

cultigen A plant that is wholly dependent on humans; a domesticate.

cultivars Wild plants fostered by human efforts to make them more productive.

culture All aspects of human adaptation, including technology, traditions, language, religion, and social roles. Culture is a set of learned behaviors; it is transmitted from one generation to the next through learning and not by biological or genetic means.

cuneiform (*cuneus*, meaning "wedge") Wedge-shaped writing of ancient Mesopotamia.

cusps The bumps on the chewing surfaces of premolar and molar teeth.

cytoplasm The portion of the cell contained within the cell membrane, excluding the nucleus. The cytoplasm consists of a semifluid material and contains numerous structures involved with cell function.

Dalton Late or transitional Paleo-Indian projectile point type that dates between 10,000 and 8,000 ya in the eastern United States.

data (*sing.*, datum) Facts from which conclusions can be drawn; scientific information.

demographic Pertaining to the size or rate of increase of human populations.

dendrochronology Archaeological dating method based on the study of yearly growth rings in ancient wood.

dental caries Erosions in teeth caused by decay; cavities.

deoxyribonucleic acid (DNA) The double-stranded molecule that contains the genetic code. DNA is a main component of chromosomes.

derived (modified) Referring to characters that are modified from the ancestral condition and thus are diagnostic of particular evolutionary lineages.

desertification Any process resulting in the formation or growth of deserts.

diffusion The idea that widely distributed cultural traits originated in a single center and were spread from one group to another through contact or exchange.

directional change In a genetic sense, the nonrandom change in allele frequencies caused by natural selection. The change is directional because the frequencies of alleles consistently increase or decrease (they change in one direction), depending on environmental circumstances and the selective pressures involved.

discoid technique A prepared-core technique in which flakes are struck toward the center of the stone core; greater efficiency of raw material use than Levallois; also called "radial core" technique.

displays Sequences of repetitious behaviors that serve to communicate an animal's emotional state. Nonhuman primate displays are most frequently associated with reproductive or agonistic behavior, and examples include chest slapping in gorillas or, in male chimpanzees, dragging and waving branches while charging and threatening other animals.

diurnal Active during the day.

divination Foretelling the future.

domestication A state of interdependence between humans and selected plant or animal species. Intense selection activity induces permanent genetic change, enhancing a species' value to humans.

dominance hierarchies Systems of social organization wherein individuals within a group are ranked relative to one another. Higher-ranking animals have greater access to preferred food items and mating partners than lower-ranking individuals. Dominance hierarchies are sometimes called "pecking orders."

dominant Describing a trait governed by an allele that can be expressed in the presence of another, different allele (i.e., in heterozygotes). Dominant alleles prevent the expression of recessive alleles in heterozygotes. (*Note:* This is the definition of *complete* dominance.)

ecofacts Natural materials that give environmental information about a site. Examples include plant and animal remains discarded as food waste and also pollen grains preserved in the soil.

ecological Pertaining to the relationships between organisms and all aspects of their environment (temperature, predators, nonpredators, vegetation, availability of food and water, types of food, disease organisms, parasites, etc.).

ecological niches Positions of species within their physical and biological environments. A species' ecological niche is defined by such components as diet, terrain, vegetation, type of predators, relationships with other species, and activity patterns, and each niche is unique to a given species. Together, ecological niches make up an ecosystem.

El Niño Periodic climatic instability, related to temporary warming of Pacific Ocean waters, which may influence storm patterns and precipitation for several years.

empirical Relying on experiment or observation; from the Latin *empiricus,* meaning "experienced."

enculturation The process by which individuals, generally as children, learn the values and beliefs of the family, peer groups, and society in which they are raised.

endemic Continuously present in a population.

endothermic (*endo,* meaning "within" or "internal") Able to maintain internal body temperature by producing energy through metabolic processes within cells; characteristic of mammals, birds, and perhaps some dinosaurs.

Enlightenment An eighteenth-century philosophical movement in western Europe that assumed a knowable order to the natural world and the interpretive value of reason as the primary means of identifying and explaining this order.

enzymes Specialized proteins that initiate and direct chemical reactions in the body.

Epipaleolithic (*epi,* meaning "after") Late Pleistocene and early Holocene period of foragers and collectors in the Near East and adjacent parts of Asia.

epochs Categories of the geological time scale; subdivisions of periods. In the Cenozoic, epochs include the Paleocene, Eocene, Oligocene, Miocene, and Pliocene (from the Tertiary) and the Pleistocene and Holocene (from the Quaternary).

estrus (es´-truss) Period of sexual receptivity in female mammals (except humans), correlated with ovulation. When used as an adjective, the word is spelled "estrous."

ethnoarchaeologists Archaeologists who use ethnographic methods to study modern peoples so that they can better understand and explain patterning in the archaeological record.

ethnoarchaeology Approach used by archaeologists to gain insights into the past by studying contemporary people.

ethnocentric Viewing other cultures from the inherently biased perspective of one's own culture. Ethnocentrism often results in other cultures being seen as inferior to one's own.

ethnographies Detailed descriptive studies of human societies. In cultural anthropology, *ethnography* is traditionally the study of non-Western societies.

eugenics The philosophy of "race improvement" through the forced sterilization of members of some groups and increased reproduction among others; an overly simplified, often racist, view that is now discredited.

evolution A change in the genetic structure of a population from one generation to the next. The term is also frequently used to refer to the appearance of a new species.

evolutionary systematics A traditional approach to classification (and evolutionary interpretation) in which presumed ancestors and descendants are traced in time by analysis of homologous characters.

experimental archaeology Research that attempts to replicate ancient technologies and construction procedures to test hypotheses about past activities.

faience (fay-ahnz´) Glassy material, usually of blue-green color, shaped into beads, amulets, and figurines by ancient Egyptians.

features Products of human activity that are usually integral to a site and therefore not portable. Examples include fire hearths and foundations.

fission-track dating Dating technique based on the natural radiometric decay (fission) of uranium-238 atoms, which leaves traces in certain geological materials.

fitness Pertaining to natural selection, a measure of the *relative* reproductive success of individuals. Fitness can be measured by an individual's genetic contribution to the next generation compared to that of other individuals. The terms *genetic fitness, reproductive fitness,* and *differential reproductive success* are also used.

fixity of species The notion that species, once created, can never change; an idea diametrically opposed to theories of biological evolution.

flexed The position of the body in a bent orientation, with arms and legs drawn up to the chest.

fluorine analysis Relative dating method that measures and compares the amounts of fluorine that bones have absorbed from groundwater during burial.

fluted point A biface or projectile point having had long, thin flakes removed from each face to prepare the base for hafting, or attachment to a shaft.

Folsom Paleo-Indian archaeological complex of the southern Great Plains, around 12,500 ya, during which long-fluted projectile points were used for bison hunting.

foragers Hunter-gatherers who live in small groups that move camp frequently to take advantage of fresh resources as they come into season, with few resources stored in anticipation of future use.

forensic anthropology An applied anthropological approach dealing with legal matters. Forensic anthropologists work with coroners and law enforcement agencies in the recovery, analysis, and identification of human remains.

founder effect A type of genetic drift in which allele frequencies are altered in small populations that are taken from, or are remnants of, larger populations.

frugivorous (fru-give´-or-us) Having a diet composed primarily of fruits.

gametes Reproductive cells (eggs and sperm in animals) developed from precursor cells in ovaries and testes.

gene A sequence of DNA bases that specifies the order of amino acids in an entire protein or, in many cases, a portion of a protein, or any functional product. A gene may be made up of hundreds or thousands of DNA bases.

gene flow Exchange of genes between populations.

gene pool The total complement of genes shared by the reproductive members of a population.

genetic drift Evolutionary changes—that is, changes in allele frequencies—produced by random factors. Genetic drift is a result of small population size.

genetics The study of gene structure and action and of the patterns of inheritance of traits from parent to offspring. Genetic mechanisms are the underlying foundation for evolutionary change.

genome The entire genetic makeup of an individual or species. In humans, it is estimated that each person possesses approximately 3 billion DNA nucleotides.

genotype The genetic makeup of an individual. Genotype can refer to an organism's entire genetic makeup or to the alleles at a particular locus.

genus (*pl.*, genera) A group of closely related species.

geological time scale The organization of earth history into eras, periods, and epochs; commonly used by geologists and paleoanthropologists.

Gilgamesh Semilegendary king and culture hero of early Uruk; reputed to have had many marvelous adventures.

glaciations Climatic intervals when continental ice sheets cover much of the northern continents. Glaciations are associated with colder temperatures in northern latitudes and more arid conditions closer to the equator, most notably in Africa.

glyphs Carved or incised symbolic figures.

grade A grouping of organisms sharing a similar adaptive pattern. Grade isn't necessarily based on closeness of evolutionary relationship, but it does contrast organisms in a useful way (e.g., *Homo erectus* with *Homo sapiens*).

Great Basin Rugged, dry plateau between the mountains of California and Utah, comprising Nevada, western Utah, southern Oregon, and Idaho.

grooming Picking through fur to remove dirt, parasites, and other materials that may be present. Social grooming is common among primates and reinforces social relationships.

habitual bipedalism Bipedal locomotion as the form of locomotion shown by hominins most of the time.

haft To equip a tool or implement with a handle or hilt.

half-life The time period in which one-half the amount of a radioactive isotope is chemically converted to a daughter product. For example, after 1.25 billion years, half the potassium-40 remains; after 2.5 billion years, one-fourth remains.

Hammurabi (ham-oo-rah´-bee) Early Babylonian king, ca. 1800–1750 B.C.

Harappa (ha-rap´-pa) A fortified city in the Indus Valley of northeastern Pakistan.

"hard hammer" percussion A direct percussion method of making stone tools that uses one rock as a hammer to knock flakes from another rock that serves as a core.

Hardy-Weinberg equilibrium A mathematical formula that calculates the predicted allele frequencies at one genetic locus in a population in which no evolution is occurring. For evolution not to occur, there must be no genetic drift, gene flow, or natural selection.

hemispheres The two halves of the cerebrum that are connected by a dense mass of fibers. (The cerebrum is the large rounded outer portion of the brain.)

hemoglobin A protein molecule that occurs in red blood cells and binds to oxygen molecules.

heterodont Having different kinds of teeth; characteristic of mammals, whose teeth consist of incisors, canines, premolars, and molars.

heterozygous Having different alleles at the same locus on members of a chromosome pair.

hieroglyphics (*hiero*, meaning "sacred," and *glyphein*, meaning "carving") The picture-writing of ancient Egypt.

historical archaeologists Archaeologists who study past societies for which a contemporary written record also exists.

Hohokam (ho-ho-kahm´) Prehistoric farming culture of southern Arizona.

Holocene The geological epoch during which we now live. The Holocene follows the Pleistocene epoch and began roughly 11,000–10,000 ya.

home-based foragers Hominins that hunt, scavenge, or collect food and raw materials from the general locality where they habitually live and bring these materials back to some central or home base site to be shared with other members of their coresiding group.

homeobox (*Hox*) genes An evolutionary ancient family of regulatory genes. *Hox* genes direct the segmentation and patterning of the overall body plan during embryonic development.

homeostasis A condition of balance, or stability, within a biological system, maintained by the interaction of physiological mechanisms that compensate for changes (both external and internal).

hominins Colloquial term for members of the tribe Hominini, which includes all bipedal hominoids back to the divergence from African great apes.

homologies Similarities between organisms based on descent from a common ancestor.

homoplasy (*homo*, meaning "same," and *plasy*, meaning "growth") The separate evolutionary development of similar characteristics in different groups of organisms.

homozygous Having the same allele at the same locus on both members of a chromosome pair.

hormones Substances (usually proteins) that are produced by specialized cells and travel to other parts of the body, where they influence chemical reactions and regulate various cellular functions.

horticulture Farming method in which only hand tools are used; typical of most early Neolithic societies.

Huaca del Sol (wah´-ka dell sole) Massive adobe pyramid built at Moche, in northern Peru.

Human Genome Project An international effort aimed at sequencing and mapping the entire human genome.

hunter-gatherers People who make their living by hunting, fishing, and gathering their food and not by producing it.

hybrids Offspring of mixed ancestry; heterozygotes.

hypothesis (*pl.*, hypotheses) A provisional explanation of a phenomenon. Hypotheses require repeated testing.

hypoxia Lack of oxygen. Hypoxia can refer to reduced amounts of available oxygen in the atmosphere (due to lowered barometric pressure) or to insufficient amounts of oxygen in the body.

index fossils Fossil remains of known age, used to estimate the age of the geological stratum in which they are found. For example, extinct marine arthropods called trilobites can be used as an index fossil of Cambrian and Ordovician geological formations.

indirect percussion The method of driving off blades and flakes from a prepared core using a bone or antler punch to press off a thin flake.

Inka People whose sophisticated culture dominated Peru at the time of the European arrival; also, the term for that people's highest ruler; also spelled Inca.

intelligence Mental capacity; ability to learn, reason, or comprehend and interpret information, facts, relationships, and meanings; the capacity to solve problems, whether through the application of previously acquired knowledge or through insight.

interglacials Climatic intervals when continental ice sheets are retreating, eventually becoming much reduced in size. Interglacials in northern latitudes are associated with warmer temperatures, while in southern latitudes the climate becomes wetter.

interspecific Between species; refers to variation beyond that seen within the same species to include additional aspects seen between two different species.

intraspecific Within species; refers to variation seen within the same species.

Kaminaljuyú (cam-en-awl-hoo-yoo´) Major prehistoric Maya site located at Guatemala City.

Kebaran Late Pleistocene hunter-gatherers of the eastern Mediterranean region and Levant.

kivas Underground chambers or rooms used for gatherings and ceremonies by pueblo dwellers.

K-selected Pertaining to an adaptive strategy whereby individuals produce relatively few offspring, in whom they invest increased parental care. Although only a few infants are born, chances of survival are increased for each one because of parental investments in time and energy. Examples of K-selected nonprimate species are birds and canids (e.g., wolves, coyotes, and dogs).

lactase persistence The ability to continue to produce the enzyme lactase in adults. Most mammals, including humans, lose this ability after they are weaned.

large-bodied hominoids Those hominoids including the great apes (orangutans, chimpanzees, gorillas) and hominins, as well as all ancestral forms back to the time of divergence from small-bodied hominoids (i.e., the gibbon lineage).

Late Pleistocene The Pleistocene stage beginning 125,000 ya and ending approximately 10,000 ya.

Laurentide (lah-ren´-tid) Pleistocene ice sheet centered in the Hudson Bay region and extending across much of eastern Canada and the northern United States.

life history traits Characteristics and developmental stages that influence reproductive rates. Examples include longevity, age at sexual maturity, and length of time between births.

locus (*pl.*, loci) (lo´-kus, lo-sigh´) The position on a chromosome where a given gene occurs. The term is sometimes used interchangeably with *gene*.

loess (luss) Fine-grained soil composed of glacially pulverized rock, deposited by the wind.

Lower Paleolithic A unit of archaeological time that begins about 2.6 mya with the earliest identified tools made by hominins and ends around 200,000 years ago.

macaques (muh-kaks´) A group of Old World monkeys comprising several species, including rhesus monkeys. Most macaque species live in India, other parts of Asia, and nearby islands.

macroevolution Changes produced only after many generations, such as the appearance of a new species.

Magdalenian A late Upper Paleolithic stone tool industry in Europe that dates to 17,000–11,000 ya.

manioc Cassava, a starchy edible root crop of the tropics.

material culture The physical manifestations of human activities, such as tools, art, and structures. As the most durable aspects of culture, material remains make up the majority of archaeological evidence of past societies.

matrilines Groups that consist of a female, her daughters, and their offspring. Matrilineal groups are common in macaques.

Maya Mesoamerican culture consisting of regional kingdoms and known for its art and architectural accomplishments; also, Native American ethnic group of southern Mexico, Guatemala, and Belize.

megafauna Literally,"large animals," those weighing over 100 pounds.

meiosis Cell division in specialized cells in ovaries and testes. Meiosis involves two divisions and results in four daughter cells, each containing only half the original number of chromosomes. These cells can develop into gametes.

Mendelian traits Characteristics that are influenced by alleles at only one genetic locus. Examples include many blood types, such as ABO. Many genetic disorders, including sickle-cell anemia and Tay-Sachs disease, are also Mendelian traits.

Mesoamerica (*meso*, meaning "middle") Geographical and cultural region from central Mexico to northwestern Costa Rica; formerly called "Middle America" in the archaeological literature.

Mesolithic (*meso*, meaning "middle," and *lith*, meaning "stone") Middle Stone Age; period of hunter-gatherers, especially in northwestern Europe.

Mesopotamia (*meso*, meaning "middle," and *potamos*, meaning "river") Land between the Tigris and Euphrates rivers, mostly included in modern-day Iraq.

metabolism The chemical processes within cells that break down nutrients and release energy. (When nutrients are broken down into their component parts, such as amino acids, energy is released and made available for the cell to use.)

Mexica (meh-shee´-ka) Original name by which the Aztecs were known before their rise to power.

microevolution Small changes occurring within species, such as a change in allele frequencies.

Middle Paleolithic Cultural period that began about 200,000 ya and ended around 30,000–40,000 years ago. Roughly the same period in sub-Saharan Africa is called the Middle Stone Age.

Middle Pleistocene The Pleistocene stage beginning 780,000 ya and ending 125,000 ya.

middens Archaeological sites or features within sites formed largely by the accumulation of domestic waste.

midline An anatomical term referring to a hypothetical line that divides the body into right and left halves.

millet Small-grained cereal grasses native to Asia and Africa.

Mississippian Referring to late prehistoric chiefdoms of the southeastern United States and southern Midwest between roughly 1,100 and 300 ya.

mitochondria (*sing.*, mitochondrion) (my´-tow-kond´-dree-uh) Structures contained within the cytoplasm of eukaryotic cells that convert energy, derived from nutrients, to a form that is used by the cell.

mitochondrial DNA (mtDNA) DNA found in mitochondria. Mitochondrial DNA is inherited only from the mother.

mitosis Simple cell division; the process by which somatic cells divide to produce two identical daughter cells.

Moche (moh´-chay) Regional state, city, and valley of the same name in northern Peru.

Mogollon (mo-go-yohn´) Prehistoric village culture of northern Mexico and southern Arizona/New Mexico.

Mohenjo-Daro (mo-henjo-dar´-o) An early Indus Valley city in south-central Pakistan.

molecule A structure made up of two or more atoms. Molecules can combine with other molecules to form more complex structures.

morphology The form (shape, size) of anatomical structures; can also refer to the entire organism.

mosaic evolution A pattern of evolution in which the rate of evolution in one functional system varies from that in other systems. For example, in hominin evolution, the dental system, locomotor system, and neurological system (especially the brain) all evolved at markedly different rates.

Mousterian A Middle Paleolithic stone tool industry associated with Neandertals and some modern *H. sapiens* groups.

multidisciplinary Pertaining to research that involves the mutual contributions and cooperation of experts from various scientific fields (i.e., disciplines).

"multimale-multifemale" groups Social groups composed of several adults and subadults of both sexes.

mutation A change in DNA. The term can refer to changes in DNA bases as well as changes in chromosome number or structure.

Naj Tunich (nah toon´-eesh) Maya sacred cave in Guatemala.

natal group The group in which animals are born and raised. (*Natal* pertains to birth.)

Natufian Referring to collector-type hunter-gatherers who established sedentary settlements in parts of the Near East after 12,000 ya.

natural selection The most critical mechanism of evolutionary change, first articulated by Charles Darwin; refers to genetic change or changes in the frequencies of certain traits in populations due to differential reproductive success between individuals.

Nebuchadnezzar (neh-boo-kud-neh´-zer) Late Babylonian king, ca. 605–562 B.C.

neocortex The more recently evolved portions of the brain's cortex that are involved with higher mental functions and composed of areas that integrate incoming information from different sensory modalities.

Neolithic (*neo*, meaning "new," and *lith*, meaning "stone") New Stone Age; period of farmers.

Neolithic revolution Childe's term for the far-reaching consequences of food production.

neural tube In early embryonic development, the anatomical structure that develops to form the brain and spinal cord.

nocturnal Active during the night.

noncoding DNA sequences Sequences that don't code for identifiable proteins but in many cases produce molecues that influence the actions of coding sequences. (The terminology is somewhat confusing. Currently, geneticists use the term *coding* to refer to sequences that code for proteins that are fairly easy to detect. *Noncoding* currently refers to sequences that seem not to have any function or that code for proteins that regulate the actions of other genes.)

nuchal torus (nuke´-ul) (*nuchal*, meaning "pertaining to the neck") A projection of bone in the back of the cranium where neck muscles attach; used to hold up the head.

nucleus A structure (organelle) found in all eukaryotic cells. The nucleus contains chromosomes (nuclear DNA).

oases (*sing.*, oasis) Permanent springs or water holes in an arid region.

Oaxaca (wah-ha´-kah) A southern Mexican state bordering the Pacific Ocean.

obligate bipedalism Bipedalism as the *only* form of hominin terrestrial locomotion. Since major anatomical changes in the spine, pelvis, and lower limb are required for bipedal locomotion, once hominins adapted to this mode of locomotion, other forms of locomotion on the ground became impossible.

Olmec Prehistoric chiefdom in the Gulf Coast lowlands of Veracruz and Tabasco, Mexico, between 3,200 and 2,400 ya.

omnivorous Having a diet consisting of many kinds of foods, such as plant materials (seeds, fruits, leaves), meat, and insects.

osteology The study of skeletal material. Human osteology focuses on the interpretation of the skeletal remains of past groups. Some of the same techniques are used in paleoanthropology to study early hominins.

Ounjougou A site populated by African hunter-gatherers who made early use of wild cereal grasses on the southern edge of the Sahara between 12,000 and 9,000 ya.

paleoanthropology The interdisciplinary approach to the study of earlier hominins—their chronology, physical structure, archaeological remains, habitats, etc.

Paleo-Indian (*paleo*, meaning "ancient") Referring to early hunter-gatherers who occupied the Americas from about 13,500 to 10,000 ya.

paleomagnetism Dating method based on the earth's shifting magnetic pole.

paleontologists Scientists whose study of ancient life-forms is based on fossilized remains of extinct animals and plants.

paleopathology The branch of osteology that studies the traces of disease and injury in human skeletal (or, occasionally, mummified) remains.

paleospecies Species defined from fossil evidence, often covering a long time span.

pandemic An extensive outbreak of disease affecting large numbers of individuals over a wide area; potentially a worldwide phenomenon.

pathogens Any agents, especially microorganisms such as viruses, bacteria, or fungi, that infect a host and cause disease.

pharaoh Title of the ruler of ancient Egypt.

phenotypes The observable or detectable physical characteristics of an organism; the detectable expressions of genotypes.

phylogenetic tree A chart showing evolutionary relationships as determined by evolutionary systematics. It contains a time component and implies ancestor-descendant relationships.

phytoliths (*phyto*, meaning "plant," and *lith*, meaning "stone") Microscopic silica structures formed in the cells of many plants.

placental A type (subclass) of mammal. During the Cenozoic, placentals became the most widespread and numerous mammals and today are represented by upward of 20 orders, including the primates.

Plano Great Plains bison-hunting culture of 11,000–9,000 ya, which employed narrow, unfluted points.

plant macrofossils Plant parts such as seeds, nutshells, and stems, preserved in the archaeological record and large enough to be clearly visible to the naked eye.

plant microfossils Small to microscopic plant remains, most falling in a range of 10 to 100 micrometers (μm), or roughly the size of individual grains of wheat flour in the bag from your grocer's shelf.

plasticity The capacity to change; in a behavioral context, the ability of animals to modify behaviors in response to differing circumstances.

Pleistocene The epoch of the Cenozoic from 1.8 mya until 10,000 ya. Frequently referred to as the Ice Age, this epoch is associated with continental glaciations in northern latitudes.

Plio-Pleistocene Pertaining to the Pliocene and first half of the Pleistocene, a time range of 5–1 mya. For this time period, numerous fossil hominins have been found in Africa.

polities The political organizations of societies or groups.

pollen Microscopic grains containing the male gametes of seed-producing plants.

polyandry A mating system wherein a female continuously associates with more than one male (usually two or three) with whom she mates. Among nonhuman primates, polyandry is seen only in marmosets and tamarins. It also occurs in a few human societies.

polychrome Many-colored.

polygenic Referring to traits that are influenced by genes at two or more loci. Examples of such traits are stature, skin color, and eye color. Many polygenic traits are also influenced by environmental factors.

polymerase chain reaction (PCR) A method of producing copies of a DNA segment using the enzyme DNA polymerase.

polymorphisms Loci with more than one allele. Polymorphisms can be expressed in the phenotype as the result of gene action (as in ABO), or they can exist solely at the DNA level within noncoding regions.

polytypic Referring to species composed of populations that differ with regard to the expression of one or more traits.

population Within a species, a community of individuals where mates are usually found.

population genetics The study of the frequency of alleles, genotypes, and phenotypes in populations from a microevolutionary perspective.

postcranial (*post*, meaning "after") In a quadruped, referring to that portion of the body behind the head; in a biped, referring to all parts of the body *beneath* the head (i.e., the neck down).

potassium-argon (K/Ar) method Dating technique based on accumulation of argon-40 gas as a by-product of the radiometric decay of potassium-40 in volcanic materials; used especially for dating early hominin sites in East Africa.

potlatch Ceremonial feasting and gift-giving event among Northwest Coast Indians.

prehensility Grasping with the hands and, in many primates, also the feet.

prehistory The several million years between the emergence of bipedal hominins and the availability of written records.

prepared-core method Pertaining to stone cores that a toolmaker shapes into a pre-planned form before striking flakes from it; enables predictable flake shape and thickness; can be efficient in the use of raw materials.

primates Members of the mammalian order Primates (pronounced "pry-may´-tees"), which includes prosimians, monkeys, apes, and humans.

primatologists Scientists who study the evolution, anatomy, and behavior of nonhuman primates. Those who study behavior in non-captive animals are usually trained as physical anthropologists.

primatology The study of the biology and behavior of nonhuman primates (prosimians, monkeys, and apes).

principle of independent assortment The distribution of one pair of alleles into gametes does not influence the distribution of another pair. The genes controlling different traits are inherited independently of one another.

principle of segregation Genes (alleles) occur in pairs (because chromosomes occur in pairs). During gamete production, the members of each gene pair separate, so that each gamete contains one member of each pair. During fertilization, the full number of chromosomes is restored, and members of gene or allele pairs are reunited.

principle of superpositioning In a stratigraphic sequence, the lower layers were deposited before the upper layers. Or, simply put, the stuff on top of a heap was put there last.

prosimians Members of a suborder of Primates, the suborder Prosimii (pronounced "pro-sim´-ee-eye"). Traditionally, the suborder includes lemurs, lorises, and tarsiers.

protein synthesis The assembly of chains of amino acids into functional protein molecules. The process is directed by DNA.

proteins Three-dimensional molecules that serve a wide variety of functions through their ability to bind to other molecules.

protohominins The earliest members of the hominin lineage, as yet only poorly represented in the fossil record; thus, the reconstruction of their structure and behavior is largely hypothetical.

public archaeology A broad term that covers archaeological research conducted for the public good as part of cultural resource management and heritage management programs; a major growth area of world archaeology.

pueblos Spanish for "town"; multiroom residence structures built by village farmers in the American Southwest; when spelled with an uppercase P, the several cultures that built and lived in such villages.

Qin Shi Huangdi (chin-shee-huangdee) First emperor of a unified China.

quadrupedal Using all four limbs to support the body during locomotion; the basic mammalian (and primate) form of locomotion.

quantitatively (quantitative) Pertaining to measurements of quantity and including such properties as size, number, and capacity.

quinoa (keen-wah´) Seed-bearing member of the genus *Chenopodium*, cultivated by early Peruvians.

rachis The short stem by which an individual seed attaches to the main stalk of a plant as it develops.

radiocarbon dating Method for determining the age of organic archaeological materials by measuring the decay of the radioactive isotope of carbon, carbon-14; also known as carbon-14 dating.

radiometric decay A measure of the rate at which certain radioactive isotopes disintegrate.

recessive Describing a trait that is not expressed in heterozygotes; also refers to the allele that governs the trait. For a recessive allele to be expressed, there must be two copies of the allele (i.e., the individual must be homozygous).

recombinant DNA technology A process in which genes from the cell of one species are transferred to somatic cells or gametes of another species.

recombination The exchange of DNA between paired chromosomes during meiosis; also called *crossing over*.

regulatory genes Genes that code for the production of proteins that can bind to DNA and modify the action of genes. Many are active only during certain stages of development.

reproductive strategies The complex of behavioral patterns that contributes to individual reproductive success. The behaviors need not be deliberate, and they can vary considerably between males and females.

reproductive success The number of offspring an individual produces and rears to reproductive age; an individual's genetic contribution to the next generation.

rhinarium (rine-air´-ee-um) (*pl.*, rhinaria) The moist, hairless pad at the end of the nose seen in most mammals. The rhinarium enhances an animal's ability to smell.

ribonucleic acid (RNA) A molecule similar in structure to DNA. Three different single-stranded forms of RNA are essential to protein synthesis.

r-selected An adaptive strategy that emphasizes relatively large numbers of offspring and reduced parental care (compared to K-selected species). *K-selection* and *r-selection* are relative terms; e.g., mice are r-selected compared to primates but K-selected compared to fish.

sagittal crest A ridge of bone that runs down the middle of the cranium like a short Mohawk. This serves as the attachment for the large temporal muscles, indicating strong chewing.

science A body of knowledge gained through observation and experimentation; from the Latin *scientia*, meaning "knowledge."

scientific method An approach to research whereby a problem is identified, a hypothesis (or hypothetical explanation) is stated, and that hypothesis is tested through the collection and analysis of data.

scientific testing The precise repetition of an experiment or expansion of observed data to provide verification; the procedure by which hypotheses and theories are verified, modified, or discarded.

sectorial Adapted for cutting or shearing; among primates, refers to the compressed (side-to-side) first lower premolar, which functions as a shearing surface with the upper canine.

sedentism The practice of residing in a single location for most or all of the year.

selective pressures Forces in the environment that influence reproductive success in individuals.

sensory modalities Different forms of sensation (e.g., touch, pain, pressure, heat, cold, vision, taste, hearing, and smell).

seriation Relative dating method that orders artifacts into a temporal series based on their similar attributes or the frequency of these attributes.

sex chromosomes The X and Y chromosomes. The Y chromosome determines maleness; in its absence, an embryo develops as a female.

sexual dimorphism Differences in physical characteristics between males and females of the same species. For example, humans are slightly sexually dimorphic for body size, with males being taller, on average, than females of the same population.

sexual selection A type of natural selection that operates on only one sex in a species. It's the result of competition for mates, and it can lead to sexual dimorphism with regard to one or more traits.

shamanism Traditional practices that mediate between the world of humans and the world of spirits.

Shang The first historic civilization in northern China; also called the Yin dynasty.

site survey The process of discovering the location of archaeological sites; sometimes called site reconnaissance.

slash-and-burn agriculture A traditional land-clearing practice whereby trees and vegetation are cut and burned. Fields are usually abandoned after a few years and another area subsequently cleared.

social stratification Class structure or hierarchy, usually based on political, economic, or social standing.

social structure The composition, size, and sex ratio of a group of animals. The social structure of a species is, in part, the result of natural selection in a specific habitat, and it guides individual interactions and social relationships.

"Soft hammer" percussion A direct percussion method of making stone tools that uses a resilient hammer or billet to gain greater control over the length, width, and thickness of flakes driven from a core.

Solutrean An Upper Paleolithic stone tool industry in southwestern France and Spain that dates to 21,000–18,000 ya.

somatic cells Basically, all the cells in the body except those involved with reproduction.

sorghum A cereal grass. Some subspecies are grown for food grains, others for their sweet, juicy stalk.

specialized Evolved for a particular function; usually refers to a specific trait (e.g., incisor teeth), but may also refer to the entire way of life of an organism.

speciation The process by which a new species evolves from an earlier species. Speciation is the most basic process in macroevolution.

species A group of organisms that can interbreed to produce fertile offspring. Members of one species are reproductively isolated from members of all other species (i.e., they can't mate with them to produce fertile offspring).

spina bifida A condition in which the arch of one or more vertebrae fails to fuse and form a protective barrier around the spinal cord.

starch grains Subcellular structures that form in all plant parts and are classifiable by family or genus; particularly abundant in seeds and tubers.

state A governmental entity that persists by politically controlling a territory; examples include most modern nations.

stelae (*sing.*, stela) (stee´-lee) Upright posts or stones, often bearing inscriptions.

stereoscopic vision The condition whereby visual images are, to varying degrees, superimposed on one another. This provides for depth perception, or the perception of the external environment in three dimensions. Stereoscopic vision is partly a function of structures in the brain.

stratigraphic Pertaining to the depositional levels, or strata, of an archaeological site.

stratigraphy Study of the sequential layering of deposits.

stratum (*pl.*, strata) A single layer of soil or rock; sometimes called a level.

stress In a physiological context, any factor that acts to disrupt homeostasis; more precisely, the body's response to any factor that threatens its ability to maintain homeostasis.

Sumerians Earliest civilization of Mesopotamia.

symbiosis (*syn*, meaning "together," and *bios*, meaning "life") Mutually advantageous association of two different organisms; also known as *mutualism*.

Tamaulipas (tah-mah-leep´-ahs) A Mexican state located on the Gulf Coast south of Texas.

taphonomy (*taphos*, meaning "grave") The study of how bones and other materials came to be buried in the earth and preserved as fossils. A taphonomist studies the processes of sedimentation, the action of streams, preservation properties of bone, and carnivore disturbance factors.

taros Species of a tropical plant with an edible starchy root.

taxonomy The branch of science concerned with the rules of classifying organisms on the basis of evolutionary relationships.

Tehuacán Valley (tay-wah-kahn´) A dry highland region on the boundary of the states of Puebla and Oaxaca in southern Mexico.

teosinte (taeo-sin´-tae) A native grass of southern Mexico, believed to be ancestral to maize.

Teotihuacán (tay-oh-tee-wah-cahn´) Earliest city-state to dominate the Valley of Mexico. It became one of the largest urban centers in the New World up to the nineteenth century.

Tenochtitlán (tay-nosh-teet-lahn´) Aztec capital, built on the future site of Mexico City.

territorial state A form of state political organization with multiple administrative centers and one or more capitals. The cities tended to house the elite and administrative classes, and food producers usually lived and worked in the surrounding hinterland.

territories Portions of an individual's or group's home range that are actively defended against intrusion, especially by members of the same species.

theories Well-substantiated explanations of natural phenomena, supported by hypothesis testing and by evidence gathered over time. Theories also allow scientists to make predictions about as yet unobserved phenomena. Some theories are so well established that no new evidence is likely to alter them substantially.

thermoluminescence (TL) (ther-mo-loo-mines´-ence) Technique for dating certain archaeological materials, such as ceramics, that release stored energy of radioactive decay as light upon reheating.

till plains Accumulations of stones, boulders, mud, sand, and silt deposited by glaciers as they melt; ground moraines.

Tiwanaku (tee-wahn-ah´-koo) Regional state, city, and valley of the same name near Lake Titicaca, in Bolivia.

Toltecs Central Mexican highlands people who created a pre-Aztec empire with its capital at Tula in the Valley of Mexico.

totem An animal or being associated with a kin-group and used for social identification; also, a carved pole representing these beings.

transhumance Seasonal migration from one resource zone to another, especially between highlands and lowlands.

transmutation The change of one species to another. The term *evolution* did not assume its current meaning until the late nineteenth century.

Tula (too´-la) Toltec capital in the Valley of Mexico; sometimes known as Tollan.

tundra Treeless plains characterized by permafrost conditions that support the growth of shallow-rooted vegetation such as grasses and mosses.

Tutankhamen (toot-en-cahm´-en) Egyptian pharaoh of the New Kingdom period, who died at age 19 in 1323 B.C.; informally known today as King Tut.

Ubaid (oo-bide´) Early formative culture of Mesopotamia, 7,500–6,200 ya; predecessor to Sumerian civilization.

uniformitarianism The theory that the earth's features are the result of long-term processes that continue to operate in the present as they did in the past. Elaborated on by Lyell, this theory opposed catastrophism and contributed strongly to the concept of immense geological time.

Upper Paleolithic Cultural period beginning roughly 30,000–40,000 ya and ending about 10,000 ya and distinguished by major technological innovations, the creation of the earliest human art widely recognized as such, and many other accomplishments. Best known from western Europe, similar industries are also known from central and eastern Europe and Africa.

variation In genetics, inherited differences among individuals; the basis of all evolutionary change.

vasoconstriction Narrowing of blood vessels to reduce blood flow to the skin. Vasoconstriction is an involuntary response to cold and reduces heat loss at the skin's surface.

vasodilation Expansion of blood vessels, permitting increased blood flow to the skin. Vasodilation permits warming of the skin and also facilitates radiation of warmth as a means of cooling. Vasodilation is an involuntary response to warm temperatures, various drugs, and even emotional states (blushing).

vectors Agents that transmit disease from one carrier to another. Mosquitoes are vectors for malaria, just as fleas are vectors for bubonic plague.

vertebrates Animals with segmented, bony spinal columns; traditionally includes fishes, amphibians, reptiles, birds, and mammals.

Wari (wah´-ree) Regional state and city of the same name in southern Peru.

Xia (shah) Semilegendary kingdom, or dynasty, of early China.

Younger Dryas A stadial between roughly 13,000 and 11,500 ya. The climate became colder and drier but did not return to full glacial conditions in higher latitudes.

Zhou (chew) Chinese dynasty that followed Shang and ruled between 1122 and 221 B.C.

ziggurat Late Sumerian mud-brick temple-pyramid.

zoonoses (*sing.*, zoonosis) Diseases that can be transmitted to humans from other vertebrates.

zoonotic (zoh-oh-no´-tic) Pertaining to a zoonosis (*pl.*, zoonoses), a disease that is transmitted to humans through contact with nonhuman animals.

zygote A cell formed by the union of an egg and a sperm cell. It contains the full complement of chromosomes (in humans, 46) and has the potential of developing into an entire organism.

Bibliography

Acosta, José de
2002   *Natural and Moral History of the Indies*. Jane E. Mangan (ed.). Durham, NC: Duke University Press.

Acsádi, G. and J. Nemeskéri.
1970   *History of Human Life Span and Mortality*. Budapest: Akadémiai Kiadó.

Adams, Robert McC.
1981   *Heartland of Cities*. Chicago: University of Chicago Press.

Adler, D. S., G. Bar-Oz, A. Belfer-Cohen, et al.
2006   "Ahead of the Game: Middle and Upper Palaeolithic Hunting Behaviors in the Southern Caucasus." *Current Anthropology*, 47:89–118.

Adovasio, James M., J. Donahue, and Robert Stuckenrath
1990   "The Meadowcroft Rockshelter Radiocarbon Chronology 1975–1990." *American Antiquity*, 55(2):348–354.

Aldred, Cyril
1998   *The Egyptians*. (Rev. Ed.) New York: Thames & Hudson.

Alemseged, Z., F. Spoor, W. H. Kimbel et al.
2006   "A Juvenile Early Hominin Skeleton from Dikika, Ethiopia." *Nature*, 443:296–301.

Alva, Walter and Christopher Donnan
1993   *Royal Tombs of Sipan*. Los Angeles: Fowler Museum of Cultural History, University of California, Los Angeles.

Ambrose, Stanley H.
2001   "Paleolithic Technology and Human Evolution." *Science*, 291:1748–1753.

Ames, K. M. and Herbert D. Maschner
1999   *Peoples of the Northwest Coast: Their Archaeology and Prehistory*. New York: Thames & Hudson.

Anikovich, M.V., A. A. Sinitsy, John F. Hoffecker et al.
2007   "Early Upper Paleolithic in Eastern Europe and Implications for the Dispersal of Modern Humans." *Science*, 315:223–229.

Armelagos, George J. and Kristin N. Harper
2005   "Genomics at the Origins of Agriculture, Part One." *Evolutionary Anthropology*, 14:68–77.

Arnold, Thomas G.
2006   *The Ice-Free Corridor: Biogeographical Highway or Environmental Cul-de-sac*. Unpublished Ph.D. dissertation. Department of Archaeology, Simon Fraser University, Burnaby, British Columbia.

Arsuaga, Juan-Luis, Carlos Lorenzo, and Ana Garcia
1999   "The Human Cranial Remains from Gran Dolina Lower Pleistocene Site (Sierra de Atapuerca, Spain)." *Journal of Human Evolution*, 37:431–457.

Arsuaga, J. L., I. Martinez, A. Garcia, et al.
1997   "Sima de los Huesos (Sierra de Atapuerca, Spain). The Site." *Journal of Human Evolution*, 33:109–127.

Ascenzi, A., I. Biddittu, P. F. Cassoli, et al.
1996   "A Calvarium of Late *Homo erectus* from Ceprano, Italy." *Journal of Human Evolution*, 31:409–423.

Asfaw, Berhane, W. Henry Gilbert, Yonnas Beyene, et al.
2002   "Remains of *Homo erectus* from Bouri, Middle Awash, Ethiopia." *Nature*, 416:317–320.

Badrian, Noel and Richard K. Malenky
1984   "Feeding Ecology of *Pan paniscus* in the Lomako Forest, Zaire." *In: The Pygmy Chimpanzee*, Randall L. Susman (ed.), New York: Plenum Press, pp. 275–299.

Bailey, G.
1975   "The Role of Molluscs in Coastal Economies." *Journal of Archaeological Science*, 2:45–62.

Balter, Michael
2005   *The Goddess and the Bull*. New York: Free Press.

———
2006   "Radiocarbon Dating's Final Frontier." *Science*, 313: 1560–1563.

Barker, Graeme
2006   *The Agricultural Revolution in Prehistory: Why Did Foragers Become Farmers?* Oxford: Oxford University Press.

Barker, Graeme, Huw Barton, Michael Bird, et al.
2007   "The Human Revolution in Lowland Tropical Southeast Asia: the Antiquity and Behavior of Anatomically Modern Humans at Niah Cave (Sarawak, Borneo)." *Journal of Human Evolution*, 52:243–261.

Bar-Oz, Guy
2004   *Epipaleolithic Subsistence Strategies in the Levant: A Zooarchaeological Perspective*. Boston, MA: Brill Academic Publishers.

Barnes, G. L.
1992   *China, Korea, and Japan: The Rise of Civilization in East Asia*. New York: Thames & Hudson.

Barnosky, Anthony, Paul L. Koch, Robert S. Feranec, Scott L. Wing, and Alan B. Shabel
2004   "Assessing the Causes of Late Pleistocene Extinctions on the Continents." *Science*, 306:70–75.

Bartlett, Thad. Q., Robert W. Sussman, and James M. Cheverud
1993   "Infant Killing in Primates: A Review of Observed Cases with Specific References to the Sexual Selection Hypothesis." *American Anthropologist*, 95(4):958–990.

Bartstra, Gert-Jan
1982   "*Homo erectus erectus*: The Search for Artifacts." *Current Anthropology*, 23(3):318–320.

Bar-Yosef, Ofer
1986   "The Walls of Jericho: An Alternative Explanation." *Current Anthropology*, 27(2):157–162.

———
1987   "Late Pleistocene Adaptations in the Levant." *In: The Pleistocene in the Old World: Regional Perspectives*, Olga Soffer (ed.), New York: Plenum, pp. 219–236.

———
1993   "The Role of Western Asia in Modern Human Origins." *In:* M. J. Aitken, et al. (eds.), q.v., pp. 132–147.

———
1994   "The Contributions of Southwest Asia to the Study of Origin of Modern Humans." *In: Origins of Anatomically Modern Humans*, M. H. Nitecki and D. V. Nitecki (eds.), New York: Plenum Press, pp. 23–66.

1998 "The Natufian Culture in the Levant, Threshold to the Origins of Agriculture." *Environmental Anthropology*, 6(5):159–177.

2004 "Eat What is There: Hunting and Gathering in the World of Neanderthals and their Neighbours." *International Journal of Osteoarchaeology*, 14:333–342.

Beadle, George W.
1980 "The Ancestry of Corn." *Scientific American*, 242:112–119.

Bearder, Simon K.
1987 "Lorises, Bushbabies and Tarsiers: Diverse Societies in Solitary Foragers." *In*: Smuts, et al. (eds.), q.v., pp. 11–24.

Begun, D. and A. Walker
1993 "The Endocast." *In*: A. Walker and R. E. Leakey (eds), q.v., pp. 326–358.

Beja-Pereira, A., G. Luikart, P. England, et al.
2003 "Gene-Culture Coevolution between Cattle Milk Protein Genes and Human Lactase Genes." *Nature Genetics*, 35:311–313.

Belfer-Cohen, Anna
1991 "The Natufians in the Levant." *Annual Review of Anthropology*, 20:167–186.

Bellwood, Peter S.
2005 *The First Farmers: The Origins of Agricultural Societies*. Malden, MA: Blackwell.

Bellwood, Peter S., C. Gamble, S. A. Le Blanc, et al.
2007 "Review Feature: *First Farmers: the Origins of Agricultural Societies*, by Peter Bellwood." *Cambridge Archaeological Journal*, 17(1):87–109.

Ben Shaul, D. M.
1962 "The Composition of the Milk of Wild Animals." *International Zoo Yearbook*, 4:333–342.

Benz, Bruce F. and Hugh H. Iltis
1990 "Studies in Archaeological Maize I: The 'Wild' Maize from San Marcos Cave Reexamined." *American Antiquity*, 55(3):500–511.

Berger, Thomas and Erik Trinkaus
1995 "Patterns of Trauma Among the Neandertals." *Journal of Archaeological Science*, 22:841–852.

Berlo, Janet (ed.)
1992 *Art, Ideology, and the City of Teotihuacán*. Washington, DC: Dumbarton Oaks.

Bermudez de Castro, J. M., J. Arsuaga, E. Carbonell, et al.
1997 "A Hominid from the Lower Pleistocene of Atapuerca, Spain. Possible Ancestor to Neandertals and Modern Humans." *Science*, 276:1392–1395.

Bermudez de Castro, J. M., M. Martinon-Torres, E. Carbonell, et al.
2004 "The Atapuerca Sites and their Contribution to the Knowledge of Human Evolution in Europe." *Evolutionary Anthropology*, 13:25–41.

Bicho, N., A. F. Carvalho, C. González-Sainz, et al.
2007 "The Upper Paleolithic Rock Art of Iberia." *Journal of Archaeological Method and Theory*, 14(1):81–151.

Binford, Lewis R.
1968 "Post-Pleistocene Adaptations." *In*: Binford, S. and L. R. Binford (eds.). *New Perspectives in Archaeology*. Chicago: Aldine, pp. 313–341.

1978 *Nunamiut Ethnoarchaeology*. New York: Academic Press.

1981 *Bones. Ancient Men and Modern Myths*. New York: Academic Press.

1983 *In Pursuit of the Past*. New York: Thames and Hudson.

Binford, Lewis R. and Chuan Kun Ho
1985 "Taphonomy at a Distance: Zhoukoudian, 'The Cave Home of Beijing Man'?" *Current Anthropology*, 26:413–442.

Binford, Lewis R. and Nancy M. Stone
1986a "The Chinese Paleolithic: An Outsider's View." *AnthroQuest*, Fall 1986(1):14–20.

1986b "Zhoukoudian: A Closer Look." *Current Anthropology*, 27(5):453–475.

Bininda-Emonds, R. P. Olaf, Marcel Cordillo, et al.
2007 "The Delayed Rise of Present-Day Mammals." *Nature*, 446:507–512

Bischoff, J. L., R. W. Williams, R. J. Rosebauer, et al.
2007 "High-Resolution U-series Dates from the Sima de los Huesos Hominids Yields 600+V/-66 kyrs: Implications for the Evolution of the Early Neanderthal Lineage." *Journal of Archaeological Science*, 34:763–770.

Boaz, N. T. and R. L. Ciochon
2001 "The Scavenging of *Homo erectus pekinensis*." *Natural History*, 110(2):46–51.

Boesch, C.
1996 "Social Grouping Tai Chimpanzees." *In*: *Great Ape Societies*. W. C. McGrew, L. Marchant, and T. Nishida (eds), Cambridge, UK: Cambridge University Press. pp. 101–113.

Boesch, C. and H. Boesch-Achermann
2000 *The Chimpanzees of the Tai Forest*. Oxford, UK: Oxford University Press.

Boesch, C. and H. Boesch
1989 "Hunting Behavior of Wild Chimpanzees in the Tai National Park." *American Journal of Physical Anthropology*, 78:547–573.

Boesch, C., P. Marchesi, N. Marchesi, et al.
1994 "Is Nut Cracking in Wild Chimpanzees a Cultural Behaviour?" *Journal of Human Evolution*, 26:325–338.

Bogucki, Peter
1988 *Forest Farmers and Stockherders: Early Agriculture and Its Consequences in North Central Europe*. Cambridge: Cambridge University Press.

Bokonyi, S.
1969 "Archaeological Problems and Methods of Recognizing Animal Domestication." *In*: *The Domestication and Exploitation of Plants and Animals*, P. J. Ucko and G. W. Dimbleby (eds.), Chicago: Aldine, pp. 207–218.

Bonnichsen, Robson, Bradley T. Lepper, Dennis Stanford, et al. (eds.)
2005 *Paleoamerican Origins: Beyond Clovis*. College Station, TX: Texas A&M University Press.

Bordaz, Jacques
1970 *Tools of the Old and New Stone Age*. Natural History Press, Garden City.

Borries, C., K. Launhardt, C. Epplen, et al.
1999 "DNA Analyses Support the Hypothesis that Infanticide is Adaptive in Langur Monkeys." *Proceedings of the Royal Society of London*, 266:901–904.

Boserup, Ester
1965 *The Conditions of Agricultural Growth*. Chicago: Aldine.

Bove, Frederick J. and Sonia Medrano Busto
2003 "Teotihuacan, Militarism, and Pacific Guatemala." *In*: Braswell (ed.), q. v., pp. 45–79.

Bower, Bruce
2006 "Evolution's Mystery Woman." *Science News*, 170:330–332.

Brace, C. L. and Ashley Montagu
1977 *Human Evolution* (2nd Ed.). New York: Macmillan.

Brace, C. Loring, H. Nelson, and N. Korn
1979   *Atlas of Human Evolution* (2nd Ed.). New York: Holt, Rinehart & Winston.

Brace, C. Loring, A. Russell Nelson, Noriko Seguchi, et al.
2001   "Old World Sources of the First New World Human Inhabitants: A Comparative Craniofacial View." *Proceedings of the National Academy of Science*, 98(4):10017–10022.

Bradley, Bruce and Dennis Stanford
2004   "The North Atlantic Ice-Edge Corridor: A Possible Palaeolithic Route to the New World." *World Archaeology*, 36(4):459–478.

————
2006   "The Solutrean-Clovis Connection: Reply to Straus, Meltzer and Goebel." *World Archaeology*, 38(4):704–714.

Brady, James E. and Andrea Stone
1986   "Naj Tunich: Entrance to the Maya Underworld." *Archaeology*, 39(6):18–25.

Braidwood, Robert J. and Bruce Howe
1960   *Prehistoric Investigations in Iraqi Kurdistan*. Studies in Ancient Oriental Civilization, No. 31. Chicago: Oriental Institute.

Braswell, Geoffrey E. (ed.)
2003   *The Maya and Teotihuacan: Reinterpreting Early Classic Interaction*. Austin: University of Texas Press.

Breuer, T. M.
2005   "First Observation of Tool Use in Wild Gorillas." *PloS Biology*, 3(11):3380.

Bromage, Timothy G. and Christopher Dean
1985   "Re-evaluation of the Age at Death of Immature Fossil Hominids." *Nature*, 317:525–527.

Brooks, Alison, et al.
1995   "Dating and Context of Three Middle Stone Age Sites with Bone Points in the Upper Semliki Valley, Zaire." *Science*, 268:548–553.

Brown, Ian
1994   "Recent Trends in the Archaeology of the Southeastern United States." *Journal of Archaeological Research*, 2(1):45–111.

Brown, M. Kathryn and Travis W. Stanton (eds.)
2003   *Ancient Mesoamerican Warfare*. Walnut Creek, CA: Altamira Press.

Brown, P., T. Sutiikna, M. K. Morwood, et al.
2004   "A New Small-Bodied Hominin from the Late Pleistocene of Flores, Indonesia." *Nature*, 431:1055–1061.

Brown, T. M. and K. D. Rose
1987   "Patterns of Dental Evolution in Early Eocene Anaptomorphine Primates Omomyidae from the Bighorn Basin, Wyoming." *Journal of Paleontology*, 61:1–62.

Brubaker, L. B., P. M. Anderson, M. E. Edwards, and A. V. Lozhkin
2005   "Beringia as a Glacial Refugium for Boreal Trees and Shrubs: New Perspectives from Mapped Pollen Data." *Journal of Biogeography*, 32(5):833–848.

Bruhns, Karen Olsen
1994   *Ancient South America*. Cambridge: Cambridge University Press.

Bruhns, Karen O., and Nancy L. Kelker
2007   "Did the Olmec Know How to Write?" *Science*, 315:1365.

Brumm, A., H. Aziz, G. D. van den Burgh, et al.
2006   "Early Stone Technology on Flores and Its Implications for *Homo floresiensis*." *Nature*, 441(7093):624–628.

Brunet, M., F. Guy, D. Pilbeam, et al.
2002   "A New Hominid from the Upper Miocene of Chad, Central Africa." *Nature*, 418:145–151.

Bruning, S. B.
2006   "Complex Legal Legacies: The Native American Graves Protection and Repatriation Act, Scientific Study, and Kennewick Man." *American Antiquity*, 71(3):501–521.

Bryan, Alan L. and Ruth Gruhn
2003   "Some Difficulties in Modeling the Original Peopling of the Americas." *Quaternary International*, 109–110:175–179.

Bryant, Vaughn M.
2003   "Invisible Clues to New World Plant Domestication." *Science*, 299:1029–1030.

Burger, Richard L.
1992   *Chavín and the Origins of Andean Civilizations*. New York: Thames & Hudson.

Butler, Declan
2006   "Yes But Will It Jump?" News. *Nature*, 439:124–125.

Butzer, Karl W.
1984   "Long-term Nile Flood Variation and Political Discontinuities in Pharaonic Egypt." *In:* Clark and Brandt (eds.), q.v., pp. 102–112.

Byers, Douglas S. (ed.)
1967   *The Prehistory of the Tehuacán Valley. Vol. 1: Economy and Subsistence*. Austin: University of Texas Press.

Cannon, Michael D. and David J. Meltzer
2004   "Early Paleoindian Foraging: Examining the Faunal Evidence for Large Mammal Specialization and Regional Variability in Prey Choice." *Quaternary Science Reviews*, 23:1955–1987.

Caramelli, David, Carlos Lalueza-Fox, Cristiano Vernesi, et al.
2003   "Evidence for Genetic Discontinuity Between Neandertals and 24,000-year-old Anatomically Modern Humans." *Proceedings of the National Academy of Sciences*, 100:6593–6597.

Carbonell, Eudald, Jose M. Bermudez de Castro, Josep M. Pares, et al.
2008   "The First Humans of Europe." *Nature*, 452:465–469.

Carter, Howard and A. C. Mace
1923   *The Tomb of Tutankhamen*. London: Cassell and Co., Ltd.

Cartmill, Matt
1972   "Arboreal Adaptations and the Origin of the Order Primates." *In: The Functional and Evolutionary Biology of Primates*, R. H. Tuttle (ed.), Chicago: Aldine-Atherton, pp. 97–122.

————
1992   "New Views on Primate Origins." *Evolutionary Anthropology*, 1:105–111.

Casson, Lionel
2001   *Everyday Life in Ancient Egypt*. Baltimore: Johns Hopkins University Press.

Catto, Norm and Gail Catto
2004   "Climate Change, Communities, and Civilizations: Driving Force, Supporting Player, or Background Noise?" *Quaternary International*, 123–125:7–10.

Cauvin, Jacques
2000   *The Birth of the Gods and the Origins of Agriculture*. Cambridge: Cambridge University Press.

Cavalli-Sforza, L. L., A. Piazza, P. Menozzi, and J. Mountain
1988   "Reconstruction of Human Evolution: Bringing Together Genetic, Archaeological, and Linguistic Data." *Proceedings of the National Academy of Sciences*, 85:6002–6006.

Chang, Kwang-chih
1980   *Shang Civilization*. New Haven: Yale University Press.

————
1986   *The Archaeology of Ancient China* (4th Ed.). New Haven: Yale University Press.

——— 2000 "Ancient China and Its Anthropological Significance." *In*: Lamberg-Karlovsky (ed.), q.v., pp. 1–11.

Chatters, James C.
1001 *Ancient Encounters : Kennewick Man and the First Americans.* New York: Simon & Schuster.

——— 2004 "Kennewick Man: A Paleoamerican Skeleton from the Northwestern U.S." *In: New Perspectives on the First Americans*, Bradley T. Lepper and Robson Bonnichsen (eds.), College Station, TX: Center for the Study of First Americans, pp. 129–135.

Chen, F-C., and Li, W-H.
2001 "Genomic Divergences Between Humans and Other Hominoids and the Effective Population Size of the Common Ancestor of Humans and Chimpanzees." *American Journal of Human Genetics*, 68:444–456.

Chen, F. C., E. J. Vallender, H. Wang, C. S. Tzeng, and W. H. Li
2001 "Genomic Divergence between Human and Chimpanzee Estimated from Large-scale Alignments of Genomic Sequences." *Journal of Heredity*, 92:481–489.

Cheng, Z., M. Ventura, X. She, P. Khaitovich, T. Graves, et al.
2005 "A Genome-wide Comparison of Recent Chimpanzee and Human Segmental Duplications." *Nature*, 437:88–93.

Childe, V. Gordon
1928 *The Most Ancient East.* London: Routledge and Kegan Paul.

——— 1934 *New Light on the Most Ancient East.* London: Kegan Paul, Trench, Trubner.

——— 1951 *Man Makes Himself* (Rev. Ed.). New York: New American Library.

The Chimpanzee Sequencing and Analysis Consortium.
2005 "Initial Sequence of the Chimpanzee Genome and Comparison with the Human Genome." *Nature*, 437:69–87.

Chisholm, J. S.
1993 "Death, Hope, and Sex: Life-history theory and the development of reproductive strategies." *Current Anthropology*, 34 (1), 1–24.

Chrisman, Donald, Richard S. MacNeish, Jamshed Mavalwala, and Howard Savage
1996 "Late Pleistocene Human Friction Skin Prints from Pendejo Cave, New Mexico." *American Antiquity*, 61(2):357–376.

Chrisman, Donald, J. Mavalwala, H. Savage, and A. Tessarolo
2003 "Friction-Skin Imprints and Hair." *In:* MacNeish and Libby, q.v., pp. 417–430.

Ciochon, Russell L. and Robert S. Corruccini (eds.)
1983 *New Interpretations of Ape and Human Ancestry.* New York: Plenum Press.

Cioffi-Revilla, Claudio and Todd Landman
1999 "Evolution of Maya Polities in the Ancient Mesoamerican System." *International Studies Quarterly*, 43:559–598.

Clark, Grahame
1972 *Star Carr: A Case Study of Bioarchaeology.* Reading, MA: Addison-Wesley.

——— 1979 *Mesolithic Prelude.* Edinburgh: Edinburgh University Press.

Clark, J. Desmond
1976 "Prehistoric Populations and Resources Favoring Plant Domestication in Africa." *In: Origins of African Plant Domestication*, J. R. Harlan, J. DeWet, and A. Stemler (eds.), The Hague: Mouton, pp. 69–84.

Clark, J. Desmond and Steven A. Brandt (eds.)
1984 *From Hunters to Farmers.* Berkeley and Los Angeles: University of California Press.

Clarke, Ronald J. and Phillip V. Tobias
1995 "Sterkfontein Member 2 Foot Bones of the Oldest South African Hominid." *Science*, 269:521–524.

Cleveland, J. and C. T. Snowdon
1982 "The Complex Vocal Repertoire of the Adult Cotton-top Tamarin (*Saguinus oedipus oedipus*)." *Zeitschrift Tierpsychologie*, 58:231–270.

Coe, Michael D.
1992 *Breaking the Maya Code.* New York: Thames & Hudson.

——— 1994 *Mexico: From the Olmecs to the Aztecs.* New York: Thames & Hudson.

——— 1999 *The Maya* (6th Ed.). New York: Thames & Hudson.

Cohen, Mark N.
1977 *The Food Crisis in Prehistory.* New Haven, CT: Yale University Press.

——— 1989 *Health and the Rise of Civilization.* New Haven, CT: Yale University Press.

Cohen, M. N. and G. J. Armelagos (eds.)
1984 *Paleopathology at the Origins of Agriculture.* Orlando: Academic Press.

Coil, James, Alejandra Korstanje, Steven Archer, Christine A. Hastorf
2003 "Laboratory Goals and Consideration for Multiple Microfossil Extraction in Archaeology." *Journal of Archaeological Science*, 30:991–1008.

Colinvaux, Paul A.
1979 *Why Big Fierce Animals Are Rare: An Ecologist's Perspective.* Princeton, NJ: Princeton University Press.

Colledge, Sue, and James Conolly (eds.)
2007 *The Origins and Spread of Domestic Plants in Southwest Asia and Europe.* Publications of the Institute of Archaeology, University College London. Walnut Creek, CA: Left Coast Press.

Colwell, Rita R.
1996 "Global Climate and Infectious Disease: The Cholera Paradigm." *Science*, 274(5295):2025–2031.

Conkey, M.
1987 "New Approaches in the Search for Meaning? A Review of the Research in 'Paleolithic Art.'" *Journal of Field Archaeology*, 14:413–430.

Conneller, Chantal
2004 "Hunter-Gatherers 'on the move'?" *Antiquity*, 78(302): 916–922.

Conroy, Glenn C.
1990 *Primate Evolution.* New York, NY: W. W. Norton.

——— 1997 *Reconstructing Human Origins. A Modern Synthesis.* New York: Norton.

Cooper, Alan, Andrew Rambaut, Vincent Macaulay, et al.
2001 "Human Origins and Ancient DNA." Letter to *Science*, 282:1655–1656.

Cordell, Linda S.
1998 *Prehistory of the Southwest.* (2nd Ed.). Orlando, FL: Academic Press.

Corvinus, Gudrun
2004 "*Homo erectus* in East and Southeast Asia, and the Questions of the Age of the Species and its Association with Stone Artifacts, with Special Attention to Handaxe-like Tools." *Quaternary International*, 117(1):141–151.

Covey, R. Alan
2003   "A Processual Study of Inka State Formation." *Journal of Anthropological Archaeology*, 22:333–357.

Cowgill, George L.
2000   "The Central Mexican Highlands from the Rise of Teotihuacan to the Decline of Tula." *In: The Cambridge History of the Native Peoples of the Americas, Vol. II: Mesoamerica, Part I*, Richard E. W. Adams and Murdo J. MacLeod (eds.). Cambridge, UK: Cambridge University Press, pp. 250–317.

———   2004   "Origins and Development of Urbanism: Archaeological Perspectives." *Annual Review of Anthropology*, 33:525–549.

Crawford, Gary W. and Chen Shen
1998   "The Origins of Rice Agriculture: Recent Progress in East Asia." *Antiquity*, 72:858–867.

Crawford, Harriet
2004   *Sumer and the Sumerians*. (2nd Ed.). Cambridge, UK: Cambridge University Press.

Crews, D. E. and G. J. Harper
1998   "Ageing as Part of the Developmental Process." *In: The Cambridge Encyclopedia of Human Growth and Development*, S. J. Ulijaszek et al. (eds.) Cambridge, UK: Cambridge University Press, pp. 425–427.

Crown, Patricia L.
1991   "Hohokam: Current Views of Prehistory and the Regional System." *In: Chaco and Hohokam Prehistoric Regional Systems in the American Southwest*, Patricia L. Crown and W. James Judge (eds.), Santa Fe: School of American Research Press, pp. 135–157.

Cummings, Michael
2000   *Human Heredity. Principles and Issues* (5th Ed.). St. Paul: Wadsworth/West Publishing Co.

Currat, M., G. Trabuchet, D. Rees, et al.
2002   "Molecular Analysis of the Beta-Globin Gene Cluster in the Niokholo Mandenka Population Reveals a Recent Origin of the Beta S Senegal Mutation." *American Journal of Human Genetics*, 70:207–223.

Curtin, Phillip D.
2002   "Overspecialization and Remedies." *In: R. H. Steckel and J. C. Rose (eds.), q.v.*, pp. 603–608.

Curtin, R. and P. Dolhinow
1978   "Primate Social Behavior in a Changing World." *American Scientist*, 66:468–475.

Cuzange, M. T., E. Delqué-Kolic, T. Goslar, et al.
2007   "Radiocarbon Intercomparison Program for Chauvet Cave." *Radiocarbon*, 49(2):339-347.

Daeschler, Edward B., Neil H. Shubin, and Farish A. Jenkins, Jr.
2006   "A Darwinian Tetrapod-Like Fish and the Evolution of the Tetrapod Body Plan." *Nature*, 440:757–763.

Dalton, Rex
2005   "Scientists Finally Get Their Hands on Kennewick Man." *Nature*, 436(7047):10.

Dart, Raymond
1959   *Adventures with the Missing Link*. New York:Harper & Brothers.

Darwin, Charles
1859   *On the Origin of Species*. A Facsimile of the First Edition, Cambridge, MA: Harvard University Press (1964).

———   1871   *The Descent of Man and Selection in Relation to Sex*. Princeton, NJ: Princeton University Press (1981).

Davies, Nigel
1983   *The Ancient Kingdoms of Mexico*. New York: Penguin.

Davis, S. and F. R. Valla
1978   "Evidence for Domestication of the Dog 12,000 Years Ago in the Natufian of Israel." *Nature*, 276:608–610.

Day, M. H. and E. H. Wickens
1980   "Laetoli Pliocene Hominid Footprints and Bipedalism." *Nature*, 286:385–387.

D'Azevedo, Warren (ed.)
1986   *Handbook of North American Indians*, vol. 11: Great Basin. Washington, DC: Smithsonian Institution Press.

Dean, M., M. Carring, C. Winkler, et al.
1996   "Genetic Restriction of HIV-1 Infection and Progression to AIDS by a Deletion Allele of the CKR5 Structural Gene." *Science*, 273:1856–1862.

De la Torre, Ignacio and Rafael Mora
2005   "Unmodified Lithic Material at Olduvai Bed I: Manuports or Ecofacts?" *Journal of Archaeological Science*, 32(2):273–285.

del Carmen Rodriguez Martinez, Maria., Ponciano Ortiz Ceballos, Michael D. Coe, et al.
2006   "Oldest Writing in the New World." *Science*, 313:1610–1614.

Delcourt, Hazel R. and Paul A. Delcourt
1991   *Quaternary Ecology: A Paleoecological Perspective*. London: Chapman & Hall.

de Lumley, Henry and M. de Lumley
1973   "Pre-Neanderthal Human Remains from Arago Cave in Southeastern France." *Yearbook of Physical Anthropology*, 16:162–168.

Demarrais, Elizabeth, Chris Gosden, and Colin Renfrew
2005   *Rethinking Materiality: The Engagement of Mind with the Material World*. Cambridge, UK: McDonald Institute of Archaeological Research.

Demuth, J. P., T. D. Bie, J. E. Stajich, N. Cristianini, and M. W. Hahn
2006   "The Evolution of Mammalian Gene Families." *PloS ONE* 1(1):e85. doi:10.1371/journal.pone.0000085.

Dene, H. T., M. Goodman, and W. Prychodko
1976   "Immunodiffusion Evidence on the Phylogeny of the Primates." *In: Molecular Anthropology*, M. Goodman, R. E. Tashian, and J. H. Tashian (eds.), New York: Plenum Press, pp. 171–195.

Dennell, Robin
1983   *European Economic Prehistory: A New Approach*. New York: Academic Press.

———   2004   *Early Hominin Landscapes in Northern Pakistan: Investigations in the Pabbi Hills*. BAR International Series 1265. Oxford, UK: British Archaeological Reports.

Dennell, Robin and Wil Roebroeks
2005   "An Asian Perspective on Early Human Dispersal from Africa." *Nature*, 438:1099–1104.

Desmond, Adrian and James Moore
1991   *Darwin*. New York: Warner Books.

de Waal, Frans
1982   *Chimpanzee Politics*. London, UK: Jonathan Cape.

———   1987   "Tension Regulation and Nonreproductive Functions of Sex in Captive Bonobos *(Pan paniscus)*." *National Geographic Research*, 3:318–335.

———   1989   *Peacemaking among Primates*. Cambridge, MA: Harvard University Press.

———
1996   *Good Natured: The Origins of Right and Wrong in Humans and Other Animals.* Cambridge, MA.: Harvard University Press.

———
1999   "Cultural Primatology Comes of Age." *Nature,* 399:635–636.

———
2007   "With a Little Help from a Friend." *PloS Biology,* 5(7):1406–1408.

de Waal, F. and F. Lanting.
1997   *Bonobo: The Forgotten Ape.* Berkeley, CA: University of California Press.

Diamond, Jared
1987   "The Worst Mistake in the History of the Human Race." *Discover,* 8(5):64–66.

———
1989   "The Accidental Conqueror." *Discover,* 10(12):71–76.

Diehl, Richard
2004   *The Olmecs: America's First Civilization.* New York: Thames & Hudson.

Diehl, Richard A. and Janet C. Berlo (eds.)
1989   *Mesoamerica after the Decline of Teotihuacán,* A.D. 700–900. Washington, DC: Dumbarton Oaks.

Diehl, Richard A. and Michael D. Coe
1996   "Olmec archaeology." *In: The Olmec World,* by M. D. Coe, R. A. Diehl, D. A. Freidel, et al. Princeton: The Art Museum, Princeton University, pp. 2–25.

Dillehay, Thomas D.
1989   *Monte Verde: A Late Pleistocene Settlement in Chile, Vol. 1: Paleoenvironment and Site Context.* Washington, DC: Smithsonian Institution Press.

———
1997   *Monte Verde: A Late Pleistocene Settlement in Chile, Vol. 2: The Archaeological Content and Interpretation.* Washington, DC: Smithsonian Institution Press.

Dincauze, Dena
1997   "Regarding Pendejo Cave: Response to Chrisman et al." *American Antiquity,* 62(3):554–555.

DiPeso, Charles C.
1974   *Casas Grandes, A Fallen Trading Center of the Gran Chichimeca.* Flagstaff: Northland Press.

Dixon, E. James
1999   *Bones, Boats, and Bison: Archaeology and the First Colonization of Western North America.* Albuquerque: University of New Mexico.

Doebley, J.
1994   "Morphology, Molecules, and Maize." *In: Corn and Culture in the Prehistoric New World,* S. Johannessen and C. A. Hastorf, (eds.), Boulder, CO: Westview Press, pp. 101–112.

Domínguez-Rodrigo, Manuel
2002   "Hunting and Scavenging by Early Humans: The State of the Debate." *Journal of World Prehistory,* 16(1):1–54.

Domínguez-Rodrigo, Manuel and Travis Rayne Pickering
2003   "Early Hominid Hunting and Scavenging: A Zooarchaeological Review." *Evolutionary Anthropology,* 12:275–282.

Dominy, N. J. and P. W. Lucas
2001   "Ecological Importance of Trichromatic Vision to Primates." *Nature,* 410:363–366.

Doran, D. M. and A. McNeilage
1998   "Gorilla Ecology and Behavior." *Evolutionary Anthropology,* 6(4):120–131.

Dressler W. W., K. S. Oths, and C. G. Gravlee
2005   "Race and Ethnicity in Public Health Research: Models to Explain Health Disparities. *Annual Review of Anthropology,* 34:231–252.

Duarte, C., J. Mauricio, P. B. Pettitt, et al.
1999   "The Early Upper Paleolithic Human Skeleton from the Abrigo do Lagar Velho (Portugal) and Modern Human Emergence in Iberia." *Proceedings of the National Academy of Sciences,* 96:7604–7609.

Dunnell, Robert C.
1982   "Science, Social Science, and Common Sense: The Agonizing Dilemma of Modern Archaeology." *Journal of Anthropological Research,* 38:1–25.

Durham, William
1981   Paper presented to the Annual Meeting of the American Anthropological Association, Washington, D.C., Dec. 1980. Reported in *Science,* 211:40.

Edmonds, M.
1999   *Ancestral Geographies of the Neolithic: Landscape, Monuments, and Memory.* London: Routledge.

Edwards, Mike
2000   "Indus Civilization: Clues to an Ancient Puzzle." *National Geographic,* 197(6):108–131.

Ehret, C.
1984   "Historical/Linguistic Evidence for Early African Food Production." *In:* J. D. Clark and S. A. Brandt (eds.), q.v., pp. 26–35.

Einwogerer, Thomas, Herwig Friesinger, Marc Handel, et al.
2006   "Upper Palaeolithic Infant Burials." *Nature,* 444(7117):285.

Emerson, Thomas E. and R. Barry Lewis (eds.)
2000   *Cahokia and the Hinterlands.* Urbana: University of Illinois Press.

Enard, W., M. Przeworski, S. E. Fisher, et al.,
2002   "Molecular Evolution of FOXP2, a Gene Involved in Speech and Language." *Nature,* 418:869–872.

Erickson, D. L., B. D. Smith, A. C. Clarke, et al.
2005   "An Asian Origin for a 10,000-year-old Domesticated Plant in the Americas." *Proceedings of the National Academy of Sciences,* 102(51):18315–18320.

Erlandson, Jon M.
1988   "The Role of Shellfish in Prehistoric Economies: A Protein Perspective." *American Antiquity,* 53:102–109.

———
2002   "Anatomically Modern Humans, Maritime Voyaging, and the Pleistocene Colonization of the Americas." *In:* "The First Americans, The Pleistocene Colonization of the New World," N. G. Jablonski (ed.), *Memoirs of the California Academy of Sciences,* 27:59–92.

Erlandson, Jon M., Michael H. Graham, Bruce J. Bourque, et al.
2007   "The Kelp Highway Hypothesis: Marine Ecology, the Coastal Migration Theory, and the Peopling of the Americas." *The Journal of Island and Coastal Archaeology* 2(2):161–174.

Etler, Dennis A. and Li-Tianyuan
1994   "New Archaic Human Fossil Discoveries in China and Their Bearing on Hominid Species Definition During the Middle Pleistocene." *In:* R. Corruccini and R. Ciochon (eds.), q.v., pp. 639–675.

Ewald, P. W.
1994   *Evolution of Infectious Disease.* New York, NY: Oxford University Press.

_____
1999 "Evolutionary Control of HIV and Other Sexually Transmitted Viruses." *In: Evolutionary Medicine*, W. R. Trevathan, E. O. Smith, and J. J. McKenna, (eds.), New York, NY: Oxford University Press.

Ezzo, Joseph A.
1993 "Human Adaptation at Grasshopper Pueblo, Arizona: Social and Ecological Perspectives." *International Monographs in Prehistory, Archaeological Series, 4.* Ann Arbor.

Fagan, Brian M.
1993 "Taming the Aurochs." *Archaeology*, 46(5):14–17.

Falgeres, Christophe, Jean-Jacques Bahain, Yugi Yokoyama, et al.
1999 "Earliest Humans in Europe: The Age of TD6 Gran Dolina, Atapuerca, Spain." *Journal of Human Evolution*, 37:345–352.

Falk, D., C. Hildebolt, K. Smith, et al.
2005 "The Brain of LB1, *Homo floresiensis*." *Science*, 308:242–245.

Fedigan, Linda M.
1983 "Dominance and Reproductive Success in Primates." *Yearbook of Physical Anthropology*, 26:91–129.

Fiedel, Stuart J.
1999 "Older Than We Thought: Implications of Corrected Dates for Paleoindians." *American Antiquity*, 64(1):95–116.

Fiedel, Stuart J. and G. Haynes
2004 "A Premature Burial: Comments on Grayson and Meltzer's 'Requiem for Overkill'." *Journal of Archaeological Science*, 31:121–131.

Firestone, R. B., A. West, J. P. Kennett, et al.
2007 "Evidence for an Extraterrestrial Impact 12,900 Years Ago that Contributed to the Megafaunal Extinctions and the Younger Dryas Cooling." *Proceedings of the National Academy of Sciences*, 104(41):16016–16021.

Fischer, Anders, Mike Richards, Jesper Olsen, et al.
2007 "The Composition of Mesolithic Food. Evidence from the Submerged Settlement on the Argus Bank, Denmark." *Acta Archaeologica*, 78(2):163–178.

Fischman, Josh
2005 "Family Ties." *National Geographic*, 207(April):16–27.

Fitzgerald, Patrick
1978 *Ancient China.* Oxford: Elsevier Phaidon.

Fleagle, John
1983 "Locomotor Adaptations of Oligocene and Miocene Hominoids and their Phyletic Implications." *In:* R. L. Ciochon and R. S. Corruccini (eds), q.v., pp. 301–324.

_____
1988/ *Primate Adaptation and Evolution.*New York:
1999 Academic Press. (2nd Ed.), 1999.

Flannery, Kent V.
1972 "The Origins of the Village As a Settlement Type in Mesoamerica and the Near East: A Comparative Study." *In: Man, Settlement and Urbanism*, P. J. Ucko, R. Tringham, and G. W. Dimbleby (eds.), London: Duckworth, pp. 23–53.

_____
1973 "The Origins of Agriculture." *Annual Review of Anthropology*, 2:217–310.

_____
1986 *Guila Naquitz: Archaic Foraging and Early Agriculture in Oaxaca, Mexico.* New York: Academic Press.

Flannery, Kent V. and Joyce Marcus
2000 "Formative Mexican Chiefdoms and the Myth of the 'Mother Culture.'" *Journal of Anthropological Archaeology*, 19:1–37.

Foley, R. A.
1991 "How Many Species of Hominid Should There Be?" *Journal of Human Evolution*, 30: 413–427.

_____
2002 "Adaptive Radiations and Dispersals in Hominin Evolutionary Ecology." *Evolutionary Anthropology*, 11 (Supplement 1):32–37.

Foley, R. A. and M. M. Lahr
1997 "Mode 3 Technologies and the Evolution of Modern Humans." *Cambridge Archaeological Journal*, 7:3–36.

Formicola, Vincenzo and Alexandra P. Buzhilova
2004 "Double Child Burial from Sunghir (Russia): Pathology and Inferences for Upper Paleolithic Funerary Practices." *American Journal of Physical Anthropology*, 124:189–198.

Fried, Morton H.
1967 *The Evolution of Political Society: An Essay in Political Anthropology.* New York: Random House.

Friedman, Florence Dunn (ed.) et al.
1998 *Gifts of the Nile: Ancient Egyptian Faience.* New York: Thames & Hudson.

Frisancho, A. Roberto
1993 *Human Adaptation and Accommodation.* Ann Arbor: University of Michigan Press.

Frison, George C.
1978 *Prehistoric Hunters of the High Plains.* New York: Academic Press.

Fritz, Gayle J.
1994 "Are the First American Farmers Getting Younger?" *Current Anthropology*, 35(3):305–309.

_____
1999 "Gender and the Early Cultivation of Gourds in Eastern North America." *American Antiquity*, 64(3):417–429.

Fritz, John M. and George Michell
2003 *Hampi.* Bombay: India Book House.

Fuller, Dorian
2006 "Agricultural Origins and Frontiers in South Asia: A Working Synthesis." *Journal of World Prehistory*, 20:1–86.

Fuller, Dorian, Ravi Korisettar, P. C. Venkatasubbaiah, Martin K. Jones
2004 "Early Plant Domestications in Southern India: Some Preliminary Archaeobotanical Results." *Vegetation History and Archaeobotany*, 13:115–129.

Galik, K., B. Senut, M. Pickford, et al.
2004 "External and Internal Morphology of the Bar1002'00 *Orrorin tugenensis* Femur." *Science*, 305:1450–1453.

Gao, Feng, Elizabeth Bailes, David L. Robertson, et al.
1999 "Origin of HIV-1 in the Chimpanzee *Pan troglodytes troglodytes*." *Nature*, 397:436–441.

Gao, Xing, Qi Wei, Chen Shen, et al.
2005 "New Light on the Earliest Hominid Occupation in East Asia." *Current Anthropology*, 46(supplement): S115–S120.

Gardner, R. Allen, B. T. Gardner, and T. T. van Cantfort (eds.)
1989 *Teaching Sign Language to Chimpanzees.* Albany: State University of New York Press.

Gibson, Jon L.
2001 *The Ancient Mounds of Poverty Point.* Gainesville, FL: University Press of Florida.

Gilbert, M. Thomas P., Dennis L. Jenkins, Anders Gotherstrom, et al.
2008 "DNA from Pre-Clovis Human Coprolites in Oregon, North America." *Science*, 320:786–789.

Gillespie, B. and R. G. Roberts
2000 "On the Reliability of Age Estimate for Human Remains at Lake Mungo." *Journal of Human Evolution*, 38:727–732.

Gingerich, Phillip D.
1985   "Species in the Fossil Record: Concepts, Trends, and Transitions." *Paleobiology*, 11:27–41.

Glassow, Michael A.
1996   *Purisimeño Chumash Prehistory*. New York: Harcourt Brace.

Goebel, Ted, Michael R. Waters, and Margarita Dikova
2003   "The Archaeology of Ushki Lake, Kamchatka, and the Pleistocene Peopling of the Americas." *Science*, 301:501–505

Goebel, Ted, Michael R. Waters, and Dennis H. O'Rourke
2008   "The Late Pleistocene Dispersal of Modern Humans in the Americas." *Science*, 319:1497–1502.

Goodall, Jane
1986   *The Chimpanzees of Gombe*. Cambridge: Harvard University Press.

Goodman, M., C. A. Porter, J. Czelusniak, et al.
1998   "Toward a Phylogenetic Classification of Primates Based on DNA Evidence Complemented by Fossil Evidence." *Molecular Phylogenetics and Evolution*, 9:585–598.

Goren-Inbar, Naama, Nira Alperson, Mordechai E. Kislev, et al.
2004   "Evidence of Hominin Control of Fire at Gesher Benot Ya'aqov, Israel." *Science*, 304:725–727.

Gossett, Thomas F.
1963   *Race, the History of an Idea in America*. Dallas: Southern Methodist University Press.

Gould, Richard A.
1977   "Puntutjarpa Rockshelter and the Australian Desert Culture." *Anthropological Papers of the American Museum of Natural History*, 54(1).

Gould, Stephen Jay
1981   *The Mismeasure of Man*. New York: W. W. Norton.

_____
1987   *Time's Arrow, Time's Cycle*. Cambridge: Harvard University Press.

_____
Gould, S. J. and N. Eldredge
1977   "Punctuated Equilibria: The Tempo and Mode of Evolution Reconsidered." *Paleobiology*, 3:115–151.

Gramly, Richard Michael
1992   *Guide to the Palaeo-Indian Artifacts of North America*. (2nd Ed.). Buffalo, NY: Persimmon Press.

Grant, B. S. and L. L. Wiseman
2002   "Recent History of Melanism in American Peppered Moths." *The Journal of Heredity*, 93(2):86–90.

Grant, P. R.
1982   "Variation in the Size and Shape of Darwin's Finch Eggs." *Auk*, 99:5–23.

_____
1986   *Ecology and Evolution of Darwin's Finches*. Princeton, NJ: Princeton University

Grant, Peter R. and B. Rosemary Grant
2002   "Unpredictable Evolution in a 30-year Study of Darwin's Finches." *Science*, 296:707–711.

Grayson, D. K.
2004   "Monte Verde, Field Archaeology, and the Human Colonization of the Americas." *In:* Madsen (ed.), q. v., pp. 379–387.

Grayson, D. K. and F. Delpech
2002   "Specialized Early Palaeolithic Hunters in Southwestern France?" *Journal of Archaeological Science*, 29:1439–1449.

_____
2003   "Ungulates and the Middle-to-Upper Paleolithic Transition at Grotte XVI (Dordogne, France)." *Journal of Archaeological Science*, 30:1633–1648.

Grayson, Donald K. and David J. Meltzer
2002   "Clovis Hunting and Large Mammal Extinction: A Critical Review of the Evidence." *Journal of World Prehistory*, 16(4):313–359.

_____
2003   "A Requiem for North American Overkill." *Journal of Archaeological Science*, 30:585–593.

_____
2004   "North American Overkill Continued?" *Journal of Archaeological Science*, 31:133–136.

Green, T. J., B. Cochran, T. W. Fenton, et al.
1998   "The Buhl Burial: A Paleoindian Woman from Southern Idaho." *American Antiquity*, 43(4):437–456.

Greene, John C.
1981   *Science, Ideology, and World View*. Berkeley: University of California Press.

Green, R. E., J. Krause, E. Ptak, A. W. Briggs, et al.
2006   "Analysis of One Million Base Pairs of Neanderthal DNA." *Nature*, 444:330–336.

Greenwood, B. and T. Mutabingwa
2002   "Malaria in 2000." *Nature*, 415:670–672.

Gregg, Susan Alling
1988   *Foragers and Farmers: Population Interaction and Agricultural Expansion in Prehistoric Europe*. Chicago: University of Chicago Press.

Gregory, J. M., P. Huybrechts, and S. C. B. Raper
2004   "Threatened Loss of the Greenland Ice Sheet." *Nature*, 428:616.

Gross, Liza
2006   *"Scientific Illiteracy and the Partisan Takeover of Biology."* PLoS Biol., 4:e167.

Grove, David C.
1989   "Olmec, What's in a Name?" *In: Regional Perspectives on the Olmec*, R. J. Sharer and D. C. Grove (eds.), Cambridge University Press, Cambridge, UK, pp. 8–14.

_____
1996   "The Formative Period in Mesoamerica." *In: The Oxford Companion to Archaeology*, Brian M. Fagan (ed.), Oxford, Oxford University Press, pp. 444–445.

Groves, Colin P.
2001a   *Primate Taxonomy*. Washington, DC: Smithsonian Institution Press.

_____
2001b   "Why Taxonomic Stability Is a Bad Idea, or Why Are There So Few (Or are there?). Evolutionary Anthropology 10:192–198.

Grün, R. and C. B. Stringer
1991   "ESR Dating and the Evolution of Modern Humans." *Archaeometry*, 33:153–199.

Grün, R., C. B. Stringer, F. McDermott, et al.
2005   "U-series and ESR Analysis of Bones and Teeth Relating to the Human Burials from Skhūl." *Journal of Human Evolution*, 49:316–334.

Guidon, N., A.-M. Pessis, Fabio Porenti, et al.
1996   "Nature and Age of the Deposits in Pedra Furada, Brazil: Reply to Meltzer, Adovasio, and Dillehay." *Antiquity*, 70:408–421.

Haas, Jonathan, and Winifred Creamer
2004   "Cultural Transformations in the Central Andean Late Archaic." *In:* Silverman (ed.), q.v., pp. 35–50.

Haas, Jonathan, Winifred Creamer, and Alvaro Ruiz
2004   "Dating the Late Archaic Occupation of the Norte Chico Region in Peru." *Nature*, 432:1020–1023.

Haas, J. D., E. A. Frongillo, Jr., C. D. Stepick, et al.
1980   "Altitude, Ethnic and Sex Difference in Birth Weight and Length in Bolivia." *Human Biology*, 52:459–477.

Haas, Jonathan, Shelia Pozorski, and Thomas Pozorski (eds.)
1987   *The Origins and Development of the Andean State.* New York: Cambridge University Press.

Haile-Selassie, Yohannes Gen Suwa, and Tim D. White
2004   "Late Miocene Teeth from Middle Awash, Ethiopia, and Early Hominid Dental Evolution." *Science*, 303:1503–1505.

Hamilton, M. J. and B. Buchanan
2007   "Spatial Gradients in Clovis-age Radiocarbon Dates across North America Suggest Rapid Colonization from the North." *Proceedings of the National Academy of Sciences*, 104(40):15625–15630.

Hanna, J. M.
1999   "Climate, Altitude, and Blood Pressure." *Human Biology*, 71:553–582.

Harlan, Jack R.
1992   *Crops and Man* (2nd Ed.). Madison, WI: American Society of Agronomy and Crop Science Society of America.

Harlow, H. F.
1959   "Love in Infant Monkeys." *Scientific American*, 200:68–74.

Harlow, Harry F. and Margaret K. Harlow
1961   "A Study of Animal Affection." *Natural History*, 70:48–55.

Harris, Edward
1989   *Principles of Archaeological Stratigraphy.* (2nd Ed.). New York: Academic Press.

Harris, J. W. K., and S. Capaldo
1993   "The Earliest Stone Tools: Their Implications for an Understanding of the Activities and Behaviour of Late Pliocene Hominids." *In: The Use of Tools by Human and Nonhuman Primates*, A. Berthelet and J. Chavaillon (eds.), Oxford, UK: Clarendon Press, pp. 196–220.

Harrison, Richard J.
1985   "The 'Policultivo Ganadero,' or Secondary Products Revolution in Spanish Agriculture, 5000–1000 B.C." *Proceedings of the Prehistoric Society*, 51:75–102.

Hart, John P. and C. Margaret Scarry
1999   "The Age of Common Beans (*Phaseolus vulgaris*) in the Northeastern United States." *American Antiquity*, 64(4):653–658.

Haury, Emil W.
1976   *The Hohokam, Desert Farmers and Craftsmen: Excavations at Snaketown*, 1964–1965. Tucson: University of Arizona Press.

Hawass, Zahi and Mark Lehner
1994   "The Sphinx: Who Built It, and Why?" *Archaeology*, 47(5):30–41.

Haynes, C. Vance
1993   "Clovis-Folsom Geochronology and Climatic Change." *In:* Soffer and Praslov (eds.), q.v., pp. 219–236.

———
1999   "Bad Weather and Good Hunters." *Discovering Archaeology*, 1(5):52.

———
2005   "Clovis, Pre-Clovis, Climate Change and Extinction." *In:* Bonnichsen et al. (eds.), q.v., pp. 113–132.

Haynes, Gary
2006   "Mammoth Landscapes: Good Country for Hunter-Gatherers." *Quaternary International*, 142–143: 20–29.

Hays, T. R.
1984   "A Reappraisal of the Egyptian Predynastic." *In:* J. D. Clark and S. A. Brandt (eds.), q.v., pp. 65–73.

Healan, Dan M. (ed.)
1989   *Tula of the Toltecs.* Iowa City, IA: University of Iowa Press.

Healan, Dan M. and James W. Stoutamire
1989   "Surface Survey of the Tula Urban Zone." *In:* Healan (ed.), q.v., pp. 203–236.

Henry, David O.
1989   *From Foraging to Agriculture: The Levant at the End of the Ice Age.* Philadelphia: University of Pennsylvania Press.

Henshilwood, C. S., F. d'Errico, M. Vanhaeren, et al.
2004   "Middle Stone Age Shell Beads from South Africa." *Science*, 304:404.

Henzi, P. and L. Barrett
2003   "Evolutionary Ecology, Sexual Conflict, and Behavioral Differentiation Among Baboon Populations." *Evolutionary Anthropology*, 12(5):217–230.

Herre, Wolf
1969   "The Science and History of Domestic Animals." *In: Science in Archaeology*, D. Brothwell and E. Higgs (eds.), New York: Frederick A. Praeger, pp. 257–272.

Hetherington, Renée, J. Vaughn Barrie, Robert G. B. Reid, et al.
2003   "Late Pleistocene Coastal Paleogeography of the Queen Charlotte Islands, British Columbia, Canada, and Its Implications for Terrestrial Biogeography and Early Postglacial Human Occupation." *Canadian Journal of Earth Science*, 40:1755–1766.

Higham, Charles and Tracey L.-D. Lu
1998   "The Origins and Dispersal of Rice Cultivation." *Antiquity*, 72:867–877.

Higham, Tom, Christopher Bronk Ramsey, Ivor Karavanic, et al.
2006   "Revised Direct Radiocarbon Dating of the Vindija G_1 Upper Paleolithic Neandertals." *Proceedings of the National Academy of Sciences*, 103:553–557.

Hodder, Ian
1990   *The Domestication of Europe.* Oxford, Blackwell.

———
1996   *On the Surface: Çatalhöyük, 1993–95.* London: David Brown. (ed.)

———
2001   "Symbolism and the Origins of Agriculture in the Near East." *Cambridge Archaeological Journal*, 11(1):107–112.

Hoffman, Michael A.
1991   *Egypt Before the Pharaohs* (Rev. Ed.). Austin: University of Texas Press.

Holloway, Ralph L.
1983   "Cerebral Brain Endocast Pattern of *Australopithecus afarensis* Hominid." *Nature*, 303:420–422.

———
1985   "The Poor Brain of *Homo sapiens neanderthalensis*." *In: Ancestors, The Hard Evidence*, E. Delson (ed.). New York: Alan R. Liss, pp. 319–324.

Holmes, C. E.
1996   "Broken Mammoth." *In:* West and West (eds.), q.v., pp. 312–318.

Houston, Stephen D.
2006   "An Example of Preclassic Mayan Writing?" *Science*, 311:1249–1250.

Howell, F. C.
1999   "Paleo-demes, Species, Clades, and Extinctions in the Pleistocene Hominin Record." *Journal of Anthropological Research*, 55:191–243.

Howell, John H.
1987   "Early Farming in Northwestern Europe." *Scientific American*, 257(5):118–126.

Hrdy, Sarah Blaffer
1977　*The Langurs of Abu.* Cambridge, MA: Harvard University Press.

Hrdy, Sarah Blaffer, Charles Janson, and Carel van Schaik
1995　"Infanticide: Let's Not Throw Out the Baby with the Bath Water." *Evolutionary Anthropology,* 3(5):151–154.

Hu, Dale J., Timothy J. Dondero, Mark A. Rayfield, et al.
1996　"The Emerging Genetic Diversity of HIV. The Importance of Global Surveillance for Diagnostics, Research, and Prevention." *Journal of the American Medical Association,* 275(3):210–216.

Hudjashou Georgi, Toomas Kivisid, Peter A. Underhill, et al.,
2007　"Revealing the Prehistoric Settlement of Australia by Y Chromosome and mtDNA Analysis." *Proceedings of the National Academy of Sciences,* 104:8726–8730.

Huysecom, E., S. Ozainne, F. Raeli, A. Ballouche, M. Rasse, and S. Stokes
2004　"Ounjougou (Mali): A History of Holocene Settlement at the Southern Edge of the Sahara." *Antiquity,* 78(301): 579–593.

Iglesias Ponce de Léon, María
2003　"Problematical Deposits and the Problem of Interaction: The Material Culture of Tikal during the Early Classic Period." *In:* Braswell (ed.), q.v., pp. 167–198.

The International SNP Map Working Group
2001　"A Map of Human Genome Sequence Variation Containing 1.42 Million Single Nucleotide Polymorphisms." *Nature,* 409:928–933.

Isbell, William H. and Alexei Vranich
2004　"Experiencing the Cities of Wari and Tiwanaku." *In:* Silverman (ed.), q.v., pp. 167–182.

Iseminger, William R.
1996　"Mighty Cahokia." *Archaeology,* 49(3):30–37.

Issar, Arie S., and Mattanyah Zohar
2004　*Climate Change—Environment and Civilization in the Middle East.* Berlin, Germany: Springer-Verlag.

IUCN (International Union for Conservation of Nature and Natural Resources)
1996/　Red List of Threatened Species. www.iucnredlist.org
2004

Izawa, K. and A. Mizuno
1977　"Palm-Fruit Cracking Behaviour of Wild Black-Capped Capuchin (*Cebus apella*)." *Primates,* 18:773–793.

Jablonski, N. G.
1992　"Sun, Skin Colour, and Spina Bifida: An Exploration of the Relationship between Ultraviolet Light and Neural Tube Defects." *Proceedings of the Australian Society of Human Biology,* 5:455–462.

Jablonski, Nina G. and George Chaplin
2000　"The Evolution of Skin Coloration." *Journal of Human Evolution,* 39:57–106.

Jacob, T., E. Indriati, R. P. Soejono, et al.
2006　"Pygmoid Australomelanesian *Homo sapiens* Skeletal Remains from Liang Bua, Flores: Population Affinities and Pathological Abnormalities." *Proceedings of the National Academy of Sciences,* 103:13421–13426.

Jacobs, Z., G. A. T. Duller, A. G. Wintle, and C. S. Heshilwood
2006　"Extending the Chronology of Deposits at Blombos Cave, South Africa, Back to 140 ka Using Optical Dating of Single and Multiple Grains of Quartz." *Journal of Human Evolution,* 51:255–273.

Jacobsson, Mattias, Sonja W. Acholz, Paul Scheet, et al.
2008　"Genotype, Haplotype and Copy-Number Variation in Worldwide Human Populations." *Nature,* 451:998–1003.

Janković, Ivor, Ivor Karavanić, James C. M. Ahern, et al.
2006　"Vindija Cave and The Modern Human Peopling of Europe." *Collegium Antropologicum,* 30:457–466.

Jantz, R. L. and D. W. Owsley
2001　"Variation Among North American Crania." *American Journal of Physical Anthropology,* 114:146–55.

Jarrige, Jean-Francois and Richard H. Meadow
1980　"The Antecedents of Civilization in the Indus Valley." *Scientific American,* 243(2):122–133.

Jensen, G. M. and L. G. Moore
1997　"The Effect of High Altitude and Other Risk Factors on Birthweight: Independent or Interactive Effects?" *American Journal of Public Health,* 87(6):1003–1007.

Jia, Lan-po
1975　*The Cave Home of Peking Man.* Peking: Foreign Language Press.

Jia, L. and W. Huang
1990　*The Story of Peking Man.* New York: Oxford University Press.

Jochim, Michael A.
1976　*Hunting-Gathering Subsistence and Settlement: A Predictive Model.* New York: Academic Press.

———
1998　*A Hunter-Gatherer Landscape: Southwest Germany in the Late Paleolithic and Mesolithic.* New York: Plenum.

Johnson, J. R., T. W. Stafford, G. J. West, et al.
2007　"Before and After the Younger Dryas: Chronostratigraphic and Paleoenvironmental Research at Arlington Springs, Santa Rosa Island, California." *EOS Transactions, American Geophysical Union,* 88(25).

Jonaitas, Aldona
1988　*From the Land of the Totem Poles.* Seattle: University of Washington Press.

Jolly, Alison
1985　*The Evolution of Primate Behavior* (2nd Ed.). New York, NY: Macmillan.

Kano, T.
1992　*The Last Ape. Pygmy Chimpanzee Behavior and Ecology.* Stanford: Stanford University Press.

Kantner, John
1999　"Anasazi Mutilation and Cannibalism in the American Southwest." *In: The Anthropology of Cannibalism,* Laurence R. Goldman, (ed.), Westport, CT: Bergin and Garvey, pp. 75–104.

Katz, D. and Suchey, J.M.
1986　"Age Determination of the Male Os Pubis." *American Journal of Physical Anthropology,* 69:427–435.

Kelly, Robert L.
1995　*The Foraging Spectrum: Diversity in Hunter-Gatherer Lifeways.* Washington, DC: Smithsonian Institution Press.

———
2003　"Maybe We Do Know When People First Came to North America; and What Does It Mean If We Do?" *Quaternary International,* 109–110:133–145.

Kembel, Silvia Rodriguez and John W. Rick
2004　"Building Authority at Chavín de Huántar: Models of Social Organization and Development in the Initial Period and Early Horizon." *In:* Silverman (ed.), q.v., pp. 51–76.

Kenoyer, Jonathan Mark
1998   *Ancient Cities of the Indus Valley Civilization.* Oxford: Oxford University Press.

Kent, Jonathan D.
1987   "The Most Ancient South: A Review of the Domestication of the Andean Camelids." *In: Studies in the Neolithic and Urban Revolutions: The V. Gordon Childe Colloquium, Mexico, 1986,* Linda Mazanilla (ed.), Oxford: B.A.R., pp. 169–184.

Kenyon, Kathleen M.
1981   *Excavations at Jericho,* Vol. 3. Jerusalem: British School of Archaeology.

Kerr, Richard A.
2008   "Experts Find No Evidence for a Mammoth-Killer Impact." *Science,* 319(5868):1331–1332.

Keynes, Randal
2002   *Darwin, His Daughter and Human Evolution.* New York: Riverhead Books.

Kimbel, W. H., T. D. White, and D. C. Johanson
1988   "Implications of KNM-WT-17000 for the Evolution of 'Robust' *Australopithecus." In: Evolutionary History of the "Robust" Australopithecines* (Foundations of Human Behavior), F. E. Grine (ed.), Somerset, NJ: Aldine Transaction, pp. 259–268.

King, Barbara J.
1994   *The Information Continuum.* Santa Fe: School of American Research.

Kislev, Mordechai, Ehud Weiss, and Anat Hartmann
2004   "Impetus for Sowing and the Beginning of Agriculture: Ground Collecting of Wild Cereals." *Proceedings of the National Academy of Sciences,* 101(9):2692–2695.

Klein, Richard G.
1999   *The Human Career: Human Biological and Cultural Origins.* (2nd Ed.) Chicago: University of Chicago Press.

Klein, Richard G. and Blake Edgar
2002   *The Dawn of Human Culture.* New York: John Wiley & Sons.

Kraeling, Carl H. and Robert McC. Adams (eds.)
1960   *City Invincible.* Chicago: University of Chicago Press.

Kramer, Andrew
1993   "Human Taxonomic Diversity in the Pleistocene: Does *Homo erectus* Represent Multiple Hominid Species?" *American Journal of Physical Anthropology,* 91:161–171.

Krause, Johannes, Carlos Lalueza-Fox, Ludavic Orlando, et al.
2007   "The Derived FOXP2 Variant of Modern Humans Was Shared with Neandertals." *Current Biology,* 17:1908–1912.

Krause, Johannes, Ludovic Orlando, David Serre, et al.
2007   "Neanderthals in Central Asia and Siberia." *Nature,* 449:902–904.

Krings, Matthias, Cristen Capelli, Frank Tscentscher, et al.
2000   "A View of Neandertal Genetic Diversity." *Nature Genetics,* 26:144–146.

Krings, Matthias, Anne Stone, Ralf W. Schmitz, et al.
1997   "Neandertal DNA Sequences and the Origin of Modern Humans." *Cell,* 90:19–30.

Kulikov, Eugene E., Audrey B. Poltaraus, and Irina A. Lebedeva
2004   "DNA Analysis of Sunghir Remains: Problems and Perspectives." Poster Presentation, European Paleopathology Association Meetings, Durham, U.K, August 2004.

Lack, David
1966   *Population Studies of Birds.* Oxford: Clarendon.

Lahr, Marta Mirazon and Robert Foley
1998   "Towards a Theory of Human Origins: Geography, Demography, and Diversity in Recent Human Evolution." *Yearbook of Physical Anthropology,* 41:137–176.

Lalani, A. S., J. Masters, W. Zeng, et al.
1999   "Use of Chemokine Receptors by Poxviruses." *Science,* 286:1968–71.

Lalueza-Fox, Carles, Hogler Römpler, David Caramelli, et al.
2007   "A Melanocortin Receptor Allele Suggests Varying Pigmentation Among Neanderthals." *Science Express,* Oct. 25, 2007.

Lamason, R. L., M-A.P.K. Mohideen, J. R. Mest, et al.
2005   "SLC24A5, a Putative Cation Exchanger, Affects Pigmentation in Zebrafish and Humans." *Science,* 310:1782–1786.

Lamberg-Karlovsky, Martha (ed.)
2000   "The Breakout: The Origins of Civilization." *Peabody Museum Monographs 9.* Cambridge, MA: Harvard University.

Lamberg-Karlovsky, C. C. and Jeremy A. Sabloff
1995   *Ancient Civilizations: The Near East and Mesoamerica.* Prospect Heights, IL: Waveland.

Lambert, Joseph
1997   *Traces of the Past: Unraveling the Secrets of Archaeology through Chemistry.* New York: Addison-Wesley Longman.

Lancaster, J. B. and C. S. Lancaster
1983   "Prenatal Investment: The Hominid Adaptation." *In:* Ortner, D. J. (ed.), *How Humans Adapt: A Biocultural Odyssey.* Washington DC: Smithsonian Institution Press.

Lanning, Edward P.
1967   *Peru Before the Incas.* Englewood Cliffs, NJ: Prentice-Hall.

Larsen, Clark Spencer
1995   "Biological Changes in Human Populations with Agriculture." *Annual Reviews of Anthropology,* 24:185–213.

———
1997   *Bioarchaeology: Interpreting Behavior from the Human Skeleton.* Cambridge: Cambridge University Press.

Lawler, Andrew
2007   "Beyond the Family Feud." *Archaeology,* 60(2):20–25.

Leakey, M. D. and R. L. Hay
1979   "Pliocene Footprints in Laetolil Beds at Laetoli, Northern Tanzania." *Nature,* 278:317–323.

Legge, Anthony J.
1972   "Prehistoric Exploitation of Gazelle in Palestine." *In: Papers in Economic Prehistory,* E. S. Higgs (ed.), Cambridge: Cambridge University Press, pp. 119–124.

Legge, Anthony J. and Peter A. Rowley-Conwy
1987   "Gazelle Killing in Stone Age Syria." *Scientific American,* 257(2):88–95.

Lehner, Mark
1997   *The Complete Pyramids.* New York: Thames & Hudson.

Lerner, I. M. and W. J. Libby
1976   *Heredity, Evolution, and Society.* San Francisco: W. H. Freeman.

Lewin, Roger
1986   "Damage to Tropical Forests, or Why Were There So Many Kinds of Animals?" *Science,* 234:149–150.

Lewis, R. Barry and Charles Stout (eds.)
1998   *Mississippian Towns and Sacred Spaces: Searching for An Architectural Grammar.* Tuscaloosa: University of Alabama Press.

Lewontin, R. C.
1972   "The Apportionment of Human Diversity." *In: Evolutionary Biology* (Vol. 6), T. Dobzhansky, et al. (eds.), New York, NY: Plenum, pp. 381–398.

Li, Jun Z., Devin M. Absher, Hua Tang, et al.
2008   "Worldwide Human Relationships Inferred from Genome-Wide Patterns of Variation." *Science*, 319:1100–1104.

Li, T. and D. A. Etler
1992   "New Middle Pleistocene Hominid Crania from Yunxian in China." *Nature*, 357:404–407.

Li, K. S., Y. Guan, J. Wang, et al.
2004   "Genesis of a Highly Pathogenic and Potentially Pandemic H5N1 Influenza Virus in Eastern Asia." *Nature*, 430:209–213.

Linnaeus, C.
1758   *Systema Naturae.*

Lohmueller, K. E., A. R. Indap, and S. Schmidt
2008   "Proportionately More Deleterious Genetic Variation in European than in African Populations." *Nature*, 451:994–997.

Lordkipanidze, David, Abesalom Vekua, Reid Ferring, et al.
2005   "The Earliest Toothless Hominin Skull. *Nature*, 434:717–718.

Lordkipandize, David, Tea Jashashuil, Abesalom Vekua, et al.
2007   "Postcranial Evidence from Early *Homo* from Dmanisi, Georgia." *Nature*, 449:305–310.

Lordkipandize D., A. Vekua, R. Ferring, P. Rightmire, et al.
2006   "A Fourth Hominid Skull from Dmanisi, Georgia." *The Anatomical Record: Part A*, 288:1146–1157.

Lowe, Gareth W.
1989   "The Heartland Olmec: Evolution of Material Culture." *In:* R. J. Sharer and D. C. Grove (eds.), q.v., pp. 33–67.

Loy, Thomas H. and E. James Dixon
1998   "Blood Residues on Fluted Points from Eastern Beringia." *American Antiquity*, 63(1):21–46.

Lucero, Lisa. J.
2003   "The Politics of Ritual: The Emergence of Classic Maya Rulers." *Current Anthropology*, 44(4):523–558.

Lynch, Thomas F.
1983   "The Paleo-Indians." *In: Ancient South Americans*, J. D. Jennings (ed.), San Francisco: W. H. Freeman, pp. 87–137.

MacKinnon, J. and K. MacKinnon
1980   "The Behavior of Wild Spectral Tarsiers." *International Journal of Primatology*, 1:361–379.

MacNeish, Richard S.
1964   "Ancient Mesoamerican Civilization." *Science*, 143:531–537.

———
1967   "A Summary of the Subsistence." *In:* D. S. Byers (ed.), q.v., pp. 290–310.

———
1978   *The Science of Archaeology?* North Scituate, MA: Duxbury Press.

MacNeish, Richard S. and Jane G. Libby
2003   *Pendejo Cave.* Albuquerque: University of New Mexico Press.

MacNeish, Richard S., et al.
1972   *The Prehistory of the Tehuacán Valley. Vol. 5: Excavations and Reconnaissance.* Austin: University of Texas Press.

Madsen, David B. (ed.)
2004   *Entering America: Northeast Asia and Beringia Before the Last Glacial Maximum.* Salt Lake City: University of Utah Press.

Maisels, C. K.
1999   *Early Civilizations of the Old World: The Formative Histories of Egypt, the Levant, Mesopotamia, India, and China.* London: Routledge.

Malik, K.
2007   "Who Owns Knowledge?" *Index on Censorship*, 36(3):156–167.

Malm, Torben
1995   "Excavating Submerged Stone Age Sites in Denmark—The Tybrind Vig Example." *In:* A. Fischer (ed.), q.v., pp. 385–396.

Manson, J. H. and R. Wrangham
1991   "Intergroup Aggression in Chimpanzees and Humans." *Current Anthropology*, 32:369–390.

Marean, Curtis W., Miryam Bar-Matthews, Jocelyn Bernatchez, et al.
2007   "Early Human Use of Marine Resources and Pigment in South Africa During the Middle Pleistocene." *Nature*, 449:905–908.

Marlar, Jennifer E. and Richard A. Marlar
2000   "Cannibals at Cowboy Wash; Biomolecular Archaeology Solves a Controversial Puzzle." *Discovering Archaeology*, 2(5):30–36.

Marris, Emma
2006   "Bushmeat Surveyed in Western Cities. Illegally Hunted Animals Turn Up in Markets from New York to London." *News@Nature.com.* doi:10.1038/news060626-10.

Martin, Robert D., Ann M. Maclaranon, James C. Phillips, and William B. Dobyns
2006   "Flores Hominid: New Species or Microcephalic Dwarf?" *The Anatomical Record: Part A*, 288:1123–1145.

Martin, Paul S.
1967   "Prehistoric Overkill." *In: Pleistocene Extinctions: The Search for a Cause*, P. S. Martin and H. E. Wright, Jr. (eds.), New Haven: Yale University Press, pp. 75–120.

———
2005   *Twilight of the Mammoths: Ice Age Extinctions and the Rewilding of America.* Los Angeles: University of California Press.

Masataka, N.
1983   "Categorical Responses to Natural and Synthesized Alarm Calls in Goeldi's Monkeys (*Callimico goeldi*)." *Primates*: 24:40–51.

Mason, J. Alden
1968   *The Ancient Civilizations of Peru* (Rev. Ed.). London: Penguin Books.

Mayr, Ernst
1970   *Population, Species, and Evolution.* Cambridge: Harvard University Press.

McBrearty, Sally and Nina G. Jablonski
2005   "First Fossil Chimpanzee." *Nature*, 437:105–108.

McDougall, I.; F. H. Brown, J. G. Fleagle
2005   "Stratigraphic Placement and Age of Modern Humans from Kibish, Ethiopia." *Nature*, 433:733–736.

McGhee, Robert
1996   *Ancient People of the Arctic.* Vancouver: University of British Columbia Press.

McGovern, Patrick E., Juzhong Zhang, Jigen Tang, et al. (eds.)
1985   *Shawnee-Minisink: A Stratified Paleoindian-Archaic Site in the Upper Delaware Valley.* Orlando: Academic Press.

McGrew, W. C.
1992   *Chimpanzee Material Culture. Implications for Human Evolution.* Cambridge: Cambridge University Press.

———
1998   "Culture in Nonhuman Primates?" *Annual Review of Anthropology*, 27:301–328.

McHenry, Henry
1988   "New Estimates of Body Weight in Early Hominids and Their Significance to Encephalization and Megadontia

in 'Robust' Australopithecines." *In:* F. E. Grine (ed.), q.v., pp. 133–148.

1992 "Body Size and Proportions in Early Hominids." *American Journal of Physical Anthropology*, 87:407–431.

McKusick, V. A. (with S. E. Antonarakis, et al.)
1998 *Mendelian Inheritance in Man.* (12th Ed.). Baltimore: Johns Hopkins University Press.

Meehan, Betty
1982 *Shell Bed to Shell Midden.* Canberra: Australian Institute of Aboriginal Studies.

Mellars, Paul
1989a "Technological Changes across the Middle-Upper Palaeolithic Transition: Economic, Social and Cognitive Perspectives." *In:* Mellars and Stringer (eds.), q. v., pp. 338–365.

1989b "Major Issues in the Emergence of Modern Humans." *Current Anthropology*, 30:349–385.

2006 "A new radiocarbon revolution and the dispersal of modern humans in Eurasia." *Nature*, 439:931–935.

Mellars, Paul and Petra Dark
1999 *Star Carr in Context: New Archaeological and Palaeoecological Investigations at the Early Mesolithic Site of Star Carr, North Yorkshire.* McDonald Institute Monographs. London: David Brown.

Mellars, Paul and C. Stringer (eds.),
1989 *The Human Revolution.* Princeton, NJ: Princeton University Press.

Meltzer, David J.
1993a "Is There a Clovis Adaptation?" *In:* Soffer and Praslov (eds.), q.v., pp. 293–310.

1993b *Search for the First Americans.* Washington, DC: Smithsonian Books.

Meltzer, David, James Adovasio, and Tom D. Dillehay
1994 "On a Pleistocene Human Occupation at Pedra Furada, Brazil." *Antiquity*, 68:695–714.

2004 "On Possibilities, Prospecting, and Patterns: Thinking about a Pre-LGM Human Presence in the Americas." *In:* Madsen (ed.), q. v., pp. 359–377.

2006 *Folsom: New Archaeological Investigations of a Classic Paleoindian Bison Kill.* Berkeley: University of California Press.

Merriwether, D. Andrew, Francisco Rothhammer, and Robert E. Ferrell
1995 "Distribution of the Four Founding Lineage Haplotypes in Native Americans Suggests a Single Wave of Migration for the New World." *American Journal of Physical Anthropology*, 98(4):411–430.

Mervis, J.
2006 "Judge Jones Defines Science—And Why Intelligent Design Isn't." *Science*, 311:34.

Mihlbachler, M. C., C. A. Hemmings, and S. D. Webb
2000 "Reevaluation of the Alexon Bison Kill Site, Wacissa River, Jefferson County, Florida." *Current Research in the Pleistocene*, 17:55–57.

Miles, H. Lyn Whire
1990 "The Cognitive Foundations for Reference in a Signing Orangutan." *In:* Parker, S. T. and K. R. Gibson (eds.) *Language and Intelligence in Monkeys and Apes: Comparative Developmental Perspectives.* New York: Cambridge University Press, pp. 511–539.

Miller, A., and C. M. Barton
2008 "Exploring the Land: A Comparison of Land-use Patterns in the Middle and Upper Paleolithic of the Western Mediterranean." *Journal of Archaeological Science*, 35:1427–1437.

Millon, René
1988 "The Last Years of Teotihuacán Dominance." *In: The Collapse of Ancient States and Civilizations.* N. Yoffee and G. Cowgill (eds.), Tucson: University of Arizona Press, pp. 102–164.

Milner, George R.
1998 *Cahokia Chiefdom: The Archaeology of a Mississippian Society.* Washington, DC:Smithsonian Institution Press.

Molnar, Stephen
1983 *Human Variation. Races, Types, and Ethnic Groups* (2nd Ed.). Englewood Cliffs: Prentice-Hall.

Montet, Pierre
1981 *Everyday Life in Egypt in the Days of Ramesses the Great.* Philadelphia: University of Pennsylvania Press.

Moore, Andrew M. T.
1985 "The Development of Neolithic Societies in the Near East." *Advances in World Archaeology*, 4:1–69.

Moore, Andrew M. T., G. C. Hillman, and A. J. Legge
2000 *Village on the Euphrates: From Foraging to Farming at Abu Hureyra.* New York: Oxford University Press.

Moore, Lorna G., et al.
1994 "Genetic Adaptation to High Altitude." *In:* Stephen C. Wood and Robert C. Roach (eds.), *Sports and Exercise Medicine.* New York: Marcel Dekker, Inc., pp. 225–262.

Moore, L. G., S. Niermeyer, and S. Zamudio
1998 "Human Adaptation to High Altitude: Regional and Life-Cycle Perspectives." *American Journal of Physical Anthropology*, Suppl. 27:25–64.

Moore, L. G. and J. G. Regensteiner
1983 "Adaptation to High Altitude." *Annual Reviews of Anthropology*, 12:285–304.

Moore, L.G., M. Shriver, L. Bemis, and E. Vargas
2006 "An Evolutionary Model for Identifying Genetic Adaptation to High Altitude." *Advances in Experimental Medicine and Biology*, 588:101–118.

Moore, L. G., S. Zamudio, J. Zhuang, et al.
2001 "Oxygen Transport in Tibetan Women During Pregnancy at 3,658 M." *American Journal of Physical Anthropology*, 114:42–53.

Moratto, Michael J.
1984 *California Archaeology.* New York: Academic Press.

Morwood, M. J., P. Brown, T. Jatmiko, et al.
2005 "Further Evidence for Small-Bodied Hominins from the Late Pleistocene of Flores, Indonesia." *Nature*, 437:1012–1017.

Morwood, M. J., R. P. Suejono, R. G. Roberts, et al.
2004 "Archaeology and Age of a New Hominin from Flores in Eastern Indonesia." *Nature*, 431:1087–1091.

Moseley, Michael E.
1975 *The Maritime Foundations of Andean Civilization.* Menlo Park: Cummings Publishing Company.

1992 *The Incas and Their Ancestors.* New York: Thames & Hudson.

Moseley, Michael E. and Kent Day (eds.)
1982 *Chan Chan: Andean Desert City.* Albuquerque: University of New Mexico Press.

Moura, A. C. de A. and P. C. Lee
2004 "Capuchin Stone Tool Use in Caatinga Dry Forest." *Science*, 306:1909.

Mourant, A. E., A. C. Kopec, and K. Domaniewska-Sobczak.
1976 *The Distribution of the Human Blood Groups and Other Polymorphisms*, 2nd Ed. London, England: Oxford University Press.

Muchmore, E. A., S. Diaz, and A. Varki
1998 "A Structural Difference between the Cell Surfaces of Humans and the Great Apes. *American Journal of Physical Anthropology*, 107:187–98.

Munro, Natalie D.
2004 "Zooarchaeological Measures of Hunting Pressure and Occupation Intensity in the Natufian: Implications for Agricultural Origins." *Current Anthropology*, 45(supplement):S5–S33.

Murdock, George Peter
1959 *Africa: Its Peoples and Their Culture History*. New York: McGraw-Hill.

Murphy, W. J., E. Elzirik, W. E. Johnson, et al.
2001 "Molecular Phylogenetics and the Origins of Placental Mammals." *Nature*, 409:614–618.

Nadel, D.
2004 "The Ohalo II Brush Huts and the Dwelling Structures of the Natufian and PPNA Sites in the Jordan Valley." *Archaeology, Ethnology and Anthropology of Eurasia*, 1(13):34–48.

Napier, John
1967 "The Antiquity of Human Walking." *Scientific American*, 216:56–66.

Napier, J. R. and P. H. Napier
1967 *A Handbook of Living Primates*. New York, NY: Academic Press.

———
1985 *The Natural History of the Primates*. London: British Museum of Natural History.

National Snow and Ice Data Center.
2007 http://nsdic.org/

Neese, R. M. and G. C. Williams
1994 *Why We Get Sick*. New York: Times Books.

Nevell, L., A Gordon, and B. Wood
2007 "*Homo floresiensis* and *Homo sapiens* Size-Adjusted Cranial Shape Variations." *American Journal of Physical Anthropology, Supplement*, 14:177–178 (Abstract).

Neves, Walter A., Rolando González-José, Mark Hubbe, et al.
2004 "Early Holocene Human Skeletal Remains from Cerca Grande, Lagoa Santa, Central Brazil, and the Origins of the First Americans." *World Archaeology*, 36(4):479–501.

Newport, S.
2007 WildlifeDirect.org. Personal communication.

News in Brief
2007 "Congolese Government Creates Bonobo Reserve." *Nature*. 450:470 doi:10.1038/450470f

Ni, Xijun, Yuanqing Wang, Yaoming Hu, and Chuankui Li
2004 "A Euprimate Skull from the Early Eocene of China." *Nature*, 427:65–68.

Nishida, T.
1991 Comments. *In:* J. H. Manson and R. Wrangham, q.v., pp. 381–382.

Nishida, T., M. Hiraiwa-Hasegawa, T. Hasegawa, and Y. Takahata
1985 "Group Extinction and Female Transfer in Wild Chimpanzees in the Mahale National Park, Tanzania." *Zeitschrift Tierpsychologie*, 67:284–301.

Nishida, T., H. Takasaki, and Y. Takahata
1990 "Demography and Reproductive Profiles." *In: The Chimpanzees of the Mahale Mountains*, T. Nishida (ed.), Tokyo: University of Tokyo Press, pp. 63–97.

Nishida, T., R. W. Wrangham, J. Goodall, and S. Uehara
1983 "Local Differences in Plant-feeding Habits of Chimpanzees between the Mahale Mountains and Gombe National Park, Tanzania." *Journal of Human Evolution*, 12:467–480.

Nissen, Hans J.
1988 *The Early History of the Ancient Near East, 9000–2000 B.C.* Chicago: University of Chicago Press.

———
2001 "Cultural and Political Networks in the Ancient Near East during the Fourth and Third Millennia B.C." *In: Uruk Mesopotamia and Its Neighbors*. Mitchell S. Rothman (ed.). Santa Fe: School of American Research Press, pp. 149–179.

Noonan, James P., G. Coop, S. Kudaravalli, D. Smith, et al.
2006 "Sequencing and Analysis of Neanderthal Genomic DNA." *Science*, 314:1113–1118.

Normille, D.
1997 "Yangtze Seen As Earliest Rice Site." *Science*, 275:309.

Nowak, Ronald M.
1999 *Walker's Primates of the World*. Baltimore: Johns Hopkins University Press.

Nowell, A.
2006 "From a Paleolithic Art to Pleistocene Visual Cultures." *Journal of Archaeological Method and Theory*, 13(4):239–249.

Oakley, Kenneth
1963 "Analytical Methods of Dating Bones." *In: Science in Archaeology*, D. Brothwell and E. Higgs (eds.). New York: Basic Books, pp. 24–34.

Oates, John F., Michael Abedi-Lartey, W. Scott McGraw, et al.
2000 "Extinction of a West African Red Colobus Monkey." *Conservation Biology*, 14(5):1526–1532.

Oates, J. F., R. A. Bergl, J. Sunderland-Groves, and A. Dunn
2007 "*Gorilla gorilla* ssp. *Diehli*. In: IUCN 2007. *2007 IUCN Red List of Threatened Species*.

O'Connell, J. F., K. Hawkes, K. D. Lupo, and N. G. Burton-Jones
2002 "Male Strategies and Plio-Pleistocene Archaeology." *Journal of Human Evolution*, 43:831–872.

Odell, George H.
1998 "Investigating Correlates of Sedentism and Domestication in Prehistoric North America." *American Antiquity*, 63(4):553–571.

Olsen, Stanley J.
1985 *Origins of the Domestic Dog: The Fossil Record*. Tucson: University of Arizona Press.

Ovchinnikov, Igor V., Anders Gotherstrom, Galina P. Romanova, et al.
2000 "Molecular Analysis of Neanderthal DNA from the Northern Caucasus." *Nature*, 404:490–493.

Owsley, Douglas W. and Richard L. Jantz
2000 "Biography in the Bones." *Discovering Archaeology*, 2(1):56–58.

Padian, Kevin and Luis M. Chiappe
1998 "The Origin of Birds and Their Flight." *Scientific American*, 278:38–47.

Page, S. E., F. Siegert, J. O. Rieley, H-D. V. Boehm, A. Jaya, and S. Limin
2002 "The Amount of Carbon Released from Peat and Forest Fires in Indonesia during 1997." *Nature*, 420:61–65.

Pagel, Mark and Ruth Mace
2004 "The Cultural Wealth of Nations." *Nature*, 428:275–278.

Pagel, M., C. Venditti, and A. Meade
2006 "Large Punctuational Contribution of Speciation to Evolutionary Divergence at the Molecular Level." *Science*, 314:119–121.

Palmer, S. K., L. G. Moore, D. Young, et al.
1999 "Altered Blood Pressure Course During Normal Pregnancy and Increased Preeclampsia at High Altitude (3100 meters) in Colorado." *American Journal of Obstetrics and Gynecology*, 189:1161–1168.

Parés, Josef M. and Alfredo Pérez-González
1995 "Paleomagnetic Age for Hominid Fossils at Atapuerca Archaeological Site, Spain." *Science*, 269:830–832.

Parfit, Michael
2000 "Hunt for the First Americans." *National Geographic*, 198(6):40–67.

Parfitt, Simon A., René W. Barendregt, Marzia Breda, et al.
2005 "The Earliest Record of Human Activity in Europe." *Nature*, 433:1003–1012.

Parpola, Asko
1994 *Deciphering the Indus Script*. Cambridge: Cambridge University Press.

Pauketat, Timothy R. and Rita P. Wright
2004 *Ancient Cahokia and the Mississippians*. Cambridge: Cambridge University Press.

Pearsall, Deborah M.
2000 *Paleoethnobotany: A Handbook of Procedures*. (2nd Ed.). San Diego, CA: Academic Press.

Pennisi, Elizabeth
2007 "No Sex Please, We're Neandertals." *Science*, 316:967.

Peres, C. A.
1990 "Effects of Hunting on Western Amazonian Primate Communities." *Biological Conservation*, 54:47–59.

Perlès, C.
2001 *The Early Neolithic in Greece*. Cambridge: Cambridge University Press.

Phillips, K. A.
1998 "Tool Use in Wild Capuchin Monkeys." *American Journal of Primatology*, 46(3):259–261.

Phillipson, David W.
1984 "Early Food Production in Central and Southern Africa." *In:* J. D. Clark and S. A. Brandt (eds.), q.v., pp. 272–280.

Pickford, Martin and Brigitte Senut
2001 "The Geological and Faunal Context of Late Miocene Hominid Remains from Lukeino, Kenya." *C. R. Acad. Sci. Paris, Sciences de la Terre et des Planètes*, 332:145–152.

Pinner, Robert W., Steven M. Teutsch, Lone Simonson, et al.
1996 "Trends in Infectious Diseases Mortality in the United States." *Journal of the American Medical Association*, 275(3):189–193.

Piperno, Dolores R.
2006 *Phytoliths: A Comprehensive Guide for Archaeologists and Paleoecologists*. Walnut Creek, CA: AltaMira Press.

———
2008 "Identifying Crop Plants with Phytoliths (and Starch Grains) in Central and South America: A Review and An Update of the Evidence." *Quaternary International*. doi:10.1016/j.quaint.2007.11.011 .

Piperno, Dolores and Deborah M. Pearsall
1998 *The Origins of Agriculture in the Lowland Neotropics*. San Diego: Academic Press.

Piperno, Dolores and Karen E. Stothert
2003 "Phytolith Evidence for Early Holocene Cucurbita Domestication in Southwest Ecuador." *Science*, 299:1054–1057.

Piperno, Dolores R., Ehud Weiss, Irene Holst, and Dani Nadel
2004 "Processing of Wild Cereal Grains in the Upper Paleolithic Revealed by Starch Grain Analysis." *Nature*, 430:670–673.

Pitulko, V. V., P. A. Nikolsky, E. Yu. Girya, et al.
2004 "The Yana RHS Site: Humans in the Arctic before the Last Glacial Maximum." *Science*, 303:52–56.

Plog, Stephen
1997 *Ancient People of the American Southwest*. New York: Thames & Hudson.

Plummer, T.
2004 "Flaked Stones and Old Bones: Biological and Cultural Evolution at the Dawn of Technology." *Yearbook of Physical Anthropology*, 47:118–164.

Pohl, Mary, E. E., Kevin O. Pope, and Christopher von Nagy
2002 "Olmec Origins of Mesoamerican Writing." *Science*, 298:1984–1987.

Pope, Kevin O., Mary E. D. Pohl, John G. Jones, et al.
2001 "Origin and Environmental Setting of Ancient Agriculture in the Lowlands of Mesoamerica." *Science*, 292:1370–1373.

Possehl, Gregory L.
1990 "Revolution in the Urban Revolution: The Emergence of Indus Urbanization." *Annual Review of Anthropology*, 19:261–282.

———
1996 *Indus Age: The Writing System*. Philadelphia: University of Pennsylvania Press.

———
1999 *Indus Age: The Beginnings*. Philadelphia: University of Pennsylvania Press.

———
2002 *The Indus Civilization: A Contemporary Perspective*. Walnut Creek, CA: Altamira Press.

Potts, Richard
1984 "Home Bases and Early Hominids." *American Scientist*, 72:338–347.

———
1991 "Why the Oldowan? Plio-Pleistocene Toolmaking and the Transport of Resources." *Journal of Anthropological Research*, 47:153–176.

———
1993 "Archeological Interpretations of Early Hominid Behavior and Ecology." *In: The Origin and Evolution of Humans and Humanness*, D. T. Rasmussen (ed.), Boston, MA: Jones and Bartlett, pp. 49–74.

Powell, K. B.
2003 "The Evolution or Lactase Persistence in African Populations." *American Journal of Physical Anthropology, Supplement*, 36:170 (Abstract).

Powell, Marvin
1985 "Salt Seed and Yields in Sumerian Agriculture." *Zeitschift für Assyriologie*, 75:7–38.

Powis, Terry G., W. Jeffrey Hurst, Maria del Carmen Rodriguez, et al.
2007 "Oldest chocolate in the New World." *Antiquity*, Vol. 81(314). December. http://www.antiquity.ac.uk/ProjGall/powis/index.html.

Pozorski, Shelia and Thomas Pozorski
1988 *Early Settlement and Subsistence in the Casma Valley, Peru*. Iowa City, IA: University of Iowa Press.

Pozorski, Thomas and Shelia Pozorski
1987 "Chavín, the Early Horizon, and the Initial Period." *In:* J. Haas et al. (eds.), q.v., pp. 36–46.

Price, T. Douglas
1995 "Social Inequality at the Origins of Agriculture." *In: Foundations of Social Inequality*, T. Douglas Price and Gary M. Feinman (eds.), New York: Plenum, pp. 129–151.

Pusey, A., J. Williams, and J. Goodall
1997 "The Influence of Dominance Rank on the Reproductive Success of Female Chimpanzees." *Science*, 277:828–831.

Rak, Y.
1983 *The Australopithecine Face*. New York: Academic Press.

Redman, Charles L.
1978 *The Rise of Civilization*. San Francisco: W. H. Freeman.

Reinhard, K. I. and Vaughan M. Bryant
1992 "Coprolite Analysis." *Archaeological Method and Theory*, 14:245–288.

Relethford, John H.
2001 *Genetics and the Search for Modern Human Origins*." New York: Wiley-Liss.

Renne, P. R., W. D. Sharp, A. L. Deino, et al.
1997 "^{40}Ar/^{39}Ar Dating into the Historic Realm: Calibration Against Pliny the Younger." *Science*, 277:1279–1280.

The Rhesus Macaque Genome Sequencing and Analysis Consortium.
2007 "Evolutionary and Biomedical Insights from the Rhesus Macaque Genome." *Science*, 316:222–234.

Rice, Don, Arthur A. Demarest, and Prudence M. Rice
2001 *The Terminal Classic in the Maya Lowlands: Collapse, Transition, and Transformation*. Boulder, CO: Westview Press.

Richards, Gary D.
2006 "Genetic, Physiologic, and Ecogeographic Factors Contributing to Variation in *Homo sapiens*: *Homo floresiensis* Reconsidered." *Journal of Evolutionary Biology*, 19:1744–1767.

Riddle, Robert D. and Clifford J. Tabin
1999 "How Limbs Develop." *Scientific American*, 280(2):74–79.

Ridley, Mark
1993 *Evolution*. Boston: Blackwell Scientific Publications.

Rightmire, G. P.
1998 "Human Evolution in the Middle Pleistocene: The Role of *Homo heidelbergensis*." *Evolutionary Anthropology*, 6:218–227.

———
2004 "Affinities of the Middle Pleistocene Crania from Dali and Jinniushan, China. *American Journal of Physical Anthropology*, Supplement 38:167 (Abstract).

Rindos, David
1984 *The Origins of Agriculture: An Evolutionary Perspective*. Orlando: Academic Press.

Roaf, Michael
1996 *Cultural Atlas of Mesopotamia and the Ancient Near East*. New York: Facts on File.

Roberts, Charlotte A. and Jane E. Buikstra
2003 *The Bioarchaeology of Tuberculosis: A Global Perspective on a Re-emerging Disease*. Gainsville: University Press of Florida.

Robinson, William J.
1990 "Tree-Ring Studies of the Pueblo de Acoma." *Historical Archaeology*, 24(3):99–106.

Rollefson, Gary O.
2001 "2001: An Archaeological Odyssey." *Cambridge Archaeological Journal*, 11(1):112–114.

Roosevelt, Anna C., et al.
1996 "Paleoindian Cave Dwellers in the Amazon: The Peopling of the Americas." *Science*, 272:373–384.

Rose, M. D.
1991 "Species Recognition in Eocene Primates." *American Journal of Physical Anthropology*, Supplement 12, p. 153.

Rothschild, Nan A.
1979 "Mortuary Behavior and Social Organization at Indian Knoll and Dickson Mounds," *American Antiquity*, 44:658–675.

Rowe, Marvin W. and Karen L. Steelman
2003 "Comment on 'Some Evidence of a Date of First Humans to Arrive in Brazil'." *Journal of Archaeological Science*, 30(10):1349–1351.

Rowley-Conwy, Peter
2004 "How the West Was Lost: A Reconsideration of Agricultural Origins in Britain, Ireland, and Southern Scandinavia." *Current Anthropology*, 45(supplement):S83–S113.

Rudran, R.
1973 "Adult Male Replacement in One-Male Troops of Purple-Faced Langurs (*Presbytis senex senex*) and its Effect on Population Structure." *Folia Primatologica*, 19:166–192.

Ruff, C. B. and Alan Walker
1993 "The Body Size and Shape of KNM-WT 15000." *In:* A. Walker and R. Leakey (eds.), q.v., pp. 234–265.

Sadr, Karim
2003 "The Neolithic of Southern Africa." *The Journal of African History*, 44(2):195–209.

Samson, M., F. Libert, B. J. Doranz, et al.
1996 "Resistance to HIV-1 Infection in Caucasian Individuals Bearing Mutant Alleles of the CCR-5 Chemokine Receptor Gene." *Nature* 382(22):722–725.

Samuels, Stephen R. (ed.)
1991 *Ozette Archaeological Project Research Reports*. Pullman, WA: Washington State University.

Sanders, William T. and Joseph Michels (eds.)
1977 *Teotihuacan and Kaminaljuyu: A Study in Prehistoric Culture Contact*. College Park: Pennsylvania State University Press.

Sanders, William T., Jeffrey R. Parsons, and Robert S. Santley
1979 *The Basin of Mexico: Ecological Processes in the Evolution of a Civilization*. New York: Academic Press.

Sandweiss, D. H., et al.
1996 "Geoarchaeological Evidence from Peru for a 5000 Years B.P. Onset of El Niño." *Science*, 273:1531–1533.

Santos, G. M., M. I. Bird, F. Parenti, et al.
2003 "A Revised Chronology of the Lowest Occupation Layer of Pedra Furada Rock Shelter, Piaui, Brazil: The Pleistocene Peopling of the Americas." *Quaternary Science Reviews*, 22(21–22):2303–2310.

Sarmiento, E. E. and J. F. Oates
2000 Cross River gorillas: A distinct subspecies, *Gorilla gorilla diehli* Matschie, 1904. *American Museum Novitates* (3304):1–55.

Sauer, Jonathan D.
1994 *Historical Geography of Crop Plants: A Select Roster*. Boca Raton: CRC Press.

Saunders, Joe W., R. D. Mandel, C. G. Sampson, et al.
2005 "Watson Brake, A Middle Archaic Mound Complex in Northeast Louisiana." *American Antiquity*, 70(4):631–668.

Savage-Rumbaugh, S.
1986 *Ape Language: From Conditioned Responses to Symbols*. New York: Columbia University Press.

Savage-Rumbaugh, S. and R. Lewin
1994 *Kanzi: The Ape at the Brink of the Human Mind*. New York, NY: John Wiley and Sons.

Savage-Rumbaugh, S., K. McDonald, R. A. Sevic, W. D. Hopkins, and E. Rupert
1986   "Spontaneous Symbol Acquisition and Communicative Use by Pygmy Chimpanzees *(Pan paniscus)*." *Journal of Experimental Psychology: General*, 115:211–235.

Savard, M., M. Nesbitt, and M. Jones
2006   "The Role of Wild Grasses in Subsistence and Sedentism: New Evidence from the Northern Fertile Crescent." *World Archaeology*, 38(2):179–196.

Savolainen, P.
2002   "Genetic Evidence for an East Asian Origin of Domestic Dogs." *Science*, 298:1610–1613.

Schele, Linda and David Freidel
1990   *A Forest of Kings*. New York: William R. Morrow.

Schele, Linda and Mary Ellen Miller
1986   *The Blood of Kings: Dynasty and Ritual in Maya Art*. Fort Worth: Kimbell Art Museum.

Schmitz, Ralf W., David Serre, Georges Bonani, et al.
2002   "The Neandertal Type Site Revisited: Interdisciplinary Investigations of Skeletal Remains from the Neander Valley, Germany. *Proceedings of the National Academy of Sciences*, 99:13342–13347.

Schoeninger, Margaret J.
1981   "The Agricultural 'Revolution': Its Effect on Human Diet in Prehistoric Iran and Israel." *Paléorient*, 7:73–92.

Schoeninger, M. J., M. J. Deniro, and H. Tauber
1983   "Stable Nitrogen Isotope Ratios of Bone Collagen Reflect Marine and Terrestrial Components of Prehistoric Human Diet." *Science*, 220:1381–1383.

Schurr, Theodore G.
2000   "The Story in the Genes." *Discovering Archaeology*, 2(1):59–60.

———
2004   "The Peopling of the New World: Perspectives from Molecular Anthropology." *Annual Review of Anthropology*, 33:551–583.

Schurr, Theodore G. and Stephen T. Sherry
2004   "Mitochondrial DNA and Y Chromosome Diversity and the Peopling of the Americas: Evolutionary and Demographic Evidence." *American Journal of Human Biology*, 16:420–439.

Schurr, T. G., et al.
1990   "Amerindian Mitochondrial DNAs Have Rare Asian Mutations at High Frequencies Suggesting a Limited Number of Founders." *American Journal of Human Genetics*, 46:613–623.

Scriver, C. R.
2001   *The Metabolic and Molecular Bases of Inherited Disease*. New York, NY: McGraw Hill.

Semaw, S., P. Renne, W. K. Harris, et al.
1997   "2.5-million-year-old Stone Tools from Gona, Ethiopia." *Nature*, 385:333–336.

Senut, Brigitte, Martin Pickford, Dominique Grommercy, et al.
2001   "First Hominid from the Miocene (Lukeino Formation, Kenya)." *C. R. Acad. Sci. Paris, Sciences de la Terre et des Planètes*, 332:137–144.

Serre, David, André Langaney, Marie Chech, et al.
2004   "No Evidence of Neandertal mtDNA Contribution to Early Modern Humans." *PloS Biology*, 2:313–317.

Seyfarth, Robert M.
1987   "Vocal Communication and Its Relation to Language." *In:* Smuts, et al. (eds.), q.v., pp. 440–451.

Seyfarth, Robert M., Dorothy L. Cheney, and Peter Marler
1980a   "Monkey Responses to Three Different Alarm Calls." *Science*, 210:801–803.

———
1980b   "Vervet Monkey Alarm Calls." *Animal Behavior*, 28:1070–1094.

Shaffer, Brian S. and Barry W. Baker
1997   "How Many Epidermal Ridges Per Linear Centimeter: Comments on Possible Pre-Clovis Human Friction Skin Prints from Pendejo Cave." *American Antiquity*, 62(3):559–560.

Shang, Hong, Haowen Tong, Shuangguan Zhang, et al.
2007   "An Early Modern Human from Tianyuan Cave, Zhoukoudian, China." *Proceedings of the National Academy of Sciences*, 104:6573–6578.

Sharer, Robert J.
1996   *Daily Life in Maya Civilization*. Westport, CT: Greenwood Press.

Sharer, Robert J. and David C. Grove (eds.)
1989   *Regional Perspectives on the Olmec*. Cambridge: Cambridge University Press.

Shea, Brian T. and Robert C. Baily
1996   "Allometry and Adaptation of Body Proportions and Stature in African Pygmies." *American Journal of Physical Anthropology*, 100:311–340

Shea, John J.
2006   "The Origins of Lithic Projectile Point Technology: Evidence from Africa, the Levant, and Europe." *Journal of Archaeological Science*, 33(6):823–846.

Sheets, Payson D.
2006   *The Ceren Site: An Ancient Village Buried by Volcanic Ash in Central America*. (2nd Ed.) Belmont, CA: Thomson Wadsworth.

——— (ed.)
2002   *Before the Volcano Erupted: The Ancient Cerén Village in Central America*. Austin: University of Texas Press.

Sherratt, A.
1981   "Plough and Pastoralism: Aspects of the Secondary Products Revolution." *In:* Ian Hodder, Glynn L. Isaac, and Norman Hammond (eds.), *Patterns of the Past: Studies in Honour of David Clarke*. Cambridge: Cambridge University Press, pp. 261–305.

Shubin, Neil H., Edward B. Daeschler, and Farish A. Jenkins, Jr.
2006   "The Pectoral Fin of *Tiktaalik roseae* and the Origin of the Tetrapod Limb." *Nature*, 440:764–771.

Shubin, Nell, Cliff Tabin, and Sean Carroll
1997   "Fossils, Genes, and the Evolution of Animal Limbs." *Nature*, 388:639–648.

Silk, J. B., S. C. Alberts, and J. Altmann
2003   "Social Bonds of Female Baboons Enhance Infant Survival." *Science*, 302:1231–1234.

Silk, J. B., S. F. Brosman, J. Vonk, et al.
2005   "Chimpanzees are Indifferent to the Welfare of Unrelated Group Members." *Nature*, 437:1357–1359.

Silverman, Helaine (ed.)
2004   *Andean Archaeology*. Malden, MA: Blackwell Publishing.

Simmons, Alan H.
1986   "New Evidence for the Use of Cultigens in the American Southwest." *American Antiquity*, 51:73–89.

Simons, E. L.
1972   *Primate Evolution*. New York: Macmillan.

Smith, Andrew
1992   "Pastoralism in Africa." *Annual Review of Anthropology*, 21:125–141.

Smith, Andrew, Penny Berens, Candy Malherbe, and Matt Guenther
2000   *The Bushmen of Southern Africa: A Foraging Society in Transition*. Athens, OH: Ohio University Press.

Smith, Bruce D.
1992   *Rivers of Change: Essays on Early Agriculture in Eastern North America*. Washington, DC: Smithsonian Institution.

———
1997   "Reconsidering the Ocampo Caves and the Era of Incipient Cultivation in Mesoamerica." *Latin American Antiquity*, 8: 342–383.

———
1999   *The Emergence of Agriculture*. (2nd Ed.) New York: W. H. Freeman.

Smith, Christopher
1998   *Late Stone Age Hunters of the British Isles*. London: Routledge.

Smith, Fred H.
1984   "Fossil Hominids from the Upper Pleistocene of Central Europe and the Origin of Modern Europeans." *In:* F. H. Smith and F. Spencer (eds.), *The Origins of Modern Humans*. New York: Alan R. Liss, pp. 187–209.

———
1989   "Modern Human Origins." *Yearbook of Physical Anthropology*, 32:35–68.

Smith, Fred H., Ivor Jankovic, and Ivor Karavanic
2002   "Migrations, Radiations and Continuity: Patterns in the Evolution of Late Pleistocene Humans. *In:* W. Hartwig (ed.), *The Primate Fossil Record*. Cambridge: Cambridge University Press, pp. 437–456.

Smith, Fred H., A. B. Falsetti, and S. M. Donnelly
2005   "The Assimilation Model, Modern Human Origins in Europe, and the Extinction of Neandertals." *Quaternary International*, 137:7–19.

Smith, F. H., E. Trinkaus, P. B. Pettitt, et al.
1999   "Direct Radiocarbon Dates for Vindija G1 and Velika Pécina Late Pleistocene Hominid Remains." *Proceedings of the National Academy of Sciences*, 96:12281–12286.

Smith, Michael E.
2003   *The Aztecs*. (2nd Ed.). Malden, MA: Blackwell Publishing.

Smith, Patricia, Ofer Bar-Yosef, and Andrew Sillen
1984   "Archaeological and Skeletal Evidence for Dietary Change During the Late Pleistocene/Early Holocene in the Levant." *In:* Cohen and Armelagos (eds.), q.v., pp. 101–136.

Smuts, Barbara
1985   *Sex and Friendship in Baboons*. Hawthorne, NY: Aldine de Gruyter.

Smuts, B., et al. (eds.)
1987   *Primate Societies*. Chicago: University of Chicago Press.

Snow, C. P.
1965   *Two Cultures and the Scientific Revolution*, (2nd Ed.). Cambridge: Cambridge University Press.

Snow, Dean R.
1980   *The Archaeology of New England*. New York: Academic Press.

———
2006   "Sexual Dimorphism in Upper Palaeolithic Hand Stencils." *Antiquity*, 80(308):390–404.

Snyder, M. and M. Gerstein
2003   "Genomics. Defining Genes in the Genomics Era." *Science*, 300:258–260.

Soffer, Olga, J. M. Adovasio, D. C. Hyland, et al.
2000   "The 'Venus' Figurines." *Current Anthropology*, 41(4):511–537.

Soffer, Olga and N. D. Praslov (eds.)
1993   *From Kostenki to Clovis: Upper Paleolithic—Paleo-Indian Adaptations*. New York: Plenum Press.

Spencer, Charles S. and Elsa M. Redmond
2004   "Primary State Formation in Mesoamerica." *Annual Review of Anthropology*, 33:173–199.

Sponheimer, M., B. H. Passey, D. J. de Ruiter, et al.
2006   "Isotopic Evidence for Dietary Variability in the Early Hominin *Paranthropus robustus*." *Science*, 314:980–982.

Spoor, F., M. G. Leakey, P. N. Gathago, et al.
2007   "Implications of New Early *Homo* Fossils from Ileret, East of Lake Turkana, Kenya." *Nature*, 448:688–691.

Stanish, Charles
2001   "The Origin of State Societies in South America." *Annual Review of Anthropology*, 30:41–64.

Steckel, Richard H. and Jerome C. Rose
2002   *The Backbone of History: Health and Nutrition in the Western Hemisphere*. New York: Cambridge University Press.

Steele, D. Gentry
2000   "The Skeleton's Tale." *Discovering Archaeology*, 2(1): 61–62.

Steele, D. Gentry and J. F. Powell
1999   "Peopling of the Americas: A Historical and Comparative Perspective." *In:* Bonnichsen R, (ed.). *Who Were the First Americans?* Corvallis, OR: Center for the Study of the First Americans, Oregon State University, pp. 97–126.

Stein, Burton
1994   *Vijayanagara*. Cambridge, UK: Cambridge University Press.

Steklis, Horst D.
1985   "Primate Communication, Comparative Neurology, and the Origin of Language Reexamined." *Journal of Human Evolution*, 14:157–173.

Stelzner, J. and K. Strier
1981   "Hyena Predation on an Adult Male Baboon." *Mammalia*, 45:106–107.

Stokstad, Erik
2002   "Oldest New World Writing Suggests Olmec Innovation." *Science*, 298:1872–1874.

Strassman, B. I. and B. Gillespie
2002   "Life-history Theory, Fertility, and Reproductive Success in Humans." *Proceedings of the Royal Society of London B*, 269:553–562.

Straus, Lawrence Guy
2005   "On the Demise of the Neandertals." *Quaternary International*, 137(1):1–5.

Straus, Lawrence Guy, D. J. Meltzer, and T. Goebel
2005   "Ice Age Atlantis? Exploring the Solutrean-Clovis 'Connection'." *World Archaeology*, 37(4):507–532.

Strier, Karen B.
2003   *Primate Behavioral Ecology*. (2nd Ed.). Boston: Allyn and Bacon.

Stringer, C. B. and P. Andrews
1988   "Genetic and Fossil Evidence for the Origin of Modern Humans." *Science*, 239:1263–1268.

Struhsaker, T. T.
1967   "Auditory Communication among Vervet Monkeys (*Cercopithecus aethiops*)." *In: Social Communication Among Primates*, S. A. Altmann (ed.), Chicago: University of Chicago Press.

———
1975   *The Red Colobus Monkey*. Chicago: University of Chicago Press.

Struhsaker, Thomas T. and Lysa Leland
1987   "Colobines: Infanticide by Adult Males." *In*: Smuts, et al. (eds.), q.v., pp. 83–97.

Surovell, Todd A., Nicole Waguespack, and P. Jeffrey Brantingham
2005   "Global Archaeological Evidence for Proboscidean Overkill." *Proceedings of the National Academy of Sciences*, 102(17):6231–6236.

Susman, Randall L. (ed.)
1984   *The Pygmy Chimpanzee. Evolutionary Biology and Behavior.* New York: Plenum.

Susman, Randall L., Jack T. Stern, and William L. Jungers
1985   "Locomotor Adaptations in the Hadar Hominids." *In: Ancestors: The Hard Evidence*, E. Delson (ed.), New York: Alan R. Liss, pp.184–192.

Sussman, Robert W.
1991   "Primate Origins and the Evolution of Angiosperms." *American Journal of Primatology*, 23:209–223.

Sussman, Robert W., James M. Cheverud, and Thad Q. Bartlett
1995   Infant Killing as an Evolutionary Strategy: Reality or Myth?" *Evolutionary Anthropology*, 3(5):149–151.

Suwa, Gen, Reikp T. Kono, Shigehiro Katoh, et al.
2007   "A New Species of Great Ape from the Late Miocene Epoch of Ethiopia." *Nature*, 448:921–924.

Swisher, C. C., W. J. Rink, S. C. Anton, et al.
1996   "Latest *Homo erectus* of Java: Potential Contemporaneity with *Homo sapiens* in Southwest Java." *Science*, 274:1870–1874.

Szalay, Frederick S. and Eric Delson
1979   *Evolutionary History of the Primates.* New York: Academic Press.

Tagg, Martyn D.
1996   "Early Cultigens from Fresnal Shelter, Southeastern New Mexico." *American Antiquity*, 61(2): 311–24.

Tattersall, Ian, Eric Delson, and John Van Couvering
1988   *Encyclopedia of Human Evolution and Prehistory.* New York: Garland Publishing.

Taylor, R. E. and M. J. Aitken
1997   *Chronometric Dating in Archaeology.* New York: Plenum.

Tenaza, R. and R. Tilson
1977   "Evolution of Long-Distance Alarm Calls in Kloss' Gibbon." *Nature*, 268:233–235.

Teresi, Dick
2002   *Lost Discoveries. The Ancient Roots of Modern Science—from the Babylonians to the Maya.* New York: Simon and Schuster.

Thieme, Hartmut
2005   "The Lower Palaeolithic Art of Hunting." *In: The Hominid Individual in Context: Archaeological Investigations of Lower and Middle Palaeolithic Landscapes, Locales and Artefacts*, Clive Gamble and Martin Porr (eds.), New York: Routledge, pp. 115–132.

Thomas, D. H., J. O. Davis, D. K. Grayson, et al.
1983   "The Archaeology of Monitor Valley 2: Gatecliff Shelter." *Anthropological Papers* 59, Pt. 1. New York: American Museum of Natural History.

Thomas, Julian
1988   "Neolithic Explanations Revisited: The Mesolithic-Neolithic Transition in Britain and South Scandinavia." *Proceedings of the Prehistoric Society* 54:59–66.

Thorne, A., R. Grün, G. Mortimer, et al.
1999   "Australia's Oldest Human Remains: Age of the Lake Mungo 3 Skeleton." *Journal of Human Evolution*, 36:591–612.

Tiemel, Chen, Yang Quan, and Wu En
1994   "Antiquity of *Homo sapiens* in China." *Nature*, 368:55–56.

Tobias, Phillip
1971   *The Brain in Hominid Evolution.* New York: Columbia University Press.

———
1983   "Recent Advances in the Evolution of the Hominids with Especial Reference to Brain and Speech." Pontifical Academy of Sciences, *Scrita Varia*, 50:85–140.

Tocheri, Matthew W., Caley M. Orr, Susan G. Larson, et al.
2007   "The Primitive Wrist of *Homo floresiensis* and Its Implications for Hominin Evolution." *Science*, 1743–1745.

Todd, T. W.
1920   "Age Changes in the Pubic Bone. I. The Male White Pubis." *American Journal of Physical Anthropology* 3:285–339.

———
1921   "Age Changes in the Pubic Bone. III. The Pubis of the White Female. *American Journal of Physical Anthropology* 4:26–39.

Traverse, Alfred
2007   *Paleopalynology.* (2nd Ed.) Dordrecht, The Netherlands: Springer.

Trigger, Bruce G.
2003   *Understanding Early Civilizations.* Cambridge, UK: Cambridge University Press.

Trigger, Bruce G., Barry J. Kemp, David O'Connor, and Alan B. Lloyd
1983   *Ancient Egypt: A Social History.* Cambridge: Cambridge University Press.

Tringham, Ruth
1971   *Hunters, Fishers, and Farmers of Eastern Europe, 6000–3000 B.C.* London: Hutchinson University Library.

Trinkaus, Erik
2005   "Early Modern Humans." *Annual Review of Anthropology*, 34:207–230.

Trinkaus, E., S. Milota, R. Rodrigo, et al.
2003   "Early Modern Human Cranial Remains from Pestera cu Oase, Romania." *Journal of Human Evolution*, 45:245–253.

Trinkaus, Erik and Pat Shipman
1992   *The Neandertals.* New York: Alfred A. Knopf.

Turner, Christy G.
1987   "Telltale Teeth." *Natural History*, 96(1):6–10.

Turner, Christy G. and Jacqueline A. Turner
1999   *Man Corn: Cannibalism and Violence in the American Southwest and Mexico.* Salt Lake City: University of Utah Press.

Van der Merwe, Nikolaas J.
1969   *The Carbon-14 Dating of Iron*, Chicago and London: University of Chicago Press.

Van Noten, Francis and Jan Raymaekers
1987   "Early Iron Smelting in Central Africa." *Scientific American*, 258:84–91.

van Schaik, C. P., M. Ancrenaz, G. Bogen, et al.
2003   "Orangutan Cultures and the Evolution of Material Culture." *Science*, 299:102–105.

Varki, A.
2000   "A Chimpanzee Genome Project Is a Biomedical Imperative." *Genome Research*, 8:1065–1070.

Vavilov, N. I.
1992   *The Origin and Geography of Cultivated Plants.* Cambridge: Cambridge University Press.

Vekua, Abesalom, David Lorkipanidze, G. Phillip Rightmire, et al.
2002   "A New Early *Homo* from Dmanisi, Georgia." *Science*, 297:85–89.

Verhoeven, Marc
2004 "Beyond Boundaries: Nature, Culture and a Holistic Approach to Domestication in the Levant." *Journal of World History*, 18(3):179–281.

Vialet, A., L. Tianyuan, D. Grimaud-Herve, et al.
2005 "Proposition de Reconstitution du Deuxième Crâne d'*Homo erectus* de Yunxian (Chine)." *Comptes rendus. Palévol*, 4:265–274.

Vigilant, L., M. Hofreiter, H. Siedel, and C. Boesch
2001 "Paternity and Relatedness in Wild Chimpanzee Communities." *Proceedings of the National Academy of Sciences*, 98:12890–12895.

Vignaud, P., P. Duringer, H. MacKaye, et al.
2002 "Geology and Palaeontology of the Upper Miocene Toros-Menalla Hominid Locality, Chad." *Nature*, 418:152–155.

Villa, Paola
1983 Terra Amata and the Middle Pleistocene Archaeological Record of Southern France. *University of California Publications in Anthropology*, Vol. 13. Berkeley: University of California Press.

Visalberghi, E.
1990 "Tool Use in Cebus." *Folia Primatologica*, 54:146–154.

Vogelsang, R.
1998 *The Middle Stone Age Fundstellen in Süd-west Namibia.* Köln: Heinrich Barth Institut.

Wagner, Daniel P. and Joseph M. McAvoy
2004 "Pedoarchaeology of Cactus Hill, a Sandy Paleoindian Site in Southeastern Virginia, U.S.A." *Geoarchaeology: An International Journal*, 19(4):297–322.

Waguespack, Nichole M.
2007 "Why We're Still Arguing About the Pleistocene Occupation of the Americas." *Evolutionary Anthropology*, 16(2):63–74.

Walker, A.
1976 "Remains Attributable to *Australopithecus* from East Rudolf." *In: Earliest Man and Environments in the Lake Rudolf Basin*, Y. Coppens, et al. (eds.), Chicago: University of Chicago Press, pp. 484–489.

———
1991 "The Origin of the Genus *Homo*." *In:* S. Osawa and T. Honjo (eds.), *Evolution of Life*. Tokyo: Springer-Verlag, pp. 379–389.

———
1993 "The Origin of the Genus *Homo*." *In:* D. T. Rasmussen (ed.), q.v., pp. 29–47.

Walker, Alan and R. E. Leakey
1993 *The Nariokotome* Homo erectus *Skeleton.* Cambridge: Harvard University Press.

Walker, Renee Beauchamp and Boyce N. Driskell (eds.)
2007 *Foragers of the Terminal Pleistocene in North America.* Lincoln: University of Nebraska Press.

Walker, J., R.A. Cliff, and A. G. Latham
2006 "U-Pb Isoptoic Age of the Stw 573 Hominid from Sterkfontein, South Africa." *Science*, 314:1592–1594.

Walsh, P. D., K. A. Abernathy, M. Bermejo, et al.
2003 "Catastrophic Ape Decline in Western Equatorial Africa." *Nature*, 422:611–614.

Ward, Peter
1994 *The End of Evolution.* New York: Bantam.

Warneken, F. and M. Tomasello
2006 "Altruistic Helping in Human Infants and Young Chimpanzees." *Science*, 311:1301–1303.

Washburn, S. L.
1963 "The Study of Race." *American Anthropologist*, 65:521–531.

Waterston, R. H., K. Lindblad-Toh, E. Birney, et al. (Mouse Genome Sequencing Consortium)
2002 "Initial Sequencing and Comparative Analysis of the Mouse Genome." *Nature*, 421:520–562.

Watson, J. B. and F. H. C. Crick
1953a "Genetical Implications of the Structure of the Deoxyribonucleic Acid." *Nature*, 171:964–967.

———
1953b "A Structure for Deoxyribonucleic Acid." *Nature*, 171:737–738.

Webster, David, AnnCorinne Freter, and Nancy Gonlin
2000 *Copán: The Rise and Fall of an Ancient Maya Kingdom.* Belmont, CA: Thomson Wadsworth.

Webb, William S.
1974 *Indian Knoll.* University of Tennessee Press, Knoxville.

Weeks, Kent R.
2001 *KV5: A Preliminary Report on the Excavation of the Tomb of the Sons of Ramesses II in the Valley of the Kings.* Cairo, Egypt: American University in Egypt Press.

Weiner, J. S.
1955 *The Piltdown Forgery.* London: Oxford University Press.

Weiner, Steve, Qinqi Xu, Paul Goldberg, Jinyi Liu, and Ofer Bar-Yosef
1998 "Evidence for the Use of Fire at Zhoukoudian, China." *Science*, 281:251–253.

Weiss, Ehud, Wilma Wetterstrom, Dani Nadel, and Ofer Bar-Yosef
2004a "The Broad Spectrum Revisited: Evidence from Plant Remains." *Proceedings of the National Academy of Science*, 101(26):9551–9555.

Weiss, Ehud, Mordechai E. Kislev, Orit Simchoni, and Dani Nadel.
2004b "Small-Grained Wild Grasses as Staple Food at the 23,000-Year-Old Site of Ohalo II, Israel." *Economic Botany*, 58(supplement): S125–S134.

Weiss, Kenneth
2003 "Come to Me My Melancholic Baby!" *Evolutionary Anthropology*, 12:3–6.

Weiss, Robin A. and Richard W. Wrangham
1999 "From *Pan* to Pandemic." *Nature*, 397:385–386.

Weiss, U.
2002 "Nature Insight: Malaria." *Nature*, 415:669.

Wendorf, Fred and Romuald Schild
1989 *The Prehistory of Wadi Kubbaniya.* Dallas, TX: Southern Methodist University.

———
1994 "Are the Early Holocene Cattle in the Eastern Sahara Domestic or Wild?" *Evolutionary Anthropology*, 3:118–128.

Wenke, Robert J.
1990 *Patterns in Prehistory : Humankind's First Three Million Years.* (3rd Ed.). New York: Oxford University Press.

West, Frederick Hadleigh and Constance West (eds.)
1996 *American Beginnings: The Prehistory and Palaeoecology of Beringia.* Chicago: University of Chicago Press.

Wheat, Joe Ben
1972 "The Olsen-Chubbuck Site: A Paleo-Indian Bison Kill." *American Antiquity*, 37:1–180.

White, Tim D.
1986 "Cut Marks on the Bodo Cranium: A Case of Prehistoric Defleshing." *American Journal of Physical Anthropology*, 69:503–509.

———
1992 *Prehistoric Cannibalism at Mancos SMTUMR-2346.* Princeton, NJ: Princeton University Press.

White, T. D., Berhane Asfaw, David DeGusta, et al.
  2003   "Pleistocene *Homo sapiens* from Middle Awash Ethiopia." *Nature*, 433:742–747.

White, Tim D., Gen Suwa, and Berhane Asfaw
  1994   "*Australopithecus ramidus*, a New Species of Early Hominid from Aramis, Ethiopia." *Nature*, 371:306–312.

———
  1995   Corrigendum (White, et al., 1994). *Nature*, 375:88.

White, T. D., Giday WoldeGabriel, B. Asfaw, et al.
  2006   "Asa Issie, Aramis and the Origin of *Australopithecus*." *Nature*, 440:883–889.

Whiten, A., J. Goodall, W. C. McGrew, et al.
  1999   "Cultures in Chimpanzees." *Nature*, 399:682–685.

Whittle, Alasdair
  1985   *Neolithic Europe: A Survey*. Cambridge: Cambridge University Press.

Wildman, Derek E., Monica Uddin, Guozhen Liu, et al.
  2003   "Implications of Natural Selection in Shaping 99.4% Nonsynonymous DNA Identity Between Humans and Chimpanzees: Enlarging Genus *Homo*." *Proceedings of the National Academy of Sciences*, 100:7181–7188.

Williams, M. A. J.
  1984   "Late Quaternary Prehistoric Environments of the Sahara." *In:* J. D. Clark and S. A. Brandt (eds.), q.v., pp. 74–83.

Wills, W. H.
  1989   *Early Prehistoric Agriculture in the American Southwest*. Santa Fe: School of American Research Press.

Wilmut, I., A. E. Schnieke, et al.
  1997   "Viable Offspring Derived from Fetal and Adult Mammalian Cells." *Nature*, 385:810–813.

Wilson, David J.
  1981   "Of Maize and Men: A Critique of the Maritime Hypothesis of State Origins on the Coast of Peru." *American Anthropologist*, 83:931–940.

Wilson, Edward O.
  1992   *The Diversity of Life*. Cambridge, MA: Harvard University Press.

Winslow, D. L. and J. R. Wedding
  1997   "Spirit Cave Man." *American History,* 32 (March/April): 74.

Wolpoff, Milford H.
  1983   "*Ramapithecus* and Human Origins. An Anthropologist's Perspective of Changing Interpretations." *In*: R. L.Ciochon and R. S. Corruccini (eds.), q.v., pp. 651–676.

———
  1984   "Evolution in *Homo erectus*: The Question of Stasis." *Paleobiology,* 10:389–406.

———
  1989   "Multiregional Evolution: The Fossil Alternative to Eden." *In:* P. Mellars and C. Stringer, (eds.) q.v., pp. 62–108.

———
  1999   *Paleoanthropology*. (2nd Ed.). New York: McGraw-Hill.

Wolpoff, M., A. G. Thorne, F. H. Smith, et al.
  1994   "Multiregional Evolutions: A World-Wide Source for Modern Human Populations." *In:* M. H. Nitecki and D. V. Nitecki (eds.), q.v., pp. 175–199.

Wolpoff, M. H., J. Hawks, D. Frayer, and K. Hunley
  2001   "Modern Human Ancestry at the Peripheries: A Test of the Replacement Theory." *Science*, 291:293–297.

Wolpoff, Milford H., Brigitte Senut, Martin Pickford, and John Hawks
  2002   "Paleoanthropology (Communication Arising): *Sahelanthropus* or 'Sahelpithecus'?" *Nature*, 419:581–582.

Woo, J.
  1966   "The Skull of Lantian Man." *Current Anthropology*, 5:83–86.

Wood, Bernard
  1991   *Koobi Fora Research Project IV: Hominid Cranial Remains from Koobi Fora*. Oxford: Clarendon Press.

———
  1992   "Origin and Evolution of the Genus *Homo*." *Nature*, 355:783–790.

———
  2002   "Hominid Revelations from Chad." News and Views, *Nature*, 418:133–135.

Wood, Bernard and Mark Collard
  1999a   "The Human Genus." *Science*, 284:65–71.

———
  1999b   "The Changing Face of Genus *Homo*." *Evolutionary Anthropology*, 8:195–207.

Wood, B. and B. G. Richmond
  2000   "Human Evolution: Taxonomy and Paleobiology." *Journal of Anatomy*, 197:19–60.

Woolley, Leonard
  1929   *Ur of the Chaldees*. London: Ernest Benn.

Wrangham, R. W. and B. B. Smuts
  1980   "Sex Differences in the Behavioural Ecology of Chimpanzees in Gombe National Park, Tanzania." *Journal of Reproduction and Fertility, Supplement*, 28:13–31.

Wrangham, R., A. Clark, and G. Isabiryre-Basita
  1992   "Female Social Relationships and Social Organization of Kibale Forest Chimps." In: *Topics in Primatology*, vol. 1, Human Origins, T. Nishida, W. McGrew, P. Marler, et al. (eds), Tokyo: Tokyo University Press, pp. 81–98.

Wrangham, R. and D. Peterson
  1996   *Demonic Males: Apes and the Origins of Human Violence*. New York, NY: Houghton Mifflin.

Wright, H. E.
  1993   "Environmental Determinism in Near Eastern Prehistory." *Current Anthropology*, 34:458–469.

Wu, Rukang and Xingren Dong
  1985   "*Homo erectus* in China." *In: Palaeoanthropology and Palaeolithic Archaeology in the People's Republic of China*, R. Wu and J. W. Olsen (eds.), New York: Academic Press, pp. 79–89.

Wu, X. and F. E. Poirier
  1995   *Human Evolution in China*. Oxford: Oxford University Press.

Wu, X., L. A. Schepartz, D. Falk, and L. Wu
  2006   "Endocranial Cast of Hexian *Homo erectus* from South China." *American Journal of Physical Anthropology*, 130:445–454.

Wuehrich, Bernice
  1998   "Geological Analysis Damps Ancient Chinese Fires." *Science*, 28:165–166.

Wurm, Stephen
  1994   "Australasia and the Pacific." *In: Atlas of the World's Languages*, Christopher Moseley, R. E. Asher, and Mary Tait (eds.), London: Routledge, pp. 25–46.

Yamei, Hon, Richard Potts, Yaun Baoyin, et al.
  2000   "Mid-Pleistocene Acheulean-like Stone Technology of the Bose Basin, South China." *Science*, 287:1622–1626.

Yan, Wenming
  1999   "Neolithic Settlements in China: Latest Finds and Research." J*ournal of East Asian Archaeology*, 1:131–147.

Yellen, John E.
  1980   *Archaeological Approaches to the Present.*New York: Academic Press.

Yellen, John E., A. S. Brooks, E. Cornelissen, et al.
1995   "A Middle Stone Age Worked Bone Industry from Katanda, Upper Semliki Valley, Zaire." *Science,* 268:553–556.

Yoffee, Norman
2005   *Myths of the Archaic State: Evolution of the Earliest Cities, States, and Civilizations.* Cambridge, UK: Cambridge University Press.

Young, Biloine Whiting and Melvin L. Fowler
2000   *Cahokia: The Great Native American Metropolis.* Urbana: University of Illinois Press.

Young, David
1992   *The Discovery of Evolution.* Cambridge: Natural History Museum Publications, Cambridge University Press.

Yudkin, J.
1969   "Archaeology and the Nutritionist." *In: The Domestication and Exploitation of Plants and Animals,* P. J. Ucko and G. W. Dimbleby (eds.), Chicago: Aldine, pp. 547–554.

Zeder, Melinda
1997   "The American Archeologist: Results of the 1994 SAA Census." *SAA Bulletin,* 15:12–17.

Zilhão, J.
2007   "The Emergence of Ornaments and Art: An Archaeological Perspective on the Origins of 'Behavioral Modernity'." *Journal of Archaeological Research,* 15(1):1–54.

Zhu, R. X., Z. S. An, R. Potts, et al.
2003   "Magnetostratigraphic Dating of Early Humans in China." *Earth Science Reviews,* 61:341–359.

Photo Credits

1, Chapter opener, Robert Glusic/Getty Images; **3,** Fig. 1, © Jon R. Holmquist, Photo Stock Source; **4,** Fig. 1-2a, Lynn Kilgore; Fig. 1-2b, NASA/Space Telescope Science Institute; Fig. 1-2c, Lynn Kilgore; Fig. 1-2d, Justin Horocks/iStockphoto; **7,** Fig. 1-3, © Russell L. Ciochon; **7,** Fig. 1-4, Lynn Kilgore; Fig. 1-5, Judith Regensteiner; **8,** Fig. 1-6, Kathleen Galvin; **8,** Fig. 1-7, Robert Jurmain; **9,** Fig. 1-8, Julie Lesnik; Fig. 1-9a, b, Lynn Kilgore; **10,** Fig. 1-10, Lorna Pierce/Judy Suchey; Fig. 1-11, Linda Levitch; **11,** Fig. 1-12, © Museum of London Archaeology; Fig. 1-13, © French Ministry of Culture; **12,** Fig. 1-14, Illinois Transportation Archaeological Research Program, University of Illinois; **13,** Fig. 1-15, Wikipedia; **14,** Fig. 1-16, Barry Lewis; **15,** Fig. 1-17, Illinois Transportation Archaeological Research Program, University of Illinois; **19,** Chapter opener, MedicalRF.com/Getty Images; **22,** Fig. 2-1, J. van (Johannes) Loon/Wikimedia Commons; **23,** Fig. 2-2, American Museum of Natural History; **25,** Fig. 2-4, Wikipedia; Fig. 2-5, With permission from the Master of Haileybury; **26,** Fig. 2-6, © National Portrait Gallery, London; Fig. 2-7, © Bettmann/Corbis; **28,** Fig. 2-10, Wolf: John Giustina/Getty Images; Dogs surrounding wolf: Lynn Kilgore and Lin Marshall; **29,** Fig. 2-11, © National Portrait Gallery, London; **31,** Fig. 2-12a, Michael Tweedie/Photo Researchers; Fig. 2-12b, Breck P. Kent/Animals Animals; **37,** Chapter opener, MedicalRF.com/Getty Images; **38,** Fig. 3-1a, b, Wikipedia; **44,** Fig. 3-6, Lynn Kilgore; **45,** Fig. 3-7, Biophoto Associates/Science Source/Photo Researchers; **50,** Fig. 3-12, Raychel Ciemma and Precision Graphics; **57,** Ray Carson, University of Florida News and Public Affairs; **58,** Fig. 3-18a–f, Lynn Kilgore; Fig. 3-18g, Robert Jurmain; **60,** Fig. 3-19, Professors P. Motta and T. Naguro/SPL/Photo Researchers, Inc.; **61,** Cellmark Diagnostics, Abingdon, UK; **65,** Fig. 3-22, Lynn Kilgore; **67,** Fig. 3-23a, b, © Dr. Stanley Flegler/Visuals Unlimited; **71,** Chapter opener, MedicalRF.com/Getty Images; **76,** Fig. 4-1a, © Peter Johnson/Corbis; Fig. 4-1b, © Charles & Josette Lenars/Corbis; Fig. 4-1c, © Gallo Images/Corbis; Fig. 4-1d, © Otto Lang, Corbis; Fig. 4-1e, Lynn Kilgore; **78,** Fig. 4-2a, b, Robert Jurmain; **82,** Fig. 4-5, © Michael S. Yamashita/Corbis; **85,** Fig. 4-7, Norman Lightfoot/Photo Researchers; **87,** Fig. 4-9, © Biophoto Associates/Photo Researchers, Inc.; **89,** Fig. 4-11a, Renee Lynn/Photo Researchers; Fig. 4-11b, George Holton/Photo Researchers; **91,** Fig. 4-12a, L. G. Moore; Fig. 4-12b, William Pratt; **95,** Fig. 4-13, Karl Ammann; **99,** Chapter opener, MedicalRF.com/Getty Images; **114,** Fig. 5-10, J. C. Stevenson/Animals Animals; **117,** Chapter opener, Jack Hollingsworth/Getty Images; **119,** Fig. 6-1a–e, Lynn Kilgore; **121,** Fig. 6-3 a, b, Lynn Kilgore; **122,** Fig. 6-4, Lynn Kilgore; **124,** Fig. 6-5 (Howler species), Raymond Mendez/Animals Animals; (Spider monkeys and muriquis), Robert L. Lubeck/Animals Animals; (Prince Bernhard's titi), Marc van Roosmalen; (Marmosets and tamarins), © Zoological Society of San Diego, photo by Ron Garrison; (Muriqui), Andrew Young; (White-faced capuchins) © Jay Dickman/Corbis; (Squirrel monkeys), © Kevin Schafer/Corbis; (Uakari), R. A. Mittermeier/Conservation International; **125,** Fig. 6-5 (Baboon species), Bonnie Pedersen/Arlene Kruse; (Macaque species), Jean De Rousseau;

(Gibbons and siamangs), Lynn Kilgore; (Tarsier species), David Haring, Duke University Primate Zoo; (Orangutans), © Tom McHugh/Photo Researchers, Inc.; (Colobus species) Robert Jurmain; (Galagos), Bonnie Pedersen/Arlene Kruse; (Chimpanzees and bonobos), Arlene Kruse/Bonnie Pedersen; (Mountain and lowland gorillas), Lynn Kilgore; (*Cercopithecus* species), Robert Jurmain; (Loris species), San Francisco Zoo; (Langur species), Joe MacDonald/Animals Animals; (Lemurs), Fred Jacobs; **126,** Fig. 6-6, © Russell L. Ciochon; **127,** Fig. 6-7a–d, Redrawn from original art by Stephen D. Nash in John G. Fleagle, *Primate Adaptation and Evolution,* 2nd ed., 1999. Reprinted by permission of publisher and Stephen Nash; Fig. 6-8, Lynn Kilgore; **131,** Fig. 6-11 (cat and calf), Lynn Kilgore; Fig. 6-12, © Victor Deak, after John G. Fleagle; **132,** Fig. 6-14, Fred Jacobs; Fig. 6-15, Fred Jacobs; Fig. 6-16, San Francisco Zoo; Fig. 6-17, Bonnie Pedersen/Arlene Kruse; **133,** Fig. 6-18, David Haring, Duke University Primate Zoo; **134,** Fig. 6-21, © Zoological Society of San Diego, photo by Ron Garrison; Fig. 6-22, Raymond Mendez/Animals Animals; **135,** Fig. 6-23, (Squirrel monkeys), © Kevin Schafer/Corbis; (Prince Bernhard's titi), Marc van Roosmalen; (Uakari), R. A. Mittermeier/Conservation International; (Muriqui), Andrew Young; (White-faced capuchins), © Jay Dickman/Corbis; **136,** Fig. 6-24, Robert L. Lubeck/Animals Animals; Fig. 6-26, Robert Jurmain; **137,** Fig. 6-27a, b, Bonnie Pedersen/Arlene Kruse; Fig. 6-28, Lynn Kilgore; Fig. 6-30, Lynn Kilgore; **139,** Fig. 6-31a Noel Rowe; Fig. 6-31b, Lynn Kilgore; **140,** Fig. 6-33a, b, Lynn Kilgore; Fig. 6-34a, b, Lynn Kilgore; **141,** Fig. 6-35a, Lynn Kilgore; Fig. 6-35b, Robert Jurmain, photo by Jill Matsumoto/Jim Anderson; **142,** Fig. 6-36, Ellen Ingmanson; **145,** Fig. 6-37, John Oates; Fig. 6-38, Karl Ammann; **146,** WildlifeDirect.org; **149,** Chapter opener, Jack Hollingsworth/Getty Images; **152,** Fig. 7-1, © Russ Mittermeir; **153,** Fig. 7-2, Lynn Kilgore; **154,** Fig. 7-3, Time Life Pictures/Getty Images; **156,** Fig. 7-4, Lynn Kilgore; Fig. 7-5, Lynn Kilgore; **157,** Fig. 7-6, Lynn Kilgore; **158,** Fig. 7-8, Curt Busse; **159,** Fig. 7-9a, Robert Jurmain; Fig. 7-9b, Meredith Small; Fig. 7-9c, d, Arlene Kruse/Bonnie Pedersen; **161,** Fig. 7-10, Alexander Klemm/iStockphoto.com; **162,** Fig. 7-11, Joe MacDonald/Animals Animals; **163,** Fig. 7-12, Peter Henzi; **164,** Fig. 7-13, Harlow Primate Laboratory, University of Wisconsin; Fig. 7-14, Lynn Kilgore; **165,** Fig. 7-15a, David Haring, Duke University Primate Center; Fig. 7–15b, Arlene Kruse/Bonnie Pedersen; Fig. 7-15c, d, Robert Jurmain; Fig. 7-15e, © Tom McHugh/Photo Researchers, Inc.; **166,** Fig. 7-16a, Lynn Kilgore; Fig. 7-16b, Manoj Shah/The Image Bank; **167,** Fig. 7-17, Tetsuro Matsuzawa; **169,** Fig. 7-18, Lynn Kilgore; **171,** Fig. 7-19, Rose A. Sevcik, Language Research Center, Georgia State University; photo by Elizabeth Pugh; **172,** Fig. 7-20, Lynn Kilgore; **175,** Chapter opener, Javier Trueba/MSF/Photo Researchers, Inc.; **179,** Fig. 8-1, NASA Goddard Space Flight Center; **180,** Fig. 8-2, Institute of Human Origins; **182,** Fig. 8-3, Barry Lewis; Fig. 8-4, Barry Lewis; **183,** Fig. 8-5, Michael L. Hargrave; Fig. 8-6, Barry Lewis; **184,** Fig. 8-7, Barry Lewis; **185,** Fig. 8-8, Illinois Transportation Archaeological Research Program, University of Illinois; Fig. 8-9, Barry Lewis; Fig. 8–10, Barry Lewis; **186,** Fig. 8-11, Dr. Colin Betts, Luther College; **187,** Fig. 8-12, Richard VanderHoek; Fig. 8-13, William Turnbaugh; **190,** Fig. 8-14, William Turnbaugh; **194,** Fig. 8-16, Beta Analytic, Inc., Darden Hood, president; **195,** Fig. 8-17, William Turnbaugh; **196,** Fig. 8-19, L.S.B. Leakey Foundation; **197,** Fig. 8-20, Robert Jurmain; Fig. 8-21, © Jeffrey Schwartz; **198,** Fig. 8-22, Robert Jurmain; **199,** Fig. 8-23, Barry Lewis; **201,** Chapter opener, Javier Trueba/MSF/Photo Researchers, Inc.; **203,** Fig. 9-1, © Russell Ciochon; **206,** Fig. 9-4, © The Natural History Museum,

Index